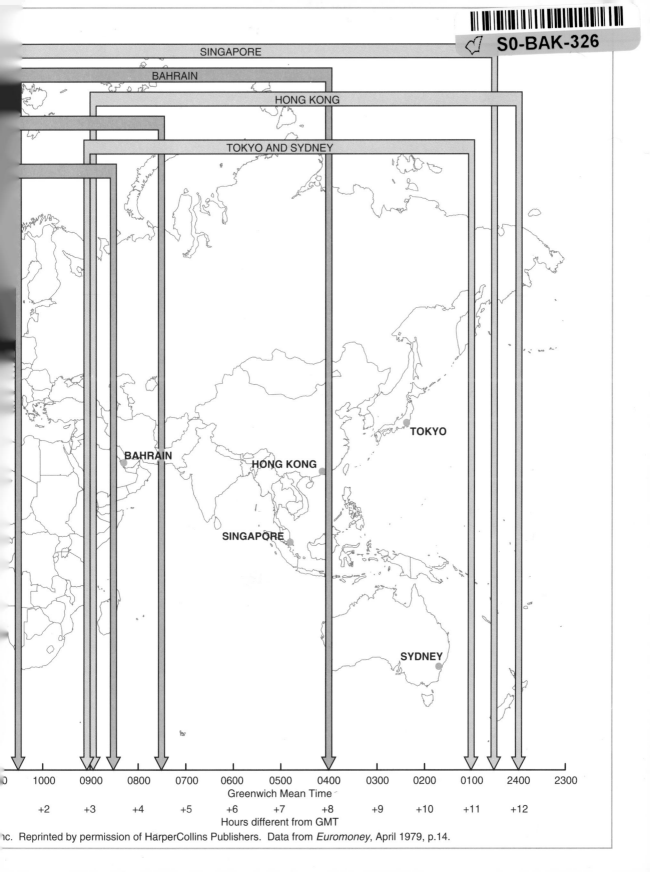

SINGAPORE

BAHRAIN

HONG KONG

TOKYO AND SYDNEY

TOKYO

BAHRAIN

HONG KONG

SINGAPORE

SYDNEY

| 1000 | 0900 | 0800 | 0700 | 0600 | 0500 | 0400 | 0300 | 0200 | 0100 | 2400 | 2300 |

Greenwich Mean Time

| +2 | +3 | +4 | +5 | +6 | +7 | +8 | +9 | +10 | +11 | +12 |

Hours different from GMT

S0-BAK-326

The Addison-Wesley Series in Finance

Chambers/Lacey
Modern Corporate Finance: Theory and Practice

Copeland
Exchange Rates and International Finance

Copeland/Weston
Financial Theory and Corporate Policy

Dufey/Giddy
Cases in International Finance

Eakins
Finance: Investments, Institutions, and Management

Eiteman/Stonehill/Moffett
Multinational Business Finance

Emery
Corporate Finance: Principles and Practice

Eng/Lees/Mauer
Global Finance

Gibson
International Finance

Gitman
Foundations of Managerial Finance

Gitman
Principles of Managerial Finance

Gitman
Principles of Managerial Finance
—Brief Edition

Gitman/Joehnk
Fundamentals of Investing

Gitman/Madura
Introduction to Finance

Megginson
Corporate Finance Theory

Melvin
International Money and Finance

Mishkin/Eakins
Financial Markets and Institutions

Moffett
Cases in International Finance

Pinches
Essentials of Financial Management

Pinches
Financial Management

Radcliffe
Investment: Concepts - Analysis - Strategy

Rejda
Principles of Risk Management and Insurance

Rejda/McNamara
Personal Financial Planning

Solnik
International Investments

Thygerson
Management of Financial Institutions

Wagner
Financial Management with the Electronic Spreadsheet

MULTINATIONAL BUSINESS FINANCE

NINTH EDITION

David K. Eiteman
University of California, Los Angeles

Arthur I. Stonehill
University of Hawaii at Manoa

Michael H. Moffett
*Thunderbird—The American Graduate School
of International Management*

With a contribution by Chuck C. Y. Kwok
University of South Carolina

Boston   San Francisco   New York
London   Toronto   Sydney   Tokyo   Singapore   Madrid
Mexico City   Munich   Paris   Cape Town   Hong Kong   Montreal

Senior Editor: Denise Clinton

Editorial Assistant: Andrea Botticelli

Production Supervisor: Patty Mahtani

Interior and Cover Design: Leslie Haimes

Art Direction: Regina Hagen

Marketing Manager: Dara Lanier

Permissions Editor: Mary Boucher

Cover Photograph: PhotoDisk © 2000

FASB Statement No. 52, Foreign Currency Translation, is copyrighted by the Financial Accounting Standards Board, 401 Merritt 7, P.O. Box 5116, Norwalk, CT 06856-5116, U.S.A. Portions are reprinted with permission. Copies of the complete document are available from the FASB.

Library of Congress Cataloging-In-Publication Data

Eiteman, David K.
  Multinational business finance / David K. Eiteman, Arthur
I. Stonehill, Michael H. Moffett; with a contribution by Chuck Kwok.—9th ed.
  p. cm.
  Includes bibliographical references and index.
  ISBN 0-201-63538-0
  1. International business enterprises--Finance.   I. Stonehill,
Arthur I.   II. Moffett, Michael H.   III. Kwok, Chuck.   IV. Title.
HG4027.5. E36 2001
658.15' 99--dc21   00–040586
                                                           CIP

1 2 3 4 5 6 7 8 9 10–CRW–0403020100

PREFACE

As the field of international finance has evolved, so has the content of ***Multinational Business Finance***. As in previous editions, we perceive the multinational enterprise to be a unique institution that acts as a catalyst and a facilitator of international trade and as an important producer and distributor in host countries where its affiliates are located. The success of a multinational enterprise continues to be dependent on its ability to recognize and benefit from imperfections in national markets for products, factors of production, and financial assets.

Also carried over from the earlier editions is the theme that volatile exchange rates may increase risk, but they also create opportunities for both investors and firms to profit, given a proper understanding of exchange risk management.

The ninth edition continues to recognize the increasing importance of global integration of money and capital markets, a trend that is creating expanded opportunities for both investors and organizations that need to raise capital. Although global integration of financial markets removes some market imperfections that impede the flow of capital internationally, excellent opportunities continue to exist for investors to increase their returns while lowering their risk through international portfolio diversification and for firms to lower their cost of capital by sourcing it internationally.

WHAT IS NEW IN THE NINTH EDITION?

In preparing this ninth edition of ***Multinational Business Finance*** a major effort was made to shorten the book and to increase the coverage of emerging market issues.

1. Although the book's length has been reduced from 854 pages to under 700 pages, four new decision cases and numerous new illustrative cases have been added.

2. The new decision cases are a reflection of the need to increase emerging market coverage.

   - The *P.T. Semen Gresik* case illustrates the valuation issues faced by a Mexican multinational (Cemex) that is considering acquiring an Indonesian cement manufacturing company in 1998.

   - The *Northwestern Paper Company* case involves a transfer pricing dispute between two foreign subsidiaries (South Korea and Indonesia) bidding on the same sale of paper to an Australian company in the mid-1990s.

   - The *Far East Trading Company* case describes the problems facing a Swedish multinational firm that has its key markets in Asia adversely affected by the emerging markets crisis in 1997.

- *Tektronix (C)* describes the case of a U.S. multinational firm that is divesting half the company in 1999. This divestment will cause problems for the foreign exchange risk-management strategies of the surviving company. Operating exposure management is particularly difficult since most of Tektronix' products are manufactured in the United States, but half of sales are exported and invoiced in local currencies.

3. Three decision cases were retained from the prior edition: *Lufthansa*, *ZAPA Chemical*, and *British Columbia Hydro*.

4. Eight decision cases from the prior edition have been transferred to a new casebook, ***Cases in International Finance***, authored by Michael Moffett and published by Addison Wesley Longman. This new casebook includes a number of other decision cases. It will be sold separately from ***Multinational Business Finance***, but its cases will be keyed to this text's contents. The new case book is being published simultaneously with this text.

5. Emerging markets are emphasized throughout the book. Extensive coverage is given to the emerging market crises of 1997–1999. The perspective of multinational firms resident in emerging markets is emphasized in the chapters on cost and availability of capital, sourcing equity globally, capital budgeting, international acquisitions, adjusting for risk in foreign investments, evaluation of performance, international portfolio investment, and working capital management. Political risk is treated throughout the book rather than in a separate chapter.

A chapter-by-chapter summary of changes follows:

PART 1. THE INTERNATIONAL FINANCIAL ENVIRONMENT

Chapter 1, International Financial Management and the Multinational Firm now includes a section on motives for foreign direct investment (FDI) that had previously appeared in our chapter on foreign investment decisions. It also has a more detailed explanation of the risks faced by multinational enterprises (MNEs). Conceptual material on political risk is treated here, while additional material on political risk has been disseminated throughout this ninth edition.

Chapter 2, The International Monetary Environment, features three illustrative cases, on Thailand, Russia, and Brazil, that highlight the emerging market crises of 1997–1999. The birth of the euro is described in detail.

Chapter 3, Foreign Exchange Rate Determination, is a revision and expansion of our old chapter on international parity conditions and balance of payments. New foreign exchange rate determinants that came to light because of the emerging market crises have been added to the traditional balance-of-payments and parity-conditions determinants of foreign exchange rates.

Chapter 4, The Foreign Exchange Market, has been revised to reflect the introduction of the euro. A revised section on foreign currency futures has been placed within the chapter rather than in an appendix, and the use of futures is compared with forward contracts.

Chapter 5, Foreign Currency Options, includes new material on the euro but is otherwise mostly unchanged.

PART 2. MEASURING AND MANAGING FOREIGN EXCHANGE EXPOSURE

Chapter 6, Transaction Exposure, now reflects the advent of the euro in all examples and end-of-chapter problems.

Chapter 7, Operating Exposure, has been revised to reflect the euro but is otherwise the same.

Chapter 8, Accounting Exposure, has been revised to reflect the euro, but is otherwise the same.

Chapter 9, Interest Rate Exposure and Swaps, has been completely rewritten. It now features a student-friendly explanation of the various types of interest rate and currency swaps.

PART 3. FINANCING THE GLOBAL FIRM

Chapter 10, Global Cost of Capital and Financial Structure, has been completely rewritten. It now features an expanded calculation of the cost of capital for Nestlé compared to a hypothetical domestic Swiss company. The former chapter on financial structure has been integrated into this chapter.

Chapter 11, Sourcing Equity Globally, has been heavily revised. It now has a greater managerial focus featuring alternative paths for a firm to follow to achieve improved global cost and availability of capital. Equity market descriptions have been updated.

Chapter 12, Sourcing Debt Globally, has been given more of a managerial focus, and the descriptive tables have been updated.

PART 4. FOREIGN INVESTMENT DECISIONS

Chapter 13, Corporate Strategy: Foreign Direct Investment and Political Risk, has been revised to include part of the former political risk chapter.

Chapter 14, Multinational Capital Budgeting, has been completely rewritten with a new greenfield investment case that is then also used in the next two chapters. The greenfield investment decision case, P.T. Semen Gresik, is about a Mexican cement producer, Cemex, considering an investment in Indonesia.

Chapter 15, International Acquisitions and Valuation, is a brand new chapter. It continues the P.T. Semen Gresik case from Chapter 14 with the Mexican producer (Cemex) now considering acquisition of an existing Indonesian cement producer (P.T. Semen Gresik). Various valuations techniques are explored.

Chapter 16, Adjusting for Risk in Foreign Investments, is another new chapter. Again utilizing the P.T. Semen Gresik case, it features the various new techniques that have been proposed to adjust the discount rate for foreign direct investments.

PART 5. MANAGING MULTINATIONAL OPERATIONS

Chapter 17, Multinational Taxation, is a very streamlined and tightened version of the eighth edition's chapter on taxation. Some of the detailed description of the U.S. taxation of foreign source income has been dropped in favor of a more generic treatment of the subject.

Chapter 18, Repositioning Funds, has been lightly revised to reflect the euro, but otherwise is the same as it was in the prior edition of this book.

Chapter 19, Working Capital Management, now includes financing working capital in addition to the management of current assets. The interface with various types of banking facilities has been moved here from its position in the import and export financing chapter in the eighth edition.

Chapter 20, Export and Import Financing, is shorter, but the topics are the same as in the prior edition. The eighth edition's section on forfaiting has been moved to the web page for this book.

Chapter 21, Evaluation of Performance, is a new chapter but is really just a shift of material from the chapter on current industry practices in the prior edition.

PART 6. ADVANCED TOPICS IN MULTINATIONAL FINANCE

Chapter 22, International Portfolio Theory and the MNE, is a new chapter that combines material from our eighth edition's chapters on the global cost of capital and the technical appendix to that chapter.

Chapter 23, Advanced Topics in Currency Risk Management, is based on a portion of the prior edition's chapter on advanced topics in multinational finance.

Chapter 24, Advanced Topics in Interest Rate Risk Management, contains the remaining portions of our eighth edition's chapter on advanced topics in multinational finance.

PEDAGOGICAL FEATURES

Multinational Business Finance, ninth edition, continues to provide an instructor-friendly package of supplements. An instructor's manual and power point slides will be provided to teachers who adopt the book for classroom use. The manual includes a disk that contains a variety of spreadsheet solutions to problems and case material, a multiple-choice test bank, and short-essay test bank.

Thanks to improved technology, we are greatly expanding our usage of Addison Wesley Longman's web page support for the text at *http://www.awl.com*. A number of "remedial" topics that were in the eighth edition have been moved to this web site. The web page will be continually updated with new illustrative cases and other relevant material as they arise.

Some chapters have in addition to new and expanded end-of-chapter questions, a separate set of Internet exercises in which students are directed to specific sources of information on the World Wide Web about current company, market, and business events. Many of these exercises have been designed to require the student to use real-time resources in the preparation of executive briefings and decision-based support.

AUDIENCE

The ninth edition of *Multinational Business Finance* is appropriate for the same audiences as the previous editions. Earlier editions have been widely used in international financial management courses in university degree programs, university-run executive education programs, and company management development programs.

Readers will find *Multinational Business Finance* most meaningful if they have the background knowledge or experience equivalent to a basic finance course. A previous course in international economics is desirable, but the text and web-site supplements are designed to cover sufficient economic material so that a separate background is not essential.

ACKNOWLEDGMENTS

The authors are very grateful to the numerous person who have provided critical comments and suggestions to improve both the current and earlier editions of this book. The ninth edition has benefitted immensely from comments we received on the previous edition, both from formal reviews and from colleagues' replies to our surveys.

REVIEWERS FOR THE NINTH EDITION

Special thanks to those who provided detailed input into the construction of the ninth edition through detailed book evaluations.

Raj Aggarwal
John Carroll University

Francesca Carrieri
McGill University

Jay Choi
Temple University

J. Markham Collins
University of Tulsa

Faramarz Damanpour
James Madison University

Robert Duvic
University of Texas at Austin

Amar Gande
Vanderbilt University

Robert Hauswald
Indiana University

Laurent Jacque
Tufts University

Chuck C. Y. Kwok
University of South Carolina

Wilbur Lewellen
Purdue University

Eva Liljeblom
Swedish School of Economis at Helsinki

William Megginson
University of Oklahoma

Chandra Mishra
Oregon State University

Devashis Mitra
University of New Brunswick

Tom O'Brien
University of Connecticut

John P. Olienyk
Colorado State University

August Ralston
Iowa State University

Lee Remmers
INSEAD

Arvind Singh
University of Arizona

Luc Soenen
California Polytechnic State University

Kishore Tandon
CUNY-Baruch College

Amiv Tavakkof
Kansas State University

Rohan Williamson
Georgetown University

Brent Wilson
Brigham Young Universtiy

Richard Wright
McGill University

K. G. Viswanathan
Hofstra University

ACADEMIC ADOPTERS SURVEYED

We take this opportunity to thank the following people for their responses to surveys of adopters of previous editions (affiliations are those at the time they provided their response):

Otto Adleberger
Essen University, Germany

Alan Alford
Northeastern University

Stephen Archer
Williamette University

Hossein G. Askari
George Washington University

Robert T. Aubey
University of Wisconsin at Madison

David Babbel
University of Pennsylvania

James Baker
Kent State University

Morten Balling
Aarhus School of Business, Denmark

Arindam Bandopadhyaya
University of Massachusetts at Boston

Ari Beenhakker
University of South Florida

Carl Beidleman
Lehigh University

Robert Boatler
Texas Christian University

Nancy Bord
University of Hartford

Finbarr Bradley
University of Dublin, Ireland

Tom Brewer
Georgetown University

Michael Brooke
University of Manchester, England

Robert Carlson
Assumption University, Thailand

Kevin Cheng
New York University

It-Keong Chew
University of Kentucky

Frederick D.S. Choi
New York University

Jay Choi
Temple University

Mark Ciechon
University of California, Los Angeles

J. Markham Collins
University of Tulsa

Alan N. Cook
Baylor University

Kerry Cooper
Texas A&M University

Robert Cornu
Cranfield School of Management, UK

Roy Crum
University of Florida

Steven Dawson
University of Hawaii at Manoa

Vijay Singal
Virginia Tech University

Luc Soenen
California Polytechnic State University

Michael Salt
San Jose State University

Marjorie Stanley
Texas Christian University

Jahangir Sultan
Bentley College

Kishore Tandon
CUNY - Bernard Baruch College

Russell Taussig
University of Hawaii at Manoa

Lee Tavis
University of Notre Dame

Norman Toy
Columbia University

Harald Vestergaard
Copenhagen Business School

K.G. Viswanathan
Hofstra University

Joseph D. Vu
University of Illinois, Chicago

Michael Williams
University of Texas at Austin

Brent Wilson
Brigham Young University

Alexander Zamperion
Bentley College

Emilio Zarruk
Florida Atlantic University

Tom Zwirlein
University of Colorado, Colorado Springs

Industry (present or former affiliation)

Paul Adaire
Philadelphia Stock Exchange

Barbara Block
Tektronix, Inc.

Holly Bowman
Bankers Trust

Payson Cha
HKR International, Hong Kong

John A. Deuchler
Private Export Funding Corporation

Kåre Dullum
Gudme Raaschou Investment Bank,
Denmark

Steven Ford
Hewlett Packard

David Heenan
Campbell Estate, Hawaii

Sharyn H. Hess
Foreign Credit Insurance Association

Aage Jacobsenl
Gudme Raaschou Investment Bank,
Denmark

Ira G. Kawaller
Chicago Mercantile Exchange

Kenneth Knox
Tektronix, Inc.

Arthur J. Obesler
Eximbank

I. Barry Thompson
Continental Bank

Gerald T. West
Overseas Private Investment Corporation

Willem Winter
First Interstate Bank of Oregon

Inevitably woven into the fabric of this book are ideas received from faculty and students at institutions all over the world where we have taught. These include our home universities of University of California, Los Angeles; Oregon State University; University of Hawaii; and Thunderbird. Our visiting stints have been at the Hong Kong University of Science and Technology; University of California, Berkeley; University of Michigan, Ann Arbor; Cranfield School of Management, United Kingdom; University of Hawaii at Manoa; Northern European Management Institute, Norway; Copenhagen Business School, Denmark; Aarhus School of Business, Denmark; Helsinki School of Economics and Business Administration, Finland; Institute for the Development of Executives, Argentina; National University of Singapore; International Centre for Public Enterprises, Yugoslavia; Beijing Institute of Chemical Engineering and Management; and Dalian University of Science & Technology, China. Further ideas came from consulting assignments in Argentina, Belgium, Canada, Denmark, Finland, Guatemala, Hong Kong, Indonesia, Japan, Malaysia, Mexico, the Netherlands, Norway, People's Republic of China, Peru, Sweden, Taiwan, the United Kingdom, and Venezuela.

We would also like to thank all those with Addison Wesley Longman who have worked so diligently on this ninth edition; Denise Clinton, Andrea Botticelli, and Patty Mahtani.

Finally, we would like to rededicate this book to our parents, the late Wilford and Sylvia Eiteman, the late Harold and Norma Stonehill, and Bennie Ruth and Hoy Moffett, who gave us the motivation to become academicians and authors. We thank our wives, Keng-Fong, Kari, and Megan, for their patience through the years spent preparing this edition.

Pacific Palisades, California　　　　　　　　　　　　　　D.K.E.
Honolulu, Hawaii　　　　　　　　　　　　　　　　　　　A.I.S.
Glendale, Arizona　　　　　　　　　　　　　　　　　　M.H.M.

ABOUT THE AUTHORS

DAVID K. EITEMAN

David K. Eiteman is Professor of Finance Emeritus at the John E. Anderson Graduate School of Management at UCLA. He has also held teaching or research appointments at the Hong Kong University of Science & Technology, Showa Academy of Music (Japan), the National University of Singapore, Dalian University (China), the Helsinki School of Economics and Business Administration (Finland), University of Hawaii at Manoa, University of Bradford (U.K.), Cranfield School of Management (U.K.), and IDEA (Argentina). He is a former president of the International Trade and Finance Association, Society for Economics and Management in China, and Western Finance Association.

Professor Eiteman received a B.B.A. (Business Administration) from the University of Michigan, Ann Arbor (1952), M.A. (Economics) from the University of California, Berkeley (1956), and a Ph.D. (Finance) from Northwestern University (1959).

He has authored or co-authored four books and twenty-nine other publications. His articles have appeared in *The Journal of Finance, The International Trade Journal, Financial Analysts Journal, Journal of World Business, Management International, Business Horizons, MSU Business Topics, Public Utilities Fortnightly*, and others.

ARTHUR I. STONEHILL

Arthur I. Stonehill is a Professor of Finance and International Business, Emeritus, at Oregon State University, where he taught for 24 years (1966–1990). During 1991–1997 he held a split appointment at the University of Hawaii at Manoa and Copenhagen Business School. From 1997 to the present he continues as a Visiting Professor at the University of Hawaii at Manoa. He has also held teaching or research appointments at the University of California, Berkeley, Cranfield School of Management (U.K.), and the North European Management Institute (Norway). He was a former president of the Academy of International Business and was a western director of the Financial Management Association.

Professor Stonehill received a B.A. (History) from Yale University (1953), an M.B.A. from Harvard Business School (1957), and a Ph.D. from the University of California, Berkeley (1965). He was awarded honorary doctorates from the Aarhus School of Business (Denmark, 1989), the Copenhagen Business School (Denmark, 1992), and Lund University (Sweden, 1998).

He has authored or co-authored eight books and twenty-three other publications. His articles have appeared in *Financial Management, Journal of International Business Studies, California Management Review, Journal of Financial and Quantitative Analysis, Journal of International Financial Management and Accounting, The Investment Analyst* (U.K.), *Nationaløkonomisk Tidskrift* (Denmark), *Sosialøkonomen* (Norway), *Journal of Financial Education*, and others.

MICHAEL H. MOFFETT

Michael H. Moffett is Associate Professor of Finance at Thunderbird, The American Graduate School of International Management. He was formerly Associate Professor of Finance at Oregon State University (1985–1993). He has also held teaching or research appointments at the University of Michigan, Ann Arbor (1991–1993), the Brookings Institution, Washington, D.C., the University of Hawaii at Manoa, the Aarhus School of Business (Denmark), the Helsinki School of Economics and Business Administration (Finland), the International Centre for Public Enterprises (Yugoslavia), and the University of Colorado, Boulder.

Professor Moffett received a B.A. (Economics) from the University of Texas at Austin (1977), an M.S. (Resource Economics) from Colorado State University (1979), an M.A. (Economics) from the University of Colorado, Boulder (1983), and a Ph.D. (Economics) from the University of Colorado, Boulder (1985).

He has authored, co-authored, or contributed to five books and a dozen other publications. His articles have appeared in the *Journal of Financial and Quantitative Analysis, Journal of Applied Corporate Finance, Journal of International Money and Finance, Journal of International Financial Management and Accounting, Contemporary Policy Issues, Brookings Discussion Papers in International Economics*, and others. He has contributed to a number of collected works, including the *Handbook of Modern Finance*, the *International Accounting and Finance Handbook*, and the *Encyclopedia of International Business*. He is also co-author of two books in multinational business with Michael Czinkota and Ilkka Ronkainen, *International Business* (fifth edition) and *Global Business* (second edition).

BRIEF CONTENTS

CONTENTS

THE INTERNATIONAL FINANCIAL ENVIRONMENT

PART 1 is an introduction to the international economic and political environment that interacts with the *multinational enterprise* (MNE).

CHAPTER 1 describes the unique foreign exchange and political risks faced by MNEs. It also analyzes cultural differences that question the universal acceptability of financial norms, such as the definitions of rate of return and risk. It concludes with an analysis of the motivations that cause MNEs to undertake *foreign direct investment* (FDI) rather than another form of international involvement.

CHAPTER 2 is a description of the international monetary system as it is now and as it evolved through history. It highlights the role of the International Monetary Fund (IMF) and the continuing argument for and against fixed exchange rates. It covers the introduction of a new currency, the *euro*, which is a composite currency for 11 of the 15 members of the European Union. The chapter concludes with three illustrative cases describing the emerging market crises in Thailand, Russia, and Brazil.

CHAPTER 3 analyzes potential exchange rate determinants including parity conditions; infrastructure; speculation; cross-border investment; and political risk. It then presents a generic *balance of payments* (BOP) statement and analyzes the managerial significance of the BOP. Traditional parity conditions are analyzed in depth. The chapter concludes with a description of forecasting practices using the BOP approach, the asset market approach, and technical analysis.

CHAPTER 4 describes the foreign exchange market itself. This includes its geographic extent, its size, market participants, types of instruments, and quotations. The chapter concludes with a description of foreign currency futures contracts and how they differ from outright forward contracts.

CHAPTER 5 describes foreign currency options. It analyzes how these options are used for speculation and details the elements of option valuation and terminology. The option premium is seen to depend on a complex calculation based on the current spot exchange rate, the specific strike rate, the forward rate, interest differentials, currency volatility, and time to maturity.

CHAPTER 1

INTERNATIONAL FINANCIAL MANAGEMENT AND THE MULTINATIONAL FIRM

This book is about international financial management with special emphasis on the *multinational firm*. The multinational enterprise (MNE) is defined as one that has operating subsidiaries, branches, and affiliates located in foreign countries. It includes firms in such traditional fields as manufacturing, mining, oil, and agriculture. It also encompasses firms in service activities such as consulting, accounting, construction, legal, advertising, entertainment, banking, telecommunications, and lodging.

MNEs are headquartered all over the world.[1] Many of them are owned by a mixture of domestic and foreign stockholders. The ownership of some firms is so dispersed internationally that they are known as *transnational corporations*. The transnationals are usually managed from a global perspective rather than from the perspective of any single country.[2]

Although *Multinational Business Finance* (MBF) emphasizes MNEs, purely domestic firms also often have significant international activities. These include the import and export of products, components, and services. Domestic firms can also license foreign firms to conduct their foreign business. They have exposure to foreign competition in their domestic market. They also have indirect exposure to international risks through their relationships with customers and suppliers. Therefore, domestic firm managers need to understand international financial risk, especially those related to foreign exchange rates and the credit risks related to trade payments.

International financial management requires an understanding of certain unique risks that are not normally a threat to domestic operations. These unique risks are related to foreign exchange risks and political risks. MNEs in particular also face other risks that can be classified as extensions of domestic finance theory. For example, the normal domestic approach to the cost of capital, sourcing debt and equity, capital budgeting, working capital management, taxation, and credit analysis needs to be modified to accommodate foreign complexities. Moreover, a number of financial instruments that are used in domestic financial management have been modified for use in international financial management. Examples are foreign currency options and futures, interest rate and currency swaps, and letters of credit.

In the rest of this chapter we identify the main risks facing MNEs. Emphasis is placed on foreign exchange and political risks that are unique to multinational operations. Then we present an international comparison of corporate goals, since this book is directed at multinationals resident in all countries, including not only Anglo-American countries but also other large industrial countries, small industrial countries, and emerging market countries. The chapter concludes with an analysis of why a firm becomes multinational in the first place and addresses the role of market imperfections in facilitating this process.

FOREIGN EXCHANGE RISKS

Foreign exchange risks can raise the cost of capital and lower the optimal debt ratios for MNEs. International portfolio investors require a *foreign exchange risk premium* when valuing the equity and debt of MNEs, especially if those firms are heavily invested in countries with volatile currencies. MNEs resident in such countries may also face a foreign exchange risk premium when they attempt to raise equity or debt abroad. Capital budgeting analyses of foreign projects often require a higher hurdle rate because of the effect of foreign exchange risk on projected cash flows and eventual repatriation of profits and capital. Working capital management is more complex for MNEs because of the impact of foreign exchange risks on moving funds among countries and managing cash, accounts receivable, and inventory. Evaluation of the performance of foreign subsidiaries is more difficult because of the need to account for foreign exchange gains and losses as well as to assign responsibilities for the results.

POLITICAL RISK

Contemporary financial analysis incorporates a *political risk premium* when foreign activities are being evaluated. Banks and investors require a higher rate of return on loans to, and bonds issued by, foreign sovereign entities or corporations when they are resident in relatively unstable countries, or even in emerging market countries. International portfolio investors also require a political risk premium in such markets. MNEs often require a higher required rate of return on foreign projects to reflect a political risk premium. Even working capital management strategies employed by MNEs reflect a political risk premium due to the potential for blocked funds, transfer pricing disagreements, and other government interference with the free flow of funds. Therefore, forecasting political risk and finding strategies to reduce its impact are major concerns of top management of MNEs.

Political risk management refers to steps taken by firms to assess the likelihood of unexpected political events, to anticipate how such events might influence corporate well-being, and to protect against loss (or to attempt to gain) from such events. Exhibit 1.1 shows that political risks can be classified along two dimensions. The first dimension distinguishes between *country-specific*, or macro, risks that affect all foreign firms in a country without regard to what they do. The second dimension is *firm-specific*, or the micro risks that are specific to an industry, a firm, or a project. Country-specific risk is of particular concern to international bankers, who often set overall limits on loans to specific countries based on their perception of country risk. Firm-specific risk is of greater concern for MNEs.

A difference exists between those political events that affect ownership of assets, such as requiring full or partial divestment, and those that affect the operations of a firm and thus its cash flows and returns. Most contemporary political risk for MNEs is firm-specific risk and affects operations rather than ownership. Consequently, political risk seldom leads to violence or a major discontinuity in the firm's operations. Most often, politically inspired changes involve constraints, such as restrictions on the free setting of prices, limitations on the use of expatriate executives or workers, or local content regulations for manufactured goods.

))) Macro Risks

Macro political risks include both expropriation and ethnic strife. *Expropriation* is defined as official government seizure of private property. It is recognized by international law as the right of any sovereign state, provided the expropriated owners are given prompt compensation at fair market value in convertible currencies. Therein lies the rub, for promptness is usually delayed by extensive negotiations and appeals. Fair market value is in the eyes of the beholder, with firms usu-

---

| **Exhibit 1.1** | *Micro-Macro Decomposition of Political Risk* |

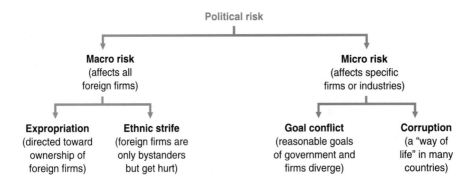

ally arguing for a "going concern" value tied to the pres-ent value of lost future cash flows. Governments frequently argue for depreciated historical book value, which is typically lower. Prompt compensation in convertible currencies is usually difficult, for the kinds of governments given to expropriation do not usually have adequate foreign exchange reserves. Hence so-called payment may be in par value of long-term bonds of dubious current market value.

The decade of the 1990s saw the sudden rise of a second type of macro political risk, caused by ethnic, racial, religious, tribal or civil strife within a country. For example, the economic hardships and disruption of the Asian Crisis contributed to tensions between ethnic and religious groups in Indonesia in 1998 and 1999. Although it is difficult to isolate the individual causes of such political upheaval, there is little doubt that the economic losses associated with the Asian Crisis fueled the fires of Indonesian discontent.

))) Micro Risks

Micro risk is the second major form of contemporary political risk. Most contemporary political risk arises from goal conflict, but political corruption—often tied to nepotism—also contributes to the risk of managing a foreign enterprise. Transparency International (TI) publishes a monthly newsletter on corruption in international business transactions. TI's Corruption Perception Index for 1999 is shown in Exhibit 1.2. This index is based on the level of corruption as perceived by persons working for MNEs and institutions. Thus it is not an index of actual corruption, but rather of perceptions. However, perceptions are what business persons act upon. The score is based on an integrity ranking, where 10 equals an entirely clean country (countries toward the top of the list) and zero equals a country where business transactions are entirely dominated by kickbacks, extortion, bribery, and similar practices. The variance measures the amount of deviation among the opinions received. These kind of indices are often used by firms to help determine a required political risk premium for the activities mentioned earlier.

The most important type of micro risk arises from a conflict between bona fide objectives of governments and private firms. Governments are normally responsive to a constituency consisting of their citizens. Firms are responsive to a constituency consisting of their owners and other stakeholders. The valid needs of these two separate sets of constituents need not be the same, but governments set the rules. Consequently, governments impose constraints on the activities of private firms as part of their normal administrative and legislative functioning.

Historically, conflicts between objectives of MNEs and host governments have arisen over such issues as the firm's impact on economic development, perceived infringement on national sovereignty, foreign control of key industries, sharing or nonsharing of ownership and control with local interests, impact on a host country's balance of payments, influence on the foreign exchange value of its currency, control over export markets, use of domestic versus foreign execu-

Exhibit 1.2			*Transparency International's Corruption Perception Index for 1999*				

Rank	Country	Score	Std Dev	Rank	Country	Score	Std Dev
1	Denmark	10.0	0.7	26	Estonia	5.7	0.5
2	Finland	9.6	0.5	27	Costa Rica	5.6	1.6
3	Sweden	9.5	0.5	28	Belgium	5.4	1.4
4	New Zealand	9.4	0.7	29	Malaysia	5.3	0.4
5	Iceland	9.3	0.9	29	Namibia	5.3	1.0
6	Canada	9.2	0.5	29	Taiwan	5.3	0.7
7	Singapore	9.1	1.0	32	South Africa	5.2	0.8
8	Netherlands	9.0	0.7	33	Hungary	5.0	1.2
8	Norway	9.0	0.7	33	Mauritius	5.0	0.8
10	Switzerland	8.9	0.6	33	Tunisia	5.0	2.1
11	Australia	8.7	0.7	36	Greece	4.9	1.7
11	Luxembourg	8.7	0.9	37	Czech Republic	4.8	0.8
11	United Kingdom	8.7	0.5	38	Jordan	4.7	1.1
14	Ireland	8.2	1.4	39	Italy	4.6	0.8
15	Germany	7.9	0.4	39	Poland	4.6	1.6
16	Hong Kong	7.8	0.5	41	Peru	4.5	0.8
17	Austria	7.5	0.8	42	Uruguay	4.3	0.9
17	United States	7.5	0.9	43	South Korea	4.2	1.2
19	Israel	7.1	1.4	43	Zimbabwe	4.2	2.2
20	Chile	6.8	0.9	45	Malawi	4.1	0.6
21	France	6.7	0.6	46	Brazil	4.0	0.4
22	Portugal	6.5	1.0	47	Belarus	3.9	1.9
23	Botswana	6.1	2.2	47	Slovak Republic	3.9	1.6
23	Spain	6.1	1.3	49	Jamaica	3.8	0.4
25	Japan	5.8	1.6	50	Morocco	3.7	1.8

Source: Transparency International, http://www.transparency.de

tives and workers, and exploitation of natural resources. Attitudes about conflicts are often colored by views about free enterprise versus state socialism, the degree of nationalism or internationalism present, or the place of religious views in determining appropriate economic and financial behavior.

WHAT IS THE GOAL OF MANAGEMENT?

The introductory course in finance is usually taught within the framework of maximizing shareholder's wealth as *the goal of management.* This perspective is dominant not only in the Anglo-American-based courses but also to some extent in basic finance courses taught in the rest of the world.[3] One has only to observe that the same textbooks, or translated versions, are used worldwide. Even when local authors write basic finance textbooks for their own national markets, they still often adopt the same prescriptive model that is used in the Anglo-American markets.

Although the idea of maximizing shareholder wealth is probably realistic both in theory and in practice in the Anglo-American markets, it is not always realistic elsewhere. Some basic differences in corporate and investor philosophies exist between the Anglo-American markets and those in the rest of the world. Therefore, one must realize that the so-called universal truths taught in basic finance courses are actually *culturally determined norms*. If management's goal is unclear, it is obviously not possible to determine what information or criteria, and ultimately what decisions, should be made in financial management.

The Shareholder Wealth Maximization Model

The Anglo-American markets are characterized by a philosophy that a firm's objective should follow the *shareholder wealth maximization* (SWM) model. More specifically, the firm should strive to maximize the return to shareholders, as measured by the sum of capital gains and dividends, for a given level of risk. Alternatively, the firm should minimize the risk to shareholders for a given rate of return.

The SWM model assumes as a universal truth that the stock market is efficient. The share price is always correct because it captures all the expectations of return and risk as seen by investors. It quickly incorporates new information into the share price. Share prices are deemed the best allocators of capital in the macro economy.

The SWM model also treats its definition of risk as a universal truth. Risk is defined as the added risk that the firm's shares bring to a diversified portfolio. The total operational risk of the firm can be eliminated through portfolio diversification by the investors. Therefore, this *unsystematic risk*, the risk of the individual security, should not be a prime concern for management unless it increases the prospect of bankruptcy. *Systematic risk*, the risk of the market in general, cannot be eliminated. This reflects risk that the share price will be a function of the stock market.

The field of *agency theory* is the study of how shareholders can motivate management to accept the prescriptions of the SWM model.[4] For example, liberal use of stock options should encourage management to think like shareholders. Whether these inducements succeed is open to debate. However, if management deviates too much from SWM objectives—of working to maximize the returns to the shareholders—the board of directors should replace them. In cases where the board is too weak or ingrown to take this action, the discipline of the equity markets could do it through a takeover. This discipline is made possible by the *one-share–one-vote rule* that exists in most Anglo-American markets.

The Corporate Wealth Maximization Model

In contrast to the SWM model, Continental European and Japanese equity markets are characterized by a philosophy that a corporation's objective should be to maximize corporate wealth.[5] Thus a firm should treat shareholders on a par with other corporate interest groups, such as management, labor, the local community, suppliers, creditors, and even the government. The goal is to earn as much as possible in the long run, but to retain enough to increase the corporate wealth for the benefit of all interest groups. This model has also been labeled the *stakeholder capitalism model.*

The definition of *corporate wealth* is much broader than just financial wealth, such as cash, marketable securities, and unused credit lines. It includes the firm's technical, market, and human resources. "Consequently, it goes beyond the wealth measured by conventional financial reports to include the firm's market position as well as the knowledge and skill of its employees in technology, manufacturing processes, marketing and administration of the enterprise."[6]

The *corporate wealth maximization* (CWM) model does not assume that equity markets are either efficient or inefficient. It does not really matter because the firm's financial goals are not exclusively shareholder-oriented. In any case, the model assumes the loyal long-term shareholder should influence corporate strategy, not the transient portfolio investor.

The CWM model assumes that *total risk*, that is, operating and financial risk, does count. It is a specific-corporate objective to generate growing earnings and dividends over the long run with as much certainty as possible, given the firm's mission statement and goals. Risk is measured more by product market variability than by short-term variation in earnings and share price. The corporate wealth maximization model was based on a study of 12 large U.S. firms. The study found that the firms actually were corporate wealth maximizers. However, shortly after Donaldson and Lorsch's 1983 book was published, the 1980s were characterized by unfriendly takeovers and leveraged buyouts of even some of the larger U.S. firms. This removed some corporate slack and free cash flow. Many of the corporate wealth maximizers were thereby transformed into shareholder wealth maximizers, and the trend continues today.

))) Corporate Governance

One might wonder why shareholders do not enforce their own objectives when management does not act as their agent. The answer is that the non-Anglo-American markets are not characterized by the corporate one-share–one-vote rule. On the contrary, dual classes of voting shares and restrictions on how many shares can be voted are the norm. Furthermore, many other anti-takeover defenses exist that make it difficult to replace management except by internal pressure from the board of directors.

Exhibit 1.3 presents a survey of takeover defenses in nine non-Anglo-American countries. It shows that dual classes of voting stock are prevalent in eight of the nine countries. The controlling class of stock is usually held by the founders, a foundation, or investors friendly to existing management. Ten other takeover defenses are listed along with the countries in which they are used. Note in particular the importance of strategic alliances (number 8) and close personal relationships (number 9).

Even without formal takeover defenses, the pattern of ownership and corporate governance in many countries has prevented the successful development of a market for corporate control. For example, in Germany and France the largest proportion of gross domestic product is originated in firms that are not publicly listed and whose shares are concentrated in few hands. Many of these firms remain private. Others are controlled by banks, other financial institutions, or other corporations. The banks often have a disproportionate influence because they can vote the proxies of their trust accounts. In Japan, ownership of many groups or *keiretsus* is internal to the group itself. Each member owns shares of the other members. A bank is typically closely involved, both in cross-ownership and as a prime lender. Therefore, an unfriendly merger or acquisition would be very difficult to implement in the ownership environments typified by Germany, France, and Japan.[7]

The emerging market case is even more illustrative. Many of the most prominent firms are owned by the government or by the relatives or friends of top government officials (so-called cronyism). They are often overstaffed because of nepotism and political payoffs. They are often over-financed by banks that are also owned by the same elite group. The emerging market crisis, starting in Asia in 1997 (see Chapter 2), may have shaken this situation considerably, thus leading to more shareholder-wealth-maximizing behavior.

Exhibit 1.3   *Survey of Takeover Defenses in Nine Non-Anglo-American Countries*

Type of Takeover Defense	Countries in Survey in Which the Defense Is Used
1. Dual classes of voting stock	Denmark, France, the Netherlands, Norway, Germany, Switzerland, Finland, Sweden
2. Restrictions on the number of shares that can be voted	Germany, Switzerland, Denmark, Finland, Norway, Sweden
3. Restrictions on foreign ownership of shares	Japan and Switzerland
4. Provisions in the corporate charter that might require a super-majority vote on a takeover bid	Japan, Switzerland, Germany
5. Selling a special issue of voting shares or convertible preferred to "stable" or "friendly" investors	France, Japan, the Netherlands, Norway, Switzerland, Germany
6. Finding a "white knight"	France, the Netherlands, Switzerland
7. Control by a foundation	Denmark, the Netherlands, Switzerland, Finland, Sweden
8. Forming a strategic alliance and/or having interlocking boards of directors	France, Japan, the Netherlands, Norway, Germany, Sweden
9. Relying on a network of close personal relationships, that is, belonging to the "establishment"	Denmark, France, Japan, the Netherlands, Norway, Switzerland, Germany, Finland, Sweden
10. Government regulations controlling competition, and monopolies	France, the Netherlands, Germany, Denmark, Norway, Finland, Sweden
11. Not disclosing ownership levels	All nine countries

The nine countries included in this survey were Denmark, France, Japan, the Netherlands, Norway, Switzerland, Germany, Finland, and Sweden. Sources: Stonehill and Dullum (1990), p. 87; Oxelheim, Stonehill, Randøy, Vikkula, Dullum, and Modén (1998), Chapter 2.

It should also be noted that a number of large multinationals resident outside the Anglo-American countries have had to tap global equity and debt markets to maintain a competitive cost and availability of capital. Since they need to attract international portfolio investors, their behavior has become more shareholder-friendly than before. Some of these firms have even converted to the one-share–one-vote system in response to shareholder demands.[8]

)))) Universal Truth or Culturally Determined Norm?

With respect to the financial goal of the firm, what is a universal truth and what is a culturally determined norm?

1. *Universal truth:* Firms are composed of competing and cooperating stake-holder groups. However, which stakeholder group dominates is a *culturally determined norm*, with a distinct but lessening difference between the Anglo-American markets and those of the rest of the world.

2. *Universal truth:* Most firms try to maximize their return. However, how that return is measured and from whose perspective is a *culturally determined norm*.

3. *Universal truth:* Most firms are risk averse. However, how that risk is measured and from whose perspective is a *culturally determined norm*.

)))) Operational Goals for MNEs

Whether a MNE is trying to maximize shareholder wealth or to maximize corporate wealth, it must be guided by operational goals suitable for various levels of the firm. For example, even if the firm's goal is to maximize shareholder value, the way in which investors value the firm is not always obvious to the firm's top management. Many top executives believe that the stock market moves in mysterious ways and is not always consistent in its conclusions. Therefore, most firms hope to receive a favorable investor response to the achievement of those operational goals that can be controlled by the firm's performance.

The MNE, because it is a collection of many business units operating in a multitude of economic environments, must determine for itself the proper balance between three common operational financial objectives:

1. Maximization of consolidated, after-tax, income

2. Minimization of the firm's effective global tax burden

3. Correct positioning of the firm's income, cash flows, and available funds

These goals are frequently inconsistent, in that the pursuit of one goal may result in a less desirable outcome in regard to another goal. Management must make decisions about the proper tradeoffs between goals about the future (which is why people, not computers, are employed as managers).

The primary operational goal of the MNE is to maximize *consolidated profits*, after-tax. *Consolidated profits* are the profits of all the individual units of the firm, originating in many different currencies but expressed in the currency of

ILLUSTRATIVE CASE

Changing Values: Satisfying Shareholders

Ulrich Hartmann, the chief executive of industrial giant Veba AG, is doing something unheard of in Germany: He's worrying about shareholder value. He has laid off thousands of workers, fired longtime managers, and closed divisions that date back to Veba's beginnings—all in the name of investors. "Our commitment," he said in last year's annual report, "is to create value for you, our shareholders."

The developments at Veba, Germany's fourth-largest company in revenue terms, underscore a trend catching hold in German boardrooms. Mr. Hartmann believes the trend will pick up in Germany, if only, he says, because the pursuit of shareholder value is in everyone's interest. "Satisfying the shareholders is the best way to make sure that other stakeholders are served as well," he says. "It does no good when all the jobs are at sick companies."

But the German public—used to a fabled "German model" of management that advocates describe as "capitalism with a human face"—remains deeply suspicious of the alternative way of doing business. "A number of people are left behind," says Norbert Wieczorek, a member of Germany's lower house of parliament and an economic expert with the opposition Social Democratic Party. "That's not the German way."

Mr. Hartmann is one of a new breed of German managers who are enthusiastically embracing the shareholder-value concept. Others are Juergen Dormann at Hoescht AG and Juergen Schrempp at Daimler-Benz AG. During a recent interview, a secretary interrupted the conversation to notify Mr. Schrempp of Daimler's opening stock price. "A year ago, no one in the company knew what the stock price was," he says. "Now," he adds, "the company keeps stockholders in mind with everything it does."

Driving companies to change are ever-growing capital requirements. Unable to raise enough money in Germany, companies are turning to foreigners. Nearly half the shares of drug companies Hoechst, Bayer AG, and Schering AG are owned by non-Germans, who want more than just a dividend check. "There is no German or French or American capital market anymore," says Veba's Mr. Hartmann. "It is a global capital market, and we all have to play by the same rules."

Adapted from Greg Steinmetz, "Changing Values: Satisfying Shareholders Is a Hot New Concept at Some German Firms," *The Wall Street Journal*, 3/6/96, p. A1, A10.

the parent company. Each of a MNE's foreign subsidiaries has its own set of traditional financial statements: (1) a statement of income, summarizing the revenues and costs accruing to the firm over the year; (2) a balance sheet, summarizing the assets employed in generating the unit's revenues, and the financing of those assets; and (3) a statement of cash flows, summarizing the individual activities of the firm that use and generate cash flows over the year. These financial statements are expressed in the local currency of the unit for tax and reporting purposes to the local government, but must be consolidated with the parent company for reporting to shareholders.

MARKET IMPERFECTIONS: A RATIONALE FOR THE EXISTENCE OF THE MULTINATIONAL FIRM

MNEs strive to take advantage of imperfections in national markets for products, factors of production, and financial assets. Imperfections in the market for products translate into market opportunities for MNEs. Large international firms are better able to exploit such competitive factors as economies of scale, managerial and technological expertise, product differentiation, and financial strength than are their local competitors. In fact, MNEs thrive best in markets characterized by international oligopolistic competition, where these factors are particularly critical. In addition, once MNEs have established a physical presence abroad, they are in a better position than purely domestic firms to identify and implement market opportunities through their own internal information network.

)))) Why Do Firms Become Multinational?

Strategic motives drive the decision to invest abroad. They can be summarized as seeking the following:

1. Markets
2. Raw materials
3. Production efficiency
4. Knowledge
5. Political safety[9]

Market seekers produce in foreign markets either to satisfy local demand or to export to markets other than their home market. U.S. automobile firms manufacturing in Europe for local consumption are an example of market-seeking motivation.

Raw material seekers extract raw materials wherever they can be found, either for export or for further processing and sale in the host country. Firms in the oil, mining, plantation, and forest industries fall into this category.

Production-efficiency seekers produce in countries where one or more of the factors of production are underpriced relative to their productivity. Labor-intensive production of electronic components in Taiwan, Malaysia, and Mexico illustrates this motivation.

Knowledge seekers operate in foreign countries to gain access to technology or managerial expertise. For example, German, Dutch, and Japanese firms have purchased U.S.-located electronics firms for their technology.

Political-safety seekers acquire or establish new operations in countries that are considered unlikely to expropriate or interfere with private enterprise. For example, Hong Kong firms invested heavily in manufacturing, services, and real estate in the United States, Canada, and Australia in anticipation of the consequences of China's 1997 takeover of the British colony.

These five types of strategic considerations are not mutually exclusive. For example, forest products firms seeking wood fiber in Brazil would also find a large Brazilian market for a portion of their output.

In industries characterized by worldwide oligopolistic competition, each of these strategic motives should be subclassified into proactive and defensive investments. *Proactive investments* are designed to enhance the growth and profitability of the firm itself. *Defensive investments* are designed to deny growth and profitability to the firm's competitors. Examples of the latter are investments that try to preempt a market before competitors establish themselves, or that attempt to capture raw material sources in order to deny them to competitors.

)))) Market Seekers and Raw Material Seekers

Market imperfections may occur naturally, but they are usually caused by policies of firms and governments. For example, market-seeking and raw-material-seeking firms in oligopolistic industries seek to create unique competitive advantages through product differentiation and/or preemptive investments to capture foreign raw material sources. Governments create market imperfections through tariff and nontariff barriers to trade, preferential purchasing policies, tax incentives, capital market controls, and similar policies.

One of the most important market imperfections created by governments was the original formation of the European Economic Community (EEC) in 1957 and the European Free Trade Area (EFTA) in 1958. These trade blocs motivated a large influx of foreign direct investment (FDI) from nonmember countries during the latter 1950s, continuing throughout the 1960s. A second wave was motivated by the prospect of the final realization of the Single European Market after 1992.

Opportunities have also been created by governments in developing countries that have large protected markets, such as Brazil, Indonesia, Nigeria, India, and China. At times they have offered MNEs "pioneer" status, which could include tax breaks, tariff protection from later entrants to the market, and subsidized local infrastructure investments. Both market-seeking and raw-material-seeking firms have received such inducements, but these benefits were more common during the colonial era when host governments were under foreign control. It should be noted, however, that government policies to create protected markets can attract FDI only if the market is sufficiently large or protected, to overcome diseconomies of scale from production units of less than optimal size.

Although government policies, oligopolistic competition, or natural barriers may create potentially large, protected markets, foreign firms operating manufacturing plants in these markets must enjoy some competitive advantages not possessed by local firms in order to be compensated for such inherent disadvantages as lack of knowledge about local customs, differing local tastes, and unfamiliar legal systems, as well as greater communication and control costs. Furthermore, the competitive advantages must allow the firm to earn a higher rate of return from FDI than would be earned by similar projects of comparable risk in the home market. If these conditions are not met, the firm will prefer to cover foreign markets through alternative modes of involvement.

))) Defensive Investments

Product and factor market imperfections also create openings for production-efficiency seekers, knowledge seekers, and political-safety seekers.

Product cycle theory. Differentiation with a time lag is the basis for the *product cycle theory*.[10] It suggests that FDI is a natural stage in the life cycle of a new product from inception to maturity and eventual decline. The socioeconomic development, economies of scale, and oligopolistic competition that are found in the most advanced industrial countries lead firms in these countries to undertake intensive research and development efforts. New technologically advanced, or distinctive, products are discovered.

The new products are first introduced in the home market. Close coordination of production and sales is required while the product is improved and the production process standardized. After a short time lag, the product is exported. As the new product reaches maturity, competition from nearly similar products narrows profit margins and threatens both export and the home markets.

At this stage foreign manufacturing locations are sought where market imperfections in the cost of factors of production create a chance for lower unit production costs. Thus the foreign investment is essentially a defensive investment designed to preserve profit margins in both export and home markets.

Examples of defensive investments can be found in many labor-intensive less-developed countries. For example, the price of labor in Mexico, Puerto Rico, China, and Indonesia is low for its productivity.[11] This feature has attracted FDI in labor-intensive industries. If laborers in these countries earn the local currency equivalent of $2.50 per hour and are as productive as their U.S. counterparts, who earn $7.50 per hour, a firm can cut its per-unit labor cost by two-thirds. Of course, other factors of production, such as shipping, tariffs, equipment, plant, and land, may cost much more in these countries, thereby offsetting the labor differential. Furthermore, over time labor costs may increase more rapidly in these countries than in the United States because of foreign demand for their services. In the meantime, however, a temporary market imperfection for labor exists and attracts FDI. Although the product cycle theory initiated the idea of defensive investments, many other theories of defensive investments followed.

Follow the Leader. According to the *follow-the-leader theory* of defensive FDI, when one competitor in an oligopolistic industry undertakes a FDI, other competitors follow very quickly with defensive FDI into that market.[12] The followers are motivated by a desire to deny any competitive advantages, such as the benefits of economies of scale, to the others.

This theory does not explain why the leader initiates the original FDI, but presumably the motivation is similar to those of the followers. For example, firms are observed entering potentially large markets prematurely with FDI, in an attempt to gain economies of scale and preempt economies of scale from the other competitors. Some of the manufacturing investments in large, growing, less-developed countries fall into this category. Even in countries where the size and growth potential of the market are permanently limited, MNEs will make direct investments or acquisitions of firms that are riskier and less profitable than themselves. There is a favorable impact on their economies of scale and diversification of risk for the firms as a whole, and denial of these advantages to other oligopolistic competitors. Multinationals sometimes make FDI of a defensive nature in the home markets of competitors, even though such investments appear in accounting statements to be unprofitable. The purpose is to disrupt the easy market share of competitors in their home market in order to reduce their economies of scale and thereby their competitiveness in other markets. U.S., European, and Japanese automobile manufacturing firms have sometimes considered defensive investments in each other's markets in this light.

Defensive investments are even more apparent in the raw-material-producing industries, such as in oil, tin, copper, bauxite, rubber, and forest products. Control over sources of raw material, and conversely denial of these sources to competitors, causes a number of preemptive, defensive-type investments, similar to those of market-seeking oligopolists.

Another characteristic that is an important motivation for FDI in raw materials is the need to develop economies of scale through both horizontal and vertical integration. The raw materials are typically just one stage in a multistage production process reaching all the way from raw materials to final consumers. The independents who perform only one stage in the process are often in a poor bargaining position. The fully integrated producers have alternative sources of supply and control the final markets. Thus, although an investment in raw materials may not be profitable in itself, it creates a real option, i.e., the opportunity for downstream profits that are not available to the independents.

Credibility. Defensive investments also occur when credibility with an existing customer base becomes important. For example, this factor motivated a Danish firm, Novo Industri, A/S (Novo), to establish a plant to manufacture industrial enzymes in North Carolina in the United States.[13] Novo enjoyed a large export market for industrial enzymes in the United States. However, enzymes are intermediate products that are used in the production of such end products as detergents and fructose. Quality control and guaranteed availability are critical in the continuous processes employed in such industries. Therefore, despite the loss of economies of scale in Denmark, and suboptimal economies of scale in the United States, Novo felt obligated to establish a manufacturing presence in the United States to maintain its credibility in the marketplace.

Growth to Survive. Another version of defensive investments suggests that firms invest abroad because they have saturated the domestic market, and any further expansion domestically would lead to destructive retaliation by the other oligopolists or antitrust action (in the United States).[14] Growth abroad, through either new investments or acquisitions, is the natural reaction of firms that have a "grow to survive" attitude. In these firms, however, there could also be an intuitive understanding that growth leads to improving economies of scale relative to competitors and therefore ultimately to superior financial performance. The current wave of mergers and acquisitions to establish a global presence provides further evidence of a growth-to-survive motivation for FDI.

Knowledge Seekers. MNEs that have been identified as knowledge seekers provide still another example of defensive investments. These are firms trying to maintain or acquire a better position in one or more of the key competitive variables. In particular, they are trying to improve managerial expertise, technology, or knowledge of product and factor markets. This goal is accomplished most efficiently by acquisition of foreign firms that already possess some of these attributes. There may also be an element of improving economies of scale and financial strength in these types of acquisitions.

Follow the Customer. The growing presence abroad of service firms is a final example of defensive investments. Banking, advertising, legal, consulting, and accounting firms have typically followed their clients abroad. Their motivation is to counter efforts by other international and local service firms to steal their clients. They are forced to invest in facilities and staff in key foreign locations both for credibility and for convenience.

SUMMARY

The field of multinational business finance is something of a blend, a *borscht*, a stew, a chowder, which blends elements of corporate finance with international economics. However, it is not merely an extension of these fields using international examples. On the contrary, it challenges some of the basic concepts of these fields.

- MNEs face unique risks that do not hamper domestic firms as much. These risks are related to *foreign exchange risks* and *political risks*.
- Foreign exchange risks for MNEs might raise their cost of capital and lower their optimal debt ratios.

- Foreign exchange risks cause MNEs to alter—typically upward—their hurdle rates for projects located in countries with volatile currencies and economies.

- MNEs face political risk premiums on their activities in unstable or emerging overseas markets. Political risk premiums may increase the cost of debt and equity for MNEs resident in such markets.

- Most political risk arises because of a conflict in goals between host governments and firms when the normal functioning of governmental administrative and legislative processes leads to regulations that influence the well-being of the firm.

- In recent years, ethnic, religious, racial, and civic strife have added another dimension to the political risks faced by MNEs.

- Most political risk events are micro in nature and project-specific, affecting only certain firms in certain industries rather than all foreign firms.

- The definitions of *rate of return* and *risk* may not be universally accepted. Indeed, they may be culturally determined norms, varying by country. In Anglo-American markets, the *shareholder wealth maximization* (SWM) model is the culturally determined norm. In non-Anglo-American markets, the *corporate wealth maximization* (CWM) model may be the culturally determined norm. There are distinct differences between these models with respect to the treatment of risk and rate of return.

- One reason that such differences exist is the one-share–one-vote rule. In the SWM model, it provides the means to discipline management in case it does not act in the shareholders' interests. In the CWM model, the one-share–one-vote rule is not the norm. Moreover, many takeover defenses exist, making it more difficult to discipline management except by internal pressure.

- MNEs are usually welcome in host countries to the extent that they transfer technology, market access, and investment capital.

- Market imperfections provide the rationale for the continued prosperity of MNEs. This rationale allows MNEs to make abnormal profits and to reduce risk though diversification.

- As MNEs become more dependent on global capital markets for financing, they may need to modify their policies of corporate governance. A trend exists for firms resident in non-Anglo-American markets to move toward being more stockholder friendly. Simultaneously, firms from the Anglo-American markets may be moving toward being more stakeholder friendly.

- The FDI decision results from a complex process involving strategic, behavioral, and economic considerations.

- The decision on whether to invest abroad at all is driven by strategic motives that can be classified as seeking markets, raw materials, production efficiency, knowledge, and political safety.

QUESTIONS

1. The Risks of Multinational Business
Multinational business is risky. Explain the difference between macro political risk, micro political risk, country-specific risk, and firm-specific risk.

2. Corporate Wealth versus Shareholder Wealth Maximization
Before executives can "manage," they must be clear on the goals to be pursued, both personal and corporate. The two major philosophies described in the chapter, shareholder wealth maximization and corporate wealth maximization, could lead a firm's management to make very different decisions.

a.   A leveraged buyout is a financial maneuver in which a group of investors gains control of a firm and then liquidates its assets (i.e., disposes of all or a part of the company's productive assets) in order to pay off the purchase price. How would this be perceived in a country that believed in corporate wealth maximization? In a country that believed in shareholder wealth maximization?

b.   In an interlocking directorate, the members of the governing board of one firm also sit on the governing board of a second firm. How is this practice likely to be perceived under the two philosophies of SWM and CWM?

c.   In some countries, labor unions are represented on boards of directors by virtue of statutes that prescribe such membership. How might this help serve the goals of either of the two philosophies? How might it be detrimental to those goals?

d.   How would each philosophy view a strategy of employing high leverage? Under which model is leverage likely to be higher?

e.   How would each philosophy view a strategy of diversification that creates a conglomerate?

f.   How would each philosophy view a strategy to achieve focus by divesting some operations?

3. Universal Principles versus Culturally Determined Norms
Explain whether the following financial tasks are actually guided by universal principles or culturally determined norms:

a.   Calculating the discount rate to be used in a capital budgeting analysis

b.   Determining the optimal mix of debt and equity for a firm's financial structure

c.   Establishing what proportion of net profits is to be distributed to shareholders and what proportion is to be retained by the firm for future growth needs (dividend policy)

4. One-Share–One-Vote versus Dual Classes of Stock
The U.S. Securities and Exchange Commission has recently reaffirmed the

desirability of U.S. firms pursuing a one-share–one-vote policy. On the other hand, many European companies have two types of share capital, A and B shares, with different voting rights. Why do you believe Europeans allow this differential in voting rights?

5. Japanese Financial Goals

It is widely believed that the goal of most large Japanese companies is to maximize corporate wealth in the long run. The survival of the firm is paramount, rather than maximizing shareholder wealth. What are the characteristics of the Japanese society and business system that have made corporate wealth maximization a more desirable goal than shareholder wealth? Is it still so today, or are Japanese firms becoming a little more shareholder-oriented?

6. MNE Motives

MNEs undertake foreign direct investment for different reasons. Match the following list of motivations with the list of MNEs (counting only the main motive).

Motives	*MNEs*
Market seekers	Hewlett-Packard
Raw material seekers	Coca Cola
Production efficiency seekers	BP Amoco
Knowledge seekers	NEC (Nippon Electric of Japan)
Political-safety seekers	Jardine Matheson (Hong Kong)

 WORLD WIDE WEB EXERCISES

Note: The Web changes rapidly, so by the time you read this, some of the URLs in this book may be out of date. If you encounter a bad URL, check this book's Web site for an update.

W1. Multinational Firms and Global Assets/Income

The differences among MNEs are striking. Using a sample of firms such as those listed here, pull from their individual web pages the proportions of their incomes that are earned outside their country of incorporation. (Note how Nestlé calls itself a "transnational company.")

Walt Disney	http://www.disney.com/
Nestlé S.A.	http://www.nestle.com/
Intel	http://www.intel.com/
Daimler-Chrysler	http://www.daimlerchrysler.de
Mitsubishi Motors	http://www.mitsubishi.com/
Nokia	http://www.nokia.com/
Royal Dutch/Shell	http://www.shell.com/

Also note the way in which international business is now conducted via the Internet. Several of the above home pages allow the user to choose the language of the presentation viewed.

W2. Corporate Governance

There is no hotter topic in business today than corporate governance. Use the following site to view recent research, current events and news items, and other information related to the relationships between a business and its stakeholders.

Corporate Governance Net   http://www.corpgov.net/

SUGGESTED READINGS

Kaplan, Steven, "Corporate Governance and Corporate Performance: A Comparison of Germany, Japan, and the U.S.," *Journal of Applied Corporate Finance*, Winter 1997, Vol. 9, No. 4, pp. 86–93.

Jensen, Michael, "Agency Cost of Free Cash Flow, Corporate Finance and Takeovers, *American Economic Review*, 76, 1986, pp. 323–329.

Jensen, Michael, and W. Meckling, "Theory of the Firm: Managerial Behavior, Agency Costs, and Ownership Structure," *Journal of Financial Economics*, No. 3, 1976, pp. 305–360.

Pedersen, Torben, and Steen Thomsen, "European Patterns of Corporate Ownership," *Journal of International Business Studies*, Vol. 28, No. 4, Fourth Quarter, 1997, pp. 759–778.

NOTES

1. For a listing of MNEs see the website for this book: *http://awl.com/eiteman/*
2. Although *Multinational Business Finance* (MBF) is written in English and usually uses the U.S. dollar in its exposition, the authors have tried to make it relevant for all multinationals by using numerous non-U.S. based multinationals as examples. In fact, almost half of MBF's sales are outside of the United States. Sales of MBF in the emerging markets in Asia, Latin America, and Eastern Europe have made up a growing market segment.
3. *Anglo-American* is defined to mean the United States, United Kingdom, Canada, Australia, and New Zealand.
4. Jensen and Meckling (1976) and Jensen (1986).
5. Donaldson and Lorsch (1983).
6. Ibid, pp. 162–163.
7. Kaplan (1997), Franks and Mayer (1997).
8. For example, in 1999, Nokia, the Finnish telecommunications company, converted all their share classes to one class with one-share–one-vote voting rights.
9. The first four classifications were suggested in Hogue (1967), pp. 1–2. They were also contained in Nehrt and Hogue (1968), pp. 43–48.
10. Vernon, 1966.

11. An empirical example of the product cycle theory, as it applies to defensive investments in offshore plants by U.S. firms, can be found in Moxon (1975).

12. A good synthesis of oligopoly theory and its relation to MNEs can be found in Knickerbocker (1973).

13. This information came from a close working relationship between one of the authors and officials of the firm.

14. For studies of the "growth" version of international oligopoly theory, see Belassa (1966) and Hymer and Rowthorn (1970).

CHAPTER 2

THE INTERNATIONAL MONETARY ENVIRONMENT

The increased volatility of exchange rates is one of the main economic developments of the past 30 years. Under the current system of partly floating and partly fixed exchange rates, the earnings of multinational firms, banks, and individual investors have been subjected to significant real and paper fluctuations as a result of changes in relative exchange rates. Policies to forecast and react to exchange rate fluctuations are still evolving as understanding of the functioning of the international monetary system grows, as accounting and tax rules for foreign exchange gains and losses become clarified, and as the economic effect of exchange rate changes on future cash flows and market values becomes recognized.

Although volatile exchange rates may increase risk, they also create profit opportunities for both firms and investors, given a proper understanding of exchange risk management. In order to manage foreign exchange risk, however, management must first understand how the international monetary system functions. The *international monetary system* can be defined as the structure within which foreign exchange rates are determined, international trade and capital flows are accommodated, and balance of payments adjustments made. It also includes all the instruments, institutions, and agreements that link together the world's currency, money markets, securities, real estate, and commodity markets.

CURRENCY TERMINOLOGY

Certain other terms need to be defined in order to increase your understanding of this chapter. All the material stems from the literature on international economics, rather than from finance or business administration in general.

- A *foreign currency exchange rate*, or simply *exchange rate*, is the price of one country's currency in units of another currency or commodity (typically gold or silver). If the government of a country—for example, Argentina—regulates the rate at which the peso is exchanged for other currencies, the system or *regime* is classified as a *fixed* or *managed exchange rate regime*. The rate at which the currency is fixed, or pegged, is frequently referred to as its *par value*. If the government does not interfere in the valuation of its currency in any way, the currency is classified as *floating* or *flexible*.

- *Spot exchange rate* is the quoted price for foreign exchange to be delivered at once, or in two days for interbank transactions. For example, ¥114/$ is a quote for the exchange rate between the Japanese yen and the U.S. dollar. It takes 114 yen to buy one U.S. dollar for immediate delivery.

- *Forward rate* is the quoted price for foreign exchange to be delivered at a specified date in the future. For example, assume the 90-day forward rate for the Japanese yen is quoted as ¥112/$. No currency is exchanged today, but in 90 days it will take 112 yen to buy one U.S. dollar. This rate can be guaranteed by a *forward exchange contract*.

- *Forward premium or discount* is the percentage difference between the spot and forward exchange rate. To calculate this, using the quotes from above, one formula is

$$\frac{S - F}{F} \times \frac{360}{n} \times 100 = \frac{\yen 114 \neq \$ - \yen 112 \neq \$}{\yen 112 \neq \$} \times \frac{360}{90} \times 100 = 7.14\%$$

where *S* is the spot exchange rate, *F* is the forward rate, and *n* is the number of days until the forward contract becomes due.

- *Devaluation* of a currency refers to a drop in foreign exchange value of a currency that is pegged to gold or to another currency. In other words, the par value is reduced. The opposite of devaluation is *revaluation*.

- *Weakening*, *deterioration*, or *depreciation* of a currency refers to a drop in the foreign exchange value of a floating currency. The opposite of weakening is *strengthening* or *appreciating*, which refers to a gain in the exchange value of a floating currency.

- *Soft* or *weak* describes a currency that is expected to devalue or depreciate relative to major currencies. It also refers to currencies whose values are being artificially sustained by their governments. A currency is considered *hard* if it is expected to revalue or appreciate relative to major trading currencies.

- *Eurocurrencies* are sometimes viewed as another kind of money, although in reality they are domestic currencies of one country on deposit in a second country. Their value is identical to that of the same currency at home. For example, a *Eurodollar* is a U.S. dollar-denominated interest-bearing deposit in a bank outside the United States. A *Euroyen* is a yen-denominated deposit in a bank outside Japan. The bank may be a foreign bank or the overseas branch of a U.S. bank.

This chapter begins with a brief history of the international monetary system from the days of the classical gold standard to the present time. This is followed by an analysis of contemporary currency regimes and the relative advantages of fixed versus floating rate systems. The most recent currency regime is the launching of the *euro*, a common currency for 11 of the 15 countries that are members of the European Union. Next comes an analysis of the emerging market crisis that began in July 1997. This crisis is illustrated through three case studies that cover the Asian, Russian, and Brazilian crises.

HISTORY OF THE INTERNATIONAL MONETARY SYSTEM

Over the ages, currencies have been defined in terms of gold and other items of value, and the international monetary system has been subject to a variety of international agreements. A brief history of these systems provides useful perspective against which to compare today's system and to evaluate weaknesses and proposed changes in the present system.

))) The Gold Standard, 1876–1913

Currencies have not always been pegged to other currencies, or to baskets of goods, or even allowed to float freely. Since the days of the Pharaohs (about 3000 B.C.), gold was used as a medium of exchange and a store of value. The Greeks and Romans used gold coins and passed on this tradition through the mercantile era to the nineteenth century. The great increase in trade during the free-trade period of the late nineteenth century led to a need for a more formalized system for settling international trade balances. One country after another set a par value for its currency in terms of gold and then tried to adhere to the "rules of the game," of what later came to be known as the classical gold standard. The *gold standard* as an international monetary system gained acceptance in Western Europe in the 1870s. The United States was something of a latecomer to the system, not officially adopting the standard until 1879.

The "rules of the game" under the gold standard were clear and simple. Each country set the rate at which its currency (paper or coin) could be converted to a weight of gold. The United States, for example, declared the dollar to be convertible to gold at a rate of $20.67/ounce of gold (a rate in effect until the beginning of World War I). The British pound was pegged at £4.2474/ounce of gold. As long as both currencies were freely convertible into gold, the dollar/pound exchange rate was:

$$\frac{\$20.67/\text{ounce of gold}}{£4.2474/\text{ounce of gold}} = \$4.8665/£$$

Because the government of each country on the gold standard agreed to buy or sell gold on demand to anyone at its own fixed parity rate, the value of each individual currency in terms of gold, and therefore the fixed parities between currencies, was set. Under this system it was very important for a country to maintain adequate reserves of gold to back its currency's value. The system also had the effect of implicitly limiting the rate at which any individual country could expand its money supply. The growth in money was limited to the rate at which additional gold could be acquired by official authorities.

The gold standard worked adequately until the outbreak of World War I interrupted trade flows and the free movement of gold. This caused the main trading nations to suspend the operation of the gold standard.

))) The Interwar Years and World War II, 1914–1944

During World War I and the early 1920s, currencies were allowed to fluctuate over fairly wide ranges in terms of gold and each other. Theoretically, supply and demand for a country's exports and imports caused moderate changes in an exchange rate about a central equilibrium value. This was the same function that gold had performed under the previous gold standard. Unfortunately, such flexible exchange rates did not work in an equilibrating manner. On the contrary, international speculators sold the weak currencies short,[1] causing them to fall further in value than warranted by the real economic factors. The reverse happened with strong currencies. Fluctuations in currency values could not be offset by the relatively thin forward exchange market except at exorbitant cost. The net result was that the volume of world trade did not grow in the 1920s in proportion to world gross national product and declined to a very low level with the advent of the Great Depression in the 1930s.

The United States adopted a *modified gold standard* in 1934 when the U.S. dollar was devalued to $35/ounce of gold from the $20.67/ounce price in effect prior to World War I. Gold was traded only with foreign central banks, not private citizens. From 1934 to the end of World War II, exchange rates were theoretically determined by each currency's value in terms of gold. During World War II and its immediate aftermath, however, many of the main trading currencies lost their convertibility into other currencies. The dollar was the only major trading currency that continued to be convertible.

))) Bretton Woods and the International Monetary Fund, 1944

In 1944, as World War II drew toward a close, the Allied Powers met at Bretton Woods, New Hampshire, in order to create a new post-war international monetary system. The *Bretton Woods Agreement* established a U.S. dollar-based international monetary system and provided for two new institutions, the International Monetary Fund and the World Bank. The *International Monetary Fund* (IMF) aids countries with balance of payments and exchange rate problems. The International Bank for Reconstruction and Development (*World Bank*) helped post-war reconstruction and since then has supported general economic development.

The IMF was the key institution in the new international monetary system, and it has remained so to the present. The IMF was established to render temporary assistance to member countries trying to defend their currencies against cyclical, seasonal, or random occurrences. It also assists countries having structural trade problems if they take adequate steps to correct their problems. However, if persistent deficits occur, the IMF cannot save a country from eventual devaluation. In recent years it has attempted to help countries facing financial crises. It has provided massive loans as well as advice to Russia and other former Russian republics, Brazil, Indonesia, and South Korea, to name but a few.

Under the original provisions of the Bretton Woods Agreement, all countries fixed the value of their currencies in terms of gold but were not required to exchange their currencies for gold. Only the dollar remained convertible into gold (at $35 per ounce). Therefore, each country decided what it wished its exchange rate to be vis-à-vis the dollar and then calculated the gold par value of its currency to create the desired dollar exchange rate. Participating countries agreed to try to maintain the value of their currencies within 1% (later expanded to 2¼%) of par by buying or selling foreign exchange or gold as needed. Devaluation was not to be used as a competitive trade policy, but if a currency became too weak to defend, a devaluation of up to 10% was allowed without formal approval by the IMF. Larger devaluations required IMF approval.

The *Special Drawing Right* (SDR) is an international reserve asset created by the IMF to supplement existing foreign exchange reserves. It serves as a unit of account for the IMF and other international and regional organizations, and it is also the base against which some countries peg the rate of exchange for their currencies.

Defined initially in terms of a fixed quantity of gold, the SDR has been redefined several times. It is currently the weighted value of currencies of the five IMF members having the largest exports of goods and services. Individual countries hold SDRs in the form of deposits in the IMF. These holdings are part of each country's international monetary reserves, along with official holdings of gold, foreign exchange, and its reserve position at the IMF. Members may settle transactions among themselves by transferring SDRs.

))) Fixed Exchange Rates, 1945–1973

The currency arrangement negotiated at Bretton Woods and monitored by the IMF worked fairly well during the post-World War II period of reconstruction and rapid growth in world trade. However, widely diverging national monetary and fiscal policies, differential rates of inflation, and various unexpected external shocks eventually resulted in the system's demise. The U.S. dollar was the main reserve currency held by central banks and was the key to the web of exchange rate values. Unfortunately, the United States ran persistent and growing deficits on its balance of payments. A heavy capital outflow of dollars was required to finance these deficits and to meet the growing demand for dollars from investors and businesses. Eventually, the heavy overhang of dollars held abroad resulted in a lack of confidence in the ability of the United States to meet its commitment to convert dollars to gold.

On August 15, 1971, President Richard Nixon was forced to suspend official purchases or sales of gold by the U.S. Treasury after the United States suffered outflows of roughly one-third of its official gold reserves in the first seven months of the year. Exchange rates of most of the leading trading countries were allowed to float in relation to the dollar and thus indirectly in relation to gold. By the end of 1971 most of the major trading currencies had appreciated vis-à-vis the dollar. This change was—in effect—a devaluation of the dollar.

In early 1973, the U.S. dollar came under attack once again, thereby forcing a second devaluation on February 12, 1973, this time by 10% to $42.22 per ounce. By late February 1973, a fixed-rate system no longer appeared feasible given the speculative flows of currencies. The major foreign exchange markets were actually closed for several weeks in March 1973. When they reopened, most currencies were allowed to float to levels determined by market forces. Par values were left unchanged. The dollar had floated downward an average of 10% by June 1973.

))) An Eclectic Currency Arrangement, 1973–Present

Since March 1973, exchange rates have become much more volatile and less predictable than they were during the "fixed" exchange rate period, when changes occurred infrequently. In general the dollar has been volatile and has weakened somewhat over the long run. On the other hand, the Japanese yen and German mark have strengthened. The emerging market currencies have been exceptionally volatile and have generally weakened.

Exhibit 2.1 summarizes the key events and external shocks that have affected currency values since March 1973. The most important shocks were, in chronological order, the oil crisis of late 1973, loss of confidence in the U.S. dollar in 1977 and 1978, the second oil crisis in 1979, formation of the European Monetary System (EMS) in 1979, diversification of foreign exchange reserves by central banks starting in 1979, and the strength of the U.S. dollar during the period 1981 to 1985, followed by a rapid decline in the value of the U.S. dollar from February 1985 until early 1988.

The 1990s were tumultuous for currencies. The EMS suffered a significant crisis and restructuring in 1992 and 1993. This was followed by a series of emerging market currency crises, including that of Mexico in 1994, Thailand in 1997 (followed by a number of other Asian currencies), Russia in 1998, and Brazil in 1999.

CONTEMPORARY CURRENCY REGIMES

The international monetary system is composed of national currencies, two artificial currencies (the SDR and the European Currency Unit—the ECU), and one

Exhibit 2.1	*World Currency Events, 1973–2000*	
Date	**Event**	**Impact**
August 1971	Dollar floated	Nixon closes the U.S. gold window, suspending purchases or sales of gold by U.S. Treasury; temporary imposition of 10% import surcharge.
December 1971	Smithsonian Agreement	Group of Ten reaches compromise whereby the US$ is devalued to $38/oz of gold; most other major currencies are appreciated versus US$.
February 1973	U.S. dollar devalued	Devaluation pressure increases on US$ forcing further devaluation to $42.22/oz of gold.
Feb–March 1973	Currency markets in crisis	Fixed exchange rates no longer considered defensible; speculative pressures force closure of international foreign exchange markets for nearly two weeks; markets reopen on floating rates for major industrial currencies.
June 1973	U.S. dollar depreciation	Floating rates continue to drive the now freely floating US$ down by about 10% by June.
Fall 1973–1974	OPEC oil embargo	Organization of Petroleum Exporting Countries (OPEC) impose oil-embargo, eventually quadrupling the world price of oil; because world oil prices are stated in US$, value of US$ recovers some former strength.
January 1976	Jamaica Agreement	IMF meeting in Jamaica results in the "legalization" of the floating exchange rate system already in effect; gold is demonetized as a reserve asset.
1977–1978	U.S. inflation rate rises	Carter administration reduces unemployment at the expense of inflation increases; rising U.S. inflation causes continued depreciation of the US$.
March 1979	EMS created	European Monetary System (EMS) is created, establishing a cooperative exchange rate system for participating members of the EEC.
Summer 1979	OPEC raises prices	OPEC nations raise price of oil once again.
Spring 1980	U.S. dollar begins rise	Worldwide inflation and early signs of recession coupled with real interest differential advantages for dollar-denominated assets contribute to increased demand for dollars.
August 1982	Latin American debt crisis	Mexico informs U.S. Treasury on Friday 13, 1982, that it will be unable to make debt service payments; Brazil and Argentina follow in months.
February 1985	U.S. dollar peaks	The U.S. dollar peaks against most major industrial currencies, hitting record highs against the Deutschemark and other European currencies.

composite currency (the euro) that replaced the 11 national European currencies on January 1, 1999. All these currencies are linked to one another via a smorgasbord of currency regimes. Exhibit 2.2 presents the various exchange rate arrangements and anchors of monetary policy. It shows that there are at least eight different exchange rate regimes.

The spectrum of exchange rate regimes runs from rigidly fixed to independently floating. The most prominent example of a rigidly fixed system is the *euro area*, in which the euro is the single currency for its 11 member countries (See

Date	Event	Impact

Exhibit 2.1   *World Currency Events, 1973–2000 (continued)*

Date	Event	Impact
February 1987	Louvre Accords	Group of Six members state they will "intensify" economic policy coordination to promote growth and reduce external imbalances.
September 1992	EMS crisis	High German interest rates induce massive capital flows into Deutschemark- denominated assets causing the withdrawal of the Italian lira and British pound from the EMS's common float.
July 31, 1993	EMS realignment	EMS adjusts allowable deviation band to ±15% for all member countries (except the Dutch guilder); U.S. dollar continues to weaken; Japanese yen reaches ¥100.25/$.
1994	EMI founded	European Monetary Institute (EMI), the predecessor to the European Central Bank, is founded in Frankfurt, Germany.
December 1994	Peso collapse	Mexican peso suffers major devaluation as a result of increasing pressure on the managed devaluation policy; peso falls from Ps3.46/$ to Ps5.50/$ within days. The peso's collapse results in a fall in most major Latin American exchanges in a contagion process (the tequila effect).
August 1995	Yen peaks	Japanese yen reaches an all-time high versus the U.S. dollar of ¥79/$; yen slowly depreciates over the following two-year period, rising to over ¥130/$.
June 1997	Asian crisis	The Thai baht is devalued in July, followed soon after by the Indonesian rupiah, Korean won, Malaysian ringgit, and Philippine peso. Following the initial exchange rate devaluations, the Asian economy plummets into recession.
August 1998	Russian crisis	On Monday, August 17, the Russian Central Bank devalued the ruble by 34%. The ruble continued to deteriorate in the following days sending the already weak Russian economy into recession.
January 1, 1999	Euro launched	Official launch date for the single European currency, the euro. 11 European Union member states elect to participate in the system, which irrevocably locks their individual currencies rates to each other.
January 1999	Brazilian real	The real, initially devalued 8.3% by the Brazilian government on January 12th, was subsequently allowed to float against the world's currencies.
January 1, 2002	Euro coinage	Euro coins and notes will be introduced in parallel with home currencies. National currencies will be phased-out during the six month period beginning January 1.

the first category, exchange arrangements with no separate legal tender, in Exhibit 2.2.) At the other extreme are 48 countries with independently floating currencies. These include many of the most developed countries such as Japan, the United States, the United Kingdom, Canada, Australia, New Zealand, Sweden, and Switzerland. However, it also includes many emerging market countries that tried to maintain fixed rates but were forced to let them float. Among these are Korea, the Philippines, Brazil, Indonesia, Mexico, Thailand, and Ecuador.

Exhibit 2.2	*Global Exchange Rate Regimes*

Regime	Participants

Exchange Arrangement (38)	**2nd Currency**	**ECCM**	**WAEMU**	**CAEMO**	**Euro Area**
	Kiribati	Antigua	Benin	Cameroon	Austria
	Marshall Islands	Barbuda	Burkina Faso	C. African Rep	Belgium
	Micronesia	Domingez	Cote d'Ivoire	Chad	Finland
	Palau	Grenada	Guinea-Bisbau	Congo, The	France
	Panama	St. Kitts/ Nevis	Mali	Equatorial Guinea	Germany
	San Marino	St. Lucia	Niger	Gibon	Ireland
		St. Vincent &	Senegal		Italy
		Grenadines	Togo		Luxembourg
					Netherlands
					Portugal
					Spain

Currency Board (8)				
	Argentina	Brunei Darussalam	China: Hong Kong	Estonia
	Bosnia Herzegovina	Bulgaria	Djibouti	Lithuania

Fixed Peg (44)	Against a Single Currency			Against a Composite
	Aruba	Iraq	Qatar	Botswana
	Bahamas, The	Jordan	Saudi Arabia	Burundi
	Bahrain	Lebanon	Syrian Arab Rep.	Fiji
	Belize	Lesotho	Swaziland	Kuwait
	Bhutan	Macedonia	Trinidad & Tobago	Latvia
	Cape Verde	Malaysia	Turkmenistan	Malta
	China, P.R.	Maldives	United Arab Emirates	Morocco
	Comoro	Namibia		Myanmar
	Egypt	Nepal		Samoa
	El Salvador	Neth Antilles		Seychelles
	Iran	Oman		Solomon Islands
				Tonga
				Vanuatu

Pegged Rate Within Horizontal Bands (7)			
	Croatia	Libya, AJ	**ERM II**
	Cyprus	Ukraine	Greece
	Iceland		Denmark

Crawling Pegs (3)	
	Angola
	Costa Rica
	Nicaragua

Crawling Bands (8)				
	Colombia	Hungary	Poland	Uruguay
	Honduras	Israel	Sri Lanka	Venezuela

Managed Floating (25)				
	Algeria	Kazakhstan	Nigeria	Slovak Republic
	Azerbaijan	Kenya	Norway	Slovenia
	Belarus	Krygyz, Rep.	Pakistan	Suriname
	Cambodia	Jamaica	Paraguay	Uzbekistan
	Czech Republic	Lao, PDR	Romania	
	Dominican Rep.	Malawi	Russian Federation	
	Ethiopia	Mauritania	Singapore	

Source: *International Financial Statistics*, International Monetary Fund, Washington DC, Monthly, July 1999.

Exhibit 2.2	*Global Exchange Rate Regimes (continued)*

Regime	Participants			
Independent *Floating* **(48)**	Afghanistan Albania Armenia Australia Brazil Canada Congo, Dem. Rep Ecuador Gambia, The Georgia Ghana Guinea Guyana	Guatemala Haiti Indonesia India Japan Korea Liberia Madagascar Mexico Moldova Mongolia Mozambique Mauritius New Zealand	Papua New Guinea Peru Philippines, The Rwanda Sao Tome & Principe Sierra Leone Somalia South Africa South Africa Sweden Switzerland Somalia Sudan Tanzania Thailand	Uganda United Kingdom United States Yemen, Rep. of Zambia Zimbabwe

ECCM is East Caribbean Common Market; WAEMU is the West African Economic and Monetary Union; CAEMO is the Central African Economic and Monetary Community. The WAEMU and CAEMO compose the CFA Franc Zone.

Exchange Arrangements with No Separate Legal Tender: The currency of another country circulates as the sole legal tender or the member belongs to a monetary or currency union in which the same legal tender is shared by the members of the union.

Currency Board Arrangements: A monetary regime based on an implicit legislative commitment to exchange domestic currency for a specified foreign currency at a fixed exchange rate, combined with restrictions on the issuing authority to ensure the fulfillment of its legal obligation.

Other Conventional Fixed-Peg Arrangements: The country pegs its currency (formally or de facto) at a fixed rate to a major currency or a basket of currencies, where the exchange rate fluctuates within a narrow margin or at most ±1% around a central rate.

Pegged Rate within Horizontal Bands: The value of the currency is maintained within margins of fluctuation around a formal or *de facto* fixed peg that are wider than ±1% around a central rate.

Crawling Pegs: The currency is adjusted periodically in small amounts at a fixed, preannounced rate or in response to changes in selective quantitative indicators.

Exchange Rates within Crawling Bands: The currency is maintained within certain fluctuation margins around a central rate that is adjusted periodically at a fixed preannounced rate or in response to change in selective quantitative indicators.

Managed Floating with No Preannounced Path for the Exchange Rate: The monetary authority influences the movements of the exchange rate through active intervention in the foreign exchange market without specifying, or pre-committing to, a pre-announced path for the exchange rate.

Independent Floating: The exchange rate is market-determined, with any foreign exchange intervention aimed at moderating the rate of change and preventing undue fluctuations in the exchange rate, rather than at establishing a level for it.

Source: *International Financial Statistics*, International Monetary Fund, Washington DC, Monthly, July 1999.

)))) Currency Boards

Exhibit 2.2 shows that eight countries, including Argentina and Hong Kong, are utilizing *currency boards* as a means of fixing their exchange rates.[2] In 1991, Argentina moved from its previous managed exchange rate of the Argentine peso to a currency board. The currency board structure fixed the Argentine peso's value to the U.S. dollar on a one-to-one basis. The fixed rate of exchange was preserved by requiring that every peso to be issued through the Argentine banking system must be backed by either gold or dollars held on account in banks in Argentina. This 100% reserve system essentially set the monetary policy of the entire country to the country's ability to obtain U.S. dollars through trade or investment. Only after dollars have been earned and held can the money supply of Argentina actually be expanded, eliminating the possibility of money supply-based sources of inflation.

An additional feature of the Argentine currency board system is the ability of all Argentines or foreigners to hold dollar-denominated accounts in Argentine banks. (Recall that this is actually a Eurodollar account, a dollar-denominated deposit in non-U.S. bank.) This presents the saver or investor with the ability to choose whether or not to hold pesos. And this right has been heavily exercised, as indicated by the magnitude of dollar-denominated bank CDs outstanding in 1998 alone.

Outstanding bank certificates of deposit by currency in Argentina (1998)

Argentine pesos	$13.6 billion	26.9%
U.S. dollars	36.9 billion	73.1%
Total	$50.5 billion	100.0%

The interest differential shown in Exhibit 2.3, the interest rate paid on dollar-denominated accounts versus peso-denominated accounts, represents a market-determined risk premium of the system itself. The differential represents continued doubt over the system's future.

)))) Dollarization

Several countries that have suffered for many years from currency devaluation, primarily as a result of inflation, have taken steps toward *dollarization*, the use of the U.S. dollar as the official currency of the country. Currently only Panama, Ecuador, and Liberia—three relatively small countries—officially use the U.S. dollar as their own. Argentina, however, may be next.

The prevalence of the U.S. dollar in Argentine society cannot be understated. Taxi drivers, restaurant owners, and ATM machines all actively utilize and dispense dollars. Virtually all rental and mortgage agreements are now denominated in dollars. Even cellular telephone contracts and payments are dollar-based.

The movement from maintaining a currency board system to dollarizing the entire economy, however, requires dramatic changes in the structure and

| **Exhibit 2.3** | *Interest Differential on Dollar- and Peso-Denominated Deposits in Argentina (basis points = 1/100 of a percent)* |

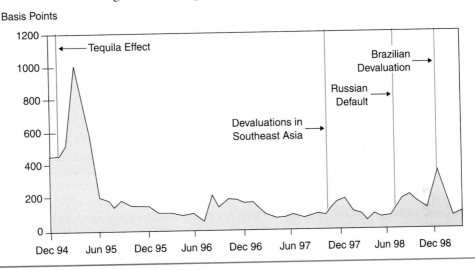

responsibilities of monetary policy authorities, both in Argentina and in the United States. Under the proposed agreement now under discussion, the U.S. Federal Reserve System would take on the responsibility of regulating and supporting the federal banking system of Argentina. This role, lender-of-last-resort, requires the Fed to ultimately ensure the liquidity and stability of the entire banking system by acting as the lender who would provide additional liquidity during times of crisis.

Although both the United States and Argentina remain highly skeptical of the current proposals under discussion, the discussion itself indicates the growing interest in the formation of a long-term currency structure in the Americas that may eventually create a euro of its own, the dollar.

⟫⟫ Fixed versus Flexible Exchange Rates

A nation's choice as to which currency regime it follows reflects national priorities about all facets of the macro economy, including inflation, unemployment, interest rate levels, trade balances, and economic growth. The choice between fixed and flexible rates may then change as priorities change.

At the risk of overgeneralization, the following observations explain why countries pursue certain exchange rate regimes. They are based on the premise that, other things being equal, countries would prefer fixed exchange rates.

- Fixed rates provide stability in international prices for the conduct of trade. Stable prices aid in the growth of international trade and lessen risks for all businesses.

- Fixed exchange rates are inherently anti-inflationary, requiring the country to follow restrictive monetary and fiscal policies. This restrictiveness, however, can often be a burden to a country wishing to pursue policies that alleviate continuing internal economic problems, such as high unemployment or slow economic growth.

- Fixed exchange rate regimes necessitate that central banks maintain large quantities of international reserves (hard currencies and gold) to be used in the occasional defense of their fixed rate. As the international currency markets have grown rapidly in size and volume, this need has become a significant burden to many nations.

- Fixed rates, once in place, may be maintained at rates that are inconsistent with economic fundamentals. As the structure of a nation's economy changes, and as trade relationships and balances evolve, the exchange rate itself should change. Flexible exchange rates allow this change to happen gradually and efficiently, but fixed rates must be changed administratively—usually too late, with too much publicity, and at too great a one-time cost to the nation's economic health.

)))) Attributes of the Ideal Currency

If the ideal currency existed in today's world, it would possess three attributes:

1. **Fixed value.** The value of the currency would be fixed in relationship to other major currencies so that traders and investors could be relatively certain of the foreign exchange value of each currency in the present and into the near future.

2. **Convertibility.** Complete freedom of monetary flows would be allowed, so that traders and investors could willingly and easily move funds from one country and currency to another in response to perceived economic opportunities or risks.

3. **Independent monetary policy.** Domestic monetary and interest rate policies would be set by each individual country so as to pursue desired national economic policies, especially as they might relate to limiting inflation, combating recessions, and fostering prosperity and full employment.

Unfortunately, these three attributes usually cannot be achieved at the same time. For example, countries whose currencies are pegged to each other are in effect agreeing to both a common inflation rate and a common interest rate policy. If inflation rates differ but the peg (i.e., fixed exchange rate) is maintained, one country's goods become cheaper in the other countries. This will lead to unemployment in the high-inflation country. If one country's interest rates are higher than the others and the peg is maintained, investors will move funds from the low-rate country to the high-rate country, creating ever more difficulty in maintaining the peg.

THE BIRTH OF A GLOBAL CURRENCY: THE EURO

The 15 members of the European Union are also members of the European Monetary System. This group has tried to form an island of fixed exchange rates among themselves in a sea of major floating currencies. Members of the EMS rely heavily on trade with each other, so the day-to-day benefits of fixed exchange rates between them are perceived to be great. Nevertheless, the EMS has undergone a number of major changes since its inception in 1979, including major crises and reorganizations in 1992 and 1993, and conversion of 11 members to the euro on January 1, 1999. In December 1991, the members of the European Union met at Maastricht, the Netherlands and concluded a treaty that changed Europe's currency future.

Timetable. The Maastricht Treaty specified a timetable and a plan to replace all individual currencies with a single currency, now called the euro. Other steps were adopted that would lead to a full European Economic and Monetary Union (EMU).

Convergence Criteria. To prepare for the EMU, the Maastricht Treaty called for the integration and coordination of the member countries' monetary and fiscal policies. Few financial market differences were to exist by the time the EMU was anticipated to start. The EMU would be implemented by a process called convergence. Before becoming a full member of the EMU, each member was originally expected to meet the following convergence criteria:

1. Nominal inflation should be no more than 1.5% above the average for the three members of the European Union (EU) with the lowest inflation rates during the previous year.

2. Long-term interest rates should be no more than 2% above the average for the three members with the lowest interest rates.

3. The fiscal deficit should be no more than 3% of gross domestic product.

4. Government debt should be no more than 60% of gross domestic product.

The convergence criteria were so tough that few, if any, of the members could satisfy them at that time, but 11 countries managed to do so just prior to 1999.

Strong Central Bank. A strong central bank, called the European Central Bank (ECB), was to be established. It has since been established in Frankfurt, Germany. The bank is modeled after the U.S. Federal Reserve System. An independent central bank dominates the continuing country central banks. The individual country central banks will regulate banks resident within their borders, but all financial market intervention and the issuance of euros will remain the sole responsibility of the ECB. The single most important mandate of the ECB is to promote price stability within the European Union.

)))) The Launch of the Euro

On January 1, 1999, 11 member states of the EU initiated the EMU. They established a single currency, the euro, which replaced the individual currencies of the participating member states.[3] On December 31, 1998, the final fixed rates between the 11 participating currencies and the euro were put into place. On January 4, 1999, the euro was officially traded. Although the result of a long-term and methodical program for the alignment of all political and economic forces in the EU, it was only the first of many steps to come. The impacts of the euro on the economic environment and on society in general within the participating countries will be dramatic. It is only now becoming apparent what some of the forces of change might be.[4]

)))) Why Monetary Unification?

According to the EU, EMU is a single currency area, now known informally as the *Euro Zone*, within the EU single market in which people, goods, services and capital move without restrictions. Beginning with the Treaty of Rome in 1957 and continuing with the Single European Act of 1987, the Maastricht Treaty of 1991–1992, and the Treaty of Amsterdam of 1997 (draft), a core set of European countries have been working steadily toward integrating their individual countries into one larger, more efficient, domestic market. Even after the launch of the 1992 Single Europe program, however, a number of barriers to true openness remained. The use of different currencies required both consumers and companies to treat the individual markets separately. Currency risk of cross-border commerce still persisted. The creation of a single currency is designed to move beyond these vestiges of separated markets.

The growth of global markets and the increasing competitiveness of the Americas and Asia drove the members of the EU in the 1980s and 1990s to take actions that would allow their residents and their firms to compete globally. The reduction of barriers across all member countries to allow economies of scale (size and cost per unit) and scope (horizontal and vertical integration) was thought to be Europe's only hope of not being left behind in the new millennium. The economic potential of the EU, as illustrated in Exhibit 2.4, is substantial. The successful implementation of a single, strong, and dependable currency for the conduct of life could well alter the traditional dominance of the U.S. dollar as the world's currency.

)))) How to Achieve Monetary Unification

If the euro is to be a successful replacement for the currencies of the 11 participating EU states, it must have a solid economic foundation. The primary driver of a currency's value is its ability to maintain its purchasing power (money is worth what money can buy). The single largest threat to maintaining purchasing power is inflation. So, Job One for the EU since the beginning has been to construct an economic system that would work to remove inflationary forces from undermining the euro.

| Exhibit 2.4 | *The European Union-15's Relative Dimensions* | | | | |

Economic Group	Population (millions)	Share of OECD GDP	Share of World Trade	Export to GDP Ratio	FX Reserves (billion $)
European Union	370	38.3%	20.9%	10.2%	349.8
Japan	125	20.5%	10.5%	9.0%	172.4
United States	263	32.5%	19.6%	8.2%	49.1

The EU11 consists of Austria, Belgium, Finland, France, Germany, Ireland, Italy, Luxembourg, the Netherlands, Portugal, and Spain. The EU15 consists of the EU11, the participants in monetary unification, plus Denmark, Greece, Sweden, and the United Kingdom. All data for 1996 with the exception of population estimates from 1995. Source: *The Financial Times.*

Fiscal Policy and Monetary Policy. The monetary policy for the EMU is conducted by the newly formed European Central Bank, which, according to its founding principles in the Maastricht Treaty, will have one singular responsibility: to safeguard the stability of the euro. Following the basic structures that were used in the establishment of the Federal Reserve System in the United States and the Bundesbank in Germany, the ECB is free of political pressures, which in history have caused monetary authorities to yield to employment pressures by inflating economies. The ECB's independence will allow it to focus simply on the stability of the currency without falling victim to history's trap.

The ECB became operational in June of 1998. It became responsible for the entire monetary policy of the 11 participating states on January 1, 1999. This institution consists of a president whose term is 8 years, assisted by a vice president and four executives from member states. The ECB's governing council sets interest rates in conjunction with the directors of the individual national central banks. These national central banks—in conjunction with the ECB—now form the European System of Central Banks (ESCB). The ECB will for the most part establish policy, and the ESCB will be responsible for implementation, regulation, and enforcement. All things considered, however, the ECB will now set only one interest rate for the whole of the EU11.[5]

Fixing the Value of the Euro. The December 31, 1998, fixing of the rates of exchange between national currencies and the euro resulted in the conversion rates shown in Exhibit 2.5. These are permanent fixes for these currencies. The United Kingdom, as it has been since the passage of the Maastricht Treaty, is skeptical of increasing EU infringement on its sovereignty. It has opted not to participate. Sweden, which has failed to see significant benefits from EU membership (although it is one of the newest members), is also skeptical of EMU participation. Denmark, like the U.K. and Sweden, has a strong political element that is highly nationalistic and has opted for now not to participate. Greece, although much in favor of participation, could not meet convergence criteria by the 1999 deadline because of the size of its fiscal deficits, national debt, and rate

Exhibit 2.5	*The Fixing of the Exchange Rates to the Euro (€), December 31, 1998*		

Previous Currency	Symbol	Per Euro	
Belgian or Luxembourg franc	BEF/LUF	40.3399	1 euro = 40.3399 BEF or LUF
Deutschemark	DEM	1.95583	1 euro = 1.95583 DEM
Spanish peseta	ESP	166.386	1 euro = 166.386 ESP
French franc	FRF	6.55957	1 euro = 6.55957 FRF
Irish punt	IEP	0.787564	1 euro = 0.787564 IEP
Italian lira	ITL	1936.27	1 euro = 1936.27 ITL
Netherlands guilder	NLG	2.20371	1 euro = 2.20371 NLG
Austrian shilling	ATS	13.7603	1 euro = 13.7603 ATS
Portuguese escudo	PTE	200.482	1 euro = 200.482 PTE
Finnish mark	FIM	5.94573	1 euro = 5.94573 FIM

of inflation. It is believed, however, that Greece will be able to reach the qualifying numbers relatively soon.

The EU has been very careful to differentiate the euro from its predecessor the ECU (the European Currency Unit). The euro is actually money, whereas the ECU was an index of money. The ECU was never legal tender under European law, whereas the euro is already legal tender (although not yet available in coins or notes). The ECU's value was based upon the composition currencies of the European Union's participants in the EMS, whereas the euro is a completely independent currency that is exchangeable into other currencies but not dependent upon them for its value. The euro is to replace all individual EMU currencies.

On January 4, 1999, the euro began trading on world currency markets. Its introduction was a smooth one, with trading heavy and relatively stable. The euro's value slid steadily in the months following its introduction, however, primarily as a result of the robustness of the U.S. economy and U.S. dollar, and continuing sluggish economic sectors in the EMU countries. But all in all, it was a good start. Exhibit 2.6 illustrates the euro's value, both before official introduction on January 1, 1999, and after.

Under the present timetable, by January 1, 2002, the individual coins and notes of the national currencies will be gradually withdrawn from circulation and replaced with euro notes and coins. This would constitute the last remaining stage of monetary unification and should not create major problems given current success.

The official abbreviation of the euro is EUR, and it has been registered with the International Standards Organization (ISO). The abbreviation is similar to the three-letter symbols used for the United States dollar, USD, and the British pound sterling, GBP. The official symbol of the euro is €.[6]

The British government has published an official fact sheet on the euro that states that the euro will affect markets in three ways: (1) countries within the euro zone will enjoy cheaper transaction costs; (2) countries within the euro zone will

Exhibit 2.6   *Daily Exchange Rates: U.S. Dollars per Euro*

Source: Pacific Exchange Rate Service, http://pacific.commerce.ubc.ca/xr ©1999 by Prof. Werner Antweiler, University of British Columbia, Vancouver, BC, Canada.

enjoy reduced currency risks and costs related to exchange rate uncertainty; and (3) all consumers and businesses both inside and outside the euro zone will enjoy price transparency and increase price-based competition.[7]

EMERGING MARKET CRISES

After a number of years of relative global economic tranquility, the second half of the 1990s was racked by a series of currency crises that shook all emerging markets. The devaluation of the Mexican peso in December 1994 served as a harbinger of crises to come. The Asian crisis of July 1997, the Russian ruble's collapse in August 1998, and more recently the fall of the Brazilian real in January 1999 provide a spectrum of emerging market economic failures, each with its own complex causes and unknown outlooks. These crises also illustrate the growing problem of capital flight and short-run international speculation in currency and securities markets. We will use each of the individual crises to focus on a specific dimension of the causes and consequences:

- **The Asian crisis of 1997.** Although this was not the collapse of any one currency, economy, or system, the complex structures combining government, society, and business throughout the Far East provide a backdrop for understanding the tenuous linkage between business, government, and society.

- **The Russian crisis of 1998**. The loss of the relatively stable ruble, once considered the cornerstone and symbol of success of President Boris Yeltsin's regime, was a potential death blow to the current Russian government and economic system. If nothing else, Russian borrowers may find themselves *persona non grata* for years to come in the international capital markets.

- **The Brazilian crisis of 1999**. Potentially the mildest of the three currency collapses, the Brazilian real's fall in January 1999 was the result of a long-expected correction in an ill-conceived currency policy. Because so many major Brazilian firms are publicly traded, this crisis serves as an excellent example of how equity markets revalue firms that are exposed to currency devaluations and vice versa.

THE ASIAN CRISIS

The roots of the Asian currency crisis extended from a fundamental change in the economics of the region, the transition of many Asian nations from net exporters to net importers. Starting as early as 1990 in Thailand, the rapidly expanding economies of the Far East began importing more than they exported, requiring major net capital inflows to support their currencies. As long as the capital continued to flow in—capital for manufacturing plants, dam projects, infrastructure development, and even real estate speculation—the pegged exchange rates of the region could be maintained. When the investment capital inflows stopped, however, crisis was inevitable.

The most visible roots of the crisis were in the excesses of capital flows into Thailand in 1996 and early 1997. With rapid economic growth and rising profits forming the backdrop, Thai firms, banks, and finance companies had ready access to capital on the international markets, finding U.S. dollar debt cheap offshore. Thai banks continued to raise capital internationally, extending credits to a variety of domestic investments and enterprises beyond that which the Thai economy could support. As capital flows into the Thai market hit record rates, financial flows poured into investments of all kinds, including manufacturing, real estate, and even equity-market margin lending. As the investment "bubble" expanded, some participants raised questions about the economy's ability to repay the rising debt. The baht came under sudden and severe pressure.

Currency Collapse

The Thai government and central bank intervened in the foreign exchange markets directly (using up precious hard currency reserves) and indirectly (by raising interest rates to attempt to stop the continual outflow). The Thai investment markets ground to a halt. This caused massive currency losses and bank failures. On July 2, 1997, the Thai central bank finally allowed the baht to float (or sink in this case). The baht fell 17% against the U.S. dollar and over 12% against the Japanese yen in a matter of hours. By November, the baht had fallen from

Baht25/US$ to Baht40/US$, a fall of about 38%. In the aftermath, the international speculator and philanthropist George Soros was the object of much criticism, primarily by the Prime Minister of Malaysia, Dr. Mahathir Mohamad, for being the cause of the crisis. Soros, however, was likely only the messenger.

Within days, in Asia's own version of the tequila effect, a number of neighboring Asian nations, some with and some without characteristics similar to Thailand's, came under speculative attack by currency traders and capital markets.[8] The Philippine peso, the Malaysian ringgit, and the Indonesian rupiah all fell within months (see Exhibits 2.7 and 2.8). In late October, Taiwan caught the markets off-balance with a surprise competitive devaluation of 15%. The Taiwanese devaluation seemed only to renew the momentum of the crisis. Although the Hong Kong dollar survived (at great expense to the central bank's foreign exchange reserves), the Korean won was not so lucky. In November the historically stable Korean won also fell victim, falling from Won900/US$ to more than Won1100/US$. By the end of November the Korean government negotiated a US$50 billion bailout of its financial sector. The only currency that had not fallen besides the Hong Kong dollar was the Chinese renminbi (Rmb), which was not freely convertible. Although the renminbi had not been devalued, there was rising speculation that the Chinese government would devalue soon for competitive reasons.

)))) Causal Complexities

The Asian economic crisis—for it was more than just a currency collapse—had many roots besides the traditional balance-of-payments difficulties. The causes

Exhibit 2.7	*The Economies and Currencies of Asia, July–Nov 1997*				
Weaker Economies	1996 Current Acct (billions US$)	Liabilities to Foreign Banks (billions US$)	Exchange Rate		
			July (per US$)	November (per US$)	% Change
Indonesia (rupiah)	−9.0	29.7	2400	3600	−33.3 %
Korea (won)	−23.1	36.5	900	1100	−18.2 %
Malaysia (ringgit)	−8.0	27.0	2.5	3.5	−28.6 %
Philippines (peso)	−3.0	2.8	27	34	−20.6 %
Thailand (baht)	−14.7	48.0	25	40	−37.5 %
Stronger Economies					
China (renminbi)	47.2	56.0	8.4	8.4	+0.0 %
Hong Kong (dollar)	0.0	28.8	7.75	7.73	+0.0 %
Singapore (dollar)	14.3	55.3	1.43	1.60	−10.6 %
Taiwan (dollar)	11.0	17.6	27.8	32.7	−15.0 %

Source: International Monetary Fund, *International Financial Statistics*, October–November, 1997.

Exhibit 2.8   *Comparative Daily Exchange Rates: Relative to U.S. Dollar*

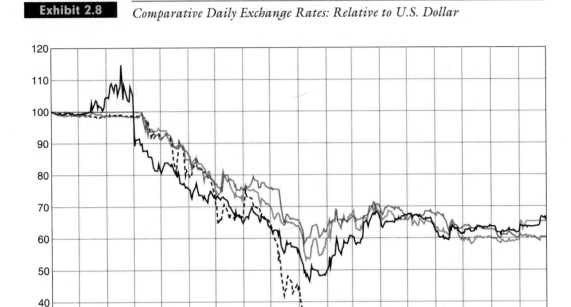

Source: Pacific Exchange Rate Service, http://pacific.commerce.ubc.ca/xr ©1999 by Prof. Werner Antweiler, University of British Columbia, Vancouver, BC, Canada. Time period shown in diagram: Apr 1, 1997 to Sept 30, 1998.

are different in each country, yet there are specific underlying similarities that allow comparison: corporate socialism, corporate governance, and banking stability and management.

Corporate Socialism. Although Western markets have long known the cold indifference of the free market, the countries of the post-World War II Asia have largely known only the good. Because of the influence of government and politics in the business arena, even in the event of failure, government would not allow firms to fold, workers to lose their jobs, or banks to close. Not, that is, until the problems reached the size seen in 1997 and business liabilities exceeded the capacities of governments to bail them out. Practices that had persisted for decades without challenge, such as lifetime employment, were now no longer sustainable. The result was a painful lesson in the harshness of the marketplace.

Corporate Governance. Many firms operating within the Far Eastern business environments are often largely controlled by either families or groups related to the governing party or body of the country. This has been labeled *cronyism.* Such control meant that the interests of minority stockholders and creditors were often secondary at best to the primary motivations of corporate management. Without a focus on "the bottom line," the bottom line deteriorated.

Banking Liquidity and Management. Bank regulatory structures and markets have been deregulated nearly without exception across the globe. The central role played by banks in the conduct of business, however, was largely ignored and underestimated. As firms across Asia collapsed, government coffers were emptied, and speculative investments made by the banks themselves failed. Without banks, the "plumbing" of business conduct was shut down. Firms could not obtain the necessary working capital financing they needed to manufacture their products or provide their services. It is this pivotal role of banking liquidity that was the focus of the IMF's bail-out efforts.

The Asian economic crisis had global impacts. What started as a currency crisis quickly became a region-wide recession.[9] The slowed economies of the region quickly caused major reductions in world demands for many products, especially commodities. World oil markets, copper markets, and agricultural products all saw severe price falls as demand fell. These price drops were immediately noticeable in declining earnings and growth prospects for other emerging economies. The problems of Russia and Brazil were reflections of those declines.

THE RUSSIAN CRISIS OF 1998

The crisis of August 1998 was the culmination of a continuing deterioration in general economic conditions in Russia. During the 1995 to 1998 period, Russian borrowers—both governmental and nongovernmental—went to the international capital markets for large quantities of capital. Servicing this debt soon became an increasing problem, as dollar debt required dollar debt-service. The Russian current account, a surprisingly healthy surplus ranging between $15 and $20 billion per year, was not, however, finding its way into internal investment and external debt service. Capital flight was accelerating, as hard-currency earnings flowed out as fast they found their way in. Finally, in the spring of 1998, even Russian export earnings were declining. Russian exports were predominantly commodity-based, and global commodity prices had been on the decline since the onset of the Asian economic crisis in the summer and fall of 1997.

The Russian currency, the ruble, operated under a *managed float.* The Central Bank of Russia allowed the ruble to trade within a band. The band, for example, was Ru5.750/$ to Ru6.350/$ in the weeks prior to August 17, 1998.[10] Mechanically, the Central Bank announced an official exchange rate each day at which it was willing to buy and sell rubles, always within the official band. In the event that the ruble's exchange rate came under pressure at the limits of the band, the Central Bank intervened in the market by buying and selling rubles—usually buying—using the country's foreign exchange and gold reserves. The stability of the ruble in the 1990s was considered the single most observable success of President Boris Yeltsin. In spite of a $4.3 billion loan from the IMF in July of 1998, the ruble came under intense pressure in August.

The August Collapse

On Friday, August 7, the Russian Central Bank announced that its hard currency reserves had fallen by $800 million in the last week of July to a level of $18.4 billion on July 31. Prime Minister Sergei Kiriyenko said that Russia would issue an additional $3 billion in foreign bonds to help pay its rising debt, a full $1 billion more than had been previously scheduled. The ruble, however, continued to trade within a very narrow range of Ru6.24/$ to Ru6.26/$.

On Monday, August 10, Russian stocks fell more than 5% as investors feared a Chinese renminbi devaluation. The Chinese currency had been the only non-Japanese Asian currency of size not devalued in 1997 and 1998. Devaluation would aid Chinese exports and cut into Russian export sales. Analysts worldwide speculated that international markets were waiting to see whether the Russian government would increase its tax revenues, as it had promised the IMF throughout the year. Russian oil companies were publicly warned by the Russian government to pay past due taxes.[11] By Wednesday, Russian financing choices were narrowing further as the government canceled the government debt auction for the third week in a row. On international markets, Russia's outstanding eurobonds due in 2001 sank in price for a sixth straight day, the yield (implicit cost of borrowing) rising 350 basis points to 23.6%. The ruble fell to Ru6.3/$.

Thursday, August 13 saw a series of press releases by senior governmental officials committing the government to stabilizing the markets and assuring the general population that all was in hand. Mikhail Zadornov, Finance Minister, said, "If we thought that devaluation was unavoidable, we would not be taking the measures we are taking now." Mr. Zadornov went on to explain that Russia expected an additional $4.3 billion from the IMF in September. Analysts believed that Russia had $23.4 billion in payments on domestic debt, and $4.5 billion due on foreign debt, throughout the remainder of the year. Despite the statements from Finance Minister Zadornov, the stock and bond markets in Moscow and St. Petersburg plummeted. Rumors regarding the likely collapse of the banking system spread.

Thursday also saw the undesired intervention of an outsider, George Soros. Soros, considered one of the world's most influential investors and most recently blamed by some for the currency crises in Asia, sent a letter to a British newspaper in which he expressed the opinion that Russia's financial situation was in a "terminal phase." Soros advocated an international bailout package of $15 billion, coupled with a devaluation of the ruble by 15 to 25%, and the creation of a currency board to maintain the ruble's new value. Soros was quoted later in the day saying the letter was intended to serve as a wake-up call to Western governments, not to proliferate panic or collapse in Russia itself. It seemed, however, to do the latter.

On Friday, August 14 the press releases and statements of commitment from senior governmental officials continued. The government stated that the "panic" was psychological, not fiscal, and repeated, as it had in recent days, that it had money to meet its obligations through the fall of the year.

> "A stable ruble is the anchor of an inflation-free economy," according to Alexander Livshits, deputy head of President Boris Yeltsin's administration. He added that the loss of a stable ruble "will start rocking our ship again. The result is well known—nausea."

The Russian Central Bank continued to trade rubles throughout Friday at Ru6.3/$, but at many unofficial exchanges throughout Moscow the rate was Ru7.0/$ or more. President Yeltsin, in a speech in the ancient city of Novgorode, stated: "There will be no devaluation—that's firm and definite." He went on to add, "That would signify that there was a disaster and that everything was collapsing. On the contrary, everything is going as it should."

"As it should" turned out to mean devaluation. On Monday, August 17 the floodgates were released. Late in the day the Russian Central Bank announced that the ruble would be allowed to fall by 34% this year, from Ru6.3/$ to about Ru9.5/$. It also postponed the payment of $43 billion in short-term domestic debt to help it through the cash crisis. As a final blow to international markets, the government announced a 90-day moratorium on all repayment of foreign debt, debt owed by Russian banks and all private borrowers, in order to avert a banking collapse.

On Tuesday, August 18 the ruble continued to fall, quickly passing the Ru9.5/$ limit for the rest of the year. Reports from Moscow to Vladivostok quoted trading at between Ru10 and Ru12 per dollar. Debate in international circles centered on whether Russia's postponement of debt service was in fact a default.

The currency's fall continued into the following week. On Thursday, August 27 Acting Prime Minister Viktor Chernomyrdin traveled to the Ukraine to meet with the visiting head of the IMF, Michael Camdessus. A sense of urgency was felt after the ruble fell from Ru10.0/$ to Ru13.0/$ the previous day alone. In related matters, the Central Bank of Russia, in an attempt to defray criticism of its management of the ruble's devaluation, disclosed that it had expended $8.8 billion in the preceding eight weeks defending the ruble's value. On Friday August 28 the Moscow currency exchange closed after 10 minutes of trading as the ruble fell.

)))) The Aftermath

It is hard to say when a crisis begins or ends, but for the Russian people and the Russian economy, the deterioration of economic conditions continues. As illustrated in Exhibit 2.9, the ruble continued to fall throughout the fall of 1998. In early December rumors that the Russian state was printing money to make long-overdue payments to state workers and pensioners added insult to injury. The tumbling ruble finally stabilized in January and February of 1999, at a rate of approximately Ru25.0/$.

The spring and early summer of 1999 saw a Russian government that battled both within and without to find ways to service the outstanding sovereign and private debts without impoverishing the country further. The domestic bonds issued by the Russian government, ruble bonds, were now in default. The primary task for survival was now the servicing of the dollar debt. Russia's outstanding Eurobonds head the list. No sovereign borrower has ever rescheduled or defaulted on outstanding Eurobonds.

What may be of more substantial concern is the toll the crisis has taken on Russian society. The collapse of the ruble and of Russia's access to the international capital markets has for many brought into question the benefits of a free-market economy, long championed by the advocates of Western-style democracy. Russia today is the world's sixth most populous country, a nuclear power, and the holder of a permanent seat on the UN Security Council. But today its economic

---

Exhibit 2.9   *Daily Exchange Rates: Russian Rubles per U.S. Dollar*

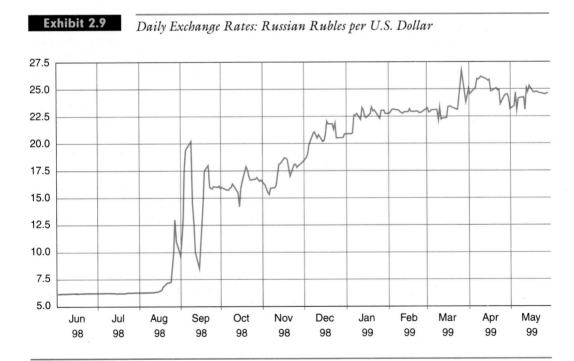

Source: Pacific Exchange Rate Service, http://pacific.commerce.ubc.ca/xr ©1999 by Prof. Werner Antweiler, University of British Columbia, Vancouver, BC, Canada.

health and credit worth places it in the same tier of global powers as the Sudan, Iraq, the Congo, and Afghanistan. To quote *The Economist*:

> A government that cannot tax its powerful citizens is in no position to protect its weakest ones. Even in the best case, changing this would take decades. Yet before the August crisis, there had been signs of hope. There was a growing middle class, particularly in large cities. The needs of the poorest were beginning to be met by a thriving, if tiny, voluntary sector. Some Russian businesses had revealed glimmerings of respect for shareholders, staff and customers. Higher standards were encouraged by a growing foreign business presence—which, miraculously, paid its taxes. Even some bits of the public sector were behaving better. Now the prospect is of almost unrelieved gloom.[12]

At the same time there is a growing cynicism over the prospects of rebirth by those outside Russia. A growing consensus in the IMF, Washington, D.C., and Brussels is that without new leadership and changes in the way in which Russia is governed, additional lending is useless. For the Russian citizens and businessmen, the crisis of August 1998 continues well into the year 2000—a Y2K problem of much more serious proportions.

THE BRAZILIAN CRISIS OF 1999

The majority of economic and financial analysts around the world never debated in 1997 and 1998 whether the Brazilian real (R$) would be devalued, only *when* and by *how much*. Since the inception of the real in July of 1994, its value had been artificially maintained by the Brazilian government in hopes of instilling stabilizing expectations for economic and financial growth. The government's inability to resolve continuing current account deficits and domestic inflationary forces, however, made the devaluation of the Brazilian real an eventuality. As illustrated in Exhibit 2.10, the pressures in 1998 intensified.

Although the Brazilian government had successfully held the value of the real quite stable for an extended period, the fact that the exchange rate had not been allowed to adjust to relative inflationary forces (for example, U.S. inflation had averaged 2.0% or less for the same period of time), coupled with stagnating economic growth, led investors to look elsewhere for economic returns. Increased volatility in the marketplace in the latter half of 1998, particularly the Russian economic collapse in August of 1998, set the stage for the devaluation of the real.

> Investors yesterday continued to take a pessimistic view of the new Brazilian currency policy, provoking frantic selling in the Brazilian stock market and prompting weakness in markets in the U.S. and Europe. But analysts said foreign investors were taking a much more negative view than domestic investors.[13]

The impact of the fall of the Brazilian real on the share prices of Brazilian firms illustrates the susceptibility of individual firms to currency risk and market risk. The impact of a currency devaluation on individual equity values should theoretically be some combination of *market risk*, in which investors of all kinds sell off securities

Exhibit 2.10   *Measures of Brazilian Economic Performance, 1995–1999*

	1995	1996	1997	1998[a]	1999[b]
Real gross domestic product growth	4.2%	2.9%	3.0%	(0.5)%	(2.5)%
Gross domestic product, GDP (billion US$)	749	779	803	753	704
Inflation: Consumer price index	23.2%	10.0%	4.8%	(1.0)%	10.5%
Nominal interest rate	53.1%	27.1%	24.7%	29.2%	30.7%
Real interest rate	24.3%	15.5%	19.0%	30.5%	21.6%
Trade balance (billion US$)	(3.4)	(5.5)	(8.4)	(5.4)	(0.5)
Trade deficit as % of GDP	7.1%	6.1%	6.1%	8.2%	7.0%
International reserves (billion US$)	51.8	60.1	52.2	40.0	36.0
Exchange rate, R$/$ (end of period)	0.972	1.039	1.117	1.207	1.700

Source: Bozano Simonsen, Brazil Research, 1999.
[a]1998 values are estimates for year.
[b]1999 values are as of February 2, 1999.

and drive the market as a whole downward, and *security risk*, in which the exposure of individual firms to currency devaluation results in some firms falling further than others. The devaluation of the Brazilian real beginning on January 12, 1999, serves as an illustrative case study in how individual firms are exposed to currency devaluation and how equity markets revalue them.

Exhibit 2.11 provides an overview of several key financial variables during the week of January 11, 1999, the week of the real crisis.

- On Monday and Tuesday, January 11 and 12, the real hovered around the bottom of its allowed trading band, R$1.21/$. Approximately $190 million in capital flowed out of the country on Monday, with the Brazilian stock markets falling 5.8%.

- On Tuesday, conditions reached crisis proportion, with nearly $1.2 billion in capital flight and a 4.9% fall in Brazilian equities.

Exhibit 2.11   *Financial Markets in the Brazilian Crisis, January 11–15, 1999*

Day & Date	Spot Exchange Rate (Real/US$)	% Change	Capital Flight (billion US$)	Brazilian equities	Brazilian equities (US$)
Mon 11	1.21	0.0%	0.19	−5.8%	−5.8%
Tue 12	1.21	0.0%	1.20	−4.9%	−4.9%
Wed 13	1.32	−8.3%	1.05	−4.4%	−12.2%
Thu 14	1.32	0.0%	1.00	−7.2%	−7.2%
Fri 15	1.43	−7.7%	0.00	+28.0%	+18.9%

Exchange rates are for close of business. Capital flight estimates as published by the Brazilian Central Bank. Brazilian equity market performance based upon local currency and U.S. dollar index values as calculated by Morgan Stanley Capital International.

- On Wednesday, January 13, the real was officially devalued by the Brazilian government, allowing its value to fall to R$1.32/$ from the previous floor of R$1.21/$ (−8.3%). An additional $1.05 billion in capital fled the country.
- Brazilian equities fell 4.4% on Wednesday and an additional 7.2% on Thursday.
- On Friday, January 15, the real was temporarily floated, allowing the currency to sink even further (closing that day at R$1.4300/$). The equity markets, however, rebounded on the news of flotation and closed up 28% on Friday.

During the following week the temporary float was made permanent and the real continued to fall in value. On Monday, January 18 the Brazilian Finance Minister was quoted as saying, "Interest rates might have to rise in the short term to limit the inflationary pressures from the devaluation." Later that same day, after the close of the financial markets in Brazil, the Central Bank announced an increase in the prime lending rate from 36% to 41%. By late April of 1999, however, the real had appreciated versus the U.S. dollar, hovering around R$1.70/$. Exhibit 2.12 provides an overview of the real's transition from heavily managed to freely floating.

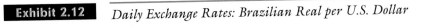

Exhibit 2.12   *Daily Exchange Rates: Brazilian Real per U.S. Dollar*

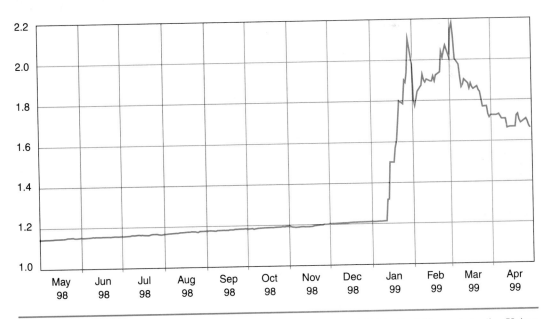

Source: Pacific Exchange Rate Service, http://pacific.commerce.ubc.ca/xr ©1999 by Prof. Werner Antweiler, University of British Columbia, Vancouver, BC, Canada.

)))) **The Brazilian Bovespa**

The Brazilian stock markets, illustrated in Exhibit 2.13 as measured by the index of the São Paulo Stock Exchange, the *Bovespa*, fell dramatically after the August 1998 Russian economic crisis. They had recovered only marginally by the time of the January 1999 real devaluation. The Bovespa did, however, recover steadily following the devaluation, illustrating some combination of the following behaviors: (1) a belief the market had become seriously undervalued as a result of overshooting through the currency crisis; (2) rising expectations regarding future business conditions as a result of or in spite of the fall of the real, versus major economic competitors; and (3) the return of foreign investors to the Brazilian markets after the crisis was considered to be over.

The comparison with the United States' S&P500 index, however, drives home the degree of volatility suffered in Brazilian equity markets during the 1998 to April 1999 period.

)))) **Corporate Currency Exposures**

The immediate sensitivity of corporate earnings and cash flows to exchange rate changes is related to both *operating cash flows* and *financing cash flows*. *Operating cash flows* are those that reflect the underlying business, the sales generated, and the costs of goods sold and services rendered. Firms generate earnings of foreign currency typically through export sales.[14] In order to analyze how susceptible corporate profitability and earnings outlooks may be affected for individual Brazilian firms, we first isolate and differentiate their operating cash flows denominated in dollars from their financing cash flows denominated in dollars.

Exhibit 2.13   *Comparison of Brazilian and North American Equity Market Performance (MSCI Indexes)*

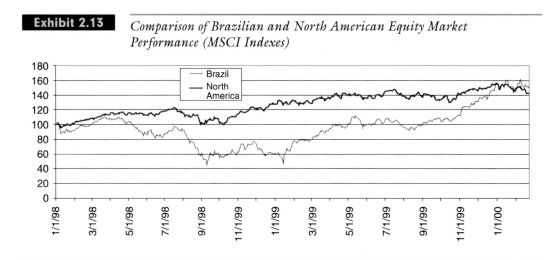

Source: Morgan Stanley Capital International (MSCI), www.msci.com.

Operating Cash Flows. The *net operating exposure* of a firm can be measured by the degree to which it earns hard currency versus the way it expends hard currency. Although many firms may have little, if any, revenue in hard currency as a result of the firm's industry, its strategic focus—or its access to international markets—and cost structures generally have some minimum exposure due to the dominance of some firms in the global marketplace in either commodities, intellectual property, or technology.

Exhibit 2.14 provides a sample of 37 Brazilian firms, in six industrial segments. Each firm's operating exposure (percentage of revenues and percentage of cost of goods sold) is identified. Aside from obvious industries having no hard currency (dollar) earnings, such as electricity and telecom, a number of the firms listed have significant proportions of their revenues in dollars. Although many firms have appreciable amounts of their costs in dollars, given that costs are a lesser proportion of revenues, the actual net cash flow exposure from operations is generally manageable.

Financing Cash Flows. The financing cash flows of a firm are typically either neutral or negative in terms of currency exposure. A firm that is domiciled in Brazil and raises all capital (specifically debt) in local currency has no hard currency obligations. If the firm maintains a proportion of its cash and marketable securities (liquid assets) in hard currency, it may actually create a net positive currency exposure position. But, more frequently, the situation is one in which the firm has borrowed some proportion of its debt from offshore, and it is then likely to have hard-currency-denominated debt-service commitments from now into the near future.

More typical of major Brazilian firms, at least those that are publicly traded, is for some proportion of both debt and cash to be dollar-denominated. Brazilian firms that have had major capital needs for financing growth in recent years were often confronted with a difficult choice: borrow locally at high rates of interest (often 20% and up) and not risk currency exposure, or borrow dollars abroad at relatively lower interest rates (sometimes as low as 10%) and risk the currency exposure of having major debt service obligations in U.S. dollars. Many choose the latter path. As illustrated by Exhibit 2.14, without exception, every one of the 37 firms included possesses some proportion of its outstanding debt in U.S. dollars. In some cases, for example in the telecom industry segment, a number of the firms have their entire debt structure in dollars.

Carlos Augusto Lira Aguiar, president of Aracruz Celulose, Brazil's biggest pulp exporter, which has net debts of about $630m–650m, said: "Our debts are in dollars and our revenues are in dollars so there is no damage."[15]

))) Equity Reactions to the Real

As noted previously, the Brazilian equity markets fell precipitously just prior to January 12, the day of the devaluation and actually recovered in the following weeks. The São Paulo Stock Exchange Index actually rose from a level of 23,223 on January 11 to 29,013 on January 27, an increase of 24.9%. In Exhibit 2.14

Exhibit 2.14 *Currency Exposure and Market Valuation Changes as a Result of the Devaluation of the Brazillian Real (millions of real)*

Industry	Company	OPERATING CASH FLOWS				FINANCING CASH FLOWS				MARKET CAPITALIZATION		
		Revenues (real)	% in US$	COGS* (real)	% in US$	Debt (real)	% in US$	Cash (real)	% in US$	Before 011299	After 012799	% Chg
Sanitation, Building Materials, & Capital Goods	Sabesp	2,666	0%	1,221	0%	3,956	38%	23	100%	1,883	905	-51.9%
	Duratex	456	10%	313	0%	269	75%	195	42%	189	129	-31.7%
	Elevadores Atlas	307	1%	162	5%	67	97%	35	100%	268	184	-31.3%
	Confab	504	70%	395	50%	71	79%	78	13%	68	54	-20.6%
	Average		20%		14%		72%		64%			-33.9%
Consumer Goods	Brahma	2,338	2%	1,574	30%	1,571	51%	780	70%	2,852	2,852	0.0%
	CBD	3,277	0%	2,128	0%	844	39%	291	60%	1,164	825	-29.1%
	Coteminas	227	15%	180	15%	112	99%	84	0%	361	280	-22.4%
	Perdilgao	893	30%	761	11%	657	49%	309	29%	249	184	-26.1%
	Sadia	1,731	23%	1,424	6%	813	87%	352	91%	347	240	-30.8%
	Souza Cruz	1,458	41%	876	0%	534	100%	941	0%	1,817	1,765	-2.9%
	Average		19%		10%		71%		42%			-18.6%
Electricity	Bandeirante	1,122	0%	1,110	17%	378	86%	17	0%	302	1,232	307.9%
	Celesc	546	0%	519	14%	164	30%	22	0%	287	206	-28.2%
	CERJ	485	0%	352	12%	678	18%	18	0%	436	163	-62.6%
	Cesp	2,530	0%	1,133	24%	6,974	58%	518	0%			
	Coelba	570	0%	429	0%	496	85%	23	0%	563	990	75.8%
	CPFL	1,089	0%	868	18%	532	21%	251	0%	1,358	1,000	-26.4%
	Light	1,397	0%	1,031	25%	2,304	94%	9	0%	1,089	432	-60.3%
	Metroplitana	2,269	0%	1,795	17%	1,738	60%	305	0%	1,324	718	-45.8%
	Average		0%		16%		57%		0%			22.9%
Oil & Gas	Petrobas	16,570	90%	10,718	55%	10,010	91%	578	10%	10,669	6,909	-35.2%

Exhibit 2.14 *Currency Exposure and Market Valuation Changes as a Result of the Devaluation of the Brazillian Real (millions of real) (continued)*

Industry	Company	OPERATING CASH FLOWS				FINANCING CASH FLOWS				MARKET CAPITALIZATION		
		Revenues (real)	% in US$	COGS* (real)	% in US$	Debt (real)	% in US$	Cash (real)	% in US$	Before 011299	After 012799	% Chg
Steel & Mining	Acesita	498	18%	405	31%	1,222	60%	474	10%	82	49	-40.2%
	Belgom Mineira	429	12%	335	14%	266	48%	15	0%	140	102	-27.1%
	Caemi	771	87%	579	33%	620	93%	166	50%	71	95	33.8%
	CSN	2,165	18%	1,327	13%	2,861	86%	1,063	75%	1,367	878	-35.8%
	CST	1,538	14%	1,065	23%	1,838	34%	292	76%	196	190	-3.1%
	CVRD	874	97%	680	44%	1,274	90%	333	0%	4,747	6,195	30.5%
	Gerdau SA	1,288	8%	892	2%	546	31%	164	70%	375	378	0.8%
	Samrco	379	100%	230	0%	449	78%	21	0%			
	Samitri	235	100%	182	50%	107	86%	43	0%	85	108	27.1%
	Usiminas	1,538	14%	1,065	23%	1,838	34%	292	76%	387	296	-23.5%
	Average		44%		20%		65%		35%			-4.2%
Telecom	Embratel	3,398	0%	2,789	0%	489	100%	637	0%	4,279	4,121	-3.7%
	Tele Celular Sul	446	0%	244	0%	53	85%	133	0%	635	576	-9.3%
	Tele Centro Sul	2,168	0%	1,685	0%	33	100%	229	0%	2,457	2,582	5.1%
	Tele Norte Leste Part.	4,533	0%	3,650	0%	352	59%	378	0%	3,757	3,790	0.9%
	Telemig Cel. Part.	385	0%	305	0%	49	100%	52	0%	340	268	-21.2%
	Telesp Cel. Part. PNB	1,436	0%	720	0%	587	100%	230	0%	1,942	2,317	19.3%
	Telesp Part	3,750	0%	2,778	0%	775	100%	871	0%	6,018	5,871	-2.4%
	TelesSudeste Cel. Part.	741	0%	448	0%	30	100%	56	0%	1,071	985	-8.0%
	Average		0%		0%		93%		0%			-2.6%

*COGS = Cost of Goods Sold
Source: Adapted from "Devaluation: Winners & Losers," Bozano, Simonsen, São Paulo, Brazil, February 1999.

the market capitalization (market price times shares outstanding) of the selected Brazilian firms moved in a direction opposite to the market index. Some shares fell by as much as 52%, which was the case for Sabesp, a sanitation firm. Others rose as much as 308%, as did Bandeirante, an electricity provider.

As with all equity value changes, there were many other individual economic and financial events occurring during this two-week period besides the real's devaluation, and in some cases, these events dominated. All things considered, however, it is clear that these individual equities suffered dramatic share price falls in the weeks following the currency's devaluation.

The theory of finance is clear: the value of an asset, such as an equity share, is the present value of the expected future cash flows arising from that asset. If a firm's ability to generate current and future cash flows and net earnings is impacted by the fall in its home currency—in this case the value of the real for these selected Brazilian firms—then the market's valuation of the firm should change accordingly. A detailed analysis of the individual firm's prospects, like that completed by investment banking analysts, would still be necessary to isolate the impacts of the real's devaluation on the valuation prospects of the individual firm.

SUMMARY

- The *international monetary system* can be defined as the structure within which foreign exchange rates are determined, international trade and capital flows are accommodated, and balance of payments adjustments made. It also includes all the instruments, institutions, and agreements that link together the world's currency, money markets, securities, real estate, and commodity markets.

- The international monetary system has evolved historically from the gold standard (1876–1913) of fixed exchange rates, to the interwar years and World War II (1914–1944) with floating exchange rates, to fixed exchange rates (1945–1973) under the Bretton Woods Agreement, to the present eclectic currency arrangement (1973–present) of fixed, floating, and managed exchange rates.

- The key monetary institution is the *International Monetary Fund* (IMF). It was first proposed in 1944 at Bretton Woods, New Hampshire, with the purpose of being a lender of last resort to countries facing temporary balance of payments difficulties.

- Contemporary currency regimes vary from rigidly fixed rates to managed floating to independently floating exchange rates.

- Several countries, such as Argentina and Hong Kong, utilize *currency boards* as a means of fixing their exchange rates. Another alternative being considered is *dollarization*, which entails the use of the U.S. dollar as the main domestic currency.

- The argument over the appropriateness of fixed rates versus flexible rates continues, as shown by the variety of currency regimes in use across the globe.

- Eleven of the 15 member countries of the European Union successfully launched a single currency effective January 1, 1999. Called the *euro*, this single currency will replace the 11 national currencies of the participant countries completely by mid-2002. The European Central Bank in Frankfurt, Germany conducts monetary policy for the 11 member countries of the EMU.

- The devaluation of the Mexican peso in 1994 and the subsequent tequila effect was a harbinger of crises to come. The second half of the 1990s was racked by a series of currency crises that shook all emerging markets.

- Three recent crises—the Asian crisis (starting in Thailand in July 1997), the Russian crisis (August 1998), and the Brazilian crisis (January 1999)—were described to demonstrate the critical roles of currencies in the global economy.

QUESTIONS

1. The Asian Crisis
The so-called Asian crisis began in Thailand in July 1997. Since then a number of other countries and regions have been affected.

a.   Explain how and why you think this crisis began.
b.   How and why did it spread to other countries and regions?
c.   What is the present status of the affected countries?
d.   What has been the recommended policy prescription by the IMF?
e.   What do you think should be done to stabilize the world's securities and currency markets?

2. The Launch of the Euro
In your opinion how do you think the euro will compete against the U.S. dollar and Japanese yen with respect to its use in denominating the following.

a. International trade transactions
b. International securities transactions
c. Central bank reserves

3. Fixed versus Floating Rate Regimes
The Argentine peso is pegged to the U.S. dollar on a one-to-one basis using a currency board. The Brazilian real floats and in 1999 it depreciated from about R1.2000/$ to above R2.000/$ (see Exhibit 2.12).

a.   Why do you think these countries adopted such different foreign exchange policies?

b. How do you think European and North American MNEs regard the different exchange rate policies? Consider how these policies influence the desirability of Argentina or Brazil as a place to make a direct investment in a manufacturing subsidiary.

c. In which of the two countries are individuals and companies more likely to flee the currency and keep excess money in foreign-bank euro or dollar deposits?

MINICASE: *Malaysian Foreign Exchange Policies*

Before the Asian currency crisis the Malaysian ringgit (RM) traded at about RM2.5000/$. In the initial months of the crisis the ringgit depreciated to above RM4.000/$. On September 1, 1998, 14 months after the crisis began, the Malaysian government introduced exchange controls intended to reduce the internationalization of the ringgit. These included:

- Requiring governmental approval for ringgit-denominated transactions with nonresidents.

- Requiring short-term inflows of capital to remain in the country for a minimum period of one year. Such funds could, however, be actively managed in terms of ringgit assets.

- Restricting travelers from bringing into the country or taking out of the country more than RM1,000—approximately $26 at the new pegged exchange rate of RM3.8000/$.

- Limiting foreign investments abroad of more than RM10,000.

- Limiting Malaysians who are traveling abroad from carrying more than RM10,000 without prior approval.

The exchange controls did not:

- Limit the repatriation of profits, dividends, interest, fees, commissions, and rental income from portfolio investments.

- Limit direct investment inflows and outflows.

The essence of these controls was to restrict the inflow of short-term portfolio flows, sometimes called "hot money," while continuing to attract long-term foreign direct investment. At the time the controls were imposed, the international investment community generally reacted with dismay and predicted that the ringgit would soon fall to RM8.00 or RM10.00 per dollar.

a. Do you think it is possible to block short-term portfolio money flows while still making a country attractive to long-term direct investors?

b. Using web sources, assess the current success or failure of Malaysia's foreign exchange policies.

WORLD WIDE WEB EXERCISES

W1. Currency ISO Symbols

In the interest of international standardization, the International Standards Organization (ISO) has created a master list of three-letter currency abbreviations for use worldwide. Those currency symbols, increasingly utilized by industry worldwide, are accessible at the web site listed below. Can you identify certain three-letter codes that are actually more confusing than the traditional symbols?

Currency ISO Symbols   http://www.xe.net/currency/iso_4217.htm

W2. The Euro prior to Launch

Use the web page listed below to determine the value of the euro before its introduction on January 1, 1999. The calculation of the euro's value before its introduction—assuming the fixed parities established by the European Union on December 31, 1998—gives some insight as to how its value has theoretically fluctuated even prior to its official launch.

Currency plots   http://pacific.commerce.ubc.ca/xr

W3. World Organizations and the Economic Outlook

The IMF, World Bank, and United Nations are only a few of the major world organizations that track, report, and aid international economic and financial development. Using these web sites and others that may be linked, briefly summarize the economic outlook for the developed and emerging nations of the world. For example, the full text of Chapter 1 of the *World Economic Outlook* published annually by the World Bank is available through the IMF's web page.

International Monetary Fund	http://www.imf.org/
United Nations	http://www.unsystem.org/
The World Bank Group	http://www.worldbank.org/
Europa (EU) Homepage	http://europa.eu.int/
Bank for International Settlements	http://www.bis.org/

SUGGESTED READINGS

Miller, Merton H., "Financial Markets and Economic Growth," *Journal of Applied Corporate Finance*, Fall 1998, Vol. 11, No. 3, pp. 8–15.

Miller, Merton H., "Some Reflections on Recent Monetary Turmoil in Eastern Europe," *Journal of Applied Corporate Finance*, 1998, Vol. 11, No. 3, pp. 49–54.

Rajan, Raghuram G., and Luigi Zingales, "Which Capitalism? Lessons From the East Asia Crisis," *Journal of Applied Corporate Finance*, Fall 1998, Vol. 11, No. 3, pp. 40–48.

Singal, Vijay, "Floating Currencies, Capital Controls, or Currency Boards: What's the Best Remedy for the Currency Crisis," *Journal of Applied Corporate Finance*, Winter 1999, Vol. 11, No. 4, pp. 49–56.

NOTES

1. *Selling short* is a speculation technique in which an individual speculator sells an asset such as a currency to another party for delivery at a future date. The speculator, however, does not yet own the asset, expecting the price of the asset to fall by the date when he must buy the asset for delivery.
2. For more details on currency boards see Culp, Hanke, and Miller (1999) and Singal (1999).
3. The 11 countries are Austria, Belgium, Finland, France, Germany, Ireland, Italy, Luxembourg, the Netherlands, Portugal, and Spain. The United Kingdom, Sweden, and Denmark chose to maintain their individual currencies. Greece did not meet the convergence criteria for membership, but may in the near future.
4. The single most comprehensive official coverage regarding the euro is available from the European Commission at http://europa.eu.int/euro/quest/.
5. As part of its development of cross-border monetary policy, the ECB has formed TARGET, the Transeuropean Automated Real-time Gross Settlement Express Transfer system. TARGET is the mechanism by which the ECB will settle all cross-border payments in the conduct of EU banking business and regulation. It will allow the ECB to quickly and costlessly conduct monetary policy and other intra-banking system capital movements.
6. According to the EU, the symbol was inspired by the Greek letter epsilon, simultaneously referring to Greece's ancient role as the source of European civilization and to its being the first letter of the word Europe.
7. A case study of how one company believes the euro will be a source of competitive advantage is "Euro case study: Siemens" at http://news.bbc.co.uk/hi/english/events/the_launch_of_emu.
8. The *tequila effect* is the term used to describe how the Mexican peso crisis of December 1994 quickly spread to other Latin American currency and equity markets, a form of financial panic termed *contagion*.
9. The magnitude of economic devastation in Asia is still largely unappreciated by Westerners. At a recent conference sponsored by the Milken Institute, a speaker noted that the preoccupation with the economic problems of Indonesia was incomprehensible since "the total gross domestic product of Indonesia is roughly the size of North Carolina." The following speaker noted, however, that the last time he had checked, "North Carolina did not have a population of 220 million people."
10. Ranges as reported by the International Monetary Fund. The band had been adjusted continually throughout 1996, 1997, and the first half of 1998. Theoretically, the Central Bank allowed the exchange rate and associated band to slide daily at a 1.5% per month rate.
11. Russian tax revenue collections averaged slightly over $1 billion per month in 1998, less than those of New York City (*The Economist*, February 6, 1999, p. 23).
12. *The Economist*, February 6, 1999, p. 25.
13. "IMF Sending Crisis Team to Brazil," *Financial Times*, Friday January 15, 1999, p. 1.
14. Firms in commodity industries, however, such as petrochemicals, sell products in all markets, which are priced in U.S. dollars. It is also important to differentiate the currency of denomination from the currency of invoice; currency of invoice is simply the currency of settlement, whereas currency of denomination is the currency in which prices are set and sales generated.
15. "Brazil Steel Group Delays New Mill," *Financial Times*, Tuesday January 19, 1999, p.19.

CHAPTER 3

FOREIGN EXCHANGE RATE DETERMINATION

What are the determinants of exchange rates? Are changes in exchange rates predictable? These are fundamental questions that managers of MNEs, international portfolio investors, importers and exporters, and government officials must deal with every day. We will focus on the needs of the MNE.

Unfortunately, there is no general theory of exchange rate determination. Instead, there are economic theories called *parity conditions* that attempt to explain long-run exchange rate determinants. Numerous other variables appear to explain short- and medium-run exchange rate determinants. A major problem is that the same set of determinants does not explain exchange rates for all countries at all times, or even for the same country at all times.

Exhibit 3.1 provides a road map to identify the potentially most important determinants that have surfaced in recent years. Many of these were observed in the emerging markets crises described in Chapter 2. Others spring from classical economic theory. Note that most determinants of the spot exchange rate are also in turn affected by changes in the spot rate. In other words, they are not only linked but mutually determined.

Parity conditions (Exhibit 3.1, upper left) are an explanation in classical economics for the long-run value of exchange rates. These conditions will be described in detail later in this chapter.

Infrastructure weaknesses (upper right) were among the big causes for the recent collapses of exchange rates in the emerging markets described in Chapter 2. On the other hand, infrastructure strengths helped explain why the U.S. dollar continues to be strong despite record balance-of-payments deficits on current account.

Speculation (lower left) contributed greatly to the emerging market crises. Some characteristics of speculation were hot money flows into and out of currencies, securities, real estate, and commodities. Uncovered interest arbitrage was a phenomenon caused by exception-

Exhibit 3.1   *Potential Foreign Exchange Rate Determinants*

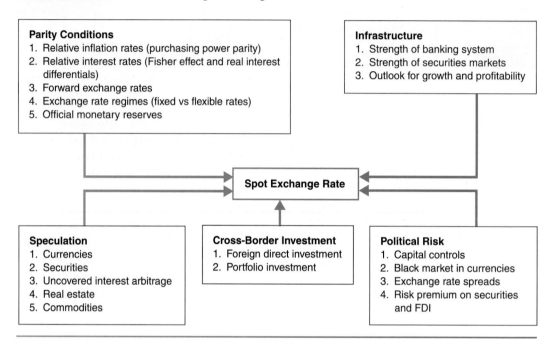

Parity Conditions
1. Relative inflation rates (purchasing power parity)
2. Relative interest rates (Fisher effect and real interest differentials)
3. Forward exchange rates
4. Exchange rate regimes (fixed vs flexible rates)
5. Official monetary reserves

Infrastructure
1. Strength of banking system
2. Strength of securities markets
3. Outlook for growth and profitability

Spot Exchange Rate

Speculation
1. Currencies
2. Securities
3. Uncovered interest arbitrage
4. Real estate
5. Commodities

Cross-Border Investment
1. Foreign direct investment
2. Portfolio investment

Political Risk
1. Capital controls
2. Black market in currencies
3. Exchange rate spreads
4. Risk premium on securities and FDI

ally low borrowing interest rates in Japan coupled with high real interest rates in the United States. It has been popular to borrow yen and invest in safe U.S. government securities, hoping that the exchange rate did not change. This is labeled the "yen carry trade."

Cross-border foreign direct investment and *international portfolio investment* into the emerging markets dried up during the recent crises. However, they have strengthened the U.S. dollar against most European currencies.

Political risks have been much reduced in recent years as capital markets became less segmented from each other and more liquid. More countries have adopted democratic forms of government. However, the emerging market crises have raised the specter of a reimposition of controls on capital flows, such as the controls imposed by Malaysia in 1998.

Cash flows motivated by any and all of the potential exchange rate determinants eventually show up in the *balance of payments* (BOP). The BOP provides a means to account for these cash flows in a standardized and systematic manner. The BOP increases the transparency of the whole international monetary environment and enables decision-makers to make more rational policy choices, in both the private and the public sectors. Therefore, the next section of this chapter describes the basics of the BOP. This discussion is followed by an analysis of parity conditions and then by forecasting considerations.

THE BALANCE OF PAYMENTS APPROACH

The International Monetary Fund defines the BOP as a statistical statement that systematically summarizes, for a specific time period, the economic transactions of an economy with the rest of the world. BOP data measures economic transactions between residents of one country and residents of all other countries. Economic transactions include exports and imports of goods and services, income flows, capital flows, and gifts and similar "one-sided" transfer payments. The net of all these transactions is matched by a change in the country's international monetary reserves.

Home-country and host-country BOP data are important to business managers, investors, consumers, and government officials because the data influences and is influenced by other key macroeconomic variables such as gross domestic product, employment, price levels, exchange rates, and interest rates. Monetary and fiscal policy must take the BOP into account at the national level.

Business managers and investors need BOP data to anticipate changes in host country economic policies that might be driven by BOP events. BOP data may be important for any of the following reasons:

- The BOP helps to forecast a country's market potential, especially in the short run. A country experiencing a serious BOP deficit is not likely to expand imports as much as it would if it were running a surplus.

- The BOP is an important indicator of pressure on a country's foreign exchange rate, and thus on the potential for a firm trading with or investing in that country to experience foreign exchange gains or losses. Changes in the BOP may presage the imposition (or removal) of foreign exchange controls.

- Changes in a country's BOP may also signal the imposition (or removal) of controls over payment of dividends and interest, license fees, royalty fees, or other cash disbursements to foreign firms or investors.

Exhibit 3.2 provides a generic BOP statement, applying to any country for any time period.[1]

MANAGERIAL SIGNIFICANCE OF BOP IMBALANCES

The significance of a deficit or surplus in the BOP has changed since the advent of floating exchange rates. Traditionally, BOP measures were used as evidence of pressure on a country's foreign exchange rate. This pressure led to governmental transactions that were compensatory in nature, forced on the government by its need to settle the deficit or face a devaluation.

))) Exchange Rate Impacts

The relationship between the BOP and exchange rates can be illustrated by use of a simplified equation that summarizes BOP data:

Exhibit 3.2	*Generic Balance of Payments*

A. Current Account

1. Net exports/imports of goods (trade balance)
2. Net exports/imports of services
3. Net income (investment income from direct and portfolio investment plus employee compensation)
4. Net transfers (sums sent home by migrants and permanent workers abroad, gifts, grants, and pensions)

A (1 through 4) = *Current account balance*

B. Capital Account (capital transfers related to the purchase and sale of fixed assets such as real estate)

C. Financial Account

1. Net foreign direct investment
2. Net portfolio investment
3. Other financial items

A + B + C = *Basic balance*

D. Net Errors and Omissions (missing data such as illegal transfers)

A + B + C + D = *Overall balance*

E. Reserves and Related Items (changes in official monetary reserves including gold, foreign exchange, and IMF position)

$$\underset{\text{Payments}}{\underset{\text{Balance of}}{BOP}} = \underset{\text{Balance}}{\underset{\text{Account}}{\underset{\text{Current}}{(X-M)}}} + \underset{\text{Balance}}{\underset{\text{Account}}{\underset{\text{Capital}}{(CI-CO)}}} + \underset{\text{Balance}^2}{\underset{\text{Account}}{\underset{\text{Financial}}{(FI-FO)}}} + \underset{\text{Balance}}{\underset{\text{Reserve}}{FXB}}$$

where: X is exports of goods and services,
M is imports of goods and services,
CI is capital inflows,
CO is capital outflows,
FI is financial inflows,
FO is financial outflows,
FXB is official monetary reserves such as foreign exchange and gold.

The effect of an imbalance in the BOP of a country works somewhat differently depending on whether that country has fixed exchange rates, floating exchange rates, or a managed exchange rate system.

Fixed Exchange Rate Countries. Under a fixed exchange rate system, the government bears the responsibility to ensure a BOP near zero. If the sum of the current and capital accounts does not approximate zero, the government is expected to intervene in the foreign exchange market by buying or selling official foreign exchange reserves. If the sum of the first two accounts is greater than zero, a surplus demand for the domestic currency exists in the world. To preserve the fixed exchange rate, the government must then intervene in the foreign exchange market and sell domestic currency for foreign currencies or gold so as to bring the BOP back near zero.

If the sum of the current and capital accounts is negative, an excess supply of the domestic currency exists in world markets. Then the government must intervene by buying the domestic currency with its reserves of foreign currencies and gold. It is obviously important for a government to maintain significant foreign exchange reserve balances to allow it to intervene effectively. If the country runs out of foreign exchange reserves, it will be unable to buy back its domestic currency and will be forced to devalue.

For fixed exchange rate countries, then, business managers use balance-of-payments statistics to help forecast devaluation or revaluation of the official exchange rate. (Recall from Chapter 2 that a change in fixed exchange rates is technically called "devaluation" or "revaluation," while a change in floating exchange rates is either "depreciation" or "appreciation.")

Floating Exchange Rate Countries. Under a floating exchange rate system, the government of a country has no responsibility to peg the foreign exchange rate. The fact that the current and capital account balances do not sum to zero will automatically (in theory) alter the exchange rate in the direction necessary to obtain a BOP near zero. For example, a country running a sizable current account deficit with the capital and financial accounts balance of zero will have a net BOP deficit. An excess supply of the domestic currency will appear on world markets. As is the case with all goods in excess supply, the market will rid itself of the imbalance by lowering the price. Thus, the domestic currency will fall in value, and the BOP will move back toward zero. Exchange rate markets do not always follow this theory, particularly in the short-to-intermediate term.

Managed Floats. Although still relying on market conditions for day-to-day exchange rate determination, countries operating with *managed floats* often find it necessary to take actions to maintain their desired exchange rate values. They therefore seek to alter the market's valuation of a specific exchange rate by influencing the motivations of market activity, rather than through direct intervention in the foreign exchange markets.

The primary action taken by such governments is to change relative interest rates, thus influencing the economic fundamentals of exchange rate determination. In the context of the equation above, a change in domestic interest rates is an attempt to alter the term $(CI - CO)$, especially the short-term portfolio component of these capital flows, in order to restore an imbalance caused by the deficit in the current account. The power of interest rate changes on international capital and exchange rate movements can be substantial. A country with a managed float that wishes to "defend its currency" may choose to raise domestic interest rates to attract additional capital from abroad. This will alter market forces and create additional market demand for the domestic currency. In this process, the government signals exchange market participants that it intends to take measures to preserve the currency's value within certain ranges. The process also raises the cost of local borrowing for businesses, however, and so the policy is seldom without domestic critics. For managed-float countries, business managers use BOP trends to help forecast changes in government policies on domestic interest rates.

PARITY CONDITIONS

As shown in Exhibit 3.1, there are many potential exchange rate determinants. Economists have traditionally isolated several of these determinants and theorized how they are linked with one another and with spot and forward exchange rates. These linkages are called *parity conditions*. They are sometimes useful in explaining and forecasting the long-run trend in an exchange rate.

PRICES, INTEREST RATES, AND EXCHANGE RATES IN EQUILIBRIUM

Exhibit 3.3 illustrates all the fundamental parity relations simultaneously by using the Japanese yen as an example. The details will be explained in the next sections of this chapter. The yen is expected to strengthen 4% versus the dollar. The spot exchange rate, ¥104/$, is forecasted to change to ¥100/$ one year from now using *purchasing power parity* (PPP, relation A), the international Fisher effect (relation C), and the forward rate (relation E). The forecasted inflation rates for Japan (1.0%) and the United States (5.0%) result in a forecast of ¥100/$. If the difference in nominal interest rates is used (international Fisher effect), the forecasted spot rate is also ¥100/$. Finally, the one-year forward rate on the Japanese yen, ¥100/$, if assumed to be an unbiased predictor of the future spot rate, also forecasts ¥100/$.

PRICES AND EXCHANGE RATES

If the identical product or service can be sold in two different markets, and no restrictions exist on the sale or transportation costs of moving the product between markets, the product's price should be the same in both markets. This is called the *law of one price*. A primary principle of competitive markets is that prices will equalize across markets if frictions or costs of moving the products or services between markets do not exist. If the two markets are two different countries, the product's price may be stated in different currency terms, but the price of the product should still be the same. Comparison of prices would only require a conversion from one currency to the other. For example,

---

Exhibit 3.3   *International Parity Relations in Equilibrium (Approximate Form)*

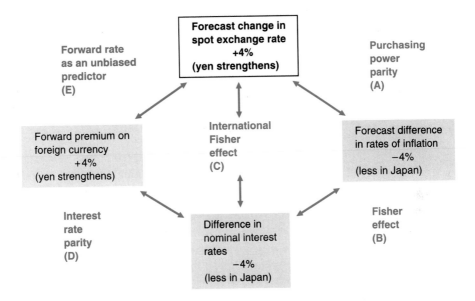

1. **Exchange Rates:**
   a. Current Spot Rate: $S_1 = ¥104/\$$
   b. Forward Rate (one year): $F = ¥100/\$$
   c. Expected Spot Rate: $S_2 = ¥100/\$$
   d. Forward Premium on yen:

   $$f^¥ = \frac{S_1 - F}{F} \times 100 = \frac{104 - 100}{100} \times 100 = +4\%$$

   e. Forecast Change in Spot Rate:

   $$\%\Delta S = \frac{S_1 - S_2}{S_2} \times 100 = \frac{104 - 100}{100} \times 100 = +4\%$$

2. **Forecast Rate of Inflation:**
   a. Japan   1%
   b. United States   5%
   c. Difference   −4%

3. **Interest on One-Year Government Security:**
   a. Japan   4%
   b. United States   8%
   c. Difference   −4%

$$P^\$ \times S = P^¥$$

where the price of the product in U.S. dollars ($P^\$$), multiplied by the spot exchange rate (S, yen per U.S. dollar), equals the price of the product in Japanese yen ($P^¥$). Conversely, if the prices of the two products were stated in local currencies and markets were efficient at competing away a higher price in one market relative to the other, the exchange rate could be deduced from the relative local product prices:

$$S = \frac{P^¥}{P^\$}$$

))) Purchasing Power Parity and the Law of One Price

If the law of one price were true for all goods and services, the purchasing power parity exchange rate could be found from any individual set of prices. By comparing the prices of identical products denominated in different currencies, we could determine the "real" or PPP exchange rate which should exist if markets were efficient.

The *hamburger standard*, as it has been christened by *The Economist* (Exhibit 3.4), is a prime example of this law of one price. Assuming that the Big Mac is indeed identical in all countries listed, it serves as one means of identifying whether currencies are currently trading at market rates that are close to the exchange rate implied by Big Macs in local currencies. For example, a Big Mac in Sweden costs SKr24.00, while the same Big Mac in the United States is $2.43. This implies a purchasing power parity exchange rate of:

$$\frac{SKr24.00}{\$2.43} = SKr9.8765/\$$$

However, on the date of the survey, the actual exchange rate was SKr8.32/$. Therefore, the Swedish krona is overvalued by:

$$\frac{SKr9.8765}{SKr8.32} = 1.187, \text{ or } \approx 19\%$$

A less extreme form of this principle would say that, in relatively efficient markets, the price of a basket of goods would be the same in each market. This formulation simply requires the replacement of the individual product's price with that of a price index. The PPP exchange rate between the two countries would then be stated:

$$S = \frac{PI^¥}{PI^\$}$$

| Exhibit 3.4 | *The Law of One Price: The Big Mac Hamburger Standard* |

Country	(1) Big Mac Price (in local currency)	(2) Actual Exchange Rate 3/30/99	(3) Big Mac Price (in dollars)	(4) Implied PPP of the Dollar	(5) Local Currency under(−)/ over(+) Valuation
United States	$2.43	—	2.43	—	—
Argentina	Peso2.50	1.00	2.50	1.03	+3
Australia	A$2.65	1.59	1.66	1.09	−32
Brazil	Real2.95	1.73	1.71	1.73	−30
Britain	£1.90	$1.61	3.07	$1.28	+26
Canada	C$2.99	1.51	1.98	1.23	−19
Chile	Peso1,250	484	2.60	518	+7
China	Yuan9.90	8.28	1.20	4.07	−51
Denmark	DKr24.75	6.91	3.58	10.19	+47
Euro area	Euro2.52	$1.08	2.71	$0.97	+11
France	FFr18.50	6.10	2.87	7.20	+18
Germany	DM4.95	1.82	2.72	2.04	+12
Italy	Lire4,500	1,799	2.50	1,852	+3
Netherlands	Fl 5.45	2.05	2.66	2.24	+10
Spain	Ptas375	155	2.43	154	0
Hong Kong	HK$10.2	7.75	1.32	4.20	−46
Hungary	Forint299	237	1.26	123	−48
Indonesia	Rupiah14,500	8,725	1.66	5,957	−32
Israel	Shekel 3.9	4.04	3.44	5.72	+42
Japan	¥294	120	2.44	121	0
Malaysia	Rm4.52	3.80	1.19	1.86	−51
Mexico	Peso19.9	9.54	2.09	8.19	−14
New Zealand	NZ$3.40	1.87	1.82	1.40	−25
Poland	Zloty5.50	3.98	1.38	2.26	−43
Russia	Ruble33.5	24.7	1.35	13.79	−44
Singapore	S$3.20	1.73	1.85	1.32	−24
South Africa	Rand8.60	6.22	1.38	3.54	−43
South Korea	Won3,000	1,218	2.46	1,235	+1
Sweden	SKr24.0	8.32	2.88	9.88	+19
Switzerland	SFr5.90	1.48	3.97	2.43	+64
Taiwan	NT$70.0	33.2	2.11	28.8	−13
Thailand	Baht52.0	37.6	1.38	21.4	−43

Source: Adapted from "Big MacCurrencies," *The Economist*, April 3, 1999, p. 66. Original quotations courtesy of McDonald's. United States Big Mac price is the average of New York, Chicago, San Francisco, and Atlanta. British and Euro area actual exchange rate and implied PPP rates quoted in U.S. dollars per currency.
Column (1): Prices in local currency; may vary by location.
Column (2): Actual exchange rate on March 30, 1999 (London quotes).
Column (3): column (1) ÷ column (2)
Column (4): column (1) ÷ $2.43 (price of Big Mac in United States).
Column (5): column (4) ÷ column (2).

where $PI^¥$ and $PI^$$ are price indices expressed in local currency for Japan and the United States, respectively. For example, if the identical basket of goods cost ¥1000 in Japan and $10 in the United States, the PPP exchange rate would be:

$$\frac{¥1000}{\$10} = ¥100/\$$$

This is the *absolute version of the theory of purchasing power parity. Absolute PPP states that the spot exchange rate is determined by the relative prices of similar baskets of goods.*

)))) Relative Purchasing Power Parity

If the assumptions of the absolute version of PPP theory are relaxed a bit more, we observe what is termed *relative purchasing power parity*. This more general idea is that PPP is not particularly helpful in determining what the spot rate is today, but that the relative change in prices between two countries over a period of time determines the change in the exchange rate over that period. More specifically, *if the spot exchange rate between two countries starts in equilibrium, any change in the differential rate of inflation between them tends to be offset over the long run by an equal but opposite change in the spot exchange rate.*

Exhibit 3.5 shows a general case of relative PPP. The vertical axis shows the percentage appreciation or depreciation of the foreign currency relative to the home currency, and the horizontal axis shows the percentage higher or lower rate of inflation in the foreign country relative to the home country. The diagonal parity line shows the equilibrium position between a change in the exchange rate and relative inflation rates. For instance, point P represents an equilibrium point where inflation in the foreign country, say Japan, is 4% lower than in the home country, say the United States. Therefore, relative PPP would predict that the yen would appreciate by 4% per annum with respect to the U.S. dollar.

The main justification for purchasing power parity is that if a country experiences inflation rates higher than those of its main trading partners, and its exchange rate does not change, its exports of goods and services will become less competitive with comparable products produced elsewhere. Imports from abroad will also become more price competitive with higher-priced domestic products. This change will lead to a deficit on *current account* in the BOP unless offset by capital and financial flows.

)))) Empirical Tests of Purchasing Power Parity

Extensive testing of both the absolute and relative versions of purchasing power parity and the law of one price has been done. The tests have, for the most part, not proved PPP is accurate in predicting future exchange rates. Goods and services do not in reality move at zero cost between countries, and in fact many goods are not "tradable," for example haircuts. Many goods and services are not

Exhibit 3.5   *Purchasing Power Parity*

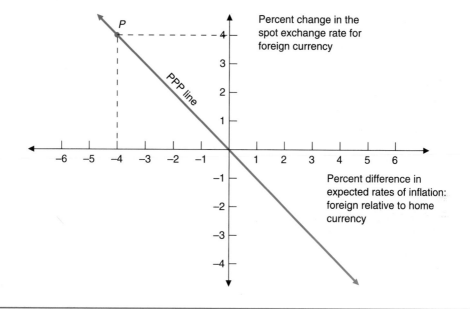

the same quality across countries, reflecting the differences in tastes and resources of the countries of their manufacture and consumption.

Two general conclusions can be made from these tests: (1) PPP holds up well over the very long run but poorly for shorter time periods; (2) the theory holds better for countries with relatively high rates of inflation and underdeveloped capital markets.[3]

On the other hand, several problems do exist with these tests:

Problem 1. Most of the tests use an index of prices such as the wholesale price index. This index may be misleading, since only goods that are traded directly affect supply and demand for foreign currencies. Nevertheless, even such non-traded goods as housing and medical costs indirectly affect the price of traded goods through their influence on the overall cost of living and thus on wage demands.

Problem 2. Tests of PPP should be based on comparing a similar market basket of goods in each country. If PPP is working, and governments do not interfere, the effective prices for a similar basket of goods should be the same in every country once exchange rates and prices have adjusted to worldwide PPP. However, because of differences in taste, level of development, and income, it is difficult to find identical market baskets among countries. Any consumption-based index is necessarily going to compare "apples and oranges."

Problem 3. Tests of PPP require a knowledge of what the market is forecasting for differential inflation rates, but the data that are available are either realized historical inflation rates or existing differential interest rates used as a proxy for expected inflation differentials.

Problem 4. Time periods for testing have seldom, if ever, been free of at least some government interference in the trade process.

Problem 5. During the 1980s and 1990s capital and financial markets were gradually deregulated worldwide. As a result, crossborder capital, financial, and speculative cash flows have grown in importance as determinants of exchange rates over PPP, especially in the short and intermediate time periods. (See Exhibit 3.1 for an illustration of nonparity determinants.)

⟫⟫⟫ Exchange Rate Indices: Real and Nominal

Any single country in the current global market trades with numerous partners. This requires tracking and evaluating its individual currency value against all other currency values in order to determine relative purchasing power, that is, whether it is "overvalued" or "undervalued" in terms of PPP. One of the primary methods of dealing with this problem is the calculation of exchange rate indices. These indices are formed by trade-weighting the bilateral exchange rates between the home country and its trading partners.

The *nominal effective exchange rate index* calculates, on a weighted average basis, the value of the subject currency at different points in time. It does not really indicate anything about the "true value" of the currency, or anything related to PPP. The nominal index simply calculates how the currency value relates to some arbitrarily chosen base period. The *real effective exchange rate index* indicates how the weighted average purchasing power of the currency has changed relative to some arbitrarily selected base period.

For example, the real effective exchange rate index for the U.S. dollar, $E_R^\$$, is found by multiplying the nominal effective exchange rate index, $E_N^\$$, by the ratio of U.S. dollar costs, $C^\$$, over foreign currency costs, C^{FC}, both in index form:

$$E_R^\$ = E_N^\$ \times \frac{C^\$}{C^{FC}}$$

A number of exchange rate indices are published on a frequent basis, such as the widely used International Monetary Fund Index, which is shown in Exhibit 3.6. It illustrates the degree to which PPP has held for five currencies during the period 1981–1998. If changes in exchange rates just offset differential inflation rates, all the real effective exchange rate indices would stay at 100. If an exchange rate strengthened more than was justified by differential inflation, its index would rise above 100, and it would be considered "overvalued" from a competitive perspective. An index value below 100 would suggest an "undervalued" currency.

As Exhibit 3.6 shows, the real effective exchange rate has varied considerably from year to year for some currencies for the long run. For example, the index of the real effective exchange rate for the U.S. dollar rose from 135.7 in 1981 to 166.0 in 1985, only to fall to 100 in 1995. The Japanese yen remained undervalued throughout the period, starting at 62.5 in 1981 and ending at 79.5 in 1997. The German mark was consistently undervalued from 1981 to 1997. The U.K. pound was consistently overvalued for the same period.

Apart from measuring deviations from PPP, a country's real effective exchange rate is an important tool for predicting upward or downward pressure

Exhibit 3.6 *International Monetary Fund's Nominal and Real Effective Exchange Rate Indices*

Year	United States Nominal[a]	Real[b]	Germany Nominal[a]	Real[b]	Japan Nominal[a]	Real[b]	United Kingdom Nominal[a]	Real[b]
1981	128.9	135.7	68.1	66.8	44.2	62.5	150.8	133.6
1982	142.7	152.4	72.1	68.3	41.4	55.1	145.2	127.4
1983	148.0	153.8	75.7	70.9	45.3	58.6	136.3	117.9
1984	158.1	161.5	75.3	69.7	47.8	60.0	131.3	112.7
1985	163.5	166.0	75.7	69.6	48.9	59.3	131.2	113.6
1986	133.0	134.3	82.2	75.5	62.4	74.5	119.6	105.0
1987	117.6	117.5	86.9	80.4	67.8	77.6	117.1	107.3
1988	109.5	110.6	86.4	80.1	75.1	81.3	124.1	115.1
1989	114.3	114.0	85.8	78.6	71.8	76.5	120.6	115.1
1990	109.1	108.0	89.4	82.8	64.7	68.6	117.8	108.3
1991	107.3	106.3	88.6	81.9	70.2	72.6	118.7	112.3
1992	105.2	105.1	91.3	85.6	73.6	73.8	114.3	114.1
1993	108.4	107.9	94.9	91.0	88.3	89.6	104.8	106.1
1994	106.4	106.4	95.1	93.4	95.2	95.8	105.2	106.0
1995	100.0	100.0	100.0	100.0	100.0	100.0	100.0	100.0
1996	105.2	105.8	97.3	98.0	86.8	84.6	101.7	103.4
1997	113.8	114.8	92.9	91.1	81.7	79.5	118.5	125.5
1998	119.3		93.1		76.5		122.5	

[a]Nominal effective exchange rate indices are derived from trade in manufactured goods with that country's major trading partners. The weights are based on relative proportions of trade for the base year of 1995, 1995=100.0.
[b]Real effective exchange rate indices are compiled from the nominal effective exchange rate index and a cost indicator of relative normalized unit labor costs in manufacturing. The reference base is 1995=100.
Source: International Monetary Fund, *International Financial Statistics*, Washington, D.C. monthly.

on its BOP and exchange rate, as well as an indicator of the desirability to produce for export from that country.

))) Exchange Rate Pass-Through

The degree to which the prices of imported and exported goods change as a result of exchange rate changes is termed *pass-through*.[4] Incomplete *exchange rate pass-through* is one reason that a country's real effective exchange rate index can deviate for lengthy periods from its PPP-equilibrium level of 100. Although PPP implies that all exchange rate changes are passed on through equivalent changes in prices to trading partners, empirical research has questioned this long-held assumption. For example, sizeable current account deficits of the United States in the 1980s and 1990s did not respond to changes in the value of the dollar.

To illustrate exchange rate pass-through, let us assume BMW produces an automobile in Germany and pays all production expense in euros. When the auto is exported to the United States, the price of the BMW in the U.S. market should simply be the euro value converted to dollars at the spot exchange rate:

$$P^\$_{BMW} = P^\unicode{x20AC}_{BMW} \times S$$

where $P^\$_{BMW}$ is the BMW price in dollars, $P^\unicode{x20AC}_{BMW}$ is the BMW price in euros, and S is the number of dollars per euro. If the euro appreciated 10% versus the U.S. dollar, the new spot exchange rate should result in the price of the BMW in the United States rising a proportional 10%. If the price in dollars increases by the same percentage change as the exchange rate, the pass-through of exchange rate changes is complete (or 100%).

If the price in dollars rises by less than the percentage change in exchange rates (as is often the case in international trade), the pass-through is *partial*, as illustrated in Exhibit 3.7. The 71% pass-through (U.S. dollar prices rise only 20% when the euro appreciated 20%) implies that BMW is absorbing a portion of the adverse exchange rate change. This absorption could result from smaller profit margins, cost reductions, or both. For example, components and raw materials imported to Germany cost less in euros when the euro appreciates. It is also likely that some time may pass before all exchange rate changes are finally reflected in the prices of traded goods, including the period over which previously signed contracts are delivered upon. It is obviously in the interests of BMW to keep the appreciation of the euro from raising the price of its automobiles in major export markets.

The concept of price elasticity of demand is useful when determining the desired level of pass-through.[5] A German product that is relatively price inelastic, meaning that the quantity demanded is relatively unresponsive to price changes, may often demonstrate a high degree of pass-through. This is so because a higher dollar price in the United States market would have little noticeable effect on the quantity of the product demanded by consumers and would, in fact, result in an

Exhibit 3.7	*Exchange Rate Pass-Through*

Pass-through is the measure of response of imported and exported product prices to exchange rate changes. Assume the price in dollars and euros of a BMW automobile produced in Germany and sold in the United States at the spot exchange rate is:

$$P^{€}_{BMW} = €35,000 \quad \times \quad S = \$1.0000/€ \quad = \quad P^{\$}_{BMW} = \$35,000$$

If the euro were to appreciate 20% versus the U.S. dollar, from \$1.0000/€ to \$1.2000/€, the price of the BMW in the U.S. market should theoretically be \$42,000. But if the price of the BMW in the U.S. does not rise by 20%—for example, to only \$40,000—then the degree of pass-through is only *partial*:

$$\frac{P^{\$}_{BMW,2}}{P^{\$}_{BMW,1}} = \frac{\$40,000}{\$35,000} = 1.1429, \text{ or a } 14.29\% \text{ increase}$$

The degree of pass-through is measured by the proportion of the exchange rate change reflected in dollar prices. In this example, the dollar price of the BMW rose only 14.29%, while the euro appreciated 20.0% against the U.S. dollar. The degree of pass-through is partial, 14.29% ÷ 20.00%, or approximately 0.71. Only 71% of the exchange rate change was passed-through to the U.S. dollar price. The remaining 29% of the exchange rate change has been absorbed by BMW.

increase in total dollar sales revenue. However, products that are relatively price elastic would respond in the opposite direction. If the 20% euro appreciation resulted in 20% higher dollar prices, U.S. consumers would decrease the number of BMWs purchased. If price elasticity for BMWs in the United States were greater than 1, total dollar sales revenue of BMWs would decline.

INTEREST RATES AND EXCHANGE RATES

We have already seen how prices of goods in different countries should be related through exchange rates. We now consider how interest rates are linked to exchange rates.

))) The Fisher Effect

The Fisher effect, named after economist Irving Fisher, states that *nominal interest rates in each country are equal to the required real rate of return plus compensation for expected inflation.* More formally:[6]

$$i = r + \pi + r\pi$$

where i is the nominal rate of interest, r is the real rate of interest, and π is the expected rate of inflation over the period of time for which funds are to be lent. The final compound term, $r\pi$, is frequently dropped from consideration due to its relatively minor value. The Fisher effect then reduces to (approximate form):

$$i = r + \pi$$

The Fisher effect applied to two different countries like the United States and Japan would be:

$$i^{\$} = r^{\$} + \pi^{\$}; \quad i^{¥} = r^{¥} + \pi^{¥}$$

where the superscripts $\$$ and $¥$ pertain to the respective nominal (i), real (r), and expected inflation (π) components of financial instruments denominated in dollars and yen, respectively. It should be noted that this requires a forecast of the future rate of inflation, not what inflation has been. Predicting the future can be difficult.

Empirical tests using ex-post national inflation rates have shown the Fisher effect to exist particularly for short-maturity government securities such as Treasury bills and notes. Comparisons based on longer maturities suffer from the increased financial risk inherent in fluctuations of the market value of the bonds prior to maturity. Comparisons of private sector securities are influenced by unequal creditworthiness of the issuers. All the tests are inconclusive to the extent that the ex-post rate of inflation does not correctly measure the ex-ante expected rate of inflation.[7]

)))) The International Fisher Effect

The relationship between the percentage change in the spot exchange rate over time and the differential between comparable interest rates in different national capital markets is known as the *international Fisher effect. Fisher-open*, as it is often termed, states that *the spot exchange rate should change in an amount equal to but in the opposite direction of the difference in interest rates between two countries.* More formally (using the dollar and yen):

$$\frac{S_1 - S_2}{S_2} \times 100 = i^{\$} - i^{¥}$$

where $i^{\$}$ and $i^{¥}$ are the respective national interest rates, and S is the spot exchange rate using indirect quotes at the beginning of the period (S_1) and the end of the period (S_2). This is the approximation form commonly used in industry. The precise formulation would be the following (see the appendix to this chapter for the complete mathematical derivation):

$$\frac{S_1 - S_2}{S_2} \times 100 = \frac{i^{\$} - i^{¥}}{1 + i^{¥}}$$

Justification for the international Fisher effect is that investors must be rewarded or penalized to offset the expected change in exchange rates. For example, if a dollar-based investor buys a 10-year yen bond earning 4% interest, compared to 6% interest available on dollars, the investor must be expecting the yen to appreciate vîs-à-vîs the dollar by at least 2% per year during the 10 years. If not, the dollar-based investor would be better off remaining in dollars. If the yen appreciates 3% during the 10 year period, the dollar-based investor would earn a bonus of 1% higher return. However, the international Fisher effect predicts that with unrestricted capital flows, an investor should be indifferent between investing in dollar or yen bonds, since investors worldwide would see the same opportunity and compete it away.

Empirical tests lend some support to the relationship postulated by the international Fisher effect, although considerable short-run deviations occur. However, a more serious criticism has been posed by recent studies that suggest the existence of a foreign exchange risk premium for most major currencies. Also, speculation in uncovered interest arbitrage, such as the "yen carry trade" described below, creates distortions in currency markets. Thus the expected change in exchange rates might be consistently more than the difference in interest rates. The following illustrative case reinforces this conclusion.

ILLUSTRATIVE CASE

The Yen Carry Trade

TOKYO—Japan's rock-bottom interest rates have international investors slowly moving back into so-called *yen carry trades*, but exchange rate volatility so far this year has kept these controversial trades from burgeoning to the levels seen last year.

Many investors got hammered last year when a sudden plunge in the yen eroded the profits gleaned from such trades, which invest cheap, yen-based funds in higher-yielding assets denominated in other currencies. Economists predict the yen's rate will probably be even more unpredictable this year than last as government policies change amid this country's economic turmoil.

If it weren't for the volatility in the currency markets, yen carry trades would look more attractive now then ever. Financial institutions in Tokyo on Tuesday were paying an annualized interest rate of 0.4% to raise yen in Tokyo money markets, almost half what the rate was a year ago and a record low rate that has seen few precedents in the industrialized, post-war world. Take that cheap yen, converted, say, into dollars, then buy short-term U.S. government securities yielding 5%, and an investor can make a tidy margin of about 4.6% minus the cost of currency conversion.

Investors the world over—but especially big U.S. hedge funds—have done variations on this trade since 1995 as the Japanese central bank pushed rates to ever lower levels in an effort to revive growth and to widen lending margins to help troubled banks. Over time, the trades grew more sophisticated as investors grew more willing to use cheap yen to leverage increasingly complicated asset purchases—purchases sometimes valued at several times the money raised. Funds raised in Tokyo zoomed from London to Kuala Lumpur in search of higher yielding securities to buy.

Then in July 1998, disaster struck. The profitability of the yen carry trade depends on the Japanese currency either remaining stable or weakening, as it generally did between 1995 and early 1998. But the yen rebounded last July, and in just two days, the dollar fell by 9% against the Japanese currency. The dollar then slid 12% more in October. As profits from the interest rate differential were eaten by currency losses, investors sold off their investments and paid back their yen.

Source: "Risky Tactic in Yen Trade Shows Life as Rates Fall," *Wall Street Journal*, 3/10/99, p. A14, A17.

》》》 Interest Rate Parity

The theory of *interest rate parity* (IRP) provides the linkage between the foreign exchange markets and the international money markets. The theory states: *The difference in the national interest rates for securities of similar risk and maturity should be equal to, but opposite in sign to, the forward rate discount or premium for the foreign currency, except for transaction costs.*

As illustrated in Exhibit 3.8, the forward premium on the Swiss franc/dollar forward exchange rate series arises from the differential between Swiss franc and U.S. dollar interest rates. Since the forward rate for any particular maturity utilizes the specific interest rates for that term, the forward premium or discount on a currency is visually obvious: The currency with the higher interest rate—in this case the U.S. dollar—will sell forward at a discount.

Exhibit 3.9 illustrates the theory of interest rate parity. Assume that an investor has $1,000,000 and several alternative but comparable Swiss franc (SF) monetary investments. If the investor chooses to invest in a dollar money market instrument, the investor would earn the dollar rate of interest. This results in $(1 + i^\$)$ at the end of the period, where $i^\$$ is the dollar rate of interest in decimal form. The investor may, however, choose to invest in a Swiss franc money market instrument of identical risk and maturity for the same period. This would require that the investor exchange the dollars for francs at the spot rate of exchange, invest the francs in a money market instrument, and at the end of the period convert the resulting proceeds back to dollars.

A dollar-based investor would compare the relative returns of starting in the top-left corner and investing in dollars (straight across the top of the box) to investing in the Swiss franc market (going around the box to the top-right corner). The comparison of returns would be:

$$(1 + i^\$) = S^{\text{SF}/\$} \times (1 + i^{\text{SF}}) \times \frac{1}{F^{\text{SF}/\$}}$$

Exhibit 3.8	*Yield Curves by Currency and the Forward Premium*

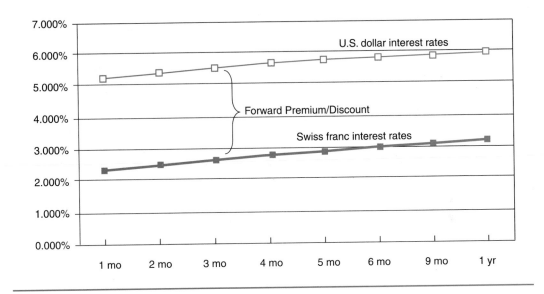

where S = the spot rate of exchange and F = the forward rate of exchange. Substituting in the spot rate (SF1.4800/$) and forward rate (SF1.4655/$) and respective interest rates ($i^\$ = 0.02$, $i^{SF} = 0.01$) from Exhibit 3.9, the interest rate parity condition is:

$$(1+.02) = 1.4800 \times (1+.01) \times \frac{1}{1.4655}$$

The left-hand side of the equation is the gross return the investor would earn by investing in dollars. The right-hand side is the gross return the investor would earn by exchanging dollars for Swiss francs at the spot rate, investing the franc proceeds in the Swiss franc money market, and simultaneously selling the principal plus interest in Swiss francs forward for dollars at the current 90-day forward rate. Ignoring transaction costs, if the returns in dollars are equal for the two alternative money market investments, the spot and forward rates are considered to be at *interest rate parity*. The transaction is "covered" because the exchange rate back to dollars is guaranteed at the end of the 90-day period. Therefore, as in Exhibit 3.9, in order for the two alternatives to be equal, any differences in interest rates must be offset by the difference between the spot and forward exchange rates (in approximate form):

$$\frac{F}{S} = \frac{(1+i^{SF})}{(1+i^\$)}, \text{ or } \frac{SF1.4655/\$}{SF1.4800/\$} = \frac{1.01}{1.02} = 0.9902 \approx 1\%$$

Exhibit 3.9   *Interest Rate Parity (IRP)*

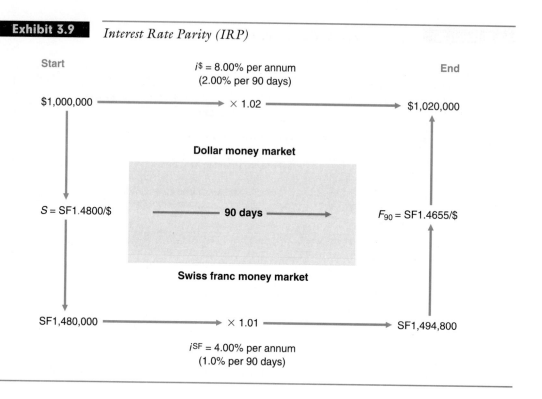

Start

$i\$ = 8.00\%$ per annum
(2.00% per 90 days)

End

$1,000,000 ——————→ × 1.02 ——————→ $1,020,000

Dollar money market

$S = SF1.4800/\$$ ———— 90 days ————→ $F_{90} = SF1.4655/\$$

Swiss franc money market

SF1,480,000 ——————→ × 1.01 ——————→ SF1,494,800

$i^{SF} = 4.00\%$ per annum
(1.0% per 90 days)

)))) Covered Interest Arbitrage

The spot and forward exchange markets are not, however, constantly in the state of equilibrium described by interest rate parity. When the market is not in equilibrium, the potential for "riskless" or arbitrage profit exists. The arbitrager who recognizes such an imbalance will move to take advantage of the disequilibrium by investing in whichever currency offers the higher return on a covered basis. This is called *covered interest arbitrage* (CIA).

Exhibit 3.10 describes the steps that a currency trader, most likely working in the arbitrage division of a large international bank, would implement to perform a CIA transaction. The currency trader, let's call him William Wong, may utilize any of a number of major Eurocurrencies which his bank possesses to conduct arbitrage investments. The morning conditions indicate to William that a CIA transaction that exchanges U.S. dollars for Japanese yen, invested in a six-month Euroyen account and sold forward back to dollars, will yield a profit of $4,638 over and above that available from a Eurodollar investment. Conditions in the exchange markets and Euromarkets change rapidly, however, so if William waits even a few minutes, the profit opportunity may disappear.[8]

This process of covered interest arbitrage drives the international currency and money markets toward the equilibrium described by interest rate parity. Slight deviations from equilibrium provide opportunities for arbitragers to make

Exhibit 3.10	*Covered Interest Arbitrage (CIA)*

Morning. William Wong, an arbitrager for Hong Kong & Shanghai Banking Corporation, Hong Kong, arrives at work Tuesday morning to be faced with the currency quotations shown in the "Morning Quotation" box below. He has access to several major Eurocurrencies for arbitrage trading. On the basis of the quotations below he decides to execute the following CIA transaction:

Step 1:   Convert $1,000,000 at the spot rate of ¥106.00/$ to ¥106,000,000 (see "Start").

Step 2:   Invest the proceeds, ¥106,000,000, in a Euroyen account for six months, earning 4.00% per annum, or 2% for 180 days.

Step 3:   Simultaneously sell the proceeds (¥108,120,000) forward for dollars at the 180-day forward rate of ¥103.50/$. This action "locks in" gross dollar revenues of $1,044,638 (see "End").

Step 4:   Calculate the cost (opportunity cost) of funds used at the Eurodollar rate of 8.00% per annum, or 4% for 180 days, with principal and interest then totaling $1,040,000. Profit on CIA at the "End" is

$$\$1,044,638 \text{ (proceeds)} - \$1,040,000 \text{ (cost)} = \$4,638$$

Morning Quotations: Hong Kong Calling the Euromarkets

small riskless profits. Such deviations provide the supply and demand forces that will move the market back toward parity (equilibrium).

Covered interest arbitrage should continue until interest rate parity is reestablished, because the arbitragers are able to earn risk-free profits by repeating the cycle as often as possible. Their actions, however, nudge the foreign exchange and money markets back toward equilibrium for the following reasons.

1. Purchase of yen in the spot market and sale of yen in the forward market narrows the premium on the forward yen. This is so because the spot yen strengthens from the extra demand and the forward yen weakens because of the extra sales. A narrower premium on the forward yen reduces the foreign exchange gain previously captured by investing in yen.

2. The demand for yen-denominated securities causes yen interest rates to fall, while the higher level of borrowing in the United States causes dollar interest rates to rise. The net result is a wider interest differential in favor of investing in the dollar.

)))) Equilibrium between Interest Rates and Exchange Rates

Exhibit 3.11 illustrates the conditions necessary for equilibrium between interest rates and exchange rates. The vertical axis shows the difference in interest rates in favor of the foreign currency, and the horizontal axis shows the forward premium or discount on that currency. The interest rate parity line shows the equilibrium state, but transaction costs cause the line to be a band rather than a thin line. Transaction costs arise from foreign exchange and investment brokerage costs on buying and selling securities. Typical transaction costs in recent years have been in the range of 0.18% to 0.25% on an annual basis. For individual transactions like William Wong's arbitrage activity in the previous example, there is no explicit transaction cost per trade; rather, the costs of the bank in supporting William's activities are the transaction costs. Point X shows one possible equilibrium position, where a 4% lower rate of interest on yen securities would be offset by a 4% premium on the forward yen.

The disequilibrium situation, which encouraged the interest rate arbitrage in the previous CIA example, is illustrated by point U. It is located off the interest rate parity line because the lower interest on the yen is –4% (annual basis), whereas the premium on the forward yen is slightly over 4.8% (annual basis). If we use the forward premium calculation presented earlier, the forward premium on the yen on an annual basis is:

$$\frac{¥106.00/\$ - ¥103.50/\$}{¥103.50/\$} \times \frac{360 \text{ days}}{180 \text{ days}} \times 100 = 4.83\%$$

The situation depicted by point U is unstable because all investors have an incentive to execute the same covered interest arbitrage. Except for a bank failure, the arbitrage gain is virtually risk free.

Some observers have suggested that political risk does exist, since one of the governments might apply capital controls that would prevent execution of the forward contract. This risk is fairly remote for covered interest arbitrage between major financial centers of the world, especially since a large portion of funds used for covered interest arbitrage is in Eurodollars. The concern may be valid for pairings with countries not noted for political and fiscal stability.

| Exhibit 3.11 | *Interest Rate Parity and Equilibrium* |

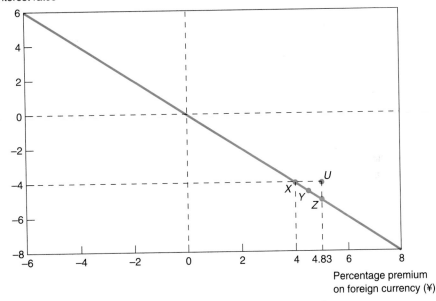

Percent difference between
foreign (¥) and domestic ($)
interest rates

Percentage premium
on foreign currency (¥)

The net result of the disequilibrium is that fund flows will narrow the gap in interest rates and/or decrease the premium on the forward yen. In other words, market pressures will cause point U in Exhibit 3.10 to move toward the interest rate parity band. Equilibrium might be reached at point Y, or at any other locus between X and Z, depending on whether forward market premiums are more or less easily shifted than interest rate differentials.

FORWARD RATE AS AN UNBIASED PREDICTOR OF THE FUTURE SPOT RATE

Some forecasters believe that for the major floating currencies, foreign exchange markets are "efficient" and forward exchange rates are *unbiased predictors* of future spot exchange rates.

Exhibit 3.12 demonstrates what this concept of unbiased prediction means in terms of how the forward rate performs in estimating future spot exchange rates. If the forward rate is an unbiased predictor of the future spot rate, the expected value of the future spot rate at time-2 equals the present forward rate for time-2 delivery, available now, $E(S_2) = F_1$.

Exhibit 3.12   *Forward Rate as an Unbiased Predictor for Future Spot Rate*

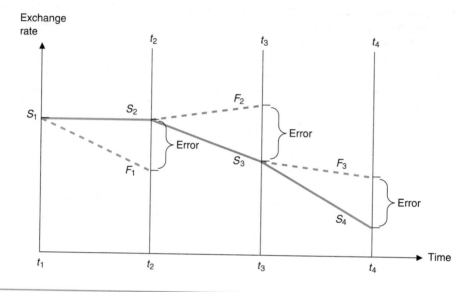

The forward rate available today ($F_{t,t+1}$), time t, for delivery at future time $t+1$, is used as a "predictor" of the spot rate of exchange that will exist on that day in the future. The forecasted spot rate for time t_2 is F_1; the actual spot exchange rate turns out to be S_2. The vertical distance between the forward rate prediction—F_1—and the actual spot rate that exists on that date—S_2—is the forecast error.

When the forward rate is termed an "unbiased predictor of the future spot rate," it means that the forward rate overestimates and underestimates the future spot rate with relatively equal frequency and amount. It therefore "misses the mark" in a regular and orderly manner. The sum of the errors equals zero.

The authors would like to thank Gunter Dufey for the original version of this clear presentation of unbiased prediction.

Intuitively this means that the distribution of possible actual spot rates in the future is centered on the forward rate. The forward exchange rate's being an unbiased predictor does not, however, mean that the future spot rate will actually be equal to what the forward rate predicts. Unbiased prediction simply means that the forward rate will, on average, overestimate and underestimate the actual future spot rate in equal frequency and degree. The forward rate may, in fact, never actually equal the future spot rate.

The rationale for this relationship is based on the hypothesis that the foreign exchange market is reasonably efficient. Market efficiency assumes that (a) all relevant information is quickly reflected in both the spot and the forward exchange markets, (b) transaction costs are low, and (c) instruments denominated in different currencies are perfect substitutes for one another.

Empirical studies of the efficient foreign exchange market hypothesis have yielded conflicting results. Nevertheless, a consensus is developing that rejects the efficient market hypothesis. It appears that the forward rate is not an unbiased predictor of the future spot rate and that it does pay to use resources to attempt to forecast exchange rates.

If the efficient market hypothesis is correct, a financial executive cannot expect to profit in any consistent manner from forecasting future exchange rates, because current quotations in the forward market reflect all that is presently known about likely future rates. While future exchange rates may well differ from the expectation implicit in the present forward market quotation, we cannot know today which way actual future quotations will differ from today's forward rate. The expected mean value of deviations is zero. The forward rate is therefore an unbiased estimator of the future spot rate.

Tests of foreign exchange market efficiency, using longer time periods of analysis, conclude that either exchange market efficiency is untestable or, if it is testable, the market is not efficient. Furthermore, the existence and success of foreign exchange forecasting services suggest that managers are willing to pay a price for forecast information even though they can use the forward rate as a forecast at no cost.[10] If the exchange market is not efficient, it would pay for a firm to spend resources on forecasting exchange rates. This conclusion is the opposite of the one in which exchange markets are deemed efficient.

THE ASSET MARKET APPROACH TO FORECASTING

So far we have analyzed the BOP approach to long-term foreign exchange rate determination. As mentioned earlier, there is an alternative approach to exchange rate forecasting called the *asset market approach*.

The asset market approach suggests that whether or not foreigners are willing to hold claims in monetary form depends partly on relative real interest rates and also on a country's outlook for economic growth and profitability. For example, during the period 1981–1985 the U.S. dollar strengthened despite growing current account deficits. This strength was due partly to relatively high real interest rates in the United States. Another factor, however, was the heavy inflow of foreign capital into the U.S. stock market and real estate, motivated by good long-run prospects for growth and profitability in the United States.

One scholar summarizes why some forecasters believe that exchange rates are more influenced by economic prospects than by the current account, as follows:

> The asset market approach. Many economists reject the view that the short-term behavior of exchange rates is determined in flow markets. Exchange rates are asset prices traded in an efficient financial market. Indeed, an exchange rate is the relative price of two currencies and therefore is determined by the willingness to hold each currency. Like other asset prices, the exchange rate is determined by expectations about the future, not current trade flows.

A parallel with other asset prices may illustrate the approach. Let's consider the stock price of a winery traded on the Bordeaux stock exchange. A frost in late spring results in a poor harvest, in terms of both quantity and quality. After the harvest the wine is finally sold, and the income is much less than the previous year. On the day of the final sale there is no reason for the stock price to be influenced by this flow. First, the poor income has already been discounted for several months in the winery stock price. Second, the stock price is affected by future, in addition to current, prospects. The stock price is based on expectations of future earnings, and the major cause for a change in stock price is a revision of these expectations.

A similar reasoning applies to exchange rates: Contemporaneous international flows should have little effect on exchange rates to the extent they have already been expected. Only news about future economic prospects will affect exchange rates. Since economic expectations are potentially volatile and influenced by many variables, especially variables of a political nature, the short-run behavior of exchange rates is volatile.[10]

We are left with an obvious dilemma as to which theory to follow. As do others, we will compromise. The consensus of opinion is that short-run exchange rate movements are determined by asset markets, interest rates, and the expectations of market participants. In the long term, however, equilibrium exchange rates are determined by PPP.

TECHNICAL ANALYSIS

Technical analysts, traditionally referred to as *chartists*, focus on price and volume data to determine past trends that are expected to continue into the future. The single most important element of time series analysis is that future exchange rates are based on the current exchange rate. Exchange rate movements, like equity price movements, can be subdivided into periods: (1) day-to-day movement that is seemingly random; (2) short-term movements extending from several days to trends lasting several months; (3) long-term movements, which are characterized by up and down long-term trends. Long-term technical analysis has gained new popularity as a result of recent research into the possibility that long-term "waves" in currency movements exist under floating exchange rates.[11]

The longer the time horizon of the forecast, the more inaccurate the forecast is likely to be. Whereas forecasting for the long-run must depend on economic fundamentals of exchange rate determination, many of the forecast needs of the firm are short- to medium-term in their time horizon and can be addressed with less theoretical approaches. Time series techniques infer no theory or causality but simply predict future values from the recent past. Forecasters freely mix fundamental and technical analysis, presumably because in forecasting, as in horseshoes and hand grenades, getting close is all that counts!

FORECASTING IN PRACTICE

Numerous foreign exchange forecasting services exist, many of which are provided by banks and independent consultants. In addition, some multinational firms have their own in-house forecasting capabilities. Predictions can be based on elaborate econometric models, technical analysis of charts and trends, intuition, and a certain measure of gall.

Whether any of the forecasting services are worth their cost depends partly on the motive for forecasting as well as the required accuracy of the forecast. For example, long-run forecasts may be motivated by a multinational firm's desire to initiate a foreign investment in Japan, or perhaps to raise long-term funds denominated in Japanese yen. Or a portfolio manager may be considering diversifying for the long term in Japanese securities. The longer the time horizon of the forecast, the more inaccurate but also the less critical the forecast is likely to be. The forecaster will typically use annual data to display long-run trends in such economic fundamentals as Japanese inflation, growth, and the BOP.

Short-term forecasts are typically motivated by a desire to hedge a receivable, payable, or dividend for perhaps a period of three months. In this case the long-run economic fundamentals may not be as important as technical factors in the marketplace, government intervention, news, and passing whims of traders and investors. Accuracy of the forecast is critical, since most of the exchange rate changes are relatively small even though the day-to-day volatility may be high.

Forecasting services normally undertake fundamental economic analysis for long-term forecasts, and some base their short-term forecasts on the same basic model. Others base their short-term forecasts on technical analysis similar to that conducted in security analysis. They attempt to correlate exchange rate changes with various other variables, regardless of whether there is any economic rationale for the correlation. The chances of these forecasts being consistently useful or profitable depend on whether we believe the foreign exchange market is efficient. The more efficient the market is, the more likely it is that exchange rates are "random walks," with past price behavior providing no clues to the future. The less efficient the foreign exchange market is, the better the chance that forecasters may get lucky and find a key relationship that holds, at least for the short run. If the relationship is really consistent, however, others will soon discover it and the market will become efficient again with respect to that piece of information.

Exhibit 3.13 summarizes the various forecasting periods, regimes, and the authors' opinions of the preferred methodologies. Opinions, however, are subject to change without notice!

SUMMARY

- Potential *foreign exchange rate determinants* can be categorized into clusters that are also influenced by exchange rates. The clusters that have been identified in this chapter are: 1) *parity conditions*; 2) *infrastructure*; 3) *speculation*; 4) *cross-border investment*; and 5) *political risk*.

Exhibit 3.13	Exchange Rate Forecasting in Practice	

Forecast Period	Regime	Recommended Forecast Methods
SHORT-RUN	*Fixed-Rate*	1. Assume the fixed rate is maintained 2. Indications of stress on fixed rate? 3. Capital controls; black market rates 4. Indicators of government's capability to maintain fixed rate? 5. Changes in official foreign currency reserves

	Floating-Rate	1. Technical methods that capture trend
		2. Forward rates as forecasts
		   a. <30 days, assume a random walk
		   b. 30–90 days, forward rates
		   c. 90–360 days, combine trend with fundamental analysis
		3. Fundamental analysis of inflationary concerns
		4. Government declarations and agreements regarding exchange rate goals
		5. Cooperative agreements with other countries

LONG-RUN	*Fixed-Rate*	1. Fundamental analysis 2. BOP management 3. Ability to control domestic inflation 4. Ability to generate hard currency reserves to use for intervention 5. Ability to run trade surpluses
	Floating-Rate	1. Focus on inflationary fundamentals and PPP 2. Indicators of general economic health such as economic growth and stability 3. Technical analysis of long-term trends; new research indicates possibility of long-term technical "waves"

- Cash flows motivated by any and all of the potential exchange rate determinants eventually show up in the *balance of payments* (BOP).

- The BOP is a statistical statement that systematically summarizes, for a specific time period, the cross-border economic transactions of an economy with the rest of the world.

- The managerial significance of the BOP depends on whether a country has a fixed, floating, or managed exchange rate system.

- Parity conditions have traditionally been used by economists to help explain the long-run trend in an exchange rate.

- Under conditions of freely floating rates, the expected rate of change in the spot exchange rate, differential rates of national inflation and interest, and forward discount or premium are all directly proportional to each other and mutually determined. A change in one of these variables has a tendency to change all of them, with a feedback on the variable that changes first.

- If the identical product or service can be sold in two different markets, and there are no restrictions on its sale or transportation costs of moving the product between markets, the product's price should be the same in both markets. This is called the *law of one price*.

- The *absolute version of the theory of purchasing power parity* states that the spot exchange rate is determined by the relative prices of similar baskets of goods.

- The *relative version of the theory of purchasing power parity* states that if the spot exchange rate between two countries starts in equilibrium, any change in the differential rate of inflation between them tends to be offset over the long run by an equal but opposite change in the spot exchange rate.

- The *Fisher effect*, named after economist Irving Fisher, states that nominal interest rates in each country are equal to the required real rate of return plus compensation for expected inflation.

- The *international Fisher effect*, or *Fisher-open* as it is often termed, states that the spot exchange rate should change in an amount equal to but in the opposite direction of the difference in interest rates between two countries.

- The *theory of interest rate parity* (IRP) states that the difference in the national interest rates for securities of similar risk and maturity should be equal to, but opposite in sign to, the forward rate discount or premium for the foreign currency, except for transaction costs.

- When the spot and forward exchange markets are not in equilibrium as described by interest rate parity, the potential for "riskless" or arbitrage profit exists. This is called *covered interest arbitrage* (CIA).

- Some forecasters believe that for the major floating currencies, foreign exchange markets are "efficient" and forward exchange rates are unbiased predictors of future spot exchange rates.

- Time-series techniques or simple use of the forward rate are forecast alternatives. Longer-term forecasting, over one year, requires a return to the basic analysis of exchange rate fundamentals such as BOP, relative inflation rates, relative interest rates, and the long-run properties of purchasing power parity.

- The asset approach to forecasting suggests that whether foreigners are willing to hold claims in monetary form depends partly on relative real interest rates and partly on a country's outlook for economic growth and profitability.

- Technical analysts (*chartists*) focus on price and volume data to determine past trends that are expected to continue into the future.

- Exchange rate forecasting in practice is a mix of both fundamental and technical forms of exchange rate analysis.

QUESTIONS

1. Polish Zloty
One year ago the exchange rate between Polish zloty and the U.S. dollar was Z3.8000/$. Since then the zloty has fallen 14% against the dollar. Price levels in the United States have not changed, but Polish prices have gone up 7%.

a. What is the nominal exchange rate today?

b. What should be the exchange rate today, based on purchasing power parity and assuming last year was "normal"?

c. Did the Polish zloty depreciate or appreciate in real terms relative to the dollar? By what percentage?

2. Pinot Noir
Pinot Noir wine is produced in the states of California (U.S.A.) and New South Wales (Australia). Equivalent bottles of Pinot Noir sell in the United States for US$22 and in Australia for A$34.

a. According to the theory of purchasing power parity, what should be the U.S. dollar/Australian dollar spot rate of exchange?

b. Suppose the price of Pinot Noir is expected to rise to $27 over the next year, while the price of a comparable bottle of Australian wine is expected to rise to A$44. What should be the one-year forward U.S. dollar/Australian dollar exchange rate?

c. Given your answers to (a) and (b) above, and given that the current interest rate in the United States is 5% for notes of a one-year maturity, what would you expect current Australian interest rates to be?

3. The Law of the One-Price Hamburger
If McDonald's hamburger prices properly measure purchasing power parity in different countries, data from Exhibit 3.4 could be used to determine proper foreign exchange rates based on the law of one price.

a. Calculate hamburger purchasing power parity exchange rates for US$/£, C$/US$, HK$/US$, and ¥/US$.

b. Which of the above currencies are overvalued and which are undervalued? What does it mean when a currency is "overvalued" or "undervalued"?

c. Using both Exhibit 3.4 in this chapter and the French franc fixing to the euro shown in Exhibit 2.5 in the previous chapter, calculate the dollar per euro rate. How does this compare with the actual exchange rate at the time the hamburgers were priced?

d. Explain precisely, using the appropriate hamburger prices from Exhibit 3.4, by how much the Chinese yuan (renminbi) is undervalued or overvalued.

4. Covered Interest Arbitrage (¥/$)

Ayako Miyake is a currency arbitrager for Atsugi Bank in Kanagawa. The spot rate this morning is ¥110.60/$, and early indications are the 90-day interest rates in the United States will rise from their current level of 4.25% per annum. The U.S. Federal Reserve Bank, the central bank, is worried about an unjustified level of the U.S. stock market and has been publically considering raising interest rates 50 basis points (½%). The 90-day forward exchange rate quoted to Miyake-san by other Japanese banks are all about the same, ¥109.80/$. The current 90-day yen interest rate is 0.5% per annum. Miyake-san has ¥400,000,000 at her disposal.

a. How much profit can Miyake-san make through covered interest arbitrage?
b. What could Miyake-san do with her ¥400 million if she wished to speculate through uncovered interest arbitrage? How much profit could she expect to make?

5. London and New York

Money and foreign exchange markets in London and New York are very efficient. You have the following information:

	London	New York
Spot exchange rate	$1.6000/£	£0.6250/$
One-year treasury bill rate	5.00%	6.00%
Expected inflation rate	2.00%	unknown

Assuming parity conditions hold:

a. Estimate inflation in the United States next year.
b. Estimate today's one-year forward exchange rate between pounds and dollars.
c. Diagram how the United Kingdom and the United States are interrelated with respect to exchange rates, interest rates, and inflation rates. Define on the diagram each of the parity conditions which cause these theoretical linkages.

6. Covered Interest Arbitrage

Henri Jacque, an arbitrager with Bank of Montreal, faces the following Canadian dollar/U.S. dollar quotes:

Spot rate:	C$1.4900/$
Six-month forward rate:	C$1.5100/$
Six-month Canadian dollar interest rate (borrowing or investing):	7.50% p.a.
Six-month U.S. dollar interest rate (borrowing or investing)	5.00% p.a.

Henri Jacque is authorized to use C$20,000,000 or its U.S. dollar equivalent. The ending profit, if any, should be realized in Canadian dollars. How can he complete covered interest arbitrage? What will be his profit?

WORLD WIDE WEB QUESTIONS

W1. Emerging Market Currencies

Although major currencies like the U.S. dollar and the Japanese yen dominate the headlines, there are nearly as many currencies as countries in the world. Many of these currencies are traded in extremely thin and highly regulated markets, making their convertibility suspect. Finding quotations for these currencies is sometimes very difficult. Starting with the Web site below, see how many African currency quotes you can find.

Emerging Markets   http://emgmkts.com/

W2. Exchange Rate Indices

JP Morgan calculates and maintains indices of many of the world's major currencies' values relative to baskets of other major currencies. Like those published by the IMF, these indices serve as more fundamental and general indicators of relative currency value. Find the most recent index values for the U.S., Japan, and Germany at the web site below.

JP Morgan Currency Indices   http://jpmorgan.com/MarketDataInd/
Forex/currIndex.html

SUGGESTED READINGS

Ohno, Kenichi, "Exchange Rate Fluctuations, PassThrough, and Market Share," *IMF Staff Papers*, Vol. 37, No. 2, June 1990, pp. 294–310.

Giddy, Ian H., and Gunter Dufey, "The Random Behavior of Flexible Exchange Rates," *Journal of International Business Studies*, Spring 1975, pp. 1–32.

NOTES

1. For a more detailed description of the balance of payments see the Addison Wesley Longman website at http://www.awl.com/.
2. Errors and omissions are assumed to be mostly uncounted, often illegal, transfers of funds. They are included here in the Financial Account.
3. For studies on the validity of PPP in the long run, see any intermediate economics textbook.
4. For a more detailed description of pass-through analysis see Magee (1973), Magee (1974), Mann (1986), and Moffett (1989).
5. Recall that the own-price elasticity of demand for any good is the percentage change in quantity of the good demanded as a result of the percentage change in the good's own price:

$$\text{Price elasticity of demand} = \epsilon_p = \frac{\%\Delta Q_d}{\%\Delta P}$$

where Q_d is quantity demanded and P is product price. If the absolute value of ϵ_p is less than 1.0 the good is relatively "inelastic," while if it is greater than 1.0 a relatively "elastic" demand is indicated.

6. This is derived from $(1 + r)(1 + \pi) - 1$.

7. Some relevant studies of the Fisher effect, the international Fisher effect, and interest rate parity include Cumby and Obstfeld (1981), Mishkin (1984), and Kaen, Simos, and Hachey (1984).

8. Note that all profits are stated in terms of the currency in which the transaction was initialized, but that a trader (in this case in Hong Kong) may conduct investments denominated in U.S. dollars, Swiss francs, or any other major convertible currency.

9. Three such studies are Goodman (1979), Levich (1980), and Bilson (1984).

10. Solnik (1996), p. 58. Reprinted with permission.

11. Engel and Hamilton (1990).

CHAPTER 3 APPENDIX

An Algebraic Primer to International Parity Conditions

The following is a purely algebraic presentation of the parity conditions explained in this chapter. It is offered to provide those who wish additional theoretical detail and definition-ready access to the step-by-step derivation of the various conditions.

The Law of One Price

The *law of one price* refers to the state in which, in the presence of free trade, perfect substitutability of goods, and costless transactions, the equilibrium exchange rate between two currencies is determined by the ratio of the price of any commodity *i* denominated in two different currencies. For example,

$$S_t = \frac{P_{i,t}^{\$}}{P_{i,t}^{SF}}$$

where $P_i^{\$}$ and P_i^{SF} refer to the prices of the same commodity *i*, at time *t*, denominated in U.S. dollars and Swiss francs, respectively. The spot exchange rate, S_t, (U.S. dollars/Swiss franc) is simply the ratio of the two currency prices.

Purchasing Power Parity

The more general form in which the exchange rate is determined by the ratio of two price indexes is termed the absolute version of *purchasing power parity (PPP)*. Each price index reflects the currency cost of the identical "basket" of goods across countries. The exchange rate that equates purchasing power for the identical collection of goods is then stated

$$S_t = \frac{P_t^{\$}}{P_t^{SF}}$$

where $P_t^{\$}$ and P_t^{SF} are the price index values in U.S. dollars and Swiss francs at time *t*, respectively. If the Greek letter π (pi) represents the rate of inflation in each country, the spot exchange rate at time *t* + 1 would be

$$S_{t+1} = \frac{P_t^{\$}(1+\pi^{\$})}{P_t^{SF}(1+\pi^{SF})} = S_t \left[\frac{(1+\pi^{\$})}{(1+\pi^{SF})} \right]$$

The change from period *t* to *t* +1 is then

$$\frac{S_{t+1}}{S_t} = \frac{\dfrac{P_t^\$(1+\pi^\$)}{P_t^{SF}(1+\pi^{SF})}}{\dfrac{P_t^\$}{P_t^{SF}}} = \frac{S_t\left[\dfrac{1+\pi^\$}{1+\pi^{SF}}\right]}{S_t} = \frac{(1+\pi^\$)}{(1+\pi^{SF})}$$

Isolating the percentage change in the spot exchange rate between periods t and $t+1$ yields

$$\frac{S_{t+1}-S_t}{S_t} = \frac{S_t\left[\dfrac{1+\pi^\$}{1+\pi^{SF}}\right]-S_t}{S_t} = \frac{(1+\pi^\$)-(1+\pi^{SF})}{(1+\pi^{SF})}$$

This equation is often approximated by dropping the denominator of the right-hand side if it is considered to be relatively close to 1. It is then stated as

$$\frac{S_{t+1}-S_t}{S_t} = (1+\pi^\$)-(1+\pi^{SF}) = \pi^\$ - \pi^{SF}$$

Forward Rates

The *forward exchange rate* is that contractual rate available to private agents through banking institutions and other financial intermediaries who deal in foreign currencies and debt instruments. The annualized percentage difference between the forward rate and the spot rate is termed the *forward premium*:

$$f^{SF} = \left[\frac{F_{t,\,t+1}-S_t}{S_t}\right] \times \left[\frac{360}{n_{t,\,t+1}}\right]$$

where f^{SF} is the forward premium on the Swiss franc, $F_{t,t+1}$ is the forward rate contracted at time t for delivery at time $t+1$, S_t is the current spot rate, and $n_{t,t+1}$ is the number of days between the contract date (t) and the delivery date ($t+1$). This is the formula for direct quotes.

Covered Interest Arbitrage (CIA) and Interest Rate Parity (IRP)

The process of *covered interest arbitrage* occurs when an investor exchanges domestic currency for foreign currency in the spot market, invests that currency in an interest-bearing instrument, and signs a forward contract to "lock in" a future exchange rate at which to convert the foreign currency proceeds (gross) back to domestic currency. The net return on CIA is

$$\text{Net return} = \left[\frac{(1 + i^{SF})F_{t,\,t+1}}{S_t}\right] - (1 + i^{\$})$$

where S_t and $F_{t,\,t+1}$ are the spot and forward rates (\$/SF), i^{SF} is the nominal interest rate (or yield) on a Swiss franc-denominated monetary instrument, and $i^{\$}$ is the nominal return on a similar dollar-denominated instrument.

If they possess exactly equal rates of return (that is, if CIA results in zero riskless profit) interest rate parity (IRP) holds and appears as

$$(1 + i^{\$}) = \left[\frac{(1 + i^{SF})F_{t,\,t+1}}{S_t}\right]$$

or alternatively

$$\frac{(1 + i^{\$})}{(1 + i^{SF})} = \frac{F_{t,\,t+1}}{S_t}$$

If the percent difference of both sides of this equation is found (the percent difference between the spot and forward rate is the forward premium), then the relationship between the forward premium and relative interest rate differentials is

$$\frac{F_{t,\,t+1} - S_t}{S_t} = f^{SF} = \frac{i^{\$} - i^{SF}}{1 + i^{SF}}$$

If these values are not equal (and thus the markets are not in equilibrium), a potential exists for riskless profit. The market will then be driven back to equilibrium through CIA by agents attempting to exploit such arbitrage potential, until CIA yields no positive return.

Fisher Effect

The *Fisher effect* states that all nominal interest rates can be decomposed into an implied real rate of interest (return) and an expected rate of inflation:

$$i^{\$} = [(1 + r^{\$})(1 + \pi^{\$})] - 1$$

where $r^{\$}$ is the real rate of return and $\pi^{\$}$ is the expected rate of inflation, for dollar-denominated assets. The subcomponents are then identifiable:

$$i^{\$} = r^{\$} + \pi^{\$} + r^{\$}\pi^{\$}$$

As with PPP, an approximation of this function has gained wide acceptance. The cross-product term of $r^{\$}\pi^{\$}$ is often very small, and therefore dropped altogether:

$$i^{\$} = r^{\$} + \pi^{\$}$$

International Fisher Effect

The *international Fisher effect* is the extension of this domestic interest rate relationship to the international currency markets. If capital, by way of covered interest arbitrage (CIA), attempts to find higher rates of return internationally resulting from current interest rate differentials, the real rates of return between currencies are equalized (e.g., $r^\$ = r^{SF}$):

$$\frac{S_{t+1} - S_t}{S_t} = \frac{(1+i^\$) - (1+i^{SF})}{(1+i^{SF})} = \frac{i^\$ - i^{SF}}{(1+i^{SF})}$$

If the nominal interest rates are then decomposed into their respective real and expected inflation components, the percentage change in the spot exchange rate is

$$\frac{S_{t+1} - S_t}{S_t} = \frac{(r^\$ + \pi^\$ + r^\$\pi^\$) - (r^{SF} + \pi^{SF} + r^{SF}\pi^{SF})}{1 + r^{SF} + \pi^{SF} + r^{SF}\pi^{SF}}$$

The international Fisher effect has a number of additional implications, if the following requirements are met: (1) capital markets can be freely entered and exited; (2) capital markets possess investment opportunities that are acceptable substitutes; and (3) market agents have complete and equal information regarding these possibilities.

Given these conditions, international arbitragers are capable of exploiting all potential riskless profit opportunities, until real rates of return between markets are equalized ($r^\$ = r^{SF}$). Thus the expected rate of change in the spot exchange rate reduces to the differential in the expected rates of inflation:

$$\frac{S_{t+1} - S_t}{S_t} = \frac{\pi^\$ + r^\$\pi^\$ - \pi^{SF} - r^{SF}\pi^{SF}}{1 + r^{SF} + \pi^{SF} + r^{SF}\pi^{SF}}$$

If the approximation forms are combined (through the elimination of the denominator and the elimination of the interactive terms of r and π), the change in the spot rate is simply

$$\frac{S_{t+1} - S_t}{S_t} = \pi^\$ - \pi^{SF}$$

Note the similarity (identical in equation form) of the approximate form of the international Fisher effect to purchasing power parity discussed previously [the only potential difference is that between ex-post and ex-ante (expected) inflation].

CHAPTER 4

THE FOREIGN
EXCHANGE MARKET

The *foreign exchange market* provides the physical and institutional structure through which the money of one country is exchanged for that of another country, the rate of exchange between currencies is determined, and foreign exchange transactions are physically completed. *Foreign exchange* means the money of a foreign country; that is, foreign currency bank balances, banknotes, checks, and drafts. A *foreign exchange transaction* is an agreement between a buyer and seller that a fixed amount of one currency is to be delivered at a specified rate in exchange for some other currency.

This chapter describes the following features of the foreign exchange market:

- The geographical extent of the foreign exchange market
- The three main functions performed by the market
- The market's participants
- The immense transaction volume that takes place daily in the foreign exchange market
- Types of transactions, including spot, forward, and swap transactions
- Methods of stating exchange rates, quotations, and changes in exchange rates
- Foreign currency futures

GEOGRAPHICAL EXTENT OF THE FOREIGN EXCHANGE MARKET

The foreign exchange market spans the globe, with prices moving and currencies trading somewhere every hour of every business day. Major world trading starts each morning in Sydney and Tokyo, moves west to Hong Kong and Singapore, passes on to Bahrain, shifts to the main European markets of Frankfurt, Zurich, and London, jumps the Atlantic to New York, goes west to Chicago, and ends up in San Francisco and Los Angeles. The market is deepest, or most liquid, early in the European afternoon, when markets of both Europe and the U.S. East Coast are open. This period is regarded as the best time to ensure the smooth execution of a very large order.

At the end of the day in California, when traders in Tokyo and Hong Kong are just getting up for the next day, the market is thinnest. During these hours, when the U.S. West Coast is awake and Europe sleeps, aggressive speculators or central banks sometimes try to move prices by trading large blocks, sometimes to influence European attitudes about particular currencies the following morning. Many large international banks operate foreign exchange trading rooms in each major geographic trading center in order to serve important commercial accounts on a 24-hour-a-day basis. The world of foreign exchange dealing is shown on the map on the front fly-leaf of this book.

In some countries, a portion of foreign exchange trading is conducted on an official trading floor by open bidding. Closing prices are published as the official price, or *fixing*, for the day, and certain commercial and investment transactions are based on this official price. Business firms in countries with exchange controls often must surrender foreign exchange earned from exports to the central bank at the daily fixing price.

Banks engaged in foreign exchange trading are connected by highly sophisticated telecommunications networks. Professional dealers and brokers obtain exchange rate quotes on desk-top computer screens and communicate with each other by telephone, computer, fax, and telex. The foreign exchange departments of many nonbank business firms also use computer networks to keep in touch with the market and to seek out the best quotations. Reuters, Telerate, and Bloomberg are the leading suppliers of foreign exchange rate information and trading systems. A recent development has been the introduction of automated "matching" systems into computerized quotation systems. Many dealers think computer-executed transactions will replace other, more conventional, trading systems in the near future.

FUNCTIONS OF THE FOREIGN EXCHANGE MARKET

The foreign exchange market is the mechanism by which we transfer purchasing power between countries, obtain or provide credit for international trade transactions, and minimize exposure to the risks of exchange rate changes.

))) Transfer of Purchasing Power

Transfer of purchasing power is necessary because international trade and capital transactions normally involve parties living in countries with different national currencies. Each party usually wants to deal in its own currency, but the trade or capital transaction can be invoiced only in one single currency. If a Japanese exporter sells Toyota automobiles to a Brazilian importer, the exporter could invoice the Brazilian importer in Japanese yen, Brazilian real, or any convenient third-country currency such as U.S. dollars. The currency would be agreed upon beforehand.

Whichever currency is used, one or more of the parties must transfer purchasing power to or from its own national currency. If the transaction is in yen, the Brazilian importer must buy yen with real. If the transaction is in real, the Japanese exporter must sell the real received for yen. If U.S. dollars are used, the Brazilian importer must exchange real for dollars and the Japanese exporter must then exchange dollars for yen. The foreign exchange market provides the mechanism for carrying out these purchasing power transfers.

))) **Provision of Credit**

Because the movement of goods between countries takes time, inventory in transit must be financed. In the case of the Toyota sale, somebody must finance the automobiles while they are being shipped to Brazil and also while they are "floored" with Toyota dealers in Brazil before final sale to a customer. The elapsed time might be anywhere from a few weeks to six months, depending on how the cars are shipped.

The Japanese exporter may agree to provide this credit by carrying the accounts receivable of the Brazilian importer, with or without interest. Alternatively, the Brazilian importer may pay cash on shipment from Japan and finance the automobiles with its local bank. The foreign exchange market provides a third source of credit. Specialized instruments, such as bankers' acceptances and letters of credit, are available to finance international trade. These documents are explained in Chapter 20.

))) **Minimizing Foreign Exchange Risk**

Neither the Brazilian importer nor the Japanese exporter may wish to carry the risk of exchange rate fluctuations. Each may prefer to earn a normal business profit on the automobile transaction without exposure to an unexpected change in anticipated profit because exchange rates suddenly change. The foreign exchange market provides "hedging" facilities for transferring foreign exchange risk to someone else. These facilities are explained in Chapter 6.

MARKET PARTICIPANTS

The foreign exchange market consists of two tiers, the interbank or wholesale market, and the client or retail market. Individual transactions in the interbank market are usually for large sums that are multiples of a million U.S. dollars or the equivalent value in other currencies. By contrast, contracts between a bank and its clients are usually for specific amounts, sometimes down to the last penny.

Five broad categories of participants operate within these two tiers: bank and nonbank foreign exchange dealers, individuals and firms conducting commercial or investment transactions, speculators and arbitragers, central banks and treasuries, and foreign exchange brokers.

)))) Bank and Nonbank Foreign Exchange Dealers

Banks, and a few nonbank foreign exchange dealers, operate in both the interbank and client markets. They profit from buying foreign exchange at a *bid* price and reselling it at a slightly higher *offer* (also called the *ask*) price. Competition among dealers worldwide narrows the spread between bid and offer and so contributes to making the foreign exchange market efficient in the same sense as in securities markets.

Dealers in the foreign exchange departments of large international banks often function as *market makers*. They stand willing at all times to buy and sell those currencies in which they specialize. They do this by maintaining an inventory position in those currencies. They trade with other banks in their own monetary centers and in other centers around the world in order to maintain inventories within the trading limits set by bank policy. *Trading limits* are important because foreign exchange departments of many banks operate as profit centers, and individual dealers are compensated on a profit incentive basis.[1] Unauthorized violation of trading limits by dealers under profit pressure increases risk and at times has caused embarrassing losses for major banks.

Small- to medium-sized banks are likely to participate but not be market makers in the interbank market. Instead of maintaining significant inventory positions, they buy from and sell to larger banks to offset retail transactions with their own customers. Of course, even market-making banks do not make markets in every currency. They trade for their own account in those currencies of most interest to their customers and become participants when filling customer needs in less important currencies.

)))) Individuals and Firms Conducting Commercial and Investment Transactions

Importers and exporters, international portfolio investors, MNEs, tourists, and others use the foreign exchange market to facilitate execution of commercial or investment transactions. Their use of the foreign exchange market is necessary but nevertheless incidental to their underlying commercial or investment purpose. Some of these participants use the market to hedge foreign exchange risk.

)))) Speculators and Arbitragers

Speculators and arbitragers seek to profit from trading in the market itself. They operate in their own interest, without a need or obligation to serve clients or to ensure a continuous market. Dealers seek profit from the spread between bid and offer in addition to what they might gain from changes in exchange rates, whereas speculators seek all their profit from exchange rate changes. Arbitragers try to profit from simultaneous exchange rate differences in different markets.

A large proportion of speculation and arbitrage is conducted on behalf of major banks by traders employed by those banks. Thus banks act both as exchange dealers and as speculators and arbitragers. (However, banks seldom admit to speculating; they characterize themselves as "taking an aggressive position"!)

))))) Central Banks and Treasuries

Central banks and treasuries use the market to acquire or spend their country's foreign exchange reserves as well as to influence the price at which their own currency is traded. They may act to support the value of their own currency because of policies adopted at the national level or because of commitments entered into through membership in joint float agreements, such as the European Monetary System which preceded introduction of the euro. Consequently their motive is not to earn a profit as such, but rather to influence the foreign exchange value of their currency in a manner that will benefit the interests of their citizens. In many instances they do their job best when they willingly take a loss on their foreign exchange transactions. As potential willing loss takers, central banks and treasuries differ in motive and behavior from all other market participants.

))))) Foreign Exchange Brokers

Foreign exchange brokers are agents who facilitate trading between dealers without themselves becoming principals in the transaction. For this service they charge a small commission. They maintain instant access to hundreds of dealers worldwide via open telephone lines. At times a broker may maintain a dozen or more such lines to a single client bank, with separate lines for different currencies and for spot and forward markets. The relationship between banks, acting as dealers, and brokers is shown in Exhibit 4.1.

The customer approaches its own bank, Citibank in New York. Citibank might buy or sell from its own inventory. Alternatively, Citibank can trade directly with Bankers Trust or Bank of New York in New York, or directly with Barclays or National Westminster in London. Alternatively, Citibank can seek quotes or place orders through a New York broker, who in turn might place the order with Bankers Trust or Bank of New York. Lastly, Citibank might contact a broker in London (or any other foreign center), who in turn would place the order with various London banks (Standard Chartered or Barclays in Exhibit 4.1), or Citibank might contact a foreign bank directly.

It is a broker's business to know at any moment exactly which dealers want to buy or sell any currency. This knowledge enables the broker quickly to find an opposite party for a client without revealing the identity of either party until after a transaction has been agreed upon. Dealers use brokers for speed and because they want to remain anonymous, because the identity of participants may influence short-term quotes.

Size of the Market

The Bank for International Settlements (BIS), in conjunction with central banks around the world, conducts a survey of currency trading activity every three years. The most recent survey, conducted in April 1998, estimated *daily* global net turnover in traditional foreign exchange market activity to be US$1,500 bil-

| Exhibit 4.1 | *Trading Combinations, New York and London* |

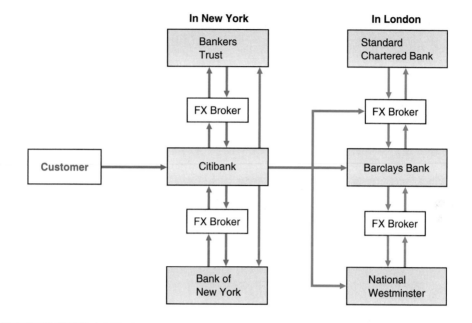

lion. (The BIS uses the French and American definition of "billion" as a thousand million.) BIS data is shown in Exhibit 4.2. The first two lines in Exhibit 4.2, spot and forwards and forex (foreign exchange) swaps, constitute what the BIS classifies as "traditional" foreign exchange market activity, while the last three lines, currency swaps and options, constitute "derivatives" market activity.

The average compound rate of growth in traditional foreign exchange activity from 1989 to 1998 was about 11%. Trading in derivatives was not significant until 1994, but in the following four years trading activity grew just over 20% per annum.

Exhibit 4.3 shows the proportionate share of foreign exchange trading for the most important national markets in the world in April 1998. The United Kingdom is the world's major foreign exchange market in traditional foreign exchange market activity with 32.3% of total world volume, followed by the United States at 17.8% and Japan at 7.5%. Indeed, more than half of all world foreign exchange trading takes place in just these three countries. Foreign exchange trading in Japan and Singapore each exceeds that of any European country except the United Kingdom, and Hong Kong is seventh in the world. Together this reflects Asia's economic importance, even in a year that was part of the Asian economic crisis.

Exhibit 4.2	*Average Daily Turnover in Global Foreign Exchange and Over-the-Counter Derivatives Markets, April of Each Year (billions of U.S. dollars)*

	1989	1992	1995	1998
Traditional FX Trading				
Spot	350	400	520	590
Forwards and forex swaps	240	420	670	900
Subtotal	590	820	1,190	1,500[a]
Derivatives FX Trading				
Outright forwards and forex swaps[b]	—	—	643	864
Currency swaps	—	—	4	10
Options	—	—	41	87
Total	590	820	1,878	2,461
Percent of Total				
Spot	59%	49%	28%	24%
Forwards and forex swaps	41	51	70	72
Currency swaps	0	0	0	0
Options	0	0	2	4
Total	100%	100%	100%	100%

[a]The BIS reports "Total reported turnover net of local double counting" as $1,982 billion. From this number the BIS subtracts $540 billion as an "adjustment for cross-border double counting," and then adds $58 billion for "estimated gaps in reporting," to arrive at the $1,500 billion figure above.
[b]Outright forwards and forex swaps are traded in both the traditional foreign exchange markets and in the over-the-counter (OTC) market. The percentages shown above are for the sum of trading in these two separate markets.
Source: Bank for International Settlements, *Central Bank Survey of Foreign Exchange and Derivatives Market Activity in April 1998.*

The distribution of derivatives market activity is similar except for one major difference. Non-Japanese Asian markets that are very important in traditional market activity are much less important in derivatives trading. One must be careful in extrapolating to the relative importance of the euro in Exhibits 4.3 and 4.4 because intra-EMU and ECU trading will be in the euro and thus no longer "foreign" exchange trading.

Exhibit 4.4 summarizes the BIS April 1998 survey results by currency, rather than by country of traditional trading activity. Because every foreign exchange transaction involves two currencies, the data cannot logically be broken down by single currency alone. Hence the sum of the world's reported transactions comes to twice the actual turnover, and the percent of total trades for each currency adds to 200%.

Net global turnover is dominated by trading in U.S. dollars and Deutschemarks, followed by Japanese yen, the U.K. pound sterling, and the Swiss franc, in that order. As noted in the last column, trading in most countries (excluding the United States) is against the U.S. dollar.

Exhibit 4.3	*Geographical Distribution of Global Traditional Foreign Exchange Market Activity, April 1998 (average daily turnover, in billions of U.S. dollars)*

		Traditional Foreign Exchange Market Activity		Derivative Market Activity	
		Amount	% Share	Amount	% Share
1	United Kingdom	$ 637.3	32.3	$ 170.8	36.0
2	United States	350.9	17.8	90.9	19.2
3	Japan	148.6	7.5	42.1	8.9
4	Singapore	139.0	7.1	11.3	2.3
5	Germany	94.3	4.8	34.4	7.3
6	Switzerland	81.7	4.1	15.8	3.3
7	Hong Kong	78.6	4.0	3.8	0.8
8	France	71.9	3.6		<1.0
9	Australia	46.6	2.4		<1.0
10	Netherlands	41.0	2.1		<1.0
11	Canada	36.8	1.9		<1.0
12	Italy	28.2	1.4		<1.0
31	Other countries	226.7	11.4		<1.0
	Total	$ 1,981.6	100.0%	$ 474.0	100.0%

Source: Bank for International Settlements, *Central Bank Survey of Foreign Exchange and Derivatives Market Activity in April 1998.*

TRANSACTIONS IN THE INTERBANK MARKET

Transactions in the foreign exchange market can be executed on a spot, forward, or swap basis. A broader definition of the foreign exchange market includes foreign currency options and futures. A *spot* transaction requires almost immediate delivery of foreign exchange. A *forward* transaction requires delivery of foreign exchange at some future date, either on an outright basis or through a futures contract. A *swap* transaction is the simultaneous purchase and sale of a foreign currency.

))) Spot Transactions

A *spot transaction* in the interbank market is the purchase of foreign exchange with delivery and payment between banks to take place, normally, on the second-following business day. The Canadian dollar settles with the U.S. dollar on the first-following business day.

The date of settlement is referred to as the *value date.* On the value date, most dollar transactions in the world are settled through the computerized Clearing House Interbank Payments Systems (CHIPS) in New York, which provides for calculation of net balances owed by any one bank to another and for payment by 6:00 P.M. that same day in Federal Reserve Bank of New York funds. Exhibit 4.2 shows that spot transactions were 24% of all foreign exchange transactions in April 1998, down from 59% in 1989.

Exhibit 4.4	*Currency Distribution of Global Traditional Foreign Exchange Market Activity, April 1998[a] (billions of U.S. dollars)*

	Amount	% Share	Traded against the Dollar(%)
U.S. dollar	$1,741.0	87.9	—
Deutschemark	602.7	30.4	68.5
French franc	102.6	5.2	80.5
Other EMU currencies	263.1	13.3	NA
Japanese yen	407.2	20.5	89.2
Pound sterling	211.9	10.7	75.2
Swiss franc	138.8	7.0	78.3
All other currencies	495.9	25.0	—
Total (double counted)	$3,963.2	200.0%	—
Total (not double counted)	$1,981.6	100.0%	

[a]Each transaction is reported twice because two currencies are involved in every trade.
Source: "Central Bank Survey of Foreign Exchange and Derivatives Market Activity, 1998," *Bank for International Settlements 69th Annual Report*, p. 117. Calculations added by authors. NA: not available.

A typical spot transaction in the interbank market might involve a U.S. bank contracting on a Monday for the transfer of £10,000,000 to the account of a London bank. If the spot exchange rate were $1.6984/£, the U.S. bank would transfer £10,000,000 to the London bank on Wednesday, and the London bank would transfer $16,984,000 to the U.S. bank at the same time. A spot transaction between a bank and its commercial customer would not necessarily involve a wait of two days for settlement.

)))) Outright Forward Transactions

An *outright forward transaction* (usually just called *forward*) requires delivery at a future value date of a specified amount of one currency for a specified amount of another currency. The exchange rate is established at the time of the agreement, but payment and delivery are not required until maturity. Forward exchange rates are normally quoted for value dates of one, two, three, six, and twelve months. Actual contracts can be arranged for other numbers of months or, on occasion, for periods of more than one year. Payment is on the second business day after the even-month anniversary of the trade. Thus a two-month forward transaction entered into on March 18 will be for a value date of May 20, or the next business day if May 20 falls on a weekend or holiday.

Note that as a matter of terminology we can speak of "buying forward" or "selling forward" to describe the same transaction. A contract to deliver dollars for euros in six months is both "buying euros forward for dollars" and "selling dollars forward for euros."

)))) **Swap Transactions**

A *swap transaction* in the interbank market is the simultaneous purchase and sale of a given amount of foreign exchange for two different value dates. Both purchase and sale are with the same counterparty. A common type of swap is a *spot against forward*. The dealer buys a currency in the spot market and simultaneously sells the same amount back to the same bank in the forward market. Since this is executed as a single transaction with one counterparty, the dealer incurs no unexpected foreign exchange risk. Swap transactions and outright forwards combined were 72% of all foreign exchange market activity in April 1998.

Forward–Forward Swaps. A more sophisticated swap transaction is called a *forward–forward swap*. A dealer sells £20,000,000 forward for dollars for delivery in, say, two months at $1.6870/£ and simultaneously buys £20,000,000 forward for delivery in three months at $1.6820/£. The difference between the buying price and the selling price is equivalent to the interest rate differential, i.e., interest rate parity, between the two currencies. Thus a swap can be viewed as a technique for borrowing another currency on a fully collateralized basis.

Nondeliverable Forwards. Created in the early 1990s, the *nondeliverable forward* (NDF) is now a relatively common derivative offered by the largest providers of foreign exchange derivatives, such as Citibank. NDFs possess the same characteristics and documentation requirements as traditional forward contracts except that they are settled only in U.S. dollars, and the foreign currency being sold forward or bought forward is not delivered. The dollar-settlement feature reflects the fact that NDFs are contracted offshore, for example, in New York for a Mexican investor, and so are beyond the reach and regulatory frameworks of the home country governments (Mexico in this case). NDFs are used primarily for emerging market currencies, currencies that typically do not have liquid money markets or Eurocurrency interest rates. Pricing of NDFs reflects basic interest differentials, as with regular forward contracts, plus an additional premium charged by the bank for dollar settlement.

Argentina is an example of one country for which NDFs play a potentially important role. Because the government of Argentina has fixed the Argentine peso to the U.S. dollar at a one-to-one rate, banks within Argentina that offer forward contracts are required to quote all forward rates at that rate. NDFs, however, because they are quoted and settled outside of Argentina, reflect a more economic-based pricing, primarily the interest differentials often observed between U.S. dollar-denominated and Argentine peso-denominated deposits (noted previously in Chapter 2). The NDF therefore reflects a market-based view of forward pricing instead of the official governmental view reflected in on-shore quotations.

Argentine peso (peso/$)	*Spot*	*3 months*	*6 months*	*12 months*
Banks in Argentina	1.00	1.00	1.00	1.00
NDFs	—	1.01	1.04	1.10

FOREIGN EXCHANGE RATES AND QUOTATIONS

A *foreign exchange rate* is the price of one currency expressed in terms of another currency. A *foreign exchange quotation* (or *quote*) is a statement of willingness to buy or sell at an announced rate.

In the retail market (including newspapers and foreign exchange booths at airports), quotes are most often given as the home currency price of the foreign currency and are also given for many currency pairs. However, this practice is not uniform worldwide. As we describe in the next section, the professional interbank market has standardized its quotation system.

)))) Interbank Quotations

Professional dealers and brokers may state foreign exchange quotations in one of two ways: (1) the foreign currency price of one dollar, or (2) the dollar price of a unit of foreign currency. Most foreign currencies in the world are stated in terms of the number of units of foreign currency needed to buy one dollar. For example, the exchange rate between U.S. dollars and Swiss franc is normally stated

SF1.5625/$, read as "1.5625 Swiss francs per dollar"

This method, called *European terms*, expresses the rate as the foreign currency price of one U.S. dollar. An alternative method is called *American terms*. The same exchange rate above expressed in American terms is

$0.6400/SF, read as "0.6400 dollars per Swiss franc"

Under American terms, foreign exchange rates are stated as the U.S. dollar price of one unit of foreign currency. Note that European terms and American terms are reciprocals:

$$\frac{1}{SF1.5625/\$} = \$0.6400/SF$$

With several exceptions, including two important ones, most interbank quotations around the world are stated in European terms. Thus, throughout the world, the normal way of quoting the relationship between the Swiss franc and U.S. dollar is SF1.5625/$; this method may also be called *Swiss terms*. A Japanese yen quote of ¥125.00/$ is in *Japanese terms*, although the expression European terms is often used as the generic name for Asian as well as European currency prices of the dollar. European terms were adopted as the universal way of expressing foreign exchange rates for most (but not all) currencies in 1978 to facilitate worldwide trading through telecommunications.

As mentioned, several exceptions exist to the use of European-terms quotes. The two most important are quotes for the euro and for the U.K. pound sterling. The euro, first traded in January 1999, and the U.K. pound sterling are both normally quoted in American terms, that is, in the U.S. dollar price of a euro or a pound sterling. Additionally, Australian dollars and New Zealand dollars are normally quoted in American terms. Sterling is quoted as the foreign currency price of one pound for historical reasons. For centuries the British pound sterling consisted of 20 shillings, each of which had 12 pence. Multiplication and division with this nondecimal currency were difficult. The custom evolved for foreign exchange prices in London, then the undisputed financial capital of the world, to be stated in foreign currency units per pound. This practice remained even after sterling changed to decimals in 1971.

American terms are used in quoting rates for most foreign currency options and futures, as well as in retail markets that deal with tourists and personal remittances. Foreign exchange traders use nicknames for major currencies. "Cable" means the exchange rate between U.S. dollars and U.K. pound sterling, the name dating from the time when transactions in dollars and pounds were carried out over the Trans-Atlantic telegraph cable. A Canadian dollar is a "loonie," named after the water fowl on Canada's one-dollar coin. "Paris" means the French franc, while "Kiwi" stands for the New Zealand dollar, "Aussie" for the Australian dollar, "Swissie" for Swiss francs, and "Sing dollar" for the Singapore dollar.

Currency amounts must be precise in foreign exchange conversations to avoid major blunders. Unfortunately, British and American English meaning differs for the word "billion." For the British, "one billion" is 1 followed by 12 zeros: i.e., 1,000,000,000,000 or a million million. In the United States and France where the system of numeration is based on groups of threes rather than fours, one billion is a thousand million, or 1,000,000,000. For the British a "trillion" is a million billions, while in American and French usage, a "trillion" is a thousand billions; i.e., the same as one British billion.[2] To avoid confusion, foreign exchange traders use the word "yard" to describe an American billion.

)))) Direct and Indirect Quotes

Foreign exchange quotes are at times described as either *direct* or *indirect*. In this pair of definitions, the home or base country of the currencies being discussed is critical.

A *direct quote* is a home currency price of a unit of foreign currency, and an *indirect quote* is a foreign currency price of a unit of home currency. The form of the quote depends on what the speaker regards as "home."

The foreign exchange quote, "SF1.5625/$" is a direct quote in Switzerland—it is the Swiss home currency (Swiss franc) price of a foreign currency (U.S. dollar). Exactly the same quotation, "SF1.5625/$," is an indirect quotation when used in the United States—it is now the foreign currency (Swiss franc) price of the home currency (U.S. dollar). The reciprocal of this quote, "$0.6400/SF," is a direct quote in the United States and an indirect quote in Switzerland.

The direct dollar quote against the Swiss franc, $0.6400/SF in the above example, may also be referred to as the "external value of the Swiss franc"—that is, the value of one Swiss franc outside Switzerland. The "internal value of the Swiss franc" is SF1.5625/$—the number of Swiss francs that can be purchased for one dollar.

))) Bid and Offer Quotations

Interbank quotations are given as a *bid* and *offer* (also referred to as *ask*). A *bid* is the price (i.e., exchange rate) in one currency at which a dealer will buy another currency. An *offer* is the price (i.e., exchange rate) at which a dealer will sell the other currency. Dealers bid (buy) at one price and offer (sell) at a slightly higher price, making their profit from the spread between the buying and selling prices.

Bid and offer quotations in the foreign exchange markets are superficially complicated by the fact that the bid for one currency is also the offer for the opposite currency. A trader seeking to buy dollars with Swiss francs is simultaneously offering to sell Swiss francs for dollars. Assume a bank makes the quotations shown in the top half of Exhibit 4.5 for the Japanese yen. The spot quotations on the first line indicate that the bank's foreign exchange trader will "buy dollars" (i.e., "sell Japanese yen") at the bid price of ¥118.27 per dollar. The trader will "sell dollars" (i.e., "buy Japanese yen") at the offer price of ¥118.37 per dollar.

As illustrated in Exhibit 4.5, however, the full *outright quotation* (the full price, to all its decimal points) is typically shown only for the current spot rate. Traders, however, tend to abbreviate when talking on the phone or putting quotations on a video screen. The first term, the bid, of a spot quotation may be given in full: that is, "118.27." However, the second term, the offer, will probably be expressed only as the digits that differ from the bid. Hence the bid and offer for spot yen would probably be printed "118.27–37" on a video screen. On

Exhibit 4.5	*Spot and Forward Quotations for the Euro, Japanese Yen, and Thai Baht*

	Term	Euro: Spot and Forward ($/€)			Yen: Spot and Forward (¥/$)			Baht: Spot and Forward (Bt/$)		
		Mid-Rate	Bid	Ask	Mid-Rate	Bid	Ask	Mid-Rate	Bid	Ask
	Spot	1.0899	1.0897	1.0901	118.32	118.27	118.37	37.585	37.560	37.610
Cash	1 week	1.0903	3	4	118.23	− 10	− 9	37.596	− 9	30
Rates	1 mo	1.0917	17	19	117.82	− 51	− 50	37.650	39	90
	2 mo	1.0934	35	36	117.38	− 95	− 93	37.739	119	189
	3 mo	1.0953	53	54	116.91	− 143	− 140	37.864	229	329
	4 mo	1.0973	72	76	116.40	− 195	− 190	37.920	310	359
	5 mo	1.0992	90	95	115.94	− 240	− 237	38.030	420	469
	6 mo	1.1012	112	113	115.45	− 288	− 287	38.145	520	600
	9 mo	1.1075	175	177	114.00	− 435	− 429	38.415	780	880
	1 yr	1.1143	242	245	112.50	− 584	− 581	38.699	1049	1179
Swap	2 yr	1.1401	481	522	106.93	− 1150	− 1129	40.050	2409	2520
Rates	3 yr	1.1679	750	810	101.09	− 1748	− 1698	41.675	3969	4210
	4 yr	1.1899	960	1039	96.82	− 2185	− 2115	43.485	5730	6070
	5 yr	1.2102	1129	1276	92.91	− 2592	− 2490	45.305	7500	7939

Source: Bloomberg, March 22, 1999. mo is month, yr is year. Mid-Rate is the numerical average of Bid and Ask.

the telephone the trader might say "118.27 (pause) 37," "118.27 to 37," or simply "27 to 37," assuming that the leading digits are already known. Traders call the part of the quote that is omitted because it seldom changes the "big figure," while the last two digits used by themselves are the "small figure."[3]

In actuality currency markets are rarely so tranquil that traders can expect consistent profit by buying at their bid and selling at their offer. If a trader quotes 118.27–37 and buys dollars at 118.27, that trader's next quote may be 118.30–40 if the trader wants to add to inventory, or 118.20–30 if the trader wants to reduce inventory. A trader's profitability depends to a large extent on ability to time individual purchases and sales. Additionally, because each dealer is a market maker (that is, stands ready to buy or sell at any time for a price), a counterparty may "hit the bid" or force the dealer to buy when the dealer's preference is to sell, or the offer may be "lifted" (accepted) when the dealer would prefer to buy.

))) Expressing Forward Quotations on a Points Basis

The spot quotations given in the top line for each currency in Exhibit 4.5 are "outright:" ¥118.27/$ for the spot bid and ¥118.37/$ for the spot ask. The forward rates are, however, typically quoted in terms of *points*, also referred to as *cash rates* and *swap rates*, depending on maturity. A *point* is the last digit of a quotation, with convention dictating the number of digits to the right of the decimal point. Currency prices for the U.S. dollar are usually expressed to four decimal points. Hence a point is equal to 0.0001 of most currencies. Some currencies, such as the Japanese yen shown in Exhibit 4.5, are quoted only to two decimal points. A forward quotation expressed in points is not a foreign exchange rate as such. Rather it is the *difference* between the forward rate and the spot rate. Consequently, the spot rate itself can never be given on a points basis.

The three-month points quotations for the Japanese yen in Exhibit 4.5 are "–143" bid and "–140" ask. The first number ("–143") refers to points away from the spot bid, and the second number ("–140") to points away from the spot ask (offer). Given the outright quotes of 118.27 bid and 118.37 ask, the outright three-month forward rates are calculated as follows:

	Bid	*Ask*
Outright spot:	¥118.27	¥118.37
plus points (3 months)	–1.43	–1.40
Outright forward:	¥116.84	¥116.97

The forward bid and offer quotations in Exhibit 4.5 for 2 years or longer are called *swap rates*. As mentioned earlier, many forward exchange transactions in the interbank market involve a simultaneous purchase for one date and sale (reversing the transaction) for another date. This swap is a way to borrow one currency for a limited time while giving up the use of another currency for the same time. In other words, it is a short-term borrowing of one currency combined with a short-term loan of an equivalent amount of another currency. The two parties could, if they wanted, charge each other interest at the going rate for each of the currencies. However, it is easier for the party with the higher-interest currency to simply pay the *net* interest differential to the other. The swap rate expresses this net interest differential on a points basis rather than as an interest rate.

)))) Forward Quotations in Percentage Terms

Forward quotations may also be expressed as the percent-per-annum deviation from the spot rate. This method of quotation facilitates comparing premiums or discounts in the forward market with interest rate differentials. However, the percent premium or discount depends on which currency is the home, or base, currency. Assume the following quotations, where the dollar is the home currency:

	Foreign Currency/ *Home Currency*	*Home Currency/* *Foreign Currency*
Spot rate	¥105.65/$	$0.009465215/¥
Three-month forward	¥105.04/$	$0.009520183/¥

Quotations Expressed in Home Currency Terms (i.e., Direct Quotations). When the home currency price for a foreign currency is used, the formula for the percent premium or discount ($f^{¥}$) is:

$$f^{¥} = \frac{\text{Forward} - \text{Spot}}{\text{Spot}} \times \frac{360}{n} \times 100$$

where n is the number of days in the contract. (n may also be the number of months, in which case the numerator is 12.) If we substitute the $/¥ spot and forward rates, as well as the number of days forward (90), we get

$$f^{¥} = \frac{0.009520183 - 0.009465215}{0.009465215} \times \frac{360}{90} \times 100 = +2.32\% \text{ p.a.}$$

The sign is positive, indicating that the forward yen is selling at a 2.32% per annum premium over the dollar.

Quotations Expressed in Foreign Currency Terms (i.e., Indirect Quotations). When the foreign currency price of the home currency is used, the formula for the percent-per-annum premium or discount becomes:

$$f^{¥} = \frac{\text{Spot} - \text{Forward}}{\text{Forward}} \times \frac{360}{n} \times 100$$

If we substitute ¥/$ spot and forward rates, as well as the number of days forward (90), we get

$$f^{¥} = \frac{105.65 - 105.04}{105.04} \times \frac{360}{90} \times 100 = +2.32\% \text{ p.a.}$$

The sign is positive, again indicating that the forward yen is selling at a 2.32% per annum premium over the dollar.

)))) Reading Newspaper Quotations

Foreign exchange rates are quoted in all major world newspapers. The manner of quotation in the *Wall Street Journal* and the *Financial Times*, the world's two major English-language business newspapers, is shown in Exhibit 4.6. Although these quotes for the pound are for the same day, they are not identical because of time zone differences and the banks surveyed for the quotes.

The *Wall Street Journal* gives American terms quotes under the heading "U.S.$ equivalent" and European terms quotes under the heading "Currency per U.S. $." Quotes are for the last two trading days and are given on an outright basis for spot, one-, three-, and six-month forwards. The heading of the table states that quotes are "selling rates," i.e., offer rates. Bid rates are not given. Quotes are for trading among banks in amounts of $1 million or more, as quoted at 4 P.M. Eastern Time by Dow Jones Telerate Inc., and other sources. The *Journal* states that retail transactions provide fewer units of foreign currency per dollar.

The Financial Times presents the latest day's spread and closing bid and ask quotes in its first two columns. One-month, three-month, and one-year forward

---

Exhibit 4.6	*What Is the Current Rate of Exchange?*

The Wall Street Journal

	U.S. $ Equivalent		Currency per U.S. $	
	Wed	Tue	Wed	Tue
Britain (Pound)	1.6125	1.6145	.6202	.6194
one-month forward	1.6128	1.6148	.6200	.6193
three-months forward	1.6138	1.6157	.6197	.6189
six-months forward	1.6159	1.6177	.6189	.6182

Source: "Currency Trading: Exchange Rates," *The Wall Street Journal*, Thursday August 12, 1999 (quotes for Wednesday August 11), p. C11.

Financial Times

	Closing Mid-point	Change on Day	Bid/Offer Spread	Day's Mid High	Low	One-month rate	%p.a.	Three-months rate	%p.a.	One-year rate	%p.a.
UK (£)	1.6101	−0.0030	097–104	1.6173	1.6089	1.6104	−0.2	1.6114	−0.3	1.6146	−0.3

Source: "Dollar Spot, Forward Against The Dollar," *Financial Times*, Thursday, August 12, 1999 (quotes for Wednesday August 11), p. 21.

rates are quoted in direct terms as well as expressed in terms of the percent-per-annum deviation from the spot rate.

))) Cross Rates

Many currency pairs are only inactively traded, so their exchange rate is determined through their relationship to a widely traded third currency. For example, a Mexican importer needs Korean won to pay for purchases in Seoul. The Mexican peso (Ps) is not quoted against the Korean won (symbol W). However, both currencies are quoted against the U.S. dollar. Assume the following quotes:

$$\text{Korean won} \qquad \text{W 1200.00/\$}$$
$$\text{Mexican peso} \qquad \text{Ps9.3750/\$}$$

The Mexican importer can buy one U.S. dollar for Ps9.3750, and with that dollar buy W1200.00. The cross rate calculation would be:

$$\frac{\text{Korean won/U.S. dollar}}{\text{Mexican pesos/U.S. dollar}} = \frac{\text{W1200.00/\$}}{\text{Ps9.3750/\$}} = \text{W128.00/Ps}$$

The cross rate could also be calculated as the reciprocal:

$$\frac{\text{Mexican peso/U.S. dollar}}{\text{Korean won/U.S. dollar}} = \frac{\text{Ps9.3750/\$}}{\text{W1200.00/\$}} = \text{Ps0.0078125/W}$$

Cross rates often appear in financial publications in the form of a matrix such as is shown in Exhibit 4.7. This matrix shows the amount of each currency (columns) needed to buy a unit of the currency of the country on the line (row).

A second use of cross rates is for businesses to validate the internal consistency of their separate foreign exchange forecasts. A dollar-per-pound exchange rate forecast for next year by a firm's European staff may be multiplied by a yen-per-pound forecast by the Japanese staff to see whether the resulting yen-per-pound cross rate is reasonable. Such cross-checking is important for maintaining consistency across foreign affiliates when drawing up corporate-wide performance budgets or setting interaffiliate transfer prices.

| Exhibit 4.7 | *Cross Rates for Selected Currencies* |

	¥	W	Ps	SF	£	$
Japan	—	9.6000	0.0750	0.0125	0.00512	0.0080
Korea	0.1041667	—	0.0078125	0.001302	0.0005333	0.000833
Mexico	13.333333	128.0000	—	0.166667	0.0682667	0.106667
Switzerland	80.0000	768.0000	6.0000	—	0.4096	0.6400
United Kingdom	195.3125	11875.000	14.648437	2.441406	—	1.6000
United States	125.00	1200.00	9.3750	1.5625	0.6250	—

))) Intermarket Arbitrage

Cross rates can be used to check on opportunities for intermarket arbitrage. Suppose the following exchange rates are quoted:

Wells Fargo	Dollars per euro	$1.0600/€
National Westminster Bank	Dollars per pound sterling	$1.5500/£
Hong Kong and Shanghai Bank	Euros per pound sterling	€1.5000/£

The cross rate between Wells Fargo and National Westminster Bank is:

$$\frac{\$1.5500/£}{\$1.0600/€} = €1.4623/£$$

This cross rate is not the same as Hong Kong and Shanghai Bank's quotation of €1.5000/£, so an opportunity exists to profit from arbitrage between the three markets. Exhibit 4.8 shows the steps in what is called *triangular arbitrage*.

A market trader with $1,000,000 can sell that sum spot to National Westminster Bank for $1,000,000 ÷ $1.5500/£ = £645,161. Simultaneously, these pounds can be sold to Hong Kong and Shanghai Bank for £645,161 × €1.5000/£ = €967,742, and then the trader immediately exchanges the euros for dollars at Wells Fargo Bank for €967,742 x $1.0600/€ = $1,025,806. The profit on one such "turn" is a risk-free $25,806. Such intermarket arbitrage can continue until exchange rate equilibrium is reestablished; that is, until the calculated cross rate equals the actual quotation, less a margin for transaction costs.

Exhibit 4.8   *Triangular Arbitrage*

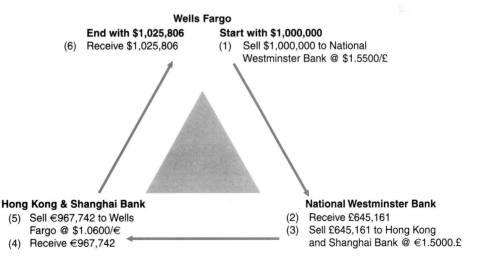

Wells Fargo

End with $1,025,806   **Start with $1,000,000**
(6)   Receive $1,025,806   (1)   Sell $1,000,000 to National
                                    Westminster Bank @ $1.5500/£

Hong Kong & Shanghai Bank   **National Westminster Bank**
(5)   Sell €967,742 to Wells   (2)   Receive £645,161
      Fargo @ $1.0600/€   (3)   Sell £645,161 to Hong Kong
(4)   Receive €967,742   and Shanghai Bank @ €1.5000.£

Two aspects should be noted: (1) Such arbitrage is practical only if the participants have instant access to quotes and executions. Hence, except in rare instances, such arbitrage is conducted only by foreign exchange traders. "Public" participation is most difficult. (2) Bank traders can conduct such arbitrage without an initial sum of money, other than their bank's credit standing, because the trades are entered into and subsequently "washed" (i.e., offset) by electronic means before the normal settlement two days later.

)))) Measuring a Change in Spot Exchange Rates

Assume that the Swiss franc, recently quoted at SF1.5625/$ (which is the same as $0.6400/SF), suddenly strengthens to SF1.2800/$ (which is the same as $0.78125/SF). What is the percent increase in the dollar value of the franc, and thus in the value of Swiss franc-denominated accounts receivable or payable held by Americans? As with forward quotations in percentage form, the home currency is critical.

Quotations Expressed in Home Currency Terms (i.e., Direct Quotations). When the home currency price for a foreign currency is used, the formula for the percent change in the foreign currency is:

$$\%\Delta = \frac{\text{Ending rate} - \text{Beginning rate}}{\text{Beginning rate}} \times 100 = \frac{\$0.78125/SF - \$0.6400/SF}{\$0.6400/SF} \times 100 = +22.07\%$$

In this instance, the Swiss franc is 22.07% stronger at the ending rate. Holders of Swiss franc receivables will receive 22.07% more dollars, but those who owe Swiss francs will have to pay 22.07% more dollars to buy them.

Quotations Expressed in Foreign Currency Terms (i.e., Indirect Quotations). When the foreign currency price of the home currency is used, the formula for the percent change in the foreign currency becomes:

$$\%\Delta = \frac{\text{Beginning rate} - \text{Ending rate}}{\text{Ending rate}} \times 100 = \frac{\text{SF1.5625/\$} - \text{SF1.2800/\$}}{\text{SF1.2800/\$}} \times 100 = +22.07\%$$

By both methods of calculation, the Swiss franc increased 22.07% in value relative to the dollar.

FOREIGN CURRENCY FUTURES

A foreign currency futures contract is an alternative to a forward contract. A foreign currency futures contract calls for future delivery of a standard amount of foreign exchange at a fixed time, place, and price. It is similar to futures contracts that exist for commodities (hogs, cattle, lumber, and so on), for interest-bearing deposits, and for gold.

Most world money centers have established foreign currency futures markets. In the United States the most important market for foreign currency futures is the International Monetary Market (IMM) of Chicago, a division of the Chicago Mercantile Exchange.

》》》 Contract Specifications

Contract specifications are established by the exchange on which futures are traded. Let's use the IMM as an example; the major features that must be standardized are the following:

- *A specific-sized contract.* Trading in each currency must be done in an even multiple of currency units.

- *A standard method of stating exchange rates.* American terms are used; that is, quotations are the U.S. dollar cost of foreign currency units, also known as direct quotes.

- *A standard maturity date.* Contracts mature on the third Wednesday of January, March, April, June, July, September, October, or December.

- *A specified last trading day.* Contracts may be traded through the second business day prior to the Wednesday on which they mature. Therefore, unless holidays interfere, the last trading day is the Monday preceding the maturity date.

- *Collateral and maintenance margins.* The purchaser must deposit a sum as an initial margin or collateral. This standard is similar to requiring a performance bond and can be met by a letter of credit from a bank, Treasury bills, or cash. In addition, a maintenance margin is required. The value of the contract is marked to market daily, and all changes in value are paid in cash daily. The amount to be paid is called the *variation margin.*

- *Settlement.* Only about 5% of all futures contracts are settled by the physical delivery of foreign exchange between buyer and seller. Most often, buyers and sellers offset their original position prior to delivery date by taking an opposite position. That is, if one buys a futures contract, that position will normally be closed out by selling a futures contract for the same delivery date. The complete buy/sell or sell/buy is called a *round turn.*

- *Commissions.* Customers pay a commission to their broker to execute a round turn and only a single price is quoted. This practice differs from that of the interbank market, where dealers quote a bid and an offer and do not charge a commission.

- *Clearing house as a counterparty.* All contracts are agreements between the client and the exchange clearing house, rather than between the two clients involved. Consequently, clients need not worry that a specific counterparty in the market will fail to honor an agreement.

))) Using Foreign Currency Futures

To illustrate the use of currency futures for speculating on currency movements, we will focus on the Mexican peso futures traded on the Chicago Mercantile Exchange (CME). Exhibit 4.9 presents Mexican peso futures quotations from the *Wall Street Journal* for Wednesday, August 11, 1999. Each contract is for 500,000 pesos and is quoted US$/peso.

Any investor wishing to speculate on the movement of the Mexican peso versus the U.S. dollar could pursue one of the following strategies.

Short Positions. If Maria Gonzalo, a speculator working for International Currency Traders, believes the Mexican peso will fall in value versus the U.S. dollar by September, she could sell a September futures contract, taking a *short position*. Maria sells one September futures contract for 500,000 pesos at the settle price listed in Exhibit 4.9, $.10535/Ps. The value of her position at maturity is then:

$$\text{Value at maturity (Short position)} = -\text{ Notional principal} \times (\text{Spot} - \text{Futures})$$

If the spot exchange rate at maturity is $.09500/Ps, the value of her position on settlement is then:

$$\text{Value} = -\text{ Ps500,000} \times (\$.09500/\text{Ps} - \$.10535/\text{Ps}) = \$5,175$$

Long Position. If Maria Gonzalo expects the peso to rise in value versus the dollar, she could take a *long position*, by buying a September futures with a price of $.10535/Ps. Her futures contract at maturity would have the following value:

$$\text{Value at maturity (Long Position)} = \text{National principal} \times (\text{Spot} - \text{Futures})$$

If the spot exchange rate at maturity is $.1100/Ps, Maria has indeed guessed right. The value of her position on settlement is then:

$$\text{Value} = \text{Ps500,000} \times (\$.11000/\text{Ps} - \$.10535/\text{Ps}) = \$2,325$$

| **Exhibit 4.9** | *Mexican Peso Futures, US$/Ps (CME)* |

Maturity	Open	High	Low	Settle	Change	Open Interest
Sept	.10410	.10540	.10410	.10535	+ 01975	14,514
Dec	.09945	.10040	.09925	.10040	+ 02000	7,374
Mar 00	.09470	.09520	.09470	.09560	+ 02000	3,816

Abstracted from *The Wall Street Journal*, Thursday, August 12, 1999, p. C14. Quotations are for close of business on Wednesday, August 11, 1999. All contracts are for 500,000 Mexican new pesos. Open interest is number of contracts outstanding.

Futures contracts could obviously be used in combinations to form a variety of more complex positions. When combining contracts, however, valuation is fairly straightforward and additive in character.

))) Foreign Currency Futures versus Forward Contracts

Foreign currency futures contracts differ from forward contracts in a number of important ways, as shown in Exhibit 4.10. As a general matter, large firms have not found futures a particularly useful device for hedging risks. In part this is so because of the constraint of fixed contract sizes and maturities, and in part it reflects the requirement for a margin deposit that must be marked to market every single day. This means either the possibility of an uncertain cash outflow every day or the maintenance of an extra cash deposit with the dealer. On the other hand, small businesses and individuals that do not have access to forward contracts with banks find futures very useful.

SUMMARY

- A foreign exchange *rate* is the price of one currency expressed in terms of another currency. A foreign exchange *quotation* is a statement of willingness to buy or sell currency at an announced price.

Exhibit 4.10   *Comparison of Foreign Currency Futures versus Forward Contracts*

Characteristic	Foreign currency futures	Forward contracts
Size of Contract	Standardized contracts per currency	Any size desired
Maturity	Fixed maturities, the longest being typically less than one year	Any maturity up to one year, sometimes longer
Location	Trading occurs on the floor of an organized exchange	Trading occurs between individuals and banks with other banks by telecommunications linkages
Pricing	Open outcry process in the "pit" by floor traders	Prices are arrived at by bid and offer quotes
Collateral	Initial margin that is marked to market value on a daily basis	No explicit collateral, but standing bank "relations" necessary
Settlement	Rarely delivered upon; settlement normally takes place through the purchase of an offsetting position	The contract is normally delivered upon, although the taking of offsetting positions possible
Commissions	Single commission covers both purchase and later sale (round trip)	Commissions gained through the bid-offer spreads provided to retail customers
Trading Hours	Traditionally traded during exchange hours; several exchanges are now moving to automated 24-hour-a-day trading	Negotiated by phone 24 hours a day through bank global networks
Counterparties	Unknown to one another due to the auction market structure	Parties are in direct contact in setting forward specifications
Liquidity	Liquid but relatively small in total sales volume and value	Liquid and relatively large in sales volume compared with that of future contracts

- Geographically, the foreign exchange market spans the globe, with prices moving and currencies traded somewhere every hour of every business day.

- The three functions of the foreign exchange market are to transfer purchasing power, provide credit, and minimize foreign exchange risk.

- The foreign exchange market is composed of two tiers: the *interbank market* and the *client market*. Participants within these tiers include bank and non-bank foreign exchange dealers, individuals and firms conducting commercial and investment transactions, speculators and arbitragers, central banks and treasuries, and foreign exchange brokers.

- Transactions within the foreign exchange market are executed either on a *spot basis*, requiring settlement two days after the transaction, or on a *forward* or *swap basis*, which requires settlement at some designated future date.

- *European terms* quotations are the foreign currency price of a U.S. dollar. *American terms* quotations are the dollar price of a foreign currency.

- Quotations can also be *direct* or *indirect*. A direct quote is the home currency price of a unit of foreign currency, while an indirect quote is the foreign currency price of a unit of home currency. Direct and indirect are *not* synonyms for American and European terms, because the home currency will change depending on who is doing the calculation, while European terms are always the foreign currency price of a dollar.

- A *cross rate* is an exchange rate between two currencies, calculated from their common relationships with a third currency. When cross rates differ from the direct rates between two currencies, *intermarket arbitrage* is possible.

- A *foreign currency futures contract* is an exchange-traded agreement calling for future delivery of a standard amount of foreign exchange at a fixed time, place, and price.

- Foreign currency futures contracts are in reality standardized forward contracts. Unlike forward contracts, however, trading occurs on the floor of an organized exchange rather than between banks and customers. Futures also require collateral and are normally settled through the purchase of an offsetting position.

QUESTIONS

1. Trading in Japanese Yen

A foreign exchange dealer in London normally quotes spot, one-month, three-months, and one-year forward. When you ask over the telephone for current quotations for the Japanese yen against the U.S. dollar, you hear:

"111.43 to 51, 52 to 48, 150 to 144, 337 to 205"

Answer the following, based on the above quotations.

a. What would you receive in dollars if you sold ¥300,000,000 spot?
b. What would it cost you to purchase ¥400,000,000 forward three-months with dollars?
c. When would you make payment for the forward transaction?
d. In New York, six-month Treasury bills yield 6% per annum. Using mid-rates (halfway between bid and ask) calculate the yield on Japanese six-month bills.
e. Verify your answer to part (c) with a hypothetical investment of $1,000,000 for six months in both countries. Use mid-rates for simplicity and ignore charges and taxes.

2. Transactions in the Foreign Exchange Market

The computer screen in a foreign exchange trading room shows the following:

Currency	Spot	1-month	3-month	6-month
Mexican peso	9.3850–80	70–80	210–215	410–440
South African rand	6.1200–300	425–445	1100–1200	1825-1900
Pound sterling	1.6320–35	40–34	105–95	190–170

a. Express all the above quotations on an outright basis.
b. You want to buy Mexican pesos three-months forward with pounds sterling. What is your effective exchange rate?
c. You read in the financial press that the South African rand has dropped 18% in value over the last ten years. What was the spot quote a decade ago?
d. What are the forward dollar/pound bid quotes as a percent per annum, from a British perspective? From an American perspective?

3. Forward Rates on the Canadian Dollar

The following outright foreign exchange quotations are given for the Canadian dollar:

	Bid (C$/US$)	Ask (C$/US$)
Spot rate	1.4868	1.4878
One-month forward	1.4866	1.4876
Three-months forward	1.4851	1.4866

a. Calculate forward quotes for both bid and ask in terms of points.
b. Express forward (bid only) exchange rates from the perspective of a trader in Montreal as an annual percentage premium or discount.
c. If a foreign exchange trader in New York calculated the annual percentage premium or discount for forward (bid only) Canadian dollars, what would that trader get? Explain why the percentages are different from those in part (b) above.

4. Currency Cross Rates

Using the *bid* spot currency quotes shown in question 2 above, answer the following:

a. What is the current cross spot rate of Mexican pesos/pounds sterling?

b. What is the current cross spot rate of pounds sterling/South African rand?

c. What is the current cross spot rate of South African rands/Mexican peso?

5. Devaluation of the Russian Ruble

Russia's currency, the ruble, is a managed float. The Central Bank of Russia announces an official exchange rate each day, along with rates at which it is willing to buy and sell. Prior to Monday, August 17, 1998, the ruble had been pegged to trade between Rb5.2700/$ and Rb7.1300/$. On August 17, 1998, new exchange rate limits of Rb6.0000/$ to Rb9.5000/$ were set. Actual rates were:

> Friday August 14, 1998: Rb6.3500/$
> Friday August 28, 1998: Rb11.0000/$
> Friday August 27, 1999: Rb24.5580/$

a. By what percent did the ruble devalue against the dollar in the two weeks from August 14, 1998, to August 28, 1998?

b. By what percent did the ruble devalue against the dollar on the year from August 28, 1998, to August 27, 1999?

c. How did this affect the personal wealth of a Russian citizen who kept his or her wealth in rubles versus dollars?

6. An Asian Triangle

The following quotations are available to you. (You may either buy or sell at the stated rates.)

Singapore bank: Singapore dollar quote for Korean won   Won714.00/S$
Hong Kong bank: HK$ quote for Singapore dollars   HK$4.70/S$
Korean bank: Korean won quote for Hong Kong dollars   Won150.00/HK$

Assume you have an initial S$1,000,000. Is triangular arbitrage possible? If so, explain the steps and compute your profit.

WORLD WIDE WEB EXERCISES

W1. What's the Euro Worth?

The European Union provides a daily tracking of the euro's value in terms of its constituent currencies. Use the following web address to find out how many Spanish pesetas the euro is worth today.

> EU's euro page
> http://europa.eu.int/comm/economy_finance/document/ecu/xecupage.htm

W2. Exchange Rates, Interest Rates, and Global Markets
The magnitude of market data can seem overwhelming on some occasions.
Use the following Bloomberg markets page to organize your mind and your
global data.

Bloomberg Financial News   http://www.bloomberg.com/markets

SUGGESTED READINGS

Zaheer, Srilata, "Circadian Rhythms: The Effects of Global Market Integration on
the Currency Trading Industry," *Journal of International Business Studies*, Vol. 26,
No. 4, Fourth Quarter 1995, pp. 699–728.

Glassman, Debra, "Exchange Rate Risk and Transactions Costs: Evidence from
Bid–Ask Spreads," *Journal of International Money and Finance*, Vol. 6, No. 4, Dec.
1987, pp. 479–491.

Sweeney, Richard J., "Beating the Foreign Exchange Market," *Journal of Finance*,
Mar. 1986, pp. 163–182.

NOTES

1. Currency trading is quite profitable for commercial and investment banks. Many of
   the major currency-trading banks in the United States derive, on average, between
   10% and 20% of their annual net income from currency trading. But currency trading
   is also very profitable for the bank's traders. The head of currency trading for
   Salomon Brothers in 1993 is purported to have received a total compensation package of $28 million; Salomon's Chief Executive Officer received only $7 million.
   Source: "Salomon's Fattest Pay Didn't Go to CEO." *Wall Street Journal*, March 29,
   1994, p. C1.
2. *The Shorter Oxford English Dictionary on Historical Principles*, 3rd Edition, Volumes I
   and II, Oxford: Clarendon Press, 1973.
3. Note that when quotations in European terms are converted to American terms, bid
   and offer reverse: the reciprocal of the bid becomes the offer, and the reciprocal of
   the offer becomes the bid.

CHAPTER 5

FOREIGN CURRENCY OPTIONS

*F*oreign currency options are instruments that have assumed increasing importance in the marketplace in recent years. They can be used to hedge the foreign exchange risk that results from commercial transactions, and they can be used for speculative purposes. Use of foreign currency options to hedge commercial transactions is covered in Chapter 6.

This chapter is presented in two parts. The first half provides a basic description of currency options, of the markets in which they are traded, and of their use for investment or speculation purposes. The second half of the chapter provides a deeper look into the forces determining option values (pricing), and how option values change with these forces.

VOCABULARY

- A *foreign currency option* is a contract giving the option purchaser (the buyer) the right, but not the obligation, to buy or sell a given amount of foreign exchange at a fixed price per unit for a specified time period (until the expiration date). In many ways buying an option is like buying a ticket to a Rolling Stones concert. The buyer has the right to attend the concert but does not have to (after all, Mick Jagger is over 50 years old). The buyer of the concert ticket risks nothing more than what was paid for the ticket. Similarly, the buyer of an option cannot lose anything more than what was paid for the option. If the buyer of the ticket decides later not to attend the concert, prior to the day of the concert the ticket can be sold to someone else who does wish to go (someone interested in the music of aging rock stars).

- There are two basic types of options, *calls* and *puts*. A *call* is an option to buy foreign currency, and a *put* is an option to sell foreign currency.

- The buyer of an option is termed the *holder*, whereas the seller of an option is referred to as the *writer* or *grantor*.

- Every option has three different price elements: (1) the exercise or strike price, the exchange rate at which the foreign currency can be purchased (call) or sold (put); (2) the premium, which is the cost, price, or value of the option itself; and (3) the underlying or actual spot exchange rate in the market.

- An *American option* gives the buyer the right to exercise the option at any time between the date of writing and the expiration or maturity date. A *European option* can be exercised only on its expiration date, not before.

- The *premium* or *option price* is the cost of the option, usually paid in advance by the buyer to the seller. In the over-the-counter market (options offered by banks), premiums are quoted as a percentage of the transaction amount. Premiums on exchange-traded options are quoted as a domestic currency amount per unit of foreign currency.

- An option whose exercise price is the same as the spot price of the underlying currency is said to be *at the money* (ATM). An option that would be profitable if exercised immediately is said to be *in the money* (ITM). An option that would not be profitable if exercised immediately is referred to as *out of the money* (OTM).

FOREIGN CURRENCY OPTIONS MARKETS

In the past decade the use of foreign currency options as a hedging tool and for speculative purposes has blossomed into a major foreign exchange activity. A number of banks in the United States and other capital markets offer flexible foreign currency options on transactions of $1 million or more. The *bank market*, or *over-the-counter market* as it is called, offers custom-tailored options on all major trading currencies for any time period up to one year. These provide a useful alternative to forward and futures contracts (discussed in the previous chapter) for firms interested in hedging foreign exchange risk on commercial transactions.

In December 1982, the Philadelphia Stock Exchange introduced trading in standardized foreign currency option contracts in the United States. The Chicago Mercantile Exchange and other exchanges in the United States and abroad have followed suit. Exchange-traded contracts are particularly appealing to speculators and individuals who do not normally have access to the over-the-counter market. Banks also trade on the exchanges because this is one of several ways they can offset the risk of options they have transacted with clients or other banks.

Increased use of foreign currency options is a reflection of the explosive growth in the use of other kinds of options and the resultant improvements in option pricing models. The original option pricing model, developed in 1973,[1] has become commercialized by numerous firms who now offer software programs and even built-in routines for hand-held calculators. Several commercial programs are available for option writers and traders to utilize.

))) Options on the Over-the-Counter Market

Over-the-counter (OTC) *options* are most frequently written by banks for U.S. dollars against pounds sterling, Deutschemarks, Swiss francs, Japanese yen, Canadian dollars, and most recently, the euro.

The main advantage of over-the-counter options is that they are tailored to the specific needs of the firm. Financial institutions are willing to write or buy options that vary by amount (notional principal), strike price, and maturity. Although the over-the-counter markets were relatively illiquid in the early years, the market has grown to such proportions that liquidity is now considered quite good. On the other hand, the buyer must assess the writing bank's ability to fulfill the option contract. Termed *counterparty risk*, the financial risk associated with the counterparty is increasingly an issue in international markets as a result of the growing use of financial contracts like options and swaps by multinational enterprise (MNE) management. (Chapter 9 provides an expanded discussion of counterparty risk.) However, firms buying and selling currency options as part of their risk management program (as detailed in Chapter 6) do so primarily in the over-the-counter market. Exchange-traded options are primarily the territory of individuals and financial institutions themselves.

A firm wishing to purchase an option in the over-the-counter market will normally place a call to the currency option desk of a major money center bank, specify the currencies, maturity, strike rate(s), and ask for an *indication*—a bid–offer quote. The bank will normally take a few minutes to a few hours to price the option and return the call.

))) Options on Organized Exchanges

Options on the physical (underlying) currency are traded on a number of organized exchanges worldwide, including the Philadelphia Stock Exchange (PHLX) and the London International Financial Futures Exchange (LIFFE).

Exchange-traded options are settled through a clearing house, so that buyers do not deal directly with sellers. The clearing house is the counterparty to every option contract and it guarantees fulfillment. Clearing-house obligations are in turn the obligation of all members of the exchange, including a large number of banks. In the case of the Philadelphia Stock Exchange, clearing-house services are provided by the Options Clearing Corporation (OCC).

The Philadelphia Stock Exchange has long been the innovator in exchange-traded options. It has in recent years continually introduced new features to its United Currency Options Market (UCOM), which have made exchange-traded options much more flexible—and more competitive—in meeting the needs of corporate clients. UCOM offers a variety of option products including cross-rate pairs (non-U.S. dollar), and European- or American-style pricing. It accepts cash settlement or traditional delivery of the currency in question via off-shore bank arrangements. It offers *customized currency options* in which the user may choose exercise price, expiration date (up to two years), and premium quotation form (units of currency or percentage of underlying value).

)))) **Currency Option Quotations and Prices**

Quotes in the *Wall Street Journal* for options on Swiss francs are shown in Exhibit 5.1. The *Journal's* quotes refer to transactions completed on the Philadelphia Stock Exchange on the previous day. Quotations are usually available for more combinations of strike prices and expiration dates than were actually traded and thus reported in the newspaper.

Exhibit 5.1 illustrates the three different prices that characterize any foreign currency option. The three prices which characterize an "August 58½ call option" (highlighted in Exhibit 5.1) are the following:[2]

1. **Spot rate.** In Exhibit 5.1, "Option and Underlying" means that 58.51 cents, or $0.5851, is the spot dollar price of one Swiss franc at the close of trading on the preceding day. This spot rate is sometimes omitted from the *Wall Street Journal* quotations.

2. **Exercise price.** The exercise price, or "Strike Price" listed in Exhibit 5.1, means the price per franc that must be paid if the option is exercised. The August call option on francs of 58½ means $0.5850/SF. Exhibit 5.1 lists nine different strike prices, ranging from $0.5600/SF to $0.6000/SF, although more were available on that date than listed here.[3]

3. **Premium.** The premium is the cost or price of the option. The price of the August 58½ call option on Swiss francs is 0.50 U.S. cents per franc, or $0.0050/SF. The September and December 58½ call did not trade on that day. The premium is the market value of the option, and therefore the terms premium, cost, price, and value are all interchangeable when referring to an option.[4]

The August 58½ call option premium is 0.50 cents per franc, and in this case, the August 58½ put's premium is also 0.50 cents per franc. As one option contract on the Philadelphia Stock Exchange consists of 62,500 francs, the total

---

Exhibit 5.1	*Foreign Currency Option Quotations (Philadelphia Stock Exchange)*

Option and Underlying	Strike Price	Calls—Last			Puts—Last		
		Aug.	Sept.	Dec.	Aug.	Sept.	Dec.
62,500 Swiss francs-cents per unit.							
58.51	56	—	—	2.76	0.04	0.22	1.16
58.51	56 1/2	—	—	—	0.06	0.30	—
58.51	57	1.13	—	1.74	0.10	0.38	1.27
58.51	57 1/2	0.75	—	—	0.17	0.55	—
58.51	58	0.71	1.05	1.28	0.27	0.89	1.81
58.51	58 1/2	0.50	—	—	0.50	0.99	—
58.51	59	0.30	0.66	1.21	0.90	1.36	—
58.51	59 1/2	0.15	0.40	—	2.32	—	—
58.51	60	—	0.31	—	2.32	2.62	3.30

Source: Adapted from the *Wall Street Journal.*

cost of one option contract for the call (as well as the put in this case) is SF62,500 × $0.0050/SF = $312.50.

FOREIGN CURRENCY SPECULATION

Speculation is an attempt to profit by trading on expectations about price changes in the future. In the foreign exchange markets, one speculates by taking an open (unhedged) position in a foreign currency and then by closing that position after the exchange rate has moved in—one hopes—the expected direction. In the following section we analyze the manner in which speculation is undertaken in spot, forward, and options markets. It is important to understand this phenomenon because speculation has a major impact on our inability to accurately forecast future exchange rates.

))) Speculating in the Spot Market

Willem Koopmans is a currency speculator in Amsterdam. He is willing to risk money on his own opinion about future currency prices. Willem may speculate in the spot, forward, or options markets. To illustrate, assume the Swiss franc is currently quoted as follows.

Spot rate:	$0.5851/SF
Six-month forward rate:	$0.5760/SF

Willem Koopmans has $100,000 with which to speculate, and he believes that in six months the spot rate for the franc will be $0.6000/SF. Speculation in the spot market requires only that the speculator believe the foreign currency will appreciate in value. Willem should take the following steps.

1. Today use the $100,000 to buy SF170,910.96 spot at $0.5851/SF.
2. Hold the SF170,910.96 indefinitely. Although the franc is expected to rise to the target value in six months, the speculator is not committed to that time horizon.
3. When the target exchange rate is reached, sell SF170,910.96 at the new spot rate of $0.6000/SF, receiving SF170,910.96 × $0.6000/SF = $102,546.57.
4. The profit is $2,546.57, or 2.5% on the $100,000 committed for six months (5.0% per annum). This ignores interest income on the Swiss francs and opportunity cost on the dollars for the moment.

The potential maximum gain is unlimited, while the maximum loss will be $100,000 if the francs purchased in step-1 drop in value to zero. Having initially undertaken a spot market speculation for six months, Willem is nevertheless not bound by that target date. He may sell the francs earlier or later if he wishes.

))) Speculating in the Forward Market

Forward market speculation occurs when the speculator believes that the spot price at some future date will differ from today's forward price for that same date.

Success does not depend on the direction of movement of the spot rate, but on the relative position of the future spot rate and the current forward rate. Given the above data and expectations, Willem Koopmans should take the following steps.

1. Today buy SF173,611.11 forward six months at the forward quote of $0.5760/SF. Note that this step requires no outlay of cash.

2. In six months, fulfill the forward contract, receiving SF173,611.11 at $0.5760/SF for a cost of $100,000.

3. Simultaneously, sell the SF173,611.11 in the spot market, receiving SF173,611.11 × $0.6000/SF = $104,166.67.

4. Profit: $4,166.67.

The profit of $4,166.67 cannot be related to an investment base to calculate a return on investment because the dollar funds were never needed. On the six-month anniversary Willem simply crosses the payment obligation of $100,000 with receipts of $104,166.67 and accepts a net $4,166.67. Nevertheless, some financial institutions might require him to deposit collateral as margin to ensure his ability to complete the trade.

In this particular forward speculation, the maximum loss is $100,000, the amount needed to buy francs via the forward contract. This loss would be incurred only if the value of the spot franc in six months were zero. The maximum gain is unlimited, since francs acquired in the forward market can in theory rise to an infinite dollar value.

Forward market speculation cannot be extended beyond the maturity date of the forward contract. However, if the speculator wants to close out the speculative operation before maturity, that speculator may buy an offsetting contract. In the above example, after, say, four months, Willem could sell SF173,611.11 forward two months at whatever forward price then existed. Two months after that he would close the matured six-month contract to purchase francs against the matured two-month contract to sell francs, pocketing any profit or paying up any loss. The amount of profit or loss would be fixed by the price at which Willem sold forward two months.

The above example is only one of several possible types of forward speculations. Note, too, that the examples given in this discussion ignored any interest earned. In a spot speculation, the speculator can invest the principal amount in the foreign money market to earn the foreign interest. In the various forward speculations, a speculator who is holding cash against the risk of loss can invest those funds in the home money market. Thus relative profitability will be influenced by interest differentials.

))) Speculating in Option Markets

Options differ from all other types of financial instruments in the patterns of risk they produce. The option owner has the choice of exercising the option or allowing it to expire unused. The owner will exercise it only when exercising is profitable, which means only when the option is in the money. In the case of a call option, as the spot price of the underlying currency moves up, the holder has the possibility of unlimited profit. On the down side, however, the holder can abandon the option and walk away with a loss, although the loss is never greater than the premium paid.

)))) Buyer of a Call

The position of Willem Koopmans as a buyer of a call is illustrated in the upper half of Exhibit 5.2. Assume that Willem purchases the August call option on Swiss francs described previously, the one with a strike price of 58½ ($0.5850/SF) and having a premium of $0.005/SF. The vertical axis measures profit or loss for the option buyer, at each of several different spot prices for the franc up to the time of maturity.

At all spot rates below the strike price of 58.5, Willem would choose not to exercise his option. This is obvious, since at a spot rate of 58.0, for example, he would prefer to buy a Swiss franc for $0.580 on the spot market than exercise his option to buy a franc at $0.585. If the spot rate remains below 58.0 until August when the option expired, Willem would not exercise the option. His total loss would be limited to only what he paid for the option, the $0.005/SF purchase price. At any lower price for the franc, his loss would similarly be limited to the original $0.005/SF cost.

Alternatively, at all spot rates above the strike price of 58.5, Willem would exercise the option, paying only the strike price for each Swiss franc. For example, if the spot rate were 59.5 cents per franc at maturity, he would exercise his call option, buying Swiss francs for $0.585 each instead of purchasing them on the spot market at $0.595 each. The Swiss francs could be sold immediately in the spot market for $0.595 each, resulting in a gross profit of $0.010/SF, or a net profit of $0.005/SF after deducting the original cost of the option of $0.005/SF. The profit to Willem, if the spot rate is greater than the strike price, with strike price $0.585, a premium of $0.005, and a spot rate of $0.595, is:

$$
\begin{aligned}
\text{Profit} &= \text{Spot rate} - (\text{Strike price} + \text{Premium}) \\
&= \$0.595/\text{SF} - (\$0.585/\text{SF} + \$0.005/\text{SF}) \\
&= \$0.005/\text{SF}
\end{aligned}
$$

More likely, Koopmans would realize the profit through executing an offsetting contract on the options exchange rather than taking delivery of the currency. Because the dollar price of a franc could rise to an infinite level (off the upper right-hand side of the page in Exhibit 5.2), maximum profit is unlimited. The buyer of a call option thus possesses an attractive combination of outcomes: limited loss and unlimited profit potential.

The *break-even price* of $0.590/SF is the price at which Willem neither gains nor loses on exercise of the option. The premium cost of $0.005, combined with

| Exhibit 5.2 | *Profit and Loss for the Buyer and Writer of a Call Option on Swiss Francs with a Premium of $0.005/SF* |

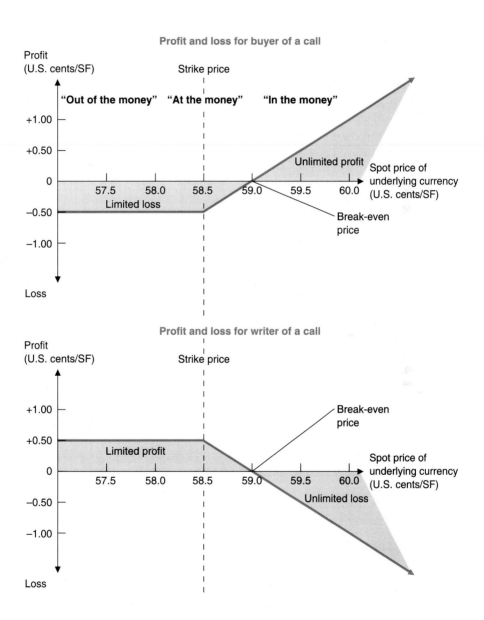

the cost of exercising the option of $0.585, is exactly equal to the proceeds from selling the francs in the spot market at $0.590. Note that Willem will still exercise the call option at the break-even price. This is so because by exercising it he at least recoups the premium paid for the option. At any spot price above the exercise price but below the break-even price, the gross profit earned on exercising the option and selling the underlying currency covers part (but not all) of the premium cost.

)))) Writer of a Call

The position of the writer (seller) of the same call option is illustrated in the bottom-half of Exhibit 5.2. If the option expires when the spot price of the underlying currency is below the exercise price of 58.5, the option holder does not exercise. What the holder loses, the writer gains. The writer keeps as profit the entire premium paid of $0.005/SF. Above the exercise price of 58.5, the writer of the call must deliver the underlying currency for $0.585/SF at a time when the value of the franc is above $0.585. If the writer wrote the option *naked*, that is, without owning the currency, that writer would now have to buy the currency at spot and take the loss. The amount of such a loss is unlimited and increases as the price of the underlying currency rises. Once again, what the holder gains, the writer loses, and vice versa. Even if the writer already owns the currency, the writer will experience an opportunity loss, surrendering against the option the same currency that could have been sold for more in the open market.

For example, the profit to the writer of a call option of strike price $0.585, premium $0.005, a spot rate of $0.595/SF is

$$\text{Profit} = \text{Premium} - (\text{Spot rate} - \text{Strike price})$$
$$= \$0.005/SF - (\$0.595/SF - \$0.585/SF)$$
$$= -\$0.005/SF$$

but only if the spot rate is greater than or equal to the strike rate. At spot rates less than the strike price, the option will expire worthless and the writer of the call option will keep the premium earned. The maximum profit that the writer of the call option can make is limited to the premium. The writer of a call option who does not own the underlying currency would have a rather unattractive combination of potential outcomes: limited profit potential and unlimited loss potential, but there are ways to limit such losses through other techniques.

)))) Buyer of a Put

Willem's position as buyer of a put is illustrated in Exhibit 5.3. The basic terms of this put are similar to those we just used to illustrate a call. The buyer of a put option, however, wants to be able to sell the underlying currency at the exercise price when the market price of that currency drops (not rises as in the case of a call option). If the spot price of a franc drops to, say, $0.575/SF, Willem will deliver francs to the writer and receive $0.585/SF. The francs can now be purchased on the spot market for $0.575 each, and the cost of the option was $0.005/SF, so he will have a net gain of $0.005/SF.

Explicitly, the profit to the holder of a put option if the spot rate is less than the strike price, with a strike price $0.585/SF and premium of $0.005/SF, and a spot rate of $0.575/SF, is:

$$\begin{aligned} \text{Profit} \ &= \text{Strike price} - (\text{Spot rate} + \text{premium}) \\ &= \$0.585/\text{SF} - (\$0.575/\text{SF} + \$0.005/\text{SF}) \\ &= \$0.005/\text{SF} \end{aligned}$$

The break-even price for the put option is the strike price less the premium, or $0.580/SF in this case. As the spot rate falls further and further below the strike price, the profit potential would continually increase, and Willem's profit could be unlimited (up to a maximum of $0.580/SF, when the price of a SF would be zero). At any exchange rate above the strike price of 58.5, he would not exercise the option and so would lose only the $0.005/SF premium paid for the put option. The buyer of a put option has an almost unlimited profit potential with a limited loss potential. Like the buyer of a call, the buyer of a put can never lose more than the premium paid up front.

⟫⟫⟫ Writer of a Put

The position of the writer of the put sold to Willem is shown in the lower-half of Exhibit 5.3. Note the symmetry of profit/loss, strike price, and break-even prices between the buyer and the writer of the put, as was the case of the call option. If the spot price of francs drops below 58.5 cents per franc, Willem will exercise the option. Below a price of 58.5 cents per franc, the writer will lose more than the premium received from writing the option ($0.005/SF), falling below break-even. Between $0.580/SF and $0.585/SF the writer will lose part, but not all, of the premium received. If the spot price is above $0.585/SF, the option will not be exercised, and the option writer pockets the entire premium of $0.005/SF. The profit earned by the writer of a $0.585 strike price put, premium $0.005, at a spot rate of $0.575, is

$$\begin{aligned} \text{Profit} \ &= \text{Premium} - (\text{Spot rate} - \text{Strike price}) \\ &= \$0.005/\text{SF} - (\$0.575/\text{SF} - \$0.585/\text{SF}) \\ &= -\$0.005/\text{SF} \end{aligned}$$

but only for spot rates that are less than or equal to the strike price. At spot rates that are greater than the strike price, the option expires out of the money and the writer keeps the premium earned up front. The writer of the put option has the same basic combination of outcomes available to the writer of a call: limited profit potential and unlimited loss potential.

Exhibit 5.3   *Profit and Loss for the Buyer and Writer of a Put Option on Swiss Francs with a Premium of $0.005/SF.*

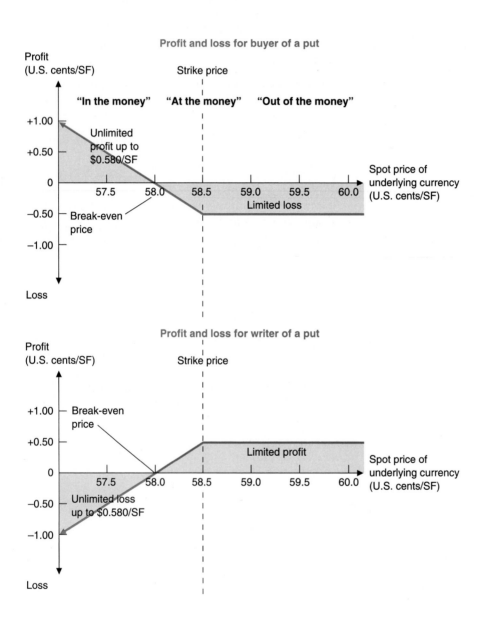

OPTION PRICING AND VALUATION

Exhibit 5.4 illustrates the profit/loss profile of a European-style call option on British pounds. The call option allows the holder to buy British pounds (£) at a strike price of $1.70/£. The value of this call option is actually the sum of two components:

Total value (premium) = Intrinsic value + Time value

Intrinsic value is the financial gain if the option is exercised immediately. It is shown by the solid line in Exhibit 5.4, which is zero until reaching the strike price, then rises linearly (one cent for each one cent increase in the spot rate). Intrinsic value will be zero when the option is out of the money—that is, when the strike price is above the market price—since no gain can be derived from exercising the option. When the spot price rises above the strike price, the intrinsic value becomes positive because the option is always worth at least this value if exercised.

In Exhibit 5.4, when the spot rate is $1.72/£, the option has an *intrinsic value* of $1.72 – $1.70/£, or 2 cents per pound. At a spot rate below $1.70/£, the option is out of the money and has no intrinsic value (and only a fool would exercise it instead of buying pounds more cheaply on the spot market).

The *time value* of an option exists because the price of the underlying currency, the spot rate, can move further and further into the money between the present time and the option's expiration date. Time value is shown in Exhibit 5.4 as the shaded area between the total value of the option and its intrinsic value. At a spot rate of $1.72/£, the option's total value is composed of the 2 cents per pound intrinsic value and 2.39 cents per pound in time value, for a total value of 4.39 cents per pound.

An investor will pay something today for an out-of-the-money option (that is, it has zero intrinsic value) on the chance that the spot rate will move far enough before maturity to move the option into the money. Consequently, the price of an option is always somewhat greater than its intrinsic value since there is always some chance that the intrinsic value will rise between the present and the expiration date.

))) Components of Option Pricing

The total value of an option is the sum of its intrinsic value, which is easy to calculate, and its time value, which depends on the market's expectations about the likelihood that the underlying currency will rise in value (for a call option) prior to maturity. On the date of maturity an option will have a value equal to its intrinsic value (zero time remaining means zero time value).

The pricing of a currency option combines six elements. For example, the European style call option on British pounds depicted in Exhibit 5.4 has a premium of $0.033/£ at a spot rate of $1.70/£. This premium is based on the following assumptions:

Exhibit 5.4	*Intrinsic Value, Time Value, and Total Value of a Call Option on British Pounds with a Strike Price of $1.70/£*

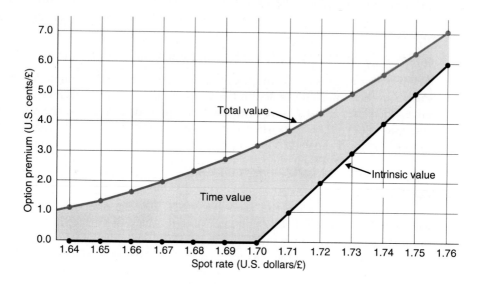

Spot ($/£)	1.64	1.65	1.66	1.67	1.68	1.69	1.70	1.71	1.72	1.73	1.74	1.75	1.76
Premium components (cents/£)													
Intrinsic value	0.00	0.00	0.00	0.00	0.00	0.00	0.00	1.00	2.00	3.00	4.00	5.00	6.00
Time value	1.12	1.37	1.67	2.01	2.39	2.82	3.30	2.82	2.39	2.01	1.67	1.37	1.12
Total value	1.12	1.37	1.67	2.01	2.39	2.82	3.30	3.82	4.39	5.01	5.67	6.37	7.12
Delta	0.27	0.28	0.32	0.36	0.41	0.45	0.50	0.55	0.59	0.63	0.68	0.71	0.75

1. Present spot rate, $1.70/£
2. Time to maturity, 90 days
3. Forward rate for matching maturity (90 days), $1.70/£
4. U.S. dollar interest rate, 8.00% per annum
5. British pound sterling interest rate, 8.00% per annum
6. Volatility, the standard deviation of daily spot price movement, 10.00% per annum

These assumptions are all that is needed to calculate the option premium. This base-case numerical example, which we will continue to use through the remainder of the chapter, assumes that both currency interest rates are the same. This means that the forward rate equals the spot rate. In the following section we will demonstrate how the value of the option—the option premium— changes as these six components change.

Currency Option Pricing Sensitivity

If currency options are to be used effectively, either for the purposes of specula- tion or risk management (covered in the coming chapters), the individual trader needs to know how option values—premiums—react to their various compo- nents. The following section will analyze these six basic sensitivities:

1. The impact of changing forward rates
2. The impact of changing spot rates
3. The impact of time to maturity
4. The impact of changing volatility
5. The impact of changing interest differentials
6. The impact of alternative option strike prices

1. Forward Rate Sensitivity

Although it is rarely noted, standard foreign currency options are priced around the forward rate because the current spot rate and both the domestic and foreign interest rates (home currency and foreign currency rates) are included in the option premium calculation.[5] Regardless of the specific strike rate chosen and priced, the forward rate is central to valuation. The option-pricing formula calcu- lates a subjective probability distribution centered on the forward rate. This approach does not mean that the market expects the forward rate to be equal to the future spot rate; it is simply a result of the arbitrage-pricing structure of options.

The forward rate focus also provides helpful information for the trader man- aging a position. When the market prices a foreign currency option, it does so without any bullish or bearish sentiment on the direction of the foreign currency's value relative to the domestic currency. If the trader has specific expectations about the future spot rate's direction, those expectations can be put to work. A trader will not be inherently betting against the market. In a following section we will also describe how a change in the interest differential between currencies, the theoretical foundation of forward rates, also alters the value of the option.

2. Spot Rate Sensitivity (Delta)

The call option on British pounds depicted in Exhibit 5.4 possesses a premium that exceeds the intrinsic value of the option over the entire range of spot rates surrounding the strike rate. As long as the option has time remaining before expi- ration, the option will possess this time-value element. This characteristic is one of the primary reasons why an American-style option, which can be exercised on any day up to and including the expiration date, is seldom actually exercised prior to expiration. If the option holder wishes to liquidate it for its value, it would normally be sold, not exercised, so any remaining time value can also be captured by the holder. If the current spot rate falls on the side of the option's strike price, which would induce the option holder to exercise the option upon expiration, the option also has an intrinsic value. The call option illustrated in Exhibit 5.4 is in the money at spot rates to the right of the strike rate of $1.70/£, at the money at $1.70/£, and out of the money at spot rates less than $1.70/£.

The vertical distance between the market value and the intrinsic value of a call option on pounds is greatest at a spot rate of $1.70/£. At $1.70/£ the spot rate equals the strike price (at the money). This premium of 3.30 cents per pound consists entirely of time value. In fact, the value of any option that is currently out of the money is made up entirely of time value. The further the option's strike price is out of the money, the lower the value or premium of the option. This is so because the market believes the probability of this option's actually moving into the exercise range prior to expiration is significantly lower than for one that is already at the money. If the spot rate were to fall to $1.68/£, the option premium falls to 2.39 cents/£—again, entirely time value. If the spot rate were to rise above the strike rate to $1.72/£, the premium rises to 4.39 cents/£. In this case the premium represents an intrinsic value of 2.00 cents ($1.72/£ – $1.70/£) plus a time-value element of 2.39 cents. Note the symmetry of time-value premiums (2.39 cents) to the left and to the right of the strike rate.

The symmetry of option valuation about the strike rate is seen by decomposing the option premiums into their respective intrinsic and time values. Exhibit 5.5 illustrates how varying the current spot rate by ± $0.05 about the strike rate of $1.70/£ alters each option's intrinsic and time values.

The sensitivity of the option premium to a small change in the spot exchange rate is called the *delta*. For example, the delta of the $1.70/£ call option, when the spot rate changes from $1.70/£ to $1.71/£, is simply the change in the premium divided by the change in the spot rate:

$$\text{Delta} = \frac{\Delta\,\text{Premium}}{\Delta\,\text{Spot rate}} = \frac{\$0.038/£ - \$0.033/£}{\$1.71/£ - \$1.70/£} = 0.5$$

Exhibit 5.5	*Decomposing Call Option Premiums: Intrinsic Value and Time Value*

Strike Rate ($/£)	Spot Rate ($/£)	Money	Call Premium (cents/£) =	Intrinsic Value (cents/£) +	Time Value (cents/£)	Delta (0 to 1)
1.70	1.75	ITM	6.37	5.00	1.37	.71
1.70	1.70	ATM	3.30	0.00	3.30	.50
1.70	1.65	OTM	1.37	0.00	1.37	.28

If the delta of the specific option is known, it is easy to determine how the option's value will change as the spot rate changes. If the spot rate changes by one cent ($0.01/£), given a delta of 0.5, the option premium would change by $0.5 \times \$0.01$, or $0.005. If the initial premium was $0.033/£, and the spot rate increased by one cent (from $1.70/£ to $1.71/£), the new option premium would be $0.033 + $0.005 = $0.038/£. Delta varies between +1 and 0 for a call option, and −1 and 0 for a put option.

Traders in options categorize individual options by their delta rather than as being in the money, at the money, or out of the money.[6] As an option moves further in the money, like the in-the-money option in Exhibit 5.5, delta rises toward 1.0 (in this case to .71). As an option moves further out-of-the-money, delta falls toward zero. Note that the out of the money option in Exhibit 5.5 has a delta of only .28.[7]

Rule of Thumb: The higher the delta (deltas of .7, or .8 and up are considered high) the greater the probability of the option expiring in the money.

))) 3. Time to Maturity: Value and Deterioration (Theta)

Option values increase with the length of time to maturity. The expected change in the option premium from a small change in the time to expiration is termed *theta*.

Theta is calculated as the change in the option premium over the change in time. If the $1.70/£ call option were to age one day from its initial 90-day maturity, the theta of the call option would be the difference in the two premiums, 3.30 cents/£ and 3.28 cents/£ (assuming a spot rate of $1.70/£):

$$\text{Theta} = \frac{\Delta\, \text{Premium}}{\Delta\, \text{Time}} = \frac{\text{cents } 3.30/£ - \text{cents } 3.28/£}{90 - 89} = .02$$

Theta is based not on a linear relationship with time, but rather on the square root of time. Exhibit 5.6 illustrates the time-value deterioration for our same $1.70/£ call option on pounds. The at-the-money strike rate is $1.70/£, and the out-of-the-money and in-the-money spot rates are $1.67/£ and $1.73/£, respectively. Option premiums deteriorate at an increasing rate as they approach expiration. In fact, most of the option premium—depending on the individual option—is lost in the final 30 days prior to expiration.

This exponential relationship between option premium and time is seen in the ratio of option values between the three-month and the one-month at-the-money maturities. The ratio for the at-the-money call option is not 3 to 1 (holding all other components constant), but rather

$$\frac{\text{Premium of 3 month}}{\text{Premium of 1 month}} = \frac{\sqrt{3}}{\sqrt{1}} = \frac{1.73}{1.00} = 1.73$$

The three-month option's price is only 1.73 times that of the one-month price, not three times it.

The rapid deterioration of option values in the last days prior to expiration is seen by once again calculating the theta of the $1.70/£ call option, but now as its remaining maturity moves from 15 days to 14 days:

$$\text{Theta} = \frac{\Delta \, \text{Premium}}{\Delta \, \text{Time}} = \frac{\text{cents } 1.37/£ - \text{cents } 1.32/£}{15 - 14} = .05$$

A decrease of one day in the time to maturity now reduces the option premium by .05 cents/£, rather than only .02 cents/£ as it did when the maturity was 90 days.

Exhibit 5.6 also illustrates the relationship between basic spot rate and option premium noted previously. The out-of-the-money call option's premium is logically smaller than the at-the-money option throughout its life, but it deteriorates at a slower rate due to its having an initially smaller level to fall from. The in-the-money option is of greater value throughout its lifetime relative to the at-the-money option, falling toward its intrinsic value (5 cents/£) at expiration. The at-the-money option, however, falls particularly quickly in the final periods prior to expiration. As any specific option ages, moving continually toward expiration, the time value will constantly decrease (assuming nothing else has changed). This situation would be illustrated by the total value line of the call option initially shown in Exhibit 5.4 collapsing inward toward the strike price of $1.70.

The implications of time-value deterioration for traders are quite significant. A trader purchasing an option with only one or two months until expiration will see the option's value deteriorate rapidly. If the trader were to then sell the option, it would have a significantly smaller market value in the periods immediately following its purchase.

At the same time, however, a trader who is buying options of longer maturities will pay more, but not proportionately more, for the longer maturity option. A six-month option's premium is approximately 2.45 times more expensive than the one-month, while the 12-month option would be only 3.46 times more expensive than the one-month. This implies that two three-month options do not equal one six-month option.

> **Rule of Thumb:** A trader will normally find longer-maturity options better values, giving the trader the ability to alter an option position without suffering significant time-value deterioration.

⟩⟩⟩ 4. Sensitivity to Volatility (Lambda)

There are few words in the financial field that are more used and abused than *volatility*. *Option volatility* is defined as the standard deviation of daily percentage changes in the underlying exchange rate. Volatility is important to option value

| Exhibit 5.6 | *Theta: Option Premium Time-Value Deterioration when the Spot Rate is $1.70/£* |

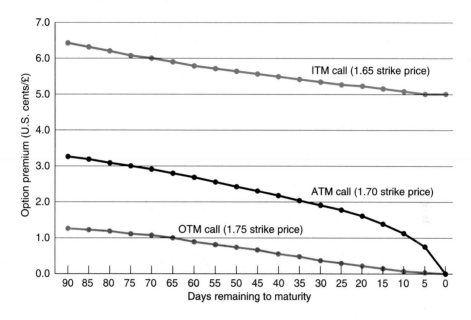

because of an exchange rate's perceived likelihood of moving either into or out of the range in which the option would be exercised. If the exchange rate's volatility is rising, and therefore the risk of the option's being exercised is increasing, the option premium would be increasing.

Volatility is stated in percent per annum. For example, an option may be described as having a 12.6% annual volatility. The percentage change for a single day can be found as follows:

$$\frac{12.6\%}{\sqrt{365}} = \frac{12.6\%}{19.105} = 0.66\% \text{ daily volatility}$$

The sensitivity of the option premium to a unit change in volatility is termed *lambda*. For our $1.70/£ call option, an increase in annual volatility of 1 percentage point—for example from 10.0% to 11.0%—will increase the option premium from $0.033/£ to $0.036/£.

$$\text{Lambda} = \frac{\Delta \text{ Premium}}{\Delta \text{ Volatility}} = \frac{\$0.036/£ - 0.033/£}{0.11 - 0.10} = 0.30$$

The primary problem with volatility is that it is *unobservable*; it is the only input into the option pricing formula that is judgmentally based by the trader pricing the option. No single correct method for its calculation exists. The problem is one of forecasting; the historical volatility is not necessarily an accurate predictor of the future volatility of the exchange rate's movement, yet there is little to go on except historical data.

Volatility is viewed three ways: *historic*, where the volatility is drawn from a recent period of time; *forward-looking*, where the historic volatility is altered to reflect expectations about the future period over which the option will exist; and *implied*, where the volatility is backed out of the market price of the option itself.

Historic volatility is normally measured as the percentage movement in the spot rate on a daily, 6-, or 12-hour basis over the previous 10, 30, or even 90 days. If option traders believe that the immediate future will be the same as the recent past, the historic volatility will equal the forward-looking volatility. If, however, the future period is expected to experience greater or lesser volatility, the historic measure must be altered for option pricing. Implied volatility is equivalent to having the answers to the test; implied volatilities are calculated by being backed out of the market option premium values traded. Since volatility is the only unobservable element of the option premium price, after all other components have been accounted for, the residual value of volatility that is *implied* by the price is used.

Option premiums are highly sensitive to volatility. As illustrated in Exhibit 5.7, the at-the-money call premium on the British pound rises linearly with currency volatility. That is, a doubling of volatility translates into a doubling of the option value. The out-of-the-money call option also gains value rapidly with rising volatility. Even though the out-of-the-money option may possess no intrinsic value at this point in time, the higher the volatility the greater the chance that the spot rate could move enough to move the option in the money. The in-the-money call option on pounds, although possessing a positive premium even at 0% volatility due to its intrinsic value, also rises in value with increased volatility due to the potential for further movements of the spot rate into the money.

Like all futures markets, option volatilities react instantaneously and negatively to unsettling economic and political events (or rumor). A doubling of volatility for an at-the-money option will result in an equivalent doubling of the option's price. Most currency option traders focus their activities on predicting movements of currency volatility in the short run, for they will move price the most. For example, option volatilities rose significantly in the months preceding the Persian Gulf War, in September 1992, when the European Monetary System was in crisis, and in July 1993, when the EMS once again was in crisis and was eventually restructured. In all instances option volatilities for major cross-currency combinations such as the SF/$ rose to nearly 20% for extended periods.

Selected implied volatilities for a number of currency pairs in January 1997 are listed in Exhibit 5.8. Volatilities are the only judgmental component that the

Exhibit 5.7   *Lambda: Option Premium Sensitivity to Volatility when the Spot Rate is $1.70/£*

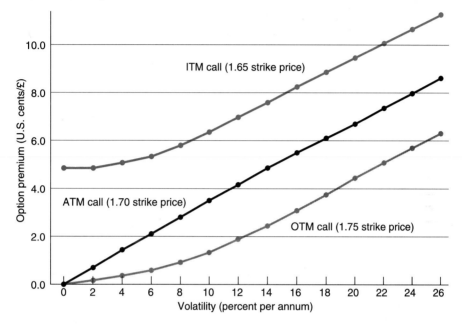

option writer contributes, and yet they play a critical role in the pricing of options. Volatilities are typically expressed in bid/offer form, reflecting whether the trader wishes to buy or sell (write) the specific option. Note also that the implied volatilities do vary over maturity (from one month to three years in Exhibit 5.8). All currency pairs have historical series that contribute to the formation of the expectations of option writers. There is a noticeable difference in relative implied volatilities, with the CAD/US$ at several maturities at 4.6%/4.9% at the low end, and the SWF/US$ at one month at 12.4%/12.8% at the high end.

> **Rule of Thumb:** Traders who believe volatilities will fall significantly in the near term will sell (write) options now, hoping to buy them back for a profit immediately after volatilities fall and cause option premiums to fall.

⟫⟫ 5. Sensitivity to Changing Interest Rate Differentials (Rho and Phi)

At the start of this section we pointed out that currency option prices and values are focused on the forward rate. The forward rate is in turn based on the theory of interest rate parity discussed in Chapter 3. Interest rate changes in either currency will alter the forward rate, which in turn will alter the option's premium or value. The expected change in the option premium from a small change in the

| Exhibit 5.8 | *Implied Volatilities in Cross Currency and Maturity, January 31, 1997* (bid/offer, percent per annum) | | | | | |

Versus US$	1 Month	3 Months	6 Months	12 Months	2 Years	3 Years
DEM	10.5/10.9	10.1/10.5	9.8/10.1	9.7/10.0	9.6/10.0	9.5/10.1
JPY	12.1/12.4	11.7/12.0	11.3/11.6	11.2/11.4	11.0/11.6	10.9/11.7
SWF	12.4/12.8	12.0/12.4	11.7/12.1	11.6/12.0	11.5/12.0	11.4/12.1
STG	10.7/11.1	10.0/10.5	9.7/10.1	9.5/9.9		
CAD	4.7/5.1	4.6/4.9	4.6/4.9	4.6/4.9		
AUD	8.0/8.6	7.4/8.2	7.0/7.5	6.6/7.1		

Cross Rates

STG/DEM	10.0/10.6	9.4/9.8	8.8/9.3	8.5/8.9		
DEM/YEN	9.2/9.8	9.1/9.7	9.1/9.7	9.1/9.6		

Source: "Implied Volatility Rates for Foreign Currency Options," Federal Reserve Bank of New York, FX Volatility, http://www.frb.org. Survey ranges of implied volatility rates, bid and asked, for at-the-money options as of 3:30 P.M. Quotes are for contracts of at least $10 million with a prime counterparty.

domestic interest rate (home currency) is called *rho*. The expected change in the option premium from a small change in the foreign interest rate (foreign currency) is called *phi*.

Continuing with our numerical example, an increase in the U.S. dollar interest rate from 8.0% to 9.0% *increases* the at-the-money call option premium on British pounds from $0.033/£ to $0.035/£. This is a *rho* value of positive 0.2:

$$\text{Rho} = \frac{\Delta \text{Premium}}{\Delta \text{U.S. dollar interest rate}} = \frac{\$0.035/£ - 0.033/£}{9.0\% - 8.0\%} = 0.2$$

A similar 1% increase in the foreign interest rate, the pound sterling rate in this case, *reduces* the option value (premium) from $0.033/£ to $0.031/£. The *phi* for this call option premium is therefore a negative 0.2.

$$\text{Phi} = \frac{\Delta \text{Premium}}{\Delta \text{Foreign interest rate}} = \frac{\$0.031/£ - 0.033/£}{9.0\% - 8.0\%} = -0.2$$

For example, throughout the 1990s U.S. dollar (domestic currency) interest rates were substantially lower than pound sterling (foreign currency) interest rates. This meant that the pound consistently sold forward at a discount versus the U.S. dollar. If this interest differential were to widen (either from U.S. interest rates falling or foreign currency interest rates rising, or some combination of both), the pound would sell forward at a larger discount. An increase in the forward discount is the same as a decrease in the forward rate (in U.S. dollars per unit of foreign currency). The option premium condition above states that the premium must increase as interest rate differentials increase (assuming spot rates remain unchanged).

Exhibit 5.9 demonstrates how European call option premiums on the British pound change with interest differentials. If we use the same call option value assumptions as before, an increase in pound sterling interest rates relative to U.S. dollar interest rates (a movement from left to right) results in a decline in call option premiums.

For the option trader, an expectation on the differential between interest rates can obviously help in the evaluation of where the option value is headed. For example, when foreign interest rates are higher than domestic interest rates, the foreign currency sells forward at a discount. This results in relatively lower call option premiums (and lower put option premiums).

Rule of Thumb: A trader who is purchasing a call option on foreign currency should do so before the domestic interest rate rises. This will allow the trader to purchase the option before its price increases.

Exhibit 5.9   *Interest Differentials and Call Option Premiums when the Spot Rate is $1.70/£*

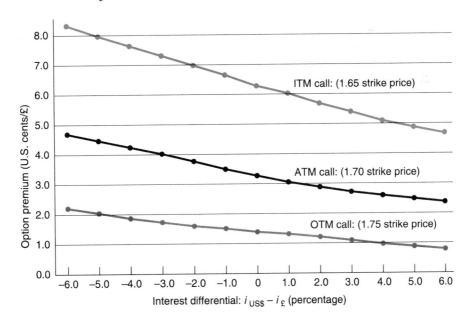

))) 6. Alternative Strike Prices and Option Premiums

The sixth and final element that is important in option valuation (but, thankfully, has no Greek alias) is the selection of the actual strike price. Although we have conducted all our sensitivity analysis using the strike price of $1.70/£ (a forward at-the-money strike rate), a firm purchasing an option in the over-the-counter market may choose its own strike rate. The question is, how to choose?

Exhibit 5.10 illustrates call option premiums required for a series of alternative strike rates above and below the forward at-the-money strike rate of $1.70/£ using our benchmark example. The option premium for the call option used throughout, the $1.70/£, is 3.3 cents/£. Call options written with strike prices less than $1.70/£, when the present spot rate is $1.70/£, are already profitable or in the money. For example, a call option with a strike rate of $1.65/£ would have an intrinsic value of $0.05/£ ($1.70/£ – $1.65/£), which the option premium must cover. The call option premium for the $1.65/£ strike rate is 6.3 cents/£, which is higher than the benchmark.

Similarly, call options on pounds at strike rates above $1.70/£ become increasingly cheap as the underlying spot rate, which is presently $1.70/£, has to move further to make them profitable. At present they have no intrinsic value. For example,

---

Exhibit 5.10   *Option Premiums for Alternative Strike Rates*

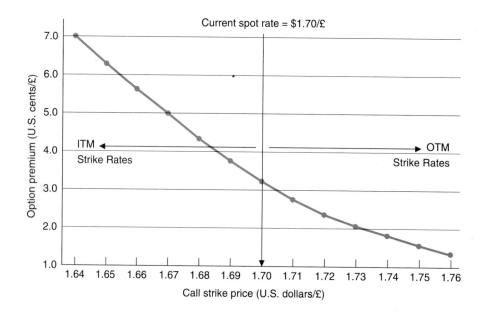

a call option on pounds with a strike rate of $1.75/£ possesses a premium of only 1.5 cents/£ because the option is at present very much out of the money. The option has no intrinsic value but time value only; intrinsic value is zero, when the spot rate is only $1.70/£.

Exhibit 5.11 briefly summarizes the various "Greek" elements and impacts discussed in the previous sections. The option premium is one of the most complex concepts in financial theory, and the application of option pricing to exchange rates does not make it any simpler. Only with a considerable amount of time and effort can the individual be expected to attain a second sense in the management of currency option positions.

Exhibit 5.11   *Summary of Option Premium Components*

Greek	Definition	Interpretation
Delta	Expected change in the option premium for a small change in the **spot rate**	The higher the delta, the more likely the option will move in the money.
Theta	Expected change in the option premium for a small change in **time to expiration**	Premiums are relatively insensitive until the final 30 or so days.
Lambda	Expected change in the option premium for a small change in **volatility**	Premiums rise with increases in volatility.
Rho	Expected change in the option premium for a small change in the **domestic interest rate**	Increases in domestic interest rates cause falling call option premiums.
Phi	Expected change in the option premium for a small change in the **foreign interest rate**	Increases in foreign interest rates cause increasing call option premiums.

SUMMARY

- *Foreign currency options* are financial contracts that give the holder the right, but not the obligation, to buy (in the case of calls) or sell (in the case of puts) a specified amount of foreign exchange at a predetermined price on or before a specified maturity date.

- The use of a currency option as a speculative device for the buyer of an option arises from the fact that an option gains in value as the underlying currency rises (for calls) or falls (for puts). The amount of loss when the underlying currency moves opposite to the desired direction is limited to the cost of the option.

- The use of a currency option as a speculative device for the writer (seller) of an option arises from the earning of the option premium on writing. If the option—either a put or call—expires out of the money (valueless), the writer of the option has earned the premium.

- *Speculation* is an attempt to profit by trading on expectations about prices in the future. In the foreign exchange market, one speculates by taking a position in a foreign currency and then closing that position after the exchange rate has moved; a profit results only if the rate moves in the direction that the speculator expected.

- *Currency option valuation*, the determination of the option's premium, is a complex combination of the current spot rate, the specific strike rate, the forward rate (which itself is dependent on the current spot rate and interest differentials), currency volatility, and time to maturity.

QUESTIONS

1. Option Premiums and Alternate Strike Prices

According to Exhibit 5.1, there are actually a variety of strike prices available on the Swiss franc. Use the strike prices and premiums quoted in the exhibit to answer the following questions.

a. If the current spot rate is 58.51 (cents/SF) and the first option strike price listed is a "56," is the August 56 put option in the money or out of the money?

b. As the strike price of the put option rises from 56 upward to 60, how does the August maturity put option premium change? Why?

c. What is the break-even exchange rate for the September maturity put option with a strike price of 59½?

2. Directional View: How Far?

Willem Koopmans—the option speculator discussed in the chapter—must hold something of a directional view when purchasing a call option on Swiss francs.

a. Assuming Willem Koopmans did indeed purchase the call option on Swiss francs with a strike price of 58.5 (cents/SF), with a premium of $0.005/SF, what exactly are his directional expectations?

b. What is Willem's break-even price if his own-cost of capital is 8%?

c. How far must the dollar depreciate (Swiss franc appreciate) before Willem has reached his view or goal?

d. At what exchange rate would Willem exercise or sell his call option? Does it matter whether he sells or exercises it? Are they the same?

3. Why in the World Would You Write an Option?

Willem is now writing put options on Swiss francs, puts with strike prices of 58.5 (cents/SF) as in Exhibit 5.3.

a. What in the world is he thinking? What is his precise directional view?
b. How far does the spot rate have to move in order for Willem to actually break even?
c. How would an increase in option volatility affect the option position he opened by writing the put options? How could he take advantage of the new higher premiums?
d. What is the limit to his profit potential?

4. Pricing Your Own Options: Call Options on British Pounds (Option.xls)
The set of assumptions used throughout the second half of this chapter assumed a spot rate of $1.70/£ , a 90-day maturity, U.S. dollar and British pound 90-day interest rates of 8.00% per annum, and a $/£ 90-day volatility of 10%. Use these assumptions and the option pricing spreadsheet, Option.xls. Answer the following questions by using alternative values in the spreadsheet.

Note: Check that all is working correctly by first using the baseline values pictured below and calculating the same option premiums (use only the European option prices and "Greeks" to answer the following questions). Also note that the $1.70/£ spot rate should be entered as 170.00 cents per pound.

a. If the spot rate suddenly changed—for example, the pound falling to $1.65/£—what would be the new 90-day call option premium?
b. If the British government responded to the falling pound by defending it with an interest rate increase, say, from 8.000% to 8.250% per annum, what would the value of the call option premium be?
c. As a result of the falling pound and the policy decision to defend it with increasing interest rates, the British Prime Minister is thought to be about to lose political support. The volatility of the dollar-pound cross rises from 10% to 12%. What is the new 90-day call option premium?

5. Time-Value Deterioration: Bodo's Dilemma
Bodo Schlegelamich is a currency speculator for a private banking house in Boston. His base currency is therefore the U.S. dollar. He is currently convinced that the euro is overvalued and wishes to take a speculative position to profit from his expectations. He will invest $1 million in his position (spent entirely on option premiums). The current spot rate is $1.0650/€. The current premiums on call and put options (U.S. cents/€) with a strike price of $1.1200/€ are the following:

Strike: $1.12/€ (U.S. cents/€)	90 days	180 days
Call options on euro: premiums	0.401	1.177
Put options on euro: premiums	6.186	6.143

a. What should Bodo do—buy a call, sell a call, buy a put, or sell a put on the euro?
b. What would be his profits or losses if he bought a 90-day call at $1.02/€, and the actual spot exchange rate in 90 days turned out to be $1.08/€?

6. Sleepless in São Paulo, Brazil

José Ballini is a currency trader and speculator for Bozano Simonsen, one of the largest investment banking firms in São Paulo. The current spot rate is R$1.7800/$, and the 360-day forward rate is R$1.8860/$. José believes the Brazilian real will actually appreciate against the U.S. dollar in the coming year.

a. What should he do with the R$500,000 he has to take a position with?

b. If the spot rate at the end of 360 days is R$1.4688/$, what was José's profit and rate of return on his investment in part (a)?

c. If the spot rate at the end of 360 days is R$1.9800/$, what was José's profit and rate of return on his investment in part (a)?

WORLD WIDE WEB EXERCISES

W1. Currency Volatilities

The single unobservable variable in currency option pricing is the volatility, since volatility inputs are the expected standard deviation of the daily spot rate for the coming period of the option's maturity. Use the New York Federal Reserve's website to obtain current currency volatilities.

Federal Reserve Bank of New York   http://ny.frb.org/pihome/statistics

W2. Currency Options and Futures Exchanges

Currency options and futures are traded in many exchanges (such as bolsas and bourses) around the world. Using the following list as a starting point, determine exactly which currencies are traded on exchanges in the forms of futures or options.

London Stock Exchange	http://www.londonstockexchange.com
Tokyo Stock Exchange	http://www.tse.or.jp/eindex.html
SBF - Paris Bourse	http://www.bourse-de-paris.fr/defaulgb.htm
Bolsa de Bogotá	http://www.bolsabogota.com.co/
Singapore Exchange	http://www.simex.com.sg/

Or for a wider spectrum of global markets:

Investor Map	http://investormap.com/global.htm

SUGGESTED READINGS

Black, Fischer, and Myron Scholes, "The Pricing of Options and Corporate Liabilities," *Journal of Political Economy*, May/June 1973, pp. 637–659.

Giddy, Ian H., and Gunter Dufey, "Uses and Abuses of Currency Options," *Journal of Applied Corporate Finance*, Vol. 8, No. 3, Fall 1995, pp. 49–57.

Huckins, Nancy White, and Anoop Rai, "Market Risk for Foreign Currency Options: Basle's Simplified Model," *Financial Management*, Vol. 28, No. 1, Spring 1999, pp. 99-109.

Melino, Angelo, and Stuart M. Turnbull, "Misspecification and the Pricing and Hedging of Long- Term Currency Options," *Journal of International Money and Finance*, Vol. 14, No. 3, June 1995, pp. 373–393.

NOTES

1. The original option pricing model was developed by Black and Scholes (1973).
2. Currency option strike prices and premiums on the U.S. dollar are quoted throughout this chapter as direct quotations ($/SF, $/¥, and so on) as opposed to the more common usage of indirect quotations used throughout the rest of the book. This is standard practice with option prices.
3. Options are available at fixed strike prices, the prices reflecting current market prices of the underlying currency at the time that option was first offered.
4. All option premiums are expressed in cents per unit of foreign currency on the Philadelphia Stock Exchange except for the French franc, which is expressed in tenths of a cent per franc, and the Japanese yen, which is expressed in hundredths of a cent per yen.
5. Recall from Chapter 4 that the forward rate is calculated from the current spot rate and the two subject currency interest rates for the desired maturity. For example, the 90-day forward rate for the call option on British pounds described above is calculated as follows:

$$F_{90} = \$1.70/\pounds \times \left[\frac{1+\left(.08 \times \dfrac{90}{360}\right)}{1+\left(.08 \times \dfrac{90}{360}\right)}\right] = \$1.70/\pounds$$

6. The full range of delta values at the bottom of Exhibit 5.4 illustrates how a call option's delta changes as the spot rate moves from out of the money to far in the money.
7. The expected change in the option's delta resulting from a small change in the spot rate is termed *gamma*. It is often used as a measure of the stability of a specific option's delta. Gamma is utilized in the construction of more sophisticated hedging strategies that focus on deltas (delta-neutral strategies).

Measuring and managing *foreign exchange exposure* is a task that involves all of top management, not just the Treasury department. It is a task that plays an important role in determining a firm's future profitability, net cash flow, and market value.

PART 2

MEASURING AND MANAGING FOREIGN EXCHANGE EXPOSURE

CHAPTER 6 analyzes how a firm should measure and manage *transaction exposure*. Transaction exposure measures changes in the value of outstanding financial obligations that exist prior to a change in exchange rates but will be settled after exchange rates change. However, in a broader sense, it includes *backlog exposure* and *quotation exposure*. Backlog exposure includes foreign-currency-denominated orders that have been accepted but not yet delivered or invoiced. Quotation exposures include foreign-currency-denominated bids that have been made but not yet accepted.

CHAPTER 7 analyzes how a firm should measure and manage *operating exposure* (also known as *economic*, *competitive*, or *strategic exposure*). Operating exposure measures the change in the present value of a firm resulting from any change in its future operating cash flows due to an unexpected change in exchange rates. The change in value depends on the effect of the exchange rate change on future sales volume, prices, or costs.

CHAPTER 8 analyzes how a firm should measure and manage *accounting exposure* (also known as *translation exposure*). Translation exposure is the potential for accounting-derived changes in owners' equity to occur because of the need to "translate" foreign-currency-denominated financial statements of foreign affiliates into a single currency to prepare worldwide consolidated financial statements.

CHAPTER 9 analyzes how a firm should measure and manage *interest rate exposure*, including *interest rate swaps*. Interest rate exposure is the potential for changes in interest rates to alter the cash flows and value of a firm. Multinational enterprises (MNEs), because they have a variety of capital sources and uses around the globe that are denominated in a variety of currencies, face particular challenges in managing the ebb and flow of interest rate movements. Interest rate swaps, financial contracts that allow firms to alter the interest rate payment structure or currency of denomination, are the primary tool used for managing these interest rate exposures.

Part II includes four decision cases (Lufthansa, Zapa Chemical and BuBa, Tektronix(C), and British Columbia Hydro), that highlight specific foreign exchange managerial challenges faced in a variety of MNEs in recent business experience.

CHAPTER 6

TRANSACTION EXPOSURE

Foreign exchange exposure is a measure of the potential for a firm's profitability, net cash flow, and market value to change because of a change in exchange rates. An important task of the financial manager is to measure foreign exchange exposure and to manage it so as to maximize the profitability, net cash flow, and market value of the firm.

TYPES OF FOREIGN EXCHANGE EXPOSURE

What happens to a firm when foreign exchange rates change? The effect can be measured in several ways. Exhibit 6.1 shows schematically the three main types of foreign exchange exposure: *transaction*, *operating*, and *accounting*.

)))) Transaction Exposure

Transaction exposure measures changes in the value of outstanding financial obligations incurred prior to a change in exchange rates but not due to be settled until after the exchange rates change. Thus it deals with changes in cash flows that result from existing contractual obligations.

)))) Operating Exposure

Operating exposure, also called *economic exposure*, *competitive exposure*, or *strategic exposure*, measures the change in the present value of the firm resulting from any change in future operating cash flows of the firm caused by an *unexpected* change in exchange rates. The change in value depends on the effect of the exchange rate change on future sales volume, prices, and costs.

Transaction exposure and operating exposure exist because of unexpected changes in future cash flows. The difference between the two is that transaction exposure is concerned with future cash flows already contracted for, while operating exposure focuses on expected (not yet contracted for) future cash flows that might change because a change in exchange rates has altered international competitiveness. The purpose of this chapter is to analyze how transaction exposure is measured and managed.

| **Exhibit 6.1** | *Conceptual Comparison of Transaction, Operating, and Accounting Foreign Exchange Exposure* |

Moment in time when exchange rate changes

Accounting exposure

Changes in reported owners' equity in consolidated financial statements caused by a change in exchange rates

Operating exposure

Change in expected cash flows arising because of an unexpected change in exchange rates

Transaction exposure

Impact of settling outstanding obligations entered into before change in exchange rates but to be settled after change in exchange rates

Time ───────────────────────────────────────▶

Accounting Exposure

Accounting exposure, also called *translation exposure*, is the potential for accounting-derived changes in owner's equity to occur because of the need to "translate" foreign currency financial statements of foreign affiliates into a single reporting currency for worldwide consolidated financial statements.

Tax Exposure

The tax consequence of foreign exchange exposure varies by country. As a general rule, however, only *realized* foreign exchange losses are deductible for purposes of calculating income taxes. Similarly, only *realized* gains create taxable income. "Realized" means that the loss or gain involves cash flows.

Losses from transaction exposure usually reduce taxable income in the year in which they are realized. Losses from operating exposure reduce taxable income over a series of future years. As will be explained in Chapter 8, losses from accounting exposure are not cash losses and so are not deductible. Some steps taken to minimize one or another of the types of exposure, such as entering into a forward exchange contract, create taxable income or loss. Other steps taken to obtain the same protection have no income tax implications. Because tax exposure is determined by the country of domicile of each affiliate, a multinational enterprise (MNE) needs to plan its foreign exchange management policies to minimize the worldwide after-tax consequences of foreign exchange losses and to maximize after-tax gains. However, since many MNEs manage foreign exchange exposures centrally, gains or losses are often not matched with the country of origin.

Why Hedge?

MNEs possess a multitude of cash flows that are sensitive to changes in exchange rates, interest rates, and commodity prices. These three financial price risks are the subject of the growing field of *financial risk management*.[1] In this chapter we will focus on the sensitivity of the individual firm's future cash flows to exchange rates alone.

Many firms attempt to manage their currency exposures through *hedging*. *Hedging* is the taking of a position, acquiring either a cash flow, an asset, or a contract (including a forward contract) that will rise (fall) in value and offset a fall (rise) in the value of an existing position. Hedging therefore protects the owner of the existing asset from loss. However, it also eliminates any gain from an increase in the value of the asset hedged against. The question remains: What is to be gained by the firm from hedging?

The value of a firm, according to financial theory, is the net present value of all expected future cash flows. The fact that these cash flows are *expected* emphasizes that nothing about the future is certain. If the reporting currency value of many of these cash flows is altered by exchange rate changes, a firm that hedges its currency exposures reduces some of the variance in the value of its future expected cash flows. *Currency risk* can therefore be defined roughly as the variance in expected cash flows arising from unexpected exchange rate changes.

Exhibit 6.2 illustrates the distribution of expected net cash flows of the individual firm. Hedging these cash flows narrows the distribution of the cash flows about the mean of the distribution. Currency hedging reduces risk. Reduction of risk is not, however, the same as adding value or return. The value of the firm depicted in Exhibit 6.2 would be increased only if hedging actually shifted the mean of the distribution to the right. In fact, if hedging is not "free," meaning that the firm must expend resources to undertake hedging activity, then hedging will add value only if the rightward shift is sufficiently large to compensate for the cost of hedging.

Hence the key question: Is a reduction in the variability of cash flows sufficient reason for currency risk management? This question is actually one inspiring

| **Exhibit 6.2** | *Impact of Hedging on the Expected Cash Flows of the Firm* |

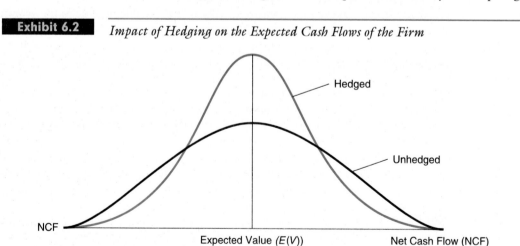

continuing debate in multinational financial management.[2] Opponents of currency hedging commonly make the following arguments:

- Shareholders are much more capable of diversifying currency risk than is the management of the firm. If stockholders do not wish to accept the currency risk of any specific firm, they can diversify their portfolios to manage the currency risk in a way that satisfies their individual preferences and risk tolerance.

- As noted above, currency risk management does not increase the expected cash flows of the firm. Currency risk management normally consumes some of a firm's resources and so reduces cash flow. The impact on value is a combination of the reduction of cash flow (which by itself lowers value) and the reduction in variance (which by itself increases value).

- Management often conducts hedging activities that benefit management at the expense of the shareholders. The field of finance called *agency theory* frequently argues that management is generally more risk-averse than shareholders. If the firm's goal is to maximize shareholder wealth, then hedging activity is probably not in the best interest of the shareholders.

- Managers cannot outguess the market. If and when markets are in equilibrium with respect to parity conditions, the expected net present value of hedging is zero.

- Management's motivation to reduce variability is sometimes driven by accounting reasons. Management may believe that it will be criticized more severely for incurring foreign exchange losses in its financial statements than for incurring similar or even higher cash costs in avoiding the foreign exchange loss. Foreign exchange losses appear in the income statement as a highly visible separate line item or as a footnote, but the higher costs of protection are buried in operating or interest expenses.

- Efficient market theorists believe that investors can see through the "accounting veil" and therefore have already factored the foreign exchange effect into a firm's market valuation.

Proponents of hedging make the following arguments:

- Reduction in risk in future cash flows improves the planning capability of the firm. If the firm can more accurately predict future cash flows, it may be able to undertake specific investments or activities that it might otherwise not consider.

- Reduction of risk in future cash flows reduces the likelihood that the firm's cash flows will fall below a necessary minimum. A firm must generate sufficient cash flows to make debt-service payments in order for it to continue to operate. This minimum cash flow point, often referred to as the *point of financial distress*, lies left of the center of the distribution of expected cash flows. Hedging reduces the likelihood of the firm's cash flows falling to or below this level.

- Management has a comparative advantage over the individual shareholder in knowing the actual currency risk of the firm.[3] Regardless of the level of disclosure provided by the firm to the public, management always possesses an advantage in the depth and breadth of knowledge concerning the real risks and returns inherent in any firm's business.

- Markets are usually in disequilibrium because of structural and institutional imperfections, as well as unexpected external shocks (such as an oil crisis or war). Management is in a better position than shareholders to recognize disequilibrium conditions and to take advantage of one-time opportunities to enhance firm value through *selective hedging*. *Selective hedging* refers to the hedging of large, singular, exceptional exposures or the occasional use of hedging when management has a definite expectation of the direction of exchange rates.

MEASUREMENT OF TRANSACTION EXPOSURE

Transaction exposure measures gains or losses that arise from the settlement of existing financial obligations whose terms are stated in a foreign currency. Transaction exposure arises from:

1. Purchasing or selling on credit goods or services when prices are stated in foreign currencies,
2. Borrowing or lending funds when repayment is to be made in a foreign currency,
3. Being a party to an unperformed foreign exchange forward contract, and
4. Otherwise acquiring assets or incurring liabilities denominated in foreign currencies.

The most common example of transaction exposure arises when a firm has a receivable or payable denominated in a foreign currency. Exhibit 6.3 demonstrates how this exposure is born. The total transaction exposure consists of *quotation*, *backlog*, and *billing exposures*. A transaction exposure is actually created at the first moment the seller quotes a price in foreign currency terms to a potential buyer (t_1). The *quotation* can be either verbal, as in a telephone quote, or in the form of a written bid or even a printed price list. With the placing of an order (t_2), the potential exposure created at the time of the quotation (t_1) is converted into actual exposure, called *backlog exposure* because the product has not yet been shipped or billed. Backlog exposure lasts until the goods are shipped and billed (t_3), at which time it becomes billing exposure. *Billing exposure* remains until actual payment is received by the seller (t_4).

))) Purchasing or Selling on Open Account

Suppose that a U.S. firm sells merchandise on open account to a Belgian buyer for €1,800,000, payment to be made in 60 days. The current exchange rate is

Exhibit 6.3	*The Life Span of a Transaction Exposure*

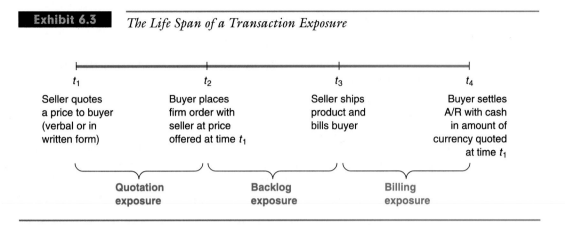

The U.S. seller expects to exchange the euros received for

$1.1200/€, and the U.S. seller expects to exchange the euros received for
€1,800,000 × $1.1200/€ = $2,016,000 when payment is received.

Transaction exposure arises because of the risk that the U.S. seller will receive something other than the $2,016,000 expected. For example, if the euro weakens to $1.0800/€ when payment is received, the U.S. seller will receive only €1,800,000 × $1.0800/€ = $1,944,000, or some $72,000 less than anticipated. If the euro should strengthen to $1.1500/€, however, the seller receives €1,800,000 × $1.1500/€ = $2,070,000, an increase of $54,000 over the amount expected. Thus exposure is the chance of either a loss or a gain.

The U.S. seller might have avoided transaction exposure by invoicing the Belgian buyer in dollars. Of course, if the U.S. company attempted to sell only in dollars it might not have obtained the sale in the first place. Avoiding transaction exposure by not having a sale is counterproductive to the well-being of the firm! Even if the Belgian buyer agrees to pay in dollars, transaction exposure is not eliminated. Instead it is transferred to the Belgian buyer, whose dollar account payable has an unknown cost in euros 60 days hence.

))) Borrowing and Lending

A second example of transaction exposure arises when funds are borrowed or loaned, and the amount involved is denominated in a foreign currency. For example, PepsiCo's largest bottler outside of the United States in 1994 was Grupo Embotellador de Mexico (Gemex). In mid-December 1994, Gemex had U.S. dollar debt of $264 million. At that time Mexico's *new peso* (NP$) was traded at NP$3.45/US$, a pegged rate that had been maintained with minor variations since January 1, 1993, when the new currency unit had been created. On December 22, 1994, the new peso was allowed to float because of economic and political events within Mexico, and in one day it sank to NP$4.65/US$. For most of the following January it traded in a range near NP$5.50/US$.

For Gemex, the increase in the peso amount of its dollar debt was:

Dollar debt in mid-December 1994:
    US\$264,000,000 × NP\$3.45/US\$ =   NP\$ 910,800,000.
Dollar debt in mid-January 1995:
    US\$264,000,000 × NP\$5.50/US\$ =   <u>NP\$1,452,000,000.</u>
Dollar debt increase measured in Mexican new pesos: NP\$ 541,200,000.

The pesos needed to repay the dollar debt increased by 59%! In U.S. dollar terms the drop in the value of the pesos caused Gemex to need the peso-equivalent of an additional US\$2,976,600 to repay. This increase in debt was the result of transaction exposure.

))) Other Causes of Transaction Exposure

When a firm buys a forward exchange contract, it deliberately creates transaction exposure. This risk is usually incurred to hedge an existing transaction exposure. For example, a U.S. firm might want to offset an existing obligation to purchase ¥100 million to pay for an import from Japan in 90 days. One way to offset this payment is to purchase ¥100 million in the forward market today for delivery in 90 days. In this manner any change in value of the Japanese yen relative to the dollar is neutralized. If the yen increases in value, an unhedged account payable would cost more dollars, a transaction loss. The forward contract, however, has already fixed the amount of dollars needed to buy the ¥100 million. Thus the potential transaction loss (or gain) on the account payable has been offset by the transaction gain (or loss) on the forward contract.

Note that foreign currency cash balances do not create transaction exposure, even though their home currency value changes immediately with a change in exchange rates. No legal obligation exists to move the cash from one country and currency to another. If such an obligation did exist, it would show on the books as a payable (e.g., dividends declared and payable) or receivable and then be counted as part of transaction exposure. Nevertheless, the foreign exchange value of cash balances does change when exchange rates change. Such a change is reflected in the consolidated statement of cash flows and the consolidated balance sheet, as will be discussed in Chapter 8.

))) Contractual Hedges

Foreign exchange transaction exposure can be managed by *contractual, operating,* and *financial hedges.* The main contractual hedges employ the forward, money, futures, and options markets. Operating and financial hedges employ the use of risk-sharing agreements, leads and lags in payment terms, swaps, and other strategies to be discussed in Chapter 7, which covers operating exposure.

At times the term *natural hedge* is used to mean either an operating hedge or some type of financial hedge, such as swaps. Strictly speaking a natural hedge arises only from the operating cash flows of the firm.

The following case illustrates how contractual hedging techniques may be used to protect against transaction exposure.

⟫⟫ Dayton Manufacturing's Transaction Exposure

Scout Finch is the chief financial officer of Dayton, a U.S.-based manufacturer of gas turbine equipment. She has just concluded negotiations for the sale of a turbine generator to Crown, a British firm, for £1,000,000. This single sale is quite large in relation to Dayton's present business. Dayton has no other current foreign customers, so the currency risk of this sale is of particular concern. The sale is made in March with payment due three months later in June. Scout has collected the following financial and market information for the analysis of her currency exposure problem.

- Spot exchange rate: $1.7640/£

- Three-month forward rate: $1.7540/£ (a 2.2676% per annum discount on the pound)

- Dayton's cost of capital: 12.0%

- U.K. three-month borrowing interest rate: 10.0% (or 2.5%/quarter)

- U.K. three-month investment interest rate: 8.0% (or 2.0%/quarter)

- U.S. three-month borrowing interest rate: 8.0% (or 2.0%/quarter)

- U.S. three-month investment interest rate: 6.0% (or 1.5%/quarter)

- June put option in the over-the-counter (bank) market for £1,000,000; strike price $1.75 (nearly at-the-money); 1.5% premium

- June put option in the over-the-counter (bank) market for £1,000,000; strike price $1.71 (out-of-the-money); 1.0% premium

- Dayton's foreign exchange advisory service forecasts that the spot rate in three months will be $1.76/£

Like many manufacturing firms, Dayton operates on relatively narrow margins. Although Scout Finch and Dayton would be very happy if the pound appreciated versus the dollar, concerns center on the possibility that the pound will fall. When Scout budgeted this specific contract, she determined that its minimum acceptable margin was at a sales price of $1,700,000. The *budget rate*, the lowest acceptable dollar per pound exchange rate, was therefore established at $1.70/£. At any exchange rate below this budget rate Dayton is actually losing money on the transaction.

Four alternatives are available to Dayton to manage the exposure:

1. Remain unhedged

2. Hedge in the forward market

3. Hedge in the money market

4. Hedge in the options market

Unhedged Position

Scout Finch may decide to accept the transaction risk. If she believes the foreign exchange advisor, she expects to receive £1,000,000 × $1.76 = $1,760,000 in three months. However, that amount is at risk. If the pound should fall to, say, $1.65/£, she will receive only $1,650,000. Exchange risk is not one-sided, however; if the transaction is left uncovered and the pound strengthens even more than forecast by the advisor, Dayton will receive considerably more than $1,760,000.

The essence of an unhedged approach is as follows.

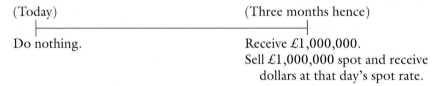

(Today)   (Three months hence)

Do nothing.   Receive £1,000,000.
                                             Sell £1,000,000 spot and receive
                                                 dollars at that day's spot rate.

Forward Market Hedge

A *forward hedge* involves a forward (or futures) contract and a source of funds to fulfill that contract. The forward contract is entered into at the time the transaction exposure is created. In Dayton's case, that would be in March, when the sale to Crown was booked as an account receivable.[4] Funds to fulfill the contract will be available in June, when Crown pays £1,000,000 to Dayton. If funds to fulfill the forward contract are on hand or are due because of a business operation, the hedge is considered "covered," "perfect," or "square" because no residual foreign exchange risk exists. Funds on hand or to be received are matched by funds to be paid.

In some situations funds to fulfill the forward exchange contract are neither already available nor due to be received later—but must be purchased in the spot market at some future date. Such a hedge is *open* or *uncovered*. It involves considerable risk because the hedger must take a chance on purchasing foreign exchange at an uncertain future spot rate in order to fulfill the forward contract. Purchase of such funds at a later date is referred to as "covering." There is an old financial saying that is appropriate for an uncovered forward obligation:

> He who sells what isn't his'n
> Must buy it back or go to prison![5]

Should Dayton wish to hedge its transaction exposure in the forward market, it will sell £1,000,000 forward today at the three-month forward quotation of $1.7540 per pound. This is a *covered* transaction in which the firm no longer has any foreign exchange risk. In three months the firm will receive £1,000,000 from the British buyer, deliver that sum to the bank against its forward sale, and receive $1,754,000. This certain sum is $6,000 less than the uncertain $1,760,000 expected from the unhedged position because the forward market quotation differs from the firm's three-month forecast. However, it would be recorded on Dayton's income statement as a *foreign exchange loss* of $10,000 ($1,764,000 as booked, $1,754,000 as settled).

The essence of a forward hedge is as follows.

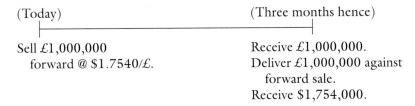

(Today)   (Three months hence)

Sell £1,000,000   Receive £1,000,000.
   forward @ $1.7540/£.   Deliver £1,000,000 against
                                                 forward sale.
                                             Receive $1,754,000.

If Scout Finch's forecast of future rates were identical to that implicit in the forward quotation, that is, $1.7540, expected receipts would be the same whether or not the firm hedges. However, realized receipts under the unhedged alternative could vary considerably from the certain receipts when the transaction is hedged.[6]

)))) Money Market Hedge

Like a forward market hedge, a *money market hedge* also involves a contract and a source of funds to fulfill that contract. In this instance the contract is a loan agreement. The firm seeking the money market hedge borrows in one currency and exchanges the proceeds for another currency. Funds to fulfill the contract—that is, to repay the loan—may be generated from business operations, in which case the money market hedge is *covered*. Alternatively, funds to repay the loan may be purchased in the foreign exchange spot market when the loan matures. In this instance the money market hedge is *uncovered* or *open*.

A money market hedge can cover a single transaction, such as Dayton's £1,000,000 receivable, or repeated transactions. Hedging repeated transactions is called *matching*. It requires the firm to match the expected foreign currency cash inflows and outflows by currency and maturity. For example, if Dayton had numerous sales denominated in pounds to British customers over a long period of time, it would have somewhat predictable U.K. pound cash inflows. The appropriate money market hedge technique would be to borrow U.K. pounds in an amount matching the typical size and maturity of expected pound inflows. Then, if the pound depreciated or appreciated, the foreign exchange effect on cash inflows in pounds would be approximately offset by the effect on cash outflows in pounds from repaying the pound loan plus interest.

The structure of a money market hedge resembles that of a forward hedge. The difference is that the cost of the money market hedge is determined by differential interest rates, while the cost of the forward hedge is a function of the forward rate quotation. In efficient markets interest rate parity should ensure that these costs are nearly the same, but not all markets are efficient at all times. Furthermore, the difference in interest rates facing a private firm borrowing in two separate national markets may be different from the difference in risk-free government bill rates or Eurocurrency interest rates in these same markets. It is the latter differential that is relevant for interest rate parity.

To hedge in the money market, Scout will borrow pounds in London at once, immediately convert the borrowed pounds into dollars, and repay the pound loan in three months with the proceeds from the sale of the generator. How much should she borrow? She will need to borrow just enough to repay both the principal and interest with the sale proceeds. The borrowing interest rate will be 10% per annum, or 2.5% for three months. Therefore, the amount to borrow now for repayment in three months is:

$$\frac{£1,000,000}{1+2.05} = £975,610$$

Scout should borrow £975,610 now and in three months repay that amount plus £24,390 of interest from the sale proceeds of the account receivable. Dayton would exchange the £975,610 loan proceeds for dollars at the current spot exchange rate of $1.7640/£, receiving $1,720,976 at once.

The money-market hedge, if selected by Dayton, actually creates a pound-denominated liability, the pound loan, to offset the pound-denominated asset, the account receivable. The money market hedge works by matching assets and liabilities according to their currency of denomination. On a simple T-account illustrating Dayton's balance sheet, the loan in British pounds is seen to offset the pound-denominated account receivable:

Assets		*Liabilities and Net Worth*	
Account receivable	£1,000,000	Bank loan	£975,610

The loan acts as a balance sheet hedge—a money market hedge, in this case—against the pound-denominated account receivable.

To compare the forward hedge with the money market hedge, we must analyze how Dayton's loan proceeds will be utilized for the next three months. Remember that the loan proceeds are received today, but the forward contract proceeds are received in three months. For comparison purposes, we must calculate either the future value in three months of the loan proceeds or the present value of the forward contract proceeds. (We will use future value for pedagogical reasons, but correct use of present value would give the same comparative results.)

Because both the forward contract proceeds and the loan proceeds are relatively certain, it is possible to make a clear choice between the two alternatives based on the one that yields the higher dollar receipts. This result, in turn, depends on the assumed rate of investment of the loan proceeds.

At least three logical choices exist for an assumed investment rate for the loan proceeds for the next three months. First, if Dayton is cash rich, the loan proceeds might be invested in U.S. dollar money market instruments that have been assumed to yield 6% per annum. Second, Scout Finch might simply use the pound loan proceeds to substitute for an equal dollar loan that Dayton would otherwise have undertaken at an assumed rate of 8% per annum. Third, Scout Finch might invest the loan proceeds in the general operations of the firm, in which case the cost of capital of 12% per annum would be the appropriate rate. The future value of the loan proceeds at the end of three months under each of these three investment assumptions

Received today	*Invested at*	*Future value in three months*
$1,720,976	6%/yr or 1.5%/quarter	$1,746,791
$1,720,976	8%/yr or 2.0%/quarter	$1,755,396
$1,720,976	12%/yr or 3.0%/quarter	$1,772,605

Because the proceeds in three months from the forward hedge would be $1,754,000, the money market hedge is superior to the forward hedge if Scout Finch used the loan proceeds to replace a dollar loan (8%) or to conduct general business operations (12%). The forward hedge would be preferable if Dayton merely invested the pound loan proceeds in dollar-denominated money market instruments at 6% annual interest.

A break-even investment rate can be calculated that would make Dayton indifferent between the forward hedge and the money market hedge. Assume that r is the unknown three-month investment rate, expressed as a decimal, that would equalize the proceeds from the forward and money market hedges. We have

$$(\text{Loan proceeds}) \, (1 + \text{rate}) = (\text{Forward proceeds})$$
$$\$1,720,976 \, (1 + r) = \$1,754,000$$
$$r = 0.0192$$

We can convert this three-month (90 days) investment rate to an annual whole percentage equivalent, assuming a 360-day financial year, as follows:

$$0.0192 \times \frac{360}{90} \times 100 = 7.68\%$$

In other words, if Scout Finch can invest the loan proceeds at a rate higher than 7.68% per annum, she will prefer the money market hedge. If she can only invest at a lower rate than 7.68%, she will prefer the forward hedge.

The essence of a money market hedge is as follows.

(Today)   (Three months hence)

├──┤

Borrow £975,610.   Receive £1,000,000.
Exchange £975,610 for   Repay £975,610 loan plus £24,390
  dollars @ $1.7640/£.   interest, for a total of £1,000,000.
Receive $1,720,976 cash.

》》》 **Options Market Hedge**

Scout Finch could also cover her £1,000,000 exposure by purchasing a put option. This technique allows her to speculate on the upside potential for appreciation of the pound while limiting downside risk to a known amount.

Given the two quotes shown earlier, Scout Finch could purchase from her bank a three-month put option on £1,000,000 at either (1) an at-the-money strike price of $1.75/£ (and a premium cost of 1.50%), or (2) an out-of-the-money strike price of $1.71/£ (and a premium cost of 1.00%). The cost of the first option with strike price of $1.75, a strike price that would be considered close to forward-at-the-money, is:[7]

$$(\text{Size of option}) \times (\text{Premium}) \times (\text{Spot rate}) = \text{Cost of option}$$
$$£1,000,000 \times 0.015 \times \$1.7640 = \$26,460$$

Because we are using future value to compare the various hedging alternatives, it is necessary to project the premium cost of the option forward three months. Once again we could justify several investment rates. We will use the cost of capital of 12% per annum or 3% per quarter. Therefore, the premium cost of the put option as of June would be $26,460(1.03) = $27,254. This is equivalent to $0.0273 per pound ($27,254 ÷ £1,000,000).

When the £1,000,000 is received in June, the value in dollars depends on the spot rate at that time. The upside potential is unlimited, the same as in the unhedged alternative. At any exchange rate above $1.75/£ Dayton would allow its option to expire unexercised and would exchange the pounds for dollars at the spot rate. If the expected rate of $1.76/£ materializes, for example, Dayton would exchange the £1,000,000 in the spot market for $1,760,000. Net proceeds would be $1,760,000 minus the $27,254 cost of the option, or $1,732,746.

In contrast to the unhedged alternative, downside risk is limited with an option. If the pound depreciates below $1.75/£, Scout Finch would exercise her option to sell (put) £1,000,000 at $1.75/£, receiving $1,750,000 gross, but $1,722,746 net of the $27,254 cost of the option. Although this downside result is worse than the downside of the forward or money market hedges, the upside potential is not limited the way it is with those hedges. Thus, whether the option strategy is superior to a forward or money market hedge depends on the degree to which management is risk-averse.

The essence of the at-the-money (ATM) option market hedge is as follows.

(Today)	(Three months hence)
Buy put option to sell pounds @ $1.75/£. Pay $26,460 for put option.	Receive £1,000,000. Either deliver £1,000,000 against put, receiving $1,750,000; or sell £1,000,000 spot if current spot rate is > $1.75/£.

We can calculate a trading range for the pound that defines the breakeven points for the option compared with the other strategies. The upper bound of the range is determined by comparison with the forward rate. The pound must appreciate enough above the $1.7540 forward rate to cover the $0.0273/£ cost of the option. Therefore the breakeven upside spot price of the pound must be $1.7540 + $0.0273 = $1.7813. If the spot pound appreciates above $1.7813, proceeds under the option strategy will be greater than under the forward hedge. If the spot pound ends up below $1.7813, the forward hedge would be superior in retrospect.

The lower bound of the range is determined by a comparison with the unhedged strategy. If the spot price falls below $1.75/£, Scout Finch will exercise her put option and sell the proceeds at $1.75/£. The net proceeds per pound will be $1.75/£ less the $0.0273 cost of the option, or $1.7221/£. If the spot rate falls below $1.7221/£, the net proceeds from exercising the option will be greater than the net proceeds from selling the unhedged pounds in the spot market. At any spot rate above $1.7221/£, the spot proceeds from the unhedged alternative will be greater.

The same basic calculations, costs, and breakeven points can be determined for the second option, the one with a strike price of $1.71/£. It has a smaller premium cost because it is out of the money. The resulting comparison of the two alternative over-the-counter options appears as follows.[8]

Put option strike price	ATM option $1.75/£	OTM option $1.71/£
Option cost (future value)	$27,254	$18,169
Proceeds if exercised	$1,750,000	$1,710,000
Minimum net proceeds	$1,722,746	$1,691,831
Maximum net proceeds	Unlimited	Unlimited
Break-even spot rate	$1.7813/£	$1.7722/£

)))) Comparison of Alternatives

The four alternatives available to Scout Finch and Dayton are shown in Exhibit 6.4. The forward hedge yields a certain $1,754,000 in three months. This is equivalent to a money market hedge if the loan proceeds are invested at 7.68% per annum. At any higher rate, such as the 12% cost of capital, the money market hedge is preferable, but at any lower rate the forward hedge is preferable.

If Scout Finch does not hedge, she can "expect" $1,760,000 in three months. However, this sum is at risk and might be greater or smaller. When the forward rate is accepted as the most likely future spot rate, the expected results from an unhedged position are identical to the certain results from the forward hedge. Under such circumstances the advantage of hedging over remaining unhedged is the reduction of uncertainty.

| Exhibit 6.4 | *Comparison of Alternative Hedging Strategies for Dayton* |

Goal: Receive maximum dollars from sale

Unhedged alternative

Wait 3 months then sell £1,000,000 for dollars
in the spot market

Result

Receive in 3 months:
1. An unlimited maximum;
2. An expected $1,760,000; or
3. A zero minimum

Forward market hedge

Sell £1,000,000 forward for dollars at once

Result

Certain receipts of $1,754,000 in 3 months

Money market hedge

1. Borrow £975,610 in U.K. @ 10%
2. Exchange for $1,720,976 at spot rate
3. Invest in U.S. for 3 months

Result

Receive $1,720,976 at once. Value in 3 months
depends on U.S. investment assumption:
1. At break-even rate of 7.68%, receive $1,754,000.
2. At cost of capital of 12% receive an expected
   $1,772,605.

Options market hedge

Purchase a 3-month put option of £1,000,000
with strike price of $1.75/£ and premium cost of
$27,254 (after 3 months)

Result

Receive in 3 months:
1. An unlimited maximum less $27,254;
2. An expected $1,760,000 less $27,254, or
   $1,732,746;
3. A minimum of $1,750,000 less $27,254, or
   $1,722,746.

The two put options offer a unique alternative. If the exchange rate moves in Dayton's favor, both options have nearly the same upside potential as the unhedged alternative except for their up-front costs. If, however, the exchange rate moves against Dayton, the put options limit the downside risk to net receipts of either $1,722,746 for the $1.75/£ strike put, or $1,691,831 for the $1.71/£ strike put.

Foreign currency options have a variety of hedging uses beyond the one illustrated here. A put option is useful to construction firms or other exporters when they must submit a fixed price bid in a foreign currency without knowing until some later date whether their bid is successful. A put option can be used to hedge the foreign exchange risk either for the bidding period alone or for the entire period of potential exposure if the bid is won. If the bid is rejected, the loss is limited to the cost of the option. In contrast, if the risk is hedged by a forward contract and the bid is rejected, the forward contract must be reversed or eventually fulfilled at an unknown potential loss or gain. The bidder has been holding what turned out to be an uncovered forward contract.

)))) Strategy Choice and Outcome

The preceding section compared hedging alternatives available to Dayton. Dayton, like all firms attempting to hedge transaction exposure, must decide on a strategy before the exchange rate changes occur. Exhibit 6.5 provides an evaluation of each potential strategy open to Dayton over a range of exchange rates that may occur at the end of the three-month period.

How will Scout Finch of Dayton choose among the alternative hedging strategies? She must select on the basis of two decision criteria: (1) the *risk tolerance* of Dayton, as expressed in its stated policies; and (2) her own *view*, or her expectation of the direction (and the distance) the exchange rate will move over the coming three-month period.

Dayton's *risk tolerance* is a combination of management's philosophy toward transaction exposure and the specific goals of treasury activities. Many firms believe that currency risk is simply a part of doing business internationally and therefore start their analysis from an unhedged baseline. Other firms, however, view currency risk as unacceptable, and they either start their analysis from a full forward contract cover baseline or simply mandate that all transaction exposures be fully covered by forward contracts regardless of the value of other hedging alternatives. The treasury in such firms operates as a cost or service center for the firm. On the other hand, if the treasury operates as a profit center, it might tolerate taking more risks.

| Exhibit 6.5 | *Valuation of Cash Flows under Various Hedging Alternatives for Dayton* |

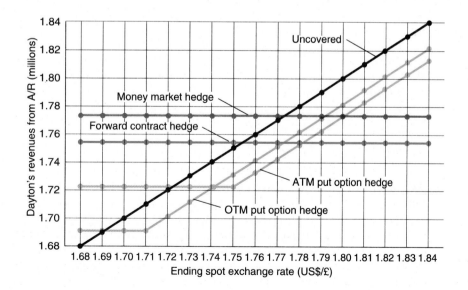

If management is willing to consider all alternatives, the firm's view of likely exchange rate changes aids in the hedging choice. As is evident from Exhibit 6.5, if the exchange rate is expected to move against Dayton— to the left of $1.76/£, the money market hedge is the clearly preferred alternative. At a guaranteed value of $1,772,605, the money market hedge is by far the most profitable choice. If the exchange rate is expected to move in Dayton's favor, to the right of $1.76/£, the choice of the hedge is more complex. Consider the following points:

- If the spot rate is expected to move to the right of $1.77/£, the unhedged alternative always provides the highest U.S. dollar value for the receivable.

- If Scout Finch is worried that her expectations may prove incorrect, the decision to remain unhedged does not assure Dayton of meeting its budgeted exchange rate of $1.70/£. This is an outcome that the firm cannot afford. The possibility always exists of a major political or economic event disrupting international currency markets unexpectedly.

- If the spot rate is expected to move to the right of $1.77/£, but not far to the right, for example to $1.78/£, the expected benefits of remaining unhedged are probably not worth the risks of remaining unhedged. The money market hedge is still the preferred choice.

- If the spot rate is expected to move far to the right of $1.76/£, such as to $1.84/£, the put option potentially would allow Dayton to enjoy the up-side movement and simultaneously provide a safety net of a minimum value if the puts are exercised.

- If the spot rate is expected to move so far to the right that Dayton considers both put options, the choice is one of tradeoffs. The $1.71/£ strike put option is significantly cheaper, but it also provides a lower level of protection ($1,691,831 minimum net proceeds as opposed to the $1,722,746 assured by the $1.75/£ strike put). You get what you pay for. The decision in this case is simplified for Dayton by the fact that the OTM put option does not assure Dayton, after premium expenses, of meeting its budgeted exchange rate of $1.70/£ (or minimum net proceeds of $1,700,000).

The final choice among hedges—if Scout Finch does expect the pound to appreciate—combines both the firm's risk tolerance, its view, and its confidence in its view. Transaction exposure management with contractual hedges requires managerial judgment.

)))) Management of an Account Payable

The Dayton Manufacturing case as discussed so far assumes a foreign-currency-denominated receivable. The management of an account payable, where the firm would be required to make a foreign currency payment at a future date, is similar but not identical in form.

If Dayton had a £1,000,000 account payable in 90 days, the hedging choices would appear as follows:

1. *Remain unhedged.* Dayton could wait 90 days, exchange dollars for pounds at that time, and make its payment. If Dayton expects the spot rate in 90 days to be $1.7600/£, the payment would be expected to cost $1,760,000. This amount is, however, uncertain; the spot exchange rate in 90 days could be very different from that expected.

2. *Forward market hedge.* Dayton could buy £1,000,000 forward, locking in a rate of $1.7540/£ and a total dollar cost of $1,754,000. This is $6,000 less than the expected cost of remaining unhedged and therefore clearly preferable to the first alternative.

3. *Money market hedge.* The money market hedge is distinctly different for a payable as opposed to a receivable. To implement a money market hedge in this case, Dayton would exchange U.S. dollars spot and invest them for 90 days in a pound-denominated interest-bearing account. The principal and interest in British pounds at the end of the 90-day period would be used to pay the £1,000,000 account payable.

   In order to ensure that the principal and interest exactly equal the £1,000,000 due in 90 days, Dayton would discount the £1,000,000 by the pound investment interest rate of 8% for 90 days to determine the pounds needed today:

$$\frac{£1,000,000}{1+\left(.08\times\dfrac{90}{360}\right)}=£980,392.16$$

This £980,392.16 needed today would require $1,729,411.77 at the current spot rate of $1.7640/£:

$$£980,392.16 \times \$1.7640/£ = \$1,729,411.77$$

Finally, in order to compare the money market hedge outcome with the other hedging alternatives, the $1,729,411.77 cost today must be carried forward 90 days to the same future date as the other hedge choices. If the current dollar cost is carried forward at Dayton's weighted average cost of capital (WACC) of 12%, the total cost of the money market hedge is $1,781,294.12.

$$\$1,729,411.77 \times\left[1+\left(.12\times\frac{90}{360}\right)\right]=\$1,781,294.12$$

This is higher than the forward hedge and therefore unattractive.

4. *Option hedge*. Dayton could cover its £1,000,000 account payable by purchasing a call option on £1,000,000. A June call option on British pounds with a near at-the-money strike price of $1.75/£ would cost 1.5% (premium) or

$$£1,000,000 \times 0.015 \times \$1.7640/£ = \$26,460$$

This premium, regardless of whether the call option is exercised or not, will be paid up-front. Its value carried forward 90 days at the WACC of 12%, as it was in the receivable example, would raise its end of period cost to $27,254.

If the spot rate in 90 days is less than $1.75/£, the option would be allowed to expire and the £1,000,000 for the payable purchased on the spot market. The total cost of the call option hedge if the option is not exercised is theoretically smaller than any other alternative (with the exception of remaining unhedged, because the option premium is still paid and lost).

If the spot rate in 90 days exceeds $1.75/£, the call option would be exercised. The total cost of the call option hedge if exercised is as follows:

Exercise call option (£1,000,000 × $1.75/£)	$1,750,000
Call option premium (carried forward 90 days)	27,254
Total maximum expense of call option hedge	$1,777,254

The four hedging methods of managing a £1,000,000 account payable for Dayton are summarized as follows:

Hedging Alternative	Cost to Dayton	Degree of Risk
1. Remain unhedged	$1,760,000	Uncertain
2. Forward hedge	$1,754,000	Certain
3. Money market hedge	$1,781,294	Certain
4. Call option hedge	$1,777,254	Maximum

As with Dayton's account receivable, the final hedging choice depends on the confidence of Scout Finch's exchange rate expectations and her willingness to bear risk. The forward hedge provides the lowest cost of making the account payable payment, which is certain. If the dollar strengthens against the pound, ending up at a spot rate less than $1.75/£, the call option could potentially be the lowest cost hedge. Given an expected spot rate of $1.76/£, however, the forward hedge appears the preferred alternative.

BASICS OF FOREIGN CURRENCY ACCOUNTING

Although we do not propose to provide an accounting text, it is still important to know the basic accounting practices that apply to certain international business practices, including foreign exchange rates. It is also important to know that, in practice, the way in which many foreign-currency-denominated transactions are recorded on the firm's books has a significant impact on how the firm views itself as being "exposed" to foreign currency movements.

⟫ Accounting for Foreign-Currency-Denominated Transactions

In the case of Dayton Manufacturing, on the date that the equipment was shipped to the British buyer, Dayton would record the sale on its books at the spot rate in effect on that date, $1.7640/£. This amount would be recorded as an account receivable due Dayton in the amount of:

$$£1,000,000 \times \$1.7640/£ = \$1,764,000$$

This sale is recorded as and expected to yield (according to accounting practices) revenue of $1,764,000. Exhibit 6.6 is an income statement that combines the export sale with sales revenue from domestic sales. If Dayton accepts the transaction risk and remains unhedged, the difference between what it was booked and what is finally received would enter Dayton's financial statements (its income statement) as a *foreign exchange gain (loss)*.[9] For example, if Dayton's foreign exchange advisor is correct and the exchange rate at the end of 90 days is $1.7600/£, the receivable would be settled at that exchange rate, resulting in a foreign exchange loss of:

A/R booked at $1.7640/£	$1,764,000
A/R settled at $1.7600/£	1,760,000
Foreign exchange gain (loss)	($ 4,000)

If the foreign exchange advisor is wrong and the spot rate at the end of the 90-day period moves in Dayton's favor to $1.7800/£, the transaction would be settled for $1,780,000, and a foreign exchange gain of $16,000 would be recorded and realized ($1,780,000 – $1,764,000 = $16,000).

Because all foreign-currency-denominated transactions must be booked at the spot rate in effect on the date of sale or purchase rather than on the date of settlement, foreign exchange gains and losses are essentially unavoidable for the firm (unless exchange rates were indeed fixed).[10] Under existing U.S. and international accounting standards and generally accepted accounting practices (GAAP), these gains and losses are reported in a firm's income statement in the period in which the gain or loss occurs.[11] These amounts are real gains and losses, and represent potential changes to net income and earnings per share that the firm may wish to monitor and manage.

⟫ Accounting for Forward Contracts as Hedges

Had Dayton decided not to accept the transaction risk but instead purchased a forward contract (sold pounds forward), the forward contract would lock-in a

Exhibit 6.6	*Dayton's Income Statement and Foreign Exchange Gains (Losses)*

Spot rate on date of export sale ($/£)	1.7640	1.7640	1.7640
Forward rate, 90 days ($/£)	1.7540	1.7540	1.7540
Ending spot rate, actual ($/£)	1.7600	1.7800	1.7600
Amount of 90-day account receivable (£)	1,000,000	1,000,000	1,000,000
Income Statement (US$)	**Uncovered: FX Advisor Is Correct**	**Uncovered: FX Advisor Is Incorrect**	**Forward Cover: Exposure Settled at Forward Rate**
Sales:			
Domestic sales	5,246,000	5,246,000	5,246,000
Export sales (single export)	1,764,000	1,764,000	1,764,000
Less cost of goods sold	(3,340,000)	(3,340,000)	(3,340,000)
Gross profit	3,670,000	3,670,000	3,670,000
Less general and administrative expenses	(565,000)	(565,000)	(565,000)
Less depreciation	(248,750)	(248,750)	(248,750)
Foreign exchange gains (losses)	(4,000)	16,000	(10,000)
Earnings before interest and taxes (EBIT)	2,852,250	2,872,250	2,846,250
Less interest expenses	(646,000)	(646,000)	(646,000)
Earnings before taxes (EBT)	2,206,250	2,226,250	2,200,250
Less U.S. corporate income taxes @ 40%	(882,500)	(890,500)	(880,100)
Net income	1,323,750	1,335,750	1,320,150
Shares outstanding	1,000,000	1,000,000	1,000,000
Earnings per share (EPS)	$1.32	$1.34	$1.32

specific exchange rate ($1.7540/£) upon settlement.[12] If the spot exchange rate on the settlement date was that forecast by Dayton's advisor, $1.7600/£, the final settlement details recorded on Dayton's books would be:

> *Receivable*
> A/R booked at $1.7640/£ $1,764,000
> A/R settled at spot rate of $1.7600/£   1,760,000
> Foreign exchange gain (loss)   ($ 4,000)
>
> *Forward Contract*
> Forward contract gain (loss)   ($ 6,000)
>   ($1,754,000 – $1,760,000)
> Total foreign exchange gain (loss)   ($ 10,000)

The foreign-currency-denominated receivable is still settled at a loss of $4,000; nothing has changed regarding its valuation. The purchase and settlement of the forward contract, however, results in an additional recognition of a $6,000 currency loss, the difference between the forward rate and the spot rate on the settlement date.

The total receipts resulting from the settlement of the receivable and the forward hedge (often referred to as the *two legs of the hedge position*) are $1,754,000. The firm receives a net dollar amount equal to that rate dictated by the forward contract. Note that this combined $10,000 loss is "locked-in," meaning that regardless of what the spot rate is at the end of the 90 day period, the combined foreign exchange gain (loss) and forward contract gain (loss) will always total a negative $10,000.[13]

))) Foreign Exchange Gains (Losses) on the Income Statement

As illustrated above, foreign-currency-denominated transactions are booked on the balance sheet of the firm at the spot exchange rate in effect on the date of the entry. If or when the transaction is settled at a later date with a different spot exchange rate, the difference between the settlement rate and the booked exchange rate results in a foreign exchange gain (loss) associated with the transaction. If the total foreign exchange gains (losses) for a firm for the current period are material in the minds of the firm's management and independent auditors, a separate line item identifies the total *currency gains* (*losses*) for the period on the firm's income statement. If not material, these gains (losses) are customarily included in *other expenses.*

Because the difference between the spot exchange rate and the forward exchange rate results from interest rate differentials between the two country currencies involved, the gains (losses) associated with the use of a forward contract may be categorized as *forward interest expenses*. This expense is ordinarily of significance only when constructing the year-end financial statements for a firm with outstanding foreign-currency-denominated transactions.

))) Hedge Accounting

Hedge accounting has a very specific meaning in corporate financial management. Hedge accounting specifies that gains and losses on hedging instruments be recognized in earnings at the same time as the effects of changes in the value of the items being hedged are recognized, assuming certain criteria are met. If a forward contract was purchased as a hedge of a foreign-currency-denominated receivable (as in the case of Dayton), changes in the value of the forward contract would only be recognized in Dayton's income when the changes in the value of the A/R were recognized (typically on settlement).

This approach seems obvious except for the possibility that the 90-day receivable was created during one year but would be settled in the following year (after December 31, the firm's end-of-year balance sheet date). Under traditional accounting practices, Dayton would have to value the forward contract and the A/R on December 31 at current market rates (the spot rate of exchange on that date) and recognize those valuation impacts in current income.[14] This process alters current income even though no real cash flow has occurred and neither the receivable nor the forward contract had been closed out. Separately, the forward premium implied by the forward rate (the difference between the originally booked spot rate and the forward rate) would be allocated as an interest expense (gain) for the current period by a day-count proportion. In this case, 45/90 days of the interest expense on the forward contract would be included in current expenses on the firm's income statement.

Many firms suggest that this practice defeats the purpose of hedging. According to FAS 52, if the transaction and hedge meet certain criteria, recognition of these changes may be deferred until the two legs of the hedge are actually settled.[15]

Meeting the criteria for the application of hedge accounting, however, is difficult for many firms. According to FAS 52, paragraph 21, a foreign currency transaction shall be considered a hedge of an identifiable foreign currency commitment provided both the following conditions are met:

1. The foreign currency transaction is designated as, and is effective as, a hedge of a foreign currency commitment.

2. The foreign currency commitment is firm.

The first condition focuses on the ability of the "hedge" such as a forward contract to act effectively as a hedge, with its value moving in the opposite direction to that of the exposure given a spot exchange rate change. This condition is typically easily met.

The second condition, however, is of a more controversial nature. For a commitment to be considered "firm," the exposure must have some type of financial certainty of occurring. For example, if a firm has sold merchandise to a foreign buyer, as in the case of Dayton, a contract exists and the seller can expect to receive the £1,000,000 as agreed. If, however, the receivable resulted from the sale of merchandise to another unit or affiliate of the same firm (for example to Dayton, UK), there must be some basis for expecting the payment to occur in the amount and on the date designated. This requirement is difficult for many firms to meet since most intra-firm sales and transactions do not have explicit contracts or penalties for nonperformance.

In summary, a firm may hedge a currency exposure in any way it deems appropriate. Taking hedging actions is a managerial decision. However, the way in which the exposure and the hedge are carried on the firm's books and recognized in income is the subject of hedge accounting principles and foreign currency accounting practices in general.

RISK MANAGEMENT IN PRACTICE

As many different approaches to exposure management exist as there are firms. A variety of surveys of corporate risk management practices in recent years in the United States, the United Kingdom, Finland, Australia, and Germany, indicates no real consensus exists regarding the best approach.[16] The following is our attempt to assimilate the basic results of these surveys and combine them with our own personal experiences in industry.

))) Which Goals?

The Treasury function of most private firms, the group typically responsible for transaction exposure management, is usually considered a cost center. It is not expected to add profit to the firm's bottom line (which is not the same thing as saying it is not expected to add value to the firm). Currency risk managers are expected to err on the conservative side when managing the firm's money.

))) Which Exposures?

Transaction exposures exist before they are actually booked as foreign-currency-denominated receivables and payables. However, many firms do not allow the hedging of quotation exposure or backlog exposure as a matter of policy. The reasoning is straightforward. Until the transaction exists on the accounting books of the firm, the probability of the exposure's actually occurring is considered to be less than 100%. Conservative hedging policies dictate that contractual hedges be placed only on existing exposures.

An increasing number of firms, however, are not only actively hedging backlog exposures but also selectively hedging quotation and *anticipated exposures*. *Anticipated exposures* are transactions for which there are—at present—no contracts or agreements between parties but that are anticipated on the basis of historical trends and continuing business relationships. Although on the surface this would appear to be overly speculative behavior on the part of these firms, it may be that hedging expected foreign currency payables and receivables for future periods is the most conservative approach for protecting the firm's future operating revenues against unexpected exchange rate changes.[17] Exhibit 6.7 reports the results of one of the most recent surveys of corporate risk management conducted by Bank of America.

))) Which Contractual Hedges?

As might be expected, transaction exposure management programs are generally divided along an "option line": those that use options and those that do not. Firms that do not use currency options rely almost exclusively on forward contracts and money market hedges. A few firms with appreciable quantities of transaction exposure actually do no hedging at all.

Proportional Hedges. Many MNEs have established rather rigid transaction exposure risk management policies that mandate proportional hedging. These policies generally require the use of forward contract hedges on a percentage (e.g., 50%, 60%, or 70%) of existing transaction exposures. As the maturity of the exposures lengthens, the percentage of forward cover required decreases. The remaining portion of the exposure is then selectively hedged on the basis of the firm's risk tolerance, view of exchange rate movements, and confidence level.

| **Exhibit 6.7** | *Bank of America Corporate FX Risk Management Survey Results* |

Translation Management

80% identify this exposure; 15% fully hedge; 15% partially or selectively hedge;
70% do not hedge; forwards used 73% of the time, options used 27%

Transaction Exposure

60% identify this exposure; 30% fully hedge; 55% partially or selectively hedge;
20% do not hedge; forwards used 83% of the time, options used 17%

Anticipated Exposure

70% identify this exposure; 2% fully hedge; 55% partially or selectively hedge;
43% do not hedge; forwards used 71% of the time, options used 29%

Contingent Exposure

52% identify this exposure; 4% fully hedge; 11% partially or selectively hedge;
85% do not hedge; forwards used 63% of the time, options used 37%

Economic Exposure

54% identify this exposure; 5% fully hedge;
95% do not hedge; forwards used 54% of the time, options used 46%

Balance Sheet Exposure

30% identify this exposure; 6% fully hedge; 15% partially or selectively hedge;
78% do not hedge; forwards used 74% of the time, options used 26%

Income Statement Exposure

44% identify this exposure; 6% fully hedge; 33% partially or selectively hedge;
61% do not hedge; forwards used 66% of the time, options used 34%

Firm Hedging Maturities

21% of hedges are for maturities of less than six months; 62% are for maturities of six months to one year;
17% are for maturities over one year

Functional Currency of Foreign Affiliates

33% USD; 66% local currency

Source: "Corporate America: FX Risk Management 1996," Global Capital Markets Group, Bank of America, Monograph 78, Winter 1996/97, pp. 1–3.

Although it is rarely acknowledged by the firms themselves, the continual use of selective hedging programs is essentially speculation against the currency markets. Significant theoretical questions remain as to whether a firm or a financial manager can consistently predict the future direction of exchange rate movements. One informed observer has noted: "it may occasionally be possible to find money lying in the street, but I would not expect to make a living at it."[18]

Forward Points. In addition to having required minimum forward-cover percentages, many firms also require full forward cover when forward rates "pay them the points." The *points on the forward rate* is the forward rate's premium or discount.

For example, using the same situation and financial assumptions as in the Dayton case, the forward rate of $1.7540/£ could be the result of the following 90-day Eurocurrency interest rates on U.S. dollars (6.80% per annum) and British pounds (9.12% per annum):

$$\text{Forward}_{90} = \$1.7640/£ \times \left[\frac{1 + \left(.0680 \times \dfrac{90}{360}\right)}{1 + \left(.0912 \times \dfrac{90}{360}\right)} \right] = \$1.7540/£$$

Because British pound interest rates are higher than U.S. dollar interest rates, the pound is selling forward at a discount. A firm such as Dayton purchasing a forward contract to sell pounds forward would itself be *paying the points.*

If U.S. dollar interest rates (6.80% per annum) were higher than British pound interest rates (6.00% per annum), the pound would be selling forward at a premium:

$$\text{Forward}_{90} = \$1.7640/£ \times \left[\frac{1 + \left(.0680 \times \dfrac{90}{360}\right)}{1 + \left(.0600 \times \dfrac{90}{360}\right)} \right] = \$1.7675/£$$

A forward rate of $1.7675/£ would allow Dayton to lock in an exchange rate for 90 days in the future, which is better than the exchange rate that would be realized even if Dayton received the British pounds today.

Many firms require that when the firm earns the forward points (as shown in this example), full forward cover be put in place. Not only is the exchange rate in the firm's favor, it also allows the firm to earn a U.S. dollar effective rate that meets its budget exchange rate, and a hedge choice that is independent of the firm's exchange rate view. Although the favorable forward rate is a result only of interest rate differences, many firms view this as riskless profit.

Bought Currency Options. A further distinction in practice can be made between those firms that buy currency options (buy a put or buy a call) and those that both buy and write currency options. Those firms that do use currency options are generally more aggressive in their tolerance of currency risk. This is a generalization, however, and in many cases firms that are extremely conservative and risk-intolerant may be hedging all existing exposures with forwards and then additionally hedging a variety of backlog and anticipated exposures with options. The currency options used by MNEs are nearly exclusively over-the-counter in origination and European in pricing style.

Hedgers with some degree of settlement risk may find it in their best interest to purchase protective options with maturities longer than the expected exposure maturity. This allows the hedger to at least recapture some of the option premium investment through resale if the exposure cash flow does indeed not occur as expected. The hedger must then determine whether the added benefits of a longer maturity and security in settlement risk coverage are worth the added expense.

Written Currency Options. Since the writer of an option has a limited profit potential with unlimited loss potential, the risks associated with writing options can be substantial. Firms that write options usually do so to finance the purchase of a second option. For example a firm such as Dayton, which is long British pounds, may write an out-of-the-money call option on pounds to partially offset the expense of purchasing an at-the-money put option on the same quantity of British pounds. These so-called *complex options* are gaining ever wider use in industry.[19]

If the hedger were actually writing options as part of its exposure management program, it would be beneficial to write relatively short-term options with rapidly deteriorating prices. This technique allows the writer to gain the benefits of the sale, the initial premium, yet in most cases rest assured that time-value deterioration will cause the value of the option to drop precipitously soon after sale, making any possible repurchase of the option affordable.

Few topics in financial management have garnered such public attention as the use and abuse of financial *derivatives* by corporations.[20] When used as a device for speculation, either with directional or volatility views, derivatives can lead to massive losses, and in some cases, the failure of the firm.[21] Derivative use by corporations, however, continues to grow.

SUMMARY

- MNEs encounter three types of currency exposure: (1) transaction exposure; (2) operating exposure; and (3) accounting (translation) exposure.

- *Transaction exposure* measures gains or losses that arise from the settlement of financial obligations whose terms are stated in a foreign currency. Transaction exposure arises from (1) purchasing or selling on credit goods or services whose prices are stated in foreign currencies; (2) borrowing or lending funds when repayment is to be made in a foreign currency; (3) being a party to an unperformed forward foreign exchange contract; and (4) otherwise acquiring assets or liabilities denominated in foreign currencies.

- Considerable theoretical debate exists as to whether firms should hedge currency risk. Theoretically, hedging reduces the variability of the cash flows to the firm. It does not increase the cash flows to the firm. In fact, the costs of hedging may potentially lower them.

- Transaction exposure can be managed by contractual techniques and certain operating strategies. *Contractual hedging* techniques include forward, futures, money market, and option hedges.

- The choice of which contractual hedge to use depends on the individual firm's currency risk tolerance, and its expectation of the probable movement of exchange rates over the transaction exposure period.

- In general, if an exchange rate is expected to move in a firm's favor, the preferred contractual hedges are probably those that allow it to participate in some up-side potential (remaining unhedged or using a currency option), but protect it against significant adverse exchange rate movements.

- In general, if the exchange rate is expected to move against the firm, the preferred contractual hedge is one that locks in an exchange rate, such as the forward contract hedge or money market hedge.

- When accounting for foreign exchange gains and losses associated with the use of a forward hedge, the gain or loss on the forward contract is reported separately from the gain or loss on the underlying position. However, hedge accounting allows gains or losses on hedging instruments to be recognized in earnings simultaneously with the gain or loss on the underlying transaction.

- Risk management in practice requires a firm's treasury department to identify its goals. Is Treasury a cost center or profit center?

- Treasury must also choose which contractual hedges it wishes to use and what proportion of the currency risk should be hedged. Additionally, treasury must determine whether the firm should buy and/or sell currency options, a strategy that has historically been risky for some firms and banks.

QUESTIONS

1. Tektronix, Inc., Account Receivable

Tektronix, Inc., an Oregon-based MNE, manufactures scientific instruments. Jerry Davies, Treasurer, needs to choose an instrument to hedge a €2,000,000 sale to Siemens in Germany, with payment due in six months. He has obtained the following quotes from Citibank.

Spot rate:	$1.0538/€
Six-month forward rate:	$1.0687/€
Six-month Euro interest rate:	3.1250% p.a.
Six-month U.S. dollar interest rate:	6.0000% p.a.
Tektronix' weighted average cost of capital:	12.00% p.a.

Six-month call option on euros at strike price $1.12/€:	$0.012/€
Six-month put option on euros at strike price $1.12/€:	$0.061/€
Six-month call option on euros at strike price $1.00/€:	$0.074/€
Six-month put option on euros at strike price $1.00/€:	$0.007/€

a. What are the costs of each alternative?

b. Diagram each alternative.

c. What are the risks of each alternative?

d. Which alternative should Jerry Davies choose if he prefers to "play it safe"?

e. Which alternative should he choose if he is willing to take a reasonable risk and he has a directional view that the euro may be appreciating versus the dollar in the coming months?

f. Which alternative should he choose if he is willing to take a reasonable risk and he has a directional view that the euro may be depreciating versus the dollar in the coming months?

g. Identify and calculate the break-even points between alternatives (exclude the $1.12/€ strike prices). Use the diagram of Dayton's alternatives in the chapter as a guide.

2. Tektronix, Inc., Account Payable

Tektronix imports some components from a Japanese supplier. Jerry Davies now needs to hedge a purchase of components for ¥80,000,000 from Tek's Japanese supplier. Payment is due in six months. He has obtained the following quotes from Citibank:

Spot rate (U.S. cents/¥):	0.8930
Six-month forward rate (U.S. cents/¥):	0.9186
Six-month yen interest rate:	0.250% p.a.
Six-month U.S. dollar interest rate:	6.000% p.a.
Textronix' weighted average cost of capital	12.00% p.a.
Six-month call option on yen at strike price 0.9090 (U.S. cents/¥):	0.037/¥ or 4.14%
Six-month put option on yen at strike price 0.9090 (U.S. cents/¥):	0.028/¥ or 3.14%

a. What are the costs of each alternative?

b. What are the risks of each alternative?

c. Which alternative should Jerry Davies choose if he prefers to "play it safe"?

d. Which alternative should he choose if he is willing to take a reasonable risk, and he has a directional view that the yen may be appreciating versus the dollar in the coming months?

3. Taj Bakeries, Ltd. (A).

On September 24 MJ Foods of Chicago sold $2,400,000 of corn oil to Taj Bakeries, Ltd. of Madras, India, payable in three months. The sale was denominated in Indian rupees at a time when the rupee traded at Rps36.96 per dollar.

During the following three months the Indian rupee dropped in value to Rps42.00 per dollar.

a. What was the percentage drop in the value of the rupee over the three months?

b. What was the dollar loss experienced by MJ Foods? When was it incurred?

c. Is the loss in part (b) above a transaction, translation, or operating loss? Explain.

4. Taj Bakeries, Ltd. (B)

The sequence of events surrounding MJ Food's sales to Taj Bakeries, Ltd., was as follows:

August 10:   Taj Bakeries, Ltd., requested a quote from MJ Foods.

August 18:   MJ Foods replied with a quote of Rps88,704,000, derived by multiplying its dollar price of $2,400,000 by the spot rate of Rps36.96/$, and payable in three months.

August 22:   Taj Bakeries placed a firm order with MJ Foods.

September 24: MJ Foods shipped the corn oil by sea and billed Taj Bakeries Rps88,704,000.

Sept. – Nov.   The Indian rupee fell steadily in value from Rps36.96/$ to Rps42.00/$. Newspaper accounts attributed this to the Indian central bank's failure to respond when "the rupee first began to wobble in September."

December 24: Taj Bakeries wired Rps88,704,000 to MJ Foods' bank, as specified in the original agreement. By mid-December the rupee had stabilized at Rps42.00/$.

a. On what date did MJ Foods first incur transaction exposure?

b. What kind of transaction exposure was this, and how much was the exposure?

c. Could MJ Foods have avoided this exposure?

d. Did the nature of the exposure change on August 22?

e. Did the nature of the exposure change on September 24?

f. Did the nature of the exposure change during October and November?

g. Did the nature of the exposure change on December 24?

5. Chalmers Incorporated

Chalmers Incorporated long ago did away with selective hedging by its treasury staff. If the date of the transaction is known with certainty, all foreign-currency-denominated cash flows must adhere to the following mandatory forward contract cover formula. Any remaining amounts may be left uncovered.

	Exposure Coverage Required by Maturity		
If Chalmers is:	*0–90 days*	*91–180 days*	*>180 days*
"paying the points forward"	75%	50%	40%
"receiving the points forward"	100%	80%	50%

Chalmers expects to receive a Mexican new peso payment of Ps.2,000,000 in four months. The spot rate is Ps.10.2400/$, and the four-month forward rate is Ps.11.0400/$:

a. What would be the amount of forward cover required?

b. If at the same time the spot rate in four months was expected to be Ps.8.1920/$, what would be the amount in pesos covered and uncovered?

c. What would be the expected total end-of-period U.S. dollar value of the position taken in part (b)?

If Chalmers were to make a Mexican new peso payment of Ps.3,000,000 in two months, the spot rate was Ps.10.3000/$, and the two-month forward rate was Ps.8.800/$:

d. What would be the amount of forward cover required?

e. If the spot rate in two months was expected to be Ps.10.0000/$, what would be the peso amount sold forward and the amount left uncovered?

f. What would be the expected total end-of-period U.S. dollar value of the payment required in part (b)?

6. Juan Garcia of Cemex

Juan Garcia, a newly minted MBA of a prestigious East Coast U.S. university, has been assigned to the treasury department at Cemex as part of his management training program's rotation. He has now been given the task of recommending a hedging strategy to protect a 10 million Singapore dollar (S$) account receivable due in three months. The recipient is Cementos de Mexico (Cemex), a large Mexican MNE that exports cement to worldwide markets. Because of the nature of its business, Cemex considers the U.S. dollar to be its functional currency rather than the Mexican new peso.

Juan Garcia has been specifically assigned as staff assistant to José Rios, Treasurer of Cemex. Mr. Garcia's first step was to collect currency and interest rate quotes from the World Wide Web to compare alternative hedging strategies. He collected the following quotes which he in turn reported to José Rios. The older and more experienced Treasurer smiled, patted Juan Garcia on the back, and said: "Do another search and talk to our bankers. These quotes are too good to be true. There is no free lunch in finance."

The original quotes collected by Juan Garcia were as follows:

Spot rate (U.S. cents/S$):	60.0000/S$
Three-month forward rate (U.S. cents/S$):	60.4658/S$
Three-month Singapore dollar interest rate:	2.5000% p.a.
Three-month U.S. dollar interest rate:	5.6250% p.a.
Three-month call option on Singapore dollars at strike price 65.000:	0.0449 or 7.48%
Three-month put option on Singapore dollars at strike price 65.000:	0.0002 or 0.03%

a. Why is José Rios suspicious of these quotes?
b. If the quotes are correct, how could Cemex benefit?
c. Which, if any, quotes seem to be reasonable?

7. Mini-Case Problem: Seattle Scientific, Inc.

Josh Miller is chief financial officer of a medium-sized Seattle-based medical device manufacturer. The company's annual sales of $40 million have been growing rapidly, and working capital financing is a common source of concern. He has recently been approached by one of his major Japanese customers, Yokasa, with a new payment proposal.

Yokasa typically orders ¥12,500,000 in product every other month and pays in Japanese yen. The current payment terms extended by Seattle Scientific are 30 days, with no discounts given for early or cash payment. Yokasa has suggested that it would be willing to pay in cash (Japanese yen) if it was given a 4.50% discount on the purchase price. Josh Miller gathered the following quotes from his bank on current spot and forward exchange rates, and estimated Yokasa's cost of capital.

Spot rate:	¥120.23/$	Yokasa's WACC	8.850%
30-Day Forward Rate:	¥119.73/$	Seattle Scientific's WACC	12.500%
90-Day Forward Rate:	¥118.78/$		
180-Day Forward Rate:	¥117.21/$		

a. What is Seattle Scientific's "cost of hedging" the yen receivable?
b. How much in U.S. dollars will Seattle Scientific receive (1) with the discount, and (2) with no discount but fully covered with a forward contract?
c. If Josh were to compare the results of part (b) in present value terms, which appears to be preferable?
d. What discount rate would Josh Miller probably try to negotiate with Yokasa?

WORLD WIDE WEB EXERCISES

W1. Dayton Manufacturing: Current Volatilities

Scout Finch wishes to price her own options, but needs current volatilities on the euro, British pound, and Japanese yen. Using the following website, collect spot rates and volatilities in order to price forward at-the-money put options for Finch's hedging analysis.

Federal Reserve Bank of New York   http://www.ny.frb.org/pihome/statistics

W2. Dayton Manufacturing : Czech koruna

Scout Finch has just received a call from her sales representative in Europe. The sales rep has been approached by a major firm in the Czech Republic. The firm would like a sales offer on a $1,000,000 turbine engine, but in local currency, the Czech koruna (CZK). The sales rep was told that prior to making any local-currency price offers, he must check with Scout Finch as to how to price it, and whether the sale could be hedged — and then at what cost.

Using the web sites listed below (and others you may find), determine current spot rates for the koruna, whether there is a forward market, and what the rates look like in the forward market. Then help the European sales rep make a Czech koruna price offer.

| Bankers Trust | http://www.bankerstrust.com/ms/fx |
| Czech Republic | http://www.czech.cz |

SUGGESTED READINGS

Bodnar, Gordon M., "1998 Wharton Survey of Financial Risk Management by U.S. Non-Financial Firms," *Financial Management*, Vol. 24, No. 4, Winter 1998, pp. 70–91.

Briys, Eric, and Francois de Varenne, "Optimal Hedging and the Partial Loss Offset," *European Financial Management*, Vol. 4, No. 3, November 1998, pp. 321–334.

Smith, Clifford W., Jr., Charles W. Smithson, and D. Sykes Wilford, "Financial Engineering: Why Hedge?" in *The Handbook of Financial Engineering*, Clifford W. Smith, Jr., and Charles W. Smithson, eds., New York: Harper Business, 1990, pp. 126–138.

Stulz, Rene M., "Rethinking Risk Management," *Journal of Applied Corporate Finance*, Vol. 9, No. 3, Fall 1996, pp. 8–24.

NOTES

1. Smith, Smithson, and Wilford (1990).
2. Smith, Smithson, and Wilford (1990), Smith and Stulz (1985), and Levi and Sercu (1991).
3. Stulz (1984), p. 127.
4. When a foreign currency-denominated sale such as this is made, it is booked at the spot rate of exchange existing on the booking date. In the case of Dayton, the spot rate on the day when it is booked as an account receivable is $1.7640/£, so the sale is recorded on Dayton's books as a sale of $1,764,000.
5. This quotation is attributed to Daniel Drew, in Bouck White, *The Book of Daniel Drew*, New York: George H. Doran Company, 1910, p. 180.
6. Belief that the forward rate is an unbiased estimate of the future spot rate does not preclude use of the forward hedge to eliminate the risk of an unexpected change in the future spot rate.
7. Recall from Chapter 5 that currency options are priced on the basis of the forward rate. An option that possesses a strike price which is the same as the forward rate is called *forward-at-the-money*.
8. The cost of the $1.71/£ strike put option = £1,000,000 × 0.010 × $1.7640 = $17,640. In future value terms, $17,640 × 1.03 = $18,169.20 ($0.018169/£). The break-even rate versus the forward rate is $1.7540 + $0.0182 = $1.7722/£.

9. This simple measurement practice imposed by accounting practices leads most firms to identify the birth of a transaction exposure as the date it is entered on the firm's balance sheet as a receivable or payable. It is important to remember, however, that the date and spot rate in effect on the date the firm agrees to the transaction—that is, the implicit contract date—gives rise to the transaction exposure economically.

10. The only other way to avoid a foreign exchange loss on a foreign-currency-denominated sale is to be paid cash at the time of sale. A cash purchase would be converted to domestic currency immediately, and no booking of receivables or foreign exchange gains (losses) is required.

11. The International Accounting Standards Committee (IASC) is a body established in 1973 by the leading professional accounting groups of the major industrial countries to formulate and promote the use of a set of global accounting standards, as well as to provide a forum for the harmonization of significant differences in practices across countries.

12. Forward contracts are off-balance sheet liabilities, meaning they are contractual commitments of the firm that do not result in specific on-balance sheet entries. They are, however, legal liabilities of the firm and are normally discussed in the footnotes to the financial statements in the firm's annual report. The Financial Accounting Standards Board (FASB) has, however, recently passed FAS #133, which will require that financial contracts such as forward contracts be on-balance sheet entries. The implementation date of the standard, however, is uncertain.

13. If, for example, the spot rate at the end of the 90-day period was $1.7800/£, the foreign exchange gain on the receivable would be $16,000, while the loss on the forward contract would total $26,000 ($1,754,000 − $1,780,000), for a net loss of $10,000 on the hedged exposure. Although the individual gains (losses) change with the ending spot rate, the net position will not (which is why the position was "hedged" initially).

14. U.S. accounting practices require the firm to value the forward contract and the receivable independently, and at current market value (market-to-market). This procedure is followed for all financial contracts or speculative instruments that any or all firms may enter into.

15. Moffett and Skinner (1995).

16. A partial listing of published research surveys on the foreign exchange management practices of firms would include the following: Batten, Mellor and Wan (1993), Australia; Canada; Hakkarainen, Kasanen, and Puttonen (1994), Finland; Edelshain (1996), United Kingdom; Belk and Glaum (1990), United Kingdom; Aggarwal and Soenen (1989), United Kingdom, Belgium and the Netherlands; Bodnar, Hayt, and Marston (1996), United States; Cezarili (1987), United States; Lessard (1991), United States; Khouri and Chan (1988), United States.

17. Anticipatory hedging programs have been the focus of considerable debate in recent years, particularly the accounting principles that apply to their use.

18. Gunter Dufey, The University of Michigan, undated verbal communication.

19. The most frequently used complex options are range forwards, participating forwards, break forwards, and average rate options. These complex options are described in detail in Chapter 23.

20. A recent article in *The Economist* provided one of the more honest definitions of a *derivative*. "Although derivatives can sometimes be complex, and can require mathematics doctorates to design and price, what they do is actually quite simple: They pro-

vide a low-cost and precise method of transferring risk from those that are exposed to it but would rather not be to those that aren't but would like to be." From "A Survey of Corporate Risk Management," *The Economist*, February 10, 1996, p. 4.

21. An abbreviated list of the derivatives-related losses of recent years would include Allied-Lyons 1991 losses from option speculation, United Kingdom; Shell Showa Sekiyu of Japan's losses in February 1993 resulting from the continual rollover of forward speculative losses from as far back as 1989; Metallgesellschaft of Germany losses related to a flawed petroleum futures hedging strategy in December 1993; Codelco of Chile's copper futures trading losses in January 1994 in which one man is credited with losing 1/2 of 1% of Chile's gross domestic product; Kashima Oil of Japan's April 1994 losses on forward speculation; Procter & Gamble, Gibson Greeting Cards, and Air Products of the United States, as well as Dharmala of Indonesia's losses in Spring 1994 on leveraged swaps purchased from Bankers Trust of the United States; and last, but not least, the failure of Barings Brothers Bank, the oldest investment bank in London at the time, because of the failed market index speculation activities of Mr. Nick Leeson in Singapore in February 1995.

DECISION CASE

Lufthansa[1]

It was February 14, 1986, and Herr Heinz Ruhnau, chairman of Lufthansa (Germany) was summoned to meet with Lufthansa's board. The board's task was to determine if Herr Ruhnau's term of office should be terminated. Herr Ruhnau had already been summoned by Germany's transportation minister to explain his supposed speculative management of Lufthansa's exposure in the purchase of Boeing aircraft.

In January 1985 Lufthansa (Germany), under the chairmanship of Herr Heinz Ruhnau, purchased twenty 737 jets from Boeing (U.S.). The agreed upon price was $500,000,000, payable in U.S. dollars on delivery of the aircraft in one year (January 1986). The U.S. dollar had been rising steadily and rapidly since 1980, and was approximately DM3.2/$ in January 1985. If the dollar were to continue to rise, the cost of the jet aircraft to Lufthansa would rise substantially by the time payment was due.

Herr Ruhnau had his own *view* or expectations regarding the direction of the exchange rate. Like many others at the time, he believed the dollar had risen about as far as it was going to go, and would probably fall by the time January 1986 rolled around. But then again, it really wasn't his money to gamble with. He compromised. He covered half the exposure ($250,000,000) at a rate of DM3.2/$, and left the remaining half ($250,000,000) uncovered.

Evaluation of the Hedging Alternatives

Lufthansa and Herr Ruhnau had the same basic hedging alternatives available to all firms:

1. Remain uncovered;
2. Cover the entire exposure with forward contracts;
3. Cover some proportion of the exposure, leaving the balance uncovered;
4. Cover the exposure with foreign currency options;
5. Obtain U.S. dollars now and hold them until payment is due.

Although the final expense of each alternative could not be known beforehand, each alternative's outcome could be simulated over a range of potential ending exchange rates. Exhibit 1 illustrates the final net cost of the first four alternatives over a wide range of potential end-of-period (January 1986) spot exchange rates.

---

1. Michael H. Moffett, 1993. Reprinted with permission. The author thanks David Eiteman and Arthur Stonehill for significant contributions. This case draws on several major sources including, "Where Options Would Have Made a Difference," Intermarket (November Supplement, 1986), pp. 20, 22; Trading in Currency Options, by William Sutton, New York Institute of Finance (1988), pp. 82–83, and The Financial Times, London (February 24, 1986).

Of course one of the common methods of covering a foreign currency exposure for firms, which involves no use of financial contracts like forwards or options, is the matching of currency cash flows. Lufthansa did have inflows of U.S. dollars on a regular basis as a result of airline ticket purchases in the United States. Although Herr Ruhnau thought briefly about matching these U.S. dollar-denominated cash inflows against the dollar outflows to Boeing, the magnitude of the mismatch was obvious. Lufthansa simply did not receive anything close to $500 million a year in dollar-earnings, or even over several years for that matter.

1: Remain Uncovered

Remaining uncovered is the maximum risk approach. It therefore represents the greatest potential benefits (if the dollar weakens versus the Deutschemark), and the greatest potential cost (if the dollar continues to strengthen versus the Deutschemark). If the exchange rate were to drop to DM2.2/$ by January 1986, the purchase of the Boeing 737s would be only DM1.1 billion. Of course if the dollar continued to appreciate, rising to perhaps DM4.0/$ by 1986, the total cost would be DM2.0 billion. The uncovered position's risk is therefore shown as that value line which has the steepest slope (covers the widest vertical distance) in Exhibit 1. This is obviously a sizable level of risk for any firm to carry. Many firms believe the decision to leave a large exposure uncovered for a long period of time to be nothing other than *currency speculation*.

Exhibit 1   *Lufthansa's Net Cost by Hedging Alternative*

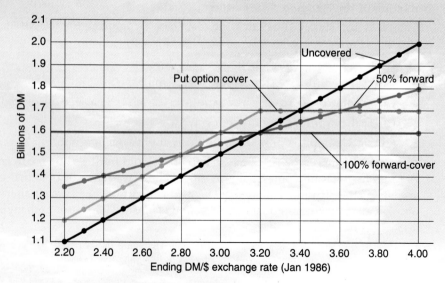

2: Full Forward Cover

If Lufthansa were very risk averse and wished to eliminate fully its currency exposure, it could buy forward contracts for the purchase of U.S. dollars for the entire amount. This would have locked in an exchange rate of DM3.2/$, with a known final cost of DM1.6 billion. This alternative is represented by the horizontal value line in Exhibit 1, the total cost of the Boeing 737s no longer has any risk or sensitivity to the ending spot exchange rate. Most firms believe they should accept or tolerate risk in their *line of business*, not in the process of payment. The 100% forward cover alternative is often used by firms as their benchmark, their comparison measure for actual currency costs when all is said and done.

3: Partial Forward Cover

This alternative would cover only part of the total exposure leaving the remaining exposure uncovered. Herr Ruhnau's expectations were for the dollar to fall, so he expected Lufthansa would benefit from leaving more of the position uncovered (as in alternative 1). This strategy is somewhat arbitrary, however, in that there are few objective methods available for determining what the proper balance (20/80, 40/60, 50/50, etc.) between covered/uncovered should be. Exhibit 1 illustrates the total ending cost of this alternative for a partial cover of 50/50: $250 million purchased with forward contracts of DM3.2/$, and the $250 million remaining purchased at the end-of-period spot rate. Note that this value line's slope is simply half that of the 100% uncovered position. Any other partial cover strategy would similarly fall between the unhedged and 100% cover lines.

Two principal points can be made regarding partial forward cover strategies such as this. First, Herr Ruhnau's total potential exposure is still unlimited. The possibility that the dollar would appreciate to astronomical levels still exists, and $250 million could translate into an infinite amount of Deutschemarks. The second point is that the first point is highly unlikely to occur. Therefore, for the immediate ranges of potential exchange rates on either side of the current spot rate of DM3.2/$, Herr Ruhnau has reduced the risk (vertical distance in Exhibit 1) of the final Deutschemark outlay over a range of ending values and the benchmark value of DM3.2/$.

4: Foreign Currency Options

The foreign currency option is unique among the hedging alternatives due to its kinked-shape value line. If Herr Ruhnau had purchased a put option on marks at DM3.2/$, he could have obtained what many people believe is the best of both worlds. If the dollar had continued to strengthen above DM3.2/$, the total cost of obtaining $500 million could be locked in at DM1.6 billion plus the cost of the option premium, as illustrated by the flat portion of the option alternative to the right of DM3.2/$.[2] If, however, the dollar fell as Herr Ruhnau had expected,

---

2. Interest expenses on the option premium are ignored in this case for simplicity of calculation.

Lufthansa would be free to let the option expire and purchase the dollars at lower cost on the spot market. This alternative is shown by the falling value line to the left of DM3.2/$. Note that the put option line falls at the same rate (same slope) as the uncovered position, but is higher by the cost of purchasing the option.

In this instance Herr Ruhnau would have had to buy put options for DM1.6 billion given an exercise price of DM3.2/$. In January 1985 when Herr Heinz Ruhnau was thinking over these alternatives, the option premium on Deutschemark put options was about 6%, equal to DM96,000,000 or $30,000,000! The total cost of the purchase in the event the put option was exercised would be DM1,696,000,000 (exercise plus premium).

It is important to understand what Herr Ruhnau would be hoping to happen if he had decided to purchase the put options. He would be expecting the dollar to weaken (ending up to the left of DM3.2/$ in Exhibit 1), therefore he would expect the option to expire without value. In the eyes of many corporate treasurers, DM96,000,000 is a lot of money for the purchase of an instrument that the hedger expects or hopes not to use!

5: Buy Dollars Now

The fifth alternative is a money market hedge for an account payable: Obtain the $500 million now and hold those funds in an interest-bearing account or asset until payment was due. Although this would eliminate the currency exposure, it required that Lufthansa have all the capital in hand now. The purchase of the Boeing jets had been made in conjunction with the ongoing financing plans of Lufthansa, and these did not call for the capital to be available until January 1986. An added concern (and what ultimately eliminated this alternative from consideration) was that Lufthansa had several relatively strict covenants in place that limited the types, amounts, and currencies of denomination of the items it could carry on its balance sheet.

Herr Ruhnau's Decision

Although Herr Ruhnau truly expected the dollar to weaken over the coming year, he believed remaining completely uncovered was too risky for Lufthansa. Few would argue this, particularly given the strong upward trend of the DM/$ exchange rate as seen in Exhibit 2. The dollar had shown a consistent three-year trend of appreciation versus the Deutschemark, and that trend seemed to be accelerating over the most recent year.

Because he personally felt so strongly the dollar would weaken, Herr Ruhnau chose to go with partial cover. He chose to cover 50% of the exposure ($250 million) with forward contracts (the one-year forward rate was DM3.2/$) and to leave the remaining 50% ($250 million) uncovered. Because foreign currency options were as yet a relatively new tool for exposure management by many firms, and because of the sheer magnitude of the up-front premium required, the foreign currency option was not chosen. Time would tell if this was a wise decision.

| **Exhibit 2** | *What Herr Ruhnau Could See: The Rise* |

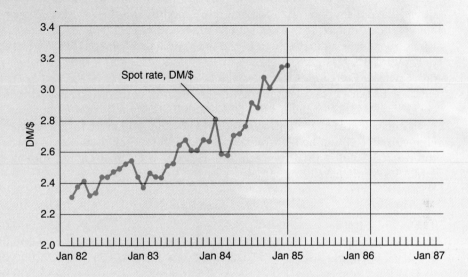

Spot rate, DM/$

| **Exhibit 3** | *What Herr Ruhnau Couldn't See: The Fall* |

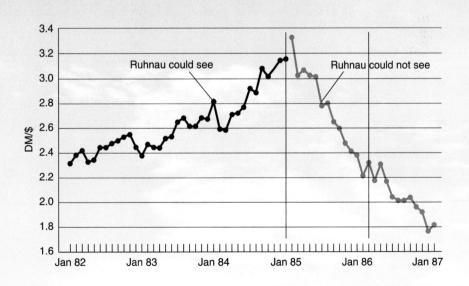

Ruhnau could see

Ruhnau could not see

How It Came Out

Herr Ruhnau was both right and wrong. He was definitely right in his expectations. The dollar appreciated for one more month, and then weakened over the coming year. In fact, it did not simply *weaken*, it plummeted. By January 1986 when payment was due to Boeing, the spot rate had fallen to DM2.3/$ from the previous year's DM3.2/$ as shown in Exhibit 3. This was a spot exchange rate movement in Lufthansa's favor.

The bad news was that the total Deutschemark cost with the partial forward cover was DM1.375 billion, a full DM225,000,000 more than if no hedging had been implemented at all! This was also DM129,000,000 more than what the foreign currency option hedge would have cost in total. The total cost of obtaining the needed $500 million for each alternative at the actual ending spot rate of DM2.3/$ would have been:

Alternative	Relevant Rate	Total DM Cost
1: Uncovered	DM2.3/$	1,150,000,000
2: Full Forward Cover (100%)	DM3.2/$	1,600,000,000
3: Partial Forward Cover	1/2(DM2.3) + 1/2(DM3.2)	1,375,000,000
4: DM Put Options	DM3.2/$ strike	1,246,000,000

Herr Ruhnau's political rivals, both inside and outside of Lufthansa, were not so happy. Ruhnau was accused of recklessly speculating with Lufthansa's money, but the *speculation* was seen as the forward contract, not the amount of the dollar exposure left uncovered for the full year. It is obvious that the term *speculation* holds an entirely new meaning when perfect hindsight is used to evaluate performance.

Case Questions

Herr Ruhnau was accused of making the following four mistakes:

1. Purchasing the Boeing aircraft at the wrong time. The U.S. dollar was at an all-time high at the time of the purchase in January 1985.

2. Choosing to hedge half the exposure when he expected the dollar to fall. If he had gone through with his instincts or expectations, he would have left the whole amount unhedged (which some critics have termed "whole hog").

3. Choosing to use forward contracts as his hedging tool instead of options. The purchase of put options would have allowed Herr Ruhnau to protect himself against adverse exchange rate movements while preserving the flexibility of exchanging DM for U.S. dollars spot if the market moved in his favor.

4. Purchasing Boeing aircraft at all. Germany, as well as the other major European Economic Community countries, has a vested interest in the joint venture Airbus. Airbus's chief rival was Boeing in the manufacture of large long-distance civil aircraft.

Given these criticisms, should the board of Lufthansa retain Herr Heinz Ruhnau as chairman? How should Ruhnau justify his actions and so justify his further employment?

DECISION CASE

ZAPA Chemical and BuBa

> ". . . there is a tendency in Europe to treat the exchange rate as a type
> of virility symbol. I, myself, have never felt the need for such a symbol."
> —British Prime Minister Margaret Thatcher

Stephanie Mayo, currency analyst for ZAPA Chemical of Cleveland, stared at her Reuters screen, her option pricing screen, and then out the window. It was Monday, September 21, 1992, and the markets seemed much calmer this morning. The French had voted *oui* by 50.95% to *non* of 49.05% to approve the Maastricht treaty the previous day. Stephanie was now debating what to do about her put option on Deutschemarks she had been holding for the last month.

The Original Exposure and Rate View

Stephanie had originally been given the exposure for management in mid-August. ZAPA Chemical had sold a specialty chemical distributorship in Stuttgart, Germany. The proceeds of the sale, approximately DM7.6 million, would be brought back to the United States sometime in November. Because of special tax and sales document filings in Germany, it could not yet be determined when exactly the funds would be available for repatriation.

The U.S. dollar had been falling like a rock since late March. The central bank of Germany, the Bundesbank, or as it is affectionately known—"BuBa," had added momentum to the drop when it had increased the German base lending rate by 75 basis points (3/4 of a percent) to 9.75% on July 16th. By August 17th, when Steph was given the exposure, the DM/$ rate looked as if it had settled down to a historically weak dollar of DM1.4649/$ (see Exhibit 1). At that time Steph had debated whether the dollar was as low as it was going to go, or just hesitating before sliding further. Steph felt there were a number of forces which could drive the dollar still lower.

- **The Bundesbank.** The Bundesbank had become very high profile in the last month as German interest rates continued to rise. The Bundesbank was slowing monetary growth to a crawl and driving interest rates up, all in an effort to stop the inflationary forces resulting from reunification. Of the many rumors emanating from the central bank, the ones about further interest rate hikes were the loudest.

Exhibit 1	*The Falling Value of the U.S. Dollar Versus the Deutschemark (Friday closing, Jan–Aug 1992)*

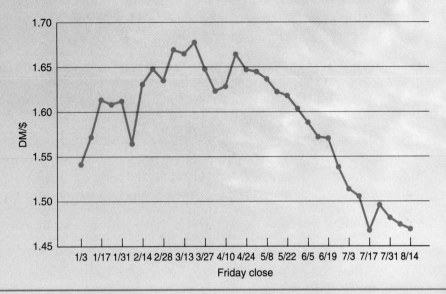

Friday close

- **Dollar-DM Interest Differentials.** The anemic growth of the U.S. economy continued. The U.S. Federal Reserve was attempting to provide needed stimulus through lower interest rates. The United States was now enjoying the lowest interest rates in twenty years. The high interest rates in Germany and the low interest rates in the U.S., an unusual scenario by any account, was resulting in a massive capital flow from dollar-denominated assets into Deutschemarks.

  Three-month Eurodollar deposits were paying 3.3125%, while similar Euro-Deutschemark deposits were paying 9.750%. And there were no signs of either rate moving toward the other.

- **The French Vote on the Maastricht Treaty.** The European Community had now painted itself into a corner with the escalating debate on the willingness of individual countries to actually pursue true European economic integration. The Maastricht Treaty had been signed by the Council of Ministers in December 1991, but had to be ratified by each country. The Treaty had formalized the steps and timetable for the adoption of a single European banking system and currency by the end of the decade. But the Danes had voted no in June 1992, when the French vote was pending. The outcome had been impossible to call. The vote was September 20th.

- **Stress in the European Monetary System (EMS).** Not only were the high German interest rates causing a strengthening of the DM versus the dollar, but for the same reasons, they were putting pressure on all EMS currencies as they tried to maintain their parities with the Deutschemark. The Italian lira and the British pound were both trading at the bottom of their allowable ranges (according to the agreed ranges within the Exchange Rate Mechanism (ERM) of the EMS) versus the Deutschemark.

To top it all off, 1992 was an election year in the United States. In mid-August President George Bush was 18 to 20 percentage points behind Democratic presidential candidate Bill Clinton in the polls. The markets had historically favored and rewarded Republican economic policies as opposed to the policies of the Democrats.

The Risk Tolerance of ZAPA

ZAPA was a rather unusual firm in its approach to currency risk management. Although the parent corporation, ZAPA Oil, did not use foreign currency options for risk management, ZAPA Chemical used them exclusively. Because of losses caused by forward contracts in the previous year, Zapa's Treasury now used foreign exchange options whenever possible. If needed, synthetic forwards were created by simply buying calls and selling puts for the same strike prices and maturities (or vice versa).

ZAPA Chemical considered Treasury a cost-center. Treasury therefore saw its primary responsibility as conservative management of exposures. Profit through currency speculation was not its purpose. In addition to an in-house aversion to forwards, the group could not write uncovered options (with their corresponding unlimited loss potential). The fiasco in 1991 at Allied-Lyons, the British food conglomerate, had sparked an internal review of all activities of international treasury at ZAPA Chemical. Allied-Lyons had suffered losses of $150 million as a result of unwise and uncontrolled currency speculation. Although ZAPA did not in any way mirror Allied-Lyons, the review had resulted in the exclusion of writing uncovered call options, as well as the requirement that the use of new instruments be allowed only after approval of the operating committee. But, all things considered, management was appreciative when the expenses of running the cost-center were lower.

Hedge Decision: August 17th

On August 17th the Deutschemark had traded around the DM1.4649/$ point all day. After discussion with her risk manager, Steph had decided that a safety net was called for. Her logic was relatively simple. First, she believed that the dollar would fall further. Most currency forecasters felt the dollar was already at bottom, but then again, they had said the same thing at the magic DM1.50/$ level. She believed the DM would move in her favor. Secondly, although she held the directional view of dollar-down, she also felt there were too many unknowns to feel secure. Currency volatility would by all guesses increase in the coming 4 to 6 weeks, with uncertainty over Bundesbank policies rising and the French vote on Maastricht forthcoming.

Before making her decision, Steph had reviewed an alternative which was not considered by ZAPA to be a true alternative: the forward. The coming volatility of the markets—and Stephanie felt sure that things would be heating up—posed many uncertainties. Selling the entire DM exposure forward would at least allow her to sleep nights. But there were two distinctly negative characteristics of the forward at this time. First, the huge interest differentials between U.S. dollar and Deutschemark assets resulted in forward rates which were extremely unattractive. The 120-day forward on August 17 was DM1.4957/$. Given the spot rate of DM1.4649/$, this was an annual discount of nearly 6.2%—expensive protection. By selling the Deutschemarks forward she would be locking in a rate which she sincerely felt was in the wrong direction from that which the spot rate would move. The forward was quite unattractive.

The safety net Steph had chosen was an out-of-the-money (OTM) put option (bank option) on Deutschemarks. Gotham Bank (NY) was willing to sell ZAPA a December put on the DM7.6 million for a premium of 1.40 cents per DM ($0.0140/DM) for a strike of 66 ($0.66/DM or DM1.5152/$). This was a total outlay of $106,400 for the DM December put option. Although seemingly a lot of money, the option price was a paltry 2.1% premium ($0.0140 ÷ $0.6600/DM) for a substantial amount of protection against a dollar rebound.

Steph, as she did with all her major stand-alone exposures, took a look at her option position versus the totally unhedged and total forward cover alternatives. Exhibit 2 reproduces her exposure valuation analysis. The put option's value

---

Exhibit 2   *Hedge Alternatives for ZAPA Chemical's DM Exposure (millions of US$)*

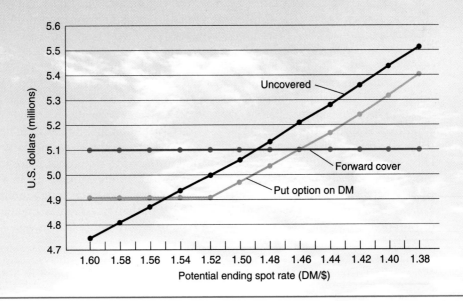

would parallel the uncovered position, but with the added benefit of a safety net if the spot rate were to actually move in the opposite direction.

Daily Position Monitoring

Given the size of the position and the tension in the markets, Steph had watched the markets and the DM put option position daily. The next two weeks yielded good news and bad news. The good news was that Steph's intuition had been right on target. The dollar had declined rapidly in the days following her put option purchase, so that the prospective dollar value of the DM7.6 million was rising by the minute. The bad news, however, was that the December 66 put option was also falling, falling in value. As the put option had moved further and further out-of-the-money, the market value of the option (the premium) had fallen.

By September 1st the U.S. dollar was at an all-time low of DM1.39/$, and the option's premium was approximately 0.50 cents per DM. The potential loss on the option was $68,400.

$$(\$.0050/DM - \$.0140/DM) \times DM7,600,000 = (\$68,400)$$

Although it was a bit unsettling when expressed in this manner, Steph recognized that this was what the corporate hedger wanted to happen when purchasing an OTM put option for protection. The U.S. dollar declined to approximately DM1.40/$ and stayed there for the first two workweeks of September. Stephanie watched and waited.

September Turbulence

The week of September 14th had been a literal nightmare. The dollar had fallen, risen, and fallen again. The British pound had been withdrawn from the ERM. The Italian lira had been first devalued by over 7%, then finally withdrawn from the ERM as it came under further pressure. The Spanish peseta had been devalued 5% in the ERM. Other currencies had come under speculative attacks on Friday. The high interest rates in Germany had continued to bleed capital out of the other major European capital markets. Exhibit 3 reviews the roller coaster of events in these turbulent times.

In Great Britain the events of the previous weeks continued to have substantial news value. With the pound still floating freely against the Deutschemark, the long-standing critics of Britain's participation in the EMS were once more making a lot of noise. The leading critic, former British Prime Minister Lady Margaret Thatcher (often known as the "iron-maiden" for her tough political stands), commented in a speech on September 20th that ". . . there is a tendency in Europe to treat the exchange rate as a type of virility symbol. I, myself, have never felt the need for such a symbol."

The cynics still seemed to have carried the day. Many EC analysts saw the Maastricht Treaty and the idea of economic integration as something of a dead

| **Exhibit 3** | *EMS in Crisis: The Events of September 1992* |

Sept 1	The U.S. dollar falls below DM1.39/$.
Sept 4	The Italian lira trades below the ERM floor. Italian central bank raises discount rate from 13.25% to 15% to protect the lira.
Sept 6	EC finance ministers and central bank governors reaffirm their unwillingness to realign the EMS and promise massive intervention to protect the status quo.
Sept 8	Finland announces that it will no longer fix the markka to the ECU following a week of increasing speculation against the markka. The markka immediately falls against the DM and the dollar. The Swedish krona is hit by speculation as capital flows accelerate out of the Nordic countries into Deutschemark-denominated assets; Swedish monetary authorities begin raising interest rates to protect the krona.
Sept 9	Swedish central bank raises interest rates from 24% to 75% and plans to raise up to ECU 31 billion to protect the krona. Bundesbank is quoted as believing the Italian lira, Spanish peseta, and British pound should be devalued.
Sept 13	The Bundesbank cuts the Lombard borrowing rate, the base bank borrowing rate, by 25 basis points, from 9.75% to 9.50%. It is the first interest rate cut by the Bundesbank in five years. Italy/EMS announce that the Italian lira will be devalued by 7.6%. The Netherlands, Belgium, Austria, and Switzerland announce that their interest rates will be allowed to fall. Sweden announces that it will lower its marginal lending rate, the rate of interest which governs overnight interest rates between banks, to 20%.
Sept 14	The currency markets react favorably, the dollar rising from Friday's close of DM1.44/$ to DM1.49/$, a 2.4% appreciation. The markets wait for more interest rate cuts from the Bundesbank.
Sept 15	Bundesbank president Helmut Schlesinger makes it clear in an interview that the German monetary authority has not changed course toward expansionary policy. The Italian lira finds itself once more under attack as no interest rate cuts follow Sunday's devaluation. Rumors abound that Giuliano Amato, the Italian Prime Minister, is about to resign. The British pound comes under increasing speculative pressure as it falls below the allowed floor value against the Deutschemark.
Sept 16	The Bank of England raises its base lending rate to defend the falling British pound. By afternoon the Bank considers a further rate increase, but instead withdraws from the Exchange Rate Mechanism (ERM) of the EMS. Sweden raises the base lending rate from 75% to 500% to stop speculators from shorting the krona. Currency volatilities and option premiums skyrocket as crisis continues.
Sept 17	The Bundesbank refuses all pressure to cut German interest rates. The Spanish peseta is devalued 5% in the European Monetary System grid. The Italian lira withdraws from the exchange rate mechanism of the EMS. Official trading in the lira is suspended until the following Tuesday. The U.S. dollar falls from the previous day's high against the Deutschemark in response to rumors that the Bundesbank may be waiting to cut interest rates until after Sunday's French vote on Maastricht.
Sept 18	Sweden announces that it will cut the bank borrowing rate from 500% to 50%. The markets remain tense as all is put on hold awaiting the results of the French referendum on Sunday the 20th.
Sept 20	The French vote on the Maastricht Treaty and its proposed monetary unification of the EC.

issue. The fundamental economic pressures which had led to the currency events of the first weeks of September were still present: extremely high interest differentials between Germany and the United States; extreme devaluation pressures on most of the currencies of the EMS versus the Deutschemark.

Steph now wished to reevaluate her put option hedge position on the DM exposure. She knew that the DM7.6 million would be repatriated to the American parent on December 15th. This would match the maturity of the DM put option's expiration. But the massive volatility in the markets in the week before the September 20th vote had sent option values straight up. Steph was wondering whether it would be better to sell her put option and either cover the position with a forward or wait a few days until the markets calmed to replace the put position.

Steph quickly downloaded data on the daily spot rate and the December put option premium value. The graphic results of the comparison are shown in Exhibit 4. The put option premium had closed at 1.95 cents per DM on Friday (September 18th), while the spot and 90-day forward rates were DM1.5015/$ and DM1.5255/$, respectively. 90-day Eurocurrency interest rates had not changed since August. Steph thought she would have to move fast if—and it was a big if— she wished to sell her option while values (and volatilities) were still high.

Exhibit 4   *Daily Changes in the DM/$ Spot Rate and the DM Put Option Premium*

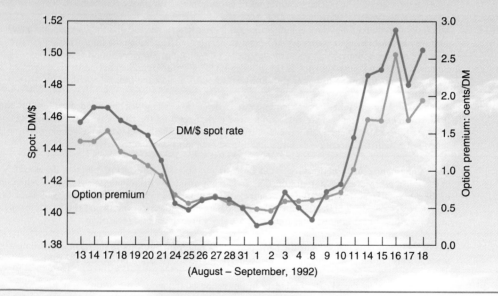

(August – September, 1992)

CHAPTER 7

OPERATING EXPOSURE

This chapter extends the concept of transaction exposure, described in Chapter 6, further into time and across the many cash flows that comprise the value of any multinational firm. *Operating exposure*, also called *economic exposure, competitive exposure,* and even *strategic exposure* on occasion, measures any change in the present value of a firm resulting from changes in future operating cash flows caused by any *unexpected* change in exchange rates. *Operating exposure analysis* assesses the impact of changing exchange rates over coming months and years on a firm's own operations and on its competitive position vis-á-vis other firms. The goal is to identify strategic moves or operating techniques the firm might wish to adopt to enhance its value in the face of unexpected exchange rate changes.

Operating exposure and transaction exposure are related in that they both deal with future cash flows. They differ in terms of which cash flows are looked at and why those cash flows change when exchange rates change.

ATTRIBUTES OF OPERATING EXPOSURE

Operating exposure of the firm requires forecasting and analyzing all the firm's future individual transaction exposures together with the future exposures of all the firm's competitors and potential competitors worldwide. A simple example may clarify the point.

A multinational enterprise (MNE) like Eastman Kodak (U.S.) possesses a number of transaction exposures at any point in time. Kodak has sales in the United States, Japan, and Europe and therefore possesses a continuing series of foreign currency receivables (and payables). Sales and expenses that are already contracted for are traditional *transaction exposures*. Sales that are highly probable based on Kodak's historical business line and market shares, but that have no legal basis yet, are *anticipated transaction exposures.*

Suppose the analysis of the firm's exposure to exchange rate changes is extended even further into the future. What are the longer-term

Case Questions

1. Should Stephanie Mayo sell the put option protection already in pla the current market rates and prices to defend your logic.

2. How have the events of September altered Stephanie's view of th exchange rate?

3. How has the volatility of the put option changed between August tember?

4. If you were the Vice President for Treasury at Zapa, what *benchmar* you use to measure Stephanie's hedging effectiveness? How would Stephanie's hedging?

exposures of Kodak to exchange rate changes? The impact on the firm's cash flows from future exchange rate changes will not only alter the domestic currency value (U.S. dollars in this case) of foreign currency cash flows; it will also change the quantity of foreign currency cash flows generated. The changes in Kodak's cash flows in the future will be dependent on how competitive it is in various markets. Kodak's international competitiveness will in turn be affected by the operating exposures of its major competitors like Fuji (Japan) and Agfa (Germany). The goal of operating exposure analysis is to predict the longer-term cash flow impact of unanticipated exchange rate changes.

))) Operating and Financing Cash Flows

The cash flows of the MNE can be divided into *operating cash flows* and *financing cash flows*. *Operating cash flows* arise from intercompany (between unrelated companies) and intracompany (between units of the same company) receivables and payables, rent and lease payments for the use of facilities and equipment, royalty and license fees for the use of technology and intellectual property, and assorted management fees for services provided. *Financing cash flows* are payments for the use of intercompany and intracompany loans (principal and interest), and stockholder equity (new equity investments and dividends). Each of these cash flows can occur at different time intervals, in different amounts, in different currencies of denomination, and with a different degree of predictability. Cash flow possibilities can be summarized as in Exhibit 7.1.

))) Expected versus Unexpected Changes in Cash Flow

Operating exposure is far more important for the long-run health of a business entity than changes caused by transaction or accounting exposure. However,

---

Exhibit 7.1   *Financial and Operating Cash Flows between a Parent and Affiliate*

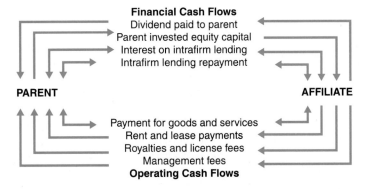

operating exposure is inevitably subjective because it depends on estimates of future cash flow changes over an arbitrary time horizon. Thus, operating exposure does not spring from the accounting process but rather derives from operating analysis. Planning for operating exposure is a total management responsibility because it involves the interaction of strategies in finance, marketing, purchasing, and production.

An *expected* change in foreign exchange rates is not included in the definition of operating exposure because both management and investors should have factored this information into their evaluation of anticipated operating results and market value. From a management perspective, budgeted financial statements already reflect information about the effect of an expected change in exchange rates. For example, under equilibrium conditions the forward rate might be used as an unbiased predictor of the future spot rate. In such a case, management would use the forward rate when preparing the operating budgets, rather than assume the spot rate would remain unchanged.

Another example is that expected cash flow to amortize debt should already reflect the international Fisher effect. The level of expected interest and principal repayment should be a function of expected exchange rates rather than existing spot rates.

From an investor's perspective, if the foreign exchange market is efficient, information about expected changes in exchange rates should be widely known and thus reflected in a firm's market value. Only unexpected changes in exchange rates, or an inefficient foreign exchange market, should cause market value to change.

From a broader perspective, operating exposure is not just the sensitivity of a firm's future cash flows to unexpected changes in foreign exchange rates, but also its sensitivity to other key macroeconomic variables. This factor has been labeled as macroeconomic uncertainty. Chapter 3 described the parity relationships between exchange rates, interest rates, and inflation rates. However, these variables are often in disequilibrium with one another. Therefore, unexpected changes in interest rates and inflation rates could also have a simultaneous but differential impact on future cash flows.

ILLUSTRATIVE CASE

Volvo Car

Volvo Car, a subsidiary of Volvo (Sweden), illustrates a MNE's sensitivity to various macroeconomic variables including exchange rates, interest rates, and prices, i.e., *macroeconomic uncertainty*. Volvo Car produces most of its cars in Sweden but buys most of its inputs from Germany. The company's most important market is the United States. Top management of Volvo Car, as well as most financial analysts, believed that a Swedish krona depreciating versus the U.S. dollar and appreciating versus the Deutschemark would be beneficial to Volvo Car. Volvo Car's cash flows were statistically analyzed for their sensitivity to relevant macroeconomic variables. However, three variables explained most of the unanticipated variability of cash flows. The three variables were:

1. The Swedish krona/Deutschemark exchange rates. A depreciating krona improved Volvo Car's cash flows.

2. The Swedish krona short-term interest rate. A reduction in this rate improved Volvo Car's cash flow due to increased demand for its cars.

3. German producer prices. An increase in these prices improved Volvo Car's cash flow.

These results reflected the fact that Volvo Car's major competitors were the German prestige car manufacturers, BMW, Mercedes, and Audi. Thus measurement of Volvo Car's long-term operating exposure depended on how its competitors were situated with respect to unexpected changes in the same key macroeconomic variables, such as foreign exchange rates, interest rates, and inflation rates.

The most recent version of macroeconomic uncertainty on future cash flows is Oxelheim and Wihlborg (1997). This case was written before the introduction of the euro.

MEASURING THE IMPACT OF OPERATING EXPOSURE

An unexpected change in exchange rates impacts a firm's expected cash flows at four levels, depending on the time horizon used.[1]

⟫⟫ Short Run

The first-level impact is on expected cash flows in the one-year operating budget. The gain or loss depends on the currency of denomination of expected cash flows. The currency of denomination cannot be changed for existing obligations, such as those defined by transaction exposure, or even for implied obligations such as purchase or sales commitments. Apart from real or implied obligations, in the short run it is difficult to change sales prices or renegotiate factor costs. Therefore, realized cash flows will differ from those expected in the budget. However, as time passes, prices and costs can be changed to reflect the new competitive realities caused by a change in exchange rates.

⟫⟫ Medium Run: Equilibrium Case

The second-level impact is on expected medium-run cash flows, such as those expressed in two- to five-year budgets, assuming parity conditions hold among foreign exchange rates, national inflation rates, and national interest rates. Under equilibrium conditions the firm should be able to adjust prices and factor costs over time to maintain the expected level of cash flows. In this case the currency of denomination of expected cash flows is not as important as the countries in which cash flows originate. National monetary, fiscal, and balance of payments policies determine whether equilibrium conditions will exist and whether firms will be allowed to adjust prices and costs.

If equilibrium exists continuously, and a firm is free to adjust its prices and costs to maintain its expected competitive position, its operating exposure may be zero. Its expected cash flows would be realized and therefore its market value unchanged because the exchange rate change was anticipated. However, it is also possible that equilibrium conditions exist but the firm is unwilling or unable to adjust operations to the new competitive environment. In such a case the firm would experience operating exposure because its realized cash flows would differ from expected cash flows. As a result, its market value might also be altered.

))) Medium Run: Disequilibrium Case

The third-level impact is on expected medium-run cash flows assuming disequilibrium conditions. In this case the firm may not be able to adjust prices and costs to reflect the new competitive realities caused by a change in exchange rates. The firm's realized cash flows will differ from its expected cash flows. The firm's market value may change because of the unanticipated results.

))) Long Run

The fourth-level impact is on expected long-run cash flows, meaning those beyond five years. At this strategic level a firm's cash flows will be influenced by the reactions of existing and potential competitors to exchange rate changes under disequilibrium conditions. In fact, all firms that are subject to international competition, whether they are purely domestic or multinational, are exposed to foreign exchange operating exposure in the long run whenever foreign exchange markets are not continuously in equilibrium.

ILLUSTRATION OF OPERATING EXPOSURE

To illustrate the consequences of operating exposure in the short- and medium-run cases, we will develop a hypothetical example of a MNE, Jefferson Controls. Exhibit 7.2 shows possible cash flows for Jefferson Controls, Inc., a U.S.-based MNE, and its wholly owned affiliates, Instruments du Rhone, S.A. in France, and Canadian Instruments, Inc. in Vancouver. The parent firm also trades directly with nonaffiliated firms in Mexico. In addition to the obvious transaction exposures arising from Jefferson Control's imports from Mexico, the firm has both operational and financial cash flows with its French and Canadian affiliates. From the perspective of Jefferson Controls, dollars invested in the subsidiary have a 20% required rate of return after taxes.

))) Base Case

Instruments du Rhone manufactures in France from European material and labor. Half of production is sold within Europe for euros, and half is exported to

Exhibit 7.2   *Cash Flows of Jefferson Controls, a U.S.-Based MNE with French and Canadian Affiliates and Trade with Mexico*

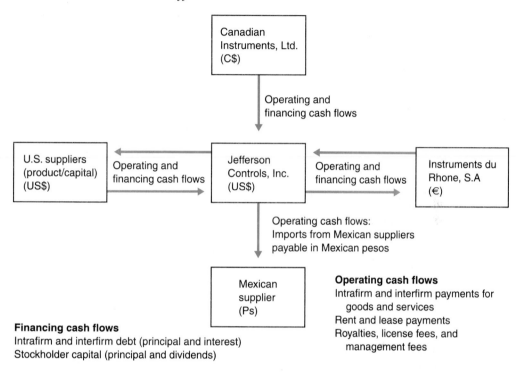

non-European countries. All sales are invoiced in euros, and accounts receivable are equal to one-fourth of annual sales. In other words, the average collection period is 90 days. Inventory is also equal to one-fourth of annual sales and is carried at direct cost, which equals 75% of sales price. Instruments du Rhone can expand or contract production volume without any significant change in per-unit direct costs or in overall general and administrative expenses. Depreciation on plant and equipment is €600,000 per year, and the corporate income tax in France is 34.00%. The December 2001 balance sheet is shown in Exhibit 7.3

In the example in Exhibit 7.3, we assume that on January 1, 2002, before any commercial activity begins, the euro unexpectedly drops 16.67% in value, from $1.2000/€ to $1.0000/€. If no devaluation had occurred, Instruments du Rhone was expected to perform in 2001 as shown in the top ¾ of Exhibit 7.3, generating a dollar cash flow from operations expressed in U.S. dollars of $2,074,320.

Operating exposure depends on whether an unexpected change in exchange rates causes unanticipated changes in sales volume, sales prices, or operating

Exhibit 7.3	*Instruments du Rhone, S.A.*

Base Case: Beginning Balance Sheet and Expected Cash Flows

Balance Sheet, December 31, 2001

Cash	€1,600,000	Accounts payable	€ 800,000
Accounts receivable	3,200,000	Short-term bank loan	1,600,000
Inventory	2,400,000	Long-term debt	1,600,000
Net plant and equipment	4,800,000	Common stock	1,800,000
		Retained earnings	6,200,000
	€12,000,000		€12,000,000

Expected Cash Flow, No Devaluation, Year 2002

Sales (1,000,000 units @ €12.80/unit)	€12,800,000
Direct costs (1,000,000 units @ €9.60/unit)	9,600,000
Cash operating expenses (fixed)	890,000
Depreciation	600,000
Pretax profit	€ 1,710,000
Income tax expenses (34.0%)	581,400
Profit after tax	€ 1,128,600
Add back depreciation	600,000
Cash flow from operations, in euros	€ 1,728,600
Times existing exchange rate: $1.2000/€	
Cash flow from operations, in U.S. dollars	$2,074,320

Case 1: Devaluation (nothing else changes)

Expected Cash Flow with Devaluation, Year 2002

Cash flow from operations, in euros	€ 1,728,600
Times existing exchange rate: $1.0000/€	
Cash flow from operations, in U.S. dollars	$1,728,600

costs. Following a euro devaluation, Instruments du Rhone might choose to maintain its domestic sales prices constant in euro terms, or it might try to raise domestic prices because competing imports are now priced higher in Europe. The firm might choose to keep export prices constant in terms of foreign currencies, in terms of euros, or somewhere in between. The strategy undertaken depends to a large measure on management's opinion about the price elasticity of demand. On the cost side, Instruments du Rhone might raise prices because of more expensive imported raw material or components, or perhaps because all domestic prices in France have risen and labor is now demanding higher wages to compensate for domestic inflation.

Instruments du Rhone's domestic sales and costs might also be partly determined by the effect of the euro devaluation on demand. To the extent that the devaluation stimulates purchases of European, including French, goods in import-competing sectors of the economy as well as greater exports of French goods, both caused by initially more competitive prices of French goods, French national income should increase. This assumes that the favorable effect of a euro devaluation on comparative prices is not immediately offset by higher domestic inflation. Thus, Instruments de Rhone might be able to sell more goods domestically because of price and income effects and internationally because of price effects.

To illustrate the effect of various post-devaluation scenarios on Instruments Jefferson's operating exposure in France, consider three simple cases:

Case 1: No change in any variable.

Case 2: Increase in sales volume; other variables remain constant.

Case 3: Increase in sales price; other variables remain constant.

To calculate the net change in present value under each of the scenarios, a five-year time horizon will be used for any change in cash flow induced by the change in the dollar/euro exchange rate.

Case 1: No Change in Any Variable.

Assume that in the five years ahead no changes occur in sale volume, sales price, or operating costs. Profits for the coming year in euros will be as expected, and cash flow from operations will be €1,728,600, as shown in Exhibit 7.3. With a new exchange rate of $1.0000/€, next year's cash flow measured in dollars will be €1,728,600 × $1.0000/€ = $1,728,600. The difference in first-year cash flow in dollars, if the euro drops 10% in value at once, will be:

Expected dollar value of first year cash flow, no devaluation:	$2,074,320
Realized dollar value of first year cash flow, with devaluation:	–1,728,600
Decrease in dollar value of first year cash flow:	$ 345,720

Instruments du Rhone thus experiences a drop of $345,720 in the dollar value of its euro cash flow. If this drop continues over the five-year time horizon, the total reduction in net cash flow will be $345,720 × 5 = $1,728,600. The discounted present value of this series of diminished dollar-value cash flows is considered later in this chapter.

Case 2: Volume Increases; Other Variables Remain Constant

Assume that, following the devaluation, sales within Europe double because French-made instruments are now more competitive with imports. Additionally, export volume doubles because French-made instruments are now cheaper in countries whose currencies have not weakened. The sales price is kept constant in euro terms because management of Instruments du Rhone has not observed any change in local French operating costs and because it sees an opportunity to increase market share.

Expected cash flow for the following year would be as described in Exhibit 7.4. The cash flow shown in the first year, however, is not available because a

Exhibit 7.4	*Instruments du Rhone, S.A.*

Case 2: Volume Doubles

Expected Cash Flow, After Devaluation, Year 2002

Sales (2,000,000 units @ €12.80/unit)	€25,600,000
Direct costs (2,000,000 units @ €9.60/unit)	(19,200,000)
Cash operating expenses (fixed)	(890,000)
Depreciation	(600,000)
Pretax profit	€4,910,000
Income tax expenses (34.0%)	(1,669,400)
Profit after tax	€3,240,600
Add back depreciation	600,000
Cash flow from operations, in euros	€ 3,840,600
Times existing exchange rate: $1.0000/€	
Cash flow from operations, in U.S. dollars	$ 3,840,600

Projected Cash Flow from Operations (2002–2006)

Year	Item	In Euros (€)	U.S. Dollars @ $1.0000/€
1	Cash flow from operations	3,840,600	
	Less required increase in working capital	(5,600,000)	
	Net cash flow, first year	(1,759,400)	(1,759,400)
2	Cash flow from operations	3,840,600	3,840,600
3	Cash flow from operations	3,840,600	3,840,600
4	Cash flow from operations	3,840,600	3,840,600
5	Cash flow from operations	3,840,600	3,840,600
	Working capital recaptured in year 5	5,600,000	5,600,000

doubling of sales volume will require additional investment in accounts receivable and in inventory. Although a portion of this additional investment might be financed by increasing accounts payable, we assume additional working capital is financed by cash flow from operations.

At the end of the first year, accounts receivable will be equal to one-fourth of annual sales, or €6,400,000. This amount is twice receivables of €3,200,000 at the end of the prior year, and the incremental increase of €3,200,000 must be financed from available cash. Year-end inventory would be equal to one-fourth of annual direct costs, or €4,800,000, an increase of €2,400,000 over the year-beginning level. Receivables and inventory together increase by €5,600,000 (i.e., €3,200,000 + €2,400,000). At the end of five years these incremental cash out-flows will be recaptured because any investment in current assets eventually rolls back into cash.

Assuming no further change in volume, price, or costs, cash inflows for the five years would be as described in the bottom half of Exhibit 7.4. In this instance the devaluation causes a major drop in first-year cash flow from the $1,728,600 anticipated in the first year without devaluation to a negative cash flow of $1,759,400. However the remaining four years' cash flow is substantially enhanced by the operating effects of the devaluation. Over time Instruments du Rhone generates significantly more cash for its owners. The devaluation produces an operating *gain* over time, rather than an operating *loss*.

The reason that Instruments du Rhone is better off in Case 2 following the devaluation is that sales volume doubled, while the per-unit dollar-equivalent sales price fell only 16.67%—the percent amount of the devaluation. In other words, the product faced a price elasticity of demand greater than 1.

)))) Case 3: Sales Price Increases, Other Variables Remain Constant

Assume the euro sales price is raised from €12.80 to €15.36 per unit to maintain the same U.S. dollar-equivalent price (the change offsets the depreciation of the euro). Assume further that volume remains constant in spite of this price increase; that customers expect to pay the same dollar-equivalent price, and local costs do not change (see Exhibit 7.5).

Exhibit 7.5	*Instruments du Rhone, S.A.*

Case 3: Sales Price Increase, No Change in Volume

Expected Cash Flow, After Devaluation, Year 2002

Sales (1,000,000 units €15.36/unit)	€15,360,000
Direct costs (1,000,000 units €9.60/unit)	(9,600,000)
Cash operating expenses (fixed)	(890,000)
Depreciation	(600,000)
Pretax profit	€4,270,000
Income tax expenses (34.0%)	(1,451,800)
Profit after tax	€2,818,200
Add back depreciation	600,000
Cash flow from operations, in euros	€ 3,418,200
Times existing exchange rate: $1.0000/€	
Cash flow from operations, in U.S. dollars	$ 3,418,200

Projected Cash Flow from Operations (2002–2006)

Year	Item	In Euros (€)	U.S. Dollars @ $1.0000/€
1	Cash flow from operations	3,418,200	
	Less required increase in working capital	(640,000)	
	Net cash flow, first year	2,778,200	2,778,200
2	Cash flow from operations	3,418,200	3,418,200
3	Cash flow from operations	3,418,200	3,418,200
4	Cash flow from operations	3,418,200	3,418,200
5	Cash flow from operations	3,418,200	3,418,200
	Working capital recaptured in year 5	640,000	640,000

Instruments du Rhone is now better off following the devaluation than it was before, because the sales price, which is pegged to the international price level, increased. However, volume did not drop. The new level of accounts receivable would be one-fourth of the new sales level of €15,360,000, or €3,840,000, an increase of €640,000 over the original increase in Case 1. No additional investment in inventory is necessary because direct costs did not change.

Cash flow for the first five years would be as shown in the bottom half of Exhibit 7.5. Expected dollar cash flow in every year exceeds the cash flow of $1,728,600 that had been anticipated with no devaluation. The increase in working capital causes first-year net cash flow to be only $2,778,200, but thereafter the cash flow is $3,418,200 per year, with an additional $640,000 in working capital recovered in the fifth year.

The key to this improvement is operating leverage. If costs are incurred in euros and do not increase after a devaluation, an increase in the sales price by the amount of devaluation will lead to sharply higher profits.

))) Other Possibilities

If any portion of sales revenues was incurred in other currencies, the situation would be different. Instruments du Rhone might leave the foreign sales price unchanged, in effect raising the euro-equivalent price. Alternatively, it might leave the euro-equivalent price unchanged, thus lowering the foreign sales price in an attempt to gain volume. Of course, it could also position itself between these two extremes. Depending on elasticities and the proportion of foreign to domestic sales, total sales revenue might rise or fall.

If some or all raw material or components were imported and paid for in hard currencies, after the devaluation of the euro, euro operating costs would increase. Another possibility is that local (not imported) euro costs would rise after a devaluation. We cannot generalize for all countries of the world, but local costs often rise with some time lag following a devaluation. In each individual country, therefore, management must estimate how devaluation will affect the firm's sales revenue, sales volume, and local costs over a future period of time.

))) Measurement of Loss

Exhibit 7.6 summarizes the change in expected cash flows for the three cases and compares them with the cash flow expected should no devaluation occur (Base Case). The top portion of the exhibit restates the expected *cash flows* (CF) for each case. The column headed CF in the lower portion shows the change in cash flow compared with the nondevaluation situation. "Chg in CF" shows the gain (loss) from these changes in future cash flows. These changes are then discounted by Jefferson Controls' weighted-average cost of capital (WACC) of 20% to obtain the present value of the gain (loss) on operating exposure.

In Case 1, in which nothing changes after the euro is devalued, Jefferson Controls incurs an operating loss on Instrument du Rhone's operations with a present value of $1,033,914. In Case 2, in which volume doubled with no price

Exhibit 7.6 Instruments du Rhône, S.A. Summary of Operating Gains and Losses Following Devaluation for Instruments du Rhône's Dollar Contribution to Its Parent Company, Jefferson Controls, U.S. (thousands of U.S. dollars)

Assumptions	Base Case	Case 1	Case 2	Case 3
Exchange rate ($/euro)	$1.2000	$1.0000	$1.0000	$1.0000
Sales volume (units)	1,000,000	1,000,000	2,000,000	1,000,000
Sales price per unit	12.80	12.80	12.80	15.36
Direct cost per unit	9.60	9.60	9.60	9.60

Year	Base Case	Case 1		Case 2		Case 3	
		Cash Flow	Chg in CF	Cash Flow	Chg in CF	Cash Flow	Chg in CF
1 (2002)	$2,074,320	$1,728,600	($345,720)	($1,759,400)	($3,833,720)	$2,778,200	$ 703,880
2 (2003)	2,074,320	1,728,600	(345,720)	3,840,600	1,766,280	3,418,200	1,343,880
3 (2004)	2,074,320	1,728,600	(345,720)	3,840,600	1,766,280	3,418,200	1,343,880
4 (2005)	2,074,320	1,728,600	(345,720)	3,840,600	1,766,280	3,418,200	1,343,880
5 (2006)	2,074,320	1,728,600	(345,720)	3,840,600	1,766,280	3,418,200	1,343,880
5 Working capital	—	—	—	5,600,000	5,600,000	640,000	640,000

Operating gain (loss):

	Base Case	Case 1	Case 2	Case 3
PV of incremental CF @ 20%		($1,033,914)	$2,866,106	$3,742,892

change after devaluation, Jefferson Controls experienced an operating gain with a present value of $2,866,106. In Case 3, in which the euro sales price was increased and volume did not change, the present value of the operating gain from devaluation was $3,742,892. An almost infinite number of combinations of volume, price, and cost could follow any devaluation, and any or all of them might take effect at once after a devaluation or only after the passage of some time.

MANAGING OPERATING EXPOSURE AT THE STRATEGIC LEVEL THROUGH DIVERSIFICATION

The objective of both operating and transaction exposure management is to anticipate and influence the effect of unexpected changes in exchange rates on a firm's future cash flows, rather than merely hoping for the best. To meet this objective, management can *diversify the firm's operating and financing base.* Management can also *change the firm's operating and financing policies* through techniques that are discussed later in this chapter.

The key to managing operating exposure at the strategic level is for management to recognize a disequilibrium in parity conditions when it occurs and to be prepositioned to react in the most appropriate way. This task can best be accomplished if a firm *diversifies* internationally both its operating and its financing bases. Diversifying operations means diversifying sales, location of production facilities, and raw material sources. Diversifying the financing base means raising funds in more than one capital market and in more than one currency.

Depending on management's risk preference, a diversification strategy permits the firm to react either actively or passively to opportunities presented by disequilibrium conditions in the foreign exchange, capital, and product markets. Such a strategy *does not* require management to predict disequilibrium but only to *recognize* it when it occurs. It *does* require management to consider how *competitors* are prepositioned with respect to their own operating exposures. This knowledge should reveal which firms would be helped or hurt *competitively* by alternative disequilibrium scenarios.

⟫⟩ Diversifying Operations

If a firm's operations are diversified internationally, management is pre-positioned both to recognize disequilibrium when it occurs and to react competitively. Consider the case where purchasing power parity is temporarily in disequilibrium. Although the disequilibrium may have been unpredictable, management can often recognize its symptoms as soon as they occur. For example, management might notice a change in comparative costs in the firm's own plants located in different countries. It might also observe changed profit margins or sales volume in one area compared to another, depending on price and income elasticities of demand and competitors' reactions.

Recognizing a temporary change in worldwide competitive conditions permits management to change its operating strategies. Management might make marginal shifts in sourcing raw materials, components, or finished products. If spare capacity exists, production runs can be lengthened in one country and reduced in another. The marketing effort can be strengthened in export markets where the firm's products have become more price-competitive because of the disequilibrium condition.

Even if management does not actively distort normal operations when exchange rates change, the firm should experience some beneficial portfolio effects. The variability of its cash flows is probably reduced by international diversification of its production, sourcing, and sales because exchange rate changes under disequilibrium conditions are likely to increase the firm's competitiveness in some markets while reducing it in others. In that case operating exposure would be neutralized.

In contrast to the internationally diversified MNE, a purely domestic firm might be subject to the full impact of foreign exchange operating exposure even though it does not have foreign currency cash flows. For example, it could experience intense import competition in its domestic market from competing firms producing in countries with undervalued currencies. Domestic and Japanese personal computer manufacturers were both made aware of this problem when Korean personal computers captured a share of the U.S. market in the late 1980s. The Korean won was probably undervalued relative to both the U.S. dollar and the Japanese yen.

A purely domestic firm does not have the option to react to an international disequilibrium condition in the same manner as a MNE. In fact, a purely domestic firm will not be positioned to recognize that a disequilibrium exists because it lacks comparative data from its own internal sources. By the time external data are available from published sources, it is often too late to react. Even if a domestic firm recognizes the disequilibrium condition, it cannot quickly shift production and sales into foreign markets in which it has had no previous presence.

)))) Diversifying Financing

If a firm diversifies its financing sources, it will be pre-positioned to take advantage of temporary deviations from the international Fisher effect. If interest rate differentials do not equal expected changes in exchange rates, opportunities to lower a firm's cost of capital will exist. However, to be able to switch financing sources, a firm must already be well known in the international investment community, with banking contacts firmly established. Once again, this is not an option for a domestic firm that has limited its financing to one capital market.

Although we recommend diversification as a strategy for foreign exchange risk management, such a strategy has a potentially favorable impact on other risks as well. In particular, it could reduce the variability of future cash flows due to domestic business cycles, provided these are not perfectly correlated with international cycles. It could increase the availability of capital, also reducing its cost, by diversifying such risks as restrictive capital market policies or government borrowing competition in the capital market. It could diversify political risks such as expropriation, war, blocked funds, or just unfavorable changes in laws that reduce or eliminate profitability. The list of advantages from international diversification can even be extended to such areas as spreading the risk of technological obsolescence and reducing portfolio risk in the context of the capital asset pricing model, but now we are preempting the diversification strategy theme that appears throughout the rest of this book.

Constraints exist that may limit the feasibility of a diversification strategy for foreign exchange risk management or one of the other risks just mentioned. For example, the technology of a particular industry may require such large economies of scale that it is not economically feasible to diversify production locations. Firms in this type of industry could still diversify sales and financing sources, however. On the other hand, the firm may be too small or too unknown to attract international equity investors or lenders. Yet it could at least diversify its sales internationally. Thus a diversification strategy can only be implemented as far as is feasible.

ILLUSTRATIVE CASE

Goodyear in Mexico

TULTILÁN, Mexico—When Hugh D. Pace, Goodyear's manager here, heard on his car radio in December 1994 that the peso had crashed, dragging the nation's economy with it, he immediately met with his managers to assess the damage. Within days, he figured that domestic demand for their tires would plunge more than 20 percent, or 3,000 a day. His choices: lay off workers or find new export markets—right away, before his warehouse overflowed.

His team members, aided by the Goodyear Tire and Rubber company headquarters in Akron, Ohio, not only found enough buyers to make up for what turned out to be a 3,500-tire drop in domestic sales, they also found spots to sell 1,600 more, setting an output record at the plant, some 15 miles north of Mexico City. A factory that had imported supplies but exported not a single tire in 1992 now ships away half its production, mostly to the United States but also to South America and Europe. "From one day to another we passed from being an importer company to an exporter company," said Marcel Miota, Mr. Pace's production chief.

Goodyear is just one of many big U.S. companies here that have compensated for the collapse of domestic demand by sending goods abroad, to the United States most of all. As the peso shriveled in value, these companies saw their labor costs, in dollars, fall by more than a third. The resulting flood into the United States of cheaper autos, televisions, and other products, including tires, is turning a U.S. $1.4 billion trade surplus with Mexico into a $15 billion deficit.

The plant got far more help from other markets than managers anticipated. They were soon able to sell 2,600 tires a day to Latin America. Though sales there have slowed, in a few months they were selling 900 tires a day to Europe and about 100 a day to Japan. All told, in 1995 the plant was turning out 16,300 tires a day, 11 percent more than the year before. Mr. Pace planned to maintain or increase exports even when the local market picks up.

In the long run, the plant will stop trying to make every type of tire the Mexican market needs and instead concentrate efficiently, like U.S. plants, on a few models. Just watch what happens to our exports then, Mr. Pace said. "We've got this magnificent opportunity now, and we cannot let go of it," he said.

Source: Adapted from Allen R. Myerson, "Out of a Crisis, An Opportunity," *The New York Times,* Tuesday, September 26, 1995, p. C 1.

MANAGING OPERATING EXPOSURE BY CHANGING OPERATING POLICIES

Operating and transaction exposures can be partially managed by adopting operating policies that deviate from normal domestic-oriented policies but that have the virtue of reducing foreign exchange exposure. The cost of adopting such policies is less obvious than the cost of making contractual arrangements because operations may become less efficient, but sometimes rethinking operating procedures leads to new efficiencies that were previously not discovered. Three of the operating policies that are commonly employed to manage operating and transaction exposures are:

1. Using leads and lags;

2. Requiring customers to share the risk through currency clauses; and

3. Using a reinvoicing center.

))) Leads and Lags: Retiming the Transfer of Funds

Firms can reduce both operating and transaction exposure by accelerating or decelerating the timing of payments that must be made or received in foreign currencies. *To lead* is to pay early. A firm holding a "soft currency" or which has debts denominated in a "hard currency" will lead by using the soft currency to pay the hard currency debts as soon as possible. The object is to pay the currency debts before the soft currency drops in value. *To lag* is to pay late. A firm holding a hard currency and having debts denominated in a soft currency will lag by paying those debts late, hoping that less of the hard currency will be needed. If possible, firms will also lead and lag their collection of receivables, collecting soft foreign currency receivables early and collecting hard foreign currency receivables later.

Leading and lagging can be done between affiliates or among independent firms. Assuming that payments will be made eventually, leading or lagging always results in changing the cash and payables position of one firm, with the reverse effect on the other firm.

Intercompany Leads and Lags. Leading or lagging between independent firms requires the time preference of one firm to be imposed to the detriment of the other firm. For example, a German firm may wish to lead in collecting its Brazilian accounts receivable that are denominated in real because it expects the real to drop in value compared with the euro. But why should the Brazilian customers prepay their accounts payable? Credit in real was part of the inducement for them to purchase from the German firm. The only way the Brazilians would be willing to pay their accounts payable early is for their German creditor to offer a discount about equal to the forward discount on the real or, in equilibrium, the difference between Brazilian and German interest rates for the period of prepayment. In equilibrium this "discount" would eliminate the benefit to Germany of collecting the "soft" currency earlier.

Intracompany Leads and Lags. Leading and lagging between related firms is more feasible because they presumably embrace a common set of goals for the consolidated group. Furthermore, periodic payments are often made between units of a MNE, providing the opportunity for many types of leads or lags. Because opportunities for leading or lagging payments depend on the requirement for payments of this nature, the device is more readily adaptable to a company that operates on an integrated worldwide basis. If each unit functions as a separate and self-sufficient entity, the motivation for leading or lagging diminishes. In the case of financing cash flows with foreign affiliates, there is an additional motivation for early or late payments to position funds for liquidity reasons.

The use of leads and lags in conjunction with intracompany family receivables is feasible only with 100% ownership of the various affiliates, because the economic effect of extended payment terms alters the relative rate of return of the various units. This practice is unfair if each unit has minority stockholders separate from the corporate family, since they do not necessarily benefit from practices that benefit the MNE as a whole. Inequities may also arise between various profit centers in a group of wholly owned affiliates unless adjustments are made to reflect a particular center's sacrifice. A necessary condition for efficient use of leads and lags is the ability of the parent to adjust its techniques for measuring profit or controlling investment in assets by its various affiliates so that the performance rating of units and managers is not changed when one unit "helps" another for the good of the overall enterprise.

Because the use of leads and lags is an obvious technique for minimizing foreign exchange exposure and for shifting the burden of financing, many governments impose limits on the allowed range. Terms allowed by governments are often subject to negotiation when a good argument can be presented. Thus some limits are subject to exceptions. For example, in the past Italy has placed no limit on export and import lags on trade payments with other OECD countries. However, a 180-day limit on export lags and a five-year limit on import lags was applied to trade with non-OECD countries.

))) Currency Clauses: Risk-Sharing

An alternative arrangement for managing a long-term cash flow exposure between firms with a continuing buyer–supplier relationship is *risk-sharing*. *Risk-sharing* is a contractual arrangement in which the buyer and seller agree to share or split currency movement impacts on payments that pass between them. If the two firms are interested in a long-term relationship that is based on product quality and supplier reliability, and not on the occasional, unpredictable, and potentially painful whims of the currency markets, a cooperative agreement to share the burden of currency risk management may be in order.

If Ford's North American operations import automotive parts from Mazda (Japan) every month, year after year, major swings in exchange rates can benefit one party at the expense of the other.[2] One potential solution would be for Ford and Mazda to agree that all purchases by Ford will be made in Japanese yen at the current exchange rate, as long as the spot rate on the date of invoice is between, say, ¥115/$ and ¥125/$. If the exchange rate is between these values on the payment dates, Ford agrees to accept whatever transaction exposure exists (because it is paying in a foreign currency). If, however, the exchange rate falls outside this range on the payment date, Ford and Mazda will *share* the difference equally.

For example, Ford has an account payable of ¥25,000,000 for the month of March. If the spot rate on the date of invoice is ¥110/$, the Japanese yen would have appreciated versus the dollar, causing Ford's costs of purchasing automotive parts to rise. Since this rate falls outside the contractual range, Mazda would agree to accept a total payment in Japanese yen which would result from a difference of ¥5/$ (i.e., ¥115 – ¥110). The payment made by Ford would be

$$\left[\frac{¥25{,}000{,}000}{¥115.00\big/\$ - \dfrac{¥5.00\big/\$}{2}}\right] = \frac{¥25{,}000{,}000}{¥112.50\$} = \$222{,}222.22$$

Ford's total payment in Japanese yen would be calculated using an exchange rate of ¥112.50/$ and would save Ford $5,050.51.[3] Both parties therefore incur costs and benefits from exchange rate movements outside the specified band. Note that the movement could just as easily have been in Mazda's favor if the spot rate had moved to ¥130/$.

The risk-sharing arrangement is intended to smooth the impact on both parties of volatile and unpredictable exchange rate movements. Of course a sustained appreciation of one currency versus the other would require the negotiation of a new sharing agreement, but the ultimate goal of the agreement is to alleviate currency pressures on the continuing business relationship. Risk-sharing agreements like these have been in use for nearly 50 years in world markets. They became something of a rarity during the 1960s when exchange rates were relatively stable under the Bretton Woods Agreement. But with the return to floating exchange rates in the 1970s, firms with long-term customer–supplier relationships across borders have returned to some old ways of maintaining mutually beneficial long-term trade.

))) Reinvoicing Centers

A *reinvoicing center* is a separate corporate subsidiary that manages in one location all transaction exposure from intracompany trade. Manufacturing affiliates sell goods to distribution affiliates of the same firm only by selling to a reinvoicing center, which in turn resells to the distribution affiliate. Title passes to the reinvoicing center, but the physical movement of goods is direct from manufacturing plant to distribution affiliate. Thus, the reinvoicing center handles paperwork but has no inventory.

As depicted in Exhibit 7.7, the Korean manufacturing unit of a MNE invoices the firm's reinvoicing center in Singapore in Korean won. However, the actual goods are shipped directly to the Japanese sales affiliate. The reinvoicing center in turn sells to (invoices) the firm's Japanese sales affiliate in Japanese yen. Consequentially, all operating units deal only in their own currency, and all transaction exposure lies with the reinvoicing center.

To avoid accusations of profit-shifting through transfer pricing, most reinvoicing centers "resell" at cost plus a small commission for their services. The resale price is frequently the manufacturer's price times the forward exchange rate for the date on which payment from the distribution affiliate is expected, although other combinations are possible. The commission covers the cost of the reinvoicing center, but does not shift profits away from operating affiliates. There are three basic benefits arising from the creation of a reinvoicing center:

1. The formation of the center allows the management of all foreign exchange transaction exposure for intracompany sales to be located in one place. Reinvoicing center personnel can develop a specialized expertise in choosing which hedging technique is best at any moment, and they are likely to obtain more competitive foreign exchange quotations from banks because they are dealing in larger transactions.

2. By guaranteeing the exchange rate for future orders, the reinvoicing center can set firm local currency costs in advance. This enables distribution affiliates to make firm bids to unrelated final customers and to protect against the exposure created by a backlog of unfilled orders. Backlog exposure does not appear on the corporate books because the sales are not yet recorded. Sales

| **Exhibit 7.7** | *Reinvoicing Center Structure* |

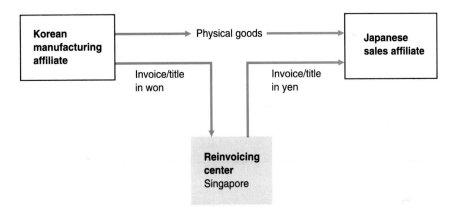

The Korean manufacturing unit ships goods directly to the Japanese sales affiliate. The invoice by the Korean unit, which is denominated in Korean won, is passed on to the reinvoicing center located in Singapore. The Singapore reinvoicing center takes legal title to the goods. It subsequently invoices the Japanese sales affiliate in the Japanese unit's own currency, Japanese yen.

subsidiaries can focus on their marketing activities and their performance can be judged without distortion because of exchange rate changes.

3. The center can manage intra-affiliate cash flows, including leads and lags of payments. With a reinvoicing center all affiliates settle intracompany accounts in their local currencies. The reinvoicing center need only hedge residual foreign exchange exposure.

The main disadvantage is one of cost relative to benefits received. One additional corporate unit must be created, and a separate set of books must be kept. The initial setup cost can be high because existing order-processing procedures must be reprogrammed. The center will have an impact on the tax status and customs duties of all affiliates, as well as on the amount of foreign exchange business directed to local banks in each country. Establishment of a reinvoicing center is likely to bring increased scrutiny by tax authorities to be sure that it is not functioning as a tax haven. Consequently, a variety of professional costs will be incurred for tax and legal advice, in addition to the costs of personnel operating the center.

MANAGING OPERATING EXPOSURE BY CHANGING FINANCING POLICIES

Operating and transaction exposures can be partially managed by adopting financing policies that offset anticipated foreign exchange exposures. Three of the financing policies commonly employed are:

1. Using natural hedges by matching currency cash flows;

2. Using back-to-back or parallel loans; and

3. Using currency swaps.

))) Natural Hedging: Matching Currency Cash Flows

One way to offset an anticipated continuous long exposure to a particular currency is to acquire debt denominated in that currency. Exhibit 7.8 depicts the exposure of a U.S. firm with continuing export sales to Canada. In order to compete effectively in Canadian markets, the firm invoices all export sales in Canadian dollars. This policy results in a continuing receipt of Canadian dollars month after month. If the export sales are part of a continuing supplier relationship, the long Canadian dollar position is relatively predictable and constant. This endless series of transaction exposures could, of course, be continually hedged with forward contracts or other contractual hedges, as discussed in the previous chapter.

But what if the firm sought out a continual use—that is an outflow—for its continual inflow of Canadian dollars? If the U.S. firm were to acquire part of its debt capital in the Canadian dollar markets, it could use the relatively predictable Canadian dollar cash inflows from export sales to service the principal and interest payments on Canadian dollar debt and be *naturally hedged*. The U.S.-based firm has hedged an operational cash inflow by creating a financial cash outflow, and so it does not have to actively manage the exposure with contractual financial instruments such as forward contracts. This form of natural hedge, sometimes referred to as *matching*, is effective in eliminating currency exposed when the exposure cash flow is relatively constant and predictable over time.

The list of potential matching strategies is nearly endless. A second alternative is for the U.S. firm to seek out potential suppliers in Canada as a substitute for raw materials or components being supplied by U.S. or other foreign firms. A third alternative, often referred to as *currency switching*, is to pay foreign suppliers with

---

Exhibit 7.8   *A U.S.-Based Firm and Matching of Canadian Dollar Cash Flows*

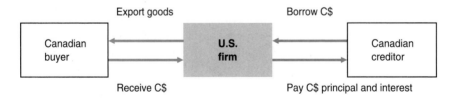

A U.S.-based firm with continuing inflows of Canadian dollars could offset, or *match*, these cash flows by creating a matching outflow. If the firm were to borrow Canadian dollar-denominated debt, it could then service this debt with the Canadian dollars earned through exports.

Canadian dollars. For example, if the U.S. firm imported components from Mexico, the Mexican firms themselves might welcome payment in Canadian dollars because they are short Canadian dollars in their multinational cash flow network.

))) Back-to-Back Loans

In a *back-to-back loan*, also referred to as a *parallel loan* or *credit swap*, two business firms in separate countries arrange to borrow each other's currency for a specific period of time. At an agreed terminal date they return the borrowed currencies. The operation is conducted outside the foreign exchange markets, although spot quotations may be used as the reference point for determining the amount of funds to be swapped. Such a swap creates a covered hedge against exchange loss, since each company, on its own books, borrows the same currency it repays. Back-to-back loans are also used at a time of actual or anticipated legal limitations on the transfer of investment funds to or from either country.

The structure of a typical back-to-back loan is illustrated in Exhibit 7.9. A British parent firm, wanting to invest funds in its Dutch affiliate, locates a Dutch parent firm that wants to invest funds in the United Kingdom. Avoiding the exchange markets entirely, the British parent lends pounds to the Dutch affiliate in the United Kingdom, while the Dutch parent lends euros to the British affiliate in the Netherlands. The two loans would be for equal values at the current spot rate and for a specified maturity. At maturity the two separate loans would each be repaid to the original lender, again without any need to use the foreign exchange markets. Neither loan carries any foreign exchange risk, and neither loan normally needs the approval of any governmental body regulating the availability of foreign exchange for investment purposes.

Exhibit 7.9   *Creation of a Back-to-Back Loan*

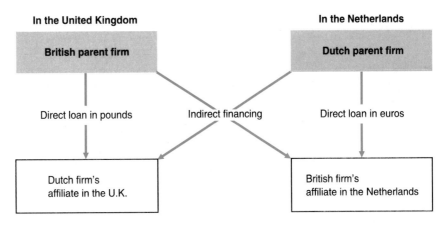

Parent company guarantees are not needed on the back-to-back loans because each loan carries the right of offset in the event of default of the other loan. A further agreement can provide for maintenance of principal parity in case of changes in the spot rate between the two countries. For example, if the pound dropped by more than, say, 6% for as long as 30 days, the British parent might have to advance additional pounds to the Dutch affiliate so as to bring the principal value of the two loans back to parity. A similar provision would protect the British if the euro should weaken. Although this parity provision might lead to changes in the amount of home currency each party must lend during the period of the agreement, it does not increase foreign exchange risk because at maturity all loans are repaid in the same currency loaned.

One fundamental impediment exists to widespread use of the back-to-back loan: It is difficult for a firm to find a partner, termed a *counterparty*, for the currency, amount, and timing desired.[6] This disadvantage has led to the rapid development and wide use of the currency swap, described next.

Currency Swaps

A *currency swap* resembles a back-to-back loan except that it does not appear on a firm's balance sheet. The term *swap* is widely used to describe a foreign exchange agreement between two parties to exchange a given amount of one currency for another and, after a period of time, to give back the original amounts swapped. Care should be taken to clarify which of the many different swaps is being referred to in a specific case.

In a currency swap, a firm and a swap dealer or swap bank agree to exchange an equivalent amount of two different currencies for a specified period of time. Currency swaps can be negotiated for a wide range of maturities up to at least 10 years. If funds are more expensive in one country than another, a fee may be required to compensate for the interest differential. The swap dealer or swap bank acts as a middleman in setting up the swap agreement.

A typical currency swap first requires two firms to borrow funds in the markets and currencies in which they are best known. For example, a Japanese firm would typically borrow yen on a regular basis in its home market (see Exhibit 7.10). If the Japanese firm were exporting to the United States and earning U.S. dollars, however, it might wish to construct a natural hedge that would allow it to use the U.S. dollars earned to make regular debt-service payments on U.S. dollar debt. If the Japanese firm is not well-known in the U.S. financial markets, it may have no ready access to U.S. dollar debt. One way in which it could, in effect, borrow dollars, is to participate in a currency swap. The Japanese firm could swap its yen-denominated debt service payments with another firm that has U.S. dollar debt service payments. The Japanese firm would then have dollar debt service without actually borrowing U.S. dollars.

Swap-dealers arrange most swaps on a "blind basis," meaning the firm does not know what firm is on the other side of the swap arrangement. The firm views the dealer or bank as its counterparty. Because the swap markets are dominated

| Exhibit 7.10 | *Creation of a Currency Swap Through a Swap Dealer* |

A Japanese firm can swap its U.S. dollar-denominated debt payments for the Japanese yen-denominated debt payments of a U.S. firm through a swap dealer. The swap dealer searches out matching currency exposures and plays the role of a middleman, providing a valuable currency management service for both firms.

by the major money center banks worldwide, the counterparty risk is thought to be acceptable. Because the swap dealer's business is arranging swaps, the dealer can generally arrange for the currency, amount, and timing of the desired swap.

Accountants in the United States treat the currency swap as a foreign exchange transaction rather than as debt and treat the obligation to reverse the swap at some later date as a forward exchange contract. Forward exchange contracts can be matched against assets, but they are entered in a firm's footnotes rather than as balance sheet items. The result is that both accounting and operating exposures are avoided, and neither a long-term receivable nor a long-term debt is created on the balance sheet. The risk of changes in currency rates to the implied collateral in a long-term currency swap can be treated with a clause similar to the maintenance-of-principal clause in a back-to-back loan. If exchange rates change by more than some specified amount, say 10%, an additional amount of the weaker currency might have to be advanced.

After being introduced on a global scale in the early 1980s, currency swaps have become one of the largest financial derivative markets in the world. Chapter 9 will provide a detailed explanation of the theory and application of currency swaps in the context of interest rate risk management.

ILLUSTRATIVE CASE

Statoil of Norway

Statoil is the state-owned oil and gas company of Norway. It is one of the largest oil companies in the world, as well as the leading trader of North Sea oil. Statoil is active in all the vertical industries associated with the petrochemical industry. Although the firm is headquartered in Norway and uses the Norwegian krone as its home currency, Statoil's primary revenues, petroleum and petroleum products, are priced and sold on world markets in U.S. dollars. Even when payment is accepted in nondollar currency, the

| **Exhibit 7.11** | *Long-Term Debt of the Statoil Group Analyzed by Currency (in millions)* |

Debt	Long-Term Debt	Currency Swap Agreements	Residual Currency Position	Average Rate of Exchange	Book Value in Norwegian Kroner
Norwegian kroner (NOK)	308	–	308	–	308
U.S. dollar (USD)	1,224	775	1,999	6.65	13,287
German marks (DEM)	684	(307)	377	367.25	1,385
Japanese yen (JPY)	65,640	(44,640)	21,000	4.44	932
French francs (FRF)	750	(400)	350	104.74	367
Swiss francs (CHF)	250	(100)	150	442.42	664
Pounds sterling (GBP)	3	(2)	1	10.96	8
Danish kroner (DKK)	400	(200)	200	90.96	182
European Currency Units (ECU)	100	(100)	0	–	–
Long-term provisions					340
Total Statoil					17,473

1. The majority of long-term loans expire over the period 1992–1998 inclusive, while a minor share runs until 2008.
2. Average rate of interest on long-term loans in 1991 was 7.6%. Average rate of exchange in foreign currency/NOK, USD and GBP are NOK per one unit. All other currencies are per 100 units.
3. Half of the loans are subject to a fixed rate of interest throughout their term.
4. The unused share of long-term loan agreements converts to NOK 5,055 million.
5. Long-term liabilities include provisions for site restoration and removal costs, NOK 281 million.

Source: *Statoil Annual Report and Accounts* 1991, p. 20.

price is based on the spot rate of a U.S. dollar petrochemical price. Costs, however, are dominated by the servicing of its outstanding debt. The petrochemical industry is an extremely capital-intensive industry, and Statoil needs large quantities of capital.

Statoil is a large firm domiciled in a small country. Although sophisticated in structure, the Norwegian capital markets alone cannot feed the voracious capital appetite of such a firm. Statoil must therefore acquire large quantities of capital on world markets.

As illustrated in Exhibit 7.11, Statoil has acquired a large quantity of its capital on world markets denominated in U.S. dollars. It has also raised capital in other major currency markets such as the Japanese yen and the German mark. To enable the cash flows coming into Statoil as revenues to service the financial outflows in each currency in which it has borrowed, Statoil has swapped large proportions of its debt into U.S. dollar payments. Note in Exhibit 7.11 how the total "currency position" of U.S. dollars is the only currency position that is increased as a result of currency swap agreements. This is a prime example of the use of currency matching to manage the operating exposure of the firm.

CONTRACTUAL APPROACHES: HEDGING THE UNHEDGEABLE

Some MNEs now attempt to hedge their operating exposure with contractual strategies. Firms like Eastman Kodak (U.S.) and Merck (U.S.) have undertaken long-term currency option positions hedges designed to offset lost earnings from adverse exchange rate changes.[5] This hedging of what many of these firms refer to as *strategic exposure* or *competitive exposure* seemingly flies in the face of traditional theory.

The ability of firms to hedge the "unhedgeable" is dependent upon *predictability*: (1) the predictability, of the firm's future cash flows; and (2) the predictability of the firm's competitors responses to exchange rate changes. Although many firms may believe they are capable of predicting their own cash flows, few in practice feel capable of accurately predicting competitor response.

Merck is an example of a firm that feels capable of both. The company possesses relatively predictable long-run revenue streams due to the product-niche nature of the pharmaceuticals industry. As a U.S.-based exporter to foreign markets, markets in which sales levels by product are relatively predictable and prices are often regulated by government, Merck believes that it can accurately predict net long-term cash flows in foreign currencies five and ten years into the future. Because of Merck's relatively undiversified operating structure (it is highly centralized in terms of where research, development, and production costs are located), it feels that it has no real alternatives but contractual hedging if it is to weather long-term unexpected exchange rate changes. Merck has purchased over-the-counter (OTC) long-term put options on foreign currencies versus the U.S. dollar as insurance against potential lost earnings from exchange rate changes. In the case of Merck, the predictability of competitor response to exchange rate changes is less pertinent given the niche-market nature of pharmaceutical products.

Eastman Kodak, the subject of this chapter's opening discussion, is another MNE that has in the past undertaken contractual hedging of its operating exposure. Kodak believes its markets are largely price-driven and is aware that its major competitor, Fuji, has a Japanese cost base. If the U.S. dollar were to strengthen in the medium- to long-term, Kodak's market share in the United States and in foreign markets would decline. Kodak also believes that whatever sales it loses, its competitors will gain. Kodak has therefore also purchased long-term put options on foreign currencies that would replace long-term earnings if the value of the U.S. dollar, its home-currency, rose unexpectedly.[6]

A significant question remains as to the true effectiveness of hedging operating exposure with contractual hedges. The fact remains that even after feared exchange rate movements and put option position payoffs have occurred, the firm is competitively disadvantaged. The capital outlays required for the purchase of such sizeable put option positions is capital not used for the potential diversification of operations, which in the long run would likely have more effectively maintained the firm's global market share and international competitiveness.

SUMMARY

- *Foreign exchange exposure* is a measure of the potential for a firm's profitability, net cash flow, and market value to change because of a change in exchange rates.

- Operating strategies for the management of transaction exposure emphasize the structuring of the firm's operations in order to create matching streams of cash flows by currency. This is termed *natural hedging.*

- *Operating exposure* measures the change in value of the firm that results from changes in future operating cash flows caused by an unexpected change in exchange rates.

- An unexpected change in exchange rates impacts a firm's expected cash flow at four levels. These are (1) short-run; (2) medium-run, equilibrium case; (3) medium-run, disequilibrium case; and (4) long-run.

- The objective of operating exposure management is to anticipate and influence the effect of unexpected changes in exchange rates on a firm's future cash flow, rather than being forced into passive reaction to such changes as was described in the Instruments du Rhone case. This task can best be accomplished if a firm diversifies internationally both its operations and its financing base.

- Strategies to change operating policies include leads and lags, currency risk sharing clauses, and reinvoicing centers.

- Strategies to change financing policies include matching currency cash flows, back-to- back loans, and currency swaps.

- Contractual approaches (i.e., options and forwards) have occasionally been used to hedge operating exposure but are costly and possibly ineffectual.

QUESTIONS

1. Paradox? Operating Gains but Transaction Losses

The possibility of a gain or loss on operating exposure concurrent with a loss or gain on transaction exposure may appear incongruous. Explain why, when the currency in which a foreign affiliate operates falls in value, the firm may have both an operating gain and a transaction loss.

2. Instruments du Rhone, S.A. (A)

Instruments du Rhone, S.A., as described in this chapter, decides not to change its domestic sales price of €12.80 per unit within Europe but to raise its export price (in euros) from €12.80 per unit to €15.36 per unit, thus preserving its original dollar-equivalent price of $15.36. Volume in both markets remains the same because no buyer perceives that the price has changed.

a. What is the impact on cash flow?

b. What is the impact on working capital needs?

c. What is the impact on the present value approach to measuring operating exposure?

3. Instruments du Rhone, S.A. (B)

Instruments du Rhone, S.A., as described in this chapter, finds that domestic costs increase in proportion to the drop in value of the euro because of local inflation and because of a rise in the cost of imported raw materials and components. This rise in costs applies to all cash costs, including direct costs and fixed cash operating costs. However, it does not apply to depreciation. Because of the increase in its costs, Instruments du Rhone increases its price in euros on both domestic and export sales from €12.80 per unit to €15.36 per unit.

a. What is the impact on cash flow?

b. What is the impact on working capital needs?

c. What is the impact on the present value approach to measuring operating exposure?

4. High-Profile Printers, Inc. (A)

High-Profile Printers, Inc. (HPP) of the United States exports computer printers to Brazil, whose currency, the real (symbol R$) has been trading at R$1.8000/US$. Exports to Brazil are currently 100,000 printers per year at the equivalent in real of $200 each. A strong rumor exists that the real will be devalued to R$2.0000/$ within two weeks. Should the devaluation take place, the real is expected to remain unchanged for another decade.

Accepting this forecast as given, HPP faces a pricing decision that must be made before any actual devaluation: HPP may either (1) maintain the same price in real and, in effect, sell for fewer dollars, in which case Brazilian volume will not change, or (2) maintain the same dollar price, raise the price in real in Brazil to compensate for the devaluation, and experience a 20% drop in volume. Direct costs in the United States are 60% of the U.S. sales price.

What would be the short-run (one-year) implication of each pricing strategy? Which do you recommend?

5. High-Profile Printers, Inc. (B)

Assume the same facts as in High-Profile Printers (A) in question 1. HPP also believes that if it maintains the same price in Brazilian real as a permanent policy, volume will increase at 10% per annum for six years. Dollar costs will not change. At the end of six years HPP's patent expires and it will no longer export to Brazil. After the real devalues to R$2.0000/US$, no further devaluation is expected.

If HPP raises the price in real so as to maintain its dollar price, volume will increase at only 4% per annum for six years, starting from the lower initial base of 80,000 units. Again dollar costs will not change, and at the end of six years HPP will stop exporting to Brazil.

HPP's weighted average cost of capital is 14%. Given these considerations, what do you recommend for HPP's pricing policy? Justify your recommendation.

6. Operating Risks in the Film Industry

Eastman Kodak (U.S.), Fuji Film (Japan), and Agfa (Germany) all compete for a share of the world film market. Each company produces entirely in its home country and exports to a worldwide array of countries. The photographic products produced by all three are essentially identical; therefore prices and/or advertising is the basis for competition.

a. How would the direction of the yen per dollar, yen per euro, and/or the euro per dollar exchange rate affect the net profits earned by each company?

b. What are some of the potential operating strategies that each company might employ to manage this operating exposure?

c. What are some of the potential contractual strategies that each company might employ to manage this operating exposure?

d. Using the Option.xls spreadsheet, what would be the premium on the appropriate option on Japanese yen, assuming a $50 million notional principal, five-year maturity, a strike price of ¥120.00/$, a spot rate of ¥120.00/$, volatility of 10.0%, and five-year euro-yen and euro-dollar interest rates of 5%? How might Kodak's Treasury finance this purchase?

7. Statoil of Norway

Statoil, the national oil company of Norway, has acquired debt capital in a variety of foreign currencies (see Exhibit 7.11). After borrowing the capital, however, Statoil swapped its currency obligations to hedge its currency exposure. As shown in Exhibit 7.11, the residual currency position in most major currencies was relatively small. Why do you think Statoil chose to reduce its long-term currency position in some currencies to near zero while leaving other currency positions essentially untouched?

8. Merck Pharmaceutical

Merck Pharmaceutical is a MNE with an enormous operating exposure problem. Merck does all of its product research and development and manufacturing in the United States. Because of the capital and technical requirements of the pharmaceutical industry, diversification of its operations is not financially practical. Once all pharmaceutical products are produced, they are distributed and sold worldwide in over 60 countries through local sales agents, offices, or affiliates. Because all local markets pay in local currencies, Merck (U.S.) ends up long in a multitude of currencies.

Pharmaceutical prices are typically regulated by host country governments. Because most individual drug companies have their own niche products, complete with patents and licenses, individual market volume sales are relatively predictable. Competition between companies is focused in the R&D stage, not in the marketplace for existing products.

a. Why does Merck have an enormous operating exposure?

b. What potential operating or contractual hedging strategies might be appropriate for Merck's long positions in foreign currencies?

c. How far into the future would these hedges need to be placed in order for Merck to yield true benefits? How effective are these strategies likely to be in the long run?

WORLD WIDE WEB EXERCISES

W1. Operating Exposure: Recent Examples

Using the following major periodicals as starting points, find a current example of a firm with a substantial operating exposure problem. To aid in your search, you might focus on businesses having major operations in countries with recent currency crises through either depreciation or major home-currency appreciation.

Financial Times	http://www.ft.com/
The Economist	http://www.economist.com/
The Wall Street Journal	http://www.wsj.com/

W2. SEC Edgar Files

In order to analyze an individual firm's operating exposure more carefully, it is necessary to have more detailed information available than in the normal annual report. Choose a specific firm with substantial international operations, for example Coca-Cola or PepsiCo, and search the Security and Exchange Commission's Edgar files for more detailed financial reports of their international operations.

Search SEC EDGAR Archives   http://www.sec.gov/cgi-bin/srch-edgar

SUGGESTED READINGS

Capel, Jeanette, "A Real Options Approach to Economic Exposure Management," *Journal of International Financial Management and Accounting*, Vol. 8, No. 2, 1997, pp. 87–113.

Harris, Trevor S., Nahun D. Melumad, and Toshi Shibano, "An Argument Against Hedging by Matching the Currency of Costs and Revenues," *Journal of Applied Corporate Finance*, Fall 1996, Vol. 9, No. 3, pp. 90–97.

He, Jia and Lilian Ng, "The Foreign Exchange Exposure of Japanese Multinational Corporations," *The Journal of Finance*, Vol. 53, No. 2, April 1998, pp. 733–753.

Lewent, Judy C., and A. John Kearney, "Identifying, Measuring, and Hedging Currency Risk at Merck," *Journal of Applied Corporate Finance*, Winter 1990, pp. 19–28.

Luehrman, Timothy A., "The Exchange Rate Exposure of a Global Competitor," *Journal of International Business Studies*, Vol. 21. No. 2, 1990, pp. 225–242.

Miller, Kent D. and Jeffrey J. Reuer, "Firm Strategy and Economic Exposure to Foreign Exchange Rate Movements," *Journal of International Business Studies*, Vol. 29, No. 3, Third Quarter, 1998, pp. 493–514.

O'Brien, Thomas J., "International Production Location and Pro Forma Financial Hedging of Exchange Rate Risk," *Journal of Applied Corporate Finance*, Fall 1998, Vol. 11, No. 3, pp. 100–108.

NOTES

1. Stonehill, Ravn, and Dullum (1982).
2. Ford is a major stockholder of Mazda, but it does not exert control over its operations. Therefore, the risk-sharing agreement is particularly appropriate; transactions between the two are both intercompany and intracompany!
3. At a spot rate of ¥110/$, Ford's costs for March would be $227,272.73. The risk-sharing agreement between Ford and Mazda allows Ford to pay $222,222.22, a savings of $5,050.51 over the cost without risk sharing. (This "savings" is a reduction in an increased cost, not a true cost reduction.)
4. Another source of concern is that of *counterparty risk*, the risk that the other party to such an agreement will not fulfill its obligations in a timely manner.
5. For a detailed explanation of Merck's operating exposure program see Lewent and Kearney (1990).
6. The magnitude of the option position depends on the nature of desired replacement. For example, if Kodak wished only to insure the lost net-earnings from exchange rate-induced losses, the option position would obviously be considerably smaller than one attempting to replace gross sales revenues. Given the premium expenses associated with long-term put option positions of this type, the former is generally favored over the latter.

CHAPTER 8

ACCOUNTING EXPOSURE

*A*ccounting exposure, also called *translation exposure*, arises because financial statements of foreign affiliates—which are stated in a foreign currency—must be restated in the parent company's reporting currency to prepare consolidated financial statements. Foreign affiliates of U.S. companies, for example, must restate local euro, pound, yen, and other currency statements into U.S. dollars so the foreign values can be added to the parent's U.S. dollar-denominated balance sheet and income statement. This accounting process is called "translation." *Translation exposure* is the potential for an increase or decrease in the parent company's net worth and reported net income caused by a change in exchange rates since the last translation.

Although the main purpose of translation is to prepare consolidated statements, translated statements are also used by management to assess the performance of foreign affiliates. Such assessment might be performed from the local currency statements, but restatement of all affiliate statements into the single "common denominator" of one currency facilitates management comparison.

OVERVIEW OF TRANSLATION

Translation, in principle, is quite simple. Foreign currency financial statements must be converted to the parent company's reporting currency for consolidation purposes. If the same exchange rate were used to remeasure each and every line item on the individual statement (income statement and balance sheet), there would be no imbalances resulting from the remeasurement. But if a different exchange rate is used for different line items on an individual statement, an imbalance results.

Why would a different exchange rate be used in remeasuring different line items? A different rate might be used because accounting principles in many countries are often a complex compromise between historical and current market valuation. Historical exchange rates may be used for certain equity accounts, fixed assets, and inventory items, while current exchange rates may be used for current assets, current

233

liabilities, income, and expense items. The question then is, what—if anything—is to be done with the imbalance? The resulting imbalance from using exchange rates is then accounted for in either current income or equity reserves.

)))) Affiliate Characterization

Most countries today specify the translation method to be used by a foreign affiliate, based on the affiliate's business operations. For example, a foreign affiliate's business can be categorized as either an integrated foreign entity or a self-sustaining foreign entity. An *integrated foreign entity* is one which operates as an extension of the parent company, with cash flows and general business lines highly interrelated with those of the parent. A *self-sustaining foreign entity* is one which operates in the local economic environment independent of the parent company. The distinction is important to the logic of translation. A foreign affiliate should be valued principally in terms of the currency that forms the basis of its economic viability.

It is not unusual to find two different foreign affiliates of a single company that are of different characters. For example, a U.S.-based manufacturer that produces sub-assemblies in the United States that are then shipped to a Spanish subsidiary for finishing, assembly, and resale in the European Union would likely characterize the Spanish affiliate as an integrated foreign entity. The dominant currency of economic operation is likely the U.S. dollar. That same U.S. parent may, however, also own an agricultural marketing business in Venezuela that has few cash flows or operations related to the U.S. parent company (or the U.S. dollar). The Venezuelan affiliate may purchase almost all materials and expend all costs of operations in Venezuelan bolivars, while selling exclusively in Venezuela. Because the Venezuelan affiliate's operations are independent of its parent, and its functional currency is the Venezuelan bolivar, it would be classified as a self-sustaining foreign entity.

)))) Functional Currency

The United States, rather than distinguishing a foreign affiliate as either integrated or self-sustaining, follows a parallel approach that requires that the functional currency of the affiliate be determined. Current U.S. translation practices are delineated in *Statement of Financial Accounting Standards Number 52*, usually referred to as FAS#52.[1]

A foreign affiliate's *functional currency* is the currency of the primary economic environment in which the affiliate operates and in which it generates cash flows. In other words, it is the dominant currency used by that foreign affiliate in its day-to-day operations.[2] Management must evaluate the nature and purpose of each of its individual foreign affiliates to decide on the appropriate functional currency for each. Exhibit 8.1 lists the indicators that the FASB uses in determining the functional currency of a foreign affiliate.

If a foreign affiliate of a U.S.-based company is determined to have the U.S. dollar as its functional currency, it is essentially an extension of the parent com-

---

Exhibit 8.1   *Economic Indicators for Determining the Functional Currency*

---

a. Cash Flow Indicators

(1) Foreign Currency—Cash flows related to the foreign entity's individual assets and liabilities are primarily in the foreign currency and do not impact the parent company's cash flows.

(2) Parent's Currency—Cash flows related to the foreign entity's individual assets and liabilities directly impact the parent's cash flows on a current basis and are readily available for remittance to the parent company.

b. Sales Price Indicators

(1) Foreign Currency—Sales prices for the foreign entity's products are not primarily responsive on a short-term basis to changes in exchange rates but are determined more by local competition or by local government regulation.

(2) Parent's Currency—Sales prices for the foreign entity's products are primarily responsive on a short-term basis to changes in exchange rates; for example, sales prices are determined more by worldwide competition or by international prices.

c. Sales Market Indicators

(1) Foreign Currency—There is an active local sales market for the foreign entity's products, although there might also be significant amounts of exports.

(2) Parent's Currency—The sales market is mostly in the parent's country or sales contracts are denominated in the parent's currency.

d. Expense Indicators

(1) Foreign Currency—Labor, materials, and other costs for the foreign entity's products or services are primarily local costs, even though there might also be imports from other countries.

(2) Parent's Currency—Labor, materials and other costs for the foreign entity's products or services, on a continuing basis, are primarily costs for components obtained from the country in which the parent company is located.

e. Financing Indicators

(1) Foreign Currency—Financing is primarily denominated in foreign currency, and funds generated by the foreign entity's operations are sufficient to service existing and normally expected debt obligations.

(2) Parent's Currency—Financing is primarily from the parent or other dollar-denominated obligations, or funds generated by the foreign entity's operations are not sufficient to service existing and normally expected debt obligations without the infusion of additional funds from the parent. Infusion of additional funds from the parent for expansion is not a factor, provided funds generated by the foreign entity's expanded operations are expected to service that additional financing.

f. Intercompany Transactions and Arrangements Indicators

(1) Foreign Currency—There is a low volume of intercompany transactions and there is not an extensive interrelationship between the operations of the foreign entity and the parent company. However, the foreign entity's operations may rely on the parent's affiliates' competitive advantages, such as patents and trademarks.

(2) Parent's Currency—There is a high volume of intercompany transactions and there is an extensive interrelationship between the foreign entity and the parent company. Additionally, the parent's currency generally would be the functional currency if the foreign entity is a device or shell corporation for holding investments, obligations, intangible assets, etc., that could readily be carried on the parent's or an affiliate's books.

Reprinted with the permission of Financial Accounting Standards Board, Stamford, Connecticut.

pany (equivalent to the designation of integrated foreign entity used by most countries). If, however, the functional currency of the foreign affiliate is determined to be different from the U.S. dollar, the affiliate is considered a separate entity from the U.S. parent (equivalent to the self-sustaining-entity designation).

))) Translation Methods

There are two basic methods for the translation of foreign affiliate financial statements employed worldwide, the *current-rate method* and the *temporal method*. Regardless of which method is employed, a translation method must designate not only at what exchange rate individual balance sheet and income statement items are remeasured but also where any imbalance is to be recorded (typically either in current income or in an equity reserve account in the balance sheet). The significance of this decision is that imbalances passed through the income statement affect the firm's current reported income, while imbalances transferred directly to the equity section of the balance sheet do not.

Current-Rate Method. The current rate method is the most prevalent in the world today. Under this method, financial statement line items are translated at the current exchange rate, with few exceptions.

- *Assets and liabilities.* All assets and liabilities are translated at the current rate of exchange; that is, at the rate of exchange in effect on the balance sheet date.
- *Income statement items.* All items, including depreciation and cost of goods sold, are translated at either the actual exchange rate on the dates the various revenues, expenses, gains, and losses were incurred or at an appropriately weighted-average exchange rate for the period.
- *Distributions.* Dividends paid are translated at the exchange rate in effect on the date of payment.
- *Equity items.* Common stock and paid-in capital accounts are translated at historical rates. Year-end retained earnings consist of the original year-beginning retained earnings, plus or minus any income or loss for the year.

Gains or losses caused by translation adjustments are not included in the calculation of consolidated net income. Rather, translation gains or losses are reported separately and accumulated in a separate equity reserve account (on the consolidated balance sheet) with a title such as *cumulative translation adjustment* (CTA).[3] If a foreign affiliate is later sold or liquidated, translation gains or losses of past years accumulated in the CTA account are reported as one component of the total gain or loss on sale or liquidation. The total gain or loss is reported as part of the net income or loss for the time period in which the sale or liquidation occurs.

The biggest advantage of the current-rate method is that the gain or loss on translation does not pass through the income statement but goes directly to a reserve account. This eliminates the variability of reported earnings due to foreign exchange translation gains or losses. A second advantage of the current-rate method is that the relative proportions of individual balance sheet accounts remain the same. Hence, the process of translation does not distort such balance sheet ratios as the current ratio or the debt-to-equity ratio. The main disadvantage of the current-rate method is that it violates the accounting principle of carrying balance sheet accounts at historical cost.[4]

Temporal Method. Under the temporal method, specific assets and liabilities are translated at exchange rates consistent with the timing of the financial item's creation.[5]

- *Monetary assets* (primarily cash, marketable securities, accounts receivable, and long-term receivables) and *monetary liabilities* (primarily current liabilities and long-term debt) are translated at current exchange rates.

- *Nonmonetary assets and liabilities* (primarily inventory and fixed assets) are translated at historical rates.

- *Income statement items* are translated at the average exchange rate for the period, except for items such as depreciation and cost of goods sold that are directly associated with nonmonetary assets or liabilities. These accounts are translated at their historical rate.

- *Distributions.* (dividends paid) are translated at the exchange rate in effect on the date of payment.

- *Equity items.* Common stock and paid-in capital accounts are translated at historical rates. Year-end retained earnings consist of the original year-beginning retained earnings plus (or minus) any income (or loss) for the year, plus (or minus) any imbalance from translation, as explained next.

Under the temporal method, gains or losses resulting from remeasurement are carried directly to current consolidated income—not to equity reserves. Hence, foreign exchange gains and losses arising from the translation process do introduce volatility to consolidated earnings.

The basic advantage of the temporal method is that foreign nonmonetary assets are carried at their original cost in the parent's consolidated statement. In most countries this approach is consistent with the original cost treatment of domestic assets of the parent firm. In practice, however, if some foreign accounts are translated at one exchange rate while others are translated at different rates, the resulting translated balance sheet will not balance. Hence, a need exists for a "plug" to remove what has been called the "dangling debit or credit."[6] The true nature of the gain or loss created by use of such a "plug" is open to question. Unrealized foreign exchange gains or losses are included in quarterly primary earnings per share (EPS), thus increasing the variability of reported earnings.

))) U.S. Translation Procedures

As mentioned previously, the United States differentiates foreign affiliates on the basis of functional currency, not affiliate characterization. The result, however, is the same. Exhibit 8.2 illustrates the translation procedures used by U.S.-based companies under current U.S. *generally accepted accounting practices* (GAAP).

- If the financial statements of the foreign affiliate of a U.S. company are maintained in U.S. dollars, translation is not required.

- If the financial statements of the foreign affiliate are maintained in the local currency and the *local currency* is the functional currency, they are translated by the *current-rate method*.

- If the financial statements of the foreign affiliate are maintained in the local currency and the *U.S. dollar* is the functional currency, they are remeasured by the *temporal method*.[7]

- If the financial statements of foreign affiliates of U.S. companies are maintained in the local currency and neither the local currency nor the dollar is the functional currency, then the statements must first be remeasured into the functional currency by the temporal method and then translated into dollars by the current-rate method.

))) Hyperinflation Countries

FAS #52 has a special provision for translating statements of foreign affiliates of U.S. companies operating in countries where cumulative inflation has been approximately 100% or more over a three-year period—the so-called *hyperinflation countries*. Financial statements of these affiliates must be translated into the reporting currency using the temporal method.

The rationale for special treatment of hyperinflation countries is to correct the problem of the "disappearing asset." If the current rate were used, depreciation would be understated relative to replacement costs, profits would be overstated in real terms, and the book value of plant and equipment would eventually nearly disappear from the balance sheet as its value diminished in reporting currency terms. Translating plant, equipment, and depreciation expenses at the historical exchange rate yields a higher asset value in the reporting currency than would use of the current (depreciated) exchange rate. This discrepancy, in turn, leads to a less distorted income statement and balance sheet. In effect, FAS #52 declares the functional currency of affiliates in hyperinflation countries to be the reporting currency (U.S. dollars for U.S. firms).

The hyperinflation standard has some precedence in business practice. Russell Taussig has stated it very well:

> When a country is plagued with hyperinflation, it often uses the U.S. dollar or other hard currency as its *de facto* functional currency for actual transactions regardless of accounting standards. For example, most Israeli retailers in 1982 priced their merchandise in U.S. dollars, not shekels. In the face of triple-digit inflation, they cannot change their prices every other day. The U.S. dollar becomes the unit of account.

Exhibit 8.2   *A Procedure Flow Chart for United States Translation Practices*

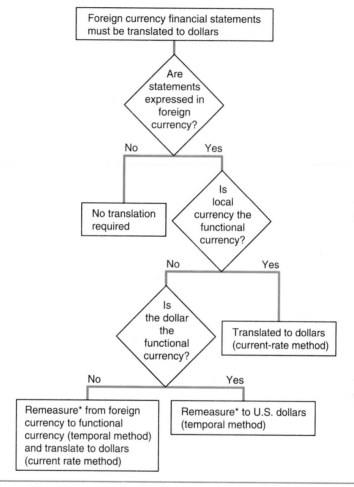

*The term remeasure means to translate as to change the unit of measure from a foreign currency to the functional currency.

Source: Frederick D.S. Choi and Gerhard G. Mueller, *International Accounting*, 3rd Edition, Englewood Cliffs, J.J., Prentice-Hall, 1998.

Also, when an Israeli holds U.S. dollars and the shekel is devalued, his holding in dollars remains the same, whereas if he holds currency in shekels and the shekel is devalued, his holding declines in purchasing power. The U.S. dollar becomes the storehouse of value. Consistent with the mercantile practice of businessmen in highly inflationary economies, the FASB promulgates the accounting standard that the home currency becomes the functional currency when inflation is rampant; otherwise, the local currency is the functional currency. Accounting standards-setting simply is patterned after accepted business practice.[8]

In summary, U.S. translation practices require the parent company to first determine the functional currency of the foreign affiliate, which then dictates whether the affiliate's financial statements will be translated by the current-rate method or remeasured by the temporal method. A final point of emphasis: the selection of the functional currency is determined by the economic realities of the affiliate's operations and is not management's discretionary selection of a procedure to obtain a desired end. Since many U.S.-based multinationals have numerous foreign affiliates, some of which are U.S. dollar-functional and some foreign currency-functional, foreign currency gains and losses may be passing through both current consolidated income and/or accruing in equity reserves.

))) International Translation Practices

As illustrated in Exhibit 8.3, many of the world's largest industrial countries—as well as the relatively newly formed International Accounting Standards Committee (IASC) – follow the same basic translation procedure.

- A foreign affiliate as an *integrated foreign entity* or a *self-sustaining foreign entity*;
- *Integrated foreign entities* are typically remeasured using the *temporal method* (or some slight variation thereof); and
- *Self-sustaining foreign entities* are translated at the *current-rate method*, also termed the *closing-rate method*.

Many different methods and practices exist, however, as we would expect when considering accounting practices across countries. For example, Switzerland allows any of four different practices (current/noncurrent, monetary/nonmonetary, modified monetary, current rate), while Mexico has no explicit recommendations for translation.

CURRENT RATE AND TEMPORAL TRANSLATION EXAMPLE

We will illustrate the use of the current rate method of translation by continuing the hypothetical example of Instruments du Rhone, S.A. from Chapter 7. This example is supplemented with an illustration of translation by the temporal method in order to demonstrate the very arbitrary nature of a translation gain or loss. Selection of the accounting method is the major factor in determining the magnitude of gain or loss. (The example that follows deals with balance sheet translation only. The somewhat more complex procedures for translating income statements are described in international accounting texts.[9])

The functional currency of Instruments du Rhone, S.A., is the euro, and the reporting currency of its parent, Jefferson Controls, is the U.S. dollar. Assume the following:

1. Plant and equipment and long-term debt were acquired, and common stock issued, by Instruments du Rhone some time in the past when the exchange

| Exhibit 8.3 | *International Comparison of Translation Methods* |

Country	Integrated Foreign Entity	Self-Sustaining Foreign Entity
United States	Financial statements are remeasured using the temporal method with adjustments included in current net income.	Current-rate method. Translation adjustments are reported as a separate component of shareholders' equity.
International	Temporal method.Translation adjustments are included in net income currently, except that translation adjustments on long-term monetary items may be deferred and amortized over the surn of the item.	Current-rate method. Translation adjustments are reported as a separate component of shareholders' equity.
Australia	Temporal method. Translation adjustments are included in current net income.	Current-rate method. Translation adjustments are reported as a separate component of shareholders' equity.
Canada	Temporal method. Translation adjustments are included in current net income.	Current-rate method. Translation adjustments are reported as a separate component of shareholders' equity.
France	Temporal method. Translation adjustments are included in current net income.	Current-rate method. Translation adjustments are reported as a separate component of shareholders' equity.
Germany	Temporal method or current-rate method is acceptable. Translation adjustments are included in net income currently if the temporal method is used and as a separate component if the current-rate method is used.	Same as for *Integrated Foreign Entity.*
Japan	Temporal method. Adjustments related to foreign subsidiaries are reported separately as an asset or a liabilitv; adjustments related to divisions or branches are included in current net income.	Same as for *Integrated Foreign Entity.*
Netherlands	Temporal method. Translation adjustments are included in current net income. The current-rate method is used if the entity utilizes current-value accounting.	Current-rate method. Translation adjustments are reported as a separate component of shareholders' equity.
United Kingdom	Temporal method. Translation adjustments are included in current net income.	Current-rate method. Translation adjustments are reported as a separate component of shareholders' equity.

Source: *Survey of International Accounting Practices,* Arthur Andersen & Co., Coopers & Lybrand, Deloitte & Touche, Ernst & Young, KPMG Peat Marwick, and Price Waterhouse, 1991.

rate was $1.2760/€. Although the euro never traded at this rate against the dollar, the historic French franc rate in use at the time the initial investment was made must be converted to a "historic euro rate" which, in effect, back-dates euro rates against the franc.

2. Inventory currently on hand was purchased or manufactured during the immediately prior quarter when the average exchange rate was $1.2180/€.

3. At the close of business on Monday, December 31, 2001, the current spot exchange rate was $1.1600/€.

4. When business reopened on January 2, 2002, after the New Year holiday, the euro had dropped 16.67% in value to reach parity with the dollar at $1.0000/€.

The example will also look at the consequences if the euro had strengthened overnight to $1.3200/€.

⑅ Current-Rate Method

The top half of Exhibit 8.4 illustrates translation loss using the current-rate method. Assets and liabilities on the pre-depreciation balance sheet are translated at the current exchange rate of $1.2000/€. Capital stock is translated at the historical rate of $1.2760/€, and retained earnings are translated at a composite rate that is equivalent to having each past year's addition to retained earnings translated at the exchange rate in effect in that year.

The sum of retained earnings and the CTA account must balance the liabilities and net worth section of the balance sheet with the asset side. For this hypothetical text example we have assumed $7,444,000 for retained earnings and a negative $136,800 for the CTA account on the balance sheet for December 31, 2001. This assumption does not affect the final measure of the increase in the CTA account because the retained earnings account is carried over at whatever arbitrary amount is assigned for this example.

As shown in the top half of Exhibit 8.4, the "just before depreciation" dollar translation reports an accumulated translation loss from prior periods of $136,800. This balance is the cumulative gain or loss from translating euro statements into dollars in prior years and had been carried separately in the CTA account.[10]

After the 16.67% depreciation, assets and liabilities are all translated at the new exchange rate of $1.0000/€. Equity accounts, including retained earnings, are translated just as they were before depreciation, and as a result, the cumulative translation loss increases to $1,736,800. The increase of $1,600,000 in this account (from a cumulative loss of $136,800 to a new cumulative loss of $1,736,800) is the translation loss measured by the current-rate method.

This translation loss is a decrease in equity, measured in the parent's reporting currency, of net exposed assets. An *exposed asset* is an asset whose value drops with the depreciation of the functional currency and rises with an appreciation of

Exhibit 8.4   *Hypothetical Case: Instruments du Rhone, S.A. Translation Loss Just after Depreciation of the Euro*

	In euros		In U.S. dollars		
			December 31, 2001 Just before		January 2, 2002 Just after
		$/euro	Depreciation	$/euro	Depreciation
Current-Rate Method					
Cash	€ 1,600,000	1.2000	$1,920,000	1.0000	$1,600,000
Accounts receivable	3,200,000	1.2000	3,840,000	1.0000	3,200,000
Inventory	2,400,000	1.2000	2,880,000	1.0000	2,400,000
Net plant and equipment	4,800,000	1.2000	5,760,000	1.0000	4,800,000
	€12,000,000		$14,400,000		$12,000,000
Accounts payable	€ 800,000	1.2000	$ 960,000	1.0000	$ 800,000
Short-term bank loan	1,600,000	1.2000	1,920,000	1.0000	1,600,000
Long-term debt	1,600,000	1.2000	1,920,000	1.0000	1,600,000
Common stock	1,800,000	1.2760	2,296,800	1.2760	2,296,800
Retained earnings	6,200,000	(a)	7,440,000	1.2000(b)	7,440,000
Cumulative translation adjustment (CTA)	–		(136,800)		(1,736,800)
	€12,000,000		$14,400,000		$12,000,000
Temporal Method					
Cash	€ 1,600,000	1.2000	$1,920,000	1.0000	$ 1,600,000
Accounts receivable	3,200,000	1.2000	3,840,000	1.0000	3,200,000
Inventory	2,400,000	1.2180	2,923,200	1.2180	2,923,200
Net plant and equipment	4,800,000	1.2760	6,124,800	1.2760	6,124,800
	€12,000,000		$14,808,000		$13,848,000
Accounts payable	€ 800,000	1.2000	$ 960,000	1.0000	$ 800,000
Short-term bank loan	1,600,000	1.2000	1,920,000	1.0000	1,600,000
Long-term debt	1,600,000	1.2000	1,920,000	1.0000	1,600,000
Common stock	1,800,000	1.2760	2,296,800	1.2760	2,296,800
Retained earnings	6,200,000	(a)	7,711,200	– (b)	7,711,200
Translation gain (loss)	–		–	(c)	(160,000)
	€ 12,000,000		$14,808,000		$13,848,000

Notes:

[a]Dollar retained earnings before depreciation are the cumulative sum of additions to retained earnings of all prior years, translated at exchange rates in each year. See text for assumptions used in this example.

[b]Translated into dollars at the same rate as before depreciation.

[c]Under the temporal method, the translation loss of $160,000 would be closed into retained earnings via the income statement rather than left as a separate line item. Hence, under the temporal method, ending retained earnings would actually be $7,711,200 − $160,000 = $7,551,200.

that currency. "Net" exposed assets in this context means exposed assets minus exposed liabilities. Net exposed assets are positive (that is, "long") if exposed assets exceed exposed liabilities; they are negative ("short") if exposed assets are smaller than exposed liabilities.

Exposure can be measured by creating a "before" and "after" translated balance sheet, as was done in Exhibit 8.4. A simpler method is to multiply net exposed assets by the percentage amount of depreciation. This calculation has

---

Exhibit 8.5   *Instruments du Rhone, S.A.*

Panel A: Translation Loss Just after a Depreciation of the Euro ($/euro)

	From $ 1.2000	to	$ 1.0000
	Current-Rate Method		*Temporal Method*
Exposed Assets			
Cash	$1,920,000		$1,920,000
Accounts receivable	3,840,000		3,840,000
Inventory	2,880,000		not exposed
Net plant and equipment	5,760,000		not exposed
Total exposed assets ("A")	$14,400,000		S5,760,000
Exposed Liabilities			
Accounts payable	$ 960,000		$ 960,000
Short-term bank loan	1,920,000		1,920,000
Long-term debt	1,920,000		1,920,000
Total exposed liabilities ("L")	S4,800,000		$4,800,000
Gain (loss) if Euro Depreciates			
Net exposed assets ("A" – "L")	$ 9,600,000		$ 960,000
Times amount of depreciation	(0.1667)		(0.1667)
Translation gain (loss)	$(1,600,000)		$(160,000)

Pand B: Translation Loss Just after an Appreciation of the Euro ($/euro)

	From $ 1.2000	to	$ 1.3200
	Current-Rate Method		*Temporal Method*
Gain (loss) if Euro Appreciates			
Net exposed assets ("A" – "L")	$9,600,000		$960,000
Times amount of appreciation	0.1000		0.1000
Translation gain (loss)	$ 960,000		$ 96,000

been done for the current-rate method in the left column of Exhibit 8.5, which illustrates that a 16.67% depreciation of the euro means that net exposed assets of $9,600,000 lose 16.67% of their value, a translation loss of $1,600,000.

Suppose instead that the euro had appreciated. If, by the end of the year, the euro had appreciated from $1.2000/€ to $1.3200/€, the appreciation would be 10%. The effect of this is seen in Panel B of Exhibit 8.5, which starts with the same net exposed assets calculated in Panel A. Under the current rate method, the U.S. parent would have a translation gain of $960,000.

))) Temporal Method

Translation of the same accounts under the temporal method shows the arbitrary nature of any gain or loss from translation. This is illustrated in the bottom half of Exhibit 8.4. Monetary assets and monetary liabilities in the pre-depreciation euro balance sheet are translated at the current rate of exchange, but other assets and the equity accounts are translated at their historic rates. For Instruments du Rhone, the historical rate for inventory differs from that for net plant and equipment because inventory was acquired more recently.

Under the temporal method, translation losses are not accumulated in a separate equity account but passed directly through each quarter's income statement. Thus, in the dollar balance sheet translated before depreciation, retained earnings were the cumulative result of earnings from all prior years translated at historical rates in effect each year, plus translation gains or losses from all prior years. In Exhibit 8.4, no translation loss appears in the pre-depreciation dollar balance sheet because any losses would have been closed to retained earnings.

The effect of the 16.67% depreciation is to create an immediate translation loss of $160,000. This amount is shown as a separate line item in Exhibit 8.4 in order to focus attention on it for this textbook example. Under the temporal method, this translation loss of $160,000 would pass through the income statement, reducing reported net income and reducing retained earnings. Ending retained earnings would in fact be $7,711,200 minus $160,000, or $7,551,200. Other countries using the temporal method do not necessarily require gains and losses to pass through the income statement.

When translation loss is viewed in terms of changes in the value of exposed accounts, as in the right column of Exhibit 8.5, the loss under the temporal method is 16.67% of net exposed assets of $960,000, or $160,000. If the euro should appreciate 10%, the translation gain to the U.S. parent would be $96,000, as shown at the bottom of the right column in Exhibit 8.5.

))) Managerial Implications

In Exhibits 8.4 and 8.5, translation loss or gain is larger under the current-rate method because inventory and net plant and equipment, as well as all monetary assets, are deemed exposed. When net exposed assets are larger, gains or losses from translation are also larger.

The managerial implications of this fact are very important. If management expects a foreign currency to depreciate, it could minimize translation exposure by reducing net exposed assets. If management anticipates an appreciation of the foreign currency, it should increase net exposed assets to benefit from a gain.

Depending on the accounting method of the moment, management might select different assets and liabilities for reduction or increase. Thus "real" decisions about investing and financing might be dictated by which accounting technique is required, when in fact the method of reporting should be neutral in its influence on operating and financing decisions.

COMPARING TRANSLATION EXPOSURE WITH OPERATING EXPOSURE

Translation gains or losses in the event of depreciation are compared with the operating gains or losses from Chapter 7 in Exhibit 8.6. Obviously translation gains or losses can be quite different from operating gains or losses, not only in magnitude but also in sign. A manager focusing only on accounting losses, in a situation such as Instruments du Rhone, might avoid France because of the likelihood of such a loss. Such a manager might fear loss of a bonus tied to reported profits, or possibly loss of a job if the investment in France were made and subsequently the translated income statement reported severe accounting losses back to the home office.

Operating exposure presents an entirely different view of the same situation. As summarized in Exhibit 8.6, France and Europe became a more (not less) desirable location for investment because of the *operating* consequences that followed depreciation in two of the three cases. This outcome illustrates the importance of focusing decisions primarily on the operating consequences of changes in

---

Exhibit 8.6   *Comparison of Accounting Exposure with Operating Exposure, Depreciation of Euro from $1.2000/€ to $1.0000/€ for Instruments du Rhone, S.A.*

Exposure	Amount	Gain or Loss
Accounting Exposure (Exhibits 8.4 and 8.5)		
Current rate method	($1,600,000)	Loss on translation
Temporal method	($160,000)	Loss on translation
Operating Exposure (in present value terms; Exhibit 7.6)		
Case 1: Depreciation of euro	($1,033,914)	Loss on operations
Case 2: Volume doubles	$2,866,106	Gain on operations
Case 3: Sales price increases	$3,742,892	Gain on operations

exchange rates, and only secondarily on the accounting-based measurements of firm performance. Chapter 21 discusses in detail this managerial debate.

CONSOLIDATION OF ACCOUNTS

Translation of statements is necessary to prepare a consolidated balance sheet and income statement.[11] It is also the first step in preparing corporate-wide exposure reports for management use.

Balance sheets for Jefferson Controls, Inc., the U.S. parent, and its two wholly owned affiliates, Instruments du Rhone, S.A., and Canadian Instruments, Ltd., are shown in Exhibit 8.7. The unconsolidated balance sheet of the parent is shown in column 1; column 2 shows the balance sheet of Instruments du Rhone; and column 3 shows the balance sheet of Canadian Instruments. All balance sheets are for December 31, 2001, before any changes in exchange rates. The symbol "C$" designates Canadian dollars.

Footnotes to Exhibit 8.7 explain details of the financial situation, including the exchange rates in effect on Monday, December 31, 2001. Jefferson Controls has £100,000 on deposit in a London bank; Canadian Instruments owes its U.S. parent C$600,000; the parent carries its investments in Instruments du Rhone and Canadian Instruments at $9,600,000 and $3,000,000, respectively. The U.S. parent company has borrowed £200,000 from a London bank; and Canadian Instruments has long-term debt denominated in euros of €500,000.

The process of creating a consolidated balance sheet from affiliate statements is shown in Exhibit 8.8. Intracompany accounts are canceled. Then remaining foreign currency accounts are translated into U.S. dollars, and the dollar amounts are added horizontally to create, in the right-hand column, the consolidated balance sheet. In this example, translation has been accomplished by the current-rate method. Details of the translation for intracompany accounts are given in the notes to Exhibit 8.8.

The net effect of consolidation is to create a worldwide consolidated balance sheet that reports, in U.S. dollar terms, assets of $32,850,000, liabilities of $14,050,000, and shareholders' equity of $18,800,000. As stated earlier, the main purpose of translation is to create such a consolidated balance sheet.

MANAGING ACCOUNTING EXPOSURE

The main technique to minimize accounting exposure is called a *balance sheet hedge*. At times some firms have attempted to hedge accounting exposure in the forward market. Such action amounts to speculating in the forward market in the hope that a cash profit will be realized to offset the noncash loss from translation. Success depends on a precise prediction of future exchange rates, for such a hedge will not work over a range of possible future spot rates. In addition, the profit from the forward "hedge" (i.e., speculation) is taxable, but the translation loss does not reduce taxable income.

| Exhibit 8.7 | *Unconsolidated Balance Sheets for Jefferson Controls, Inc., and Its French and Canadian Affiliates, December 31, 2001 (in thousands of currency units)* |

	Jefferson Controls (parent only)	Instruments du Rhone	Canadian Instruments
Assets			
Cash	$800,000[a]	€1,600,000	C$825,000
Accounts receivable	2,400,000[b]	3,200,000	1,350,000
Inventory	3,000,000	2,400,000	1,800,000
Net plant and equipment	7,000,000	4,800,000	4,500,000
Investment in subsidiaries:			
Instruments du Rhone	9,600,000[c]		
Canadian Instruments	3,000,000[d]		
	$25,800,000	€12,000,000	C$8,475,000
Liabilities and Net Worth			
Accounts payable	$2,000,000	€800,000	C$1,500,000[b]
Short-term bank loan	2,000,000[e]	1,600,000	1,200,000[f]
Long-term debt	3,000,000	1,600,000	1,275,000[g]
Capital stock	4,000,000	1,800,000	1,200,000
Retained earnings	14,800,000	6,200,000	3,300,000
	$25,800,000	€12,000,000	C$8,475,000

Assumed Exchange Rates and Cross Rates, Monday, December 31, 2001

	Canadian Dollar	*U.K. Pound*	*U.S. Dollar*	*Euroland Euro*
Canada	–	£0.4167	$ 0.6667	€0.5747
United Kingdom	C$ 2.4000	–	$1.6000	€1.3793
United States	C$ 1.5000	£0.6250	–	€0.8621
Euroland	C$ 1.7400	£0.7250	$ 1.2000	–

[a]U.S. parent has £100,000 in a London bank, carried on its books as $160,000. This amount is part of the total cash balance of $800,000 shown on the parent's books.

[b]Canadian Instruments owes the U.S. parent C$600,000, included in accounts payable and carried on the U.S. books at $400,000 (C$600,000 ÷ C$1.5000/$). Remaining accounts receivable (parent's books) and accounts payable (Canadian Instrument's books) are in U.S. and Canadian dollars, respectively.

[c]The U.S. parent carries its 100% ownership of Instruments du Rhone at $9,600,000, which is the sum of capital stock (€1,800,000) and retained earnings (€6,200,000) times the exchange rate $1.2000/€.

[d]The U.S. parent carries its 100% ownership of Canadian Instruments at $3,000,000, which is the sum of capital stock (C$1,200,000) and retained earnings (C$3,300,000) divided by C$1.5000/$.

[e]The U.S. parent has borrowed, on a short-term basis, £200,000 from a London bank, carried on its books as $320,000. Remaining parent short-term bank debt is denominated in U.S. dollars.

[f]Canadian Instruments' short-term bank loan consists of £400,000, carried on Canadian books as C$960,000 (£400,000 × C$2.40/£.)

[g]Canadian Instruments' long-term debt consists of €500,000, carried on Canadian books as C$870,000 (€500,000 × C$1.7400/€).

| Exhibit 8.8 | *Consolidated Balance Sheets for Jefferson Controls, Inc., December 31, 2001 (accounts translated into U.S. dollars with intracompany accounts removed)* |

	Jefferson Controls (parent only)	Instruments du Rhone	Canadian Instrument	Consolidated Balance Sheet
Assets				
Cash	$ 800,000[a]	$1,920,000	$550,000	$3,270,000
Accounts receivable	2,000,000[b]	3,840,000	900,000	6,740,000
Inventory	3,000,000	2,880,000	1,200,000	7,080,000
Net plant and equipment	7,000,000	5,760,000	3,000,000	15,760,000
Investment in subsidiaries:				
Instruments du Rhone	– [c]			
Canadian Instruments	– [c]			
				$32,850,000
Liabilities and Net Worth				
Accounts payable	$2,000,000	$ 960,000	$600,000[e]	$3,560,000
Short-term bank loan	2,000,000[d]	1,920,000	$800,000	4,720,000
Long-term debt	3,000,000	1,920,000	850,000	5,770,000
Capital stock	4,000,000	– [c]	– [c]	4,000,000
Retained earnings		– [c]	– [c]	14,800,000
				$32,850,000

[a]The U.S. parent has £100,000 on deposit in a London bank, carried on its books as $160,000. This amount is part of the total cash balance of $800,000 shown on the parent's books, and for consolidation purposes is carried at its U.S. dollar value on the parent's books.
[b]$2,400,000 – $400,000 intracompany debt = $2,000,000.
[c]Investments in affiliates cancel with the equity of the affiliates in consolidation. If the carrying value on the books of the parent is not equal to the translated equity value of the affiliate, the difference is closed to retained earnings.
[d]Includes £200,000 carried at $300,000.
[e]Original Canadian account payable of $1,500,000 less intracompany debt of C$600,000 to U.S. parent leaves C$900,000, which is translated at the current exchange rate of C$1.5000/$ into US$600,000.

>>> **Balance Sheet Hedge Defined**

A *balance sheet hedge* requires an equal amount of *exposed* foreign currency assets and liabilities on a firm's consolidated balance sheet. If this can be achieved for each foreign currency, net accounting exposure will be zero. A change in exchange rates will change the value of exposed liabilities in an equal amount but in a direction opposite to the change in value of exposed assets. If a firm translates by the temporal method, a zero net exposed position is called *monetary balance*. Complete monetary balance cannot be achieved under the current-rate method because total assets would have to be matched by an equal amount of debt, but the equity section of the balance sheet must still be translated at historic exchange rates.

The cost of a balance sheet hedge depends on relative borrowing costs. If foreign currency borrowing costs, after adjusting for foreign exchange risk, are higher than parent currency borrowing costs, the balance sheet hedge is costly, and vice versa. Normal operations, however, already involve decisions about the magnitude and currency denomination of specific balance sheet accounts. Thus, balance sheet hedges are a compromise in which the denomination of balance sheet accounts is altered, perhaps at a cost in terms of interest expense or operating efficiency, to achieve some degree of foreign exchange protection.

))) Balance Sheet Hedge Illustrated

To illustrate a balance sheet hedge, let us return again to the accounting exposure previously identified for Instruments du Rhone and its parent, Jefferson Controls. Earlier data from Exhibit 8.4 is restated in a different format in Exhibit 8.9.

Instruments du Rhone expects the euro to drop 16.67% in value from its year-beginning value to a new exchange rate of $1.0000/€. Under the current rate method, the expected loss is 16.67% of the exposure of $9,600,000, or $1,600,000. Under the temporal method, the expected loss is 16.67% of the exposure of $960,000, or $160,000.

To achieve a balance sheet hedge, Jefferson Controls must either (1) reduce exposed euro assets without simultaneously reducing euro liabilities or (2) increase euro liabilities without simultaneously increasing euro assets. One way to do this is to exchange existing euro cash for dollars. If Instruments du Rhone does not have large euro cash balances, it can borrow euros and exchange the borrowed euros for dollars. Another European affiliate (if one existed) could borrow euros and exchange them for dollars, That is, the essence of the hedge is for the parent or any of its affiliates to create euro debt and exchange the proceeds for dollars.

Current-Rate Method. Under the current-rate method, as much as €9,600,000 should be borrowed. The initial effect of this first step is to increase both an exposed asset (cash) and an exposed liability (notes payable) on the balance sheet of Instruments du Rhone, with no immediate effect on *net* exposed assets. The required follow-up step can take two forms: (1) Instruments du Rhone could exchange the acquired euros for U.S. dollars and hold those dollars itself or (2) it could transfer the borrowed euros to Jefferson Controls, perhaps as a euro dividend or as repayment of intracompany debt. Jefferson Controls could then exchange the euros for dollars. In some countries, of course, local monetary authorities will not allow their currency to be so freely exchanged.

Another possibility is for Jefferson Controls or a sister affiliate to borrow the euros, thus keeping the euro debt entirely off Instrument du Rhone's books. However, the second step is still essential to eliminate euro exposure; the borrowing entity must exchange the euros for dollars or other unexposed assets. Any such borrowing should be coordinated with all other euro borrowings to avoid the possibility that one affiliate is borrowing euros to reduce accounting exposure

| | Exhibit 8.9 | *Instruments du Rhone, S.A., Balance Sheet Exposure* |

	Balance Sheet Accounts	Current Rate Exposure	Monetary/ Nonmonetary Exposure
Assets			
Cash	€ 1,600,000	€ 1,600,000	€ 1,600,000
Accounts receivable	3,200,000	3,200,000	3,200,000
Inventory	2,400,000	2,400,000	
Net plant and equipment	4,800,000	4,800,000	
Total assets	€ 12,000,000		
Exposed assets		€ 12,000,000	€ 4,800,000
Liabilities and Capital			
Accounts payable	€ 800,000	€ 800,000	€ 800,000
Short-term bank debt	1,600,000	1,600,000	1,600,000
Long-term debt	1,600,000	1,600,000	1,600,000
Capital stock	1,800,000		
Retained earnings	6,200,000		
Total liabilities and net worth	€ 12,000,000		
Exposed liabilities		€ 4,000,000	€ 4,000,000
Net exposed assets in euros		€ 8,000,000	€ 800,000
Times exchange rate ($/€)		1.2000	1.2000
Net exposed assets in dollars		$ 9,600,000	$ 960,000
Times amount of depreciation		×(0.1667)	×(0.1667)
Expected translation gain (loss)		$(1,600,000)	$ (160,000)

at the same time that another affiliate is repaying euro debt. (Note that euros can be "borrowed" by simply delaying repayment of existing euro debt; the goal is to increase euro debt, not borrow in a literal sense.)

Temporal Method. If translation is by the temporal method, only the much smaller amount of €960,000 need be borrowed. As before, Instruments du Rhone could use the proceeds of the loan to acquire U.S. dollars. However, Instruments du Rhone could also use the proceeds to acquire inventory or fixed assets in Europe. Under the temporal method these assets are not regarded as exposed and do not drop in dollar value when the euro devalues.

))) When Is a Balance Sheet Hedge Justified?

If a firm's subsidiary is using the local currency as the functional currency, the following circumstances could justify using a balance sheet hedge:

1. The foreign affiliate is about to be liquidated, so that value of its CTA would be realized.

2. The firm has debt covenants or bank agreements that state the firm's debt/equity ratios will be maintained within specific limits.

3. Management is evaluated on the basis of certain income statement and balance sheet measures that are affected by translation losses or gains.

4. The foreign affiliate is operating in a hyperinflationary environment.

If a firm is using the parent's home currency as the functional currency of the foreign affiliate, all transaction gains/losses are passed through to the income statement. Hedging this consolidated income to reduce its variability may be important to investors and bond rating agencies.

⟫ Choice between Minimizing Transaction or Accounting Exposure

Management will find it almost impossible to offset both accounting and transaction exposure at the same time. Reduction of one exposure usually changes the amount of the other exposure. For example, the easiest way to offset accounting exposure is to require the parent and all affiliates to denominate all exposed assets and liabilities in the parent's reporting currency. For U.S. firms and their affiliates, all assets and liabilities would be held in dollars. In this case, a firm would have no accounting exposure, but each affiliate would have its own transaction exposure.

To illustrate, assume that a U.S. parent instructs its Japanese affiliate to bill an export to the parent in dollars. The account receivable on the Japanese affiliate's books is shown as the yen equivalent of the dollar amount, and yen profit is recorded at the time of sale. If, before the parent pays dollars to the Japanese affiliate, the yen appreciates 5%, the parent still pays only the contracted dollar amount. The Japanese affiliate receives 5% fewer yen than were expected and booked as profit. Hence, the Japanese affiliate will experience a 5% foreign exchange loss on its dollar-denominated accounts receivable. Lower yen profit will eventually be translated into lower dollar profit when the affiliate's income statement is consolidated with that of the parent. Eventually the consolidated U.S.-based MNE will show a foreign exchange loss—on dollars!

Similar reasoning will show that if a firm chooses to eliminate transaction exposure, accounting exposure might even be increased. The easiest way to be rid of transaction exposure is to require the parent and all affiliates to denominate all accounts subject to transaction exposure in its local currency. Thus, every affiliate would avoid transaction gains or losses. However, each affiliate would be creating net accounting exposure by being either long or short in terms of local currency-exposed assets or liabilities. The consolidated financial statement of the parent firm would show accounting exposure in each local currency.

As a general matter, firms seeking to reduce both types of exposure usually reduce transaction exposure first. They then recalculate accounting exposure (which may have changed) and decide whether any residual accounting exposure can be reduced without creating more transaction exposure. Taxes complicate the decision to seek protection against transaction or accounting exposure. Transaction losses are normally considered "realized" losses and are therefore deductible from pretax income. However, accounting losses are only "paper" losses, involving no cash flows, and are not deductible from pretax income. It is highly debatable whether protective techniques that necessitate cash payments, and so reduce net cash flow, should be incurred to avoid noncash losses.

SUMMARY

- *Accounting exposure* results from translating foreign-currency-denominated statements of foreign affiliates into the parent's reporting currency so the parent can prepare consolidated financial statements. Accounting exposure is the potential for loss or gain from this translation process.

- The two basic procedures for translation used in most countries today are the *current-rate method* and the *temporal method*.

- Technical aspects of translation include questions of when to recognize gains or losses in the income statement, the distinction between functional and reporting currency, and the treatment of affiliates in hyperinflation countries.

- The main technique for managing accounting exposure is a *balance sheet hedge*. Its use calls for having an equal amount of exposed foreign currency assets and liabilities.

- Even if management chooses to follow an active policy of hedging accounting exposure, it is nearly impossible to offset both transaction and translation exposure simultaneously. If forced to choose, most managers will protect against transaction losses because these are realized cash losses, rather than protect against accounting losses.

QUESTIONS

1. Florida-Pure, K.K.

Florida-Pure, K.K., the Japanese affiliate of a U.S. beverage company, mixes and bottles citrus drinks for sale in the Japanese domestic market. Florida-Pure K.K.'s June 30 balance sheet is:

Assets		Liabilities and Net Worth	
Cash	¥90,000,000	Accounts payable	¥45,000,000
Accounts receivable	135,000,000	One-year bank loan	45,000,000
Inventory	135,000,000	Long-term yen bonds	90,000,000
Net plant and	180,000,000	Capital stock	180,000,000
equipment		Retained earnings	180,000,000
	¥540,000,000		¥540,000,000

Exchange rates for translating Florida Pure's balance sheet into U.S. dollars are:

¥100/$ Historic exchange rate at which plant and equipment, long-term bonds, and common stock were acquired or issued.

¥120/$ June 30 exchange rate. Inventory was purchased at this rate.

¥125/$ July 1 exchange rate after overnight drop in value of yen from ¥120/$ to ¥125/$.

Assuming no change in balance sheet accounts between June 30 and July 1, calculate the translation gain or loss by the current-rate method (or by the temporal method, if more appropriate). Explain translation loss in terms of changes in the value of exposed accounts.

2. Instruments du Rhone (C)

Using facts in this chapter for Instruments du Rhone, assume the exchange rate on January 2, 2002, in Exhibit 8.4 is $0.9918/€ rather than $1.0000/€. Recalculate Instruments du Rhone's translated balance sheet for January 2, 2002, with the new exchange rate, using both the current-rate method and temporal method.

a. Current-rate method: What would be the new value of the CTA account? What was the translation gain or loss?
b. Temporal method: What would be the translation gain/loss?
c. Had the euro appreciated versus the U.S. dollar to, say, $1.2500/€, instead of dropping in value, what would be the current rate's CTA value and the temporal method's translation gain or loss?

3. Instruments du Rhone (D)

Exhibits 8.7 and 8.8 in this chapter combine to create the consolidated balance sheet for Jefferson Controls, Inc. Instead of the rates used in the chapter, assume current rates are as reflected in the following table of cross rates. (Any uneven rate obtained as the reciprocal of an even rate is carried to 6 decimal places.)

	Canadian Dollar	U.K. Pound	U.S. Dollar	Euro
Canada	—	£0.367647	$0.6250	€0.529661
United Kingdom	C$2.7200	—	$1.7000	€1.440678
United States	C$1.6000	£0.588235	—	€0.847458
Euro	C$1.8880	£0.694118	$1.1800	—

a. Recalculate the entries for Exhibit 8.7, the December 31, 2001, unconsolidated balance sheets for Jefferson Controls, Inc., and its French and Canadian affiliates.

b. Recalculate Exhibit 8.8's consolidated balance sheet for Jefferson Controls, Inc., for December 31, 2001.

c. How have the values of Instruments du Rhone and Canadian Instruments changed in the eyes of Jefferson Controls compared with the chapter case?

4. Cuzco Carpets, S.A.

Cuzco Carpets, S.A., is the Peruvian subsidiary of the U.S. firm, Carolina Fabrics, Inc. Cuzco Carpets manufactures high-quality carpets from llama wool and sells its finished carpets to its U.S. parent. The rate of exchange between the Peruvian new sole and the dollar is NS3.2000/$. This is also the historic rate at which fixed assets and inventory were purchased and at which capital stock was issued. Unconsolidated balance sheets for both parent and subsidiary are as follows:

	Carolina Fabrics	Cuzco Carpets
Assets		
Cash	$2,880,000	NS 32,000,000
Accounts receivable	5,600,000	40,000,000[a]
Inventory	7,320,000	48,000,000
Net plant & equipment	24,000,000	60,000,000
Investment in Cuzco Carpets	14,200,000	—
	$54,000,000	NS180,000,000
Liabilities and Net Worth		
Accounts payable	$10,000,000[a]	NS36,000,000
Accrued wages	6,000,000	34,560,000
Long-term debt	18,000,000	64,000,000
Capital stock	14,000,000	3,840,000
Retained earnings	6,000,000	41,600,000
	$54,000,000	NS180,000,000

[a]Carolina Fabrics owes Cuzco Carpets NS28,000,000, denominated in Peruvian new soles, for purchases of carpets imported into the United States. This sum is included in Carolina Fabric's accounts payable as NS28,000,000 ÷ NS3.2000/$ = $8,750,000.

a. Does Carolina Fabrics have any transaction exposure? If so, where and how much? What would be the effect should the new sol devalue from NS3.2/$ to NS4.0/$?

b. Does Carolina Fabrics have any translation exposure? If so, where and how much? What would be the effect should the new sol devalue from NS3.2/$ to NS4.0/$?

c. Prepare consolidated balance sheets for Carolina Fabrics and Cuzco Carpet, both before and after a devaluation from NS3.2/$ to NS4.0/$. Use the current-rate method.

WORLD WIDE WEB EXERCISES

W1. Changing Accounting Practices: FASB
The Financial Accounting Standards Board (FASB) promulgates standard practices for the reporting of financial results by companies in the United States. It also, however, often leads the way in the development of new practices and emerging issues around the world. One major such issue today is the valuation and reporting of financial derivatives and derivative agreements by firms. Use the FASB's home page and the web pages of several of the major accounting firms and other interest groups around the world to see current proposed accounting standards and the current state of reaction to the proposed standards.

FASB home page   http://raw.rutgers.edu/raw/fasb/
Treasury Management Association   http://www.tma.org/

W2. Nestlé's Financial Statements and Exchange Rates
Using Nestlé's web page, check Current Press Releases for more recent financial results, including what the company reports as the primary currencies and average exchange rates used for translation of international financial results during the most recent period.

Nestlé: The World Food Company   http://www.nestlepress.com

SUGGESTED READINGS

Aliber, R. Z., and C. P. Stickney, "Accounting Measures of Foreign Exchange Exposure: The Long and Short of It," *Accounting Review*, Jan. 1975, pp. 44–57.

Ball, Ray, "Making Accounting International: Why, How, and How Far Will It Go?" *Journal of Applied Corporate Finance*, Vol. 8, No. 3, Fall 1995, pp. 19–29.

Houston, Carol Olson, "Translation Exposure Hedging Post SFAS No. 52," *Journal of International Financial Management and Accounting*, Vol. 2, Nos. 2 and 3, Summer and Autumn 1990, pp. 145–170.

Ruland, Robert G., and Timothy S. Doupnik, "Foreign Currency Translation and the Behavior of Exchange Rates," *Journal of International Business Studies*, Fall 1988, pp. 461–476.

NOTES

1. *Statement of Financial Accounting Standards Number 52* is also referred to as SFAS#52 and FASB#52. It was issued by the Financial Accounting Standards Board (FASB) in December 1981, superseding FAS#8, which had been in effect since 1975. The FASB determines accounting policy for U.S. firms.

2. It is important to note that the geographic location of a foreign affiliate and its functional currency may be different. The Singapore affiliate of a U.S. firm may find that its functional currency is the U.S. dollar (*integrated* affiliate), the Singapore dollar (*self-sustaining* affiliate), or a third currency such as the British pound (also a *self-sustaining* affiliate).

3. There are a multitude of different names used for this reserve account adjustment. In Spain, for example, the CTA is termed the *diferencias de conversión.*

4. For example, foreign assets purchased with dollars and then recorded on an affiliate's statements at their foreign currency historical cost are translated back into dollars at a different rate. Thus, they are reported in the consolidated statement in dollars at something other than their historical dollar cost.

5. The *temporal method* assumes that a number of individual assets such as inventory and net plant and equipment are restated regularly to reflect market value. If these items were not restated, but carried at historical cost, the temporal method becomes the *monetary/nonmonetary method* of translation, an approach that is still used by a number of countries today.

6. Mueller, Gernon, and Meek (1987).

7. Terminology is tricky. Under U.S. accounting and translation practices, use of the current rate method is termed "translation," while use of the temporal method is termed "remeasurement."

8. Taussig (1983), pp. 145–146.

9. See, for example, Frederick D.S. Choi and Gerhard G. Mueller, *International Accounting*, 3rd edition, Englewood Cliffs, N.J.: Prentice-Hall, Inc., 1998.

10. Statements from 1998 and earlier would have originally been French franc statements, translated into euros after January 1, 1999, when the euro was introduced.

11. The consolidated statement of cash flow is constructed from the consolidated balance sheet and income statement, not directly from the individual financial statements of the parent and affiliates.

DECISION CASE

Tektronix (C)

In October 1999, Jerry Davies, Treasurer, Tektronix (Tek) and Randahl Finnessy, Worldwide Cash Manager, needed to make some urgent decisions about Tek's foreign exchange risk management strategy.

On June 24, 1999, Tek had announced its decision to split itself into two separate, publicly traded companies. One company would be comprised of Tek's Measurement Business Division (MBD) and would retain the Tektronix name. The other company would be comprised of Tek's Color Printing and Imaging Division (CPID) with a new name to be announced later. It would be capitalized with an initial public offering (IPO) of 15% of its shares. The remaining shares would be distributed tax-free to Tek's existing shareholders. Tek also announced that it intended to sell or find a strategic alliance for its Video and Networking Division, excluding Video Tele.com business unit, which had just been merged into MBD.

On August 10, 1999, Tek announced that it had agreed to sell its video and networking division to a private investment group. Tek will retain a 10% interest in this group.

On September 22, 1999 Tek announced that it had agreed to sell its Color Printing and Imaging Division (CPID) to Xerox Corp. for $950 million in cash. The purchase would enable Xerox to become second only to Hewlett-Packard in the office color printing market with about a 30% market share.

The deal was expected to close within 60 days subject to regulatory approval. However, regulatory approval could be complicated. Tek would need approvals from the Federal Trade Commission, the Department of Justice (antitrust), and the Securities and Exchange Commission. They would also need to receive approvals from each country where a subsidiary was located. It could happen that approval would be received in the United States but be delayed somewhat abroad. This would leave the status of the individual foreign subsidiaries in limbo, both with respect to their eventual financial structures and foreign exchange exposure. It would be necessary in any case to adopt a transition strategy for these activities. In the worst case, the whole sale of CPID to Xerox might fall through.

Jerry Davies and Randahl Finnessy would remain with the surviving Tektronix Inc., which would be comprised of the existing Measurement Business Division (MBD) headquartered in Beaverton, Oregon. The divestment would result in a new foreign exchange risk profile for Tek that differed from the existing combined profile. It meant rethinking the strategies and instruments to be used in managing the new operating, transaction, and accounting exposures. The instruments that had been used by the combined company included matching cash flows, forward contracts, foreign currency options, a risk sharing agreement, a multilateral netting program, and a reinvoicing center.

THE DECISION TO DIVEST

The decision to split up was motivated by the need to improve focus. This generic strategy is the current fad in the academic literature, and it is promoted heavily by management consultants and security analysts. Management would be able to focus its efforts on a single business line of competency. Shareholders and analysts would gain transparency; the ability to analyze and invest in a pure business line—a *pure play*.

Tek's timing was motivated by its recent stock price performance. As shown in Exhibit 1, it had underperformed the market, as measured by the S&P500, since March 1998. (Appendix 1 illustrates Tek's share price alone.)

If the Tek/Xerox deal was approved, by all regulatory bodies, numerous strategic and financial decisions needed to be made. Dividing up Tek to gain focus is a divestment strategy that could reverse some of the economies of scale

| Exhibit 1 | *Tektronix (TEK) Share Price Performance versus the S&P500* |

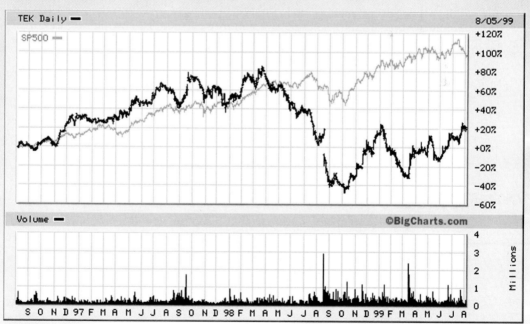

Source: www.Hoovers.com

and synergies that accrue to firms from mergers and acquisitions. The immediate problem being analyzed by Jerry Davies and Randahl Finnessy related to the foreign exchange risk management strategy, but other financial repercussions were also important. Among these was the question of what to do with the sale proceeds from Xerox; net proceeds after taxes were forecast to be $700 million. Should these funds be returned to the shareholders? If so, should it be done via dividends or share repurchases?

Another option would be to pay down corporate debt, but this depended on the eventual new optimal capital structure. Tek had recently been put on *credit watch* by one of the bond rating agencies because of its non-recurring losses in the last two fiscal years. However, its overall debt was modest and quite manageable given expected cash flows.

Still another option for use of some of the sales proceeds was to acquire other measuring instruments companies. Hewlett-Packard's spinoff, Agilent, dominated the worldwide measuring instruments industry. Tek was in second place. There were several other companies that were smaller but significant competitors, and numerous small measuring instruments components.

The optimal debt strategy for the foreign sales subsidiaries was also to be determined. That decision depended on the division of existing debt and assets between Tek and Xerox. In fact, some of the subsidiaries might end up too small to justify a stand-alone status. They would need to be combined with each other. One alternative might be to pool the accounts receivable for the subsidiaries located in the eurozone. These could be monetized by selling them to a separate company that would have Tek as a minority partner. This would increase Tek's cash and remove the receivables from the reported consolidated balance sheet. That would replace trying to borrow locally by many small Tek subsidiaries.

In addition to the financial repercussions of a divestment strategy, there could be serious effects on strategies in marketing, production, distribution, research and development, human resources and other links in the value chain. These are beyond the scope and responsibility of Treasury executives but are obviously critical to the overall success of a divestment strategy. In summary, there is a price to pay for pursuing a divestment strategy, but gains could accrue from a strategy that focuses a company more narrowly on its core competencies.

BACKGROUND

Tek is a U.S. corporation, headquartered in Wilsonville, Oregon. Until the proposed divestment it designed, manufactured, and marketed worldwide three major product lines: measurement instruments, color printing and imaging products, and video and networking products. Tek had 7571 employees worldwide as of May 31, 1999, and maintained operations in 29 countries outside the United States (see Appendix 2). Tek's stock is listed on the New York Stock Exchange under the symbol TEK.

Products and Markets

A description of Tek's products and markets, excluding the video and networking division, is presented in Exhibit 2. About half of Tek's sales are outside the United States. Europe, the Pacific, Japan, and the Americas are the most important markets in declining order of importance. About 45% of total sales in 1999 was produced by MBD, 39% by CPID, and the remaining 16% by the Video and Networking Division.

Exhibit 2	*Tektronix's Products and Markets at a Glance*

Measuring Instruments

Fiscal 1999 Facts		*Geographic Sales (in millions)*	
Sales (thousands):	$844,882	Japan	$59.2
Headquarters:	Beaverton	Europe	$226.6
Number of employees:	3,600	Americas	$38.0
		Pacific	$112.3
		United States	$408.8

Principal Products

Protocol analyzers and simulators
Network monitoring systems
Transmission and cable test products
RF and communication products through alliances
Windows-based logic analyzers and systems
Broad range of oscilloscopes and accessories

Global Market Focus

Focuses on high-growth segments; communications, computers, and semiconductors.Includes telecommunications public network equipment manufacturers and operators; electronic design engineers and prototype developers; television equipment manufacturers; content providers; broadcasters; cable network providers.

Color Printing and Imaging

Fiscal 1999 Facts		*Geographic Sales (in millions)*	
Sales (thousands):	$725,334	Japan	$15.9
Headquarters:	Wilsonville	Europe	$243.4
Number of employees:	2,100	Americas	$35.4
		Pacific	$42.8
		United States	$387.9

Principal Products

Phaser workgroup color printers use either color laser or solid ink printing technology. Also market a complete line of printer consumable products such as ink, toner, and transparencies.

Global Market Focus

Business office market; graphic arts/publishing; science/engineering data analysis; and on-demand printing.

Source:*Tektronix Annual Report, 1999.*

Financial Results

In fiscal 1998 and 1999 (year ending May 31), Tek took nonrecurring pretax charges of $79 million and $120 million, respectively. In 1999 diluted earnings per share fell to a negative ($1.07) from $1.60 in 1998 and $2.29 in 1997. The decline in earnings was mainly due to the downturn in Asian markets, flat U.S. markets, and restructuring to cut costs and to anticipate the split-up. Exhibit 3 presents selected financial data for the 1995-1999 period.

FOREIGN OPERATIONS

Tek was founded in 1946, but had already established its first foreign distribution agreement (in Sweden) by 1948. In the succeeding years Tek established numerous sales subsidiaries, a 50–50 joint venture with Sony of Japan (Sony–Tek), and for a period, manufacturing facilities in the U.K., the Isle of Guernsey, and The Netherlands. The latter have been replaced more recently by manufacturing facilities in Berlin (Germany), Padova (Italy), and Penang (Malaysia). It also has a joint venture in China. Despite the large number of foreign entities, Tek still manufactures 85% of the value of its production in the United States and only 15% abroad. However, foreign sales account for 50% of Tek's total sales.

MBD products are mostly produced and exported from Beaverton, Oregon (Tek's original location), but specialized products are manufactured in Berlin with support from Padova. CPID products mostly originate in Wilsonville, Oregon, although the purpose of acquiring manufacturing facilities in Penang, Malaysia, was to shift some color-printing manufacturing to that location. The Video and Networking Division that will be divested also had foreign sales, but it transacted all of its business in U.S. dollars, both with respect to sales and purchases. Therefore, its sales are expected to have a neutral effect on any foreign exchange exposure strategy.

Exhibit 4 shows how Tek (Oregon) is related to its foreign operating affiliates. Tek also utilizes a Foreign Sales Corporation (FSC), located in Vancouver, British Columbia, that enables it to reduce U.S. taxes on export sales from the United States. All exports with U.S. content greater than 50% go through the FSC.

The majority of Tek's exports from Oregon utilize its reinvoicing center, Tek Europe International (TEI). The products are invoiced to TEI in U.S. dollars but TEI then invoices the foreign subsidiaries in local currency. Thus, the foreign exchange risk is assumed by TEI and is managed at Tek's Wilsonville, Oregon, headquarters. TEI is a legal entity that has no physical presence. Its transfer prices to foreign subsidiaries are adjusted for each country to reflect the customary local margins in each location. The margins employed by local independent distributors are used as a proxy for customary local margins. Tek (Oregon) both buys and sells to Sony–Tek (Japan). Sony–Tek sells to their own customers in Japan and the rest of Asia. Yangzhong buys from Tek (Oregon) and sells in China. It also manufactures and sells some of its own product types in China.

Exhibit 3	*Selected Financial Data, Tektronix 1995–1999 (in millions, except per share and employees; returns are based on average net assets)*				

	1999	1998	1997	1996	1995
Net sales	$1,861.5	$2,085.8	$1,940.1	$1,768.9	$1,498.0
Gross margin	38.2%	41.5%	42.9%	41.9%	45.3%
Excluding NRC	39.7%	43.3%	42.9%	41.9%	45.3%
R&D expenses	11.0%	9.7%	9.7%	9.3%	11.1%
Selling, G&A expenses	25.8%	24.4%	24.8%	24.8%	26.7%
Operating margin	(3.7)%	5.5%	8.5%	8.1%	7.7%
Excluding NRC	2.8%	9.3%	8.5%	8.1%	7.7%
Pretax margin	(4.0)%	5.9%	8.7%	8.0%	7.4%
Excluding NRC	2.4%	9.7%	8.7%	8.0%	7.4%
Earnings margin	(2.7)%	3.9%	5.9%	5.6%	5.4%
Excluding NRC	1.7%	6.5%	5.9%	5.6%	5.4%
Net earnings (loss)	$(51.2)	$82.3	$114.8	$99.6	$81.6
Excluding NRC	$30.8	$135.2	$114.8	$99.6	$81.6
Basic earnings (loss)per share	$(1.07)	$1.63	$2.32	$2.00	$1.67
Excluding NRC	$0.65	$2.68	$2.32	$2.00	$1.67
Diluted earnings per share	$(1.07)	$1.60	$2.29	$1.95	$1.64
Excluding NRC	$0.64	$2.63	$2.29	$1.95	$1.64
Weighted-average shares outstanding:					
Basic	47.7	50.4	49.5	49.8	48.9
Diluted	47.7	51.3	50.2	51.0	49.8
Dividends per share	$0.48	$0.46	$0.40	$0.40	$0.40
Cash and cash equivalents	$39.7	$120.5	$142.7	$36.6	$31.8
Total assets	$1,359.4	$1,389.2	$1,316.7	$1,328.5	$1,218.3
Long-term debt	$150.7	$150.7	$151.6	$202.0	$105.0
Total debt	$266.4	$156.1	$157.7	$246.6	$192.6
Total capitalization	$621.6	$784.9	$771.3	$675.3	$604.2
Return on equity	(7.3)%	10.6%	15.9%	15.6%	15.2%
Excluding NRC	4.0%	16.8%	15.9%	15.6%	15.2%
Ending shares outstanding	46.9	50.3	50.1	49.0	49.6
Book value per share	$13.25	$15.59	$15.39	$13.77	$12.18
Capital expenditures	$107.5	$155.1	$112.0	$106.7	$103.8
Depreciation expense	$71.4	$65.9	$59.6	$47.1	$40.9
Square feet in use	3.7	4.0	3.8	4.1	4.3
Employees	7,571	8,630	8,392	7,929	7,712
Net sales per employee (000s)	$246.1	$241.7	$231.2	$223.1	$194.2
Revenue from new products	71%	74%	73%	67%	62%

NRC = non-recurring charges.

Source: www.Tektronix.com

| **Exhibit 4** | *Organization of Tek (Oregon) and Its Foreign Affiliates* |

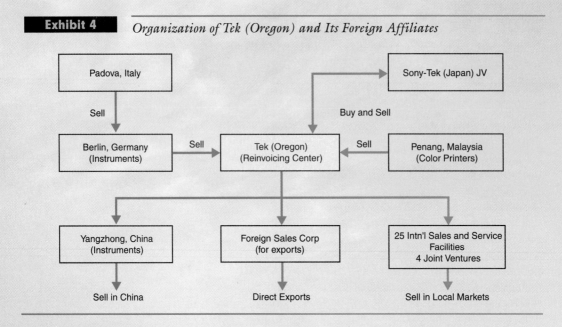

FOREIGN EXCHANGE EXPOSURE

Manufacturing in Oregon and selling abroad in local currencies creates significant structural operating and transaction exposures. When the U.S. dollar strengthens relative to its foreign sales locations, Tek's products become less price competitive. If prices are maintained in local currency terms, foreign exchange losses occur when the local currency proceeds are converted to dollars. If prices are maintained in U.S. dollar terms, foreign sales decline. This phenomenon led to large losses on foreign sales during the 1980–1985 period, when the U.S. dollar appreciated by as much as 50% against European currencies. It is also partly responsible for the most recent losses due to declining sales in Asian markets, where local currencies plunged in value. The U.S. dollar has even strengthened somewhat compared to the euro, but not yet to the point of the 1980–1985 disaster.

Exhibit 5 presents Tek's foreign exchange exposures as of May 31, 1999. *Equity exposure* measures the net exposed assets of Tek's foreign affiliates from an accounting exposure perspective. It is the dollar value of the shareholder equity account on the balance sheet of the foreign affiliates. Gains and losses on equity exposure are placed in an equity reserve account. *Earnings exposure* is a measure of Tek's existing transaction exposure. *Backlog exposure* measures foreign-currency-denominated contracts or orders that have been accepted by Tek but not yet delivered or invoiced. *Current exposure* is foreign exchange contracts for vendor payables. *Anticipated exposure* springs from expected future transactions, not actually contracted for, which in this case are primarily an ongoing commitment for Tek to import components from a major Japanese supplier.

Exhibit 5	*Tektronix Foreign Exchange Exposures, Fiscal Year-end 1999, and Foreign Exchange Losses in Recent Years (thousands of US dollars)*

	Equity	Earnings	Backlog	Current	Anticipated
European Exposures					
Belgian francs	$2,543	$839	$673		
Danish krone	1,655	497	851	1,675	
Deutschemark	33,935	4,072	7,236		
Dutch guilder	1,372	926	713		
Italian lira	17,923	3,838	4,500		
Austrian shilling	2,125	3,838	547		
British pound	72,888	371	8,073		
French franc	23,658	4,859	4,052		
Norwegian krone	374	2,900	191		
Spanish peseta	8,255	0	2,669		
Swedish krona	926	3,126	1,007		
Swiss franc	15,199	132	1,267		
Total European	$180,853	$25,398	$31,780	$1,675	—
AM/PAC Exposures					
Australian dollar	$5,894	$2,301	$5,152		
Brazilian real	9,135	−6,170	207		
Canadian dollar	10,362	2,805	3,329		
Japanese yen	1,682	1,004	12,744	995	50,000
Mexican peso	3,982	−380	81		
Total AM/PAC	$31,055	−$439	$21,514	$995	$50,000
Exposure Summary					
European	$180,853	$25,398	$31,780	$1,675	—
AM/PAC	31,055	-439	21,514	995	50,000
Total exposure	$211,908	$24,959	$53,294	$2,670	$50,000

Foreign Exchange Gains and Losses (thousands of U.S. dollars)

1995	($2,230)
1996	($1,341)
1997	($753)
1998	($278)
1999	($3,448)

Source: Tektronix Treasury Group.

Tek has experienced modest foreign exchange losses every year (1995–1999) despite efficient risk-management programs. Not every exposure is hedged since that would be very costly. The main reason for Tek's continuing foreign exchange losses is its *operating exposure*. Some transaction gains (losses) could also result from the use of the U.S. dollar as the functional currency for Sony–Tek and Tek's Hong Kong subsidiary. All the other foreign subsidiaries use their local currency as the functional currency, so that the foreign exchange gains and losses on these subsidiaries are closed to an equity reserve account (the Cumulative Translation Adjustment or CTA) and do not affect earnings. Appendix 3 presents the functional currency designation and buy currency for each of Tek's subsidiaries.

Operating Exposure

All of the foreign exchange exposures shown in Exhibit 5 are positive because Tek has structural foreign currency operating exposure. Tek produces mainly in Oregon (U.S.), but sells half of its output abroad. Most foreign sales are invoiced in foreign currencies. The imbalance is most severe in Europe even though Tek manufactures to a limited extent in Berlin, Germany (which sources inputs from Padova, Italy). Centralized manufacturing in Oregon has the advantages of gaining economies of scale, close coordination with Tek's R&D activities, and the supporting external infrastructure that has built up over the years.

Tek's main worldwide competitors are predominantly much larger MNEs that can and do enjoy economies of scale in multiple foreign manufacturing locations. For example, Hewlett-Packard (HP) is the longtime competitor that most closely matches Tek in both product lines and historical development. HP, based in Palo Alto, California, has manufacturing plants in 20 foreign countries besides the United States. HP is therefore not as severely affected by operating exposure as is Tek.

In March 1999 HP also announced a strategy to "sharpen its focus." It, too, will split into two companies, named Agilent and Hewlett-Packard. Agilent will focus on the traditional measuring instruments products and markets. It has existing sales of $7 billion (much larger than all of Tek combined). The other company, keeping the HP name, will focus on computer and printing operations with sales of $40 billion worldwide.

Exhibit 6 is an attempt to profile Tek compared to its competitors from the perspective of foreign exchange operating exposure. In addition to HP, Siemens is an immense European MNE, with particularly strong manufacturing in Germany and the Netherlands. However, it has its own operating exposure that depends on the fortunes of the euro. In the color printing and imaging sector, Tek faces giant U.S.-based MNEs such as Xerox, Eastman Kodak, Compaq, and, of course, HP. These MNEs all have multiple manufacturing operations worldwide even though they are headquartered in the United States. It should be noted, however, that some elements of the value chain are equally exposed, especially among Tek's U.S. competitors. These elements include the location of administration and a large part of research and development in the United States. All firms also source a number of their major inputs and much of their equipment at world prices. They all have access to a global cost and availability of capital, shown by their listing on the NYSE, NASDAQ, and European stock exchanges (Siemens). They all sell worldwide and therefore have ongoing exposure to foreign currency receipts.

| Exhibit 6 | Profile of Tek's Global Competitors and Their Structural Operating Exposures |

	Main Listing Exchange	1998 Sales (millions)	1998 Income (millions)	1998 Employees	Main Mfg. Locations	Admin. & R&D Locations	Equipment Source
Measurement							
Tektronix (U.S.)	NYSE	$ 1,863	$ (51)	8,630	U.S.	U.S.	Global
Hewlett-Packard (U.S.)	NYSE	$47,061	$ 2,945	124,600	Global	U.S.	Global
Siemens (Germany)	European	$70,551	$ 550	416,000	Ger/Neth	Germany	Global
National Instruments (U.S.)	NYSE	$274	$37	1,658	U.S.	U.S.	not avail
Color Printers							
Tektronix (U.S.)	NYSE	$ 1,863	$ (51)	8,630	U.S.	U.S.	Global
Hewlett-Packard (U.S.)	NYSE	$47,061	$ 2,945	124,600	Global	U.S.	Global
Compaq Computer (U.S.)	NYSE	$31,169	$(2,743)	71,000	U.S.	U.S.	Global
Eastman Kodak (U.S.)	NYSE	$13,406	$ 1,390	86,200	Global	U.S.	Global
Xerox (U.S.)	NYSE	$19,449	$ 395	92,700	Global	U.S.	Global
Lexmark (U.S.)	NYSE	$ 3,021	$ 243	8,800	U.S.	U.S.	Global

Foreign Exchange Risk Management

Tek uses a number of complementary strategies to manage its foreign exchange risk. The most important tools are: (1) matching cash flows; (2) risk sharing; (3) forward contracts and currency options; (4) reinvoicing; and (5) multilateral netting.

Matching Cash Flows

As a combined company Tek has been able to mitigate part of its Japanese yen exposure by natural matching of cash flows. CPID imports components from a major supplier in Japan and is invoiced in yen. MBD and CPID have healthy sales invoiced in yen. These yen cash flows can be matched at the present time, but not in the future after the split up. Wherever possible, Tek tries to match cash flows as a primary foreign exchange risk-management technique.

At the moment, most of Tek's sales in Japan are through Sony-Tek. The sales to SonyTek are invoiced in U.S. dollars. If necessary it might be possible to change some of these sales to be invoiced in yen. Video Tele.com, which was carved out of the Video and Networking Division before its sale, was established as a new start-up subsidiary in Japan. Its charter is to sell measuring instruments for Tek in Japan. Their products would not compete directly with the Sony-Tek products. Video Tele.com's initial financing came from extended accounts payable to Tek, overdraft privileges, and short term loans. This business was expected to grow and eventually do some local manufacturing. That would require more yen and help to offset the yen proceeds from Tek's sales to Japan. The heavy yen obligations from sourcing color printer components in Japan would disappear with the divestment of CPID. The color printer manufacturing facility in Penang, Malaysia would also become irrelevant from the perspective of natural matching cash flows.

Tek had recently bought out their Chinese joint venture partner in Yangzhong (China) and was expecting to expand manufacturing operations in China. This would require additional financing, foreign exchange exposure, and altered cash flows. Tek also expected to increase its manufacturing operations in Germany. This would require added financing and also alter cash flows.

Risk Sharing

CPID also had a risk-sharing agreement with its major Japanese supplier that it canceled a few years ago. The agreement required Tek to assume the foreign exchange risk for the Japanese yen/U.S. dollar (¥/$) exchange rate for a limited range of movement. Beyond the range, Tek and its Japanese supplier shared the foreign exchange risk for the ¥/$. It worked in favor of the Japanese supplier when the yen was at ¥165/$, but badly for Tek. After the risk-sharing agreement was canceled, the yen strengthened to around ¥114/$. Tek needs to come up with a replacement for this agreement, especially without future matching yen cash flows. Appendix 4 illustrates the typical structure Tek uses in its currency risk-sharing agreements.

Forward Contracts, Currency Options, and Reinvoicing

Tek's policy is for TEI, the reinvoicing center, to hedge selectively with forward contracts where natural currency matching strategies are ineffective. It can only hedge known commercial exposures including backlog exposures. It cannot hedge anticipated exposures. At the end of 1999 and 1998, the notional amounts of Tek's currency contracts were $75.3 million and $127.4 million, respectively.

TEI has also utilized covered options but does not write any uncovered options. In general, Tek has historically been quite conservative when it comes to the use of exotic financial instruments to hedge foreign exchange exposures. This approach is in tune with its other historical financial policies, which favor a low debt ratio and a high level of risk aversion.

Multilateral Netting

Tek employs an internal multilateral netting system to minimize the transaction cost of too many small infrequent internal transfers of cash between operating units and between countries. The birth of the euro should greatly simplify the netting process for subsidiaries located in the Euro-zone (11 participating countries). At one time Tek used Citibank in London to run its multilateral netting system. Since this is a very low cost operation, loss of volume through the divestment would not warrant any changes in the present system.

Decision Time

Jerry Davies and Randahl Finnessy need to propose a foreign exchange risk management strategy for the surviving Tek. Its implementation would be determined by the outcome of the regulatory approval process. In the meantime it would be necessary to define a transition strategy.

| Appendix 1 | *Tektronix Share Price, 1997–1999* |

Source: Hoovers, www.Hoovers.com

| Appendix 2 | *Tektronix Corporate Information* |

Corporate Office

Tektronix, Inc., Wilsonville, Oregon

Manufacturing	**Subsidiary Companies**	**Joint Ventures**
Beaverton, Oregon	England	Japan (Sony/Tek)
Chelmsford, Massachusetts	Wilsonville, Oregon	China (Yangzhong)
Nevada City, California	Beaverton, Oregon	Madison, Wisconsin
Penang, Malaysia	The Netherlands	Beaverton, Oregon
Wilsonville, Oregon	Agana, Guam	
Yangzhong, China	Bangalore, India	
Berlin, Germany	Penang, Malaysia	
	Padova, Italy	
	Berlin, Germany	

International Sales and Service

Argentina	France	Norway
Australia	Germany	Poland
Austria	Hong Kong	Singapore
Belgium	India	Spain
Brazil	Italy	Sweden
Canada	Japan	Switzerland
China (PRC)	Korea	Taiwan (ROC)
Denmark	Mexico	United Kingdom
Finland	The Netherlands	

| **Appendix 3** | *Functional and Buy Currencies for Tektronix Subsidiaries* |

Subsidiary	Functional Currency	Buy Currency	Subsidiary	Functional Currency	Buy Currency
Asia (U.S.)	USD	USD	Berlin (CTE)	DEM	DEM
Australia	AUD	AUD	Bouwerij (Neth's)	NLG	NLG
Beijing	CNY	CNY	Denmark	DKK	DKK
Brazil	BRL	BRL	Europe B.V. (Neth's)	NLG	NLG
Canada	CAD	CAD	Europe Ltd. (U.K.)	GBP	GBP
China	CNY	CNY	Finland	FIM	FIM
Fed Systems (U.S.)	USD	USD	France	FRF	FRF
FSC (U.S.)	USD	USD	Germany	DEM	DEM
GV Japan	JPY	JPY	Holding Co. (U.K.)	GBP	GBP
Hong Kong	USD	USD	Italy	ITL	ITL
India	INR	INR	Norway	NOK	NOK
India Engineering	INR	INR	Poland	PLZ	PLZ
International (U.S.)	USD	USD	Research Ltd. (U.K.)	GBP	GBP
Korea	KRW	KRW	Spain	ESP	ESP
Mexico	MXP	MXP	Sweden	SEK	SEK
Singapore	SGD	SGD	Switzerland	CHF	CHF
Sony/Tek (Japan)	USD	USD	TEI EAME (U.S.)	USD	USD
Taiwan	TWD	TWD	TEI Americas (U.S.)	USD	USD
TDC (U.S.)	USD	USD	TEI Pacific (U.S.)	USD	USD
YTK (Yangzhong)	CNY	CNY	Tek Holland (Neth's)	NLG	NLG
Austria	ATS	ATS	UK	GBP	GBP
Belgium	BEF	BEF			

Note: "Functional Currency" is identified by Tek in accordance with guidelines provided by FAS#52. "Buy Currency" is the currency of denomination for purchases from Tek (Oregon) or other suppliers.

| **Appendix 4** | *Currency Risk-Sharing Agreement for the Japanese Yen/U.S. Dollar (Sample structure used by Tektronix)* |

1. Payment in dollars

Prices for products are set in Japanese yen.Payments for products will be made in U.S.dollars at an adjusted foreign exchange rate (yen per U.S.dollar).The adjusted foreign exchange rate shall be calculated monthly for each month 's shipments based on the following formula:

$$\frac{\text{Price in Japanese yen}}{[(\text{Average JPY spot rate } + \text{ JPY base rate}) \times 1/2\ ]}$$

Base rate = Value of Japanese yen per one U.S.dollar at contract signing

Average spot rate = Based on the New York edition of *The Wall Street Journal*, the yen-to-dollar exchange rate for the calendar month two months prior to the actual shipments, e.g., for shipments for the month of April 1999, the average exchange rate for the month of February 1999, will be used.

2. Payment in yen

The U.S. dollar base unit price (BUP)for each item uses a base exchange rate (BER)(value of Japanese yen per one U.S.dollar at contract signing) to determine the yen price.On four (4)consecutive Tuesdays in each month of December, March, June, and September, SELLER shall record the spot JPY rate as published in the New York edition of *The Wall Street Journal*.The average rate of these four Tuesdays shall be defined as the average exchange rate (AER).

If the difference between the AER and the BER for a specific item is greater than 5%, then the price of that item for the calendar quarter following the month of each calculation shall be adjusted using the following yen-based formula:

If *AER* – *BER* > (some amount of foreign currency), then
    Revised BUP Price = $BUP \times AER / [\ ((AER + BER) \times 1/2\ ]$
Else,
    If *BER* – *AER* > (some amount of foreign currency), then
        Revised BUP Price = $BUP \times AER / [(AER + BER) \times 1/2\ ]$

After the revised BUP price is calculated, it is applied against the BER to determine the new JPY payment.

If the absolute value of the difference between the AER and the BER for a specific item is greater than (some amount of foreign currency)/Dollar, then BUYER and SELLER shall upon the request of either or both meet and discuss a revision of the BER and/or the BUP.

Source: Tektronix Treasury Group.

CHAPTER 9

INTEREST RATE EXPOSURE AND SWAPS

The management of *financial risks*—exchange rates (FX), interest rates (I/R), and commodity prices (CP)—is a rapidly expanding area of multinational financial management. All three of these financial prices introduce risk into the cash flows of the firm. The identification, measurement, and management of interest rate risk now receives roughly the same high level of attention and effort as that focused on foreign exchange risk just a few years ago. In this chapter we provide an overview of interest rate risk management as practiced by international treasurers today. Many of the same basic management processes we observed earlier in foreign exchange risk management have their parallels in interest rate risk management.

DEFINING INTEREST RATE RISK

All firms—domestic or multinational, small or large, leveraged or unleveraged—are sensitive to interest rate movements in one way or another. Although a variety of interest rate risks exist in theory and in industry, this book focuses on the financial management of the firm, so we will limit our discussion to the interest rate risks associated with the multinational firm.[1]

The single largest interest rate risk of the nonfinancial firm is debt service. The debt structure of the multinational firm possesses differing maturities of debt, different interest rate structures (such as fixed- versus floating-rate), and different currencies of denomination. Interest rates are currency-specific. Each currency has its own interest rate yield curve and credit spreads for borrowers. Therefore, the multicurrency dimension of interest rate risk for the multinational is a serious concern. As illustrated in Exhibit 9.1, even the interest rate calculations vary on occasion across currencies and countries.

The second most prevalent source of interest rate risk for the multinational firm lies in its holdings of interest-sensitive securities. As opposed to debt, which falls on the right-hand side of the firm's balance sheet, the marketable securities portfolio of the firm falls on the left-hand side. This portfolio represents potential earnings or interest in-

Exhibit 9.1	*International Interest Rate Calculations*

International interest rate calculations differ by the number of days used in the period's calculation and the country's determination of how many days there are in a year (for financial purposes). The following example highlights how the different methods result in different one-month payments of interest on a $10 million loan, 5.500% per annum interest, for an exact period of 28 days.

Practice	Day Count in Period	$10 million @ 5.500% per annum		
		Days/Year	Days Used	Interest Payment
International	Exact number of days	360	28	$42,777.78
British	Exact number of days	365	28	$42,191.78
Swiss (Eurobond)	Assumed 30 days/month	360	30	$45,833.33

Adapted from "Hedging Instruments for Foreign Exchange, Monday Market, and Precious Metals," Union Bank of Switzerland, 41–42.

flows to the firm. The ever-increasing pressures on competitiveness have pushed financial managers to tighten their management of both the left- and right-hand sides of the firm's balance sheet.

Whether it is on the left or the right, the *reference rate* of the interest calculation merits special attention. A *reference rate*—for example, U.S. dollar LIBOR—is the rate of interest used in a standardized quotation, loan agreement, or financial derivative valuation. LIBOR, the London Interbank Offered Rate, is by far the most widely used and quoted. LIBOR is officially defined by the British Bankers Association (BBA). U.S. dollar LIBOR is the mean of 16 multinational banks' interbank offered rates as sampled by the BBA at approximately 11 A.M. London time in London. Similarly, the BBA calculates the Japanese yen LIBOR, euro LIBOR, and other currency LIBOR rates at the same time from samples of banks.

The interbank interest rate market is not, however, confined to London. Most major domestic financial centers construct their own interbank offered rates for local loan agreement purposes. These rates include PIBOR (Paris Interbank Offered Rate), MIBOR (Madrid Interbank Offered Rate), SIBOR (Singapore Interbank Offered Rate), and FIBOR (Frankfurt Interbank Offered Rate), to name but a few.

MANAGEMENT OF INTEREST RATE RISK

))) The Management Dilemma

Treasurers and financial managers of all types must resolve a basic management dilemma prior to undertaking any form of interest rate risk management: the dilemma of risk and return. Treasury has traditionally been considered a service center (cost center) and is therefore not expected to take positions that incur risk in the expectation of profit. Its activities are rarely managed or evaluated as profit centers. Treasury management practices are therefore predominantly conservative, but opportunities to reduce costs or actually earn profits are not to be ignored. History, however, is littered with examples in which financial managers have strayed from their fiduciary responsibilities in the expectation of profit. Unfortunately, much of the time, they have only realized a loss.[2] It is this dilemma, combined with the wider use of financial derivatives, that has helped more and more firms realize the value of well-constructed policy statements (see Exhibit 9.2).

Both foreign exchange and interest rate risk management must focus on managing existing or anticipated cash flow exposures of the firm. As in foreign exchange exposure management, the firm cannot undertake informed management or hedging strategies without forming expectations—a *directional* and/or *volatility view*—of interest rate movements. Fortunately, interest rate movements have historically shown more stability and less volatility than exchange rates. And as with exchange rates, financial management has frequently preferred to err on the conservative side in order to improve the predictability of commitments and cash flows. This, in turn, improves the strategic decision-making capability of the firm.

Once management has formed expectations about future interest rate levels and movements, it must choose the appropriate implementation, a path that includes the selective use of various techniques and instruments.

Exhibit 9.2   *Treasury Policy Statements*

The major derivative disasters of the 1990s highlighted the need for the proper construction and implementation of corporate financial management policy statements. Policy statements are, however, frequently misunderstood by those writing and enforcing them. A few helpful fundamentals may be in order.

- *A policy is a rule, not a goal.* A policy is intended to limit or restrict management actions, not set priorities or goals. For example, "Thou shalt not write uncovered options" is a policy. "Management will pursue the lowest cost of capital at all times" is a goal.

- *A policy is intended to restrict some subjective decision-making.* Although at first glance this aspect seems to indicate that management is not to be trusted, it is actually intended to make management's decision-making easier in potentially harmful situations. For example, in 1993 Bankers Trust was offering leveraged swaps. The total downside risk was unquantifiable or quantifiable only by the creditors themselves (proprietary). A policy stating that all derivative positions must be quantifiable by the borrower alone would have eliminated the judgment call of management.

- *A policy is intended to establish operating guidelines independently of staff.* Although many policies may appear overly restrictive given the specific talents of financial staff, the fiduciary responsibility of the firm needs to be maintained independently of the specific personnel on-board. Changes in personnel frequently place new managers in uncomfortable and unfamiliar surroundings. Errors in judgment may result. Proper policy construction provides a constructive and protective base for management's learning curve.

))) Credit Risk and Repricing Risk

Before we describe the management of the most common interest rate pricing risks, we need to distinguish between *credit risk* and *repricing risk*. *Credit risk*, sometimes termed *roll-over risk*, is the possibility that a borrower's credit-worth, at the time of renewing a credit, will be reclassified by the lender. This can result in changing fees, higher interest rates, reduced credit-line commitments, or even denial. *Repricing risk* is the risk of changes in interest rates charged (earned) at the time a financial contract's rate is reset.

Consider the following three different debt strategies being considered by a corporate borrower. Each is intended to provide $1 million in financing for a three-year period.

- *Strategy #1*: Borrow $1 million for three years at a fixed rate of interest.

- *Strategy #2*: Borrow $1 million for three years at a floating-rate, LIBOR + 2%, to be reset annually.

- *Strategy #3*: Borrow $1 million for one year at a fixed rate; then renew the credit annually.

Although the lowest cost of funds is always a major selection criteria, it is not the only one. If the firm chooses strategy #1, it assures itself of the funding for the full three years at a known interest rate. It has maximized the predictability of cash flows for the debt obligation. What it has sacrificed, to some degree, is the ability to enjoy a lower interest rate in the event that interest rates fall over the period. It, of course, has also eliminated the risk that interest rates could rise over the period, thus increasing debt servicing costs.

Strategy #2 offers what strategy #1 did not, flexibility (repricing risk). It too assures the firm of full funding for the three-year period. This eliminates credit risk. Repricing risk is, however, alive and well in strategy #2. If LIBOR changes dramatically by the second or third year, the LIBOR rate change is passed through fully to the borrower. The spread, however, remains fixed (reflecting the credit standing that has been locked in for the full three years). Flexibility comes at a cost in this case, the risk that interest rates could go up as well as down.

Strategy #3 offers more flexibility and more risk. First, the firm is borrowing at the shorter end of the yield curve. If the yield curve is positively sloped, as is commonly the case in major industrial markets, the base interest rate should be lower. But the short end of the yield curve is also the more volatile. It responds to short-term events in a much more pronounced fashion than longer-term rates. The strategy also exposes the firm to the possibility that its credit rating may change dramatically by the time of credit renewal, for better or worse. Noting that credit ratings in general are established on the premise that a firm can meet its debt-service obligations under worsening economic conditions, firms of high credit worth (investment grades) may view strategy #3 as a more relevant alternative than those of lower quality (speculative grades). It is not a strategy for firms that are financially weak.

Although it gives only a partial picture of the complexity of funding decisions within the firm, this example aids in demonstrating the many ways credit risks and repricing risks are inextricably intertwined. *Interest rate exposure* is a complex concept, and the proper measurement of the exposure prior to its management is critical. We now proceed to describe the interest rate risk of the most common form of corporate debt, floating-rate loans.

))) Floating-Rate Loans

Floating-rate loans are a widely used source of debt for firms worldwide. They are the source of the single largest and most frequently observed corporate interest rate exposure.

Exhibit 9.3 depicts the costs and cash flows for a three-year floating-rate loan taken out by Puebla Corporation. The loan, with a principal of US$10 million, will be serviced with annual interest payments and total principal repayment at the end of the three-year period.

- The loan is *priced* at U.S. dollar LIBOR + 1.500% (note that the cost of money, interest, is often referred to as *price*). The LIBOR base will be reset each year on an agreed-upon date (say, two days prior to payment). Whereas the LIBOR component is truly floating, the spread of 1.500% is actually a fixed component of the interest payment that is known with certainty for the life of the loan.

- When the loan is drawn down initially, at time year 0, an up-front fee of 1.500% is charged by the lender. This fee results in a reduction in the net proceeds of the loan by US$150,000. Although the loan agreement states $10,000,000, and that Puebla will be required to repay the full $10,000,000, the actual net proceeds to the firm are only $9,850,000.

- The actual interest cost of the loan will not be known by Puebla until the loan has been completely repaid. This reflects the fact that the firm may forecast what LIBOR will be for the life of the loan, but it will not know with certainty until all payments have been completed. This is not only an interest rate risk, but it is also an actual cash flow risk associated with the interest payment. (A fixed interest rate loan has *interest rate risk*, in this case opportunity cost, which does not result in putting actual cash flows at risk.)

Exhibit 9.3 illustrates what the *all-in-costs* (AIC) of the loan are under a number of different sensitivities. The AIC is found by calculating the internal rate of return (IRR) of the total cash flows for repayment. The baseline analysis assumes that LIBOR remains at 5.000% for the life of the loan. Including the up-front fees, the AIC to Puebla is 7.072% (or 6.500% flat without fees). If, however, LIBOR were to rise steadily over the three-year period by 25 basis points (0.25%) per year, the AIC of the loan would rise to 7.565%. If LIBOR were to fall by the same 25 basis points per year, the AIC would fall to 6.578%. It is important to remember, however, that it is only the LIBOR component of the loan price that is the true source of cash flow risk.

| Exhibit 9.3 | *Puebla Corporation's Costs and Cash Flows in Servicing a Floating-Rate Loan* |

The expected interest rates and cash flows associated with a three-year $10,000,000 floating-rate loan. Puebla pays an initiation fee of 1.500% of principal up-front (which reduces proceeds).

Loan Interest Rates	Year-0	Year-1	Year-2	Year-3	
LIBOR (floating)	5.000%	5.000%	5.000%	5.000%	
Spread (fixed)		1.500%	1.500%	1.500%	
Total interest payable		6.500%	6.500%	6.500%	
Interest Cash Flows on Loan					
LIBOR (floating)		($500,000)	($500,000)	($500,000)	
Spread (fixed)		(150,000)	(150,000)	(150,000)	
Total interest		($650,000)	($650,000)	($650,000)	
Loan proceeds (repayment)	$9,850,000			($10,000,000)	
Total loan cash flows	$9,850,000	($650,000)	($650,000)	($10,650,000)	
IRR of total cash flows	7.072% "all-in-cost" (AIC)				

Sensitivities to LIBOR	LIBOR (yr-0)	LIBOR (yr-1)	LIBOR (yr-2)	LIBOR (yr-3)	AIC
Baseline case above	5.000%	5.000%	5.000%	5.000%	7.072%
LIBOR rises 25 basis points/yr		5.250%	5.500%	5.750%	7.565%
LIBOR falls 25 basis points/yr		4.750%	4.500%	4.250%	6.578%

Note. The effective cost of funds (before-tax) for Puebla, the all-in-cost (AIC), is found by determining the internal rate of return (IRR) of the total cash flows associated with the loan. The all-in-cost of the original loan agreement, without fees, is 6.500%.

If Puebla Corporation decided, after it had taken out the loan, that it wished to manage the interest rate risk associated with the loan agreement, it has a number of management alternatives:

- **Refinancing.** Puebla could go back to its lender and restructure and refinance the entire agreement. This is not always possible, and when it is, it is often expensive.

- **Forward Rate Agreements (FRAs).** Puebla could lock in the future interest rate payments with FRAs (see below), much the same way as exchange rates are locked in with forward contracts.

- **Interest Rate Futures.** Although foreign currency futures are rarely used by companies for foreign exchange risk management, interest rate futures have gained substantially more acceptance. Puebla could lock in the future interest rate payments by taking an interest rate futures position.

- **Interest Rate Swaps.** Puebla could enter into an additional agreement with a bank or swap dealer in which it exchanged cash flows in such a way that the interest rate payments on the floating-rate loan would become fixed.

))) Forward Rate Agreements

A *forward rate agreement* (FRA) is an interbank-traded contract to buy or sell interest rate payments on a notional principal. These contracts are settled in cash. The buyer of an FRA obtains the right to effectively lock in an interest rate for a desired term that begins at a future date. The contract specifies that the seller of the FRA will pay the buyer the increased interest expense on a nominal sum (the notional principal) of money if interest rates rise above the agreed rate, but the buyer will pay the seller the differential interest expense if interest rates fall below the agreed rate. Maturities are typically 1, 3, 6, 9, and 12 months, much like traditional forward contracts for currencies.

For example, Puebla may decide that it wishes to lock in the first interest payment (due at the end of the year 1) and so buys an FRA which locks in a total interest payment of 6.500%. If LIBOR rises above 5.000% by the end of year 1, Puebla would receive a cash payment from the FRA seller that would reduce the interest rate to 5.000%. Similarly, if LIBOR were to fall during year 1 to below 5.000% (not what Puebla expects to happen), Puebla would make a cash payment to the seller of the FRA, effectively raising its LIBOR payment to 5.000% and the total loan interest to 6.500%.

Like foreign currency forward contracts, FRAs are useful on individual exposures. They are contractual commitments of the firm that allow little flexibility to enjoy favorable movements, such as when LIBOR is falling as described above. In addition to locking in future floating-rate interest payments, FRAs are also used by firms that plan to invest in securities at future dates but fear that interest rates might fall prior to the investment date. Because of the limited maturities and currencies available, however, FRAs are not widely used outside the largest industrial economies and currencies.

))) Interest Rate Futures

Unlike foreign currency futures, *interest rate futures* are relatively widely used by financial managers and treasurers of nonfinancial companies. Their popularity stems from the relatively high liquidity of the interest rate futures markets, their simplicity of use, and the rather standardized interest rate exposures most firms possess. The two most widely used futures contracts are the Eurodollar futures traded on the Chicago Mercantile Exchange (CME) and the U.S. Treasury Bond Futures of the Chicago Board of Trade (CBOT).[3]

To illustrate the use of futures for managing interest rate risks, we will focus on the three-month Eurodollar futures contracts. Exhibit 9.4 presents Eurodollar futures prices for the coming two years (they actually trade 10 years into the future) on April 30, 1999. The yield of a futures contract is calculated from the *settlement price* (closing price). For example, a financial manager, examining the Eurodollar quotes in Exhibit 9.4, for a March 2000 contract, would see that the settlement price on the previous day was 94.76, an annual yield of 5.24%:

Exhibit 9.4	*Eurodollar Futures Prices*					
Maturity	Open	High	Low	Settle	Yield	Open Interest
June	94.99	95.01	94.98	95.01	4.99	455,763
Sept	94.87	94.97	94.87	94.96	5.04	535,932
Dec	94.60	94.70	94.60	94.68	5.32	367,036
Mar 00	94.67	94.77	94.66	94.76	5.24	299,993
June	94.55	94.68	94.54	94.63	5.37	208,949
Sept	94.43	94.54	94.43	94.53	5.47	168,961
Dec	94.27	94.38	94.27	94.36	5.64	130,824

Abstracted from *The Wall Street Journal*, Friday April 30, 1999, p. C16. Only regular quarterly maturities are shown. All contracts are for $1million; points of 100%. Open interest refers to number of contracts outstanding.

$$Yield = (100.00 - 94.76) = 5.24\%$$

Since each contract is for a three-month period (a quarter) and a notional principal of $1 million, each basis point is actually worth $2500 (.01 × $1,000,000 × 90/360).

If this financial manager were interested in hedging a floating-rate interest payment due in March 2000, he would need to *sell a futures* or take a *short position*. It is referred to as a short position because he is selling something that he does not own (as in shorting common stock). If interest rates rise by March 2000—as the manager fears—the futures price will fall and he will be able to close the position at a profit.[4] This profit will roughly offset the losses associated with rising interest payments on his debt. If the manager is wrong, however, and interest rates actually fall by the maturity date causing the futures price to rise, the resulting loss will wipe-out the "savings" derived by making a lower floating-rate interest payment than he expected. So, by selling the March 2000 futures contract, the manager will be effectively locking in an interest rate of 5.24%.

As mentioned previously, the most common interest rate exposure of the nonfinancial firm is interest payable on debt. It is not, however, the only interest rate risk. As more and more firms aggressively manage their entire balance sheet, the interest earnings from the left-hand side are under increasing scrutiny. If financial managers are expected to continue to earn higher interest on interest-bearing securities, they may well find a second use of the interest rate futures market: the locking in of future interest earnings. Exhibit 9.5 provides an overview of these two basic interest rate exposures and the strategies needed for successful management with interest rate futures.

Interest Rate Swaps

Swaps are contractual agreements to exchange or swap a series of cash flows. These cash flows are most commonly the interest payments associated with debt service, such as the floating-rate loan described above.

| Exhibit 9.5 | *Interest Rate Futures Strategies for Common Exposures* |

Exposure or Position	Futures Action	Interest Rates Change	Position Outcome
Paying interest on future date	Sell a Futures. (short position)	If rates go up . . .	Futures price falls; short earns a profit.
		If rates go down . . .	Futures price rises, short earns a loss.
Earning interest on future date	Buy a Futures. (long position)	If rates go up . . .	Futures price falls; long earns a loss.
		If rates go down . . .	Futures price rises, long earns a profit.

- If the agreement is for one party to swap its fixed interest rate payment for the floating interest rate payments of another, it is termed an *interest rate swap*.

- If the agreement is to swap currencies of debt service obligation—for example, Swiss franc interest payments in exchange for U.S. dollar interest payments—it is termed a *currency swap*.

In either case, however, the swap serves to alter the firm's cash flow obligations, as in changing floating-rate payments into fixed-rate payments associated with an existing debt obligation. The swap itself is not a source of capital but rather an alteration of the cash flows associated with payment. What is often termed the *plain vanilla swap* is an agreement between two parties to exchange fixed-rate for floating-rate financial obligations. This type of swap forms the largest single financial derivative market in the world, with over $25 trillion in existing agreements at the end of 1998.[5]

The two parties may have various motivations for entering into the agreement. For example, a corporate borrower of good credit standing, who has existing floating-rate debt service payments, may believe that interest rates are about to rise. In order to protect the firm against rising debt-service payments, the company's Treasury may enter into a swap agreement to *pay fixed* and *receive floating*. This means the firm will now make fixed interest rate payments and receive from the swap counterparty floating interest rate payments. The floating-rate payments that the firm receives are used to service the debt obligation of the firm, so that the firm, on a net basis, is now making fixed interest rate payments. Using derivatives, it has synthetically changed floating-rate debt into fixed-rate debt. It has done so without going through the costs and intricacies of refinancing existing debt obligations. Similarly, a firm with fixed-rate debt that expects interest rates to fall can change fixed-rate debt to floating-rate debt. In this case, the firm would enter into a *pay floating/receive fixed* interest rate swap. Exhibit 9.6 presents a summary table of the recommended interest rate swap strategies for firms holding either fixed-rate debt or floating-rate debt.

| | Exhibit 9.6 | *Interest Rate Swap Strategies* |

Position	Expectation	Interest Rate Swap Strategy
Fixed-Rate debt	Rates to go up . . .	Do nothing.
	Rates to go down . . .	Pay floating receive fixed.
Floating-Rate debt	Rates to go up . . .	Pay fixed receive floating.
	Rates to go down . . .	Do nothing.

The cash flows of an interest rate swap are interest rates applied to a set amount of capital termed the *notional principal*. These swaps are also referred to as *coupon swaps*. Firms entering into interest rate swaps set the notional principal so that the cash flows resulting from the interest rate swap cover their interest rate management needs.

Interest rate swaps are contractual commitments between a firm and a swap dealer completely independent of the interest rate exposure that is being swapped. That is, the firm may enter into a swap for any reason it sees fit and then swap a notional principal that is less than, equal to, or even greater than the total position being managed. For example, a firm with a variety of floating-rate loans on its books may enter into interest rate swaps for only 70% of the existing principal of debt it carries, if it wishes. The reason for entering into a swap, and the swap position the firm enters, are purely up to management's discretion.

⟫ Puebla Corporation: Swapping to Fixed Rates

Puebla Corporation's existing floating-rate loan is now the source of some concern to its Treasurer. Recent events have led the Treasurer to believe that interest rates, specifically LIBOR, may be rising in the three years ahead. Since the loan agreement is relatively new (Puebla is still in the first year of the loan and has yet to make an interest payment), refinancing is considered too expensive at this point. The Treasury staff believes that a pay fixed/receive floating interest rate swap may be the better alternative for fixing future interest rates now. Upon contacting several of its primary banks, Puebla is quoted a fixed rate of 5.750% against LIBOR. If Puebla enters into the swap agreement, for the next three years it will receive LIBOR and pay out 5.750% on a notional principal of $10 million. A quick analysis of the combined existing loan and pay fixed/receive floating swap undertaken by the Treasury group is presented in Exhibit 9.7.

The swap agreement would be a separate agreement from the existing loan; it would not replace but rather would supplement it. Puebla would still be responsible for making all payments on the floating-rate loan. (Note that the swap agreement applies only to the interest payments on the loan and does not include the principal repayment.) But the part of the payment that Puebla is concerned about—the LIBOR base rate—would now be offset by the receipt of a cash flow of LIBOR from the swap bank. That would leave Puebla responsible for the pay-

| Exhibit 9.7 | Puebla Corporation's Interest Rate Swap to Pay Fixed/Receive Floating | | | |

Loan Interest Rates	Variability	Year-1	Year-2	Year-3
LIBOR (floating)	Could go up or down	−5.000%	−5.000%	−5.000%
Spread (fixed)	Fixed	−1.500%	−1.500%	−1.500%
Total interest payable		−6.500%	−6.500%	−6.500%
Swap Interest Rates				
Pay fixed	Fixed	−5.750%	−5.750%	−5.750%
Receive floating LIBOR	Could go up or down	+5.000%	+5.000%	+5.000%
Combined Loan and Swap Position				
LIBOR on loan	Paying	−5.000%	−5.000%	−5.000%
Spread (fixed)	Paying	−1.500%	−1.500%	−1.500%
Pay fixed on swap	Paying	−5.750%	−5.750%	−5.750%
Receive floating LIBOR on swap	Receiving	+5.000%	+5.000%	+5.000%
Net interest due after swap	Net payment	−7.250%	−7.250%	−7.250%

Note: On the date the interest rate swap agreement is made, the actual LIBOR rates for all years (1, 2, and 3), are unknown. However, on the basis of the expectations of swaps traders, the present value of the floating-rate cash flow streams and fixed-rate cash flow streams are equal on the agreement date.

ment of the 1.500% fixed spread on the loan plus the fixed payment to the swap bank of 5.750%. This would combine to create a total fixed interest rate payment of 7.250% on the $10 million debt.

The question that remains for Puebla's Treasury staff is whether this is a good deal. Puebla now has a fixed-rate debt of $10 million for three years. If current market rates quoted to Puebla by its lenders were at fixed rates above 7.250%, the answer would be *yes* and Puebla would be well advised to secure the swap agreement now, assuming its goal is to lock in fixed rates of interest for the coming three years.

Currency Swaps

Since all swap rates are derived from the yield curve in each major currency, the fixed to floating-rate interest rate swap existing in each currency allows firms to swap across currencies. Exhibit 9.8 lists the swap rates for the euro, the U.S. dollar, the Japanese yen, and the Swiss franc as published in the *Financial Times*. These swap rates are based on the government security yields in each of the individual currency markets, plus a credit spread applicable to investment grade borrowers in the respective markets.

Note that the swap rates in Exhibit 9.8 are not rated or categorized by credit ratings. This is so because the swap market itself does not carry the credit risk associated with individual borrowers. We saw this in the previous interest rate swap example when Puebla, which borrowed on its own at LIBOR plus a spread of 1.500% (the spread representing the credit spread specific to the borrower),

| Exhibit 9.8 | | *Interest Rate and Currency Swap Quotes* | | | | | | | |

	Euro-€		Swiss franc		U.S. dollar		Japanese yen	
Years	Bid	Ask	Bid	Ask	Bid	Ask	Bid	Ask
1	2.99	3.02	1.43	1.47	5.24	5.26	0.23	0.26
2	3.08	3.12	1.68	1.76	5.43	5.46	0.36	0.39
3	3.24	3.28	1.93	2.01	5.56	5.59	0.56	0.59
4	3.44	3.48	2.15	2.23	5.65	5.68	0.82	0.85
5	3.63	3.67	2.35	2.43	5.73	5.76	1.09	1.12
6	3.83	3.87	2.54	2.62	5.80	5.83	1.33	1.36
7	4.01	4.05	2.73	2.81	5.86	5.89	1.55	1.58
8	4.18	4.22	2.91	2.99	5.92	5.95	1.75	1.78
9	4.32	4.36	3.08	3.16	5.96	5.99	1.90	1.93
10	4.42	4.46	3.22	3.30	6.01	6.04	2.04	2.07
12	4.58	4.62	3.45	3.55	6.10	6.13	2.28	2.32
15	4.78	4.82	3.71	3.81	6.20	6.23	2.51	2.56
20	5.00	5.04	3.96	4.06	6.29	6.32	2.71	2.76
25	5.13	5.17	4.07	4.17	6.29	6.32	2.77	2.82
30	5.19	5.23	4.16	4.26	6.28	6.31	2.82	2.88
LIBOR	3.0313	3.0938	1.3125	1.4375	4.9375	5.0625	0.1250	0.2188

Source: *The Financial Times*, Tuesday, March 30, 1999, p. 27. Bid and ask spreads as of close of London business. US$ is quoted against three-month LIBOR; Japanese yen against six-month LIBOR; Euro and Swiss franc against six-month LIBOR.

swapped out of the LIBOR component only. The fixed spread, a credit risk premium, was still borne by the firm itself.[6]

The usual motivation for a currency swap is to replace cash flows scheduled in an undesired currency with cash flows in a desired currency. The desired currency is probably the currency in which the firm's future operating revenues (inflows) will be generated. Firms often raise capital in currencies, in which they do not possess significant revenues or other natural cash flows. The reason they do so is cost; specific firms may find capital costs in specific currencies attractively priced under special conditions. Having raised the capital, however, the firm may wish to swap its repayment into a currency in which it has future operating revenues.

The utility of the currency swap market to a multinational corporation is significant. A multinational firm wishing to swap a 10-year fixed 6.04% U.S. dollar cash flow stream could swap to 4.46% fixed in euro, 3.30% fixed in Swiss francs, or 2.07% fixed in Japanese yen. It could swap not only from fixed dollars to fixed rates, but to floating LIBOR rates in the various currencies as well. All are possible at the rates quoted in Exhibit 9.8.

))) Puebla Corporation: Swapping Floating Dollars into Fixed-Rate Swiss Francs

We return to Puebla Corporation to demonstrate how it might utilize a currency swap. If Puebla, after raising $10 million in floating-rate financing and subsequently swapping into fixed-rate payments, decides that it would prefer to make its debt service payments in Swiss francs, it could enter into a currency swap. Puebla may have recently signed a sales contract with a Swiss buyer that will be paying francs to Puebla over the next three-year period. This would be a natural inflow of Swiss francs for the coming three years, and Puebla may decide it wishes to match the currency of denomination of the cash flows through a currency swap.

Puebla Corporation now enters into a three-year *receive U.S. dollars and pay Swiss francs* currency swap. Both interest rates are fixed. Puebla will pay 2.01% (ask rate) fixed Swiss franc interest and receive 5.56% (bid rate) fixed U.S. dollars.

As illustrated in Exhibit 9.9, the three-year currency swap entered into by Puebla is different from the plain vanilla interest rate swap described above in two important ways:

1. The spot exchange rate in effect on the date of the agreement establishes what the notional principal is in the target currency. The target currency is the currency Puebla is swapping into, in this case, the Swiss franc. The $10,000,000 notional principal converts to a Sfr15,000,000 notional principal. This is the principal that is used to establish the actual cash flows Puebla is committing to making (2.01% × Sfr15,000,000 = Sfr301,500).

2. The notional principal itself is part of the swap agreement. In the interest rate swaps described previously, since both interest payment cash flows were based on the same U.S. dollar notional principal, there was no need to include the principal in the agreement. In a currency swap, however, because the notional principals are denominated in two different currencies, and the exchange rate between those two currencies will change over the life of the swap, the notional principals are actually part of the swap agreement.

| **Exhibit 9.9** | *Puebla Corporation's Currency Swap: Pay Swiss Francs and Receive U.S. Dollars* | | | |

Swap Component	Year-0	Year-1	Year-2	Year-3
Will receive fixed US$ at this rate:		5.56%	5.56%	5.56%
on a notional principal of:	$10,000,000			
Puebla will receive cash flows:	↑ ⟶	$556,000 ⟶	$556,000 ⟶	$10,556,000
Exchange rate	Sfr.1.5000/$			
	↓			
Puebla will pay fixed SFR at this rate:		2.01%	2.01%	2.01%
on a notional principal of:	Sfr15,000,000			
Puebla will pay cash flows:	⟶	Sfr301,500 ⟶	Sfr301,500 ⟶	Sfr15,301,500

The pay fixed US$ rate of 5.56% is the three-year bid rate in Exhibit 9.8. The receive fixed Swiss franc rate of 2.01% is the three-year ask rate from Exhibit 9.8. Once Puebla Corporation determines the notional principal of $10,000,000, the current spot rate is used to determine the notional principal for the Swiss franc side of the swap (or vice versa depending on Puebla's goals). The present value of each side of the swap at inception is $10,000,000 (Sfr15,000,000).

At the time of the swap's inception, both positions have the same net present value. Puebla's swap commits it to three future cash payments in Swiss francs, and, in turn, it will receive three payments in U.S. dollars. The payments are set. Financing accounting practices will require Puebla to regularly track and value its position; *mark-to-market* the swap on the basis of current exchange rates and interest rates. If after the swap was initiated the Swiss franc were to appreciate versus the dollar, and if Puebla were paying francs, the firm would record a loss on the swap for accounting purposes. (Similarly, the swap dealer's side of the transaction would record a gain.) At the same time, if interest rates in Swiss franc markets were rising, and Puebla's swap commits it to a fixed rate of 2.01%, then a gain would result from the interest component of the swap's value. In short, gains and losses on the swap, at least for accounting purposes, will persist throughout the swap's life.[7]

))) Unwinding Swaps

As with all original loan agreements, it may happen that at some future date the partners to a swap may wish to terminate the agreement before it matures. If, for example, after one year Puebla Corporation's Swiss sales contract is terminated, Puebla would no longer need the swap as part of its hedging program. Puebla could terminate or *unwind* the swap with the swap dealer.

Unwinding a currency swap requires the discounting of the remaining cash flows under the swap agreement at current interest rates, then converting the target currency (Swiss francs here) back to the home currency of the firm (U.S. dollars for Puebla). If Puebla has two payments remaining on the swap agreement of Sfr301,500 and Sfr15,301,500 (an interest-only payment, and a principal and interest payment), and the two-year fixed rate of interest for francs is now 2.000%, the present value (PV) of Puebla's commitment in Swiss francs is:

$$PV(Sfr) = \frac{Sfr\ 301,500}{(1.020)^1} + \frac{Sfr\ 15,301,500}{(1.020)^2} = Sfr\ 15,002,912$$

At the same time, the present value of the remaining cash flows on the dollar-side of the swap is determined using the current two-year fixed-dollar interest rate, which is now 5.500%:

$$PV(\$) = \frac{\$556,000}{(1.055)^1} + \frac{\$10,556,000}{(1.055)^2} = \$10,011,078$$

Puebla's currency swap, if unwound at this time, would yield a present value of net inflows (what it receives under the swap) of $10,011,078 and a present value of outflows (what it pays under the swap) of Sfr15,002,912. If the spot exchange rate is now Sfr1.4650/$, the net settlement of this currency swap will be:

$$\text{Settlement} = \$10{,}011{,}078 - \frac{\text{Sfr } 15{,}002{,}912}{\text{Sfr } 1.4650/\$} = (\$229{,}818)$$

Puebla makes a cash payment to the swap dealer of $229,818 to terminate the swap. Puebla *lost* on the swap largely as a result of the appreciation of the Swiss franc (the interest rates barely changed). Since Puebla had promised to pay in the currency that was now stronger in value—the franc—unwinding the swap was costly. The swap, however, was entered into as a *hedge* rather than as a *financial investment*.

))) Counterparty Risk

Counterparty risk is the potential exposure any individual firm bears that the second party to any financial contract will be unable to fulfill its obligations under the contract's specifications. Concern over counterparty risk has risen in the interest rate and currency swap markets as a result of a few large and well-publicized swap defaults. Rapid growth in the currency and interest rate financial derivatives markets has actually been accompanied by a surprisingly low default rate to date, particularly in a global market, which is, in principle, unregulated.

Counterparty risk has long been one of the major factors that favor the use of exchange-traded rather than over-the-counter derivatives. Most exchanges, like the Philadelphia Stock Exchange for currency options or the Chicago Mercantile Exchange for Eurodollar futures, are themselves the counterparty to all transactions. This allows all firms to have a high degree of confidence in buying or selling exchange-traded products quickly and with little concern over the credit quality of the exchange itself. Financial exchanges typically require a small fee of all traders on the exchanges to fund insurance funds created expressly for the purpose of protecting all parties. Over-the-counter products, however, are direct credit exposures to the firm because the contract is generally between the buying firm and the selling financial institution. Most financial derivatives in today's world financial centers are sold or brokered only by the largest and soundest financial institutions. This structure does not mean, however, that firms can enter continuing agreements with these institutions without some degree of real financial risk and concern.

A firm entering into a currency or interest rate swap agreement retains ultimate responsibility for the timely servicing of its own debt obligations. Although a swap agreement may constitute a contract to exchange U.S. dollar payments for euro payments, the firm that actually holds the dollar debt is still legally responsible for payment. The original debt remains on the borrower's books. In the event a swap counterparty does not make the payment as agreed, the firm legally holding the debt is still responsible for debt service. In the event of such a failure, the euro payments would be stopped, by the right of *offset*, and the losses associated with the failed swap would be mitigated.

The real exposure of an interest or currency swap is not the total notional principal, but the mark-to-market values of differentials in interest or currency interest payments (replacement cost) since the inception of the swap agreement. This differential is similar to the change in swap value discovered by unwinding a swap. This amount is typically only 2% to 3% of the notional principal.

Option-Based Instruments and Techniques

Interest rate risk management in practice employs some of the newer option-based instruments and techniques. These are analyzed in Chapter 24, Advanced Topics in Interest Rate Risk Management. Topics include interest rate caps, floors, collars, and swaptions.

ILLUSTRATIVE CASE

A Three-Way Back-to-Back Cross-Currency Swap

Individual firms often find special demands for their debt in select markets, allowing them to raise capital at several basis points lower there than in other markets. Thus a growing number of firms are confronted with debt service in currencies that are not normal for their operations. The result has been a use of debt issuances coupled with swap agreements from inception. The three-way swap of a Canadian province, depicted in Exhibit 9.10, a Finnish export agency, and a multilateral development bank is a case in point.

The Finnish Export Credit agency, the Province of Ontario, Canada, and the Inter-American Development Bank all possessed ready access to particular sources of capital but wished debt service in another. The investment banking house of Goldman Sachs, acting as matchmaker, brought all parties together and aided in the negotiation of both borrowing rates and swap rates.

- Finnish Export Credit (FEC) had not raised capital in the Canadian dollar Euromarkets before this and would be well-received if issuing there. FEC, however, had a need for increased debt service payments in U.S. dollars at this time, not Canadian dollars.

- The Province of Ontario, Canada, needed Canadian dollars, but due to the size of provincial borrowings in the recent past, it knew that further issues would push up the cost of funds. The province, however, was considered an attractive credit by the U.S. dollar Euromarkets.

- Inter-American Development Bank (IADB), like FEC, had a need for additional U.S. dollar-denominated debt service. It had, however, already raised the majority of its capital in the dollar markets, but it was a welcome newcomer to the Euro-Canadian dollar market.

Exhibit 9.10   *A Three-Way Back-to-Back Cross-Currency Swap*

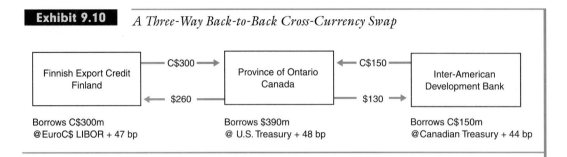

Borrows C$300m
@EuroC$ LIBOR + 47 bp

Borrows $390m
@ U.S. Treasury + 48 bp

Borrows C$150m
@Canadian Treasury + 44 bp

> Each borrower determined its initial debt amounts and maturities with the needs of the currency swap expressly in mind. Then, in conjunction with Goldman Sachs, each negotiated the best pricing for its individual debt commitments. Simultaneous with debt issuance and placement, the three parties swapped the proceeds and debt service payment streams for their desired debt profiles. Each party was therefore able to issue debt in the market in which its debt would be well-received, and thus at lower cost, and then swap into the desired currency. All parties borrowed where they had a comparative advantage and then swapped into their desired currency at a lower all-in-cost than they could have achieved by direct debt issuance in that currency.

SUMMARY

- The increasing volatility of world interest rates, combined with the increasing use of short-term and variable-rate debt by firms worldwide, has led many firms to actively manage their *interest rate risks.*

- The primary sources of interest rate risk to a multinational nonfinancial firm are short-term borrowing and investing, as well as long-term sources of debt.

- The techniques and instruments used in interest rate risk-management in many ways resemble those used in currency risk-management: the old tried-and-true methods of lending and borrowing, combined with the new methods of option-based derivatives (discussed further in Chapter 23).

- The primary instruments and techniques used for interest rate risk-management include forward rate agreements (FRAs), forward swaps, interest rate futures, and interest rate and currency swaps.

- The interest rate and currency swap markets allow firms that have limited access to specific currencies and interest rate structures to gain access at relatively low costs. This access in turn allows these firms to manage their currency and interest rate risks more effectively.

QUESTIONS

1. Interest Rate Practices
What would be the one-month interest payment due on a principal of ¥150 million at 2.375% annual interest assuming the following interest rate practices?

a. 360 days per year, 28 days per month
b. 365 days per year, 28 days per month
c. 360 days per year, 30 days per month

2. Financial Price Risk and Management Perception
Interest rates and exchange rates are theoretically equivalent in their relative impacts on the value of a firm. Yet interest rate risk is commonly considered by management as a "necessary evil" of doing business, whereas exchange rate risk is perceived as unusual and troublesome.

a. What characteristics of these two risks do you think lead management to perceive them in this way?
b. If managers handle financial price risks as they perceive them, how will these differing perceptions alter their management of exchange rate and interest rate risk?

3. Puebla Corporation's Floating-Rate Loan
Exhibit 9.3 provided an analysis of Puebla Corporation's all-in-cost (AIC) of servicing a floating rate loan. Recalculate the loan's AIC, using the same assumptions, with the exception that the loan would have a four-year maturity rather than a three-year maturity.

4. Eurodollar Interest Rate Futures
Use Exhibit 9.4 to answer the following questions.

a. How is the yield for the June 2000 Eurodollar interest rate future calculated?
b. A financial manager wishing to hedge the interest the firm would receive on a $12.5 million principal in September 2000 would take what type of a position?
c. A financial manager with a floating rate loan whose interest payment is due in December 1999 would enter into what type of a position? Explain how it would hedge the firm's interest rate exposure.

5. Kyocera's Currency Swap
Kyocera is a Japanese MNE that operates in at least 12 countries around the world but has little name recognition outside Japan. It has traditionally raised all capital in its home market and therefore has substantial quantities of long-term yen-denominated debt.

As a result of its global expansion, the firm now faces substantial long foreign currency positions, particularly in U.S. dollars. It has decided that it wishes to manage this long dollar position by entering into a cross-currency interest rate swap to pay dollars and receive yen. Use the data presented in Exhibit 9.8 to answer the following questions:

a. What would be the annual swap payments on a ¥500 million notional principal, four-year maturity currency swap, in both yen (receive yen) and U.S. dollars (pay dollars)?

b. Calculate the annual cash flows associated with the currency swap in part (a) for the entire lifespan of the swap agreement, including both principal and interest. Use the structure of Exhibit 9.9 as a template. Assume a spot exchange rate of ¥114.80/$.

c. Assume that the day following the swap agreement in part (a), Kyocera changes its mind and wishes to unwind the currency swap. If all interest rates are the same, but the exchange rate has changed from ¥114.80/$ to ¥112.00/$, what is the cost or profit of unwinding the swap?

6. Unwinding Puebla's Swap

What would be the result of Puebla's swap (the example used in this chapter) if the exchange rate at the time of unwinding were SF1.4260/$ and the two year fixed rate of interest on Swiss francs were 2.375%? Remember Puebla has two Swiss franc payments remaining. Would Puebla gain or lose this amount on the swap?

MiniCase: *McDonald's Corporation's British Pound Exposure*

McDonald's Corporation has investments in over 100 countries. It considers its equity investment in foreign affiliates as capital that is at risk, subject to hedging depending on the individual country, currency, and market.

British Subsidiary as an Exposure

McDonald's parent company has three different pound-denominated exposures arising from its ownership and operation of its British subsidiary. First, the British subsidiary has equity capital, which is a pound-denominated asset of the parent company. Secondly, in addition to the equity capital invested in the British affiliate, the parent company provides intracompany debt in the form of a four-year £125 million loan. The loan is denominated in British pounds and carries a fixed 5.30% per annum interest payment. Third, the British subsidiary pays a fixed percentage of gross sales in royalties to the parent company. This too is pound-denominated. The three different exposures sum to a significant exposure problem for McDonald's.

An additional technical detail further complicates the situation. When the parent company makes an intracompany loan like that to the British subsidiary, according to U.S. accounting and tax law practices it must designate whether the loan is considered to be *permanently invested* in that country. (Although on the surface it seems illogical to consider four years permanent, the loan itself could simply be continually rolled over by the parent company and never actually be repaid.) If it is not considered permanent, the foreign exchange gains and losses related to the loan flow directly to the parent company's profit and loss statement (P&L), according to FAS #52. If, however, the loan is designated as permanent, the foreign exchange gains and losses related to the intracompany loan would flow only to the CTA (cumulative translation adjustment) on the consolidated balance sheet. To date, McDonald's has chosen to designate the loan as permanent. The functional currency of the British affiliate for consolidation purposes is the local currency, the British pound.

Brian Moore is both the Manager for Financial Markets/Treasury and a McDonald's shareholder. He is currently reviewing the existing hedging strategy employed by McDonald's against the pound exposure. The company has been hedging the pound exposure by entering into a cross-currency U.S. dollar/British pound sterling swap. The current swap is a seven-year swap to receive dollars and pay pounds. Like all cross-currency swaps, the agreement requires McDonald's-U.S. to make regular pound-denominated interest payments and a bullet principal repayment (notional principal) at the end of the swap agreement. McDonald's considers the large notional principal payment a hedge against the equity investment in its British affiliate.

According to FAS #52, a company may elect to take the interest associated with a foreign-currency-denominated loan and carry that directly to the parent company's P&L This has been done in the past, and McDonald's has benefitted from the inclusion of this interest payment.

FAS #133, *Accounting for Derivative Instruments and Hedging Activities*, issued in June 1998, was originally intended to be effective for all fiscal quarters within fiscal years beginning after June 15, 1999 (for most firms this meant January 1, 2000). The new standard, however, was so complex and potentially of such material influence to U.S.-based MNEs that the Financial Accounting Standards Board has been approached by dozens of major firms and asked to postpone mandatory implementation. The standard's complexity, combined with the work loads associated with Y2K (year 2000) risk controls, persuaded the Financial Accounting Standards Board to delay FAS #133's mandatory implementation date indefinitely.

Brian Moore, however, still wishes to consider the impact of FAS #133 on the hedging strategy currently employed. Under FAS #133, the firm will have to mark-to-market the entire cross-currency swap position, including principal, and carry this to *other comprehensive income (OCI)*. OCI, however, is actually a form of income required under U.S. GAAP and is reported in the footnotes to the financial statements, but not in the income measure used in reported earnings per share. Although McDonald's has been carrying the interest payments on the swap to income, it has not previously had to carry the present value of the swap principal to OCI. In Brian Moore's eyes, this poses a substantial material risk to OCI.

Brian Moore wished to reconsider the current strategy. He began by listing the pros and cons of the current strategy, comparing these to alternative strategies, and then deciding what if anything should be done about it at this time.

Financial values have been altered in this case to preserve confidentiality. The case is based on conversations between Mr. Brian Moore and the authors.

 ## WORLD WIDE WEB EXERCISES

W1. Current Interest Rates and Yield Curves
Use the New York Federal Reserve Bank's web page for recent interest rates on all maturities of U.S. dollar-denominated debt issues. Historical data is also available so that it is relatively easy to plot how the Treasury's constant maturity yields have changed from week to week and month to month for maturities varying between 3 months and 10 years.

Federal Reserve Bank of New York   http://www.ny.frb.org/
Board of Governors of the Federal Reserve
                          http://www.bog.frb.fed.us/releases/h15/current

W2. The International Swaps and Derivatives Association (ISDA)
The ISDA is the primary global organization that attempts to both standardize the use of interest rate and cross-currency swaps and track the market's size. Use ISDA's web site to find out which type of interest rate derivative is growing the fastest—the plain vanilla interest rate swap, the cross currency swap, or the various types of interest rate options.

International Swaps & Derivatives Association   http://www.isda.org

W3. Emerging Markets & Debt
Many firms are now expanding operations into the emerging markets of Latin America, Eastern Europe, Africa, and Asia and are therefore creating new demands for debt. Use the following web pages to learn more about the instruments of many emerging markets. In particular, find the most recent quotes on Brady Bonds, one of the most widely traded emerging market debt instruments in the world.

Emerging Markets Companion http://www.emgmkts.com/
J.P. Morgan & Company, Inc.   http://www.jpmorgan.com/

SUGGESTED READINGS

Brown, Keith C., and Donald J. Smith, "Default Risk and Innovations in the Design of Interest Rate Swaps," *Financial Management*, Vol. 22, No. 2, Summer 1993, pp. 94–105.

Ho, T.S., Richard C. Stapleton, and Marti G. Subrahmanyam, "The Risk of a Currency Swap: A Multivariate Binomial Methodology, *European Financial Management*, Vol. 4, No. 1, March 1998, pp. 9–28.

Smith, Clifford W., Jr., Charles W. Smithson, and Lee MacDonald Wakeman, "The Market for Interest Rate Swaps," *Financial Management*, Winter 1988, pp. 34–44.

Solnik, Bruno, "Swap Pricing and Default Risk: A Note," *Journal of International Financial Management and Accounting*, Vol. 2, No. 1, Spring 1990, pp. 79–91.

NOTES

1. For example, banking institutions focus on the management of *basis risk*, the mismatching of interest rate bases for associated assets and liabilities. Because of the nature of bank assets and liabilities, the sensitivity in the value of all bank assets and liabilities to interest rates is significant.
2. An abbreviated list of derivatives-related losses would include Allied Lyons (U.K., 1991), Shell Showa Sekiya (Japan, 1993), Metallgesellschaft (Germany, 1993), Codelco (Chile, 1994), Kashima Oil (Japan, 1994), Procter & Gamble (U.S., 1994), Dharmala (Indonesia, 1994), Barings Brothers (U.K. and Singapore, 1995).
3. Interestingly, the third largest volume of a traded futures contract in the latter 1990s was the U.S. dollar/Brazilian real currency futures contract traded on the Bolsa de Mercadorias y Futuros in Brazil.
4. Obviously interest rate futures positions could be—and are on a regular basis—purchased purely for speculative purposes. Although speculation is not the focus of the managerial context here, one can clearly see how any speculator with a directional view on interest rates could take positions in expectations of profit.
5. The International Swap and Derivatives Association (ISDA) monitors market size and performance. For the latest in market measurements see the ISDA web page at http://www.isda.org.
6. For example, lower-rated firms may pay spreads of 3% or 4% over LIBOR, while some of the world's largest and most financially sound multinational firms may actually raise capital at rates of LIBOR – 0.40%. The swap market does not differentiate the rate by the participant; all swap at fixed rates versus LIBOR in the respective currency.
7. The currency swaps described here are *nonamortizing swaps*. A *nonamortizing swap* repays the entire principal at maturity, rather than over the life of the swap agreement (*amortizing*). Swap dealers will, of course, be more than happy to provide the firm with the form of its choice. We use nonamortizing swap examples throughout this chapter for simplicity of presentation (we hope).

DECISION CASE

British Columbia Hydro

"Treasury cannot be seen as a passive activity," Bell says. "Once we isolated treasury as a separate subset of our business and set some goals for it, it helped our people view problems in a fresh way. If you think of it in terms of opportunities, it may be the biggest profit centre you have got in your company, particularly if you are capital intensive."

Larry Bell, CEO, British Columbia Hydro Intermarket, September 1989.

British Columbia Hydroelectric and Power Authority (BC Hydro) is a Provincial Crown Corporation, a wholly owned subsidiary of the Province of British Columbia. BC Hydro is the fifth largest Canadian utility, generating, transmitting, and distributing electricity to more than one million customers in British Columbia. The fact that it is a government-owned utility does not change its need to manage treasury operations against financial risks.

BC Hydro has substantial exposure to financial risk. Larry Bell, as Chairman of BC Hydro, was determined to do something about the financial price risks—the movements of exchange rates, interest rates, and commodity prices—facing the firm. It was now March 1988, and the time for discussion had ended and the time for decisions had come.

Financial Exposures

Upon taking over as Chairman of BC Hydro in late 1987, Larry Bell started at the ground up in his analysis of the firm's financial exposures. Bell was formerly British Columbia's Deputy Minister of Finance, and therefore not a newcomer to issues in financial management. His first step was to isolate those major business and financial forces driving net income (revenues and operating costs) and the balance sheet (asset and liability component values).

BC Hydro was—at least by financial standards—relatively simple in financial structure. The firm's revenues came from power sales. Power sales were in turn divisible into residential and small business (60%), and transmission sales (40%). Residential power use was extremely stable, so that 60% of all revenues of BC Hydro were easily predictable. However, the same could not be said of transmission sales. This was power sold to large industrial users, users who numbered only 80 at that time. The power use of these 80 industrial users was determined by their business needs, and needs were highly cyclical. BC Hydro's sales were predominantly domestic, with only about 5% of all revenues generated from power sales to utilities across the border in the United States.

The cost structure of BC Hydro was also relatively simple—debt service. Debt service dominated operating expenses, averaging 55% of operating expenses over the mid-1980s. (Debt service rarely constitutes more than 15% of operating expenses in typical corporate financial structures.) Power generation, however, is extremely capital intensive. The requirements for capital are met primarily by debt.

In 1987 BC Hydro had approximately C$8 billion in debt outstanding. Unfortunately, BC Hydro was a victim of its own attractiveness. It had been a direct beneficiary of the need for U.S.-based investors to diversity their exposures in the late 1970s and early 1980s. It had tapped the U.S. dollar debt markets at extremely attractive rates for the time. But now it was faced with the servicing of this U.S. dollar-denominated debt, a full-half of its total debt portfolio. Much of the U.S. dollar debt had been acquired when the U.S. dollar was weaker (approximately C$1/US$) and both U.S. and Canadian interest rates were higher. As shown in Exhibit 1, the appreciation of the U.S. dollar had resulted in an increase in the Canadian dollar debt equivalent of C$750 million. Equity amounted to approximately C$540 million. BC Hydro was highly leveraged to say the least.

BC Hydro had followed the general principles of conservative capital structure management. It had financed long-term assets with long-term debt. The match of asset and liability maturities was quite good, but the currency of denomination was not. This currency mismatch constituted an enormous potential exposure to the financial viability of the firm.

Isolating the Issues

In early 1988 Chairman Larry Bell called in Bridgewater Associates, a Connecticut financial consulting firm, for help. Bob Prince and Ray Dalio (president) of Bridgewater, along with senior management of BC Hydro and representatives of

---

Exhibit 1   *Currency Composition and Exchange Rate Impacts on British Columbia Hydro's Liabilities and Net Worth*

Debt and Equity by Currency of Denomination		Initial Values (Canadian Dollars)	March 1988 (Canadian Dollars)
Debt	Canadian dollar-denominated	4,000,000,000	4,000,000,000
	U.S. dollar-denominated	3,250,000,000	4,000,000,000
Equity		540,000,000	540,000,000
Total liabilities and net worth		7,790,000,000	8,540,000,000
Exchange rate related gains (losses)			(750,000,000)

Source: BC Hydro and Moodys Canada. Initial values of debt are Canadian dollar equivalents, regardless of original currency of denomination, on original date of issuance.

the BC Ministry of Finance met at Whistler Mountain, British Columbia. The purpose of the retreat was to first identify the primary financial risk issues facing BC Hydro, and secondly to propose preliminary solutions. Chairman Bell encouraged an open exchange of ideas.

> We have to do what makes sense economically. We'll deal with the accounting and regulatory hurdles after they've been resolved. If someone wanted to point out that our legislation wouldn't allow us to trade in futures, that's fine. The legislature sits every year.[1]

Bell felt that consideration of institutional or legal constraints would prevent the analysis from getting to the core issues. The group proceeded to isolate two basic questions that had to be addressed prior to moving forward:

1. Does BC Hydro want to eliminate all financial risk, or only manage it?
2. BC Hydro is in the business of providing power. Is it also in the business of trading or speculating in the financial markets?

Discussion was heated on these points and ended with no clear agreement initially. Ray Dalio of Bridgewater pushed the discussion by arguing that the interest rate and foreign exchange problems the firm was saddled with were the direct result of a simple basic problem: the lack of a plan.

> BC Hydro hadn't thought through its financial activities strategically. They were thinking about running their business, not asset-liability management. You can't take that approach in a volatile economic environment.

The participants agreed to move on to a detailed discussion and analysis of the BC Hydro's financial exposures without resolving these first two issues.

Financial Price Risks

Financial risk management focuses on how the movement of financial prices (interest rates, exchange rates, and commodity prices) affect the value of the firm. Isolating these impacts on any individual firm requires the evaluation of how revenues and costs, both operational and financial, change with movements in these prices. Bridgewater Associates and BC Hydro's staff conducted a number of statistical studies to find what economic forces were at work in the costs and revenues of the firm.

Revenues. The results were quite clear. The 60% of power sales going to the 1.25 million small business and residential consumers was extremely stable, and was therefore insensitive to movements in interest rates, or other business cycle indicators such as unemployment or inflation. In fact, residential power use was sensitive primarily to population size. The 40% of power sales to the large industrial users was, however, very cyclical. Closer analysis of the industrial users indicated

---

[1]Intermarket, September 1989, p. 26.

that these users were sensitive to basic commodity prices (pulp, paper, chemicals mining, etc.). Statistically speaking, transmission sales were found to be heavily dependent on movements in commodity prices (positively related) and industrial production (positively related).

Costs. A closer look at the cost structure of BC Hydro also revealed a number of clear economic forces at work. Operating expenses were dominated by debt service, over 55% of the total. The remaining 45% of operating costs possessed little variable content. Although business conditions for industrial users could decline, the nature of the utility industry still required that operations continue with little change in operating expenses achievable.

Secondly, since 55% of operating expenses were debt service, costs could potentially move directly with interest rates. But BC Hydro's practice over the past decade had been to finance long-term assets with long-term debt, and long-term debt at fixed rates obviously did not move with shorter-cycle interest rate movements. Long-term interest rates were locked in. And interest rates (short-term and long-term rates) had in general been falling in both the United States and Canada since the early 1980s.

Short-term interest rates move with commodity prices. Because increases in commodity prices frequently lead to more inflation, and interest rates and bond yields must in turn move with changes in inflation, significant commodity price increases translated directly into rising interest rates.

It was now clear that if BC Hydro's revenues and cost structures were to be managed against underlying economic or financial forces, protection would be needed against commodity prices. Exhibit 2 illustrates how power sales moved positively with commodity price changes. At the same time, it also shows how short-term interest rates moved with commodity price changes, but long-term interest rates did not. Since BC Hydro was financed nearly exclusively with long-term debt, its present debt structure was not enjoying the fruits of these correlated movements (lower commodity prices and interest rates).

Currency Exposure. BC Hydro was facing an enormous foreign currency exposure. The fact that revenues were 95% Canadian dollar-denominated, while C$4 billion of total long-term debt was U.S. dollar-denominated, meant that debt-service was completely exposed to currency risk. The firm earned only 5% of its revenues in U.S. dollars, and therefore had no "natural way" of obtaining the foreign currency it needed to service debt. As Exhibit 3 illustrates, although the U.S. dollar had risen versus the Canadian dollar steadily between 1980 and 1986, the Canadian dollar had regained some ground in the past two years.

By 1988 Larry Bell estimated that BC Hydro had realized C$350 million in foreign currency losses on its U.S. dollar debt, all of which passed through current income. The remaining exposure still approached C$400 million depending on the direction of the exchange rate movement. Something had to be done

| Exhibit 2 | *British Columbia Hydro's Revenue and Cost Sensitivity to Commodity Price Changes* |

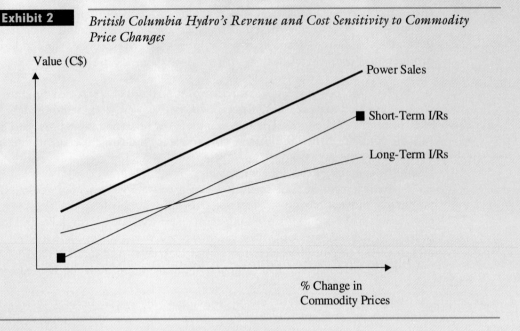

quickly. The urgency of the issue was particularly acute given that the total equity of BC Hydro amounted to only C$540 million!

The outstanding U.S. dollar debt was to be repaid in single "balloon" payments upon maturity. BC Hydro therefore had an enormous amount of cash flowing into a sinking fund for debt principal repayment. The funds were presently being reinvested in Canadian bonds, yielding short-term current rates on Canadian debt instruments.

Proposed Risk Management Strategies

Several alternative solutions were put forward for both the revenue-cost risks and the foreign currency risks. It seemed the solutions would have to be independently constructed.

The basic revenue-cost mismatch, the fact that BC Hydro held little short-term debt which would parallel the movement of revenues with commodity prices, was attacked first. The obvious solution was to increase the proportion of short-term debt. Although this approach would clearly increase the matching of commodity price cycles, it would do the opposite with regard to asset-liability maturity matching. It was argued that 60% of all power revenues were still very stable, and that the debt structure of the entire utility should not be reworked in order to pursue risk management goals. The critics of the short-term debt approach also emphasized that historical correlations might not hold up in the future. Movements of revenues and short-term interest rates correlated with commodity price movements may not hold true. The debate was heated.

| Exhibit 3 | *The Canadian Dollar/U.S. Dollar Exchange Rate, 1980–1987 (C$/US$)* |

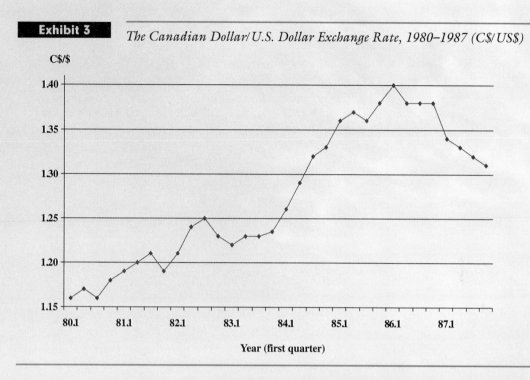

The foreign currency exposure problem was at first glance, simple. The easiest and most risk-averse approach would simply be to buy U.S. dollars forward. There was little risk in that the debt-service schedule was known exactly in terms of amounts and timing, and the resulting forward cover would eliminate the currently risk.

Several senior finance ministry officials suggested a currency-interest rate swap instead. All agreed that both would work equally well. However, they were not certain that as a Crown Corporation they would be allowed to enter into a swap agreement. Late in the afternoon of the weekend retreat an additional detail was also recognized, that the signing of a forward contact (or series of forward contracts) to cover the U.S. dollar debt-service would require BC Hydro to recognize and realize (pass through the income statement) the total currency loss remaining, approximately C$500 million. This was obviously unacceptable.

A second alternative put forward by Ray Dalio of Bridgewater Associates was to move all sinking-fund capital out of Canadian dollar bonds into a similar risk category of U.S. dollar-denominated securities. This would result in the security values moving in the opposite direction of the U.S. dollar debt, thus offsetting adverse (or favorable) exchange rate changes; a natural hedge. But, this also meant that BC Hydro, a Crown Corporation, would be intentionally constructing an enormous uncovered foreign currency position. This met with considerable opposition by representatives of the British Columbia Ministry of Finance.

The participants returned from the quiet wilderness setting of Whistler Mountain to the hustle and bustle of Vancouver. It was now March 1988; Larry Bell needed a decision soon.

> "When I came to BC Hydro, because half our costs are associated with debt servicing, there were significant opportunities that could be shaken loose in a proactive treasury operation," he recalls. "As a manager, I shouldn't run this company unless I exploited all of those opportunities."

FINANCING THE GLOBAL FIRM

PART 3 analyzes how firms can utilize the global capital market to minimize their cost of capital and maximize availability. Gaining a global cost and availability of capital is key to whether a firm can be competitive in both its domestic and its foreign markets.

CHAPTER 10 analyzes how a firm needs to attract international portfolio investors, especially if it is resident in a segmented or illiquid capital market. Chapter 10 also analyzes how a MNE manages its consolidated financial structure and the financial structures of its foreign affiliates.

CHAPTER 11 analyzes the strategic steps necessary to attract international investors to purchase and hold a firm's equity. The strategy includes the choice of markets in which to cross-list the firm's shares and to issue equity. Euro-equity issues and American Depositary Receipts are included in the choices of equity issuances described.

CHAPTER 12 explores the methods and choices available to a MNE to raise long-term debt on international markets. It analyzes the foreign exchange risks that arise because of issuing foreign-currency-denominated debt. It also describes the main debt instruments available, including international syndicated loans, Euronotes, Euro-commercial paper, Euro-medium-term notes, and international bonds.

CHAPTER 10

GLOBAL COST OF CAPITAL
AND FINANCIAL STRUCTURE

How can firms utilize the global capital market to minimize their cost of capital and maximize capital's availability? *The cost of capital and its availability are keys to whether a firm can be competitive in both domestic and global markets.* The current spate of cross-border mergers and acquisitions was triggered in part by a lowered cost of capital and the need to achieve economies of scale in both commercial and financial activities. The tremendous increases in stock prices in most developed and some developing countries during the 1990s were indicative of a declining cost of capital. This declining capital cost has provided the financial fuel to energize the mergers and acquisitions market, support a rapid growth in foreign direct investment projects, and increase the number of capital investment projects that can meet lower hurdle rates.

The ability of a firm to achieve a globally competitive cost and availability of capital depends on its success at attracting international portfolio investors. This, in turn, depends on firm-specific characteristics, a regulatory environment that permits unrestricted cross-border investment flows, and a financial strategy that creates market liquidity and global pricing for the firm's securities, whether or not its domestic market is segmented from other capital markets. Exhibit 10.1 illustrates the spectrum of possibilities.

Firm-specific characteristics that attract international portfolio investors are partly, but not totally, dependent on the firm's financial strategy. The motivation for international portfolio investment is introduced in the next section of this chapter. The illustrative case about Nestlé (Switzerland) in the next section of the chapter, demonstrates how international portfolio investment is factored into the calculation of the cost of capital.

If a firm is forced to source its long-term debt and equity in a highly illiquid domestic securities market, it will probably have a relatively high cost of capital and limited availability of capital. Firms resident in some emerging capital markets are in this category. The same is true of firms that are too small to gain access even to their own national se-

Exhibit 10.1   *Dimensions of the Cost of Availability of Capital Strategy*

Firm-Specific Characteristics

Firm's securities appeal only to domestic investors

Firm's securities appeal to international portfolio investors

Market Liquidity for Firm's Securities

Illiquid domestic securities market and limited international liquidity

Highly liquid domestic market and broad international participation

Effect of Market Segmentation on Firm's Securities

Segmented domestic securities market that prices shares according to domestic standards

Access to global securities market that prices shares according to international standards

curities markets. Family-owned firms are also in the same boat, because they choose not to utilize securities markets to source their long-term capital needs. Firms resident in many of the small industrial country capital markets, such as the smaller European markets, often source their long-term debt and equity in partially liquid domestic securities markets. Their cost and availability of capital is better than in the illiquid market case. However, those firms that are able to tap highly liquid markets are likely to achieve a global cost and availability of capital. In addition to firms resident in the United States and United Kingdom, firms from all over the world, including those in emerging markets, have followed financial strategies to tap these markets to gain liquidity that rewards them with a global cost and availability of capital. Analysis of the liquidity effect follows the section on international portfolio investment in this chapter.

Firms resident in a *segmented capital market* must devise a strategy to escape dependence on that market for their long-term debt and equity needs. Capital markets become segmented because of such factors as regulatory controls, perceived political risk, foreign exchange risk, lack of transparency, asymmetric information, cronyism, insider trading, and other market imperfections. Nevertheless, numerous firms have been able to escape their own segmented markets by sourcing their long-term capital needs abroad. The impact of segmented markets on a firm's cost and availability of capital is analyzed after the coverage of the liquidity effect. An illustrative case on Novo Industri (Denmark) later in the chapter shows how a firm can successfully escape from its illiquid and segmented home capital market in order to achieve a global cost and availability of capital.

Once a firm achieves a global cost and availability of capital, it pays a price to maintain it because of the need to retain the loyalty of its international portfolio investors. Agency costs arise due to the need to maintain a higher level of disclosure, sponsor a continuing investor-relations program, and follow internationally acceptable standards for its financial structure. Agency costs due to high disclosure and investor relations are discussed in Chapter 12. This chapter continues with an analysis of a firm's optimal financial structure, given its commitment to attracting international portfolio investors. It then analyzes whether or not a MNE has a higher or lower weighted-average cost of capital than its domestic counterpart. The chapter concludes with an analysis of the optimal financial structure for MNE affiliates.

THE DEMAND FOR FOREIGN SECURITIES: THE ROLE OF INTERNATIONAL PORTFOLIO INVESTMENT

Gradual deregulation of equity markets during the past three decades not only elicited increased competition from domestic players but also opened up markets to foreign competitors. International portfolio investment and cross-listing of equity shares on foreign markets have become commonplace.

What motivates portfolio investors to purchase and hold foreign securities in their portfolio? The answer lies in an understanding of domestic portfolio theory and how it has been extended to handle the possibility of global portfolios. More specifically, it requires an understanding of the principles of portfolio risk reduction, portfolio rate of return, and foreign currency risk. These principles are explained in detail in Chapter 22 but are introduced here in a more intuitive manner.

)))) Portfolio Composition

Both domestic and international portfolio managers are *asset allocators*. Their objective is to maximize a portfolio's rate of return for a given level of risk or to minimize risk for a given rate of return. International portfolio managers can choose from a larger bundle of assets than can portfolio managers limited to domestic-only asset allocations. As a result, internationally diversified portfolios often have a higher expected rate of return and nearly always have a lower level of portfolio risk, since national securities markets are imperfectly correlated with one another.

Portfolio asset allocation can be accomplished along many dimensions, depending on the investment objective of the portfolio manager. For example, portfolios can be diversified according to the type of securities. They can be composed only of stocks or bonds or a combination of both, and they can be diversified by industry or by size of capitalization (small-cap, mid-cap, and large-cap stock portfolios).

For our purposes, the most relevant dimensions are diversification by country, geographic region, stage of development, or a combination of these (global). An example of diversification by country is the Korea Fund. It was at one time the only vehicle for foreign investors to hold South Korean securities, but foreign ownership restrictions have more recently been liberalized. A typical regional diversification would be one of the many Asian funds. These performed exceptionally well until the "bubble" burst in Japan and Southeast Asia during the second half of the 1990s. Portfolios composed of emerging market securities are examples of diversification by stage of development. They are composed of securities from different countries, geographic regions, and stage of development.

ILLUSTRATIVE CASE

Nestlé

Nestlé, the Swiss-based multinational firm that produces and distributes a variety of confectionary products, serves as an excellent example of how the global cost of capital may differ in the eyes of the potential investor, and of a domestic investor.

The traditional capital asset pricing model (CAPM) approach to estimating the cost of equity—*the required return by stockholders investing in the firm today*—is based on adding a risk-premium to a risk-free rate of return. The estimate of what rate of return stockholders will require of Nestlé for the coming, say, one-year period, $k_e^{\text{Nestlé}}$, would be expressed as:

$$k_e^{\text{Nestlé}} = k_{\text{rf}} + (k_{\text{m}} - k_{\text{rf}})\beta_{\text{Nestlé}}$$

where k_{rf} is the risk-free rate of return, k_{m} is the average or index return for the market, and $\beta_{\text{Nestlé}}$ is the beta measure of Nestlé's risk versus that of the market.[1] The risk-free rate, k_{rf}, is typically a government debt issuance yield, k_{m} is the average return for the market, and beta is estimated from both historical data of the firm's returns relative to the market and the forecast for it and like firms for the prospective investment period. All rates of return are in the home currency of the investor—in this case, the Swiss franc.

Whereas traditional risk theory emphasized the total risk of expected returns, the capital asset pricing model emphasizes only the *systematic risk* of expected returns. *Systematic risk* is a function of the total variability of expected returns of the firm relative to the market index and the degree to which the variability of expected returns of the firm is correlated to the expected returns on the market index. Systematic risk is the risk of the market itself, risk which cannot be diversified away. Beta, $\beta_{Nestlé}$ in this case, is CAPM's representation of systematic risk.

Estimating the required return on Nestlé, a prospective Swiss investor might assume a risk-free return of 3.3% (index of Swiss government bond issues, in Swiss francs), an average return on a portfolio of Swiss equities of 10.2% (*Financial Times Swiss Index*, in Swiss francs), and a $\beta_{Nestlé}$ of 0.885. An investor would then expect Nestlé to yield 9.4065% for the coming year.[2]

$$k_e^{Nestlé} = k_{rf} + (k_m - k_{rf})\beta_{Nestlé} = 3.3\% + (10.2\% - 3.3\%)\,0.885 = 9.4065\%$$

There are a number of problems with this traditional domestic CAPM approach. First, it assumes that investors in the Swiss market, and potentially in Nestlé, hold portfolios that are limited to stocks available in the Swiss market alone—purely domestic portfolios. If Swiss investors held internationally diversified portfolios instead, both the expected market return k_m, and the beta-estimate for Nestlé itself, would be defined and determined differently.

A Swiss investor may hold a *global portfolio*, rather than a domestic portfolio.[3] Given the trends toward deregulation and integration of international capital markets, the Swiss investor's portfolio expectations would be more accurately represented by a global portfolio index rather than by a purely domestic index.

In the case of Nestlé, for the same time period as before, a global portfolio index such as the *Financial Times* index in Swiss francs (FTA–Swiss) would show a market return of 13.7% (as opposed to the domestic Swiss index return of 10.2%). In addition, a beta for Nestlé estimated on Nestlé's returns versus the global portfolio index would be much smaller, 0.585 (as opposed to the 0.885 found previously). The return expected on Nestlé by an internationally diversified Swiss investor would then be:

$$k_e^{Nestlé} = k_{rf} + (k_m - k_{rf})\beta_{Nestlé} = 3.3\% + (13.7\% - 3.3\%)\,0.585 = 9.384\%$$

Admittedly, this is not a lot of difference in the end (Exhibit 10.2 summarizes the values and results of the comparison). However, given the magnitude of change in both the values of the market return average and the beta for the firm, it is obvious that the final result could easily have varied by several hundred basis points. The proper construction of the investor's portfolio and the proper portrayal of the investor's perceptions of risk and opportunity cost are clearly important to identifying the global cost of a company's equity capital.

Exhibit 10.2	*Estimating the Global Cost of Equity for Nestlé (Switzerland)*

Domestic Portfolio for Swiss Investor	Global Portfolio for Swiss Investor
k_{rf} = 3.3% (Swiss bond index yield)	k_{rf} = 3.3% (Swiss bond index yield)
k_m = 10.2% (Swiss market portfolio in SF)	k_m = 13.7% (*Financial Times* global index in SF)
$\beta_{Nestlé}$ = 0.885 (Nestlé versus Swiss market portfolio)	$\beta_{Nestlé}$ = 0.585 (Nestlé versus FTA-Swiss index)

$$k_{Nestlé} = k_{rf} + (k_m - k_{rf})\,\beta_{Nestlé}$$

Required return on Nestlé:	Required return on Nestlé:
$k_e^{Nestlé}$ = 9.4065%	$k_e^{Nestlé}$ = 9.3840%

Source: All values are taken from Rene Stulz, "The Cost of Capital in Internationally Integrated Markets: The Case of Nestlé," *European Financial Management*, Vol. 1, No. 1, March 1995, pp. 11–22.

In order to find Nestlé's weighted-average cost of capital, k_{wacc}, we assume it pays 4.00% for its debt, has a debt/total capitalization of 35%, and pays income taxes at the Swiss rate of 20%:

$$k_{wacc}^{Nestlé} = k_e \frac{E}{V} + k_d(1-t)\frac{D}{V},$$

where k_e = risk-adjusted cost of equity, k_d = before-tax cost of debt, t = marginal tax rate, E = market value of Nestlé's equity, D = market value of Nestlé's debt, and V = total market value of Nestlé's securities ($E + D$). Substituting the numbers above yields

$$k_{wacc}^{Nestlé} = 9.384\%(.65) + 4.000\%(1 - .20)(.35) = 7.2196\%$$

Nestlé's weighted-average cost of capital would be 7.2196%.

This section draws upon the work of Stulz (1995, pp. 11–22).

THE LINK BETWEEN COST AND AVAILABILITY OF CAPITAL

Nestlé's WACC was calculated assuming that equity and debt capital would always be available at the same required rate of return even if Nestlé's capital budget expands. This is a reasonable assumption considering Nestlé's excellent access to international portfolio investors in global capital markets. It is a bad assumption, however, for firms resident in illiquid or segmented emerging capital markets, for small domestic firms, and for family-owned firms resident in any capital market.

))))   Improving Market Liquidity

Although no consensus exists about the definition of *market liquidity*, we can observe it by noting the degree to which a firm can issue a new security without depressing the existing market price, as well as the degree to which a change in price of its securities elicits a substantial order flow.

In the domestic case, an underlying assumption is that total availability of capital to a firm is determined at any time by supply and demand in the domestic capital markets. A firm should always expand its capital budget by raising funds in the same proportion as its optimal financial structure. As its budget expands in absolute terms, however, its marginal cost of capital will eventually increase. In other words, a firm can only tap the capital market for some limited amount in the short run before suppliers of capital balk at providing further funds, even if the same optimal financial structure is preserved. In the long run this may not be a limitation, depending on market liquidity.

In the multinational case, a firm is able to improve market liquidity by raising funds in the Euromarkets (money, bond and equity), by using directed security issues in individual national capital markets, and by tapping local capital markets through foreign affiliates. Such activity should logically expand the capacity of a MNE to raise funds in the short run over what might have been raised if the firm were limited to its home capital market. This situation assumes that the firm's optimal financial structure is preserved.

)))) Market Segmentation

A national capital market is *segmented* if the required rate of return on securities in that market differs from the required rate of return on securities of comparable expected return and risk that are traded on other national securities markets (New York and London, for example). On the other hand, if all capital markets are fully integrated, securities of comparable expected return and risk should have the same required rate of return in each national market after adjusting for foreign exchange risk and political risk. This definition applies to both equity and debt, although it often happens that one or the other may be more integrated than its counterpart.

A national securities market can be efficient in a domestic context and yet segmented in an international context. According to finance theory, a market is *efficient* if security prices in that market reflect all available relevant information and adjust quickly to any new relevant information. Therefore, the price of an individual security reflects its intrinsic value and any price fluctuations will be "random walks" around this value. This view assumes that transaction costs are low, that many participants are in the market, and that these participants have sufficient financial strength to move security prices. Empirical tests of market efficiency have been conducted on most of the major European securities markets and in Japan, Canada, and the United States. The results show that most of these markets are reasonably efficient.

An efficient national securities market might very well correctly price all securities traded in that market on the basis of information available to the investors who participate in that market. However, if that market is segmented, foreign investors would not be participants. Thus, securities in the segmented market would be priced on the basis of domestic rather than international standards.

In the rest of this chapter and the next chapter we will use the term *MNE* to designate all firms that have access to a global cost and availability of capital. This includes qualifying MNEs, whether they are located in highly developed or emerging markets. It also includes large firms that are not multinational but have access to global capital markets. They, too, could be located in highly developed or emerging capital markets. We will use the term *domestic firm* (DF) to mean all firms that do not have access to a global cost and availability of capital, no matter where they are located.

Availability of capital depends on whether a firm can gain liquidity for its debt and equity securities and a price for those securities based on international rather than national standards. In practice this means that the firm must define a strategy to attract international portfolio investors and thereby escape the constraints of its own illiquid or segmented national market. Such a strategy will be illustrated shortly in the Novo case.

)))) Measures of Market Liquidity and Segmentation

In practice, hardly any capital market is totally illiquid and segmented. Instead, there is a spectrum of possibilities. The Milken Institute Capital Access Index is one of the best of recent attempts to identify the extent to which firms resident in individual emerging capital markets have access to foreign sources of capital. Exhibit 10.3 is an illustration of this index. The Milken Institute describes its methodology as follows:

> The Milken Institute Capital Access Index focuses on market factors alone and not on political ideologies. We examine empirical market factors regulating the entry and exit, origin and destination of capital flows. Thus, our rankings focus less upon macroeconomic policies and issues than do other economic rankings, and more upon recent revolutions in corporate finance theory and practice. The ability to tap capital markets and structure corporate finances to facilitate business growth strategies is key. Obviously, the macroeconomic environment can constrain or enhance that capacity, but this index focuses upon finance variables that link microeconomic behavior to macroeconomic performance.
>
> We measure capital access according to the depth, breadth, and liquidity of markets. Risk measures include the volatility of interest rates, currencies, and equity prices. These risk factors have the greatest impact upon foreign portfolio flows, domestic capital formation, firm formation, and aggregate growth. Even though we do not incorporate political factors per se, some policy information can be gleaned by examining our government-control factors, which are indicative of the role of the state in determining patterns of economic performance.
>
> The Milken Institute Capital Access Index is an equally weighted index of 17 variables, divided into three categories: quantitative, risk, and qualitative.[4]

| Exhibit 10.3 | *The Milken Institute Capital Access Index: Ranking of Emerging Capital Markets* |

Country	Score	Rank	Quantitative Measures	Risk Measures	Qualitative Measures
Singapore	100.0	1	97.7	78.3	100.0
Taiwan	96.3	2	89.9	100.0	23.6
Hong Kong	92.9	3	100.0	66.3	92.7
South Africa	81.2	4	76.0	74.5	52.7
Chile	80.0	5	86.8	71.7	29.1
Israel	76.6	6	65.9	76.1	43.6
Greece	72.9	7	65.9	69.0	45.5
Argentina	72.0	8	50.3	75.0	56.4
China	72.0	8	77.5	97.3	0.0
Panama	71.4	10	50.4	64.1	89.1
Malaysia	70.8	11	75.2	65.8	21.8
Turkey	70.2	12	72.9	57.1	52.7
Peru	69.2	13	51.2	68.5	60.0
Brazil	66.5	14	71.3	63.0	14.5
Morocco	65.5	15	60.5	67.4	20.0
India	64.3	16	66.7	71.2	0.0
Czech Republic	64.0	17	59.7	66.8	14.5
Philippines	62.2	18	57.4	56.0	45.5
Hungary	60.6	19	43.4	73.9	9.1
Ecuador	59.7	20	54.3	51.6	52.7
Mexico	56.0	21	66.7	44.6	25.5
Thailand	56.0	21	82.9	40.8	9.9
Slovak Republic	50.8	23	45.0	54.9	10.9
Nigeria	49.8	24	48.1	40.2	47.3
Venezuela	45.2	25	45.7	39.7	27.3
Poland	44.3	26	29.5	69.6	0.0
Egypt	43.1	27	56.6	59.2	0.0
Indonesia	37.8	28	56.6	26.3	0.0
Korea	20.6	29	51.9	39.1	0.0
Russia	18.2	30	42.6	32.1	0.0
Bulgaria	9.8	31	22.5	21.7	0.0

Quantitative Measures: Government spending/GDP; Equity market capitalization/GDP; Debt market capitalization/GDP; Government debt/GDP.

Risk Measures: Interest-rate spread between U.S. Treasury bonds and domestic debt; Stock market activity; Short-term interest-rate volatility; Currency volatility; 90-day interest rates; Velocity of M1 money supply; Equity market liquidity; IPOs as a share of total issues.

Qualitative Measures: Moody's bank strength rankings; IMF program; Capital controls; Allowed foreign ownership; Capital gains tax.

Source: *http://www.milken-inst.org* (1998). Milken Institute. Reprinted with permission.

THE EFFECT OF LIQUIDITY AND MARKET SEGMENTATION ON THE MARGINAL COST OF CAPITAL

The degree to which capital markets are illiquid or segmented has an important influence on a firm's marginal cost of capital. This relationship is illustrated in Exhibit 10.4, which shows the transition from a domestic to a global marginal cost of capital.

Exhibit 10.4 shows that the MNE has a given marginal return on capital at different budget levels, represented in the line DD'. This demand is determined by ranking potential projects according to net present value or internal rate of return. Percentage rate of return to both users and suppliers of capital is shown on the vertical scale. If the firm is limited to raising funds in its domestic market, the line SS_D shows the marginal domestic cost of capital (vertical axis) at various budget levels (horizontal axis). Remember that the firm continues to maintain the same debt ratio as it expands its budget, so that financial risk does not change. The optimal budget in the domestic case is $40 million, where the marginal return on capital (MRR) just equals the marginal cost of capital (MCC_D). At this budget the marginal domestic cost of capital, k_D, would be equal to 20%.

If the MNE has access to additional sources of capital outside an illiquid domestic capital market, the marginal cost of capital should shift to the right (the line SS_F). In other words, foreign markets can be tapped for long-term funds at times when the domestic market is saturated because of heavy use by other bor-

---

Exhibit 10.4   *Market Liquidity, Segmentation, and the Marginal Cost of Capital*

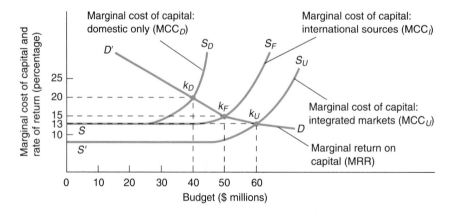

A MNE that raises capital on international markets shifts the marginal cost of capital from SS_D to SS_F due to the favorable effect on the liquidity of its securities. If, however, the firm not only escapes the illiquid domestic capital market but also is successful in having its securities integrated and priced on international markets, the marginal cost of capital shifts down and farther right to $S'S_U$. The firm now has access to lower-cost capital over the entire budget range.

rowers or equity issuers or when the market is unable to absorb another issue of the MNE in the short run. Exhibit 10.4 shows that by a tap of foreign capital markets, the marginal international cost of capital, k_F, has been reduced to 15%, even while an additional $10 million has been raised. This statement assumes that about $20 million is raised abroad, since only about $30 million could be raised domestically at a 15% cost of capital.

If the MNE is located in a capital market that is both illiquid and segmented, the line SS_D represents the decreased marginal cost of capital if the MNE gains access to other equity markets. As a result of the combined effects of greater availability of capital and international pricing of the firm's securities, the marginal cost of capital, k_U, declines to 13% and the optimal capital budget climbs to $60 million.

Most of the tests of market segmentation suffer from the usual problem for model builders—namely, the need to abstract from reality in order to have a testable model. In our opinion, a realistic test would be to observe what happens to a single security's price when it has been traded only in a domestic market, is discovered by foreign investors, and then is traded in a foreign market. Arbitrage should keep the market price equal in both markets. However, if during the transition we observe a significant change in the security's price uncorrelated with price movements in either of the underlying securities markets, we can infer that the domestic market was segmented.

In academic circles, tests based on case studies are often considered to be "casual empiricism," since no theory or model exists to explain what is being observed. Nevertheless, something may be learned from such cases, just as scientists learn from observing nature in an uncontrolled environment. Furthermore, case studies that preserve real-world complications may illustrate specific kinds of barriers to market integration and ways in which they might be overcome.

Unfortunately, few case studies have been documented where a firm has escaped from a segmented capital market. In practice, escape usually means being listed on a foreign stock market such as New York or London and/or selling securities in foreign capital markets. We will illustrate what can be learned from a case study by using the example of Novo Industri A/S, a Danish firm.

ILLUSTRATIVE CASE

Novo Industri A/S (Novo)

Novo is a Danish multinational firm that produces industrial enzymes and pharmaceuticals (mostly insulin). In 1977, Novo's management decided to "internationalize" its capital structure and sources of funds. This decision was based on the observation that the Danish securities market was both illiquid and segmented from other capital markets. In particular, the lack of availability and high cost of equity capital in Denmark resulted in Novo having a higher cost of capital than its main multinational competitors, such as Eli Lilly (U.S.), Miles Laboratories (U.S.—a subsidiary of Bayer, Germany), and Gist Brocades (The Netherlands).

Apart from the cost of capital, Novo's projected growth opportunities signaled the eventual need to raise new long-term capital beyond what could be raised in the illiquid Danish market. Since Novo is a technology leader in its specialties, planned capital investments in plant, equipment, and research could not be postponed until internal financing from cash flow became available. Novo's competitors would preempt any markets not served by Novo.

Even if an equity issue of the size required could have been raised in Denmark, the required rate of return would have been unacceptably high. For example, Novo's price/earnings ratio was typically around 5; that of its foreign competitors was well over 10. Yet Novo's business and financial risk appeared to be about equal to that of its competitors. A price/earnings ratio of 5 appeared appropriate for Novo only within a domestic Danish context when Novo was compared with other domestic firms of comparable business and financial risk.

If Denmark's securities markets were integrated with world markets, we would expect foreign investors to rush in and buy "undervalued" Danish securities. In that case, firms like Novo would enjoy an international cost of capital comparable to that of their foreign competitors. Strangely enough, no Danish governmental restrictions existed that would have prevented foreign investors from holding Danish securities. Therefore, we must look to investor perception as the main cause of market segmentation in Denmark at that time.

At least six characteristics of the Danish equity market were responsible for market segmentation: (1) asymmetric information base of Danish and foreign investors; (2) taxation; (3) alternative sets of feasible portfolios; (4) financial risk; (5) foreign exchange risk; and (6) political risk.

Asymmetric Information

Certain institutional characteristics of Denmark caused Danish and foreign investors to be uninformed about each other's equity securities. The most important information barrier was the Danish regulation that prohibited Danish investors from holding foreign private sector securities. Therefore, Danish investors had no incentive to follow developments in foreign securities markets or to factor such information into their evaluation of Danish securities.

As a result, in the efficient market sense Danish securities might have been priced correctly, but incorrectly relative to one another, considering a combined foreign and Danish information base. Another detrimental effect of the regulation was that foreign securities firms did not locate offices or personnel in Denmark, since they had no product to sell. Lack of a physical presence in Denmark reduced the ability of foreign security analysts to follow Danish securities.

A second information barrier was lack of enough Danish security analysts following Danish securities. Only one professional Danish securities analysis service was published (*Børsinformation*), and that was in the Danish language. A few Danish institutional investors employed in-house analysts, but their findings were not available to the public. Almost no foreign security analysts followed Danish securities because they had no product to sell and the Danish market was too small (small-country bias).

Other information barriers included language and accounting principles. Naturally, financial information was normally published in Danish, using Danish accounting principles. A few firms, such as Novo, published English versions, but almost none used U.S. or British accounting principles or attempted to show any reconciliation with such principles.

Taxation

Danish taxation policy had all but eliminated investment in common stock by individuals. Until a tax law change in July 1981, capital gains on shares held for over two years were taxed at a 50% rate. Shares held for less than two years or for "speculative" purposes were taxed at personal income tax rates, with the top marginal rate being 75%. In contrast, capital gains on bonds were tax free. This situation resulted in bonds being issued at deep discounts because the redemption at par at maturity was considered a capital gain. Thus, most individual investors held bonds rather than stocks. This factor reduced the liquidity of the stock market and increased the rate of return required on stocks if they were to compete with bonds.

Feasible Set of Portfolios

Because of the prohibition on foreign security ownership, Danish investors had a very limited set of securities from which to choose a portfolio. In practice, Danish institutional portfolios were composed of Danish stocks, government bonds, and mortgage bonds. Since Danish stock price movements are closely correlated with each other, Danish portfolios possessed a rather high level of systematic risk. In addition, government policy had been to provide a relatively high real rate of return on government bonds after adjusting for inflation. The net result of taxation policies on individuals, and attractive real yields on government bonds, was that required rates of return on stocks were relatively high by international standards.

From a portfolio perspective, Danish stocks provided an opportunity for foreign investors to diversify internationally. If Danish stock price movements were not closely correlated with world stock price movements, inclusion of Danish stocks in foreign portfolios should reduce these portfolios' systematic risk. Furthermore, foreign investors were not subject to the high Danish income tax rates, since they are normally protected by tax treaties that typically limit the tax to 15% on dividends and capital gains. As a result of the international diversification potential, foreign investors might have required a lower rate of return on Danish stocks than would Danish investors, other things being equal. However, other things may not be equal because foreign investors may have perceived Danish stocks to carry more financial, foreign exchange, and political risk than their own domestic securities.

Financial, Foreign Exchange, and Political Risks

Financial leverage utilized by Danish firms was relatively high by U.S. and U.K. standards but not abnormal for Scandinavia, Germany, Italy, or Japan. In addition, most of the debt was short term with variable interest rates. Just how foreign investors viewed financial risk in Danish firms depended on what norms they followed in their home countries. We know from Novo's experience in tapping the Eurobond market in 1978 that Morgan Grenfell, its British investment banker, advised Novo to maintain a *debt ratio* (debt/total capitalization) closer to 50% rather than the traditional Danish 65% to 70%.

Foreign investors in Danish securities are subject to foreign exchange risk. Whether this is a plus or a minus factor depends on the investor's home currency, the investor's perception of the future strength of the Danish krone, and the impact of foreign exchange risk on a firm's operating exposure. Based on personal contacts with foreign investors and bankers, Novo's management did not believe foreign exchange risk was a factor in Novo's stock price because its operations were perceived as being well diversified internationally.

From the same interviews, with respect to political risk, Denmark was perceived as a stable Western democracy but with the potential to cause periodic problems for foreign investors. In particular, Denmark's national debt was regarded as too high for comfort, although this judgment had not yet shown up in the form of risk premiums on Denmark's Eurocurrency syndicated loans. The other threat perceived by foreign investors was that Denmark would move toward implementing *economic democracy* in a more substantial manner. Economic democracy would result in a mandatory profit-sharing plan whereby a central fund, governed by labor unions, would eventually become a major shareholder in private-sector firms. Despite these general concerns about Denmark's political situation, investors in Novo in particular indicated that their evaluation of Novo's prospects was not influenced by political risk.

The Road to Internationalization

Although Novo's management in 1977 wished to escape from the shackles of Denmark's segmented and illiquid capital market, many barriers had to be overcome. It is worthwhile to describe some of these obstacles, since they typify the barriers faced by other firms from segmented markets that wish to internationalize their capital sources.

Closing the Information Gap. Novo had been a family-owned firm from its founding in the 1920s by the two Pederson brothers until 1974, when it went public and listed its B shares on the Copenhagen Stock Exchange. The A shares were held by the Novo Foundation; they were sufficient to maintain voting control. However, Novo was essentially unknown in investment circles outside Denmark. To overcome this disparity in the information base, Novo increased the level of its financial and technical disclosure in both Danish and English versions.

The information gap was further closed when Morgan Grenfell successfully organized a syndicate to underwrite and sell a $20 million convertible Eurobond issue for Novo in 1978. In connection with this offering, Novo listed its shares on the London Stock Exchange to facilitate conversion and to gain visibility. These twin actions were the key to dissolving the information barrier, and, of course, they also raised a large amount of long-term capital on favorable terms, capital that would have been unavailable in Denmark.

Despite the favorable impact of the Eurobond issue on availability of capital, Novo's cost of capital actually increased when Danish investors reacted negatively to the potential dilution effect of the conversion right. During 1979, Novo's share price declined from around Dkr300 per share to around Dkr200–225 per share.

The Biotechnology Boom. During 1979, a fortuitous event occurred. Biotechnology began to attract the interest of the U.S. investment community, with several sensationally oversubscribed stock issues by such start-up firms as Genentech and Cetus. Thanks to the domestic information gap, Danish investors were unaware of these events and continued to value Novo at a low price/earnings ratio of 5, compared with over 10 for its established competitors and 30 or more for potential new competitors.

In order to profile itself as a biotechnology firm with a proven track record, Novo organized a seminar in New York City on April 30, 1980. Soon after the seminar a few sophisticated individual U.S. investors began buying Novo's shares and convertibles through the London Stock Exchange. Danish investors were only too happy to supply this foreign demand. Therefore, despite relatively strong demand from U.S. and British investors, Novo's share price increased only gradually, climbing back to the

Dkr300 level by mid-summer. However, during the following months foreign interest began to snowball, and by the end of 1980 Novo's stock price had reached the Dkr600 level. Moreover, foreign investors had increased their proportion of share ownership from virtually nothing to around 30%. Novo's price/earnings ratio had risen to around 16, which was now in line with that of its international competitors but not with the Danish market. At this point we must conclude that Novo had succeeded in internationalizing its cost of capital. Other Danish securities remained locked in a segmented capital market. Exhibit 10.5 shows that the movement in the Danish stock market in general did not parallel the rise in Novo's share price, nor could it be explained by movement in the U.S. or U.K. stock markets as a whole.

Improving Liquidity: Sponsoring the ADR System. Novo wanted to improve the liquidity of its shares held by U.S. investors and to increase the availability of capital by tapping the U.S. new issue market. In 1981 Novo sponsored an American Depositary Receipts (ADR) program in the United States, had its shares quoted on the over-the-counter market (NASDAQ), and retained Goldman Sachs to advise it about a U.S. stock issue. The firm split its shares five for one in the U.S. market by issuing five times as many ADRs as there were underlying Danish kroner shares held in the bank.

A Directed Share Issue in the United States. During the first half of 1981, under the guidance of Goldman Sachs and with the assistance of Morgan Grenfell and Copenhagen Handelsbank, Novo prepared a prospectus for SEC registration of a U.S. share offering and eventual listing on the New York Stock Exchange. The main barriers encountered in this effort, which would have general applicability, were connected with preparing financial statements that could be reconciled with U.S. accounting principles and meeting the higher level of disclosure required by the SEC. In particular, industry segment reporting was a problem from both a disclosure perspective and an accounting perspective, because the accounting data were not available internally in that format. As it turned out, the investment barriers in the U.S. were relatively tractable though expensive and time consuming to overcome.

The more serious barriers were caused by a variety of institutional and governmental regulations in Denmark. The latter were never designed so that firms could issue shares at market value, since Danish firms typically issued stock at par value with preemptive rights. By this time, however, Novo's share price, driven by continued foreign buying, was so high that virtually nobody in Denmark thought it was worth what foreigners were willing to pay. In fact, prior to the time of the share issue in July 1981, Novo's share price had risen to over Dkr1500 before settling down to a

Exhibit 10.5   *Novo's B-Share Prices Compared with Stock Market Indices*

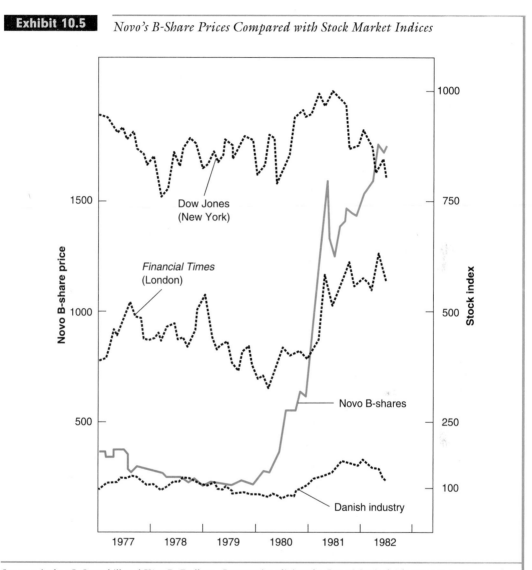

Source: Arthur I. Stonehill and Kåre B. Dullum, *Internationalizing the Cost of Capital: The Novo Experience and National Policy Implications*, London: John Wiley, 1982, p. 73. Reprinted with permission.

level around Dkr1400. Foreign ownership had increased to over 50% of Novo's shares outstanding!

Market segmentation was very apparent during the first half of 1981. Published and unpublished reports by Danish security analysts, bankers, and the popular press consistently claimed that Novo was seriously overvalued, while their foreign counterparts were consistently touting Novo as being undervalued. The difference in views was based partly on investor perceptions of the importance of biotechnology and Novo's role in this field.

Stock Market Reactions. One final piece of evidence on market segmentation can be gleaned from the way Danish and foreign investors reacted to the announcement of the proposed $61 million U.S. share issue on May 29, 1981. Novo's share price dropped 156 points the next trading day in Copenhagen, equal to about 10% of its market value. As soon as trading started in New York, the stock price immediately recovered all its loss. The Copenhagen reaction was typical for an illiquid market. Investors worried about the dilution effect of the new share issue, since it would increase the number of shares outstanding by about 8%. They did not believe that Novo could invest the new funds at a rate of return that would not dilute future earnings per share. They also feared that the U.S. shares would eventually flow back to Copenhagen if biotechnology lost its glitter.

The U.S. reaction to the announcement of the new share issue was consistent with what one would expect in a liquid and integrated market. U.S. investors viewed the new issue as creating additional demand for the shares as Novo became more visible due to the selling efforts of a large aggressive syndicate. Furthermore, the marketing effort was directed at institutional investors who were previously under-represented among Novo's U.S. investors. They had been under-represented because U.S. institutional investors want to be assured of a liquid market in a stock in order to be able to get out, if desired, without depressing the share price. The wide distribution effected by the new issue, plus SEC registration and a New York Stock Exchange listing, all added up to more liquidity and an international cost of capital.

Effect on Novo's Weighted-Average Cost of Capital. During most of 1981 and the years thereafter, Novo's share price was driven by international portfolio investors transacting on the New York and London stock exchanges. This changed Novo's weighted-average cost of capital and lowered its marginal cost of capital. Unlike Nestlé's, Novo's systematic risk was reduced from its previous level, which was determined by Danish institutional investors that were nondiversified internationally and by the Novo Foundation. However, its appropriate debt ratio level was also reduced to match the standards expected by international portfolio investors trading in the United States, United Kingdom, and other important markets. In essence, the U.S. dollar became Novo's functional currency when shares were being evaluated by international investors. Theoretically, its revised weighted-average cost of capital should have become a new reference hurdle rate when evaluating new capital investments in Denmark or abroad.

Other firms that follow Novo's strategy are also likely to have their weighted-average cost of capital become a function of the requirements of international portfolio investors. Firms resident in some of the emerging market countries have already experienced "dollarization" of trade and financing for working capital. This phenomenon might be extended to long-term financing and the weighted-average cost of capital.

We have described the Novo experience in hopes that it can be a model for other firms wishing to escape from segmented and illiquid home equity markets. However, a word of caution is advised. Novo had an excellent operating track record and a very strong worldwide market niche in two important industry sectors. This record continues to attract investors in Denmark and abroad. Other companies would also need to have such a favorable track record to attract foreign investors.

The Novo case material is a condensed version of Arthur Stonehill and Kåre B. Dullum, *Internationalizing the Cost of Capital in Theory and Practice: The Novo Experience and National Policy Implications*, Copenhagen: Nyt Nordisk Forlag Arnold Busck, 1982; and New York: Wiley, 1982. Reprinted with permission.

THE COST OF CAPITAL FOR MNEs COMPARED TO DOMESTIC FIRMS

Is the weighted-average cost of capital for MNEs higher or lower than for their domestic counterparts? The answer is a function of the marginal cost of capital, the relative after-tax cost of debt, the optimal debt ratio, and the relative cost of equity.

)))   Availability of Capital

We saw earlier in this chapter that international availability of capital to MNEs, or to other large firms that can attract international portfolio investors, may allow them to lower their cost of equity and debt compared with most domestic firms. In addition, international availability permits a MNE to maintain its desired debt ratio, even when significant amounts of new funds must be raised. In other words, a MNE's marginal cost of capital is constant for considerable ranges of its capital budget. This statement is not true for most domestic firms. They must either rely on internally generated funds or borrow short and medium term from commercial banks.

As an illustration of the effect of availability of capital on optimal financial structure and the marginal cost of capital, Exhibit 10.6 presents a graphic comparison between a MNE with a global cost of capital and a firm that has a domestic cost of capital.

In Exhibit 10.6 a MNE is depicted as enjoying a constant marginal cost of capital at all levels of its likely capital budget. Thus it is able to raise funds in the proportion desired for minimizing its cost of capital (k_{wacc}^{MNE}). In this example the

| **Exhibit 10.6** | *Cost of Capital and Financial Structure: Constant versus Rising Marginal Cost of Capital* |

a. Multinational firm with global cost of capital

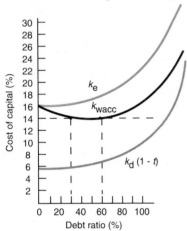
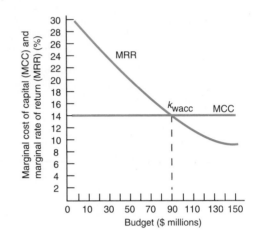

b. Domestic firm with domestic cost of capital

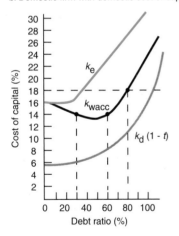
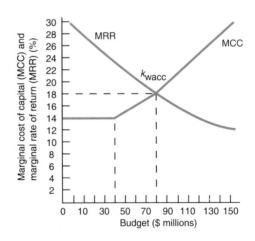

Key:

$$k_{wacc} = k_e \frac{E}{V} + k_d(1-t)\frac{D}{V}, \text{ weighted-average cost of capital}$$

k_e	=	risk-adjusted cost of equity,	D	=	market value of the firm's debt,
k_d	=	before-tax cost of debt,	V	=	total market value of the firm's securities $(E + D)$
t	=	marginal tax rate,	MRR	=	marginal rate of return
E	=	market value of the firm's equity,	MCC	=	marginal cost of capital

MNE can minimize its cost of capital by choosing any debt ratio between 30% and 60%, which is the lowest (flat) part of its cost of capital curve. If it chooses 45%, for example, it can raise all the funds it needs in the proportion of 45% debt and 55% equity without raising the cost of these funds. Even if internally generated funds are insufficient to maintain this proportion, it can sell new equity at about the same price as its existing equity. The optimal capital budget for the MNE in this example happens to be $90 million (Exhibit 10.6a). At this point its marginal return on capital just equals its marginal cost of capital. In other words, if the MNE ranks all capital budgeting projects according to their *internal rate of return* (IRR), the last project to be accepted would be the one whose IRR just equals the firm's 14% marginal weighted average after-tax cost of capital ($k_{\text{wacc}}^{\text{MNE}}$).

The domestic firm cannot raise funds in the proportions desired to minimize its cost of capital ($k_{\text{wacc}}^{\text{Dom}}$). Yet it is assumed to have the same relationship between its cost of capital ($k_{\text{wacc}}^{\text{Dom}}$) and its debt ratios as the MNE. In other words, the left-hand graphs are identical (Exhibit 10.6b). Furthermore, both firms are assumed to face the same opportunities, represented by the marginal return on capital curves. The difference is that the domestic firm can maintain its optimal debt ratio range (30% to 60%) only for capital budgets up to $40 million (Exhibit 10.6b right side). At that point it has committed all its internally generated funds plus the optimal proportion of additional debt. If it wishes to reach its optimal budget, which is $80 million, it must borrow the remaining $40 million. It cannot raise $40 million in its national equity market, except perhaps at exorbitant rates or with unacceptable loss of control. Nevertheless, despite increasing its debt ratio to 80%, and its cost of capital ($k_{\text{wacc}}^{\text{Dom}}$) to 18%, it should borrow the additional $40 million in order to realize its profit potential. Its profit potential is maximized at the point in the capital budget where the marginal return on capital (MRR) equals the marginal cost of capital (MCC, Exhibit 10.6b right side).

Note that not only does the domestic firm have a higher marginal cost of capital, with 18% compared with 14% for the MNE, but its optimal capital budget is lower, $80 million compared with $90 million for the MNE.

⟫⟩ Financial Structure, Systematic Risk, and the Cost of Capital for MNEs

Recent empirical research has suggested that, contrary to previous beliefs, MNEs may actually have a higher weighted-average cost of capital and systematic risk and lower debt ratio than their domestic counterparts. This textbook, and most other textbooks, have traditionally argued that theoretically MNEs should be in a better position than their domestic counterparts to support higher debt ratios because their cash flows are diversified internationally. The probability of a firm's covering fixed charges under varying conditions in product, financial, and foreign exchange markets should improve if the variability of its cash flows is minimized.

By diversifying cash flows internationally, the MNE might be able to achieve the same kind of reduction in cash flow variability as portfolio investors receive from diversifying their security holdings internationally. The same argument applies—namely, that returns are not perfectly correlated between countries. For example, in 1999 Japan was in recession, but the United States was experiencing rapid growth. Therefore, we might have expected returns, on either a cash flow or an earnings basis, to be depressed in Japan while being favorable in the United States. A MNE with operations located in both these countries could rely on its strong U.S. cash inflow to cover debt obligations, even if its Japanese affiliate produced weak net cash inflows.

Despite the theoretical elegance of this hypothesis, recent empirical studies have come to the opposite conclusion.[5] Despite the favorable effect of international diversification of cash flows, bankruptcy risk for MNEs was about the same as for domestic firms. However, MNEs faced higher agency costs, political risk, foreign exchange risk, and asymmetric information. These have been identified as the factors leading to lower debt ratios.

Even more surprising, one of these studies found that U.S.-based MNEs have a higher level of systematic risk than do their domestic counterparts.[6] The same factors caused this phenomenon as caused the lower debt ratios for MNEs. The study concluded the increased standard deviation of cash flows from internationalization more than offset the lower correlation from diversification.

More formally, the systematic risk term, β_j, is defined as:

$$\beta_j = \frac{\rho_{jm}\sigma_j}{\sigma_m}$$

where ρ_{jm} is the correlation coefficient between security j and the market; σ_j is the standard deviation of the return on firm j; and σ_m is the standard deviation of the market return. The MNE's systematic risk could increase if the decrease in its correlation coefficient, ρ_{jm}, due to international diversification, is more than offset by an increase in σ_j, its standard deviation due to the risk factors above. This conclusion is consistent with the observation that many MNEs use a higher hurdle rate to discount expected foreign project cash flows. In essence, they are accepting projects they consider to be riskier than domestic projects, thus potentially skewing upward their perceived systematic risk. At the least, MNEs need to earn a higher rate of return than their domestic equivalents in order to maintain their market value.

A very recent study found that for emerging market MNEs, internationalization actually allowed them to carry a higher level of debt and lowered their systematic risk. This is because the emerging market MNEs are investing in more stable economies abroad, a strategy that lowers their operating, financial, foreign exchange, and political risks. The reduction in risk more than offsets their increased agency costs and leads to the emerging market MNEs enjoying higher leverage and lower systematic risk than their U.S.-based MNE counterparts.[7] In order to apply these research findings to practice, we now return to the Nestlé case introduced earlier in this chapter.

ILLUSTRATIVE CASE

Nestlé Revisited

Exhibit 10.2 showed that from the perspective of a Swiss investor with a global portfolio, Nestlé's expected rate of return on equity, $k_{Nestlé}$, was 9.3840%. Its weighted-average cost of capital, k_{wacc}, was 7.2196%.

Assume that Swiss Confectionary is a domestic Swiss firm that sells confectionary products that compete with Nestlé's but that are sold only in Switzerland. Swiss Confectionary is owned by Swiss institutional investors as part of their global portfolios. If the research conclusions for U.S.-based MNEs cited above are also correct for MNEs based in other highly developed capital markets, Swiss Confectionary, as a domestic firm, could have a lower systematic risk and higher debt ratio than Nestlé, a multinational firm. Both firms are in the same industry but Nestlé is much larger, has better growth opportunities, and has access to long-term debt. Otherwise, they face the same values for the Swiss bond index (risk-free rate), tax rate (20%), and expected rate of return for the market. However, because of its much smaller size, and lack of access to global debt markets, Swiss Confectionary must pay 6% for its debt compared to Nestlé's 4%. On the other hand, according to the research results, it could justify a higher debt ratio, say, 45%, compared to Nestlé's 35%. Furthermore, its systematic risk might be lower than Nestlé's. Assume Swiss Confectionary's beta is 0.500 compared to Nestlé's 0.585. The required rate of return on Swiss Confectionary by a global Swiss investor would be:

$$k_e^{Swiss} = k_{rf} + (k_m - k_{rf})\beta_{Swiss} = 3.3\% + (13.7\% - 3.3\%)\,0.500 = 8.50\%$$

The required rate of return by a Swiss investor on Swiss Confectionary would be 8.50% compared to Nestlé's 9.3840%. Swiss Confectionary's weighted-average cost of capital would be:

$$k_{wacc}^{Swiss} = k_e \frac{E}{V} + k_d(1-t)\frac{D}{V} = 8.50\%(.55) + 6.00\%(1-.20)(.45) = 6.835\%$$

Swiss Confectionary's weighted average cost of capital would be 6.835% compared to Nestlé's 7.2196%. This assumes that both firms are operating in the flat part of their marginal cost of capital curves (Exhibit 10.6), and that there are no market liquidity or segmentation constraints in Switzerland.

SOLVING A RIDDLE: IS THE WEIGHTED-AVERAGE COST OF CAPITAL FOR U.S.-BASED MNES REALLY HIGHER THAN FOR THEIR DOMESTIC COUNTERPARTS?

The riddle is that the U.S.-based MNE is supposed to have a lower marginal cost of capital (MCC) than a domestic firm because of the MNE's access to a global cost and availability of capital. On the other hand, the empirical studies mentioned above show that the U.S.-based MNE's weighted-average cost of capital is actually higher than that of a comparable domestic firm because of agency costs, foreign exchange risk, political risk, asymmetric information, and other complexities of foreign operations.

The answer to this riddle lies in the linkage between the cost of capital, its availability, and the opportunity set of projects. As the opportunity set of projects increases, eventually the firm needs to increase its capital budget to the point where its marginal cost of capital is increasing. The optimal capital budget would still be at the point where the rising marginal cost of capital equals the declining rate of return on the opportunity set of projects. However, this would be at a higher weighted-average cost of capital than would have occurred for a lower level of the optimal capital budget.

To illustrate this linkage Exhibit 10.7 depicts the situation facing Nestlé and Swiss Confectionary. This time, however, there are two different demand schedules based on the opportunity set of projects for both Nestlé and Swiss Confectionary. The line D_1D_1' shows a modest set of potential projects. It intersects the MCC for both Nestlé and Swiss Confectionary at its flat section (point A for Swiss Confectionary). Both firms would have the same WACC as calculated previously (7.2196% for Nestlé and 6.8350% for Swiss Confectionary).

The line D_2D_2' shows a more aggressive set of potential projects. It intersects the MCC for Swiss Confectionary at a MCC of 8.000% and an optimal budget of 300 million Swiss francs compared to 200 million Swiss francs for the modest opportunity set of projects (line D_1D_1'). At these budget levels Nestlé still has a 7.2196% MCC. The line D_4D_4' intersects Nestlé's MCC of capital at 8.000% too, but this is at an optimal budget of 6 billion Swiss francs (point E), compared to its previous optimal budget of 5 billion Swiss francs when facing the modest opportunity set of projects (line D_3D_3').

The argument presented in Exhibit 10.7 is that Swiss Confectionary actually has a lower MCC than Nestlé (7.2196%) up to a budget level of 250 million Swiss francs (point B in Exhibit 10.7). Past this point, however, Swiss Confectionary's MCC rises rapidly due to its lack of access to global capital markets.

In order to extend this conclusion to the general case, it would be necessary to know under what conditions a domestic firm would be willing to undertake the optimal capital budget despite increasing its marginal cost of capital. At some point the MNE might also have an optimal capital budget at the point where its MCC is rising.

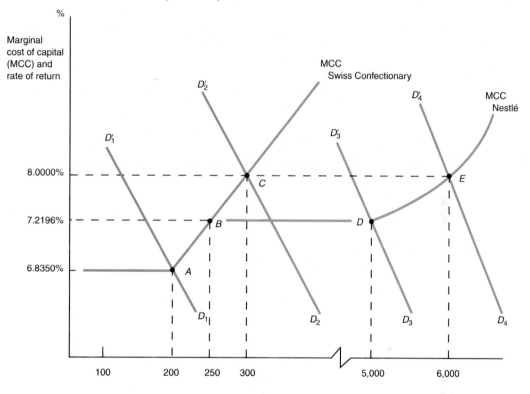

Exhibit 10.7 *The Marginal Cost of Capital and Optimal Budget for Nestlé and Swiss Confectionary*

Empirical studies show that neither mature domestic firms nor MNEs are typically willing to assume the higher agency costs or bankruptcy risk associated with higher MCCs and capital budgets. In fact, most mature firms demonstrate some degree of corporate wealth-maximizing behavior. They are somewhat risk-averse and tend to avoid returning to the market to raise fresh equity. They prefer to limit their capital budgets to what can be financed with free cash flows. Indeed, they have a so-called pecking order that determines the sources of funds they intend to tap and in what order.[8] This behavior motivates shareholders to monitor management more closely. They may tie management's compensation to stock performance (options). They may also require other types of contractual arrangements that are collectively part of agency costs.

In conclusion, if both MNEs and domestic firms do actually limit their capital budgets to what can be financed without increasing their MCC, then the empirical findings that MNEs have higher WACC stands. If the domestic firm has such good growth opportunities that it chooses to undertake despite an increasing marginal cost of capital, then the MNE will have a lower WACC.

FINANCIAL STRUCTURE OF FOREIGN AFFILIATES

If we accept the theory that minimizing the cost of capital for a given level of business risk and capital budget is an objective that should be implemented from the perspective of the consolidated MNE, then the financial structure of each affiliate is relevant only to the extent that it affects this overall goal. In other words, an individual affiliate does not really have an independent cost of capital. Therefore, its financial structure should not be based on an objective of minimizing its own independent cost of capital.

Financial structure norms for firms vary widely from one country to another but cluster together for firms domiciled in the same country. This statement is the conclusion of a long line of empirical studies that have investigated this question, from 1969 to the present.[9] Most of these international studies concluded that country-specific environmental variables are key determinants of debt ratios. Among these variables are historical development, taxation, corporate governance, bank influence, existence of a viable corporate bond market, attitude toward risk, government regulation, availability of capital, and agency costs.

Many other institutional differences also influence debt ratios in national capital markets, but firms that are trying to attract international portfolio investors must pay attention to debt-ratio norms expected by these investors. Since many international portfolio investors are influenced by the debt ratios that exist in the Anglo-American markets, there is a trend toward more global conformity. MNEs and other large firms dependent on attracting international portfolio investors are beginning to adopt similar debt-ratio standards, even if national standards continue to be used by domestic firms.

)))) Should Local Affiliates of MNEs Be Influenced by Local Financial Structure Norms?

Within the given constraint of minimizing its consolidated worldwide cost of capital, should a MNE take differing country debt-ratio norms into consideration when determining its desired debt-ratio for foreign affiliates?

For definition purposes, the debt considered here should be only what is borrowed from sources outside the MNE. This debt would include local and foreign currency loans as well as Eurocurrency loans. The reason for this definition is that parent loans to foreign affiliates are often regarded as equivalent to equity investment both by host countries and by investing firms. A parent loan is usually subordinated to other debt and does not create the same threat of insolvency as an external loan. Furthermore, the choice of debt or equity investment is often arbitrary and subject to negotiation between host country and parent firm.

The main advantages of a finance structure for foreign affiliates that conforms to local debt norms are as follows:

1. A localized financial structure reduces criticism of foreign affiliates that have been operating with too high a proportion of debt (judged by local standards), often resulting in the accusation that they are not contributing a fair share of risk capital to the host country. At the other end of the spectrum, it would improve the image of foreign affiliates that have been operating with too little debt and thus appear to be insensitive to local monetary policy.

2. A localized financial structure helps management evaluate return-on-equity investment relative to local competitors in the same industry. In economies where interest rates are relatively high as an offset to inflation, the penalty paid reminds management of the need to consider price-level changes when evaluating investment performance.

3. In economies where interest rates are relatively high because of a scarcity of capital, the penalty paid for borrowing local funds reminds management that unless return on assets is greater than the local price of capital—that is, unless there is negative leverage—they are probably misallocating scarce domestic resources. This factor may not appear to be relevant to management decisions, but it will certainly be considered by the host country in making decisions with respect to the firm.

The main disadvantages of localized financial structures are as follows:

1. A MNE is expected to have a comparative advantage over local firms in overcoming imperfections in national capital markets through better availability of capital and the ability to diversify risk. Why should it throw away these important competitive advantages to conform to local norms that are established in response to imperfect local capital markets, historical precedent, and institutional constraints that do not apply to the MNE?

2. If each foreign affiliate of a MNE localizes its financial structure, the resulting consolidated balance sheet might show a financial structure that does not conform to any particular country's norm. The debt ratio would be a simple weighted average of the corresponding ratio of each country in which the firm happened to operate. This feature could increase perceived financial risk and thus the cost of capital for the MNE, but only if two additional conditions are present:

    a. The consolidated debt ratio must be pushed completely out of the discretionary range of acceptable debt ratios in the flat area of the cost of capital curve, shown previously in Exhibit 10.2.

    b. The MNE must be unable to offset high debt in one foreign affiliate with low debt in other foreign or domestic affiliates at the same cost. If the international Fisher effect is working, replacement of debt should be possible at an equal after-tax cost after adjusting for foreign exchange risk. On the other hand, if market imperfections preclude this type of replacement, the possibility exists that the overall cost of debt, and thus the cost of capital, could increase for the MNE if it attempts to conform to local norms.

3. The debt ratio of a foreign affiliate is in reality only cosmetic, since lenders ultimately look to the parent and its consolidated worldwide cash flow as the source of repayment. In many cases, debt of affiliates must be guaranteed by the parent firm. Even if no formal guarantee exists, an implied guarantee usually exists since almost no parent firm would dare to allow an affiliate to default on a loan. If it did, repercussions would surely be felt with respect to the parent's own financial standing, with a resulting increase in its cost of capital.

)))) A Compromise Solution

In our opinion a compromise position is possible. Both multinational and domestic firms should try to minimize their overall weighted-average cost of capital for a given level of business risk and capital budget, as finance theory suggests. However, if debt is available to a foreign affiliate at equal cost to that which could be raised elsewhere, after adjusting for foreign exchange risk, then localizing the foreign affiliate's financial structure should incur no cost penalty and also allow the advantages listed above.

Naturally, if a particular foreign affiliate has access to subsidized local debt at a lower cost, after adjusting for foreign exchange risk, the MNE should borrow all it can through that foreign affiliate. The reverse would be true if the foreign affiliate had access only to higher-cost debt than available elsewhere. Nothing should be borrowed externally through that foreign affiliate.

These disequilibrium situations for a foreign affiliate can occur only in imperfect or segmented markets because otherwise the international Fisher effect would eliminate any such opportunities. The fact that opportunities to lower the cost of debt do exist its simply evidence of market imperfections or segmentation.

In summary, a MNE should probably follow a policy of borrowing at lowest cost, after adjusting for foreign exchange risk, anywhere in the world without regard to the cosmetic impact on any particular affiliate's financial structure. This policy assumes that local regulations permit this practice. The objective for a MNE is the same as that for a domestic firm, namely, to minimize its consolidated cost of capital for a given level of business risk and capital budget. On the other hand, if conforming to host country debt norms does not require a cost penalty but merely replaces debt in one affiliate by debt in another, worthwhile advantages can be realized. These advantages include better public relations with host country monetary authorities and more realistic evaluation of performance of foreign affiliates relative to competition with host country firms.

SUMMARY

- Gaining access to global capital markets should allow a firm to lower its cost of capital. This can be achieved by increasing the market liquidity of its shares and by escaping from segmentation of its home capital market.

- A firm is able to increase its market liquidity by raising debt in the Euromarket, by selling security issues in individual national capital markets and as Euroequities, and by tapping local capital markets through foreign affiliates. Increased market liquidity causes the marginal cost of capital line to "flatten out" to the right. This results in the firm's being able to raise more capital at the same low marginal cost of capital and thereby justifies investing in more capital projects. The key is to attract international portfolio investors.

- A national capital market is segmented if the required rate of return on securities in that market differs from the required rate of return on securities of comparable expected return and risk that are traded on other national securities markets.

- *Capital market segmentation* is a financial market imperfection caused by government constraints and investor perceptions. The most important imperfections are: (1) asymmetric information; (2) transaction costs; (3) foreign exchange risk; (4) takeover defenses; (5) small-country bias; (6) political risk; and (7) regulatory barriers.

- If a firm is resident in a segmented capital market, it can still escape from this market by sourcing its debt and equity abroad. The result should be a lower marginal cost of capital, improved liquidity for its shares, and a larger capital budget.

- The experience of Novo is a possible model for firms resident in small or emerging markets that are partially segmented and illiquid.

- Access to international capital markets permits the MNE to maintain its desired debt ratio even when significant amounts of new funds must be raised. Its marginal cost of capital is constant for much wider ranges of its capital budget compared with a domestic competitor that does not have access to international capital markets.

- MNEs should be in a better position than domestic firms to support higher debt ratios because their cash flows are diversified internationally. Agency costs, however, are higher for MNEs, as are foreign exchange risks, political risks, asymmetric information, and the complexity of international operations. As a result, MNEs have a lower debt ratio than their domestic counterparts. Furthermore, for the same reasons, MNEs appear to have a higher systematic risk and weighted-average cost of capital, except when domestic firms have an optimal capital budget that is affected by its rising marginal cost of capital.

■ The MNE should choose a capital structure that minimizes its cost of capital from the perspective of the consolidated firm. The financial structure of each affiliate is relevant only to the extent it affects this overall goal. An individual affiliate does not have an independent cost of capital.

QUESTIONS

1. Nestlé's WACC

Assume that Nestlé is updating its weighted-average cost of capital. The firm has altered its capital structure in recent years and wishes to use the revised relative weights of debt and equity in its capitalization with current costs of debt and equity.

As discussed above, Nestlé can calculate its cost of capital from the traditional "domestic portfolio" approach or one that is based on the "global portfolio" approach. Nestlé's CFO, Dr. Mario Corti, has now collected recent values for all alternative portfolios, as well as receiving a new estimate of its beta from one of its major banks, Union Bank of Switzerland (UBS). The cost of debt is 4%.

Component	Symbol	Domestic Portfolio	Global Portfolio	Revised Beta Global Portfolio
Risk free rate	k_{rf}	3.5%	3.5%	3.5%
Market return	k_m	10.0%	12.5%	12.5%
Beta	$\beta_{Nestlé}$	0.950	0.625	0.556

a. Calculate Nestlé's cost of equity for the three different portfolio data sets.

b. UBS's new beta estimate was found using a methodology in which the beta itself is a moving average of how the individual security's covariance with the global market "trends" over time. It assumes that the trend will continue, and that Nestlé's beta will continue to fall in value. What are the implications of the falling beta for Nestlé's cost of capital?

c. If Nestlé's debt/total capitalization has recently changed from 35% to 45%, how has its weighted-average cost of capital changed according to the three different portfolio constructions?

2. Novo's Lessons?

It is obvious that Novo served as a role model for other Nordic multinationals to attain a global cost and availability of capital. Does it follow that the Nordic experience could be relevant for MNEs resident in emerging markets using the Acer Group (www.acer.com),

a. Is the Taiwan market segmented or partially segmented from global equity markets?

b. Is the Acer Group's stock priced according to domestic standards or international standards?

c. If it is priced according to domestic standards, what strategies could the firm adopt to attain a global cost and availability of capital?

d. What, if any, government regulations need to be changed to encourage inward international portfolio investment in the selected emerging market?

3. L'Oreal

L'Oreal is a well known-French MNE specializing in cosmetics and fragrances. Its 1998 sales were €10.9 billion ($12 billion), with profits of €681 million ($749 million), and a return on equity of 15.1%. L'Oreal's Chief Financial Officer is concerned about how the introduction and conversion to the euro will affect L'Oreal's weighted-average cost of capital.

As part of the Eurozone (Euroland), would all firms be accorded a regional benchmark capital cost? If so, it would probably be adjusted for specific company and project risk, but probably not for country risk.

Since the introduction of the euro, the European Central Bank has determined monetary policy and thus the level of interest rates for all of Euroland. Differences in interest rates among the member countries have disappeared. This, in turn, should have an impact on the cost of equity. Furthermore, the equity markets in the Eurozone are becoming more closely correlated with each other.

a. Is the systematic risk of L'Oreal now different? How should this affect its cost of equity?

b. What does country risk mean for members of the Eurozone?

c. Track the convergence of interest rates within the Eurozone. What appears to be the benchmark risk-free rate of interest?

d. Track the equity performance of Euroland firms or a Euroland share price index. Are shareholder returns also converging?

e. Track the correlation coefficients for equity returns among the 11 member countries. Are these also converging?

f. Do you expect the weighted-average cost of capital to increase or decrease for L'Oreal? Why?

WORLD WIDE WEB EXERCISES

W1. International Diversification via Mutual Funds

All major mutual fund companies now offer a variety of internationally diversified mutual funds. The degree of international composition across funds, however, differs significantly. Use the web sites listed below, and any others of interest, to:

a. Distinguish between international funds, global funds, worldwide funds, and overseas funds.

b. Determine how international funds have been performing, in U.S. dollar terms, relative to mutual funds offering purely domestic portfolios.

Fidelity	http://www.fidelity.com/funds/
T. Rowe Price	http://www.troweprice.com/
Merrill Lynch	http://www.ml.com/
Scudder	http://www.scudder.com/
Kemper	http://www.kemper.com/

W2. Center for Latin American Capital Markets Research

Although most of the Latin American markets have suffered significant falls in trading following the Mexican peso crisis of December 1994 and the Brazilian real crisis in January 1999, many of these markets may still be some of the most undervalued in the world. If you were given the task of investing US$ 1 million in a single equity market in Latin America, which one would you invest in? Use the World Wide Web to find recent market performance statistics to support your choice.

Center for Latin American Capital Markets Research
http://www.netrus.net/users/gmorles/

SUGGESTED READINGS

Domowitz, Ian, Jack Glen, and Ananth Madhavan, "Market Segmentation and Stock Prices: Evidence from an Emerging Market," *Journal of Finance*, Vol. 52, No. 3, June 1997, pp. 1059–1085.

Lee, Kwang Chul, and Chuck C.Y. Kwok, "Multinational Corporations vs. Domestic Corporations: International Environmental Factors and Determinants of Capital Structure," *Journal of International Business Studies*, Summer 1988, pp. 195–217.

Rajan, Raghuram, and Luigi Zingales, "Debt, Folklore, and Cross-Country Differences in Financial Structure," *Journal of Applied Corporate Finance*, Winter 1998, Vol. 10, No. 4, pp. 102–107.

Reeb, David M., Chuck C. Y. Kwok, and H. Young Baek, "Systematic Risk of the Multinational Corporation," *Journal of International Business Studies*, Second Quarter 1998, pp. 263–279.

Stulz, Rene M., "Does the Cost of Capital Differ Across Countries? An Agency Perspective," *European Financial Management*, Vol. 2, 1996, pp. 11–22.

Wald, John K., "How Firm Characteristics Affect Capital Structure: An International Comparison," *Journal of Financial Research*, Vol. 22, No. 2, Summer 1999, pp. 161–187.

NOTES

1. Beta may take a value of less than 1.0 if the firm's returns are less volatile than the market, 1.0 if the same as the market, or greater than 1.0 if more volatile—or risky—than the market.

2. CAPM analysis assumes that the required return estimated is an indicator of what is necessary to keep an investor's capital invested in the equity considered. If the equity's return does not reach the expected return, CAPM assumes that individual investors will liquidate their holdings.

3. We follow Stulz' (1995) preference here for describing the internationally diversified portfolio as the *global portfolio* rather than the *world portfolio*. The distinction is important. The *world portfolio* would be an index of all securities in the world. However, even with the increasing trend of deregulation and financial integration, there are still a number of securities markets that remain segmented/restricted in their access. Those securities actually available to an investor would then be defined as the *global portfolio*.

4. Source: Milken Institute, *Capital Access Index*, Fall 1998, at http://www.milken-inst.org.

5. Lee and Kwok (1988), Michel and Shakad (1986), Fatemi (1988), Prowse (1990), Burgman (1996), Doukas and Pantzalis (1998), Reeb, Kwok, and Baek (1998), and Chen, Cheng, He, and Kim (1997).

6. Reeb, Kwok, and Baek (1998).

7. Kwok and Reeb (1999).

8. Donaldson (1969) and (1984), and Jensen (1986).

9. See the following references in the bibliography in the back of this book: Stonehill and Stitzel (1969), Remmers, Stonehill, Wright, and Beckhuissen (1974), Toy, Stonehill, Remmer, Wright, and Beckhuissen (1974), Stonehill et al. (1975), Shapiro (1978), Errunza (1979), Aggarwal (1981), Stanley (1981), Collins and Sekely (1983), Sarathy and Chatterjee (1984), Wright and Suzuki (1985), Kester (1986), Sekely and Collins (1988), Lee and Kwok (1988), Hodder and Senbet (1990), Aggarwal (1990), Prowse (1990), Boris (1990), Frankel and Montgomery (1991), Burgman (1996), and Rajan and Zingales (1995) and (1998a).

CHAPTER 11

SOURCING EQUITY GLOBALLY

Chapter 10 analyzed why gaining access to global capital markets should lower a firm's marginal cost of capital and increase its availability by improving the market liquidity of its shares and by overcoming market segmentation. In order to implement such a lofty goal the firm must design a strategy that will ultimately attract international investors. This means identifying and choosing among alternative paths to access global markets. Usually this strategy requires some restructuring of the firm, improving the quality and level of its disclosure, and making its accounting and reporting standards more transparent to foreign potential investors. The Novo case in Chapter 10 provides a good illustration of the steps that need to be taken and the barriers that might be faced.

The main focus of this chapter is on firms resident in less liquid markets or in segmented markets. They are the ones that need to tap liquid and unsegmented markets in order to attain the global cost and availability of capital. These are firms that are typically resident in emerging markets and many of the smaller industrial country markets. Firms resident in the United States and United Kingdom already have full access to their own domestic liquid and unsegmented markets. Although they too source equity and debt abroad, such sourcing is unlikely to have as favorable an impact on their cost and availability of capital. In fact, it is often motivated only by the need to fund large foreign acquisitions rather than domestic or foreign operations.

This chapter starts with the design of a strategy to source both equity and debt capital globally. It then describes depositary receipts. These are the most important instruments that facilitate cross-border trading in securities.[1] The chapter continues with the specifics of crosslisting and selling equity issues abroad. (Selling of debt issues abroad is delayed until the next chapter.) It concludes with an analysis of alternative instruments to source equity abroad.

DESIGNING A STRATEGY TO SOURCE EQUITY AND DEBT GLOBALLY

Designing a capital sourcing strategy requires management to agree upon a long-run financial objective and then choose among the various alternative paths to get there. Exhibit 11.1 is a visual presentation of alternative paths toward the objective of attaining a global cost and availability of capital.

Normally, the choice of paths and implementation is aided by an early appointment of an investment bank as official advisor to the firm. Investment bankers are the persons in touch with potential foreign investors and knowledgeable about what these investors are currently requiring. They can also help navigate the various institutional requirements and barriers that must be surmounted. Their services include advising whether, when, and where a crosslisting should be initiated. They usually prepare the required stock prospectus if an equity issue is desired, help to price the issue, and maintain an aftermarket to prevent the share price from falling below its initial price.

)))) Alternative Paths

With reference to Exhibit 11.1, most firms raise their initial capital in their own domestic market. Next it is tempting to skip all the intermediate steps and drop to the bottom line, a Euro equity issue in global markets. This is the time when a good investment bank advisor will offer a "reality check." Most firms that have only raised capital in their domestic market are not well known enough to attract foreign investors. Remember from Chapter 10 that Novo was advised by its investment bankers to start with a convertible Eurobond issue and simultaneously crosslist its shares (and the bonds) in London. This recommendation was made despite the fact that Novo had an outstanding track record with respect to growth, profitability, and dominance of two worldwide market niches (insulin and industrial enzymes).

Exhibit 11.1 shows that most firms should start sourcing abroad with an international bond issue. It could be placed on a less prestigious foreign market. This could be followed by an international bond issue in a target market or in the Eurobond market. The next step might be to crosslist and issue equity in one of the less prestigious markets to attract international investor attention. The next step could be to crosslist shares on a highly liquid prestigious foreign stock exchange such as London (LSE), NYSE, or NASDAQ. The ultimate step would be to place a directed equity issue in a prestigious target market or a Euro equity issue in global equity markets.

)))) Depositary Receipts

Depositary receipts (depositary shares) are negotiable certificates issued by a bank to represent the underlying shares of stock, which are held in trust at a foreign custodian bank. *Global depositary receipts* (GDRs) refer to certificates traded outside the United States. *American depositary receipts* (ADRs) refer to certificates

Exhibit 11.1   *Alternative Paths to Internationalize the Cost and Availability of Capital*

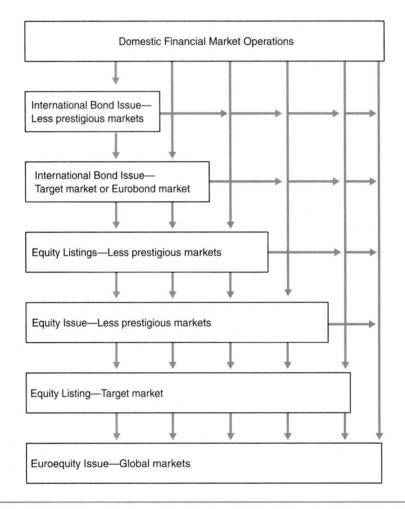

Source: Lars Oxelheim et al, *Corporate Strategies to Internationalize the Cost of Capital*, Copenhagen: Copenhagen Business School Press, 1998, p. 119.

traded in the United States and denominated in U.S. dollars. ADRs are sold, registered, and transferred in the United States in the same manner as any share of stock, with each ADR representing some multiple of the underlying foreign share. This multiple allows the ADRs to possess a price per share appropriate for the U.S. market (typically between $20 and $50 per share) even if the price of the foreign share is inappropriate when converted to U.S. dollars directly. Exhibit 11.2 illustrates the underlying issuance structure of an ADR.

Exhibit 11.2   *The Mechanics of American Depositary Receipts*

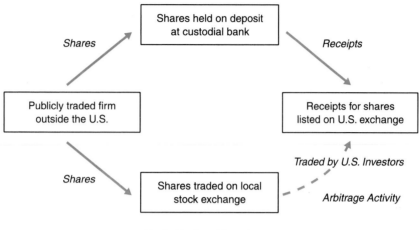

ADRs can be exchanged for the underlying foreign shares, or vice versa, so arbitrage keeps foreign and U.S. prices of any given share the same after adjustment for transfer costs. For example, investor demand in one market will cause a price rise there, which will cause an arbitrage rise in the other market even when investors there are not as bullish on the stock.

ADRs convey certain technical advantages to U.S. shareholders. Dividends paid by a foreign firm are passed to its custodial bank and then to the bank that issued the ADR. The issuing bank exchanges the foreign currency dividends for U.S. dollars and sends the dollar dividend to the ADR holders. ADRs are in registered form, rather than in bearer form. Transfer of ownership is facilitated because it is done in the United States in accordance with U.S. laws and procedures. In the event of death of a shareholder, the estate need not go through probate in a foreign court system. Normally, trading costs are lower than when buying or selling the underlying shares in their home market. Settlement is usually faster in the United States. Withholding taxes are simpler because they're handled by the depositary bank.

ADRs are either *sponsored* or *unsponsored*. Sponsored ADRs are created at the request of a foreign firm wanting its shares traded in the United States. The firm applies to the Securities and Exchange Commission (SEC) and a U.S. bank for registration and issuance of ADRs. The foreign firm pays all costs of creating such sponsored ADRs. If a foreign firm does not seek to have its shares traded in the United States but U.S. investors are interested, a U.S. securities firm may initiate creation of the ADRs. Such an ADR would be unsponsored, but the SEC still requires that all new ADR programs, even unsponsored ones, must be approved by the firm itself.

Exhibit 11.3 summarizes the characteristics of ADRs in the United States. It shows three levels of commitment, distinguished by the necessary accounting standards, SEC registration requirement, time to completion, and costs. Level I ("over the counter" or pink sheet) is the easiest to satisfy. It facilitates trading in foreign securities that have been acquired by U.S. investors, but the securities are not registered with the SEC. It is the least costly approach but might have a minimal impact on liquidity.

Level II applies to firms that want to list existing shares on the NYSE, ASE, or NASDAQ markets. They must meet the full registration requirements of the SEC. This means reconciling their financial accounts with those used under U.S. GAAP, and that raises the cost considerably. Level III applies to the sale of a new equity issued in the United States. It too requires full registration with the SEC and an elaborate stock prospectus. This is the most expensive alternative but is the most likely to improve the stock's liquidity and ability to escape from home market segmentation. So-called 144a programs will be described later in this chapter.

Exhibit 11.3	*Characteristics of Depositary Receipt Programs Traded in the United States*			
	Level I	**Level II**	**Level III**	**144A**
Primary exchange	OTC pink sheets	NYSE, AMEX or NASDAQ	NYSE, AMEX or NASDAQ	PORTAL
Accounting standards	Home country	U.S. GAAP	U.S. GAAP	Home country
SEC registration	Exempt	Full registration	Full registration	Exempt
Share issuance	Existing shares only (public offering)	Existing shares only (public offering)	New equity capital raised (public offering)	New equity capital raised (private offering)
Time to completion	10 weeks	10 weeks	14 weeks	16 days
Costs	≤ $25,000	$200,000–700,000	$500,000–2,000,000	$250,000-500,000

Foreign securities traded in the U.S. are required to perform periodic reporting under the 1934 Exchange Act, provided that the company's equity securities are held of record by 500 or more persons, of which 300 or more are U.S. residents. This requires quarterly reporting, filing the form 20-F in U.S. Generally Accepted Accounting Principles. Level I and 144A DRs are eligible for a 12g3-2(b) exemption from this requirement, and only have to supply to the SEC copies of information that the company makes public in its home country. Privately placed Depositary Receipts are also eligible for the 12g3-2(b) exemption. They trade between Qualified Institutional Buyers under SEC Rule 144A, which provides a safe harbor exemption from the registration requirements of the Securities Act of 1933. Source: Global Offerings of Depositary Receipts, A Transaction Guide (The Bank of New York, 1995). Reprinted in Miller (1999).

WHERE SHOULD A FIRM CROSSLIST AND RAISE EQUITY ON A FOREIGN MARKET?

According to the alternative paths depicted in Exhibit 11.1, a firm needs to choose one or more stock markets on which to crosslist its shares and sell new equity. Just where to go depends mainly on the firm's specific motives and the willingness of the host stock market to accept the firm. By crosslisting and selling its shares on a foreign stock exchange, a firm typically tries to accomplish one or more of the following objectives:

1. Improve the liquidity of its existing shares and support a liquid secondary market for new equity issues in foreign markets.

2. Increase its share price by overcoming mispricing in a segmented and illiquid home capital market.

3. Increase the firm's visibility and political acceptance to its customers, suppliers, creditors, and host governments.

4. Establish a secondary market for shares used to acquire other firms in the host market.

5. Create a secondary market for shares that can be used to compensate local management and employees in foreign affiliates.[2]

))) Improving Liquidity

Quite often foreign investors have acquired a firm's shares through normal brokerage channels, even though the shares are not listed in the investor's home market or are not traded in the investor's preferred currency. Crosslisting is a way to encourage such investors to continue to hold and trade these shares, thus marginally improving secondary market liquidity. This listing is usually done through ADRs.

Firms domiciled in countries with small illiquid capital markets often outgrow these markets and are forced to raise new equity abroad. Listing on a stock exchange in the market in which funds are to be raised is typically required by the underwriters to ensure post-issue liquidity in the shares.

The introductory section of this chapter suggested that firms start by crosslisting in a less prestigious market, followed by listing an equity issue in that market (see Exhibit 11.1). In order to maximize liquidity, however, the ideal is to crosslist and issue equity in a prestigious market and eventually to be able to offer a global equity issue.

Exhibit 11.4 describes selected stock exchange size characteristics (in 1998). The stock exchanges shown are divided into three categories to help identify which are the illiquid markets and which are the liquid prestigious markets. Exhibit 11.5 compares global equity markets with respect to P/E ratios, yields, and domestic inflation rates.

)))) Size of the Market

In order to maximize liquidity, it is desirable to crosslist and/or sell equity in the "Most Liquid" category of Exhibit 11.4. The columns entitled "Value of Share Trading" and "Gross New Capital Raised by Domestic Companies" are indicators of the overall ability of the market to provide liquidity and availability of capital.

London (LSE), NYSE, and NASDAQ are clearly the most liquid and prestigious markets. LSE has the highest value for foreign shares traded, followed by NYSE and NASDAQ. However, both NYSE and NASDAQ have much higher trading liquidity for domestic shares and for combined domestic and foreign shares.

Although the number of listed foreign firms on the NYSE is relatively small, their individual trading volume is typically quite large relative to their home markets. For example, Telefonos de Mexico was the most actively traded stock on the NYSE in 1994 and 1995.

The value of NASDAQ's trading volume is biased toward a few large firms. Market concentration of the top 5 percent of the largest companies ranked by trading value was almost 79 percent in 1998. This compares to 51 percent for the NYSE and 60 percent for LSE. Although NASDAQ used to attract smaller but growing firms, these have now become giants, especially in the high-tech fields. Listings include Microsoft, Intel, Apple Computer, Dell Computer, and Amazon.

Germany and Paris have fairly liquid markets for domestic shares but a much lower level of liquidity for trading foreign shares. On the other hand, Germany and Paris are quite appropriate target markets for firms resident in the EU, especially those that have adopted the euro. They are also used as supplementary crosslisting locations for firms that are already crosslisted on LSE, NYSE, or NASDAQ. However, as on NASDAQ, 5 percent of the listed firms ranked by trading volume in Germany account for almost 86 percent of the total trading value.

Tokyo has fallen on hard times. It is now in only fourth place for total market capitalization and sixth place for trading volume and is nearly unusable as a location for foreign firms to gain liquidity. Tokyo had only 52 foreign firms crosslisted in 1998, compared to 67 in 1996. Trading in foreign shares is at a lower level than in four of the markets shown in the "Semi-Liquid" category.

)))) Semi-Liquid and Least Liquid Markets

In the "Semi-Liquid" and "Least Liquid" categories of Exhibit 11.4, only Stockholm can provide reasonable liquidity for foreign firms, but it is not the major source for raising new equity capital, even by domestic firms. The "Least Liquid" markets, as expected, offer no value to foreign firms and very little liquidity to their own domestic firms. This is, of course, why some firms resident in these illiquid markets are dependent on raising equity in more liquid foreign markets. Those that can meet the stringent qualifications of the "Most Liquid" markets

Exhibit 11.4	*Selected Stock Exchange Size Characteristics Categorized by Market Liquidity, 1998*

Exchanges	Number of Companies		Market Capitalization (millions of USD)		Value of Share Trading (millions of USD)		Gross New Capital Raised by Domestic Companies (millions of USD)
	Domestic	Foreign	Domestic	Foreign	Domestic	Foreign	
Most Liquid							
London	1,957	466	2,372,738	4,665,753	1,043,659	1,842,569	17,431
NYSE	2,278	391	10,271,900	479,633	6,722,420	561,362	156,346
Nasdaq	4,627	441	2,527,970	127,732	5,294,889	215,849	33,409
Deutsche Börse (Ger)	741	2,784	1,093,962	NA	1,393,297	98,499	23,337
Paris	914	183	991,484	417,969	2,013,003	40,297	29,832
Switzerland	432	193	689,199	NA	653,478	33,478	7,540
Spain	1,122	12	402,163	NA	1,056,000	1,198	11,318
Tokyo	1,838	52	2,495,757	NA	750,024	675	11,814
Semi-Liquid							
Taiwan	437	0	260,498	–	892,154	1,113	10,462
Italy	239	4	569,732	69,351	485,935	572	11,456
Amsterdam	212	144	603,182	NA	384,965	1,934	39,643
Toronto	1,384	49	543,394	189	331,537	311	10,381
Brussels	146	122	245,657	2,475,869	228,265	NA	2,761
Stockholm	258	18	278,708	19,034	203,413	26,548	895
Hong Kong	665	15	343,567	6,845	205,972	179	4,766
Australia	1,162	60	328,929	210,255	159,213	1,788	18,111
Korea	748	0	114,593	–	145,061	–	9,901
Brazil	1,116	2	160,886	–	139,584	–	18,412
Least Liquid							
Singapore	312	37	96,473	64,509	58,509	–	NA
Kuala Lumpur	728	3	95,561	589	26,525	303	428
Mexico	191	4	91,746	20,944	30,817	–	4,292
Thailand	418	0	34,118	–	30,879	–	8,126
Jakarta	287	0	22,078	NA	10,637	–	1,028
Philippines	221	0	34,911	NA	10,198	–	462
Buenos Aires	131	0	45,333	–	26,052	–	930
Santiago	287	0	51,866	–	4,412	–	1,006

NA: Not Available.

1. Converted to U.S. dollars at month end exchange rate except Gross Amount of New Capital Raised, which is at year-end rate.

2. Investment funds are included in the value of share trading but not in any other category.

3. Whenever a country is listed instead of a city it signals that several stock exchanges have been combined. For example, Spain combines both the Barcelona and Madrid stock exchanges.

Source: Federation Internationale des Bourses de Valeur (FIBV) Statistics, http://www.fibv.org.

Exhibit 11.5	*Comparison of Global Equity Markets: P/E Ratios, Yields, and Domestic Inflation Rates*

Time zone	Exchange	Price-Earning Ratio		Gross Dividend Yield		Inflation Rate		Total Return	
		1998	1997	1998 %	1997 %	1998 %	1997 %	1998 %	1997 %
North	Amex	32.5	21.7	1.3	1.2	1.6	1.7	1.9	20.8
America	Chicago	NA	NA	NA	NA	1.6	1.7	NA	NA
	Mexico	16.2	17.9	2.9	1.4R	18.6	15.7	−21.4	57.0
	Montreal	24.1	19.6	2.9	2.1	0.9	1.6	0.8	17.4
	Nasdaq	37.2	26.4	NA	NA	1.6	1.7	NA	NA
	NYSE	27.2	23.9	NA	1.7	1.6	1.7	NA	32.0
	Toronto	28.5	22.9	1.7	1.6	0.9	1.6	−1.5	14.6
	Vancouver	NA	NA	NA	NA	0.9	1.6	NA	NA
South	Buenos Aires	13.0	16.0	3.6	2.9	0.7	0.3	−20.9	27.6
America	Lima	NA	NA	4.3	3.8	6.0	6.5	−25.5	NA
	Rio de Janeiro	10.2	11.1	9.4	4.0	1.8	7.7	−38.2	43.2
	Santiago	12.7	13.6	5.4	3.8	4.7	6.0	−19.6	1.6
	Sao Paulo	15.2	12.5 R	NA	NA	1.8	7.7	−33.5	44.8
Europe, Africa,	Amsterdam	22.4	20.2 R	2.0	2.3	2.0	2.3	20.7	43.8
Middle East	Athens	27.2	12.4 R	1.6	2.9	3.9	4.8	86.6	61.4
	Barcelona	19.6	17.8	2.4	3.1	1.4	2.0	35.0	43.1
	Bilbao	NA	NA	NA	2.7	1.4	2.0	NA	48.3
	Brussels	23.3	17.3	1.9	3.1	0.6	1.6	43.5	36.2
	Copenhagen	NA	NA	NA	NA	1.7	2.1	NA	NA
	Germany	30.6	27.8	1.3	1.7	0.8	1.8	16.3	44.9
	Helsinki	22.6	12.4 R	1.7	2.7 R	0.9	1.8	70.2	35.0
	Irish	21.3	19.1	1.6	2.0	2.9	1.5	24.8	50.7
	Istanbul	8.8	24.4	0.4	1.6	65.9	99.1	−24.3	255.2
	Italy	25.0	24.7	1.4	1.7	1.5	1.5	42.4	59.9
	Johannesburg	19.4	16.8	3.3	2.7	9.0	6.1	−9.1	−4.1
	Lisbon	22.2	22.5 R E	2.6	3.0	2.8	2.2	26.2	32.6
	Ljubljana	17.5	14.6	2.8	3.3	2.7	9.4	24.2	22.0

would normally opt for that alternative. Others must settle for the "Semi-Liquid" markets, that is, for the less prestigious markets depicted earlier in Exhibit 11.1.

))) Availability of Capital and Market Depth

The availability of capital is another indicator of the depth of the liquidity of the market. The NYSE is by far the most important location in the column labeled "Gross New Capital Raised by Domestic Companies" in Exhibit 11.4. NASDAQ, Paris, Germany, and, surprisingly, Amsterdam are also good locations to sell new equity.

Overall market liquidity is shown in Exhibit 11.4, but additional characteristics contribute to the liquidity of individual stocks. These include market-making

Exhibit 11.5

Comparison of Global Equity Markets: P/E Ratios, Yields, and Domestic Inflation Rates (continued)

Time zone	Exchange	Price-Earning Ratio 1998	1997	Gross Dividend Yield 1998 %	1997 %	Inflation Rate 1998 %	1997 %	Total Return 1998 %	1997 %
	London	23.3	19.2	2.8	3.2	1.8	3.6	17.3	27.9
	Luxembourg	NA	NA	2.3	2.2	0.4	2.1	10.6	26.9
	Madrid	26.1	22.2 R	1.5	2.3 R	1.4	2.0	38.7	44.5
	Oslo	16.8	16.7	2.1	2.5 R	2.4	2.3	−26.7	31.5
	Paris	NA	NA	2.1	2.2	0.3	1.0	30.6	26.7
	Stockholm	21.0	22.0	2.2	2.1	−1.1	1.6	12.4	25.9
	Switzerland E	19.7	28.7 R E	1.5	1.1	−0.2	0.4	15.4	55.0
	Tehran	3.0	4.9	NA	NA E	17.5	17.3 R	NA	NA
	Tel–Aviv	13.4	13.6	NA	2.4	8.6	7.0	NA	37.6
	Vienna	12.7	13.7 R	2.1	1.9	0.9	1.3	−2.5	15.4
	Warsaw	13.6	16.1 R	0.9	1.3 R	8.6	13.2	−12.0	2.3
Asia, Pacific	Australian	20.8	19.5	3.5	3.9	1.6	−0.2	11.0	20.2
	Colombo	9.0	12.5	4.5	3.2 E	9.9	9.6	−10.4	NA
	Hong Kong	10.7	12.1	3.7	3.5	2.8	4.8	− 14.6	−15.7
	Jakarta	4.1	10.6 R	NA	NA	77.6	11.1	NA	NA
	Korea	27.8	NA	0.8	2.8	7.5	4.5	50.3	−39.4
	Kuala Lumpur	−130.6	10.3	2.7	3.1	5.3	6.3	1.3	−48.9
	New Zealand	37.6	15.3	4.0	4.7	0.4	0.8	−3.3	18.3
	Osaka	122.1	41.6	1.1	1.2	0.6	2.3	−6.5	−14.7
	Philippine	15.8	9.5 R	0.5	1.3	10.4	6.1	5.8	−39.7
	Singapore	19.0	15.2	1.8	NA	NA	2.0	NA	NA
	Taiwan	NA	27.0	NA	2.9	NA	2.8	−21.6	21.0
	Thailand	10.4	6.6	1.3	6.0	8.1	5.6	−3.2	−49.2
	Tokyo	103.1	37.6	1.2	1.0	0.6	2.3	−6.3	−19.1

Total Return = Stock index performance + Gross dividend yield. For SE with stock return indexes, Total Return = Stock index performance.
NA: Not Available E: Estimate R: Revised.
Source: Federation Internationale des Bourses de Valeur (FIBV)

activities, transaction costs, fairness, and crisis management. At one end of the spectrum is the NYSE, where assigned *specialists* are responsible for ensuring a liquid, low-cost, fair, and orderly market. At the other end of the spectrum is the LSE where *market makers*, formerly called *jobbers*, voluntarily make an active market in some, but not all, listed shares.

))) The New York Stock Exchange

About one-third of the members who are allowed to trade on the floor of the New York Stock Exchange (NYSE) are specialists. They are organized into specialist groups, each of which is assigned a certain number of the listed shares exclusively.

Market-Making Activities. It is the specialists' affirmative obligation to ensure that their assigned shares enjoy a liquid, low-cost, fair, and orderly market at all times, even when a crisis arises. To ensure a liquid market, the specialists must risk their own capital to buy shares when the public wants to sell and sell shares when the public wants to buy.

Transaction Costs. To guarantee low transaction costs, the NYSE regulates the spread between one transaction and the next. The specialists do not act as brokers for the public in their assigned shares, but they trade with other floor members who represent the public. Negotiated commissions are the lowest in the world.

Fairness. Fairness is guaranteed in several ways. Orders from the public are executed chronologically. About 75 percent of the orders come in through a computerized system but are executed by the responsible specialist. Large orders (the other 25 percent) come to the specialist manually through the other floor brokers. These orders are executed during the day by the specialist dealing with other floor brokers, professional floor traders, and the specialist's own capital account. Fairness is also enhanced by a 200-person staff whose function is surveillance. A very sophisticated computer-based surveillance system searches continually for evidence of insider trading.

Limit Orders. Although the specialist groups have a quasi-monopoly on their assigned stocks, they experience competition from professional floor traders, customer day traders, and limit orders. A *limit order* is an order to buy or sell a share at a specified price. For example, suppose a public investor wants to buy 1000 shares of IBM at a price no higher than $50 per share at a time when IBM is selling at $55 per share. If and when IBM ever falls to $50 per share, that investor's order will be executed by the specialist in chronological sequence and, of course, ahead of any purchase by the specialist at that price.

Crisis Management. In deciding where to list to improve share liquidity, a firm should consider not only how a market functions under normal conditions but also whether liquidity remains even during a stock market crisis. The world experienced major stock market crises in 1987 and 1989. Most analysts believe the specialist-driven NYSE system did a better job of crisis management during those episodes than did competing dealer-driven markets.

))) The London Stock Exchange

The London Stock Exchange (LSE) experienced its "Big Bang" in October 1986, an event that moved trading from the floor of the exchange upstairs to computer screens in a dealer-driven market. The former distinction between brokers and jobbers (market makers) was abolished, along with fixed commissions. Entry restrictions were removed, opening securities firms up to foreign ownership and greatly increased competition.

Market-Making Activities. Competing dealer/brokers trade with the help of a screen quotation system modeled after the NASDAQ system in the United States. Foreign shares are grouped together on the International Stock Exchange (ISE) but quoted on SEAQ International (Stock Exchange Automated Quotation System). Domestic British firms are quoted on SEAQ Domestic.

In contrast to the NYSE, there are no assigned specialists, but market makers voluntarily make a liquid market in the shares of their choice. Since market makers compete for many of the active shares, nobody has an exclusive affirmative obligation to ensure a liquid, low-cost, fair, or orderly market. It is expected that these attributes will evolve from the level of competition.

Limit Orders. One competitive element that is missing is official limit orders. Members of the public can give limit orders to their brokers, but there is no guarantee these will actually be executed chronologically or even at the exact limit-order price.

A Comparison of the LSE and the NYSE. If we compare the LSE to the NYSE, liquidity in the most actively traded shares is similar, but the NYSE specialists system results in a more liquid market for the least popular shares. Transaction costs as measured by spreads are lower on the NYSE. The LSE spreads are roughly comparable to the spreads on NASDAQ. On the other hand, the cost of listing and disclosure requirements are less onerous on the LSE than on the NYSE. In terms of fairness, the NYSE is superior because orders are executed chronologically, whereas on the LSE a buyer or seller has to shop from dealer to dealer. Crisis management in practice has been more effective on the NYSE than on any other exchanges, including LSE. Despite the more favorable liquidity attributes of the NYSE, more foreign firms list on the LSE, and the trading volume in those shares is higher than foreign-listed shares on the NYSE. The ease and cost of listing, lower required disclosure levels, and less-frequent reporting requirements have apparently tilted the scale toward the LSE for firms that might have trouble overcoming these barriers. However, for those firms that are willing to pay the price, a listing on the NYSE should improve the liquidity of their shares more than would a similar listing elsewhere.

FAVORABLE EFFECT ON SHARE PRICE?

Does merely crosslisting on a foreign stock exchange have a favorable impact on share prices? It depends on the degree to which markets are segmented.

If a firm's home capital market is segmented, the firm could theoretically benefit by crosslisting in a foreign market if that market values the firm or its industry more than does the home market. This was certainly the situation experienced by Novo when it listed on the NYSE in 1981 (see Chapter 10). However, most capital markets are becoming more integrated with global markets. Even emerging markets are less segmented than they were just a few years ago.

Even as early as the 1969–1982 period, when markets were more segmented than today, a research study found a positive share price effect for foreign firms that listed on the NYSE, ASE, or NASDAQ.[3] A more recent study found that share prices increased for foreign firms that crosslisted their shares in ADR form on the NYSE and ASE during the period 1982–1992.[4] The authors concluded that crosslisting in the United States enhanced share value by reducing the overall effect of segmentation among different national securities markets. The most recent and most comprehensive study consisted of 181 firms from 35 countries that instituted their first ADR program in the United States over the period 1985–1995.[5] The author measured the stock price impact of the announcement of a crosslisting in the United States. The study found significant positive abnormal returns around the announcement date. These returns were retained in the immediate following period. As expected, the study showed that the abnormal returns were greater for firms resident in emerging markets, with a low level of legal barriers to capital flows, than the abnormal returns of firms resident in developed markets. Firms resident in emerging markets with heavy restrictions on capital flows received some abnormal returns, but not as high as firms resident in the other markets. This difference was due to the limited perceived liquidity of firms resident in markets with too many restrictions on capital flows.

It is well known that a new equity issue made simultaneously with a crosslisting has a more favorable impact on stock price than does crosslisting alone. This is so because the new issue creates an instantly enlarged shareholder base. Marketing efforts by the underwriters prior to the issue engender higher levels of visibility. Post-issue efforts by the underwriters to support at least the initial offering price also reduce investor risk.

The study of 185 firms crosslisting in the United States contained 30 firms that initiated new equity issues (Level III ADRs). The author found a statistically significant abnormal return for these firms, even higher than for the firms that just crosslisted (Levels 1 and II).[6] Furthermore, the highest abnormal return was for Chilean firms (8.23 percent). The Chilean market has one of the highest levels of restrictions affecting foreign investors.

)))) Other Objectives for Crosslisting and New Equity Issues

Increasing Visibility and Political Acceptance. MNEs list in markets where they have substantial physical operations. Commercial objectives are to enhance their corporate image, advertise trademarks and products, get better local press coverage, and become more familiar with the local financial community in order to raise working capital locally.

Political objectives might include the need to meet local ownership requirements for a multinational firm's foreign joint venture. Local ownership of the parent firm's shares might provide a forum for publicizing the firm's activities and how they support the host country. This objective is the most important one for Japanese firms. The Japanese domestic market has both low cost capital and high availability. Therefore, Japanese firms are not trying to increase the stock price, the liquidity of their shares, or the availability of capital.

Potential for Share Swaps with Acquisitions. Firms that follow a strategy of growth by acquisition are always looking for creative ways to fund these acquisitions rather than just by paying cash. Offering their shares as partial payment is considerably more attractive if those shares have a liquid secondary market. In that case, the target's shareholders have an easy way to convert their acquired shares to cash if they do not prefer a share swap. However, a share swap is often attractive as a tax-free exchange.

Compensating Management and Employees. If a MNE wishes to use stock options and share purchase compensation plans for local management and employees, local listing would enhance the perceived value of such plans. It should reduce transaction and foreign exchange costs for the local beneficiaries.

BARRIERS TO LISTING AND SELLING EQUITY ABROAD

Although a firm may decide to crosslist and/or sell equity abroad, certain barriers exist. The most serious barrier is the future commitment to providing full disclosure of operating results and balance sheets, as well as to a continuous program of investor relations.

))) The Commitment to Disclosure and Investor Relations

A decision to crosslist must be balanced against the implied increased commitment to full disclosure and to a continuing investor relations program. For firms resident in the Anglo-American markets, listing abroad might not appear to be much of a barrier. For example, the SEC's disclosure rules for listing in the United States are so stringent and costly that any other market's rules are mere child's play. Reversing the logic, however, non-U.S. firms must really think twice before crosslisting in the United States. Not only are the disclosure requirements breathtaking, but also a continuous demand for timely quarterly information is required by U.S. investors. As a result, the foreign firm must provide a costly continuous investor relations program for its U.S. shareholders, including frequent "road shows" and the time-consuming personal involvement of top management.

))) Disclosure Is a Double-Edged Sword

The U.S. school of thought is that the worldwide trend toward requiring fuller and more standardized financial disclosure of operating results and balance sheet positions may have the desirable effect of lowering the cost of equity capital.

> Increased firm disclosure tends to improve the subjective probability distributions of a security's expected return streams in the mind of an individual investor by reducing the uncertainty associated with the return stream. For firms which generally outperform the industry average, it is also argued that improved financial disclosure will

tend to increase the relative weighting which an investor will place on favorable firm statistics relative to the firm. Both of the foregoing effects will entice an individual to pay a larger amount for a given security than otherwise, thus lowering a firm's cost of capital.[7]

The other school of thought is that the U.S. level of required disclosure is an onerous, costly burden. It chases away many potential listers, thereby narrowing the choice of securities that are available to U.S. investors at reasonable transaction costs. At year-end 1998, only 391 foreign firms were listed on the NYSE, whereas 466 foreign firms were listed on the LSE, and 2,784 foreign firms were listed on the German stock exchanges.[8]

A study of 203 internationally traded shares concluded that there is a statistically significant relationship between the level of financial disclosure required and the market on which the firms chose to list.[9] The higher the level of disclosure required, the less likely that a firm would list in that market. However, for those firms that do list despite the disclosure and cost barriers, the payoff could be needed access to additional equity funding of a large factory or an acquisition in the United States. Daimler-Benz took the painful step of crosslisting on the NYSE prior to raising equity in the United States to fund a new auto plant and, as it turned out later, to merge with Chrysler Corporation.

ILLUSTRATIVE CASE

Daimler-Benz (A)

New York—Foreign companies are falling in love with American finance. The latest illustration of the widespread appeal of U.S. capital markets is Daimler-Benz AG's decision to list its shares on the New York Stock Exchange, beginning today. To qualify for listing, the diversified German auto maker had to undertake a costly, excruciating revision of its accounting practices that $2\frac{1}{2}$ weeks ago caused a $592 million first-half loss, the company's first since World War II.

American investment bankers who stand to profit by arranging financing for foreign companies are understandably gleeful. That Daimler was willing to subject itself to America's rigorous accounting rules to get on the Big Board makes a fundamental shift in the way U.S. financial markets are viewed abroad, they say.

With all the foreign interest in listing stock on U.S. markets, why the hoopla about Daimler's decision? As with other German and Swiss giants, Daimler's long history of steady profits can be attributed partly to its ability to massage its financial statements through off-the-books "hidden reserves." Whenever product demand slackens and operating losses develop, these companies tap the reserves, built up from earlier earnings, to offset the loss and show a modest profit.

But "hidden reserves" are anathema to the SEC, which has steadfastly maintained that the only way Daimler or any other German or Swiss company could get a Big Board listing was to disclose the reserves and their effects on profits. For three acrimonious years, that issue had stalemated negotiations between the SEC and several big German companies. Finally, last March, Daimler broke, pushed by its need for capital.

Arthur Levitt Jr. [SEC Chairman] says he is concerned about the enormous costs that foreign companies face when translating their financial data to the U.S. format. "I regard foreign listings as one of my top two priorities," says Mr. Levitt, who also hopes to increase public confidence in the debt markets.

If Mr. Levitt doesn't make it easier for foreign companies to enter the U.S. markets, they will go elsewhere, some observers say. "There are some 200 global companies with multibillion-dollar sales, which would easily qualify for listing on the New York Stock Exchange—and that is where they belong," says William Freund, a former chief economist at the Big Board. "But unless they have a financial reason like Daimler-Benz, I don't think they will. And if they don't, the New York Stock Exchange will be consigned to a secondary role among world markets."

Adapted from Anita Raghavan and Michael R. Sesit,"Financing Boom: Foreign Firms Raise More and More Money in the U.S. Markets," 10/5/93, A1, A9, Reprinted by permission of *The Wall Street Journal*, © 1993, Dow Jones & Co., Inc. All rights reserved worldwide.

ALTERNATIVE INSTRUMENTS TO SOURCE EQUITY IN INTERNATIONAL MARKETS

Alternative instruments to source equity in international markets include the following:

- Sale of a *directed public share issue* to investors in a target market
- Sale of a *Euroequity public issue* to investors in more than one market, including both foreign and domestic markets
- *Private placements* under SEC Rule 144a
- Sale of shares to *private equity* funds
- Sale of shares to a foreign firm as part of a *strategic alliance*

))) Directed Public Share Issues

A *directed public share issue* is defined as one which is targeted at investors in a single country and underwritten in whole or in part by investment institutions from that country. The issue might or might not be denominated in the currency of the target market. The shares might or might not be crosslisted on a stock exchange in the target market.

Improving liquidity. The $61 million U.S. share issue by Novo in 1981 (Chapter 10) was a good example of a successful directed share issue that both improved the liquidity of Novo's shares and lowered its cost of capital. Novo repeated this success in 1983 with a $100 million share issue at $53 per share (ADR), compared to $36 per share two years earlier.

Funding Acquisitions or Capital Investments. A directed share issue might be motivated by a need to fund acquisitions or major capital investments in a target foreign market. This is an especially important source of equity for firms resident in smaller capital markets that have outgrown that market. A foreign share issue, plus crosslisting, can provide it with improved liquidity for its shares and the means to use those shares to pay for acquisitions.

Nycomed, a small but well respected Norwegian pharmaceutical firm, was an example of this type of motivation of a directed share issue combined with crosslisting. Nycomed's commercial strategy for growth is to leverage its sophisticated knowledge of certain market niches and technologies within the pharmaceutical field by acquiring other promising firms that possess relevant technologies, personnel, or market niches. Europe and the United States have provided fertile hunting grounds. The acquisitions were paid for partly with cash and partly with shares. Norway is too small a home capital market to fund these acquisitions for cash or to provide enough liquidity to minimize Nycomed's marginal cost of capital.

Nycomed responded to the challenge by selling two successful directed share issues abroad. In June 1989 it crosslisted on the LSE (quoted on SEAQ International) and raised the equivalent of about $100 million in equity from foreign investors there. Then in June 1992 it crosslisted on the NYSE and raised about $75 million with a share issue directed at U.S. investors.

))) Euroequity Public Issue

The gradual integration of the world's capital markets and increased international portfolio investment have spawned the emergence of a very viable Euroequity market. A firm can issue equity that is underwritten and distributed in multiple foreign equity markets, sometimes simultaneously with distribution in the domestic market. The same financial institutions that had previously created an infrastructure for the Euronote and Eurobond markets were responsible for the Euroequity market.[10] The term Euro does not imply that the issuers or investors are located in Europe. Euroequity is a generic term for international equity issues originating and sold anywhere in the world.

The Euroequity market has been able to absorb single equity issues ranging in size from less than $10 million to over $13 billion. It has also accepted B shares (low vote), preference shares, equity warrants, and hybrid instruments.

))) Euroequity and Privatizations

The largest and most spectacular recent issues have been in conjunction with a wave of privatizations of government-owned enterprises. The Thatcher government in the United Kingdom created the model when it privatized British Telecom in December 1984. That issue was so large that it was necessary and desirable to sell *tranches* to foreign investors in addition to the sale to domestic investors. A *tranche* is an allocation of shares, typically to underwriters that are expected to sell to investors in their designated geographic markets. The objective is both to raise the funds and to ensure post-issue worldwide liquidity. Unfortunately, in the case of British Telecom the issue, in retrospect, was underpriced. Most of the foreign shares, especially those placed in the United States, flowed back to London, leaving a nice profit behind for the U.S. underwriters and investors. Nevertheless, other large British privatization issues followed British Telecom, most notably British Steel in 1988.

Euroequity privatization issues have been particularly popular with international portfolio investors because most of the firms are very large, with excellent credit ratings and profitable quasi-government monopolies at the time of privatization. The British privatization model has been so successful that numerous others have followed. One of the largest Euroequity issues was by Deutsche Telekom A.G. It was privatized by an initial public offering of $13.3 billion in November 1996.

Even government-owned firms in emerging capital markets have implemented privatization with the help of foreign tranches.

- Telefonos de Mexico, the giant Mexican telephone company, completed a $2 billion Euroequity issue in 1991. It acquired U.S.-based Southwestern Bell as a 10% shareholder, numerous other foreign institutional and individual investors, and a very liquid listing on the NYSE.

- One of the largest Euroequity offerings by a firm resident in a "Least Liquid" market (see Exhibit 11.4) was the 1993 sale of shares for $3.04 billion by YPF Sociedad Anónima, Argentina's state-owned oil company. About 75% of its shares were placed in tranches outside Argentina, with 46% in the United States alone. Its underwriting syndicate represented a virtual who's who of the world's leading investment banks.

It appears that many of the privatized firms have performed well after being privatized. A recent study of privatization concluded that privatized firms showed strong performance improvements without reducing employment security. The firms in the study had been fully or partially privatized via public equity issues during the period 1961–1990. After privatization, the firms increased real sales, raised capital investment levels, improved efficiency, and expanded their employment. With respect to financial performance, their profitability improved, debt levels were lowered, and dividend payments increased.[11]

))) Private Placement under SEC Rule 144A

One type of directed issue that has a long history as a source of both equity and debt is the private placement market. A *private placement* is the sale of a security to a small set of qualified institutional buyers. Traditionally, the investors are insurance companies and investment companies. Since the securities are not registered for sale to the public, investors have typically followed a "buy and hold" policy. In the case of debt, terms are often custom-designed on a negotiated basis. On the other hand, equities are usually the same as the publicly traded versions except that they are unregistered. Private placement markets now exist in most countries.

In April 1990, the SEC approved Rule 144A. It permits *qualified institutional buyers* (QIBs) to trade privately placed securities without the previous holding period restrictions and without SEC registration.[12] Simultaneously, the SEC modified its Regulation S to permit foreign issuers to tap the U.S. private placement market through an SEC Rule 144A issue, also without SEC registration. A screen-based automated trading system called PORTAL was established by the National Association of Securities Dealers (NASD) to support the distribution of primary issues and to create a liquid secondary market for these unregistered private placements.

Since SEC registration has been identified as the main barrier to foreign firms wishing to raise funds in the United States, SEC Rule 144A placements are proving attractive to foreign issuers of both equity and debt securities. Atlas Copco, the Swedish multinational engineering firm, was the first foreign firm to take advantage of SEC Rule 144A. It raised $49 million in the United States through an ADR equity placement as part of its larger $214 million Euroequity issue in 1990. Since then, several billion dollars a year have been raised by foreign issuers with private equity placements in the United States. However, it does not appear that such placements have a favorable effect on either liquidity or stock price.[13]

))) Private Equity Funds

Many mature family-owned firms resident in emerging markets are unlikely to qualify for a global cost and availability of capital even if they follow the strategy suggested in this chapter. Although they might be consistently profitable and growing, they are still too small, too invisible to foreign investors, lacking in managerial depth, and unable to fund the upfront costs of an internationalization strategy. For these firms private equity funds may be a solution.

Private equity funds are usually limited partnerships of institutional and wealthy individual investors that raise their capital in the most liquid capital markets, especially the United States. They then invest the private equity fund in mature, family-owned firms located in emerging markets. The investment objective is to help these firms to restructure and modernize in order to face increasing competition and the growth of new technologies. Sometimes they fund family-owned firms that need to be connected with foreign MNEs, joint venture partners, or strategic alliances. They also can fund privatized government-owned firms.

Private equity funds differ from traditional venture capital funds. The latter usually operate mainly in highly developed countries. They typically invest in high-technology start-ups with the goal of exiting the investment with an *initial public offering* (IPO) placed in those same highly liquid markets. Very little venture capital is available in emerging markets, partly because it would be difficult to exit with an IPO in an illiquid market. The same exiting problem faces the private equity funds, but they appear to have a longer time horizon, to invest in already mature and profitable companies, and are content with growing them through better management and mergers with other firms.

The Exxel Group is an example of a successful private equity fund. Its founder and CEO, Juan Navarro, is the so-called "buyout king of Argentina," with plans to expand into the rest of South America. It was reported that as of 1998 the Exxel Group controlled 38 companies with combined annual sales of $3 billion and profits of $500 million.[14]

)))) Strategic Alliances

Strategic alliances are normally formed by firms that expect to gain synergies from one or more of the following joint efforts. They might share the cost of developing technology or pursue complementary marketing activities. They might gain economies of scale or scope or a variety of other commercial advantages. However, one synergy that may sometimes be overlooked is the possibility for a financially strong firm to help a financially weak firm to lower its cost of capital by providing attractively priced equity or debt financing.

ILLUSTRATIVE CASE

Bang & Olufsen and Philips N.V.

One excellent example of financial synergy was provided by the crossborder strategic alliance of Philips N.V. of the Netherlands with Bang and Olufsen (B & O) of Denmark in 1990. Philips N.V. is one of the largest multinational firms in the world and the leading consumer electronics firm in Europe. B & O is a small European competitor but with a nice market niche at the high end of the audio-visual market.

Philip's Motivation

Philips was a major supplier of components to B & O, a situation it wished to continue. It also wished to join forces with B & O in the upscale consumer electronics market, where Philips did not have the quality image enjoyed by B & O. Philips was concerned that financial pressure might force B & O to choose a Japanese competitor for a partner. That would be very unfortunate. B & O had always supported Philips' political efforts to gain EU support to make the few remaining European-owned consumer electronics firms more competitive vîs-à-vîs their strong Japanese competitors.

B & O's Motivation

B & O was interested in an alliance with Philips to gain more rapid access to its new technology and assistance in converting that technology into B & O product applications. B & O wanted assurance of timely delivery of components at large volume discounts from Philips itself, as well as access to Philip's large network of suppliers under terms enjoyed by Philips. Equally important, B & O wanted to get an equity infusion from Philips to strengthen its own shaky financial position. Despite its commercial artistry, in recent years B & O had been only marginally profitable, and its publicly traded shares were considered too risky to justify a new public equity issue either in Denmark or abroad. It had no excess borrowing capacity.

The Strategic Alliance

A strategic alliance was agreed upon that would give each partner what it desired commercially. Philips agreed to invest DKK342 million (about $50 million) to increase the equity of B & O's main operating subsidiary. In return it received a 25% ownership of the expanded company.

When B & O's strategic alliance was announced to the public on May 3, 1990, the share price of B & O Holding, the listed company on the Copenhagen Stock Exchange, jumped by 35% during the next two days. It remained at that level until the Gulf War crisis temporarily depressed B & O's share price. The share price has since recovered and the expected synergies eventually materialized.

Source: Abstracted from *The Strategic Alliance of Bang & Olufsen and Philips N.V.*, Thunderbird Case Series, 1999.

If we evaluate what happened, it is obvious that an industrial purchaser might be willing to pay a higher price for a firm that will provide it some synergies than would a portfolio investor who does not receive these synergies. Portfolio investors are pricing firm's shares based only on the normal risk versus return tradeoff. They cannot normally anticipate the value of synergies that might accrue to the firm from an *unexpected* strategic alliance partner. The same conclusion should hold for a purely domestic strategic alliance, but this example happens to be a cross-border alliance.[15]

SUMMARY

Designing a *capital sourcing strategy* requires management to agree upon a long-run financial objective. Management then must choose among the various alternative paths to get there, including where to crosslist its shares, and where to issue new equity, and in what form. A firm *crosslists* its shares on foreign stock exchanges for one or more of the following reasons. It might wish to:

- Improve the liquidity of its existing shares by using depositary receipts.

- Increase its share price by overcoming mispricing by a segmented, illiquid home capital market.

- Support a new equity issue sold in a foreign market.

- Establish a secondary market for shares used in acquisitions.

- Increase the firm's visibility and political acceptance to its customers, suppliers, creditors, and host governments.

- Create a secondary market for shares that will be used to compensate local management and employees in foreign affiliates.

Barriers to listing include an increased commitment to full disclosure and a continuing investor relations program. The choice of where to crosslist depends on the motive for listing.

- If it is to support a new equity issue or to establish a market for share swaps, the target market should also be the listing market.

- If it is to increase the firm's commercial and political visibility or to compensate local management and employees, the target market should be the market in which the firm has significant operations.

- The major liquid stock markets are New York, London, Tokyo, Frankfurt, and Paris. The choice among these five markets depends on the market's size and the sophistication of its market-making activities, including competitive transaction costs and competent crisis management.

A firm can lower its cost of capital and increase its liquidity by selling its shares to foreign investors in one or more of four alternative ways:

- Sale of a directed share issue to investors in one particular foreign equity market

- Simultaneous sale of a Euroequity share issue to foreign investors in more than one market, including both foreign and domestic markets

- Sale of shares to a foreign firm as part of a strategic alliance

QUESTIONS

1. Firms from Countries with Segmented Equity Markets
What advantages accrue to firms in emerging market countries from increasing the transparency of their financial performance so as to qualify for selling equity securities in the major financial markets of the world? What are some of the disadvantages?

2. Firms from Countries with Highly Developed Equity Markets
What advantages accrue to firms, such as Daimler-Benz (Illustrative Case in this chapter) that are from countries with highly developed equity markets,

from qualifying to list their shares directly on the New York or London stock exchanges?

3. American Depositary Receipts

ADRs are designed so that U.S. investors can invest in equity positions of foreign firms without the difficulty of executing an order on a foreign exchange, of converting foreign currency dividends into dollars, of handling a bearer equity certificate, and—for the investor's heirs—of going through probate in a foreign court in the event of death. Why would an Argentine investor choose to invest in ADRs of Argentine corporations traded in the United States instead of buying the underlying shares directly in Buenos Aires?

4. P/E Ratios around the Globe

Exhibit 11.5 reported market P/E ratios for equity markets across the globe. Using the data reported in the exhibit, answer the following questions:

a. Which three markets provide the highest capitalization for a currency unit of earnings on average?

b. Which three markets provide the lowest capitalization for a currency unit of earnings on average?

c. Which markets in 1997 and 1998 provided the highest average return after inflation?

 ## World Wide Web Exercises

W1. American Depositary Receipts

American Depositary Receipts now make up more than 10% of all equity trading on U.S. stock exchanges. As more companies based outside the United States list on U.S. markets, the need to understand the principal forces that drive ADR values increases with each trading day. Begin with Deutsche Morgan Grenfell's detailed description of the ADR process and current ADR trading activity, as described in its web site.

a. Prepare a briefing for senior management in your firm, encouraging them to consider internationally diversifying the firm's liquid asset portfolio with ADRs

b. Identify whether the ADR program level (I, II, III, 144A) has any significance as to which securities you believe the firm should consider

Global Value	http://www.global-value.com/gv/
Bank of New York	http://www.bankofny.com/
JP Morgan's ADR Center	http://adr.com
Stock City	http://www.stockcity.com/
American Depository Receipts	http://www.site-by-site.com/adr/toc.htm

W2. Institutional Ownership of ADRs

Use the JP Morgan ADR Center web site to find the largest individual owners of major ADRs traded in New York. Include Nokia, Telefonos de Mexico, Toyota, Siemens, and Philips in your search.

JP Morgan's ADR Center   http://adr.com

W3. Cost of Capital Calculator

Ibbotson and Associates of Chicago is one of the leading providers of quantitative estimates of the cost of capital across markets. Use the following web site—specifically its Cost of Capital Center—to prepare an overview of the major theoretical approaches and the numerical estimates they yield for cross-border costs of capital.

Ibbotson & Associates   http://www.ibbotson.com/

SUGGESTED READINGS

Boubakri, Narjess and Jean Claude Cosset, "The Financial and Operating Performance of Newly Privatized Firms: Evidence from Developing Countries," *The Journal of Finance*, Vol. 53, No. 3, June 1998, pp. 1081–1110.

Chan, Su Han, John W. Kensinger, Arthur Keown, and John D. Martin, "When Do Strategic Alliances Create Shareholder Value," *Journal of Applied Corporate Finance,* Spring 1999, Vol. 12, No. 1, pp. 82–87.

Dewenter, Kathryn L., and Paul H. Malatesta, "Public Offerings of State-Owned and Privately-Owned Enterprises: An International Comparison," *The Journal of Finance*, Vol. 52, No. 4, August 1997, pp. 1659–1670.

Domowitz, Ian, Jack Glen, and Ananth Madhavan, "International Cross Listing and Order Flow Migration: Evidence from an Emerging Market," *The Journal of Finance*, Vol. 53, No. 6, December 1998, pp. 2001–2027.

Foerster, Stephen R., and G. Andrew Karolyi, "The Effects of Market Segmentation and Investor Recognition on Asset Prices: Evidence From Foreign Stock Listing in the United States," *The Journal of Finance*, Vol. 54, No. 3, June 1999, pp. 981–1013.

Jorion, Philippe, and William N. Goetzmann, "Global Sock Markets in the Twentieth Century," *The Journal of Finance*, Vol. 54, No. 3, June 1999, pp. 953–980.

Miller, Darius P., "The Market Reaction to International Cross-Listings: Evidence from Depositary Receipts," *Journal of Financial Economics*, 51, 1999, pp. 103–123.

Saudagaran, Shahrokh M. and Gary C. Biddle, "Foreign Listing Location: A Study of MNEs and Stock Exchanges in Eight Countries," *Journal of International Business Studies*, Vol. 26, No. 2, Second Quarter 1995, pp. 319–341.

Sundaram, Anant K., and Dennis E. Logue, "Valuation Effects of Foreign Company Listings on U.S. Exchanges," *Journal of International Business Studies,* Vol. 27, No. 1, First Quarter 1996, pp. 67–88.

NOTES

1. For a comprehensive description of depositary receipts and their use in cross-listing and new equity issues, see Miller (1999).
2. Research on the motivation for foreign listings is reported in Saudagaran and Biddle (1995).
3. Alexander, Eun, and Janakiramanan (1988).
4. Sundaram and Logue (1996), p. 67.
5. Miller (1999).
6. Ibid, pp. 117–118.
7. Choi (1973), p. 279.
8. *Federation Internationale des Bourses de Valeur (FIBV) Statistics 1998.*
9. Saudagaran and Biddle (1992).
10. The Euronote and Eurobond markets are described in the next chapter.
11. Megginson, Nash, and Randenbough (1994).
12. A qualified institutional buyer is an entity (other than a bank or saving and loan) that owns and invests on a discretionary basis $100 million in securities of nonaffiliates. Banks and savings and loans must meet this test but also have a minimum net worth of $25 million. The SEC has estimated that about 4000 QIBs exist, composed mainly of investment advisors, investment companies, insurance companies, pension funds, and charitable institutions.
13. Boubakri and Cosset (1998), and confirmed by a more recent study by Miller (1999).
14. *Business Week*, June 22, 1998, pp. 64–66. See also the Harvard Business School case entitled "The Exxel Group: September 1995," Boston, MA: Harvard Business School Publishing, 1997 (case number 9-297-068 Rev. November 14, 1997.)
15. A favorable impact on the share price of firms receiving equity infusions was also reported in studies of strategic alliances by firms resident in the United States. See Chan, Kensinger, Keown, and Martin (1997) and (1999).

CHAPTER 12

SOURCING DEBT GLOBALLY

Cross-border financial markets are an increasingly important source of debt capital for MNEs. Chapter 10, which opened this section, described why a MNE needed to source its capital globally in order to lower its cost of capital. Chapter 11 described the issues and method by which a MNE can go outside its home country for equity capital. This chapter explores the methods and choices the MNE may use to raise long-term debt on international markets.

The first part of this chapter details the common financial guidelines that firms follow when acquiring long-term debt. In addition to the normal concerns, however, debt capital that is denominated in foreign currency has unique international facets. These may be either good or bad. The second part of the chapter provides a cursory overview of the major debt markets and instruments available to the MNE—that is, the menu of choices. The third and final section provides a short but detailed analysis of the financial decision-making that goes into the selection of a specific debt issue when it is sourced in three different currency markets.

DEBT MANAGEMENT AND FUNDING GOALS

The MNE that is raising debt capital on the international markets must—as it must always do in a domestic market—determine the quantity of funds needed per issuance, the maturity of the issuance, and the type of repayment stream to be used. In addition to these customary domestic dimensions of debt issuance is the question of currency of denomination. So how does the firm determine what types of debt it wants?

))) Currency Matching

The MNE possesses a continuing series of foreign-currency-denominated assets. The firm may wish to fund these assets with liabilities of not only the same maturity structure, but also the same currency of denomination. This is the basic *operating strategy* for transaction exposure management first discussed in Chapter 6.

The question is whether the currency of debt is to be the currency of denomination of assets and liabilities (the balance sheet), which is of critical significance, or the currency of denomination of cash flows (the income statement) of the firm. A firm that is acquiring debt denominated in a specific currency for asset/liability matching is focusing on *accounting exposures* (Chapter 8). A firm interested primarily in the matching of currency of denomination of cash flows arising from assets and liabilities is interested primarily in potential *transaction* and *operating exposures* (Chapters 6 and 7). As we concluded in Part II, the primary emphasis of multinational financial management should be based on cash flow value, and not on accounting conventions and practices that have no real cash flow impact.

Potential benefits arise from diversifying the sources of long-term debt in terms of capital cost. If the firm intentionally diversifies debt sourcing across currencies (as we saw with Statoil of Norway in Chapter 7), care must be taken that these cost benefits gained initially from diversification do not disappear as the debt is repaid. As the following section describes, the currency risks associated with foreign-currency-denominated debt are significant and must be managed from the time of the debt issuance.

))) Foreign Exchange Risk and the Cost of Debt

When a firm issues foreign-currency-denominated debt, its effective cost equals the after-tax cost of repaying the principal and interest in terms of the firm's own currency. This amount includes the nominal cost of principal and interest in foreign currency terms, adjusted for any foreign exchange gains or losses.

For example, if a U.S.-based firm borrows Sfr1,500,000 for one year at 5.00% interest, and during the year the franc appreciates from an initial rate of Sfr1.5000/$ to Sfr1.4400/$, what is the dollar cost of this debt ($k_d^{\$}$)? The dollar proceeds of the initial borrowing are calculated at the current spot rate of Sfr1.5000/$:

$$\frac{\text{Sfr1,500,000}}{\text{Sfr1.5000}/\$} = \$1,000,000$$

At the end of one year, the U.S.-based firm is responsible for repaying the Sfr1,500,000 principal plus 5.00% interest, or a total of Sfr1,575,000. This repayment, however, must be made at an ending spot rate of Sfr1.4400/$:

$$\frac{\text{Sfr1,500,000} \times 1.05}{\text{Sfr1.4400}/\$} = \$1,093,750$$

The actual dollar cost of the loan's repayment is not simply 5.00%, which was paid in Swiss franc interest, but 9.375%.

$$\frac{\$1,093,750}{\$1,000,000} = 1.09375$$

The dollar cost is higher than expected due to appreciation of the Swiss franc against the U.S. dollar.

This total home currency cost is actually the result of the combined percentage cost of debt and the percentage change in the foreign currency's value. The total cost of borrowing Swiss francs by a U.S. dollar-based firm, $k_d^\$$, can be found by multiplying 1 plus the Swiss franc interest expense, k_d^{Sfr}, by 1 plus the percentage change in the Sfr/$ exchange rate, s:

$$k_d^\$ = [\,(1 + k_d^{Sfr}) \times (1 + s)\,] - 1$$

where $k_d^{Sfr} = 5.00\%$ and $s = 4.1667\%$.[1]

The total expense is:

$$k_d^\$ = [\,(1 + .0500) \times (1 + .041667)\,] - 1 = .09375$$

The total percentage cost of debt capital is 9.375%, not simply the foreign currency interest payment of 5%. The after-tax cost of this Swiss franc-denominated debt, when the U.S. income tax rate is 34%, is:[2]

$$k_d^\$ (1 - t) = 9.375\% \times 0.66 = 6.1875\%$$

ILLUSTRATIVE CASE

Borrowing with 20–20 Hindsight

MNEs have discovered that borrowing foreign-currency-denominated bonds on a long-term basis creates considerable exposure to transaction gains or losses. Exhibit 12.1 compares a sample of foreign-currency-denominated bonds issued by firms in a wide variety of countries during 1989–1990, as shown in columns (1) and (2). Column (3) shows the firm's expected cost in home currency terms at the time of issuance. Column (4) shows that about 10 years later—June 1, 1999—the realized cost was different from the expected cost (again, in home currency terms). Column (5) shows the difference between expected and realized costs, which was, of course, due to changes in exchange rates. Note that foreign exchange exposure worked both favorably (negative differences) and unfavorably (positive differences) for the sample firms. And note specifically the disastrous impact of Turkey's currency devaluation on its cost of funds in home currency terms: +73.86%!

Exhibit 12.1	*Costs of Borrowing in Foreign-Currency-Denominated Bonds (percentage)*				
Issuer	(1) Home Country	(2) Date of Issue	(3) Cost of Funds: Time of Issue	(4) Cost of Funds as of 6/1/99	(5) Cost Differences
Deutsche Bank Finance	Germany	5/24/89	9.59	7.24	–2.35
Republic of Austria	Austria	7/10/89	8.46	6.73	–1.73
Den Danske Bank	Denmark	2/16/89	9.93	8.46	–1.47
Electricite de France	France	4/18/89	9.50	8.22	–1.28
Japan Finance Corp.	Japan	4/4/89	9.63	8.70	–0.93
British Telecom Finance	Britain	7/13/89	8.46	8.33	–0.13
Alcan Aluminum Ltd.	Canada	7/20/89	9.89	11.38	+1.49
Finnish Export Credit Ltd.	Finland	2/1/89	9.68	12.16	+2.48
Banca Commerciale Italiana	Italy	3/10/89	9.37	12.07	+2.70
Government of Malaysia	Malaysia	9/19/90	10.29	13.10	+2.81
Kingdom of Thailand	Thailand	8/1/89	8.70	11.87	+3.17
Republic of Turkey	Turkey	8/30/89	10.25	84.11	+73.86

Source: Steven M. Dawson, based on calculation methods in "Eurobond Currency Selection: Hindsight," *Financial Executive*, November 1993, p. 73. "Cost of Funds: Time of Issue" is the expected home currency cost given coupon, new issue price, and maturity. "Cost of Funds as of 6/1/99" is cost in home-country currency given the U.S. bank transfer exchange rate at time of each interest or principal payment. Payments after June 1, 1999, are assumed made at the June 1 exchange rate.

INTERNATIONAL DEBT MARKETS: INSTRUMENT CHOICES

The international debt markets offer the borrower a variety of different maturities, repayment structures, and currencies of denomination. The three major sources of debt funding on the international markets are *international commercial bank loans*, the *Euronote market*, and the *international bond market*.

A MNE will normally need debt in a variety of maturities, payment structures, and currencies; therefore it often uses all three markets—in addition to its traditional domestic funding base. The following sections describe the basic attributes of these markets and instruments, as well as their relative advantages and disadvantages for meeting the funding needs of the individual MNE.

EUROCURRENCIES

As mentioned in Chapter 2, *Eurocurrencies* are domestic currencies of one country on deposit in a second country. Eurodollar time-deposit maturities range from call money and overnight funds to longer periods. Certificates of deposit are usually for three months or more and in million-dollar increments. A *Eurodollar deposit* is not a demand deposit; it is not created on the bank's books by writing loans against required fractional reserves, and it cannot be transferred by a check drawn on the bank having the deposit. Eurodollar deposits are transferred by wire or cable transfer of an underlying balance held in a correspondent bank located within the United States. A domestic analogy in most countries is the transfer of deposits held in nonbank savings associations. These are transferred by having the association write its own check on a commercial bank.

Any convertible currency can exist in "Euro-" form.[3] The *Eurocurrency market* includes Euromarks (Deutschemarks deposited in banks outside Germany), Eurosterling (British pounds deposited outside the United Kingdom), and Euroyen (Japanese yen deposited outside Japan), as well as Eurodollars. The exact size of the Eurocurrency market is difficult to measure because it varies with daily decisions by depositors about where to hold readily transferable liquid funds, and particularly about whether to deposit dollars within or outside the United States.[4]

Eurocurrency markets serve two valuable purposes: (1) Eurocurrency deposits are an efficient and convenient money market device for holding excess corporate liquidity, and (2) the Eurocurrency market is a major source of short-term bank loans to finance corporate working capital needs, including the financing of imports and exports.

Banks in which Eurocurrencies are deposited are called *Eurobanks*. A *Eurobank* is "a financial intermediary that simultaneously bids for time deposits and makes loans in a currency other than that of the currency in which it is located."[5] Eurobanks are major world banks that conduct a Eurocurrency business in addition to all other banking functions. Thus, the Eurocurrency operation that qualifies a bank for the name *Eurobank* is, in fact, a department of a large commercial bank, and the name springs from the performance of this function.

)))) History of the Eurodollar Market

The modern Eurodollar market was born shortly after World War II. Eastern European holders of dollars, including the various state trading banks of the Soviet Union, were afraid to deposit their dollar holdings in the United States because these deposits might be attached by U.S. residents with claims against communist governments. Therefore, Eastern European holders deposited their dollars in Western Europe, particularly with two Soviet banks: the Moscow Narod-ny Bank in London and the Banque Commerciale pour l'Europe du Nord in Paris. These banks redeposited the funds in other Western banks, especially in London. Additional dollar deposits were received from various central banks in Western Europe, which elected to hold part of their dollar reserves in this form to obtain a higher yield. Commercial banks also placed their dollar balances in the market for the same reason, and because specific maturities could be negotiated in the Eurodollar market. Additional dollars came to the market from European insurance companies with a large volume of U.S. business. Such companies found it financially advantageous to keep their dollar reserves in the higher-yielding Eurodollar market. Various holders of international refugee funds also supplied funds.

Although the basic causes of the growth of the Eurodollar market are economic efficiencies, a number of unique institutional events during the 1950s and 1960s also helped it grow. In 1957, British monetary authorities responded to a weakening of the pound by imposing tight controls on U.K. bank lending in sterling to nonresidents of the United Kingdom. Encouraged by the Bank of England, U.K. banks turned to dollar lending as the only alternative that would allow them to maintain their leading position in world finance. Although New York was "home base" for the dollar and had a large domestic money and capital market, international trading in the dollar centered in London because of that city's expertise in international monetary matters and its proximity in time and distance to major customers.

Additional support for a European-based dollar market came from the balance-of-payment difficulties of the United States during the 1960s, which temporarily segmented the U.S. domestic capital market from those of the rest of the world. Ultimately, however, the Eurocurrency market continues to thrive because it is a large international money market relatively free of governmental regulation and interference.

INTERNATIONAL BANK LOANS

International bank loans have traditionally been sourced in the Eurocurrency markets. Eurodollar bank loans are also called *Eurodollar credits* or simply *Eurocredits*. The latter title is broader because it encompasses nondollar loans in the Eurocurrency market.

The key factor attracting both depositors and borrowers to the Eurocurrency syndicated loan market is the narrow interest rate spread within that market. The difference between deposit and loan rates is often less than 1%. The narrower spread of the Euromarkets, compared to domestic markets, is illustrated in Exhibit 12.2 for Eurodollars.

Interest spreads in the Eurodollar market are small for a number of reasons. Low lending rates exist because the Eurodollar market is a "wholesale" market, where deposits and loans are made in amounts of $500,000 or more on an unsecured basis. Borrowers are usually large corporations or government entities that qualify for low rates because of their credit standing and because the transaction size is large.

In addition, overhead assigned to the Eurodollar operation by participating banks is small. Deposit rates are higher in the Eurodollar market than in the U.S. domestic market because banks need not comply with U.S. reserve requirements. These reserve requirements, although significantly smaller than in the past, require that a certain percentage of funds be held in non-interest-earning form, raising the cost of banking operations. A second cost avoided in the Eurocurrency and Eurodollar markets is the assessment of deposit insurance fees, such as Federal Deposit Insurance Corporation (FDIC) assessments paid on deposits in the United States.

| Exhibit 12.2 | *Comparative Spreads between Lending and Deposit Rates: The Eurodollar Market* |

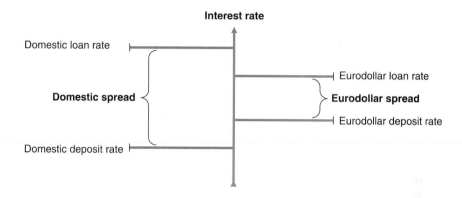

Eurodollar deposit rates are higher and Eurodollar loan rates are lower than their corresponding domestic deposit and loan rates due to the absence of banking restrictions such as reserve requirements and deposit insurance fees, and the wholesale nature of the market.

))) Eurocredits

Eurocredits are bank loans to MNEs, sovereign governments, international institutions, and to other banks, denominated in Eurocurrencies and extended by banks in countries other than the country in whose currency the loan is denominated. Because of the large size of these loans, the lending banks form a *syndicate* or group in order to diversify their risk.

The basic borrowing interest rate for Eurodollar loans has long been tied to the London Interbank Offered Rate (LIBOR), which is the deposit rate applicable to interbank loans within London. In the early 1980s, however, use of this LIBOR base was supplemented by use of a U.S. money market rate base. Consequently, both rates serve as the base for different credits. Borrowers usually pay a premium over the base rate, determined by their creditworthiness and the terms of the credit.

Eurodollars are lent for both short- and medium-term maturities, with transactions for six months or less regarded as routine. Most Eurodollar loans are for a fixed term with no provision for early repayment.

Standby Eurodollar credits are of two types: a *Eurodollar line of credit* and a *Eurodollar revolving commitment.* Under a *Eurodollar line of credit,* a bank promises to lend Eurodollars up to the credit limit, with the interest rate determined by market conditions when the loan is made. Because the line of credit can be canceled by the bank at any time, the arrangement is essentially one of preparing for borrowing in advance.

Under a *Eurodollar revolving commitment*, a bank agrees to lend for a period of perhaps three to five years by accepting a series of sequential notes of short maturity. For example, the borrower may renew a series of 180-day notes at each maturity at the interest rate then in effect. Banks charge a fee of about 0.5% per annum on the unused portion of such a revolving, nonrevocable commitment.

))) Structure of a Syndicated Credit

The syndication of loans has enabled banks to spread the risk of very large loans among a number of banks. Syndication has been particularly important because many large MNEs need credit in excess of a single bank's loan limit.

A *syndicated bank credit* is arranged by a lead bank on behalf of its client. Before finalizing the loan agreement, the lead bank seeks the participation of a group of banks, with each participant providing a portion of the total funds needed. The lead manager bank will work with the borrower to determine the amount of the total credit, the floating-rate base and spread over the base rate, maturity, and fee structure for managing the participating banks. The syndicated loan may or may not be totally underwritten by the participating banks. In the case of loans which are undersubscribed, the amount of credit may be altered to reflect market demand. When a loan is oversubscribed, allotment is required. The periodic expenses of the syndicated credit are composed of two elements:

1. The actual interest expense of the loan, normally stated as a spread in basis points over a variable-rate base such as LIBOR

2. The commitment fees paid on any unused portions of the credit. The spread paid by the borrower is considered the *risk premium*, reflecting the general business and financial risk applicable to the borrower's repayment capability.

Spreads in the syndicated loan market have typically varied from as little as $1/16$% to over $2^{1/2}$% (paid by the government of Brazil in 1981 and 1982 on what were then termed "jumbo loans" of $1 billion or more). The size and nature of the commitment fees paid depends on whether the syndicated loan is a revolving credit or term credit. If it is a term credit, the borrower has a specified draw-down time schedule for the loan, and there is usually no associated commitment fee. If, however, the credit is in the form of a revolving credit, the participating banks have theoretically set aside capital that must be paid for if unused. Exhibit 12.3 illustrates the structure and pricing of a syndicated credit for Irish Aerospace.

THE EURONOTE MARKET

The *Euronote market* is the collective term used to describe short- to medium-term debt instruments sourced in the Eurocurrency markets. Although there are a multitude of differentiated financial products, they can be divided into two major groups—*underwritten facilities* and *nonunderwritten facilities*. The under-written facilities are used for the sale of Euronotes in a number of different forms.

Exhibit 12.3	*Pricing and Structure of a Syndicated Eurocredit*

Borrower: Irish Aerospace, GPA Airbus, GPA Fokker, GPA Jetprop, GPA Rolls
Amount: US$1.25 billion; Revolving loans/guarantees/letters of credit
Terms: 8 years at 93.75 basis points over LIBOR, with a margin of 7/8% for GPA Airbus drawings
Arranger: Citicorp Investment Bank
Lead Managers
& Underwriters: Citibank, Chase Investment Bank, Toronto-Dominion Bank, Citibank (Channel Islands) for a syndicate of Japanese leasing companies, Credit Suisse, Societe Generale (London), Amsterdam-Rotterdam Bank, Bank of Nova Scotia, Bank of Tokyo International, Daiwa Bank, IBJ, Irish Intercontinental Bank/Kredeitbank International Group, Mitsubishi Trust & Banking, National Westminster Bank, Swiss Bank, Tokai Bank

A typical syndicated loan of this type would have up-front fees totaling 1.5% of the principal. The fees would be divided between three groups: (1) the lead arranger bank(s), which organizes the loan and participants; (2) the lead managing and underwriting banks, which aid in the syndication of the loan; and (3) the participating banks, which actually provide the capital.

If the 1.5% total fee was subdivided equally among the three groups, the proceeds of the loan after expenses of issuance and arrangement are:

$$\$1,250,000 - [\ (0.005 + 0.005 + 0.005) \times \$1,250,000,000\ ] = \$1,231,250,000$$

The debt service payments over the 8-year period prior to principal repayment are LIBOR + 93.75 basis points; assuming an initial LIBOR rate of 9.00% (reset every six months for semi-annual debt service payments):

$$\left[\frac{0.0900 + 0.009375}{2} \right] \times \$1,250,000,000 = \$62,109,375.$$

The effective annual cost is thus:

$$\left[\frac{\$62,109,375}{\$1,231,250,000} \right] \times 2 \times 100 = 10.09\%$$

Source: Adapted from "Syndicated Loans," *Euromoney*, November 1989, p.165. Reprinted with permission.

The nonunderwritten facilities are used for the sale and distribution of *Euro-commercial paper* (ECP) and *Euro-medium-term notes* (EMTNs).

⟫⟫⟫ Facilities for Euronotes

A major development in international money markets has been the establishment of facilities for sales of short-term, negotiable, promissory notes—*Euronotes*. Among the facilities for their issuance are revolving underwriting facilities (RUFs), note issuance facilities (NIFs), and standby note issuance facilities (SNIFs). These facilities are provided by international investment and commercial banks. They reflected the movement toward securitization that first hit both domestic and international financial markets after the onset of the debt crisis in the early 1980s.

The RUFs, NIFs, and SNIFs all constitute medium-term (three- to seven-year) commitments by commercial and investment banks to underwrite and distribute the Euronotes. A typical structure might include between one and three arranger banks who would organize a group of participating banks to take shares of the total commitment. The arranger banks would keep relatively small shares for themselves and earn fees for their services. The arrangers and participating banks would stand ready to buy the borrower's notes in the event the notes could not be placed in the market at previously guaranteed rates (usually stated as a maximum interest expense). The Euronote is a substantially cheaper source of short-term funds than syndicated loans, because the notes are placed directly with the investor public, and the securitized and underwritten form allow the ready establishment of liquid secondary markets. The banks receive substantial fees up front for their underwriting and placement services.

Euro-Commercial Paper

Euro-commercial paper, like the commercial paper (CP) issued in domestic markets around the world, is a short-term debt obligation of a corporation or bank. Maturities are typically one, three, and six months. The paper is normally sold at a discount or, occasionally, with a stated coupon. Although the market is capable of supporting issues in any major currency, over 90% of issues outstanding are denominated in U.S. dollars. Exhibit 12.4 shows typical yield calculations for ECP, along with a number of factors relevant to specific ECP currency issues.

The typical ECP issue has changed from the completely underwritten issues of the early years to nonunderwritten issues similar to commercial paper issued in the United States. Unlike domestic commercial paper markets, the ECP market did not place much importance on quality of issuer as measured by ratings until recently.

The ECP market is in competition with domestic markets of the same instrument. The increasing concern for quality ratings of issuers in the ECP market has reduced the comparative advantage to some borrowers of issuing internationally (ECP) rather than in their domestic market. For example, the United States domestic commercial paper market has always been considered less cosmopolitan because domestic borrowers normally raise funds at lower cost than foreign issuers in the United States. This situation is changing. As financial deregulation continues in both Japan and Europe, domestic commercial paper markets may increasingly constitute effective competition for ECP. Lower-quality borrowers may now find their domestic market to be their most reasonably priced source of such debt.

Euro-Medium-Term Notes

The *Euro-medium-term note* market began in 1986 with two major issues, a $160 million dollar facility for First Interstate Bank (U.S.) and a $200 million facility established for Nordic Investment Bank. The EMTN effectively bridges the maturity gap between ECP and the longer-term and less flexible international

| **Exhibit 12.4** | *Pricing and Structure of Euro-Commercial Paper* |

The proceeds of the issuance of Euro-Commercial Paper (ECP) at a discount by corporate borrowers is calculated as follows:

$$\text{Market price} = \frac{\text{Face value}}{1 + \left[\left(\dfrac{N}{360}\right) \times \left(\dfrac{Y}{100}\right)\right]}$$

where Y is yield in annual percent and N is days remaining until maturity.

For example, the market price (proceeds) of the sale of a $1,000 face-value 90-day ECP priced to yield 8.0 percent annually (reflecting current market yields on similar debt securities for comparable credit ratings) would be:

$$\text{Market price} = \frac{\$1,000}{1 + \left[\left(\dfrac{90}{360}\right) \times \left(\dfrac{8.0}{100}\right)\right]} = \$980.39$$

The calculation of the market price varies by the currency of denomination's day-count convention. For example, the British pound-sterling-denominated ECP market uses a 365-day financial year instead of the U.S. dollar's 360-day year.

bond. Although many of the notes were initially underwritten, most EMTNs are now nonunderwritten.

The rapid initial growth of the EMTN market followed directly on the heels of the same basic instrument, which began in the U.S. domestic market in 1982. With SEC Rule #415 instituted in 1982, the SEC allowed a U.S. corporation to obtain a *shelf registration* for debt issues. This meant that once the registration was obtained, the corporation could issue notes on a continuous basis without having to obtain new registrations for each additional issue. This, in turn, allowed a firm to sell short- and medium-term notes through a much cheaper and more flexible issuance facility than ordinary bonds. Although the European version does not, of course, have the problem of registration such as is required for domestic notes, its success to date has been a result of the same basic features that have given the MTN in the United States its advantages over the traditional bond.

The EMTN's basic characteristics are similar to a bond, with principal, maturity, and coupon structures and rates being comparable. The EMTN's typical maturities range from as short a time as nine months to a maximum of 10 years. Coupons are typically paid semiannually, and coupon rates are comparable to those of similar bond issues. The EMTN does, however, have three unique characteristics. First, the EMTN is a facility allowing continuous issuance over a period of time, unlike a bond issue, which is essentially sold all at once. Second, because EMTNs are sold continuously, in order to make debt service (coupon redemption) manageable, coupons are paid on set calendar dates regardless of the

| **Exhibit 12.5** | *Structure and Pricing of a Euro-Medium-Term Note* |

Euro-medium-term notes (EMTNs), because they are shelf-registered with fixed coupon and maturity dates, result in some rather awkward valuations. For example, let us assume a EMTN is issued on November 1, 1999, in the denomination of US$1000. The note matures on June 15, 2001, with set coupon dates of May 1 and November 1 each year. The coupon is 7.0% per annum and is paid semi-annually to the bearer.

Since the note is issued on November 15, 1999, and the next scheduled coupon payment is on May 1 of 2000, the first coupon period is only 165 days and therefore the buyer will not receive the full coupon payment (only 165/180 percent of the $35.00 semi-annual coupon). The full valuation of this specific issue off-the-shelf appears as follows:

Cash Flow	Date	Number of Days since Prev. Date	Days as Percentage of 180 Days	Amount of Cash Flow
First coupon	1 May 2000	165	92%	$ 32.08
Second coupon	1 Nov 2000	180	100%	$ 35.00
Third coupon	1 May 2001	180	100%	$ 35.00
Final coupon	15 June 2001	45	25%	$ 8.75
Principal	15 June 2001	45	25%	$1000.00

Note that the final time period, the one following the third coupon payment, is only 45 days. This results in a final coupon payment of $8.75 (45/180 × $35.00). The principal of US$1000 is also fully repaid upon the specified maturity date.

The market price (P) or present value of the EMTN on November 1, 1999—the date of issuance—yielding 6% annually (a 3.0% semi-annual discount factor) would be calculated in the following way:

$$P = \frac{\$32.08}{(1+.03)^{0.92}} + \frac{\$35.00}{(1+.03)^{1.92}} + \frac{\$35.00}{(1+.03)^{2.92}} + \frac{\$8.75}{(1+.03)^{3.17}} + \frac{\$1000}{(1+.03)^{3.17}} = \$1,008.31.$$

This amount, net of any issuance fees (if any), would constitute the proceeds of the issue to the firm.

date of issuance. Finally, EMTNs are issued in relatively small denominations, from $2 million to $5 million, making medium-term debt acquisition much more flexible than the large minimums customarily needed in the international bond markets. Exhibit 12.5 details the pricing and structure of a sample EMTN issue.

THE INTERNATIONAL BOND MARKET

The international bond market sports a rich array of innovative instruments created by imaginative investment bankers, who are unfettered by the usual controls and regulations governing domestic capital markets. Indeed, the international bond market rivals the international banking market in terms of the quantity and cost of funds provided to international borrowers.

All international bonds fall within two generic classifications, *Eurobonds* and *foreign bonds*. The distinction between categories is based on whether the borrower is a domestic or a foreign resident, and whether the issue is denominated in the local currency or a foreign currency.

A *Eurobond* is underwritten by an international syndicate of banks and other securities firms and is sold exclusively in countries other than the country in whose currency the issue is denominated. For example, a bond issued by a firm resident in the United States, denominated in U.S. dollars but sold to investors in Europe and Japan (not to investors in the United States), is a Eurobond.

A *foreign bond* is underwritten by a syndicate composed of members from a single country, sold principally within that country, and denominated in the currency of that country. The issuer, however, is from another country. A bond issued by a firm resident in Sweden, denominated in dollars, and sold in the United States to U.S. investors by U.S. investment bankers is a foreign bond. Foreign bonds have nicknames: foreign bonds sold in the United States are "Yankee bonds"; foreign bonds sold in Japan are "Samurai bonds"; and foreign bonds sold in the United Kingdom are "Bulldogs."

Eurobond Market

Eurobonds are issued by multinational corporations, large domestic corporations, sovereign governments, governmental enterprises, and international institutions. They are offered simultaneously in a number of different national capital markets, but not in the capital market or to residents of the country in whose currency the bond is denominated. Almost all Eurobonds are in bearer form with call provisions and sinking funds.

The syndicate that offers a new issue of Eurobonds might be composed of underwriters from a number of countries, including European banks, foreign branches of U.S. banks, banks from offshore financial centers, investment and merchant banks, and nonbank securities firms. In the United States, commercial banks may not underwrite corporate securities, but their foreign subsidiaries may do so. This distinction does not exist in most of the world, where commercial banks also act as major underwriters and distributors of new issues of securities.

The Straight Fixed-Rate Issue

The *straight fixed-rate issue* is structured like most domestic bonds, with a fixed coupon, set maturity date, and full principal repayment upon final maturity. Coupons are normally paid annually, rather than semiannually, primarily because the bonds are bearer bonds and annual coupon redemption is more convenient for the holders.

The Floating-Rate Note

The *floating-rate note (FRN)* was the new instrument of fashion on the international bond scene in the early 1980s. The FRN normally pays a semi-annual coupon that is determined using a variable-rate base. A typical coupon would be set at some fixed spread over LIBOR. This structure, like most variable-rate interest-bearing instruments, was designed to allow investors to shift more of the interest rate risk of a financial investment to the borrower. It was a popular instrument in the early 1980s when world markets were characterized by relatively high and unpredictable interest rates. Although many FRNs have fixed maturities, a number of major issues since 1985 are perpetuities. The principal will never be repaid. Thus they provide many of the same financial functions as equity.

)))) The Equity-Related Issue

The most recent major addition to the international bond markets is the *equity-related issue*. The equity-related international bond resembles the straight fixed-rate issue in practically all price and payment characteristics, with the added feature that it is convertible to stock prior to maturity at a specified price per share (or alternatively, number of shares per bond). The borrower is able to issue debt with lower coupon payments due to the added value of the equity conversion feature.

Japanese borrowers have contributed to the rapid development of this instrument. The increase of Japanese stock prices in the late 1980s allowed Japanese borrowers to issue substantial equity-related debt at low interest rates. Investors were attracted to the potential capital gains from such instruments, particularly since a large portion of issues were dollar-denominated with detachable warrants. This allowed the separate development of a market for the warrants, the equivalent of long-dated call options on Japanese yen equities. The market outlook, however, has become uncertain given the introduction of a registration requirement by the Japanese Ministry of Finance and the collapse of the Japanese stock market. Exhibit 12.6 provides a sample of the structure of a convertible bond issue in Japanese yen by a British firm, Glaxo Holdings, plc.

)))) Unique Characteristics of Eurobond Markets

Although the Eurobond market evolved at about the same time as the Eurodollar market, the two markets exist for different reasons, and each could exist independently of the other. The Eurobond market owes its existence to several unique factors, some of which have changed recently. Three of the original factors still of importance are absence of regulatory interference, less stringent disclosure practices, and favorable tax treatment.

Absence of Regulatory Interference. National governments often impose tight controls on foreign issuers of securities denominated in the local currency and sold within their national boundaries. However, governments in general have less stringent limitations for securities denominated in foreign currencies and sold within their markets to holders of those foreign currencies. In effect, Eurobond sales fall outside the regulatory domain of any single nation.

Less Stringent Disclosure. Disclosure requirements in the Eurobond market are much less stringent than those of the Securities and Exchange Commission (SEC) for sales within the United States. U.S. firms often find that the registration costs of a Eurobond offering are less than those of a domestic issue and that

| **Exhibit 12.6** | *A New Issuance of Glaxo Holdings plc, International Convertible Bonds* |

Shelf Sale

¥20 Billion, Japanese Yen, Convertible Bonds, First Series   **Rating:** Aaa

Offering Price:	100.
Underwriters:	A syndicate led by The Nomura Securities Co., Ltd.
Yield:	Current: 4.30% Maturity: 4.30%.
Interest:	4.30% annually.
Interest Payment Dates:	March 28 and September 28, commencing September 28, 1991.
Maturity:	28 September 1998.
Call Features:	The bonds may be called in the 12-month period beginning September 28, 1994, at 103. Thereafter, the price declines 1.0 annually, to 100 on or after September 28, 1997. The bonds may be redeemed in whole, not in part. In the event of a change in the laws of the United Kingdom, or a subdivision thereof, which would require the company to make additional payments for tax reasons, the company may redeem the bonds in whole at 100.
Conversion Feature:	The initial conversion price will be ¥1299 per share, but will be subject to adjustment for certain events. The initial number of ordinary shares to be issued upon conversion will be determined by dividing the Japanese yen principal amount of the bond by the fixed exchange rate of ¥236 = £1. The pound sterling principal amount will then be divided by the conversion price per share. The shares may be converted at any time between August 1, 1991, and September 22, 1998.
Purpose:	General corporate purposes. The proceeds will be used for investment in or loans to an affiliate of the company in Japan.
Form:	Bearer form, with coupons.
Denomination:	¥1 million.
Governing Law:	Japanese law.
Tax Treatment:	U.K. taxation.
Security:	The bonds are unsecured obligations of the company, ranking *pari passu* with all other unsecured, unsubordinated obligations of the company.
Proceeds to Company:	Approximately ¥19.6 billion.
Remaining Shelf Balance:	¥80 billion.

Source: Adapted from *Moody's Bond Survey*, August 19, 1991, p. 4644. Reprinted with permission.

less time is needed to bring a new issue to market. Non-U.S. firms often prefer Eurodollar bonds over bonds sold within the United States because they do not wish to undergo the costs of disclosure or need to register with the SEC However, the SEC has relaxed disclosure requirements for certain private placements (Rule #144A), which is expected to improve the attractiveness of the U.S. domestic bond and equity markets (see Chapter 11 for more details).

Favorable Tax Status. Eurobonds offer tax anonymity and flexibility. Interest paid on Eurobonds is generally not subject to an income withholding tax. As we might suspect, Eurobond interest is not always reported to tax authorities. Prior to June 1984, U.S. corporations issuing Eurobonds were required to withhold up to 30% of each interest payment to foreigners for U.S. income taxes. The rate depended on the foreigner's country of residence and the bilateral tax treaty between that country and the United States. U.S. corporations wishing to issue Eurobonds had to do so through offshore finance affiliates, typically in the Netherlands Antilles, in order to avoid this tax. In 1984, however, the U.S. tax laws were revised to exempt foreign holders of bonds issued by U.S. corporations from any withholding tax. U.S. corporations found it feasible for the first time to sell Eurobonds directly to foreigners. Repeal of the U.S. withholding tax caused other governments, including those of France, Germany, and Japan, to liberalize their tax rules as a defensive measure to avoid an outflow of capital from their markets.

Eurobonds are usually issued in bearer form, meaning that the name and country of residence of the owner is not on the certificate. To receive interest, the bearer cuts an interest coupon from the bond and turns it in at a banking institution listed on the issue as a paying agent. European investors are accustomed to the privacy provided by bearer bonds and are very reluctant to purchase registered bonds, which require holders to reveal their names before they receive interest. Bearer bond status, of course, is also tied to tax avoidance.

))) Rating of Eurobonds and Other International Issues

Purchasers of Eurobonds do not only rely on bond-rating services or on detailed analyses of financial statements. General reputation of the issuing corporation and its underwriters has been a major factor in obtaining favorable terms. For this reason, larger and better-known MNEs, state enterprises, and sovereign governments are able to obtain the lowest interest rates. Firms whose names are better known to the general public, possibly because they manufacture consumer goods, are often believed to have an advantage over equally qualified firms whose products are less widely known.

Rating agencies, such as Moody's and Standard & Poor's (S&P's), provide ratings for selected international bonds. Moody's ratings for international bonds imply the same creditworthiness as for domestic bonds of U.S. issuers. Moody's limits its evaluation to the issuer's ability to obtain the necessary currency to repay the issue according to the original terms of the bond and excludes any assessment of risk to the investor caused by changing exchange rates. Exhibit 12.7 lists Moody's sovereign ceilings for foreign currency ratings by country as of August 1999.

Moody's rates international bonds upon request of the issuer for a fee paid by the issuer. Based on supporting financial statements and other material obtained from the issuer, a preliminary rating is made. The issuer is then informed and given an opportunity to comment. After Moody's determines its final rating, the issuer may decide not to have the rating published. Consequently, a disproportionately large number of published international ratings fall into the highest categories, since issuers about to receive a lower rating often decide not to have the rating published.

Exhibit 12.7 *Moody's Investors Service's Sovereign Ceilings for Foreign Currency Ratings for Selected Countries (August 1999)*

Country	Bonds & Notes		Bank Deposits		Country	Bonds & Notes		Bank Deposits	
	L.T.	S.T.	L.T.	S.T.		L.T.	S.T.	L.T.	S.T.
Argentina	Ba3	P-1	Aaa	P-1	Lithuania	Ba1	NP	Ba2	NP
Australia	Aa2	P-1	Aa2	P-1	Luxembourg	WR	WR	WR	WR
Brazil	B2	NP	Caa1	NP	Malaysia	Baa3	NP	Baa1	NP
Bulgaria	B2	NP	B3	NP	Mexico	Ba2*	NP	B1*	NP
Canada	Aa2	P-1	Aa2	P-1	New Zealand	Aa2	P-1	Aa2	P-1
Cayman Islands	Aa3	P-1	Aa3	P-1	Norway	Aaa	P-1	Aaa	P-1
Chile	Baa1	P-2	Baa1	P-2	Oman	Baa2	P-2	Baa2	P-2
China	A3	P-2	Baa2	P-3	Pakistan	Caa1	NP	Ca	NP
Colombia	Baa3	–	Ba1	NP	Peru	Ba3	NP	B1	NP
Croatia	Baa3	P-3	Ba1	NP	Philippines	Ba1	NP	Ba2	NP
Czech Republic	Baa1	P-2	Baa1	P-2	Poland	Baa3	–	Ba1	NP
Denmark	Aa1	P-1	Aa1	P-1	Romania	B3	NP	Caa1	NP
Euroland	Aaa	P-1	Aaa	P-1	Russia	B3	NP	Ca	NP
Greece	A2	P-2	A2	P-2	Singapore	Aa1	P-1	Aa1	P-1
Hong Kong	A3	P-1	A3	P-1	Slovakia	Ba1	NP	Ba2	NP
Hungary	Baa1	P-2	Baa1	P-2	Slovenia	A3	P-2	A3	P-2
Iceland	Aa3	P-1	Aa3	P-1	South Africa	Baa3	–	Ba1	NP
India	Ba2	NP	Ba3	NP	Sweden	Aa2	P-1	Aa2	P-1
Indonesia	B3	NP	Ca	NP	Switzerland	Aaa	P-1	Aaa	P-1
Israel	A3	P-2	A3	P-2	Taiwan	Aa3	P-1	Aa3	P-1
Japan	Aa1	P-1	Aa1	P-1	Thailand	Ba1	NP	B1	NP
Kazakstan	B1	NP	B2	NP	United States	Aaa	P-1	Aaa	P-1
Korea	Baa3	NP	Baa2	NP	Uruguay	Baa3	P-3	Baa3	P-3
Kuwait	Baa1	P-2	Baa1	P-2	United Kingdom	Aaa	P-1	Aaa	P-1
					Venezuela	B2	NP	Caa1	NP

*Under review for possible up-grading.
** Under review for possible down-grading.
L.T. is long term, S.T. is short term
All EU-11 members of the euro (Euroland) are rated together. Long-term bond ratings, from highest to lowest: Aaa, Aa, and A are highest grade (investment grade); Baa, Ba, and B are medium-grade (speculative grade); Caa, Ca, and C are poorest grade. Moody's also applies numerical modifiers (1, 2, and 3) within each rating classification, with 1 being in the higher end of the rating grade. Short term ratings, from highest to lowest: P-1, P-2, P-3, and NP (not prime).
Source: Moody's Investors Services, http:www.moodys.com/repldata/ratings/ratsov.htm.

Moody's review of political risk includes study of the government system, the social environment, and the nation's external relations. Its review of economic risk looks at debt burden, international liquidity, balance of payments flexibility, economic structure, growth performance, economic management, and economic outlook. Moody's also evaluates the bonds of sovereign-supported entities by looking first at their creditworthiness on a stand-alone basis, and then looking at the extent to which sovereign support either enhances or diminishes the borrower's financial strength. Credit ratings are critical to borrowers and investors alike. A MNE's credit rating determines its cost of funds.

EMERGING MARKETS AND BRADY BONDS

One of the most lasting elements of the so-called debt crisis of the early 1980s is the *Brady Bond market*. The dollar-denominated syndicated loans extended to Latin American borrowers in the late 1970s and early 1980s constituted a serious problem not only for the borrowers when they could not meet debt service requirements, but also for the lenders, those multinational banks that found themselves heavily exposed. Then Secretary of the U.S. Treasury Nicholas Brady led the conversion of these bank loans into securitized instruments—*Brady bonds*—which could be traded in the marketplace. This created a liquid market for these debt instruments and allowed both debtors and creditors to move out of the market if they wished.

Brady bonds have a number of special features. First, the maturity of the debt obligations has generally lengthened considerably over the original agreements, alleviating much of the debt service pressure. Secondly, the interest obligations of the securities were substantially lower than the original loan agreements, again, to make debt service less burdensome. Most importantly, however, was the collateral created by the home country government and often accompanied by some form of guarantee to investors by the IMF or World Bank. This provided a more secure credit standing to the newly created and issued securities. Each country's Brady restructuring is slightly different. Typically, the home government purchases U.S. government securities, such as zero-coupon U.S. treasury bonds, for a fraction of the outstanding security principals. The U.S. Treasury bonds are then held in escrow outside the debtor country (typically in the United States) as collateral against the outstanding securities. Since nearly all Brady bonds are "bullet" amortizations, their principals are repaid in a single payment upon maturity. The zero-coupon bond collateral grows to match the bullet principal.

In addition to the critical role these bonds played in alleviating the crisis pressures for both debtors and creditors, they have also served as something of a barometer of emerging market creditworth and economic health. Since all Brady bonds are dollar-denominated, they often provide proxies of the cost of dollar-debt for emerging market nations, and they are frequently used by MNEs as benchmarks of the cost of capital in these tumultuous markets. Chapter 16 will provide additional detail on the theory and practice of using such costs of capital in assessing risk of foreign investments. Crises in Mexico (1994) and Brazil (1999) have proven something of a test of the Brady bond market. In both cases the market fell, the appropriate response to potentially worsening repayment capability of heavily indebted emerging countries. Yet, the Brady bond market maintained its liquidity, allowing market participants to measure and manage their risk exposures.

SUMMARY

- *Cross-border financial markets* are an increasingly important source of capital for MNEs, sovereign entities, and international institutions.

- The main components of the international debt markets are bank syndicated loans, Euronotes, and Eurobonds.

- Syndicated loans, known as *Eurocredits*, are bank loans to business firms, sovereign entities, international institutions, and other banks.

- The basic borrowing rate on syndicated loans is a variable rate of interest based on LIBOR.

- The *Euronote market* is the collective term used to describe short- to medium-term debt instruments sourced in the Eurocurrency markets.

- *Euro-commercial paper* is a short-term debt obligation similar to domestic commercial paper but sourced in the Eurocurrency markets.

- *Euro-medium-term notes* bridge the maturity gap between Euro-commercial paper and Eurobonds. Their terms of repayment are similar to bonds but they have a shorter maturity.

- A *Eurobond* is underwritten by an international syndicate of financial institutions and is sold exclusively in countries other than the country in whose currency the bond is denominated. By comparison, an *international bond* is underwritten by a syndicate of members from a single country for an issuer from a foreign country. It is sold principally within the syndicate's country and is denominated in that country's currency.

- Eurobonds can be straight fixed-rate issues, floating rate notes, or equity-related issues.

- Eurobonds are attractive because of the absence of regulatory interference, less stringent disclosure requirements, and a favorable tax status due to their bearer form.

- The cost of foreign-currency-denominated debt includes the nominal cost of principal and interest in foreign currency terms, adjusted for any foreign exchange gains or losses. This creates transaction exposure that can be risky.

- The creation of the *Brady bond market* of former syndicated loans to emerging market countries with dollar debt-service difficulties has added significantly to the creditworth and capital liquidity of emerging markets in the 1990s.

QUESTIONS

1. Grupo Milano

Grupo Milano is a multinational manufacturer of small gasoline-generator motor scooters located in Italy. Most of its cash flow is generated in euros.

Grupo Milano wishes to access the international debt markets for short-term capital, which it hopes will be cheaper than the bank credit it has been using for many years.

If Grupo Milano issues a total principal of €400,000,000 in Euro-commercial paper (ECP) at a discount, with the following characteristics, what are the total proceeds to Grupo Milano of the following issues?

Issue	Notional Principal	Yield
90-day ECP	€250,000,000	7.40%
180-day ECP	€150,000,000	7.80%

2. Iowa Grain Syndicate

Iowa Grain Syndicate exports large quantities of corn and wheat to Russia and eastern Europe. The Syndicate was quoted a borrowing rate of 9% p.a. in Chicago, but borrowed €3,000,000 for one year at 6% interest in Frankfurt in order to save on interest costs. During the year the euro appreciated 8% from its initial rate of $1.2000/€. Was it wise for the Syndicate to borrow in Frankfurt instead of Chicago? What was its all-in-cost?

3. Eurodollars

The Egyptian Solidarity Fund is holding a 60-day US$1,000,000 certificate of deposit in a New York bank on which it is earning 4%. A Beirut bank offers to pay 4.5% if the Egyptian Solidarity Fund will transfer the funds to Beirut, to be held in the form of a 30-day U.S. dollar-denominated certificate of deposit (i.e., a Eurodollar deposit).

a. What happens to the underlying dollar deposit in the New York bank?
b. How can the Beirut bank afford to pay an interest rate one-half of one percent above the rate paid by the New York bank?

4. Euro-Medium-Term Note (EMTN)

Exhibit 12.5 illustrates the pricing of a Euro-medium-term note. Assume that an EMTN is sold on March 25, 2001, with a maturity on September 30, 2003, and with set coupon dates of June 30 and December 31. The coupon rate is 8% but the issue is sold to yield 6%. Calculate the price at which the note should be sold.

5. Kelly & Murphy, Inc.

Kelly & Murphy, Inc., wishes to raise $4,000,000 in U.S. dollars with debt financing. The funds, needed to augment working capital, will be repaid with interest in one year. Ms. Kelly, the Treasurer of Kelly & Murphy, is considering three alternatives:

a. Borrow U.S. dollars from Wells Fargo Bank at 7%
b. Borrow British pounds from National Westminster at 12%
c. Borrow Japanese yen from Tokomori Credit Bank at 4%

If Kelly & Murphy borrow a foreign currency, the company will remain uncovered; that is, it will simply change foreign currency for dollars at today's spot rate and buy the needed foreign currency back one year later at the spot rate then in effect. Kelly & Murphy has no foreign operations.

Ms. Kelly estimates the pound will depreciate 4% relative to the dollar and the yen will appreciate 2% relative to the dollar during the coming year. Corporate tax rates are 34% in the United States, 36% in the United Kingdom, and 38% in Japan.

From which bank should Kelly & Murphy borrow, and what is its projected after-tax cost of borrowing from each source?

6. Wilford Merchandising Company

Wilford Merchandising Company wants to borrow $100 million or the foreign currency equivalent for five years. The following alternatives are available:

a. *Borrow in U.S. dollars:* Borrow dollars at 7% per annum with bonds sold at par. Expenses of the issue will be 2.5% of the amount borrowed.
b. *Borrow in euros:* Borrow euros at 8% per annum with bonds sold at "99." Expenses of the issue will be 3.0% of the amount borrowed. The current exchange rate is $1.2500/€ and the euro is expected to depreciate against the dollar by 2% per year.
c. *Borrow in Japanese yen:* Borrow yen at 4% per annum. The bonds would be sold at par, and expenses would be 3.0% of the face value of the issue. The current exchange rate is ¥110.00/$, and the yen is expected to appreciate against the dollar by 2% per annum.

Evaluate the cost of each alternative and make a recommendation to the chief financial officer regarding the source of debt capital that is likely to be least expensive for the five-year period.

7. Norsk Finance A/S

Norsk Finance A/S, a national mortgage company headquartered in Oslo, Norway, is offering residential customers the opportunity to refinance their mortgages from Norwegian krone to Swiss francs. Nora Nielsen is considering the opportunity. The major attraction is that Swiss franc interest rates are over 4% per annum lower than comparable maturity Norwegian mortgage rates, and Nora has a new home mortgage of NOK920,000. The mortgage rates Norsk Finance is currently offering for a 10-year refinancing are:

Currency of denomination	*Rates (per annum)*
Norwegian krone	7.500%
Swiss francs	3.250%

The Norwegian krone and Swiss franc are both currencies that are not part of the euro. Both currencies are still effectively freely floating on world currency markets. The current spot exchange rate is NOK5.6400/SFR. The long-term expectations for inflation rates in the two countries (from a recent OECD study) are 1.000% per annum in Switzerland and 2.500% per annum in Norway. Morgan Stanley Capital International recently completed its own study of the outlook for various currencies and concluded that the Norwegian krone may depreciate at roughly 4% per annum versus the Swiss franc in the coming decade. Assume that the mortgage payments are annual and amortized.

a. What are the expected interest, principal, and total payments per year for the two alternative mortgage rates and currencies?

b. How do the two different mortgage payments compare if the NOK/SFR exchange rate were to (1) remain fixed, (2) change according to purchasing power parity, and (3) change according to recent Morgan Stanley expectations?

c. What is the present value, in Norwegian krone terms, of the different mortgage rates and scenarios?

d. What would you advise Nora Nielsen to do?

WORLD WIDE WEB EXERCISES

W1. Sovereign Credit Ratings Criteria
The evaluation of credit risk and all other relevant risks associated with the multitude of borrowers on world debt markets requires a structured approach to international risk assessment. Check both Standard & Poor's and Moody's criteria described in depth on their web pages to differentiate the various risks (such as local currency risk, default risk, currency risk, and transfer risk) with major sovereign ratings worldwide.

Standard & Poor's	http://www.standardpoor.com/ratings
Moody's	http://www.moodys.com/

W2. Brady Bonds and Emerging Markets
Emerging markets have repeatedly been beaten down with every major international financial crisis, whether it be the Mexican peso (1994), the Thai baht (1997), the Russian ruble (1998), or the Brazilian real (1999). Use the web sites listed below to prepare an analysis of why these markets come under such severe pressure when a crisis occurs somewhere else around the globe.

Brady Network	http://www.bradynet.com
Emerging Markets	http://www.emgmkts.com

SUGGESTED READINGS

Hill, Claire A., "Securitization: A Financing Strategy for Emerging Market Firms," *Journal of Applied Corporate Finance*, Fall 1998, Vol. 11, No. 3, pp. 55–65.

Cantor, Richard, and Frank Packer, "Sovereign Risk Assessment and Agency Credit Ratings," *European Financial Management*, Vol. 2, 1996.

Codogne, Lorenzo, "Assessing Bond Market Developments Post-Euro," *Journal of Applied Corporate Finance*, Fall 1998, Vol. 11, No. 3, pp. 66–81.

Johnson, Greg, and Thomas Funkhouser, "Yankee Bonds and Cross-Border Private Placements," *Journal of Applied Corporate Finance*, Fall 1999, Vol. 10, No. 3, pp. 34–45.

NOTES

1. The percentage change in the value of the Swiss franc versus the U.S. dollar, when the home currency is the U.S. dollar is:

$$\frac{S_1 - S_2}{S_2} \times 100 = \frac{\text{Sfr}1.5000/\$ - \text{Sfr}1.4400/\$}{\text{Sfr}1.4400/\$} \times 100 = +4.1667\%$$

2. The added 4.1667% cost of this debt in terms of U.S. dollars would be reported as a foreign exchange transaction loss, and it would be deductible for tax purposes.
3. Note that this use of the expression "Euro-" should not be confused with the new common European currency called the *euro*.
4. Eurocurrency statistics are provided both in the *Annual Report of the Bank for International Settlements* (BIS), in Basle, Switzerland, and by Morgan Guaranty Trust Company of New York in its bimonthly *World Financial Markets*.
5. Dufey and Giddy (1978).

FOREIGN INVESTMENT DECISIONS

PART 4 is an analysis of the *foreign direct investment* (FDI) decision process from strategy to implementation and is intended to be used as an integrated module. It builds on Chapter 1, which described the strategic reasons that motivated firms to become multinational enterprise (MNEs). Chapter 1 also described the foreign exchange and political risks faced by MNEs. Foreign exchange risk management has already been analyzed in Part II.

CHAPTER 13 describes the decision process that eventually leads to FDI rather than alternative modes of foreign involvement. It also suggests strategies for political risk management related to FDI.

CHAPTER 14 analyzes capital budgeting for a greenfield project located abroad. *Greenfield* means that the project starts with bare ground and builds up from there. The numerical illustration is of Cemex of Mexico evaluating a greenfield project in Indonesia, Indonesia Semen (Cement).

CHAPTER 15 analyzes FDI via international *mergers and acquisitions* (M&A). This topic requires an understanding of the techniques employed to value firms, and of the typical practices of MNEs in M&A. The chapter builds upon the previous case study, P.T. Semen Gresik.

    The introduction of this new chapter reflects the growing importance of M&A among international activities. Between 55% and 60% of FDI during the 1985–95 period was through M&A rather than through traditional greenfield investments.*

CHAPTER 16 concludes Part IV with a detailed analysis of how MNEs can adjust for risk when investing internationally. Also new to this edition, this chapter focuses on different dimensions of foreign risk, qualitative and quantitative measures of foreign risk, and how to adjust expected cash flows and/or discount rates to reflect the different risks borne by a MNE that invests in foreign projects.

*Dunning (1998), p. 50. The original source is UNCTAD 1997.

CHAPTER 13

CORPORATE STRATEGY: FOREIGN DIRECT INVESTMENT AND POLITICAL RISK

This chapter analyses the decision whether, where, and how to undertake *foreign direct investment* (FDI). It also describes political risk management strategies that start before FDI and end with operating strategies after FDI takes place.

Exhibit 13.1 provides a roadmap to explain the FDI sequence. In order to undertake FDI a firm must develop a competitive advantage that is suitable for exploitation abroad. It then needs to decide where to produce in order to satisfy the demand for its products. It could produce at home and export, or it could produce abroad. Producing abroad can be accomplished through a licensing agreement or management contract. However, if the firm wants to control its assets abroad, it can choose between a joint venture and a wholly owned affiliate. The wholly owned affiliate (also called FDI) could be either a *greenfield investment* or an acquisition of a foreign enterprise. A *greenfield investment* is a project that starts with bare ground and builds up from there.

DOES THE FIRM HAVE A SUSTAINABLE COMPETITIVE ADVANTAGE IN THE HOME MARKET?

In deciding whether to invest abroad, management must first determine whether the MNE has some sustainable competitive advantage that enables it to compete effectively in its home market. The competitive advantage must be firm-specific, transferable, and powerful enough to compensate the firm for the potential disadvantages of operating abroad (foreign exchange risks, political risks, and increased agency costs).

Based on observations of firms that have successfully invested abroad, some of the competitive advantages enjoyed by MNEs are (1) economies of scale and scope arising from their large size; (2) managerial and marketing expertise; (3) superior technology based

Exhibit 13.1	*The Foreign Direct Investment Decision Sequence*

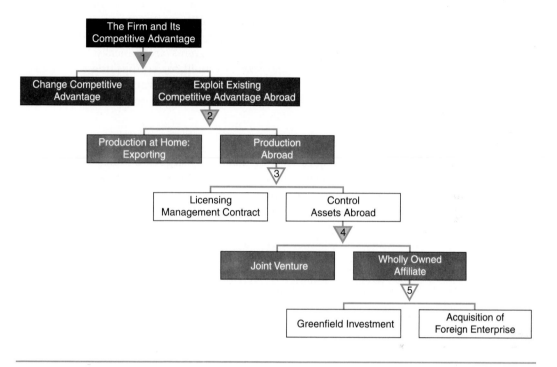

Source: Adapted from Gunter Dufey and R. Mirus, "Foreign Direct Investment: Theory and Strategic Considerations," unpublished, University of Michigan, 1985. Reprinted with permission.

on a heavy emphasis on research; (4) financial strength; (5) differentiated products; and sometimes (6) competitiveness of their home markets.

)))) Economies of Scale and Scope

Economies of scale and scope can be developed in production, marketing, finance, research and development, transportation, and purchasing. In each of these areas there are significant competitive advantages to being large, whether because of international or domestic operations. Production economies can come from the use of large-scale, automated plant and equipment or from an ability to rationalize production through worldwide specialization. For example, some automobile manufacturers, such as Ford, decentralize manufacturing by producing engines in one country, transmissions in another, and bodies in another and then by assembling still elsewhere, with the location often being dictated by comparative advantage.[1] Marketing economies occur when firms are large enough to use the most efficient advertising media to create worldwide brand identification, as well as to establish worldwide distribution, warehousing, and servicing systems. Financial economies derive from access to the full range of financial instruments and sources of funds, such as the Eurocurrency, Euroequity, and Eurobond markets. In-house research and development programs are typically restricted to large firms because of the minimum-size threshold for establishing a laboratory and scientific staff. Transportation economies accrue to firms that can ship in carload or shipload lots. Purchasing economies come from quantity discounts and market power.

Managerial and Marketing Expertise

Managerial expertise includes skill in managing large industrial organizations from both a human and technical viewpoint. It also encompasses knowledge of modern analytical techniques and their application in functional areas of business. Managerial expertise can be developed through prior experience in foreign markets. In most empirical studies, multinational firms have been observed to export to a market before establishing a production facility there. Likewise, they have prior experience sourcing raw materials and human capital in other foreign countries through either imports, licensing, or FDI. In this manner the MNEs can partially overcome the supposed superior local knowledge of host country firms.

Technology

Technology includes both scientific and engineering skills. It is not limited to MNEs, but firms in the most industrialized countries have an advantage in terms of access to continuing new-technology spin-offs from the military and space programs. Empirical studies have confirmed that technology plays an important role for MNEs.[2]

Financial Strength

Financial strength is demonstrated by achieving and maintaining a global cost and availability of capital, as explained in Chapter 10. This is a critical competitive cost variable for funding FDI and other foreign activities. MNEs that are resident in liquid and unsegmented capital markets are normally blessed with this attribute. However, as shown in Chapter 10, MNEs that are resident in small industrial or emerging market countries can follow a proactive strategy of seeking foreign portfolio and corporate investors. In order to be successful, these firms must receive the cooperation of both home and foreign government regulators. The regulators must not impose capital controls that prevent or discourage foreign investors from purchasing securities across borders.

Small- and medium-sized firms often lack the characteristics that attract foreign (and maybe domestic) investors. They are too small or unattractive to achieve a global cost of capital. This limits their ability to fund FDI, and their higher marginal cost of capital reduces the number of foreign projects that can generate the higher required rate of return.

))) Differentiated Products

Firms create their own firm-specific advantages by producing and marketing differentiated products.[3] Such products originate from research-based innovations or heavy marketing expenditures to gain brand identification. Furthermore, the research and marketing process continues to produce a steady stream of new differentiated products. It is difficult and costly for competitors to copy such products, and they always face a time lag if they try. Having developed differentiated products for the domestic home market, the firm may decide to market them worldwide, a decision consistent with the desire to maximize return on heavy research and marketing expenditures.

))) Competitiveness of the Home Market

A strongly competitive home market can sharpen a firm's competitive advantage relative to firms located in less competitive home markets. This phenomenon is known as the "diamond of national advantage."[4] The diamond has four components:

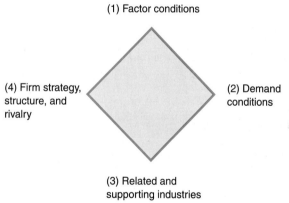

(1) Factor conditions

(4) Firm strategy, structure, and rivalry

(2) Demand conditions

(3) Related and supporting industries

Success of a firm to compete in a particular industry depends partly on the availability of factors of production (land, labor, capital, and technology) appropriate for that industry. Countries that are either naturally endowed with the appropriate factors or able to create them will probably spawn firms that are both competitive at home and potentially competitive abroad. For example, a well-educated work force in the home market creates a competitive advantage for firms in certain high-tech industries.

Firms facing sophisticated and demanding customers in the home market are able to hone their marketing, production, and quality control skills. Japan is such a market.

Firms in industries that are surrounded by a critical mass of related industries and suppliers will be more competitive because of this supporting cast. For example, electronic firms that are located in centers of excellence, such as in the San Francisco Bay area, are surrounded by efficient, creative suppliers and enjoy access to educational institutions at the forefront of knowledge.

A competitive home market forces firms to fine-tune their operational and control strategies for their specific industry and country environment. For example, Japanese firms learned how to organize to implement their famous "just-in-time" inventory control system. One key was to use numerous subcontractors and suppliers that were encouraged to locate near the final assembly plants.

In some cases home country markets have not been large or competitive, but MNEs that are located there have nevertheless developed global niche markets served by foreign subsidiaries. Global competition in oligopolistic industries substitutes for domestic competition. For example, a number of MNEs resident in Scandinavia, Switzerland, and the Netherlands fall in this category. Examples are Novo Nordisk (Denmark), Norske Hydro (Norway), Nokia (Finland), L.M. Ericsson (Sweden), Astra (Sweden), ABB (Sweden/Switzerland), Roche Holding (Switzerland), Royal Dutch Shell (the Netherlands), Unilever (the Netherlands), and Philips (the Netherlands).

Emerging market countries have also spawned aspiring global MNEs in niche markets while still lacking competitive home country markets. Some of these are traditional exporters in natural resource fields such as oil, agriculture, and minerals, but they are in transition to becoming MNEs. They typically start with foreign sales subsidiaries, joint ventures, and strategic alliances. Examples are Petrobras (Brazil), YPF (Argentina), and Cemex (Mexico). Another category of firms are those that have been recently privatized in the telecommunications industry. Examples are Telefonos de Mexico and Telebras (Brazil). Still others started as electronic component manufacturers but are transitioning into manufacturing abroad. Examples are Samsung Electronics (Korea), Hyundai (Korea), and Taiwan Semiconductor (Taiwan).

THE OLI PARADIGM AND INTERNALIZATION

The *OLI paradigm* is an attempt to create an overall framework to explain why MNEs rely on FDI rather than serving foreign markets through alternative modes such as licensing, joint ventures, strategic alliances, management contracts, and exporting.[5]

The "O" in OLI stands for *owner-specific advantages*. As described earlier, a firm must have competitive advantages in its home market. These must be firm-specific, not easily copied, and in a form that allows them to be transferred to foreign subsidiaries. For example, economies of scale and financial strength are not necessarily firm-specific because they can be achieved by many other firms. Certain kinds of technology can be purchased, licensed, or copied. Even differentiated products can lose their advantage to slightly altered versions, given enough marketing effort and the right price.

The "L" in OLI stands for *location-specific advantages*. These are typically market imperfections or genuine comparative advantages that attract FDI to particular locations. These factors might include a low-cost but productive labor force, unique sources of raw materials, a large domestic market, defensive investments to counter other competitors, or centers of technological excellence.[6]

The "I" in OLI stands for *internalization*. According to the theory, the key ingredient for maintaining a firm-specific competitive advantage is possession of proprietary information and control of the human capital that can generate new information through expertise in research. Needless to say, once again large research-intensive firms are most likely to fit this description.

Why does possession of information lead to FDI? In the words of one of the theory's proponents:

> Information is an intermediate product par excellence. It is the oil which lubricates the engine of the MNE . There is no proper market for the sale of information created by the MNE and therefore no price for it. There are surrogate prices; for example, those found by evaluating the opportunity cost of factor inputs expended in the production and processing of a new research discovery or by an ex post evaluation of the extra profits generated by that discovery, assuming all other costs to remain the same. Yet there is no simple interaction of supply and demand to set a market price. Instead the MNE is driven to create an internal market of its own in order to overcome the failure of an external market to emerge for the sale of information. This internal market of the MNE is an efficient response to the given exogenous market imperfection in the determination of the price of information. Internalization allows the MNE to solve the appropriability problem by assigning property rights in knowledge to the MNE organization.
>
>   The creation of an internal market by the MNE permits it to transform an intangible piece of research into a valuable property specific to the firm. The MNE will exploit its advantage in all available markets and will keep the use of information internal to the firm in order to recoup its initial expenditures on research and knowledge generation. Production by subsidiaries is preferable to licensing or joint ventures since the latter two arrangements cannot benefit from the internal market of an MNE. They would therefore dissipate the information monopoly of the MNE, unless foreign markets were segmented by effective international patent laws or other protective devices.[7]

Minimizing transactions costs is the key factor in determining the success of an internalization strategy. Wholly owned FDI reduces the agency costs that arise from asymmetric information, lack of trust, and the need to monitor foreign partners, suppliers, and financial institutions. Self-financing eliminates the need to observe specific debt covenants on foreign subsidiaries that are financed locally or by joint venture partners. If a multinational firm has a low global cost and high availability of capital, why share it with joint venture partners, distributors, licensees, and local banks, all of whom probably have a higher cost of capital?[8]

WHERE TO INVEST?

The decision about where to invest is influenced by economic and behavioral factors, as well as the stage of a firm's historical development. The decision about where to invest abroad for the first time is not the same as where to reinvest abroad. A firm learns from its first few investments abroad, and this influences subsequent investments.

In theory, a firm should identify its competitive advantages. Then it should search worldwide for market imperfections and comparative advantage, until it finds a country where it expects to enjoy a competitive advantage large enough to generate a risk-adjusted return above the firm's hurdle rate.

In practice, firms have been observed to follow a sequential search pattern as described in the behavioral theory of the firm.[9] Human rationality is bounded by our ability to gather and process all the information that would be needed to make a perfectly rational decision based on all the facts. This observation lies behind two related behavioral theories of FDI. They are described next as the *internationalization process theory* and *international network theory*.

The Internationalization Process

The decision to invest abroad for the first time is often a stage in a firm's development process. The firm first develops a competitive advantage in its home market and eventually finds that it can grow profitably by exporting to foreign markets. At some point it experiences a stimulus from the external environment that leads it to consider production abroad.

In a classic study of the foreign investment decision process in 38 market-seeking U.S. firms that had considered investing in Israel, the following external stimuli were important.

1. An outside proposal, provided it comes from a source that cannot be easily ignored. The most frequent sources of such proposals are foreign governments, the distributors of the company's products, and its clients, or a powerful member of the firm's board of directors.

2. Fear of losing a market.

3. The "bandwagon" effect: very successful activities abroad of a competing firm in the same line of business, or a general belief that investment in some area is "a must."

4. Strong competition from abroad in the home market.[10]

The sequence and intensity of investigation, including the motivating force, was the major determinant of the FDI decision.

The behavioral approach to analyzing the FDI decision has been further developed by the so-called Swedish School of economists.[11] They have rather successfully explained not only the initial decision to invest abroad but also later decisions to reinvest elsewhere and to change the structure of a firm's international involvement over time. Based on the internationalization process of a large sample of Swedish MNEs, they observed that these firms tended to invest first in countries that were not too far distant in "psychic" terms. Close psychic distance meant countries with a cultural, legal, and institutional environment similar to Sweden's. Examples of such countries are Norway, Denmark, Finland, Germany, and the United Kingdom. The initial investments were modest in size, to minimize the risk of an uncertain foreign environment. As the Swedish firms learned from their initial investments, they became willing to take greater risks with respect to both the psychic distance of the countries and the size of the investments.

))) Multinational Firms in a Network Perspective

As the Swedish MNEs grew and matured, so did the nature of their international involvement. Today, each MNE is perceived as being a member of an *international network*, with nodes based in each of the foreign subsidiaries, as well as the parent firm itself.[12] Centralized (hierarchical) control has given way to decentralized (heterarchical) control.[13] Foreign subsidiaries compete with each other, and the parent, for expanded resource commitments, thus influencing the strategy and reinvestment decisions. Many of these MNEs have become political coalitions with competing internal and external networks. Each subsidiary (and the parent) is embedded in its host country's network of suppliers and customers. It is also a member of a worldwide network based on its industry. Finally, it is a member of an organizational network under the nominal control of the parent firm. Complicating matters still further is the possibility that the parent itself may have evolved into a *transnational firm*, i.e., one that is owned by a coalition of investors located in different countries.

Asea Brown Boveri (ABB) is an example of a Swedish-Swiss firm that has passed through the international evolutionary process all the way to being a transnational firm. ABB was formed through a merger of Sweden-based ASEA and Switzerland-based Brown Boveri in 1991. Both firms were already dominant players internationally in the electrotechnical and engineering industries. ABB has literally hundreds of foreign subsidiaries that are managed on a very decentralized basis. ABB's "flat" organization structure and transnational ownership encourage local initiative, quick response, and decentralized FDI decisions. Although overall strategic direction is the legal responsibility of the parent firm, foreign subsidiaries play a major role in all decision-making. Their input in turn is strongly influenced by their own membership in their local and worldwide industry networks.

HOW TO INVEST ABROAD: MODES OF FOREIGN INVOLVEMENT

So far the analysis has concentrated on success characteristics and where to establish majority-owned FDI subsidiaries abroad. However, there are several alternative modes of foreign involvement (mergers and acquisitions are treated separately in Chapter 15). The main choices are:

1. Entering a joint venture with one or more local partners
2. Forming one or more strategic alliances

3. Licensing a foreign firm

4. Undertaking a management contract for a foreign firm.

5. Doing traditional exporting

)))) Joint Venture

A joint venture between a MNE and a host country partner is a viable strategy if, and only if, the MNE finds the right local partner. Some of the obvious advantages of having a compatible local partner are as follows:

1. The local partner understands the customs, mores, and institutions of the local environment. This understanding might take years for a MNE to acquire on its own with a 100%-owned greenfield subsidiary.

2. The local partner can provide competent management, not just at the top but also with respect to middle management.

3. If the host country requires that foreign firms share ownership with local firms or investors, 100% foreign ownership is not a realistic alternative to a joint venture.

4. The local partner's contacts and reputation enhance access to the host country's capital markets.

5. The local partner may possess technology that is appropriate for the local environment or perhaps can be used worldwide.

6. The public image of a firm that is partially locally owned may improve its sales possibilities if the purpose of the investment is to serve the local market.

Despite this impressive list of advantages, joint ventures are not as common as foreign subsidiaries that are 100%-owned by a MNE because MNEs fear interference by the local partner in certain critical decision areas. Indeed, what is optimal from the viewpoint of the local venture may be suboptimal for the multinational operation as a whole. The most important potential conflicts are these:

1. Political risk is increased rather than reduced if the wrong partner is chosen. Imagine the standing of joint ventures undertaken with the family or associates of Suharto in Indonesia or Ferdinand Marcos in the Philippines just before their fall from power. The local partner must be credible and ethical, or the venture is worse off for being a joint venture.

2. Local and foreign partners may have divergent views about the need for cash dividends, or about the desirability of growth financed from retained earnings versus new financing.

3. Transfer pricing on products or components bought from or sold to related companies creates a potential for conflict of interest.

4. Control of financing is another problem area. A MNE cannot justify its use of cheap or available funds raised in one country to finance joint venture operations in another country.

5. Ability of a firm to rationalize production on a worldwide basis can be jeopardized.

6. Financial disclosure of local results might be necessary with locally traded shares, whereas if the firm is wholly owned from abroad, such disclosure is not needed. Disclosure gives nondisclosing competitors an advantage in setting strategy.

7. Valuation of equity shares is difficult. How much should the local partner pay for its share? What is the value of contributed technology, or of contributed land in a country like China where all land is state owned? It is highly unlikely that foreign and host country partners have similar opportunity costs of capital, expectations about the required rate of return, or similar perceptions of appropriate premiums for business, foreign exchange, and political risks. Insofar as the venture is a component of the portfolio of each investor, its contribution to portfolio return and variance may be quite different between them.

))) Strategic Alliances

Strategic alliances are currently in vogue. The definition of strategic alliance is unclear because it connotes different meanings to different observers. In one form of cross-border strategic alliance, two firms exchange a share of ownership with one another. This was the case for the Bang & Olufsen and Philips strategic alliance described in Chapter 11. A strategic alliance can be a takeover defense if the prime purpose is for a firm to place some of its stock in stable and friendly hands. If that is all that occurs, it is just another form of portfolio investment.

In a more comprehensive strategic alliance, in addition to exchanging stock, the partners establish a separate joint venture to develop and manufacture a product or service. Numerous examples of such strategic alliances can be found in the automotive, electronics, telecommunications, and aircraft industries. Such alliances are particularly suited to high-tech products where the cost of research and development is high and timely introduction of improvements is important.

A third level of cooperation might involve joint marketing and servicing agreements wherein each partner represents the other in certain markets. Some observers believe such arrangements begin to resemble the cartels that were prevalent in the 1920s and 1930s. Because they reduce competition, cartels have been banned by international agreements and many national laws.

It remains to be seen whether the current wave of strategic alliances with and between partners in the European Union are stable and durable. It seems as if most firms feel they should be treating the EU internal market as if it were a United States of Europe. Strategic alliances are a quick way to get EU-wide coverage. This is particularly attractive to firms that have historically served the EU markets through exports, licensing, or minor FDI in assembly and service facilities. Specifically, firms located in Norway, Israel, and Switzerland are feeling the pressure to become "insiders." Strategic alliances with EU partners have also been popular with firms from the United States, Japan, Canada, and Australia. After the euphoria associated with the internal market wears off, it is possible many of these hurried strategic alliances will be dissolved and replaced in a more deliberate manner by traditional types of FDI.

)))) Licensing and Management Contracts as Alternatives to Foreign Direct Investment

In recent years a number of host countries have demanded that MNEs sell their services in "unbundled form" rather than only through FDI. For instance, host countries would like to purchase managerial expertise and knowledge of product and factor markets through management contracts, and they would like to gain technology through licensing agreements.

Licensing is a popular method for domestic firms to profit from foreign markets without the need to commit sizable funds. Since typically the foreign producer is wholly locally owned, political risk is minimized.

The main disadvantage of licensing is that license fees are likely to be lower than FDI profits, although the return on the marginal investment might be higher. Other disadvantages include possible loss of quality control, establishment of a potential competitor in third-country markets, possible improvement of the technology by the local licensee (which then enters the original firm's home market), and possible loss of opportunity to enter the licensee's market with FDI later. Yet another disadvantage is the risk the technology will be stolen. Finally, agency costs are likely to be high.

MNEs have not typically used licensing of independent firms. On the contrary, most licensing arrangements have been with their own foreign affiliates or joint ventures. License fees have been a way to spread the corporate research and development cost among all operating units and a means of repatriating profits in a form typically more acceptable to some host countries than dividends.

Management contracts are similar to licensing insofar as they provide for some cash flow from a foreign source without significant foreign investment or exposure. Management contracts probably lessen political risk because it is easy to repatriate the managers. International consulting and engineering firms have traditionally conducted their foreign business on the basis of a management contract.

Whether licensing and management contracts are cost-effective compared to FDI depends on the price host countries are willing to pay for the unbundled services. If the price were high enough, many firms would prefer to take advantage of market imperfections in an unbundled way, particularly in view of the lower political, foreign exchange, and business risks. Since we observe MNEs continuing to prefer FDI, we must assume that the price for selling unbundled services is still too low.

Why is the price of unbundled services too low? The answer may lie in the synergy created when services are bundled as FDI in the first place. Managerial expertise is often dependent on a delicate mix of organizational support factors that cannot be transferred abroad efficiently. Technology is a continuous process, but licensing usually captures only the technology at a particular point in time. Most important of all, however, economies of scale cannot be sold or transferred in small bundles. By definition they require large-scale operations. How can even a relatively large operation in a small market achieve the same economies of scale as a large operation in a large market?

Despite the handicaps, some MNEs have successfully sold unbundled services, such as managerial expertise and technology to the OPEC countries. In this case, however, the Organization of Petroleum Export Countries (OPEC) are both willing and able to pay a price high enough to approach the returns on FDI (bundled services) while receiving only the lesser benefits of the unbundled services.

))) Exporting

Domestic firms usually start any foreign involvement with traditional exports through domestic or foreign sales agents and distributors. As the export business grows, the next step might be to establish foreign sales offices and eventually sales branches or subsidiaries. Depending on the importance of their foreign business relative to their domestic business, many firms are quite satisfied to continue as exporters rather than become involved with other modes of servicing their foreign markets.

There are several advantages to limiting a firm's activities to exports. It avoids the unique risks facing FDI, joint ventures, strategic alliances, and licensing. Political risks are minimal. Agency costs, such as monitoring and evaluating foreign units, are avoided. However, foreign exchange risks still exist. The amount of front-end investment is typically lower than in other modes of foreign involvement.

There are also disadvantages. A firm is not able to internalize and exploit the results of its research and development as effectively as in FDI. The firm also risks losing markets to imitators and global competitors that might be more cost efficient in production abroad and distribution. As these firms capture foreign markets, they might become so strong that they can export back into the domestic exporter's own market. Remember that defensive FDI is often motivated by the need to prevent this kind of predatory behavior as well as to preempt foreign markets before competitors can get started.

POLITICAL RISK MANAGEMENT

The best approach to political risk management is to anticipate problems and negotiate understandings ahead of time. Different cultures apply different ethics to the question of honoring prior "contracts," especially when they were negotiated with a previous administration. Nevertheless, pre-negotiation of all conceivable areas of conflict provides a better basis for a successful future for both parties than does overlooking the possibility that divergent objectives will evolve over time.

))) Negotiating Investment Agreements

An *investment agreement* spells out specific rights and responsibilities of both the foreign firm and the host government. The presence of MNEs is as often sought by development-seeking host governments as is a particular foreign location sought by a MNE. All parties have alternatives, so bargaining is appropriate.

An investment agreement should spell out policies on financial and managerial issues, including the following:

- The basis on which fund flows, such as dividends, management fees, royalties, patent fees, and loan repayments, may be remitted
- The basis for setting transfer prices
- The right to export to third-country markets
- Obligations to build, or fund, social and economic overhead projects, such as schools, hospitals, and retirement systems
- Methods of taxation, including the rate, the type of taxation, and how the rate base is determined
- Access to host-country capital markets, particularly for long-term borrowing
- Permission for 100% foreign ownership versus required local ownership (joint venture) participation
- Price controls, if any, applicable to sales in the host-country markets
- Requirements for local sourcing versus import of raw materials and components
- Permission to use expatriate managerial and technical personnel, and to bring them and their personal possessions into the country free of exorbitant charges or import duties
- Provision for arbitration of disputes
- Provisions for planned divestment, should such be required, indicating how the going concern will be valued and to whom it will be sold

))) Investment Insurance and Guarantees: OPIC

MNEs can sometimes transfer political risk to a home-country public agency through an investment insurance and guarantee program. Many developed countries have such programs to protect investments made by their nationals in developing countries.

The U.S. investment insurance and guarantee program is managed by the government-owned Overseas Private Investment Corporation (OPIC), organized in 1969 to replace earlier programs. OPIC's stated purpose is to mobilize and facilitate the participation of U.S. private capital and skills in the economic and social progress of less-developed friendly countries and areas, thereby complementing the developmental assistance of the United States. OPIC offers insurance coverage for four separate types of political risk, which have their own specific definitions for insurance purposes:

- *Inconvertibility* is the risk that the investor will not be able to convert profits, royalties, fees, or other income, as well as the original capital invested, into dollars.

- *Expropriation* is the risk that the host government takes a specific step that for one year prevents the investor or the foreign affiliate from exercising effective control over use of the property.

- *War, revolution, insurrection, and civil strife* coverage applies primarily to the damage of physical property of the insured, although in some cases inability of a foreign affiliate to repay a loan because of a war may be covered.

- *Business income* coverage provides compensation for loss of business income resulting from events of political violence that directly cause damage to the assets of a foreign enterprise.

Operating Strategies after the FDI Decision

Although an investment agreement creates obligations on the part of both foreign investor and host government, conditions change and agreements are often revised in the light of such changes. The changed conditions may be economic, or they may be the result of political changes within the host government. The firm that sticks rigidly to the legal interpretation of its original agreement may well find that the host government first applies pressure in areas not covered by the agreement and then possibly reinterprets the agreement to conform to the political reality of that country. Most MNEs, in their own self-interest, follow a policy of adapting to changing host-country priorities whenever possible.

The essence of such adaptation is anticipating host-country priorities and making the activities of the firm of continued value to the host country. Such an approach assumes the host government acts rationally in seeking its country's self-interest and is based on the idea that the firm should initiate reductions in goal conflict. Future bargaining position can be enhanced by careful consideration of policies in production and logistics, marketing, finance, organization, and personnel.

Local Sourcing. Host governments may require foreign firms to purchase raw material and components locally as a way to maximize value-added benefits and to increase local employment. From the viewpoint of the foreign firm trying to adapt to host-country goals, local sourcing reduces political risk, albeit at a trade-off with other factors. Local strikes or other turmoil may shut down the operation, and such issues as quality control, high local prices because of lack of economies of scale, and unreliable delivery schedules become important. Often the foreign firm acquires lower political risk only by increasing financial and commercial risk.

Facility Location. Production facilities may be located so as to minimize risk. The natural location of different stages of production may be resource-oriented, footloose, or market-oriented. Oil, for instance, is drilled in and around the Persian Gulf, Russia, Venezuela, and Indonesia. No choice exists for where this activity takes place. Refining is footloose; a refining facility can easily be moved to another location or country. Whenever possible, oil companies have built refineries in politically safe countries, such as Western Europe or small islands (such as Singapore or Curacao), even though costs might be reduced by refining nearer the oil fields. They have traded off reduced political risk and financial exposure for possibly higher transportation and refining costs.

Control of Transportation. Control of transportation has been an important way to reduce political risk. Oil pipelines that cross national frontiers, oil tankers, ore carriers, refrigerated ships, and railroads have all been controlled at times to influence the bargaining power of both nations and companies.

Control of Technology. Control of key patents and processes is a viable way to reduce political risk. If a host country cannot operate a plant because it does not have technicians capable of running the process or of keeping up with changed technology, abrogation of an investment agreement with a foreign firm is unlikely. Control of technology works best when the foreign firm is steadily improving its technology.

Control of Markets. Control of markets is a common strategy to enhance a firm's bargaining position. As effective as the OPEC cartel was in raising the price received for crude oil by its member countries in the 1970s, marketing was still controlled by the international oil companies. OPEC's need of the oil companies limited the degree to which its members could dictate terms. In more recent years, OPEC members have established some marketing outlets of their own, such as Kuwait's extensive chain of Q8 gas stations in Europe.

Control of export markets for manufactured goods is also a source of leverage in dealings between foreign-owned firms and host governments. The MNE would prefer to serve world markets from sources of its own choosing, basing the decision on considerations of production cost, transportation, tariff barriers, political risk exposure, and competition. The selling pattern that maximizes long-run profits from the overall viewpoint of the worldwide firm rarely maximizes exports, or value added, from the perspective of the host countries. Some will argue that if the same plants were owned by local nationals and were not part of a worldwide integrated system, more goods would be exported by the host country. The contrary argument is that self-standing local firms might never obtain foreign market share because they lack economies of scale on the production side and are unable to market in foreign countries.

Brand Name and Trademark Control. Control of a brand name or trademark can have an effect almost identical to that of controlling technology. It gives the MNE a monopoly on something that may or may not have substantive value but quite likely represents value in the eyes of consumers. Ability to produce for and market under a world brand name is valuable for local firms and thus represents an important bargaining attribute for maintaining an investment position.

Thin Equity Base. Foreign affiliates can be financed with a thin equity base and a large proportion of local debt. If the debt is borrowed from locally owned banks, host government actions that weaken the financial viability of the firm also endanger local creditors.

Multiple-source Borrowing. If the firm must finance with foreign source debt, it may borrow from banks in a number of countries rather than just from home-country banks. If, for example, debt is owed to banks in Tokyo, Frankfurt, London, and New York, nationals in a number of foreign countries have a vested interest in keeping the borrowing affiliate financially strong. If the multinational is U.S. owned, a fallout between the United States and the host government is less likely to cause the local government to move against the firm if it also owes funds to these other countries.

SUMMARY

- In order to invest abroad, a firm must have a sustainable *competitive advantage* in the home market. This must be strong enough and transferable enough to overcome the disadvantages of operating abroad.

- Competitive advantages stem from economies of scale and scope arising from large size, managerial and marketing expertise, superior technology, financial strength, differentiated products, and competitiveness of the home market.

- The *OLI paradigm* is an attempt to create an overall framework to explain why MNEs choose FDI rather than serve foreign markets through alternative modes, such as licensing, joint ventures, strategic alliances, management contracts, and exporting.

- The theory of *internalization* holds that firms having a competitive advantage because of their ability to generate valuable proprietary information can capture the full benefits of innovation only through FDI.

- The decision about where to invest is influenced by economic and behavioral factors, as well as the stage of a firm's historical development.

- Behavioral studies show that the FDI decision is often motivated by a strong stimulus from the external environment, or from within an organization on the basis of personal biases, needs, and commitments of individuals and groups. The investigation process itself, particularly the choice of projects to be investigated, is a major determinant of the FDI decision.

- *Psychic distance* plays a role in determining the sequence of FDI and later reinvestment. As firms learn from their early investments, they venture further afield and are willing to risk larger commitments.

- Alternative (to 100%-owned foreign subsidiaries) modes of foreign involvement exist. They include joint venture, strategic alliances, licensing, management contracts, and traditional exporting.

- The success of a joint venture depends primarily on the right choice of a partner. For this reason and because of a number of issues related to possible conflicts in decision making between a joint venture and a multinational parent, the 100%-owned foreign subsidiary approach is most common. Joint venture is not as popular as other modes of foreign investment.

- The completion of the European Internal Market at end-of-year 1992 induced a surge in cross-border entry through strategic alliances. Although some forms of strategic alliances share the same characteristics as joint ventures, they often also include an exchange of stock.

- Licensing enables a firm to profit from foreign markets without a major front-end investment. However, disadvantages include limited returns, possible loss of quality control, and potential of establishing a future competitor.

- Exporting avoids political risk but not foreign exchange risk. It requires the least upfront investment, but the firm might eventually lose markets to imitators and global competitors that might be more cost-efficient in production abroad and distribution.

- The best approach to political risk management is to anticipate problems and negotiate understandings ahead of time.

- An investment agreement prior to entry details specific rights and responsibilities of both the foreign firm and the host government.

- In some countries MNEs can purchase political risk insurance through investment insurance and guarantee programs. In the United States this is available through the OPIC.

- Political risk can also be reduced by the choice of operating strategies after the FDI is started.

- Operating strategies include the location of facilities, control of transportation and distribution, control of the technology, control of markets, control of brand name and trademark, and using a thin equity base with heavy local borrowing (or multiple source borrowing).

QUESTIONS

1. Daimler-Chrysler Merger
In 1998 Chrysler Corporation of the United States and Daimler-Benz of Germany announced a merger of their two firms. Evaluate whether or not the following theoretical synergies from a merger apply to Daimler-Chrysler:

a. Greater economies of scale than previously existed

b. A pooling of managerial and marketing expertise that would improve their efficiency and effectiveness

c. A combination of research capability and superior technology such that, joined together, the new firm will possess a competitive advantage

d. Greater financial strength due to the increase in size and established home location in both Europe and the United States

e. Ability to sell more cars together than had been possible as two separate companies, due to differentiated products from each of the firms

2. Japanese Property Investments in the United States

In the late 1980s and early 1990s, many Japanese financial institutions and firms from a variety of industries invested in U.S. real estate such as hotels, office buildings, and golf courses. Such property was cheap in Japanese eyes, relative to comparable properties in Japan. Did these foreign investments by large Japanese firms fit into the competitive advantage categories suggested at the beginning of this chapter? What do you suppose was the driving force behind such investments?

3. Pequot Indians and Foxwood High-Stakes Bingo and Casino

Firms often find it difficult to find capital for new and riskier investments. In 1992 the Pequot Indians of Ledyard, Connecticut (U.S.) wished to build and operate a casino on their reservation but could not find the necessary capital. After an extended search, a joint-venture agreement was concluded with the Gentry Group, a Malaysian conglomerate with casino and gaming industry experience in the highland casinos of Malaysia. The result was formation of the Foxwood High-Stakes Bingo and Casino.

Why would an international joint-venture partner, such as the Malaysian investment group in this case, see the investment returns differently from a similar U.S.-based venture-capital group?

4. Management Contracts versus Foreign Direct Investment

What are the relative merits of management contracts compared with foreign direct investments? Answer this question both from the perspective of a host country and from the perspective of a firm that has the management contract.

5. Joint Ventures

What are the advantages and disadvantages of joint ventures from the viewpoint of each of the following?

a. A multinational firm
b. A local joint-venture partner
c. The host country

6. Licensing versus Foreign Direct Investment

Compare licensing to foreign direct investment from the viewpoint of:

a. The licensor (multinational firm)

b. The licensee (host country firm)

c. The host country

7. Strategy in the Service Industries

Most service industries, such as accounting, law, advertising, consulting, and banking, have become multinational. What motivates these industries to establish offices abroad? What theories apply?

WORLD WIDE WEB EXERCISES

W1. International Capital Flows: Public and Private

Major multinational organizations (some of which are listed below) attempt to track the relative movements and magnitudes of global capital investment. Using these web pages and others you may find, prepare a two-page executive briefing on the question of whether capital generated in the industrialized countries is finding its way to the less-developed and emerging markets. Is there some critical distinction between "less-developed" and "emerging?"

The World Bank	http://www.worldbank.org/
OECD	http://www.oecd.org/
European Bank for Reconstruction	http://www.ebrd.org/

W2. Overseas Private Investment Corporation

The Overseas Private Investment Corporation (OPIC) provides long-term political risk insurance and limited-recourse project-financing aid to U.S.-based firms investing abroad. Using the organization's web page, answer the following questions:

a. Exactly what types of risk will OPIC insure against?

b. What financial limits and restrictions are there on this insurance protection?

c. How should a project be structured to aid in its approval for OPIC coverage?

Overseas Private Investment Corp	http://www.opic.gov/

W3. International Management and Strategy Consultancies

The management consulting industry has been one of the primary resources utilized by MNEs throughout the world in the 1990s to design and develop their corporate strategies. The web pages of the following firms provide some insight into the industry, the job opportunities available for professionals in consulting, as well as some interesting features such as the Boston Consulting Group's online interactive case study.

A.T. Kearney	http://www.atkearney.com/
Bain and Company	http://www.bain.com/
Booze, Allen & Hamilton	http://www.bah.com/
Boston Consulting Group	http://www.bcg.com/
McKinsey & Company	http://www.mckinsey.com/

SUGGESTED READINGS

Buckley, Peter J., "The Limits of Explanation: Testing the Internalization Theory of the Multinational Enterprise," *Journal of International Business Studies*, Summer 1988, pp. 181–193.

Dunning, John H., "Location and the Multinational Enterprise: A Neglected Factor?," *Journal of International Business Studies*, Vol. 29, No. 1, First Quarter 1998, pp. 45–66.

Dunning, John H., "The Eclectic Paradigm of International Production: A Restatement and Some Possible Extensions," *Journal of International Business Studies*, Spring 1988, pp. 1–32.

Mishara, Chandra S. and David H. Gobeli, "Managerial Incentives, Internalization, and Market Valuation of Multinational Firms, "*Journal of International Business Studies*, Vol. 29, No. 3, Third Quarter 1998, pp. 583–598.

Wells, Louis T., Jr., "Multinationals and the Developing Countries," *Journal of International Business Studies*, Vol. 29, No. 1, First Quarter, 1998, pp. 101–114.

NOTES

1. *Comparative advantage* was the original cornerstone of international trade theory. It explained the relative competitiveness of nations with respect to trade. It is still a relevant theory to help explain why particular countries are most suitable for FDI by MNEs, especially with respect to location of rationalized production, service, and research and development facilities. An explanation of comparative advantage can be found in any economics or international economics textbook.
2. Gruber, Mehta, and Vernon (1967), Hirsch (1967), and Hirsch (1973).
3. Caves (1971), and Vernon (1966).
4. Porter (1990).
5. The OLI paradigm and theory of internalization has its origins in transactions cost theory, which was first introduced by Coase (1937). The theory was further developed by Williamson (1975) and (1985). Its international dimension was first developed by Buckley and Casson (1976) and Dunning (1977).
6. For a good summary of locational factors, see Dunning (1998).
7. Rugman (1980).
8. Dunning (1988).
9. Simon (1963).
10. Aharoni (1966).
11. The internationalization process theory was first introduced by two Swedish scholars, Johansen and Weidersheim-Paul (1975), and further developed by Johansen and Vahlne (1977).
12. An excellent explanation of network theory as applied to multinational firms, written by one of its Swedish pioneers, can be found in Forsgren (1989).
13. Heterarchical control systems of multinational firms was first described by Hedlund (1994).

CHAPTER 14

MULTINATIONAL CAPITAL BUDGETING

This chapter describes in detail the issues and principles related to the buying and selling of real productive assets in foreign countries, generally referred to as *multinational capital budgeting*.

Although the original decision to undertake an investment in a particular foreign country may be determined by a mix of strategic, behavioral, and economic decisions, the specific project, as well as all reinvestment decisions, should be justified by traditional financial analysis. For example, a production efficiency opportunity may exist for a U.S. firm to invest abroad, but the type of plant, mix of labor and capital, kinds of equipment, method of financing, and other project variables must be analyzed within the traditional financial framework of discounted cash flows. Consideration must also be given to the impact of the proposed foreign project on consolidated net earnings, cash flows from affiliates in other countries, and the market value of the parent firm.

Multinational capital budgeting, like traditional domestic capital budgeting, focuses on the cash inflows and outflows associated with prospective long-term investment projects. Multinational capital budgeting techniques are used in traditional FDI analysis, such as for the construction of a manufacturing plant in another country, as well as in the growing field of international mergers and acquisitions.

Capital budgeting for a foreign project uses the same theoretical framework as domestic capital budgeting—with a few very important differences. The basic steps are as follows:

1. Identify the initial capital invested or put at risk.
2. Estimate the cash flows to be derived from the project over time, including an estimate of the terminal or salvage value of the investment.
3. Identify the appropriate discount rate for determining the present value of the expected cash flows.

4. Apply traditional capital budgeting decision criteria such as net present value (NPV) and internal rate of return (IRR) to determine the acceptability of or priority ranking of potential projects.

FOREIGN COMPLEXITIES

Capital budgeting for a foreign project is nevertheless considerably more complex than the domestic case. Several factors contribute to this greater complexity.

- Parent cash flows must be distinguished from project cash flows. Each of these two types of flows contributes to a different view of value.

- Parent cash flows often depend on the form of financing. Thus, cash flows cannot be clearly separated from financing decisions, as is done in domestic capital budgeting.

- Additional cash flows generated by a new investment in one foreign affiliate may be in part or in whole taken away from another affiliate, with the net result that the project is favorable from a single affiliate's point of view but contributes nothing to worldwide cash flows.

- Remittance of funds to the parent must be explicitly recognized because of differing tax systems, legal and political constraints on the movement of funds, local business norms, and differences in the way financial markets and institutions function.

- Cash flows from affiliates to the parent can be generated by an array of nonfinancial payments, including payment of license fees and payments for imports from the parent.

- Differing rates of national inflation must be anticipated because of their potential to cause changes in competitive position, and thus changes in cash flows over a period of time.

- The possibility of unanticipated foreign exchange rate changes must be kept in mind because of possible direct effects on the value to the parent of local cash flows, as well as indirect effects on the competitive position of the foreign affiliate.

- Use of segmented national capital markets may create an opportunity for financial gains or may lead to additional financial costs.

- Use of host-government subsidized loans complicates both capital structure and the ability to determine an appropriate weighted-average cost of capital for discounting purposes.

- Political risk must be evaluated because political events can drastically reduce the value or availability of expected cash flows.

- Terminal value is more difficult to estimate because potential purchasers from the host, parent, or third countries, or from the private or public sector, may have widely divergent perspectives on the value to them of acquiring the project.

Since the same theoretical capital budgeting framework is used to choose among competing foreign and domestic projects, a common standard is critical. Thus, all foreign complexities must be quantified as modifications to either expected cash flow or the rate of discount. Although in practice many firms make such modifications arbitrarily, readily available information, theoretical deduction, or just plain common sense can be used to make less arbitrary and more reasonable choices.

))) Project versus Parent Valuation

A strong theoretical argument exists in favor of analyzing any foreign project from the viewpoint of the parent. Cash flows to the parent are ultimately the basis for dividends to stockholders, reinvestment elsewhere in the world, repayment of corporate-wide debt, and other purposes that affect the firm's many interest groups. However, since most of a project's cash flows to its parent, or to sister affiliates, are financial cash flows rather than operating cash flows, the parent viewpoint usually violates a cardinal concept of capital budgeting, namely, that financial cash flows should not be mixed with operating cash flows. Often the difference is not important because the two are almost identical, but in some instances a sharp divergence in these cash flows will exist. For example, funds that are permanently blocked from repatriation, or "forcibly reinvested," are not available for dividends to the parent company stockholders or for repayment of parent corporate debt. Therefore, shareholders will not perceive the blocked earnings as contributing to the value of the firm, and creditors of the parent company will not count on them in calculating interest coverage ratios and other evidence of ability to service debt.

Evaluation of a project from the local viewpoint serves some useful purposes but should be subordinated to evaluation from the parent's viewpoint. In evaluating a foreign project's performance relative to the potential of a competing project in the same host country, we must pay attention to the project's local return. Almost any project should at least be able to earn a cash return equal to the yield available on host government bonds with a maturity the same as the project's economic life, if a free market exists for such bonds. Host government bonds ordinarily reflect the local risk-free rate of return, including a premium equal to the expected rate of inflation. If a project cannot earn more than such a bond yield, the parent firm should buy host government bonds rather than invest in a riskier project—or, better yet, invest somewhere else!

If the theory of FDI is correct, multinational firms should invest only if they can earn a risk-adjusted return greater than local-based competitors can earn on the same project. If they are unable to earn superior returns on foreign projects, their stockholders would be better off buying shares in local firms, where possible, and letting those companies carry out the local projects.[1]

The attention paid to project returns in the various survey results probably reflects emphasis on maximizing reported consolidated net earnings per share as a corporate financial goal. As long as foreign earnings are not blocked, they can be consolidated with the earnings of both the remaining affiliates and the parent.[2] Even in the case of temporarily blocked funds, some of the most mature multinational firms do not necessarily eliminate a project from financial consideration. They take a very long-run view of world business opportunities.

If reinvestment opportunities in the country where funds are blocked are at least equal to the parent firm's required rate of return (after adjusting for anticipated exchange rate changes), temporary blockage of transfer may have little practical effect on the capital budgeting outcome because future project cash flows will be increased by the returns on forced reinvestment. Since large multinationals hold a portfolio of domestic and foreign projects, corporate liquidity is not impaired if a few projects have blocked funds; alternate sources of funds are available to meet all planned uses of funds. Furthermore, a long-run historical perspective on blocked funds does indeed lend support to the belief that funds are almost never permanently blocked. However, waiting for the release of such funds can be frustrating, and sometimes the blocked funds lose value because of inflation or unexpected exchange rate deterioration while blocked, even though they have been reinvested in the host country to protect at least part of their value in real terms.

In conclusion, most firms appear to evaluate foreign projects from both parent and project viewpoints. The parent's viewpoint gives results closer to the traditional meaning of net present value in capital budgeting. Project valuation provides a closer approximation of the effect on consolidated earnings per share, which all surveys indicate is of major concern to practicing managers. To illustrate the foreign complexities of multinational capital budgeting, we analyze a hypothetical market-seeking foreign direct investment by Cemex in Indonesia.

ILLUSTRATIVE CASE

Cemex (A)

It is early in 1998. Cementos Mexicanos, Cemex, is considering the construction of a cement manufacturing facility on the Indonesian island of Sumatra. The project, Semen Indonesia,[3] would be a wholly owned greenfield investment with a total installed capacity of 20 million metric tonnes per year (mmt/y). Although large by Asian production standards, Cemex believes that its latest cement manufacturing technology would be most efficiently utilized with a production facility of this scale.

Cemex has three driving reasons for the project: (1) the firm wishes to initiate a productive presence of its own in Southeast Asia, a relatively new market for Cemex; (2) the long-term prospects for Asian infrastructure development and growth appear very good over the longer term; and (3) there are positive prospects for Indonesia to act as a produce-for-export site as a result of the fall of the Indonesian rupiah (Rp) from 1997 to 1998.

Cemex, as the world's third-largest cement manufacturer, is a MNE headquartered in an emerging market but competing in a global arena. The firm competes in the global marketplace for both market share and capital. The international cement markets, similar to markets in commodities like oil, is a dollar-based market. For this reason, and for comparisons against its major competitors in both Germany and Switzerland, Cemex considers the U.S. dollar as its functional currency.

Cemex's shares are listed in both Mexico City and New York (OTC: CMXSY). The firm has successfully raised capital—both debt and equity—outside Mexico in U.S. dollars. Its investor base is increasingly global, with the U.S. share turnover rising rapidly as a percentage of total trading. As a result, its cost and availability of capital is internationalized and dominated by U.S. dollar investors. Ultimately, the Semen Indonesia project will be evaluated—in both cash flows and capital cost—in U.S. dollars.

Overview

A road-map of the complete multinational capital budgeting analysis for Cemex in Indonesia is illustrated in Exhibit 14.1. The basic principle is that, starting at the top-left, the parent company invests U.S. dollar-denominated capital, which in turn flows clockwise through the creation and operation of an Indonesian subsidiary, which then generates cash flows that are eventually returned in a variety of forms to the parent company—in U.S. dollars. The first step is to construct a set of pro forma financial statements for Semen Indonesia, all in Indonesian rupiah (Rp). The next step is to create two capital budgets, the *project viewpoint* and *parent viewpoint*.

Only one year will be required to build the physical plant and prepare for operations. Actual business operations will commence in year 1. The Indonesian government has only recently deregulated the heavier industries to allow foreign ownership. The following analysis is conducted assuming that purchasing power parity (PPP) holds for the Rp/US$ exchange rate for the life of the Indonesian project. This is a standard financial assumption made by Cemex for its foreign investments.[4] The projected inflation rates for Indonesia and the United States are 30% per annum and 3% per annum, respectively.

Financial Assumptions

The following series of financial statements is based on these assumptions.

Capital Investment. Although the cost of building new cement manufacturing capacity anywhere in the industrial countries is now estimated at roughly $150/tonne of installed capacity, Cemex believed that it could build

Exhibit 14.1   *A Road-Map to the Construction of Semen Indonesia's Capital Budget*

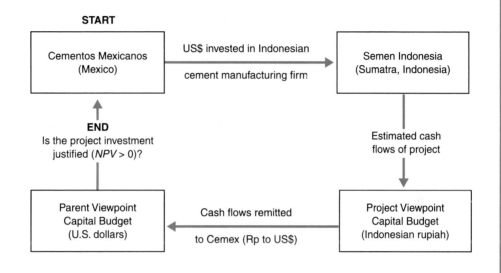

a state-of-the-art production and shipment facility on the island of Sumatra at roughly $110 per tonne (see Exhibit 14.2). Assuming a 20 mmt/y capacity and a year-0 average exchange rate of Rp10,000/$, this cost still constitutes an investment of Rp22 trillion or U.S. $2.2 billion. It would include an investment of Rp17.6 trillion in plant and equipment, giving rise to an annual depreciation charge of Rp1.76 trillion if we assume a 10-year straight-line depreciation schedule. The relatively short depreciation schedule is one of the policies of the Indonesian tax authorities meant to attract foreign investment.

Financing. This massive investment would be financed with 50% equity, all from Cemex, and 50% debt, 75% from Cemex and 25% from a bank consortium arranged by the Indonesian government. Cemex's own U.S. dollar-based weighted-average cost of capital (WACC) was currently estimated at 11.98%. The WACC on a local Indonesian level in rupiah terms, for the project itself, was estimated at 33.257%.[5]

The explicit debt structures, including repayment schedules, are presented in Exhibit 14.3. The loan arranged by the Indonesian government, part of the government's economic development incentive program, is an eight-year loan, in rupiah, at 35% per annum interest, fully amortizing. The interest payments are fully deductible against corporate tax liabilities.

The majority of the debt, however, is being provided by the parent company, Cemex. After raising the capital from its financing subsidiary,

Exhibit 14.2	*Investment and Financing of the Semen Indonesia Project (all values in 000S unless otherwise noted)*

INVESTMENT		FINANCING	
Average exchange rate, Rp/$	10,000	Equity	Rp 11,000,000,000
Cost of installed capacity, $/tonne	$110	Debt	
Installed capacity	20,000	Rupiah debt	2,750,000,000
Investment in US$	$2,200,000	US$ debt, Rp	8,250,000,000
Investment in rupiah	22,000,000,000	Total	Rp 22,000,000,000
Plant and equipment, Rp	17,600,000,000		
Annual depreciation, Rp	1,760,000,000		

COSTS OF CAPITAL: CEMEX

Risk-free rate	6.000%	Cemex beta	1.500
Credit premium	2.000%	Equity risk premium	7.000%
Cost of debt	8.000%	Cost of equity	16.500%
Cost of debt, after tax	5.200%	Percent equity	60%
Percent debt	40%	WACC	11.980%

COSTS OF CAPITAL: SEMEN INDONESIA

Risk-free rate	33.000%	Semen Indonesia beta	1.000
Credit premium	2.000%	Equity risk premium	6.000%
Cost of rupiah debt	35.000%	Cost of equity	40.000%
Cost of debt, after tax	24.500%	Percent equity	50%
Cost of US$ debt	38.835%		
Cost of US$ debt, after tax	27.184%		
Percent debt	50%	WACC	33.257%

Assumes corporate income tax rates of 35% and 30% in Mexico and Indonesia, respectively. The cost of the US$ loan is stated in rupiah terms assuming purchasing power parity and U.S. dollar and Indonesian rupiah inflation rates of 3% and 30%, respectively, throughout the subject period.

Cemex will relend the capital to Semen Indonesia. The loan is denominated in U.S. dollars, five years maturity, with an annual interest rate of 10%. Because the debt will have to be repaid from the rupiah earnings of the Indonesian enterprise, the pro forma financial statements are constructed so that the expected costs of servicing the dollar debt are included in the firm's pro forma income statement. The dollar loan, if the rupiah follows the purchasing power parity forecast, will have an effective interest expense in rupiah terms of 38.835%. This is found by determining the internal rate of return of repaying the dollar loan in full in rupiah (see Exhibit 14.3).

Revenues. Given the current existing cement manufacturing in Indonesia, and its currently depressed state as a result of the Asian crisis, all sales are based on export. The 20 mmt/y facility is expected to operate at only 40% capacity (producing 8 million metric tonnes). Cement produced will be sold in the export market at $58/tonne (delivered). Note also that, at least for the conservative baseline analysis, no increase in the price received over time is assumed.

Exhibit 14.3	*Semen Indonesia's Debt Service Schedules and Foreign Exchange Gains/Losses (millions of Rp and US$)*					

Spot rate (Rp/$)	10,000	12,621	15,930	20,106	25,376	32,028
Project year	**0**	**1**	**2**	**3**	**4**	**5**
Indonesian loan @ 35% for 8 years						
Principal	2,750,000					
Interest payment		(962,500)	(928,921)	(883,590)	(822,393)	(739,777)
Principal payment		(95,939)	(129,518)	(174,849)	(236,046)	(318,662)
Total payment		(1,058,439)	(1,058,439)	(1,058,439)	(1,058,439)	(1,058,439)
Cemex loan @ 10% for 5 years						
Principal (US$)	825					
Interest payment (US$)		(82.5)	(69.0)	(54.1)	(37.8)	(19.8)
Principal payment (US$)		(135.1)	(148.6)	(163.5)	(179.9)	(197.8)
Total payment		(217.6)	(217.6)	(217.6)	(217.6)	(217.6)
Scheduled at Rp10,000/$:						
Interest payment		(825,000)	(689,867)	(541,221)	(377,710)	(197,848)
Principal payment		(1,351,329)	(1,486,462)	(1,635,108)	(1,798,619)	(1,978,481)
Total payment		(2,176,329)	(2,176,329)	(2,176,329)	(2,176,329)	(2,176,329)
Actual (at current spot rate):						
Interest payment		(1,041,262)	(1,098,949)	(1,088,160)	(958,480)	(633,669)
Principal payment		(1,705,561)	(2,367,915)	(3,287,494)	(4,564,190)	(6,336,691)
Total payment		(2,746,823)	(3,466,864)	(4,375,654)	(5,522,670)	(6,970,360)
CFs in Rp on						
Cemex loan:	8,250,000	(2,746,823)	(3,466,864)	(4,375,654)	(5,522,670)	(6,970,360)
IRR of CFs:	38.835%					
FX losses on debt interest:		(216,262)	(409,082)	(546,940)	(580,770)	(435,821)

IRR: Internal rate of return

Costs. The cash costs of cement manufacturing (labor, materials, power, and so on) are estimated at Rp115,000/tonne for 1999, rising at about the rate of inflation, 30% per annum. Additional production costs of Rp20,000/tonne for year-1 are also assumed to rise at the rate of inflation. As a result of all production being exported, loading costs of $2.00/tonne and shipping of $10.00/tonne must also be included. Note that these costs are originally stated in U.S. dollars, and for the purposes of Semen Indonesia's income statement, they must be converted to rupiah terms. This is so because both ship-loading and shipping costs are international services governed by contracts denominated in dollars. As a result, they are expected to rise over time only at the U.S. dollar rate of inflation (3%).

Semen Indonesia's pro forma income statement is illustrated in Exhibit 14.4. This is the typical financial measurement of the profitability of any business, whether domestic or international. The baseline analysis assumes only a capacity utilization rate of 40% (year-1), 50% (year-2), and 60% in the following years. Management believes this is necessary since existing in-country cement manufacturers are only averaging 40% at this time.

Additional expenses in the pro forma financial analysis include license fees paid by the subsidiary to the parent company of 2.0% of sales, and general and administrative expenses for Indonesian operations of 8.0% per annum (and growing an additional 1% per annum). Foreign exchange gains and losses are those related to the servicing of the U.S. dollar-denominated

Exhibit 14.4	*Semen Indonesia's Pro Forma Income Statement (millions of rupiah)*					
Exchange Rate (Rp/$)	10,000	12,621	15,930	20,106	25,376	32,038
Project year	**0**	**1**	**2**	**3**	**4**	**5**
Sales volume		8,000	10,000	12,000	12,000	12,000
Sales price (US$)		58	58	58	58	58
Sales price (Rp)		732,039	923,933	1,166,128	1,471,808	1,857,627
Total revenue		5,856,311	9,239,325	13,993,541	17,661,751	22,291,530
Less cash costs		(920,000)	(1,495,000)	(2,332,200)	(3,031,860)	(3,941,418)
Less other production costs		(160,000)	(260,000)	(405,600)	(527,280)	(685,464)
Less loading costs		(201,942)	(328,155)	(511,922)	(665,499)	(865,149)
Less shipping costs		(1,009,709)	(1,640,777)	(2,559,612)	(3,327,495)	(4,325,744)
Total production costs		(2,291,650)	(3,723,932)	(5,809,334)	(7,552,134)	(9,817,774)
Gross profit		3,564,660	5,515,393	8,184,207	10,109,617	12,473,756
Gross margin		61%	60%	58%	57%	56%
Less license fees		(117,126)	(184,787)	(279,871)	(353,235)	(445,831)
Less general and administrative		(468,505)	(831,539)	(1,399,354)	(1,942,792)	(2,674,984)
Plus foreign exchange gains (losses)		(216,262)	(409,082)	(546,939)	(580,770)	(435,821)
EBITDA		2,762,767	4,089,985	5,958,043	7,232,819	8,917,120
Less depreciation and amortization		(1,760,000)	(1,760,000)	(1,760,000)	(1,760,000)	(1,760,000)
EBIT		1,002,767	2,329,985	4,198,043	5,472,819	7,157,120
Less interest on Cemex debt		(825,000)	(689,867)	(541,221)	(377,710)	(197,848)
Less interest on local debt		(962,500)	(928,921)	(883,590)	(822,393)	(739,777)
EBT		(784,733)	711,196	1,963,323	2,990,901	4,353,647
Less income taxes (30%)		–	–	(809,909)	(1,281,815)	(1,865,847)
Net income		(784,733)	711,197	1,963,323	2,990,901	4,353,647
Net income (US$)		(62)	45	98	118	136
Return on sales		–13%	8%	14%	17%	20%

EBITDA = earnings before interest, taxes, depreciation, and amortization; EBIT = earnings before interest and taxes; EBT = earnings before taxes. Tax credits resulting from current period losses are carried forward toward next year's tax liabilities. Dividends are not distributed in the first year of operations as a result of losses, and are distributed at a 50% rate in the years 2000–2003.

debt provided by the parent and are drawn from the bottom of Exhibit 14.3. In summary, the subsidiary operation is expected to begin turning an accounting profit in its second year of operations (2000), with profits rising with margins as capacity utilization increases over time.

Project Viewpoint Capital Budget

The capital budget for the Semen Indonesia manufacturing project from a project viewpoint is shown in Exhibit 14.5. The net cash flow, or *free cash flow* as it is often referred to, is found by summing EBITDA (earnings before interest, taxes, depreciation, and amortization), recalculated taxes,[6] and changes in net working capital (the sum of the net additions to receivables, inventories, and payables necessary to support sales growth). The initial investment of Rp22 trillion is the total capital invested to support these earnings. Although receivables average 50 to 55 days sales outstanding (DSO) and inventories 65 to 70 DSO, payables and trade credit are also relatively long at 114 DSO in the Indonesian cement industry. On net, Semen Indonesia expects to add approximately 15 net DSO to its investment with sales growth. The elements remaining to complete the project viewpoint's capital budget are the terminal value (discussed below) and the discount rate of 33.257% (the firm's WACC).

Terminal value. The terminal value (TV) of the project represents the continuing value of the cement manufacturing facility in the years after year-5, the last year of the detailed pro forma financial analysis shown here. This

---

Exhibit 14.5   *Semen Indonesia's Capital Budget: Project Viewpoint (millions of rupiah)*

Exchange Rate (Rp/$)	10,000	12,621	15,930	20,106	25,376	32,038
Project year	**0**	**1**	**2**	**3**	**4**	**5**
EBITDA		2,762,767	4,089,985	5,958,043	7,232,819	8,917,120
Less recalculated taxes		(828,830)	(1,226,996)	(1,787,413)	(2,169,846)	(2,675,136)
Net operating cash flow		1,933,937	2,862,990	4,170,630	5,062,973	6,241,984
Less additions to NWC		(240,670)	(139,028)	(436,049)	(289,776)	(626,314)
Initial investment	(22,000,000)					
Terminal value						18,769,117
Free cash flow (FCF)	(22,000,000)	1,693,267	2,723,962	3,734,581	4,773,197	24,384,787
NPV	(10,300,045)					
IRR	13.5 %					

NWC = net working capital. NPV = net present value. Discount rate is Semen Indonesia's WACC of 33.257%. IRR = internal rate of return, the rate of discount yielding an NPV of exactly zero. Values in exhibit are exact and are rounded to the nearest million.

value, like all asset values according to financial theory, is the present value of all future free cash flows that the asset is expected to yield. The TV is then calculated as the present value of a perpetual net operating cash flow (NOCF) generated in the fifth year by Semen Indonesia, the growth rate assumed for that net operating cash flow (g), and the firm's weighted-average cost of capital (k_{wacc}):

$$\text{Terminal value} = \frac{NOCF_5\,(1 + g)}{k_{wacc} - g} = \frac{Rp6,241,984\,(1 + 0)}{.33257 - 0} = Rp18,769,117 \text{ or } Rp18.8 \text{ trillion}$$

The assumption that $g = 0$, in other words, that net operating cash flows will not grow past year-5, is probably not true, but it is considered a prudent assumption for Cemex to use when estimating future cash flows so far into the future.

The results of the capital budget from the project viewpoint indicate a negative net present value (NPV) of –Rp10,300,045 million (or about Rp10.3 trillion) and an internal rate of return (IRR) of only 13.5% compared to the 33.257% cost of capital. These are the returns that the project would yield to a local or Indonesian investor in Indonesian rupiah. The project, from this viewpoint, is not acceptable.

Repatriating Cash Flows to Cemex

As described in the section preceding the case, a foreign investor's assessment of a project's returns depends on the actual cash flows that are returned to it, in its own currency. For Cemex, this means that the investment must be analyzed in terms of what U.S. dollar cash inflows and outflows are associated with the investment over the life of the project, after-tax, discounted at its appropriate cost of capital.

This *parent viewpoint capital budget* is built in two steps. First, the individual cash flows are isolated, adjusted for any withholding taxes imposed by the Indonesian government, and converted to U.S. dollars.[7] Mexico does not tax repatriated earnings since they have already been taxed in Indonesia.[8] The second step, the actual parent viewpoint capital budget, combines these U.S. dollar after-tax cash flows with the initial investment to determine the net present value of the proposed Semen Indonesia subsidiary in the eyes (and pocketbook) of Cemex. This is illustrated in Exhibit 14.6, which shows all incremental earnings to Cemex from the prospective investment project.

Parent Viewpoint Capital Budget

Finally, all cash flow estimates are now constructed to form the parent viewpoint's capital budget, as detailed in Exhibit 14.6. The cash flows generated by Semen Indonesia from its Indonesian operations, dividends, license fees,

Exhibit 14.6		*Semen Indonesia's Remittance and Capital Budget: Parent Viewpoint (millions of US$)*				
Exchange Rate (Rp/$)	10,000	12,621	15,930	20,106	25,376	32,038
Project year	**0**	**1**	**2**	**3**	**4**	**5**
Dividend Remittance						
Dividends paid (Rp)		–	355,598	981,662	1,495,451	2,176,823
Less withholding tax			(53,340)	(147,249)	(224,318)	(326,524)
Net dividend remitted (Rp)		–	302,259	834,412	1,271,133	1,850,300
Net dividend remitted (US$)		–	19.0	41.5	50.1	57.8
License Fees Remittance						
License fees remitted (Rp)		117,126	184,787	279,871	353,235	445,831
Less withholding tax		(5,856)	(9,239)	(13,994)	(17,662)	(22,292)
Net dividend remitted (Rp)		111,270	175,547	265,877	335,573	423,539
Net license fees remitted (US$)		8.8	11.0	13.2	13.2	13.2
Debt Service Remittance						
Promised interest paid (US$)		82.5	69.0	54.1	37.8	19.8
Less withholding tax @ 10%		(8.25)	(6.90)	(5.41)	(3.78)	(1.98)
Net interest remitted (US$)		74.25	62.09	48.71	33.99	17.81
Principal payments remitted (US$)		135.1	148.6	163.5	179.9	197.8
Capital Budget: Parent Viewpoint (millions of US$)						
Dividends		–	19.0	41.5	50.1	57.8
License fees		8.8	11.0	13.2	13.2	13.2
Debt service		209.4	210.7	212.2	213.9	215.7
Total earnings		218.2	240.7	266.9	277.2	286.7
Initial investment	(826.1)					
Terminal value						586.0
Free cash flow (FCF)	(826.1)	218.2	240.7	266.9	277.2	872.7
NPV	219.2					
IRR	26.8 %					

NPV calculated using a company-determined discount rate of WACC + foreign investment premium of 11.98% + 6.00% = 17.98%.

debt service payments, and terminal value are now valued in U.S. dollar terms after-tax.

Cemex's weighted-average cost of capital is 11.980%. If the firm were undertaking an investment of the same relative degree of risk as the firm itself, a simple discount rate of 11.980% might be adequate. Cemex, however, generally requires new investments to yield an additional 3% over the cost of capital for domestic investments, and 6% more for international projects. The discount rate for Semen Indonesia's cash flows repatriated to Cemex will therefore be discounted at 11.98% + 6.00%, or 17.98%. The project's baseline analysis indicates a NPV of US$219.2 million and an IRR of 26.8%, which means that it is an acceptable investment from the parent's viewpoint.

Most corporations require that new investments more than cover the cost of the capital employed in their undertaking. It is therefore not unusual for the firm to require a hurdle rate of 3% to 6% above its cost of capital in order to identify potential investments that will literally add value to stockholder wealth.[9] For foreign projects, as discussed previously, there are additional agency costs and foreign exchange-related risks and costs that also must be adjusted for. Chapter 16 will focus on the alternative methods of adjusting for risk in foreign investments.

An issue of significant debate in the parent's viewpoint is *terminal value*. The entire capital budget from the parent's viewpoint is constructed of cash flows remitted from the Indonesian subsidiary to the parent company Cemex—with the lone exception of terminal value. This is not a cash flow, but a theoretical value for the business in the post-year-5 period. Many multinational firms require valuation of cash flows only and do not include the terminal value. In this case, if the terminal value were eliminated from consideration, the project would not meet investment criteria because its NPV would fall to ($96.9 million), with an IRR of 13.0%.

Sensitivity Analysis

So far the project investigation team has used a set of "most likely" assumptions to forecast rates of return. It is now time to subject the most likely outcome to *sensitivity analysis*. The same probabilistic techniques are available to test the sensitivity of results to political and foreign exchange risks as are used to test sensitivity to business and financial risks. Popular techniques include using decision tree analysis, reducing cash flows to certainty equivalents, adjusting the discount rate to reflect the degree of riskiness of the project, and measuring the statistical dispersion of expected returns. Many decision-makers feel more uncomfortable about the necessity to guess probabilities for unfamiliar political and foreign exchange events than they do about guessing their own more familiar business or financial risks. Therefore, it is more common to test sensitivity to political and foreign exchange risk by simulating what would happen to net present value and earnings under a variety of "what if" scenarios.

Political Risk

What if Indonesia should impose controls on the payment of dividends or license fees to Cemex? The impact of blocked funds on the rate of return from Cemex's perspective would depend on when the blockage occurs, what reinvestment opportunities exist for the blocked funds in Indonesia, and when the blocked funds would eventually be released to Cemex. We could simulate various scenarios for blocked funds and rerun the cash flow analysis in Exhibit 14.6 to estimate the effect on Cemex's rate of return.

What if Indonesia should expropriate Semen Indonesia? The effect of expropriation would depend on the answers to the following questions.

- When will the expropriation occur, in terms of number of years after the business began operation?

- How much compensation will the Indonesian government pay, and how long after expropriation will payment be made?

- How much debt is still outstanding to Indonesian lenders, and will the parent, Cemex, have to pay this debt because of its parental guarantee?

- What are the tax consequences of the expropriation?

- What are the future cash flows foregone?

Many expropriations eventually result in some form of compensation to the former owners. This compensation can come from a negotiated settlement with the host government or from payment of political risk insurance by the parent government. Negotiating a settlement takes time, and the eventual compensation is sometimes paid in installments over a further period of time. Thus, the present value of the compensation is often much lower than its nominal value. Furthermore, most settlements are based on book value of the firm at the time of expropriation rather than the firm's market value.

Repayment of parent-guaranteed local debt usually takes first claim on any compensation funds paid. If Cemex had guaranteed Semen Indonesia's debt to Indonesian lenders, they would be paid before Cemex could receive any settlement funds. In fact, the settlement agreement would probably provide for this arrangement. Alternatively, Cemex might have refused to guarantee Semen Indonesia's debt, protecting itself in the case of an expropriation but probably causing Semen Indonesia to have to pay a higher rate of interest and making the subsidiary less profitable to its parent.

If no compensation agreement is negotiated, Semen Indonesia, as an independently incorporated subsidiary of Cemex, might default on its debt. Cemex would not be obligated for Semen Indonesia's own debt, lacking a parent guarantee. As a practical matter, this is likely to occur only when the affiliate's debt is borrowed locally, as in the case of Semen Indonesia. If Semen Indonesia had borrowed from, say, Singaporean banks, parent Cemex would feel an obligation to repay the debt even if not technically obligated.

The tax consequences of expropriation would depend on the timing and amount of capital loss recognized by Mexico. This loss would usually be based on the uncompensated book value of the Indonesian investment. However, there is often some doubt as to when a write-off is appropriate for tax purposes, particularly if negotiations for a settlement drag on. In some ways a nice clear expropriation without hope of compensation, such as occurred in Cuba in the early 1960s, is preferred to a slow "bleeding to death" in protracted negotiations. The former leads to an earlier use of the tax shield and a one-shot write-off against earnings, whereas the latter tends to depress earnings for years, as legal and other costs continue and no tax shelter is achieved.

Foreign Exchange Risk

The project team assumed that the Indonesian rupiah would depreciate versus the U.S. dollar at the purchasing power parity rate (approximately 20.767% per year in the baseline analysis). What if the rate of rupiah depreciation were greater? Although this would make the assumed cash flows to Cemex worth less in dollars, operating exposure analysis would be necessary to determine whether the cheaper rupiah made Semen Indonesia more competitive. For example, since Semen Indonesia's exports to Taiwan are denominated in U.S. dollars, a weakening of the rupiah versus the dollar could result in greater rupiah earnings from those export sales. This would serve to somewhat offset the imported components that Semen Indonesia purchases from the parent company, which are also denominated in U.S. dollars. Semen Indonesia is somewhat representative of firms today that have both cash inflows and outflows denominated in foreign currencies, providing a partial natural hedge against currency movements.

What if the rupiah should *appreciate* against the dollar? The same kind of economic exposure analysis is needed. In this particular case, we might guess that the effect would be positive on both local sales in Indonesia and the value in dollars of dividends and license fees paid to Cemex by Semen Indonesia. Note, however, that an appreciation of the rupiah might lead to more competition within Indonesia from firms in other countries with now lower-cost structures, lessening Semen Indonesia's sales.

Other Sensitivity Variables

The project rate of return to Cemex would also be sensitive to a change in the assumed terminal value, the capacity utilization rate, the size of the license fee paid by Semen Indonesia, the size of the initial project cost, the amount of working capital financed locally, and the tax rates in Indonesia and Mexico. Since some of these variables are within the control of Cemex, it is still possible that the Semen Indonesia project could be improved in its value to the firm, although already acceptable.

The greenfield investment analysis described here is hypothetical.

PROJECT FINANCE

One of the hottest topics in international finance today is *project finance*.[10] *Project finance* refers to the arrangement of financing for long-term capital projects, large in scale, long in life, and generally high in risk. This is a very general definition, however, since there are many different forms and structures that fall under this generic heading.

Project finance is not new. Examples go back centuries and include many famous early international businesses such as the Dutch East India Company. These entrepreneurial importers financed their trade ventures to Asia on a voyage-by-voyage basis, with each voyage's financing being like venture capital; investors would be repaid when the shipper returned and the fruits of the Asian marketplace were sold at the docks to Mediterranean and European merchants. If all went well, the individual shareholders of the voyage received back their initial investment plus healthy profits.

Project finance is used widely today in the development of large-scale infrastructure projects in China, India, and many other emerging markets. Although each individual project has unique characteristics, most are highly leveraged transactions, with debt making up more than 80 percent of the total financing. Equity is a small component of project financing for two reasons: first, the simple scale of the investment project often prevents a single investor or even a collection of private investors from being able to fund it; secondly, many of these projects involve subjects traditionally funded by governments—such as electrical power generation, dam building, highway construction, and energy exploration, production, and distribution.

This level of debt, however, places an enormous burden on cash flow for debt service. Therefore, project financing usually requires a number of additional levels of risk reduction. The lenders involved in these investments must feel secure that they will be repaid; bankers are not by nature entrepreneurs, and do not enjoy entrepreneurial returns from project finance.

There are four basic properties that are critical to the success of a project financing.

1. Separability of the project from its investors. The project is established as an individual legal entity, separate from the legal and financial responsibilities of its individual investors. This structure not only serves to protect the assets of equity investors, it also provides a controlled platform upon which creditors can evaluate the risks associated with the singular project, assess the ability of the project's cash flows to service debt, and be assured that the debt service payments will automatically be allocated by and from the project itself rather than by a decision of managers within the sponsors.

2. Long-lived and capital intensive singular projects. Not only must the individual project be separable and large in proportion to the financial resources of its owners, its business line must be singular in its construction, operation, and size (capacity). The size is set at inception and is seldom, if ever, changed over the project's life.

3. Cash flow predictability from third-party commitments. An oil field or electric power plant produces a homogeneous commodity product that can produce predictable cash flows if third-party commitments to take and pay can be established. In addition to revenue predictability, nonfinancial costs of production need to be controlled over time, usually through long-term supplier contracts with price adjustment clauses based on inflation. The predictability of net cash inflows to long-term contracts eliminates much of the individual project's business risk, allowing the financial structure to be heavily debt-financed and still remain safe from financial distress.

The predictability of the project's revenue stream is essential in securing project financing. Typically, contract provisions that are intended to ensure adequate cash flow include the following clauses: quantity and quality of the project's output; a pricing formula that enhances the predictability of adequate margin to cover operating costs and debt service payments; and a clear statement of the circumstances that permits significant changes in the contract such as *force majeure* or adverse business conditions.

4. Finite projects with finite lives. Even with a longer-term investment, it is critical that the project have a definite ending point at which all debt and equity have been repaid. Because the project is a stand-alone investment in which its cash flows go directly to the servicing of its capital structure, and not to reinvestment for growth or other investment alternatives, investors of all kinds need assurances that the project's returns will be attained in a finite period. There is no capital appreciation, but only cash flow.

Examples of project finance include some of the largest individual investments undertaken in the past three decades, such as British Petroleum's financing of its interest in the North Sea, and the Trans-Alaska Pipeline. The Trans-Alaska Pipeline was a joint venture between Standard Oil of Ohio, Atlantic Richfield, Exxon, British Petroleum, Mobil Oil, Philips Petroleum, Union Oil, and Amerada Hess. Each of these projects were at or above $1 billion, and represented capital expenditures that no single firm would or could attempt to finance.[11] Yet, through a joint venture arrangement, the higher-than-normal risk absorbed by the capital employed could be managed.

SUMMARY

- Capital budgeting for foreign projects involves many complexities that do not exist in domestic projects.
- A foreign project should be judged on its net present value from the viewpoint of funds that can be freely remitted to the parent.
- Comparison of a project's net present value to similar projects in the host country is useful for evaluating expected performance relative to potential.
- Rates of return were calculated from both the project's viewpoint and the parent's viewpoint, for an illustrative example, Semen Indonesia.
- Once the most likely outcome has been determined, a sensitivity analysis is normally undertaken. Foreign project returns are particularly sensitive to

changes in assumptions about exchange rate developments, political risk, and the way the repatriation of funds is structured.

QUESTIONS

1. Semen Indonesia

a. According to the assumptions in this baseline case, the project rate of return is negative and the parent rate of return is positive. Should the project be accepted?

b. Are there assumptions that could be reasonably changed to make the project rate of return positive and improve the parent rate of return as well?

c. Are there any external benefits or costs that could change the two project rates of return?

d. If Cemex were a U.S.-based firm, rather than being based in Mexico, would this capital budgeting analysis lead to different results? What are the key differences?

e. Is there a better way to calculate the cash flows or the discount rate used in the case to adjust for the many risks of the investment?

2. Santa Clara Electronics

Questions a–i are all based on the following scenario for Santa Clara Electronics, Inc.

Santa Clara Electronics, Inc. of California exports 24,000 sets of low-density light bulbs per year to Argentina under an import license that expires in five years. In Argentina the bulbs are sold for the Argentine peso equivalent of $60 per set. Direct manufacturing costs in the United States and shipping together amount to $40 per set, and there are no other costs. The market for this type of bulb in Argentina is stable, neither growing nor shrinking, and Santa Clara holds the major portion of the market.

The Argentine government has invited Santa Clara to open a manufacturing plant so imported bulbs can be replaced by local production. If Santa Clara makes the investment, it will operate the plant for five years and then sell the building and equipment to Argentine investors at net book value at the time of sale plus the value of any net working capital. (Net working capital is the amount of current assets less any portion financed by local debt.) Santa Clara will be allowed to repatriate all net income and depreciation funds to the United States each year.

Outlay: Santa Clara's anticipated cash outlay, in dollars, in 2001 would be:

Building and equipment	$1,000,000
Net working capital	1,000,000
Total	$2,000,000

All investment outlays will be made in 2001, and all operating cash inflows will occur at the end of years 2002 through 2006. The Argentine peso is tied to the U.S. dollar through Argentina's currency board, so no change in exchange rates is expected.

Depreciation and investment recovery. Building and equipment will be depreciated over five years on a straight-line basis. At the end of the fifth year, the $1,000,000 of net working capital may also be repatriated to the United States, as may the remaining net book value of the plant.

Sales price of bulbs. Locally manufactured bulbs will be sold for the Argentine peso equivalent of $60 per set.

Operating expenses per set of bulbs:

Materials purchased in Argentina (dollar equivalent)	$20 per set
Materials imported from Santa Clara Electronics	10 per set
Variable costs	$30 per set

Transfer prices. The $10 transfer price per set for raw material sold by the parent consists of $5 of direct costs incurred in the United States and $5 of pretax profit to Santa Clara. There are no other operating costs in either Argentina or the United States.

Taxes. The corporate income tax rate is 40% in both Argentina and the United States (combined federal and state).

Discount rate: Santa Clara Electronics uses a 15% discount rate to evaluate all domestic and foreign projects.

a. Using the data given, calculate annual project cash flows for the years 2002 through 2006.

b. Using the data given, calculate annual cash flows to the parent for the years 2002 through 2006. Cash inflows to Santa Clara consist of
   i   profit on component sales to Argentina, less taxes,
   ii   dividends remitted from Argentina at 100% of net profit,
   iii funds equal to depreciation charges, remitted to the United States,
   iv   cash received from liquidating building and equipment, if any,
   v   cash flow losses due to the ending of export sales of bulbs manufactured in the United States.

c. Using the data given, calculate the net present value of the project.

d. Santa Clara learns that Matsubara Electronics of Japan will make a similar investment in Argentina should Santa Clara decide not to invest. Matsubara would be protected by the Argentine government from competitive imports. Using the data given, how would this information affect your analysis and recommendations?

e. After the analysis in part (d) above, you discover the following: The anticipated investment of $1,000,000 in building and equipment includes the book value of some surplus equipment now in the United

States, which Santa Clara intended to ship to Argentina and factor in at its book value of $400,000. However, that equipment could have been sold in the United States for $800,000 after all taxes. In other words, the equipment is worth $800,000 instead of $400,000. How would this information affect your analysis and recommendations?

f. Assume the conditions of part (d) above. Argentina reduces income taxes charged to foreign firms from 40% to 20%, for a period of 10 years, in order to attract foreign investment. How would this information affect your analysis and recommendations?

g. How would your analysis and recommendation differ if Santa Clara expected to have a permanent presence in Argentina, and if it expected long-run growth opportunities in Argentina?

h. Assume the conditions of part (d) above. Imports from parent Santa Clara are paid for at once. However, Argentina blocks all other cash remittances to the United States until the end of the fifth year, at which time all free cash may be repatriated. Liquid funds investment in Argentina earn 3% per annum, compounded annually, after Argentine taxes. How would this information affect your analysis and recommendation?

i. Assume the conditions of part (h) above. Santa Clara is able to enter into an arrangement to use operating free cash flow (depreciation plus net income) to purchase canned beef for shipment to and ultimate sale in the United States. The Argentine cost of canned beef is charged against Argentine earnings at full cost. The supply of canned beef is unlimited, but U.S. demand is such that it can be sold only at 80% of its Argentine purchase price. How would this opportunity affect your analysis and recommendations in part (d) above?

3. Brussels Mustard Company

Brussels Mustard Company (BMC) of Belgium has been exporting French-style mustard to the United States for many years and has developed a good reputation. Costs within the European Union have now risen so that BMC is no longer price competitive in the United States. Hence, it is considering purchasing an existing U.S. food factory and converting it into a manufacturing plant for the U.S.

If purchased, the new wholly owned subsidiary will have the following attributes:

- The initial ($t = 1$) sales price per container will remain $20.
- First-year production and sales will be 1 million containers per year, and physical sales will grow at 10% per annum for the first three years and then stabilize forever. First-year production costs will be $15 per container. Administrative costs will be $1 million per year, and depreciation will be $1 million per year.

- Prices and costs in future years will rise with U.S. inflation as follows:
  a. 4.00% p.a. for raw materials and labor
  b. 3.00% p.a. for sales prices
  c. No change for administrative costs or depreciation
- BMC will use 15% for its weighted-average cost of capital.
- The value of the U.S. factory to BMC at the end of the third year is assumed to be equal to an infinite stream of third-year dividends, discounted at 20% p.a. The higher discount rate is because of the perceived greater risk in the future.
- Production is for sale. Hence production volume equals sales volume. All sales are for cash.
- Corporate tax rate in the United States: 35%; Corporate tax rate in Belgium: 40%
- Current and expected exchange rates are:

  $t_1 = \$1.1000/€$
  $t_2 = \$1.2000/€$
  $t_3 = \$1.3000/€$

- BMC plans to have its U.S. subsidiary pay 80% of its profit back to the parent.

What is the maximum U.S. purchase price BMC can afford to pay for the U.S. affiliate?

WORLD WIDE WEB EXERCISES

W1. Project Finance
Project finance analysis and lending is a highly specialized area in which many banks and other financial service providers are trying to build additional expertise. Use the following sites to construct a briefing on services currently available in this area.

Milbank: Project Finance	http://www.milbank.com/03_practice12.html
First Chicago Capital Markets	http://fccm.com/
Nomura Project Finance International	http://npfi.com.hk/
General Electric Capital Services	http://www.ge.com/gec/
World Bank	http://worldbank.org/

W2. Emerging Markets: China
Long-term investment projects such as electrical power generation require a thorough understanding of all attributes of doing business in that country, including import/export restrictions, labor relations, supplier financing, tax rules, depreciation schedules, currency properties and restrictions, and sources of short-term and long-term debt, to name a few. China is currently the focus of investment and market penetration strategies of multinational firms worldwide. Using the web (you might start with the web sites listed below), build a

data base on doing business in China, and prepare an update of several of the factors, such as average receivables outstanding and currency convertibility, discussed in this chapter.

Ministry of Foreign Trade and Economic Cooperation, PRC
http://www.chinamarket.com.cn/
China Investment Trust & Investment Corporation
http://www.citic.com/
ChinaNet Investment Pages   http://www.business-china.com/invest

SUGGESTED READINGS

Brealey, Richard A., Ian A. Cooper, and Michael A. Habib, "Using Project Finance to Fund Infrastructure Investments," *Journal of Applied Corporate Finance*, Fall 1996, Vol. 9, No. 5, pp. 25–38.

Dixit, Avinash K., and Robert S. Pindyck, "The Options Approach to Capital Investment," *Harvard Business Review*, May/Jun 1995, pp. 105–115.

Keck, Tom, Eric Levengood, and Al Longfield, "Using Discounted Cash Flow Analysis in an International Setting: A Survey of Issues in Modeling the Cost of Capital," *Journal of Applied Corporate Finance*, Fall 1998, Vol. 11, No. 3, pp. 82–99.

Lessard, Donald R., "Evaluating International Projects: An Adjusted Present Value Approach," in *International Financial Management: Theory and Application*, Donald R. Lessard, ed., New York: Wiley, 1985, pp. 570–584.

NOTES

1. Apart from these theoretical arguments, surveys over the last 30 years show that in practice multinational firms continue to evaluate foreign investments from both the parent and project viewpoint. Responses of multinational firms to surveys by Stonehill and Nathanson (1968), Baker and Beardsley (1973), Oblak and Helm (1980), Bavishi (1981), Kelly and Philippatos (1982), and Stanley and Block (1983) reveal that firms calculate and evaluate rates of return by using cash flows to and from the parent alone, as well as to and from the foreign project alone. In their study of 121 U.S. multinational firms, conducted in the early 1980s, Stanley and Block found that 48% of their 121 respondents evaluate foreign projects on the basis of the project's cash flows, 36% on the basis of parent cash flows, and 16% on both.
2. U.S. firms must consolidate foreign affiliates that are over 50% owned. If an affiliate is between 20% and 50% owned, it is usually consolidated on a pro-rata basis. Affiliates less than 20% owned are normally carried as unconsolidated investments.
3. *Semen* is Indonesian for the English word "cement."
4. Assuming an initial spot rate of Rp10,000/US$, and Indonesian and U.S. inflation rates of 30% and 3% per annum, respectively, for the life of the project, forecasted spot exchange rates follow the usual PPP calculation. For example, the forecasted exchange rate for year 1 of the project would be:

$$\text{Spot rate (year} - 1) = \text{Rp}10,000/\text{US\$} \times \frac{1+.30}{1+.03} = \text{Rp}12,621/\text{US\$}$$

5. The cost of equity for both Cemex and Semen Indonesia is found using the capital asset pricing model (CAPM):

$$k_e = k_{rf} + (k_m - k_{rf})\,\beta$$

6. Note that EBITDA, not EBT, is used in the capital budget, which contains both depreciation and interest expense. Depreciation and amortization are noncash expenses of the firm, and therefore contribute positive cash flow. Because the capital budget creates cash flows that will be discounted to present value with a discount rate, and the discount rate includes the cost of debt—interest—we do not wish to subtract interest twice. Therefore, taxes are recalculated on the basis of EBITDA. The firm's cost of capital used in discounting also includes the deductibility of debt interest in its calculation.

7. Statutory withholding taxes on international transfers are set by bilateral tax treaties, but individual firms may negotiate lower rates with governmental tax authorities. In the case of Semen Indonesia, dividends will be charged a 15% withholding tax, interest payments 10%, and license fees 5%.

8. The United States does levy a contingent tax on repatriated earnings of foreign source income. This is a complex calculation and is covered in Chapter 17.

9. A NPV of zero means the investment is "acceptable," but NPV values that exceed zero are literally the present value of wealth that is expected to be added to that of the firm and its shareholders.

10. The authors would like to thank James L. Mills for helpful input on this section.

11. Project finance has been employed in many other industries and applications as well. For example, R&D Limited Partnerships (RDLP) were common in the 1980s, such as Cummins Engine's $20 million financing of a new form of diesel engine. Other firms such as Genentech and Amgen have utilized similar financing arrangements in which a finite project was financed with large proportions of nonrecourse debt.

DECISION CASE

P.T. Semen Gresik

Mismanagement, poor regulation or simple inertia had left more than half of state-owned enterprises "unhealthy." State-appointed managers ran companies like fiefdoms; bloated, failing industries were kept alive more from national pride than economic sense. As 1997 came to a close, 164 state firms were reporting a combined pre-tax profit of just $1.2 billion. Yet state enterprises employed more than 700,000 Indonesians and were worth some $60 billion. They were overseen by touchy ministers and entrenched managers. They were wrapped in a mythology of development. Slimming down or selling off these sacred cows meant playing with fire.

"Anatomy of a Deal," by Jose Manuel Tesoro, *AsiaWeek*, January 22, 1999.

On July 6, 1998, the Indonesian government announced that Cementos Mexicanos (Cemex) was the *preferred bidder* for the largest government-owned cement company—PT Semen Gresik. The first round of bidding had pitted Cemex against Holderbank of Switzerland and Heidelberger of Germany, two of the largest cement manufacturing firms in the world. And a mere seven weeks had passed since the resignation of President Suharto, a turning-point in Indonesia's political and economic future.

In a surprise announcement on August 20th, Cemex was informed that its first-round bid would have to be restructured, the primary change being a maximum of 14% of ownership passing from the government to Cemex. Then, as *preferred bidder*, Cemex would wait for the other first round bidders to submit second bids no later than September 28th. If their second bids were superior to that of Cemex's first bid, Cemex would have the right to match theirs if it wished. In the event the second bids did not match that of Cemex, Cemex would automatically be declared the winner. Cemex was required to bid in the second round. The vice president for finance of Cemex, Hector Medina, and his acquisition staff and consultants now had only a few weeks to finalize their position.

INDONESIAN PRIVATIZATION

The entire process of selling-off Indonesian state firms was directed by Mr. Tanri Abeng, a former deal-maker in Indonesia's private sector and thought to be well-suited for the position as a result of his lack of ties with politicians. Abeng's background encouraged foreign investors to believe that Indonesia's government was serious about its privatization program. Abeng had previously held positions as the head of Indonesian operations for Union Carbide (United States), Heineken (the Netherlands), and finally the Bakrie Group, a diversified Indonesian conglomerate. After being named State Enterprises Minister in 1997 by then-President Suharto, he was given a very ambitious revenue target: raise $1.5 billion from the sale of stakes in selected Indonesian state-owned enterprises.

Abeng moved quickly, placing 12 government-owned companies up for sale. The 12 included port-operator *Pelindo*, highway and airport operators, mining companies, agricultural plantations, and telecommunications companies—including *Indosat*. These 12 possessed assets of 461 trillion rupiah ($50.6 billion). By early June of 1998 Abeng had arranged for nine different investment banking firms to act as financial advisors and agents to the 12 companies on the auction block.

Goldman Sachs's Indonesian partner, Bahana, was hired to represent the Indonesian cement producer Semen Gresik. In May Abeng appointed Goldman Sachs and Lehman Brothers senior advisors to the Indonesian government in its privatization drive. Exhibit 1 summarizes the firms.

The Indonesian privatization drive was the direct result of the economic crisis in which Indonesia was currently mired, and the subsequent promises made by President Suharto to the International Monetary Fund (IMF) in order to obtain economic and financial assistance. The structural reform program agreement signed with the IMF required Indonesia and President Suharto to open the Indonesian economy to outside investors and market forces. Under the terms of the agreement, Indonesia would sell stakes in four firms by the end of 1998, all 12 companies by the end of 1999.

Exhibit 1	*Indonesian Enterprises Slated for Privatization and Their Financial Partners*

State-Owned Company	Industry	Financial Adviser
1. Telekomunikasi Indonesia	Telecommunications	Merrill Lynch, Lehman Brothers
2. Indonesia Satellite (Indosat)	Telecommunications	Goldman Sachs
3. Semen Gresik	Cement	Goldman Sachs
4. Tambang Timah	Tin mining	Morgan Stanley, Banque Paribas
5. AnekaTambang	Gold mining	Morgan Stanley, Banque Paribas
6. Tambang Batubara Bukit Asam	Gold mining	Morgan Stanley, Banque Paribas
7. Jasa Marga	Toll road operator	Lehman Brothers
8. Pelabuhan II (Pelindo II)	Port operator	Goldman Sachs
9. Pelabuhan III (Pelindo III)	Port operator	Credit Suisse First Boston
10. Angkasa Para II	Airport manager	UBS/SBC Warburg Dillon Read
11. Perkebunan Nuisantra IV	Plantation	Jardine Fleming
12. Krakatoa Steel	Steel	Salomon Smith Barney

The World Bank would supervise the privatization process implemented by the government. In stage one, each bidder—upon the completion of due diligence—would submit a binding offer for shares in the company based on directives given by the government (typically on how much of the government's share was actually up for sale). The winning bid would combine financial, social (employment guarantees), and environmental dimensions. The winning bidder of stage one would then enter into a provisional sales agreement with the government. Third parties were then allowed to submit bids in a second stage to improve upon the winning bidder's offer. The winning bidder of stage one was then given the right to match the better offer if it wished in order to win the bid.

Many of these state-owned enterprises were already publicly traded—minority shares—so that market values did exist for these firms. However, these market capitalizations had been severely degraded following the onslaught of the Asian economic crisis. Markets, in addition to the individual equities traded in these markets, had fallen across Asia. For example, official forecasts for the Indonesian economy expected a 10% fall in total gross domestic product (GDP) for 1998.[1]

Cemex S.A. de C.V.

Founded in 1906, Cementos Mexicanos S.A. (Cemex) is the largest cement manufacturer in the Americas and the third largest cement producer in the world, just behind Holderbank of Switzerland and Lafarge of France. Based in Monterey, Mexico, Cemex has operations in 22 countries and trade relations with over 60 countries worldwide. Cemex is the market leader in Mexico, Spain, Venezuela, Panama, the Dominican Republic, with a rapidly expanding presence in Colombia, the Caribbean, the southwestern portion of the United States, and most recently the Philippines. Exhibit 2 provides an overview of Cemex's recent financial results. (Appendix 1 provides additional Cemex results.)

Cemex has a corporate strategy which provides much of the impetus for its Asian expansion: 1) to leverage its core cement and ready-mix concrete franchise; 2) to concentrate on developing markets; and 3) to maintain high growth by applying free cash flow toward selective investments that further its geographic diversification. This strategy was focused on repositioning the company from being a dominant regional producer to a true global player in the cement industry.

Most notable regarding Cemex's performance had been its ability to maintain its operating and EBITDA margins over the tumultuous 1990s. Consistently higher than all of its European-based global competitors, the source of its efficiencies rests with a capable combination of relatively new vintage capital facilities, pricing-power and market dominance in its primary markets, and a progres-

---

1. The magnitude of this depression and economic collapse is seen when this 10% fall is compared with the deepest recessions in recent U.S. economic history—when GDP fell by a mere 2% during the 1930s.

Exhibit 2	Selected Consolidated Financial Results of Cemex SA (December 31, millions of constant pesos)				
	1993	**1994**	**1995**	**1996**	**1997**
Net sales	25,759	27,687	33,924	35,540	38,464
Operating income	6,269	7,431	8,100	8,482	9,088
Majority net income	4,637	4,951	10,045	10,319	7,725
Earnings per share (EPS)	4.39	4.60	7.81	7.95	6.01
Operating margin (%)	24.4	26.8	23.9	23.8	23.6
EBITDA	8,120	9,471	10,786	11,483	12,116
EBITDA margin (%)	31.6	34.2	31.8	32.3	31.5

EBITDA = earnings before interest, taxes, depreciation and amortization.

Source: Cemex, http://wwwcemex.com.

sive management group and strategy which focuses on customer satisfaction and service (a rare concept in cement markets). The bottom line in all commodity-based industries, however, was operating excellence. Cemex consistently attained margins, even in new acquisitions, which competitors could not match.[2]

Cemex had little experience in Asia, but it did possess significant experience of its own in surviving an economic crisis. The devaluation of the Mexican peso in December 1994 and the resulting Mexican economic crisis of 1995 had provided Cemex with some in-house insights into enterprise value. Cemex's own price-to-book value had plunged to 1.16 in March 1995 following the fall of the peso, yet Cemex was able to recover remarkably quickly from this discounting by the equity markets. It hoped to use some of these insights into market valuation in expanding its presence in Asia when Asian cement stocks were themselves trading at significant discounts to what their true values likely were.

> "This is most definitely the right time to buy in Asia. The current crisis in Asia has resulted in a fall in value per tonne of capacity for cement companies to US$100 per tonne from US$500 per tonne."
>
> Lorenzo Zambrano, Chairman, Cemex[3]

Cemex's first direct operating activities in Asia commenced with its acquisition of a 30% stake in Rizal Cement of the Philippines in September 1997 for US$100 million. Although Cemex itself had aspirations of expanding across Asia, and the Asian economic crisis had made many firms throughout the Far East relatively cheap, many analysts had grave concerns over the ability of Cemex to digest more acquisitions in the region rapidly. Nonetheless, Cemex continued to pour

---

2. Operating margins expanded by 18 percentage points in Spain after Cemex acquiring Valenciana and Sanson, and 19 percentage points in Venezuela after acquiring Vencemos.

3. *The Financial Times*, November 7, 1997.

over the possibilities in the region, paying significant attention to the movements of its major global competitors.[4] In early 1998 Cemex directed Goldman Sachs to find a company in Indonesia in which the firm might acquire a strategic stake. Exhibit 3 provides an overview of the major cement manufacturing firms across the region, their recent earnings and share price performance, and several measures of cement producer valuation.

Valuation

> Value, in our opinion, should be the guiding principle in such turbulent times. While stock prices in efficient markets naturally respond to day-to-day changes in life, this should not cloud the fact that the underlying assets possess an intrinsic economic value. When the market price falls below that value, a profit opportunity arises. . . . Is there value in the Indonesian cement sector and, if there is, when is it going to be realised?[5]

In addition to most of the traditional valuation techniques (price to earnings, price to free cash flow, earnings per share growth) there are typically additional techniques useful in specific industries. Two such techniques widely used in the cement industry are *enterprise value to capacity* and *enterprise value to EBITDA* (earnings before interest, taxes, depreciation and amortization).

Enterprise value to capacity is a frequently used method of valuation in the cement industry, and is calculated by dividing *enterprise value (EV)* (the total of market capitalization and net debt) by the existing installed capacity of the cement producer. Because of standardized technology across countries, EV/capacity provides a very clear indicator of how different companies may be described as under- or over-valued. Industry experts estimated the *set-up costs* (*replacement cost*) in Asia to be roughly US$160/tonne for a standard 1.5 million metric tons per year (mmt/y) production facility.

Enterprise value to EBITDA is a more common measure of value used across all industries, and focuses on the market's current market capitalization to the current pre-financing and tax based operating earnings of the firm. Similarly, price to free cash flow (P/FCF) and price-to-earnings (PE) ratios also provide market values to firm cash flows and earnings by more standard methodologies.

As illustrated in Exhibit 3, the lowest EV/capacity in Asia at the moment were the producers in Indonesia (52), South Korea (52), and Malaysia (55). The lowest EV/EBITDA values were found in a different subset of countries, with the lowest being the Philippines (4.1), South Korea (6.1), and India (7.2). The cement producers of Indonesia and Thailand had suffered negative earnings in

---

4. Within months of the start of the Asian crisis Holderbank (Switzerland) and Blue Circle (United Kingdom) were both moving on properties in Malaysia and the Philippines, while LaFarge (France) moved to expand into the Philippines and India.

5. Indonesian Research–Building Materials Sector, "On the Brink of Value Realization," Indosuez W.I. Car Securities Limited, June 22, 1998, p. 5.

Exhibit 3   *Cement Producers in Asia*

Firm	Market Cap (US$ million)	EV/ Capacity	EV/ EBITDA	Price/ FCF	Price/ Earnings	Earnings Per Share Price 1997	1998E	Change	Share (EPS) Performance 12 mo.	Relative
INDIA										
Associated Cement	460.0	77	12.4	22.1	142.4	56.2	9.2	–84%	3%	6%
Gujarat Ambuja Cement	433.5	128	8.0	11.5	12.4	18.0	18.6	3%	–10%	–8%
India Cement	97.8	64	4.3	4.3	4.9	12.8	12.0	–6%	–8%	–6%
Madras Cement	102.7	73	4.2	3.8	5.8	642.7	572.2	–11%	–59%	–58%
Average		86	7.2	10.4	41.4				–19%	–17%
INDONESIA										
Indocement	957.9	39	12.6	15.8	(27.9)	(371.1)	(123.8)	improved	38%	82%
Semen Gresik	461.9	53	8.5	11.4	56.0	(90.2)	121.0	improved	–14%	14%
Semen Cibinong	49.5	65	5.5	0.5	(1.1)	2.0	(334.0)	–16800%	–61%	–48%
Average		52	8.9	9.2	9.0				–12%	16%
THAILAND										
Siam Cement	926.6	190	7.2	4.1	(1.5)	(440.3)	(37.5)	improved	–48%	–23%
Siam City Cement	338.3	97	9.8	10.0	(3.7)	(96.0)	(36.6)	improved	–2%	44%
TPI Polene	71.7	150	15.2	(1.3)	(1.3)	(53.4)	(28.4)	improved	–79%	–68%
Average		146	10.7	4.3	(2.2)				–43%	–16%
MALAYSIA										
Cement Industries	69.6	26	9.3	11.5	(91.3)	52.7	(2.3)	–104%	–70%	–44%
Kedah Cement	109.4	93	5.1	2.7	4.0	28.3	26.5	–6%	–76%	–55%
Malayan Cement	238.9	45	20.1	11.0	6.7	29.8	10.0	–66%	–56%	–17%
Average		55	11.5	8.4	(26.9)				–67%	–38%
PHILIPPINES										
Alsons	54.0	40	4.0	4.6	4.4	0.6	0.5	–17%	–74%	–56%
Davao Union Cement	19.3	56	3.0	2.0	1.9	0.4	0.3	–25%	–89%	–81%
Fortune Cement	120.6	96	6.2	7.2	10.0	0.4	0.4	0%	–66%	–44%
Hi Cement	60.3	39	3.1	3.1	5.8	0.7	0.5	–29%	–68%	–47%
Average		58	4.1	4.2	5.5				–74%	–57%
TAIWAN										
Asia Cement	1,716.2	228	10.1	8.9	13.9	2.3	2.4	4%	–23%	–33%
Taiwan Cement	1,343.7	147	14.1	14.1	25.4	1.2	1.4	17%	–38%	–46%
Average		188	12.1	11.5	19.7				–30%	–40%
SOUTH IOREA										
Hanil Cement	65.4	25	4.2	3.0	11.5	2,186.5	2,031.0	–7%	–48%	–29%
Ssaang)ong Cement	84.8	70	8.0	2.1	11.5	529.2	392.3	–26%	–60%	–45%
Tong Yang Cement	35.5	62	6.0	1.5	6.8	1,151.0	1,061.7	–8%	–59%	–45%
Average		52	6.1	2.2	9.9				–56%	–40%

Enterprise Value (EV) calculated as total market capitalization plus net debt.

Source: Constructed by authors from Paribas Asia Equity and other sources. All values are estimates for 1998 unless otherwise stated. Market capitalization as of March 2, 1998.

| Exhibit 4 | *Bagged Cement Prices and Cash Costs Across Asia, June 1998* |

Country	Ex-Factory Price (US$/tonne)	Cash Costs (US$/tonne)	Margin (US$/tonne)	Gross Margin (per tonne)
Pakistan	55	29	26	47%
Malaysia	40	26	14	35%
India	46	27	19	41%
Philippines	39	23	16	41%
Korea	39	28	11	28%
Taiwan	54	30	24	44%
Thailand	38	20	18	47%
Indonesia	16	10	6	38%
Average	41	24	17	40%

Source: Indosuez W.I. Carr Securities, June 12, 1998.

1997 and 1998, although the expectations for 1998 were for significant improvement (although still negative for these two countries). The other manufacturers across the region seemed to be still sliding, at least as far as expected earnings for 1998 went. Share price performance for cement manufacturers since the inception of the crisis in June 1997 was, however, unambiguously disastrous.

The prospects of the Indonesian cement industry were not clear. In March the Indonesian government announced it would deregulate the local guideline price system (HPS), and the Indonesian Cement Association (ASI) would assume responsibility for supervision of cement distribution and control of cement prices. This was expected to result in price wars as excess supply of cement was expected to continue through the year 2002. Prices could fall by 10% to Rp139,500 per tonne. Because cement is a bulk commodity with high transportation costs, markets are typically geographically defined. Prices therefore vary significantly from one region or country to another.

The Asian currency crisis had led to a significant differentiation—some would say *distortion*—of relative costs and prices across the Asian cement industry. As seen in Exhibit 4, cash costs ranged from a low of $10/tonne in Indonesia to $30/tonne in Taiwan. At the same time, prices were also the lowest in Indonesia, currently falling to $16/tonne, while Pakistan and Taiwan earned $55 and $54/tonne, respectively. The result was an Indonesian industry which was the lowest cost, but also relatively low in gross margin.

The large discrepancies in costs and prices had led many of the world's largest cement producers to consider something long forgotten, large scale low-cost production and international distribution through exports. For example, the Taiwanese cement market may be quite vulnerable to Indonesian exports. Assuming cash production costs in Indonesia of $10/tonne, loading costs (on both ends) of $2/tonne, and shipping costs to Kaohsiung (Taiwan) from East Java (Indonesia) of $10/tonne, Indonesian exports could severely undercut domestic Taiwanese producers.[6] Several analysts argued that even the United States cement markets may be vulnerable to Indonesian exports if shipping costs between Indonesia and the U.S. could be kept at $35 to $40/tonne. Cement prices in the U.S. hovered just below $75/tonne. Semen Gresik was currently in the process of a significant upgrading of its port facilities to increase its export capabilities. (Appendix 2 provides a discounted cash flow valuation of PT Semen Gresik.)

PT Semen Gresik

> We believe that Gresik would be on the top of the list of acquisition targets for foreign cement players. The partial sell-down of the government's 65% stake will represent a unique opportunity for the foreign players to take a meaningful stake in the Indonesian cement industry (previously closed). However, in our view this foreign interest is dependent on, at a minimum, gaining management control.[7]

Semen Gresik began producing cement in 1957 by exploiting large and readily accessible limestone deposits in East Java, and was the first government-owned cement producer in Indonesia to go public, issuing 35% of its shares on the Jakarta exchange in July 1991. The ownership structure had not changed since 1991, with 65% of the shares held by the Indonesian government and 35% free float on the Jakarta exchange. The current Indonesian privatization program was focused on maximizing the revenues per share received by the government for some proportion of the 65% held by the government.

Semen Gresik had become the largest Indonesian cement producer, as measured by installed capacity, in September 1995 when it had purchased Semen Padang (West Sumatra) and Semen Tonasa (South Sulawesi) for a total of $476 million. The three companies still operated separately, maintaining independent administrative structures. Although this added substantial capacity to Semen Gresik's resources, it was also an unpopular government-directed consolidation as fears arose over possibilities of layoffs and reorganizations away from the outer island/provinces.

The Indonesian market, however, like all cements markets around the globe, was regional in nature. The largest markets in Indonesia were Jakarta—dominated by Indocement—and West Java—dominated by Semen Cibinong. Regardless of which region the individual producer dominated, the Asian crisis had hit all the major producers. Indocement and Cibinong were expected to only reach 37% and 27% capacity utilization rates in 1998, respectively. All producers were expected to see 1998 annual sales volumes fall by roughly 40% from the previous year. Exhibit 5 provides an overview of the major Indonesian cement producers as of July 1998.

Semen Gresik's management of the Asian economic crisis had, however, been relatively successful. As a result of rising input costs (roughly 10% of Gresik's production costs were imported), the firm—all three operational units—had

---

6. Export cost estimates drawn primarily from Indosuez I.D. Carr Securities, June 12, 1998, p. 11.

7. Ibid, p. 17.

Exhibit 5	*Indonesia's Major Cement Manufacturers*			
	Semen Gresik	Indocement	Semen Cibinone	Semen Andalas
Installed capacity (mmt/y)	17.0	15.5	10.5	1.2
Market share	43%	35%	17%	5%
Dominant market in Indonesia	East Java	Jakarta	West Java	–
1997 sales (mmt)	11.7	9.5	4.6	1.4
1998e sales (mmt)	7.0	5.7	2.8	0.8
Change in sales, 1997 to 1998	–40%	–40%	–39%	–43%
1998e capacity utilization	41%	37%	27%	67%
Costs comparison:				
Production costs (Rp/tonne)	135,478	145,956	155,009	na
Production costs (US$/tonne)	13.6	14.6	15.5	na
Cash costs (Rp/tonne)	115,949	117,844	129,411	na
Cash costs (US$/tonne)	11.6	11.8	12.0	na
Debt in Rupiah (billion)	Rp 1,792	Rp 391	Rp 40	na
Debt in U.S. dollars (million)	$226	$889	$903	na
Primary owner	Government	Private	Prvate	Government
Minority owner	Market	None	Holderbank	None
Status	Privatizing	Partner?	Stable	Privatizing

na=not available.

Costs for Semen Gresik are numerical average of the three primary production facilities.

Source: Deutsche Bank Research, Mexican Special Report, July 6, 1998, p. 5.

increased its ex-factory prices by over 40% in the spring of 1998, to an average of Rp 229,000 per tonne (US$23/tonne at the then current exchange rate of Rp 10,000/$). Appendices 3 and 4 provide recent and pro forma income statements, cash flows, and balance sheets for Semen Gresik.

BIDDING FOR SEMEN GRESIK

Tari Abeng believed that Semen Gresik was the proper choice to begin the state's privatization program. President Suharto agreed, and allowed Abeng to proceed without interference.[8] The firm was considered one of the best managed government-run enterprises, and had shown some resiliency in the declining business conditions suffered by most in the current crisis. Gresik was not only the largest Indonesian cement producer, it was generally regarded as potentially the most efficient, particularly with so much of its existing capacity using the latest technology, and being of such a recent vintage.[9]

---

8. Krakatoa Steel had actually been the first privatization subject but had run into a variety of delays resulting in a still-born privatization program.

9. Roughly 30% of Semen Gresik's installed capacity had come on-line in 1996 and 1997.

In the midst of rising political tension throughout Indonesia—focused primarily on the push for President Suharto's resignation—Abeng initiated negotiations on May 5th with three of the world's largest cement manufacturers: Holderbank, Heidelberger, and Cemex. Holderbank, fresh off the acquisition of Union Cement (Philippines) and Siam City (Thailand), appeared the most aggressive. Cemex's due diligence team of 30 professionals arrived in Indonesia six days later. On May 17th, President Suharto resigned. After a temporary pause in the process, Abeng proceeded with the privatization process. Heidelberg withdrew at this stage, leaving only Cemex and Holderbank to pursue the allotted two-week period of due diligence. On June 19th, both companies filed their bids. Holderbank offered $0.96/share, roughly $200 million. The Cemex bid was much higher—$1.38/share—a potential investment of $287 million (both bids were for 207.6 million shares).

At this point Tari Abeng's gamesmanship became apparent. Departing from the original privatization program outlined by the World Bank, Abeng invited both bidders to up their bids at this point without revealing the bids submitted by either party. While Cemex confirmed its existing bid, Holderbank increased its bid to $1.21/share, or $251 million. Cemex was officially declared the winner and the *preferred bidder* for the final stage two.

Cemex's winning stage one bid was actually a complex combination offer:

1. A bid of $1.38/share for 35% of Semen Gresik's shares held by the Indonesian government. Given a current share price of Rp 9,150 (about $0.63/share at the current exchange rate of Rp14,500/$), this represented nearly a 100% premium.

2. An announced intention to purchase an additional 16% of the company's shares on the open market, bringing its total constructed position to 51%.

3. A five-year put option to the Indonesian government to sell its remaining shares to Cemex at a base price of $1.38/share plus an 8.2% annual premium.

4. A one-off payment of $129 million to the Indonesian government in 2006 if Semen Gresik's performance surpassed specific expectations.

5. A contribution of approximately $50 million to the on-going port facilities upgrade and capacity expansion of Semen Gresik (bringing it up to 17.5 mmt/y capacity; see Appendix 5).

This purchase of 207.6 million shares would reap the government approximately $287 million.[10] If the additional 16% were tendered at roughly the same price, the total investment for control of Semen Gresik by Cemex would total $417.5 million. This was approximately one-quarter of what Indonesia had promised the IMF to raise through privatization—in just the first of the 12 firm sales.

---

10. Semen Gresik had 35% of its shares publicly issued, totaling 593,200,000 shares. 65% of Gresik's share ownership was held by the Indonesian government, totaling 1,101,700,000 shares.

Growing Opposition

Meanwhile, social and political tensions were rising over the falling employment levels of the Indonesian economy. A number of prominent Indonesian government officials raised questions regarding the wisdom of selling valuable Indonesian assets to foreign interests, particularly in light of the control these powers would exert over the companies and their employees. The management of Semen Gresik itself had previously been under pressure to ensure employment levels at its Tonasa and Padang subsidiaries (acquired in 1995), and now the prospect of this parent becoming further subordinated itself was not a popular one.

A second area of debate arose over the process itself. A number of prominent bankers in Jakarta were quoted in the press as questioning both the transparency of the process directed by Abeng, and the ethics of the process. At the center of the controversy was whether the investment banking firm—Goldman Sachs—was not actually playing both sides of the street. Goldman Sachs represented both the potential buyer (Cemex) and the seller (the Indonesian government). By mid-July the controversy reached its zenith, the pressure resulting in Goldman Sachs resigning as Cemex's advisor:

> "Goldman Sachs decided to withdraw in the interest of transparency. We didn't think there was anything illegal in what Goldman Sachs was doing. The bank simply wanted to avoid further public debate over its role."
>
> Sofyan Djalil, Special Assistant to Minister of State Enterprises

Cemex immediately replaced Goldman with Jardine Fleming. Despite the resignation, Goldman Sachs' relationship with Bahana remained controversial. As described by Goldman Sachs, the relationship was "a joint operating agreement with no current cross-ownership." In principle, the problem was one of suspicion in an environment which could not at this time allow suspicion to arise.[11]

A third debate, one which erupted literally days after the culmination of the first stage, was the announcement by the Jakarta Stock Market's watchdog organization—*Bapepam*—of a probe into insider trading in Semen Gresik shares. Evidence put forward to suggest the possibility was that Gresik shares had risen 57% in the month of June while the general market fell. On the day of bid submission (June 19th), a record 62 million shares of Gresik were traded, closing above Rp8,700/share for the first time. Bapepam announced that the investigation would focus on the trading activities at Jardine Fleming (now associated with Cemex), Bahana (aligned with Goldman Sachs), and the state-controlled investment bank Danareksa Securities.

Although the bids submitted by the two companies were for shares held by the Indonesian government, and the actual bids submitted secretly, both compa-

---

11. The sensitivity of this topic is summarized well by Michael Vatikiotis in an article in the *Far Eastern Economic Review*: "*Indonesians cannot be accused of cynicism if they say that these investment banks are guilty of the same kind of collusion and nepotism which brought down the Suharto regime,*" from "Bankiing on Big Names," *Far Eastern Economic Review*, November 19, 1998.

nies had been quite public in their plans to acquire additional shares sold on the open market in combination with a winning bid. Both firms wished to acquire control of Gresik, and that would have to be done by combining government shares with free-floating shares. The investigation into insider trading continued for months with no violations ever substantiated. The bidding process would continue.

Indonesia Backs Off

For months rumors had been circulating in West Sumatra that the new owners of Semen Gresik would lay off nearly half the 3,000 employees of Semen Padang's operations. Cemex's acquisition team had, during the due diligence process in which the team had direct contact with present Gresik management and labor, guaranteed that no one would be laid off before the year 2000. Demonstrations intensified in West Sumatra and Jakarta, however, after the first round of bidding. Protests in Jakarta grew in size and fervor, and by late July were occurring nearly daily (eventually resulting in the posting of signs designating a "Demonstration Area"). Rumors that management at Semen Padang paid demonstrators in both West Sumatra and Jakarta were denied by employees.

The governor of West Sumatra then threatened to remove certain land rights and concessions provided to Semen Padang if control of Semen Gresik was allowed to pass to foreign investors.[12] The final tide turned when Azwar Anas, a former army general, former West Sumatra governor, and former CEO of Semen Padang (prior to acquisition in 1995) took the unofficial lead in opposing the privatization. On August 11th Tanri Abeng was called to testify before the Economic Committee of Indonesia's Supreme Advisory Council. Here Abeng finally capitulated to the growing pressure.

> I was able to grasp that the real reason behind the resistance is purely emotional and cultural. Nothing to do with economics. From there on, I knew, no way. We are fighting a losing battle if we push so hard.
>
> Tanri Abeng, August 12th

Abeng informed Cemex that the sale of Semen Gresik would have to be restructured and the second round of bidding would be postponed. Speculation on the structure of the new sale intensified, and in a conference call with Morgan Stanley Dean Witter, the Managing Director of Semen Gresik stated that he believed the company would still be sold as one, and not broken up into the individual units (Semen Padang, Semen Tonasa, Semen Gresik). It was also rumored that the winning bidder would be required to make a tender offer to the public minority shareholders at the same price as the bid price, but only if taking more than a 20% position from the government.

---

12. The opposition parties became more and more public with their demands and threats, promising they would occupy the properties of Semen Padang in the event of foreign acquisition.

Final Bids

On August 20th Tanri Abeng's Office of State Enterprises announced that the government would entertain bids for only 14% of Semen Gresik rather than the original 35% offered, assuring that the government would remain the controlling shareholder after the sale. Tanri Abeng's office informed Cemex that its stage one bid would have to be restructured, keeping its preferred bidder status, and then the second round bids would be accepted. It was now up to Cemex to determine what it wished to do in its restructured stage one bid. Competitor bids were due no later than September 28th, a little more than five weeks from now.

Appendix 1   *Selected Consolidated Financial Results of Cemex SA*
(millions of constant pesos)

Income Statement Information	1993	1994	1995	1996	1997	1998
Net Sales	25,729	27,687	33,924	35,540	38,464	42,720
Cost of Sales	15,512	15,968	20,689	21,550	23,571	24,701
Gross Profit	10,217	11,719	13,235	13,990	14,893	18,019
Operating Expenses	3,948	4,288	5,135	5,518	5,805	6,360
Operating Income	6,269	7,431	8,100	8,472	9,088	11,659
Comprehensive Financing Costs	221	(213)	7,498	5,588	1,611	(1,309)
Other Income (Expenses)	(895)	(1,754)	(2,142)	(1,801)	(1,396)	(1,506)
Income BeforeTaxes & Others	5,595	5,464	13,456	12,259	9,303	8,844
Minority Interest	861	595	1,440	1,256	1,083	391
Majority Net Income	4,637	4,951	10,045	10,319	7,725	7,952
Earnings Per Share (EPS)	4.39	4.60	7.81	7.95	6.01	6.30
Dividends Per Share (DPS)	0.81	0.83	0.87	na	na	1.18
Number of Shares Outstanding	1,056	1,077	1,286	1,303	1,268	1,258

Balance Sheet Information

	1993	1994	1995	1996	1997	1998
Cash and Temporary Investments	2,900	6,385	4,691	4,316	3,862	4,027
Net Working Capital	5,285	6,954	7,498	6,452	5,971	6,320
Property, Plant & Equipment (net)	39,145	53,944	65,337	60,646	60,976	60,805
Total Assets	71,212	104,027	110,738	104,998	103,878	103,551
Short Term Debt	6,073	8,534	11,515	8,609	6,674	10,948
Long-Term Debt	25,455	41,059	40,135	41,757	40,213	31,049
Total Liabilities	35,723	56,546	60,901	59,197	56,198	52,682
Minority Interests	6,845	10,158	11,758	10,562	11,992	12,384
Stockholders Equity, ex Minority	28,644	37,323	38,079	35,239	35,689	38,484
Total Stockholders Equity	35,489	47,481	49,837	45,801	47,681	50,868
Book Value Per Share	27.12	34.65	29.62	27.15	27.80	30.49

Other Financial Data

	1993	1994	1995	1996	1997	1998
Operating Margin	24.4%	26.8%	23.9%	23.8%	23.6%	27.3%
EBITDA Margin	31.6%	34.2%	31.8%	32.3%	31.5%	34.4%
EBITDA	8,120	9,471	10,786	11,483	12,116	14,697
Cash Earnings	4,950	5,873	3,020	4,993	7,316	10,263
Cash Earnings Per Share	4.69	5.45	2.35	3.85	5.70	8.13

Source: Cemex SA, http://wwwcemex.com

Appendix 2	*Discounted Cash Flow Valuation of the PT Semen Gresik Group*

Assumptions	Value		Assumptions	Value
Cost of capital:			FX rate (Rp/$)	13,000
Risk-free rate	33.7%		Inflation	29.4%
Equity risk prmium	6.0%		Tax rate	30.0%
Beta	1.20		Growth rate of operating CF	30.4%
After-tax cost of debt	23.6%		Terminal value growth rate	5.0%
Cost of equity	40.9%		WC/sales	14.0%
Percentage debt	50%			
Percentage equity	50%			
Weighted average cost of capital	32.2%			

Billions of Rp	1998	1999	2000	2001	2002
Assumed growth rate	16%	27%	20%	20%	20%
EBIT	458.0	614.0	736.8	884.2	1,061.0
Add depreciation & amortization	261.0	276.0	276.0	276.0	276.0
EBITDA	719.0	890.0	1,012.8	1,160.2	1,337.0
Less changes in net working capital	(19.0)	(21.8)	(17.2)	(20.6)	(24.8)
Less capital expenditure	(40.0)	(40.0)			
Terminal value					74,680.1
Total Free Cash Flow	660.0	828.2	995.6	1,139.5	75,992.3
Present value factor	1.0000	0.7562	0.5718	0.4324	0.3270
Present value of free cash flow	660.0	626.2	569.3	492.7	24,845.8
Cumulative present value	27,194.0				

Enterprise value	27,194.0		Terminal value as % of total EV	90%
Less net debt	(4,113.5)		Implied Price to FCF (1998):	58.9
Less minority interests	(23.1)			
Equity value, total	23,057.4			
Shares outstanding (millions)	593.2			
Fair value of equity per share	38,869			
In US dollars	$ 2.99			

Capital cost assumptions from Paribas Asia Equity, "Semen Gresik," August 1998, p.3

| **Appendix 3** | *PT Semen Gresik's Historical and Pro Forma Income and Cash Flows (billion rupiah)* | | | |

Statement of Income	1996	1997	1998e	1999e
Sales by unit:				
Gresik	625	608	874	1,189
Tonasa	235	465	437	522
Padang	485	495	511	607
Non-cement	17	20	20	20
Total net sales	1,362	1,588	1,842	2,338
Growth in net sales (%)		17%	16%	27%
COGS Gresik	(365)	(377)	(534)	(734)
COGS Tonasa	(144)	(290)	(289)	(345)
COGS Padang	(273)	(286)	(277)	(317)
Total cost of goods sold	(782)	(953)	(1,100)	(1,396)
Gross profit	580	635	742	942
Gross margin (% of net sales)	43%	40%	40%	40%
Less selling, general & admin expenses	(259)	(313)	(284)	(328)
Operating profit	321	322	458	614
Less net interest	(43)	(101)	(279)	(535)
Contributions from subsidiaries	3	4	5	6
Others	5	9	10	10
Non-operating income	(35)	(89)	(264)	(519)
Pretax profit	286	234	194	95
Less Indonesian taxes	(65)	(44)	(29)	(11)
Minorities	(4)	(5)	(6)	(6)
Net profit	217	185	159	78
Return on sales (%)	16%	12%	9%	3%
Effective tax rate (%)	23%	19%	15%	12%

Cash Flow (billion rupiah)	1996	1997	1998e	1999e
Profit before interest & taxes	321	322	458	614
Depreciation & amortization	138	180	261	276
Associated adjustments	(3)	(4)	(5)	(6)
Change in net working capital	156	(466)	(96)	(144)
Operating Cash Flow	612	32	618	740
Taxes paid	(65)	(44)	(29)	(11)
Interest paid	(43)	(101)	(279)	(535)
Capitalised interest	(92)	(178)	(187)	(263)
Forex gains (losses)	–	(286)	(674)	–
Cash earnings	412	(577)	(551)	(69)
Dividends paid	(65)	(65)	(74)	–
Net capex (disposal)	(592)	(1,337)	(648)	(60)
Change in share capital	–	–	–	–
Others	(248)	–	–	–
Change in net debt	(493)	(1,979)	(1,273)	(129)
Ending cash (debt)	(1,003)	(2,982)	(4,255)	(4,384)

Source: Barings, March 3, 1998.

Appendix 4   *PT Semen Gresik's Balance Sheet (billions of rupiah)*

Assets	1992	1993	1994	1995	1996	1997
Cash & banks	336	140	52	275	220	461
Accounts receivable	14	5	17	145	179	238
Inventory	30	45	82	175	228	323
Other current	8	19	20	54	81	82
Total current assets	388	209	171	649	708	1,104
Fixed assets	108	109	769	1,471	2,090	2,282
Investments	14	3	6	45	14	14
Other assets	383	649	60	1,186	1,418	2,037
Total assets	893	970	1,006	3,351	4,230	5,437

Liabilities & Net Worth						
Trade payables	–	8	17	41	76	82
Accounts payable	6	21	17	62	309	414
Taxes payable	4	14	4	32	49	51
Other payables	17	4	18	70	47	–
Long-term debt (current)	–	40	79	287	227	93
Notes payable	–	–		–	136	–
Current liabilities	27	87	135	492	844	640
Long-term debt	182	181	139	532	900	2,339
Minorities	–	10	11	14	18	20
Share capital	148	148	148	593	593	593
Revaluation surplus	240	240	240	1,252	1,252	1,252
Reserves	293	302	333	468	622	600
Shareholders' funds	681	690	721	2,313	2,467	2,445
Total capital	863	881	871	2,859	3,385	4,804
Net assets (Total assets – current liabilities)	866	883	871	2,859	3,386	4,797

Source: Barings, March 3, 1998.

Appendix 5	*Installed Capacity of the PT Semen Gresik Group (million metric tons/year)*				

	1994	1995	1996	1997	1998
Semen Gresik (Java):					
Gresik I	500	500	500	208	208
Gresik II	1,300	1,300	1,300	1,300	1,300
Tuban I	575	2,300	2,300	2,300	2,300
Tuban II	–	–	–	2,300	2,300
Tuban III	–	–	–	–	2,400
Total	2,375	4,100	4,100	6,108	8,508
Semen Padang (Sumatra, acquired 1995):					
Indatung I	254	254	254	254	254
Indatung II	660	660	660	660	660
Indatung III	660	660	660	660	660
Indatung IV	1,620	1,620	1,620	1,620	1,620
Indatung V	–	–	–	–	2,300
Total	3,194	3,194	3,194	3,194	5,494
Semen Tonasa (Sulawesi, acquired 1995):					
Tonasa I	–	–	–	–	–
Tonasa II	590	590	590	590	590
Tonasa III	590	590	590	590	590
Tonasa IV	–	–	2,300	2,300	2,300
Total	1,180	1,180	3,480	3,480	3,480
Total under Gresik Ownership	2,375	8,474	10,774	12,782	17,482
Percent change (%)	32%	257%	27%	19%	37%

Source: Morgan Stanley Dean Witter, June 22, 1998, p. 4, and ING Barings, March 3, 1998, p. 2.

Appendix 6

PT Semen Gresik's Share Price and Market Capitalization for Selected Dates (1998)

Date	Share Price (Rp)	Exchange Rate (Rp/$)	Implied Price (US$)	Market Capitalization (Rp thousands)	Market Capitalization (US$ millions)
Feb 3	6,775	9,750	$0.69	3,997,250	410
March 3	5,600	9,300	$0.60	3,304,000	355
June 19	9,150	14,500	$0.63	5,398,500	372
July 6	9,150	14,700	$0.62	5,398,500	367
July 10	9,150	14,600	$0.63	5,398,500	370
Aug 18	10,775	12,000	$0.90	6,357,250	530
Aug 21	8,750	12,000	$0.73	5,162,500	430
Aug 28	10,500	13,000	$0.81	6,195,000	477

Note: Market capitalization on the basis of the following shares outstanding: 593,200,000

Appendix 7

Daily Exchange Rates: Indonesian Rupiah per U.S. Dollar

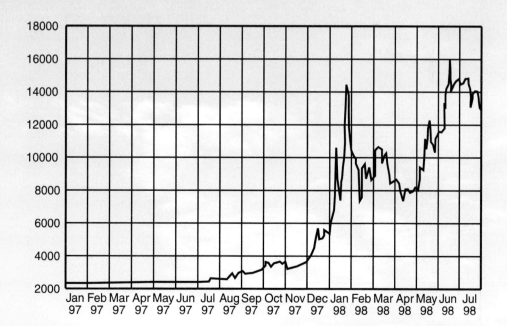

Appendix 8   *PT Semen Gresik Share Price, April 1–August 24, 1998*

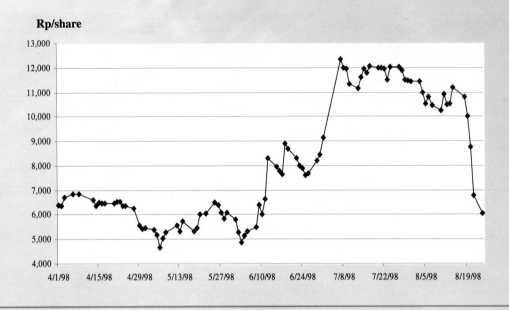

CHAPTER 15

INTERNATIONAL ACQUISITIONS AND VALUATION

The 1980s and 1990s were characterized by a spate of mergers and acquisitions (M&As), with both domestic and foreign partners. Cross-border mergers have played an important role in this activity. The 1992 completion of the European Union's Internal Market stimulated many of these investments, as European, Japanese, and U.S. firms jockeyed for stronger market positions within the EU. However, the weak value of the U.S. dollar in the early 1990s, long-run U.S. growth prospects, and political safety in the United States motivated more takeovers of U.S. firms by foreign firms, particularly from the United Kingdom and Japan, than vice versa. This was a reversal of historical trends in which U.S. firms were net buyers of foreign firms rather than net sellers to foreign firms.

The latter half of the 1990s saw a number of mega-mergers between multinationals such as Daimler-Chrysler and Exxon-Mobil, which virtually changed the entire competitive landscapes of their respective global markets. The 1990s also saw the rise of enterprise privatizations in many emerging markets, giving rise to many growth opportunities for MNEs to gain access to previously closed markets of enormous potential. As illustrated in Exhibit 15.1, the growth in M&A activity—both domestically and cross-border—accelerated rapidly at the end of the 1990s. The Asian economic crisis did not, however, result in permanently "discounted" valuations, as reflected in falling merger and acquisition activity in 1998.

International mergers, acquisitions, and strategic alliances, all face similar challenges: *they must value the target enterprise on the basis of its projected performance in its market.* This process of enterprise valuation combines elements of strategy, management, and finance. Strategically, it is the potential core competencies and competitive advantages of the target firm that attract the acquisition. An enterprise's potential value is a combination of the intended strategic plan and the commensurate operational effectiveness to be implemented post-acquisition.[1]

| Exhibit 15.1 | *Global and Asian Merger and Acquisition Activity, 1990–1998* |

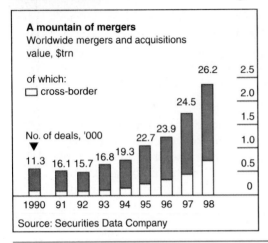

A mountain of mergers
Worldwide mergers and acquisitions
value, $trn

of which:
☐ cross-border

No. of deals, '000
▼

11.3 16.1 15.7 16.8 19.3 22.7 23.9 24.5 26.2

1990 91 92 93 94 95 96 97 98

Source: Securities Data Company

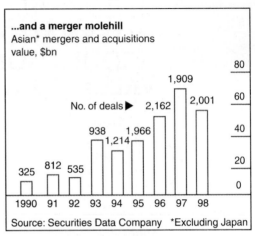

...and a merger molehill
Asian* mergers and acquisitions
value, $bn

No. of deals ▶

325 812 535 938 1,214 1,966 2,162 1,909 2,001

1990 91 92 93 94 95 96 97 98

Source: Securities Data Company   *Excluding Japan

©1999 the Economist Newspaper Group, Inc. Reprinted with permission. Further reproduction prohibited.
www.economist.com.

Whereas previous chapters have discussed the theoretical use of cross-border expansion for the growth of the MNE (Chapter 13) and the capital budgeting process (Chapter 14), this chapter focuses on the process of completing an international acquisition transaction. In addition to detailing both the valuation techniques employed and the management of the acquisition process, we describe both the theory and the application of calculating discount rates for foreign investments and acquisitions.

INTERNATIONAL ACQUISITION

As opposed to greenfield investment, a *cross-border acquisition* has a number of significant advantages. First and foremost, it is quicker. Greenfield investment frequently requires extended periods of physical construction and organizational development. Acquiring an existing firm shortens the time required to gain a presence and facilitates competitive entry into the market. Second, it may be a cost-effective way of gaining competitive advantages such as technology, brand names valued in the target market, and logistical and distribution advantages, while simultaneously eliminating a local competitor. Third, specific to cross-border acquisitions, international economic, political, and foreign exchange conditions may result in market imperfections allowing target firms to be undervalued. Many enterprises throughout Asia have been the target of acquisition as a result of the Asian economic crisis' impact on their financial health. Many enterprises were in dire need of capital injections from so-called *white knights*, for competitive survival.

Cross-border acquisitions are not, however, without their pitfalls. As with all acquisitions—domestic or international—there are the frequent problems of paying too high a price or suffering a method of financing that is too costly. Meshing different corporate cultures can be traumatic. Management of the post-acquisition process is frequently characterized by downsizing to gain economies of scale and scope in overhead functions. This results in nonproductive impacts on the firm as individuals attempt to save their own jobs. Internationally, additional difficulties arise from host governments intervening in price, financing, employment guarantees, market segmentation, and general nationalism and favoritism. In fact, the ability to complete international acquisitions successfully may itself be a test of competency of the MNE in the twenty-first century.

The Acquisition Process

The process of acquiring an enterprise anywhere in the world has three common elements: (1) identification and valuation of the target; (2) negotiating the tender and its acceptance; and (3) management of the post-acquisition transition.

Mergers and acquisitions have long been considered the realm of high-flying investment bankers and deal-makers. But the investment banking enterprise requires an enormous work effort in the key elements of market analysis, competitive evaluation, and financial detail. The due-diligence process alone can be an extremely arduous undertaking. In the end, successful acquisitions require successful completion of all three key elements listed above. The value of an acquisition may not be reflected in the spreadsheets, but in the future lines of business and competencies created in the post-merger enterprise.

Valuation

Identification of potential acquisition targets, discussed in both Chapter 1 ("seekers") and Chapter 13 (alternatives for foreign market entry) requires a well-defined corporate strategy and focus. The identification of the *target market* precedes the identification of the *target firm*. Entering a highly developed market offers the widest choice of publicly traded firms with relatively well defined markets and publicly disclosed financial and operational data. Emerging markets frequently require the services of acquisition specialists who can aid in the identification of firms—generally privately held firms—that not only possess promising market prospects but may be amenable to suitors. Emerging markets pose additional problems, including scant financial data, limited access to management, government restrictions on foreign purchases, and few firms that are publicly traded. The growth of privatization programs in emerging markets in the latter half of the 1990s did, however, provide a number of new targets for cross-border acquisitions that would have been unavailable in previous times.

Once identification has been completed, the process of valuing the target begins. A variety of valuation techniques are widely used in international business today, each with its relative merits. In addition to the fundamental methodologies of *discounted cash flow* (DCF) and *multiples* of earnings and cash flows, there is also a variety of industry-specific measures that focus on the most significant elements of value in business lines.[2] In the field of valuation, "more is better." The completion of a variety of alternative valuations for the target firm aids in gaining a more complete picture of what price must be paid to complete the transaction, and also in determining whether the price is attractive.

ILLUSTRATIVE CASE

Valuing P.T. Semen Gresik of Indonesia

The following valuation analysis uses the case study preceding this chapter, P.T. Semen Gresik, as the basis for this numerical example. Valuing Semen Gresik poses a number of additional financial challenges beyond the typical challenges frequently found in emerging markets, such as high rates of inflation and currency volatility.

Valuation by Discounted Cash Flow

The most common valuation technique, discounted cash flow (DCF) requires that a complete set of pro forma financial statements be constructed for the target firm—in this case, P.T. Semen Gresik. Following the capital budgeting principles detailed in the previous chapter (Chapter 14), the expected future earnings, free cash flows, and DCF valuation is presented in Exhibit 15.2. The total value of the enterprise is found first by discounting all free cash flows, then by deducting creditor and minority interest to determine the residual equity value. This is called *sequential valuation*.

Free cash flow. Prediction of *free cash flow* (FCF) is defined as follows:

$$FCF = EBITDA - Taxes - Chg\ NWC - Capex$$

where *EBITDA* is estimated earnings before interest, taxes, depreciation, and amortization; Taxes are taxes payable after interest is deducted; Chg *NWC* is change in net working capital; and *Capex* is any capital expenditure currently planned by the firm. The resulting *FCF* is the cash flow available to the owners of capital (shareholders and creditors) after all expenses, payments to government, and necessary maintenance investments have been made.

Cost of capital. The discount rate utilized in Exhibit 15.2 is based upon the estimated weighted-average cost of capital for Semen Gresik in Indonesian rupiah. This is a particularly troublesome value in an economy suffering relatively high inflation, in this case approximately 30% per year.

The government issues debt that is indexed to yield a 3% real rate of return over and above inflation, 30% + 3%, or 33%. This is the local currency

Exhibit 15.2   *Discounted Cash Flow Valuation of P.T. Semen Gresik*

Billions of Indonesian rupiah	1998	1999	2000	2001	2002
Assumed growth in EBIT	16%	27%	20%	20%	20%
EBIT	458.0	614.0	736.8	884.2	1061.0
Add depreciation & amortization	261.0	276.0	276.0	276.0	276.0
EBITDA	719.0	890.0	1,012.8	1,160.2	1,337.0
Less taxes (30%)	(215.7)	(267.0)	(303.8)	(348.0)	(401.1)
Less changes in working capital	(19.0)	(21.8)	(17.2)	(20.6)	(24.8)
Less capital expenditure	(40.0)	(40.0)	–	–	–
Free cash flow (FCF)	444.3	561.2	691.8	791.5	911.1
Terminal value					18,222.8
FCF for discounting	444.3	561.2	691.8	791.5	19,133.9
Present value (PV) factor	1.0000	0.7556	0.5709	0.4313	0.3259
PV of FCF	444.3	424.0	394.9	341.4	6,236.0
Cumulative PV of FCF	7,840.6				
Enterprise value (EV)	7,840.6		Terminal value makes up 76% of EV		
Less net debt	(4,113.5)				
Less minority interests	(23.1)				
Equity value	3,704.0				
Shares outstanding (millions)	593.2				
Fair value of equity per share	Rp 6,244				

Notes: Depreciation and amortization as scheduled for 1998 and 1999, assumed constant thereafter. Working capital grows to maintain 14% of EBIT. Capital expenditures (Capex) is as scheduled in 1998 and 1999, with no expenditures currently planned after that date. Terminal value is a multiple of 20 of the year 2002's net operating cash flow. Discount factor is Semen Gresik's rupiah cost of capital, 32.350%.

risk-free rate of interest. The risk-free rate serves as the basis for the firm's before-tax cost of debt and as input into the Capital-Asset Pricing Model (CAPM) utilized to calculate a cost of equity for the firm. The firm pays 2% over and above the risk-free rate for debt, or 35% (33% + 2%). If an effective corporate income tax rate of 30% is assumed, Semen Gresik's after-tax cost of debt is:

$$k_d\,(1 - \text{Tax}) = 35\%\,(1 - .30) = 24.5\%$$

The cost of equity for Semen Gresik is obtained using the CAPM. The firm's beta (β) over the past 60 months (typical period for beta analysis) has averaged 1.2. The Indonesian market equity risk premium (RPM)—the average equity market return over and above the risk-free rate—is currently 6.0%. Semen Gresik's cost of equity is:

$$k_e = k_{rf} + \beta RPM = 33.0\% + 1.20\,(6.0\%) = 40.2\%$$

With a 50% debt-to-capital ratio (equal parts debt and equity), Semen Gresik's weighted-average cost of capital (WACC) is:

$$WACC = (\% \text{ debt})\,k_d(1 - \text{Tax}) + (\% \text{ equity})k_e$$
$$= (.50)24.5\% + (.50)40.2\% = 32.35\%$$

Although this appears to be a very high discount rate, it discounts cash flows that are also growing with inflation, although imperfectly.

Note that the earnings and cash flows of Semen Gresik are not assumed to rise as rapidly as inflation. Although it would be theoretically convenient to assume so, the actual earnings outlook is estimated independently of inflation. This difference in rates, where inflation is rising faster than earnings, is an example of real operating exposure previously discussed in Chapter 7.

Terminal value. Although the pro forma earnings and cash flows are only estimated through the year 2002, clearly the firm will continue to operate further into the future. The terminal value is intended to capture in an approximate manner this continuing business value. In the previous chapter on multinational capital budgeting, the terminal value was estimated on the basis of a perpetuity of net operating cash flow.

An alternative method frequently used in valuation analysis is to assume some multiple of net operating cash flow in the final year considered. In this case, with an assumed multiple of 20, the terminal value for Semen Gresik is estimated as Rp18,222.8 (20 × Rp9,111.1 with internal rounding not shown here). This technique is particularly applicable in leveraged buyouts (LBOs) and private equity ventures, where the real value and purpose of the initial purchase is the eventual sale of the enterprise at a future date.

Equity value. The present value of all future expected cash flows is the total enterprise value. Semen Gresik's equity value is then found by deducting the net debt due creditors and any minority interests. Total equity value divided by total shares outstanding (including shares held by the Indonesian government) is the fair value of equity per share.

The DCF valuation shown in Exhibit 15.2 is only a starting point. A number of assumptions have been made in order to derive a price of Rp6,244 per share, and these "value drivers" should be analyzed further utilizing sensitivity analysis. Exhibit 15.3 below illustrates how this DCF

| Exhibit 15.3 | *Sensitivity Analysis on DCF Value Drivers for P.T. Semen Gresik: Equity Value per Share (rupiah)* |

Earnings Growth	Terminal Value Multiple	Cost of Capital	Equity Value per Share	
15%	20	32.35%	5,257	
20%	20	32.35%	6,244	Baseline
25%	20	32.35%	7,309	
30%	20	32.35%	8,454	
35%	20	32.35%	9,684	
20%	10	32.35%	1,238	
20%	15	32.35%	3,741	
20%	20	32.35%	6,244	Baseline
20%	25	32.35%	8,747	
20%	30	32.35%	11,250	

value per equity share changes as these value drivers are changed. Clearly, after a variety of DCF sensitivity studies, an average fair value can be approximated.

Valuation by Multiples of Earnings and Cash Flows

The valuation of businesses of all kinds, small or large, domestic or multinational, goods or services, has long been as much art as science. The use of *multiples*, in which a ratio for the subject firm is compared to comparable ratios for competitors or recent acquisitions, is one of these more artistic processes. Similar in logic to ratio analysis used in traditional financial analysis, it simply presents how the firm stacks up against industry comparables. Some of the most widely used measures include the price/earnings per share (P/E) ratio, the price/free cash flow (PFCF) ratio, the market-to-book (M/B) ratios, and a variety of ratios that compare enterprise value (EV) to either earnings or cash flows.[3] Each of these ratios includes a market-determined value—price—either explicitly in the numerator or used in calculating market capitalization. This price is then combined with values taken from the firm's own financials, in the form of either earnings (e.g., earnings per share), cash flow (e.g., free cash flow), or market capitalization.

P/E ratio. The P/E ratio is by far the most widely used of the valuation ratios. As discussed in Chapter 11 on sourcing equity globally, equity markets themselves are frequently compared in terms of market averages of P/E. Simply stated, the *P/E ratio* is an indication of what the market is willing to pay for a unit of earnings. But more importantly, it is an indication of how secure the market's perception is about the future earnings and cash flow of the firm.[4] Markets do not pay for past or present earnings. An investor purchasing a share today is taking a long position on the basis of what earnings are expected to do in the future—from that moment on.

The current share price of Semen Gresik at the time of the case, Rp10,500, when combined with expected earnings for the following year (1999) on a per share basis, Rp78 billion divided by 593,200,000 shares (Appendix 3 in the PT Semen Gresik case), implies a PE ratio of nearly 80!

$$P/E \text{ ratio} = \frac{\text{Current market price}}{\text{Earnings per share}} = \frac{\text{Rp}10,500}{\left(\dfrac{\text{Rp}78,000,000,000}{593,200,000 \text{ shares}}\right)} = 80$$

Clearly the market at the time of the case believed either that Semen Gresik's earnings would be relatively riskless into the future or that the earnings were artificially low at the present time as a result of the Asian and Indonesian economic crises.[5]

An added feature of the P/E ratio is its ability to separate what the management of a firm has direct responsibility for—earnings—from what the market thinks about the quantity and quality of those earnings—the *multiple*.

$$Market\ price = EPS_{management} \times PE_{market}$$

In the case of Semen Gresik, the assessment of the marketplace, at least in the month prior to the final bids for the Indonesian government's sale of its shares to foreign suitors, was highly aggressive. P/E ratios for the global cement industry rarely fall outside a narrow range between 10 and 14.

M/B Ratio. The market-to-book (M/B) ratio is nearly as widely used in valuation as is the P/E ratio. The M/B ratio provides some measure of the market's assessment of the employed capital per share versus what the capital cost. It is calculated as the ratio of share price to book value per share:[6]

$$M/B \text{ ratio} = \frac{\text{Current share price}}{\text{Book value per share}} = \frac{\text{Rp}10,500}{\text{Rp}4,492} = 2.34$$

With a ratio of 2.34, Semen Gresik was considered comparable if not high by industry standards. The 1998 average for cement manufacturers in emerging markets ranged from a low of 0.3 (several Colombian firms) to a high of 2.7 (Lima Cement, Peru), averaging 1.0. Cemex's own M/B ratio hovered around 1.0 for most of the year. The average M/B ratio for the six largest cement groups in the world for 1998 was only 1.7.

Exhibit 15.4	*Valuing Semen Gresik Using the U.S. Dollar as the Functional Currency*			
Date	**Share Price (Rp)**	**Exchange Rate (Rp/$)**	**Share Price (US$)**	**Capitalization (US$)**
June 19, 1998	9,150	14,500	0.63	374,329,655
July 10, 1998	9,150	14,600	0.63	371,765,753
August 18, 1998	10,775	12,000	0.90	532,644,167
August 28, 1998	10,500	13,000	0.73	432,541,667

The *book value* of a firm is the value of common stock as recorded on the firm's balance sheet plus the retained earnings (cumulative capital reinvested from earnings). If the M/B ratio exceeds 1, it implies that the firm's equity is currently valued in excess of what stockholders invested in the firm. Like the P/E ratio, the magnitude of the M/B ratio, as compared to its major competitors, reflects the market's perception of the quality of the firm's earnings, management, and general strategic opportunities.

Functional Currency and Valuation

The P.T. Semen Gresik case also raises one of the truly international questions in valuation, the significance of functional currency of denomination. In Chapter 8 the functional currency of a foreign affiliate was defined as the currency that dominated the economic cash flows of the firm. In the case of Semen Gresik, the Indonesian rupiah may not be the functional currency of either the firm or the industry; the functional currency may be the U.S. dollar. If this is the case, it is the interaction of earnings and price in local currency terms (Indonesian rupiah) with the exchange rate of the functional currency (rupiah/dollar) that reflects value.

Exhibit 15.4 provides a series of alternative valuations of Semen Gresik shares as a function of the exchange rate. If the U.S. dollar is indeed the relevant currency of denomination for the true valuation of Semen Gresik, much of the volatility in the share price as determined on the Jakarta exchange over the months prior to privatization reflects offsetting movements to the exchange rate itself. Note that the share prices illustrated here, ranging between Rp9,150 and Rp10,775, are considerably higher than the DCF valuation of Rp6,244 we derived previously.

ILLUSTRATIVE CASE

How High a Hurdle?

It did raise some eyebrows at first. When Aegon, a Dutch life insurer, bought Transamerica, a San Francisco-based insurer, Aegon said it was expecting a return of only 9% from the deal, well below the 11% "hurdle rate" it once proclaimed as its benchmark. Had this darling of the stock market betrayed its devoted investors for the sake of an eye-catching deal?

Not at all. Years of falling interest rates and rising equity valuations have shrunk the cost of capital for firms such as Aegon. So companies that regularly adjust the hurdle rates they use to evaluate potential projects and acquisitions are not cheating their shareholders. Far from it: they are doing their investors a service. Unfortunately, such firms are rare in Europe. "I don't know many companies at all who lowered their hurdle rates in line with interest rates, so they're all under investing," says Greg Milano, a partner at Stern Stewart, a consultancy that helps companies estimate their cost of capital.

This has a huge impact on corporate strategy. Companies generally make their investment decisions by discounting the net cash-flows a project is estimated to generate to their present value. If that net present value is positive, the project should, in theory, make shareholders better off. But the entire decision rests on the accuracy of both the cash-flow forecasts and the discount rate. Set the rate even a sliver too high, and good projects appear bad; set it too low and bad investments look appealing.

This makes it all the more surprising that some companies pay little attention to the impact on the discount rate of changes in their cost of capital. Steve Hodge, Treasurer of Shell, an Anglo-Dutch oil giant, says that a difference of only one percentage point in the discount rate can change the value of , say, an oil-refinery with a 15-year life by hundreds of millions of dollars. Nonetheless, Shell left its hurdle rates unchanged for two decades, and now intends to keep them at present levels for years to come.

Generally speaking, says Paul Gibbs, an analyst at J.P. Morgan, an American bank, finance directors in America often review their hurdle rates; in continental Europe they do so sometimes, and in Britain, rarely. As a result, the Confederation of British Industry, a big-business lobby, worries about under investment, and officials at the Bank of England grumble about firms' reluctance to lower hurdles.

But many managers remain deeply skeptical about the theory behind discount rates. Even though it spits out percentages to several decimal points, the capital-asset pricing model, as the conceptual framework for calculating the rates is controversial in itself. "The whole basis of setting hurdle rates is flawed," says Mr. Hodge. "If you change the hurdle rate you're hiding away a management decision in a piece of spurious arithmetic."

POST MERGER AND ACQUISITION MANAGEMENT

Although the headlines and flash of investment banking activities are typically focused on the valuation and bidding process in an acquisition transaction, the post-transaction management is probably more critical. An acquiring firm can pay too little or too much, but if the management post-transaction is not managed effectively, the entire return on the investment is squandered. Post-merger management is the period in which the motivations for the transaction must be realized. Those reasons, more effective management, synergies arising from the new combination, and the injection of capital at a cost and availability previously out of the reach of the acquisition target must be effectively implemented after the transaction. The biggest problem, however, is nearly always corporate culture.

As painfully depicted in the following illustrative case of British Petroleum and Amoco, the clash of corporate cultures, personalities, and the human beings who make up the core competencies of their respective enterprises pose both the biggest risk and the biggest potential gain from international mergers and acquisitions.

ILLUSTRATIVE CASE

Post-Merger Management: The 'Merger' of British Petroleum and Amoco

A popular joke in Amoco hallways goes: What's the British pronunciation of BP-Amoco? BP–the Amoco is silent.

LONDON—BP and Amoco called it a merger of equals. But over coffee and sandwiches one day in the BP cafeteria here, Amoco Corp. executives discovered that British Petroleum PLC had other plans.

During a conference of 20 top executives from both companies last fall, Rodney Chase, then BP's deputy chief executive, unveiled the blueprint for the merged company. It would be led by BP management, run with BP's structure and infused with BP's do-or-die culture. Anyone who didn't agree was welcome to join the 10,000 other workers who were being fired.

In Chicago during negotiations, Mr. Browne [BP's chief executive] and Amoco Chief Executive Lawrence Fuller wrestled with the question of management control. It was clear that BP would be the acquirer, since it was larger, but Mr. Fuller wondered whether the two companies could combine the "best of both" management worlds. Mr. Browne was unequivocal. "It was not negotiable for us," he said in a recent interview. "We had developed a structure and systems that had worked for us, and we were anxious to apply it to a larger company."

Indeed, at the heart of BP is an unusual management structure and culture that it aims to stamp on other companies. The system grew from the company's near-fatal crisis in 1992, when then-CEO Robert Horton was ousted in a boardroom coup, the company's dividend was cut in half and a single quarter's loss topped $1 billion. The subsequent restructuring essentially turned the company into a giant family of entrepreneurial small businesses.

The system clashed badly with Amoco. More like a classic pyramid, Amoco had strict reporting lines and heavy internal bureaucracy. Managers often spent months negotiating contracts with internal businesses. Amoco's executive suite on the 30th floor in Chicago was a formal corridor of closed doors and strict schedules. BP's fourth-floor suite in London is an open-plan space with glass walls, where top executives breeze in and out of each other's offices.

Company memos began showing up with British spellings, prompting complaints in the BP Amoco newsletter about use of the words "organisation" and "labour." BP jargon was lost on some Amoco executives. In meetings, BP's managers lived on "hard targets" that had to be met, while Amoco talked about "aspirations" that were only occasionally reached. BP raved about "peer groups," while Amoco talked about "strategic-planning councils."

The culture clash came to a head in the cafeteria meeting last fall at BP headquarters. While most managers expected BP would dominate the merged company, few anticipated that its grip would be so strong. During the all-day conference, Amoco managers argued the case for a centralized structure, while their BP counterparts said it wouldn't work. "You're not interested at all in our ideas," said one Amoco executive. Another said: "We weren't prepared for this." Sensing a crisis, Mr. Fuller stood up, a BP executive says, and gave his troops a final order: "We're going to use the BP systems, and that's that."

REAL-OPTION ANALYSIS

The *discounted cash flow* (DCF) approach used in the valuation of P.T. Semen Gresik—and capital budgeting and valuation in general—has long had its critics. Investments that have long lives, cash flow returns in later years, or possess levels of risk higher than those typical of the firm's current business activities, are often rejected by traditional DCF financial analysis. More importantly, when MNEs evaluate competitive projects, traditional DCF financial analysis is typically unable to capture the *strategic options* that an individual investment option may offer. This has led to the development of *real-option theory* (OPT) or *real-asset analysis*. OPT is the application of option theory to capital budgeting decisions.

OPT is a different way of thinking about investment values. Although difficult to describe simply, OPT is a cross between decision-tree analysis and pure option-based valuation. It is particularly useful when analyzing investment projects that will follow very different value-paths at decision points in time where management decisions are made regarding project pursuit. This wide range of potential outcomes is at the heart of OPT theory.

Real option valuation also allows the analysis of a number of managerial decisions that in practice characterize many major capital investment projects:

1. The option to defer
2. The option to abandon
3. The option to alter capacity
4. The option to start-up or shut-down (switching)

OPT treats cash flows in terms of future value in a positive sense, whereas DCF treats future cash flows negatively (on a discounted basis). OPT is a particularly powerful device when addressing potential investment projects with extremely long life spans, or investments that do not commence until future dates. OPT acknowledges the sequence in time of how information is gathered and utilized by management to develop a capital project. Management learns from active and passive knowledge gathering and then utilizes that knowledge in making subsequent decisions.

OPT, like DCF and other investment analysis techniques, is simply a tool. OPT and DCF are complementary. Both methods should be employed in the analysis of potential investments, and information gathered from both.

Finally, OPT is not a simple technique to be implemented. The analyst must have an enormous amount of technical facility to implement the technique correctly. Like most techniques derived from financial theory, it is a powerful technique that can be easily abused. And as with other applications of option theory in international finance, a large investment of effort is required to educate the users of OPT information in the proper interpretation of results.

ILLUSTRATIVE CASE

Keeping Your Options Open

"Those who can, do, those who cannot, teach." Many a manager has at time been tempted to borrow this aphorism to put woolly professors in their place. Company bosses find it especially hard to resist grumbling about academic otherworldliness whenever they are deciding where to invest their shareholders' money. To evaluate potential projects, they almost invariably have to resort to a theory of corporate finance called the "Capital-asset Pricing Model" (CAPM). Yet real-life managers tend not to like this model, for the simple reason that it ignores the value of real-life managers. So they might welcome some recent academic work. In the ivory tower, they are talking about ditching the CAPM for a rival, called "real-options theory," that places managers at its very core.

To see why bosses are likely to prefer this new approach, consider what is wrong with the traditional model. The CAPM involves forecasting all the cash flows of an investment project and discounting them to their net present value (NPV). Getting the cash-flow projections right (or even close) is staggeringly difficult. But it is even trickier to choose the correct discount rate. Conceptually, that rate is the opportunity cost of not investing in another project of similar systematic risk (i.e., risk that, in a large portfolio, cannot be diversified away). So the higher a project's risk, the higher its discount rate and the lower its NPV. But in practice, setting discount rates at the right level is almost impossible. The CAPM often spits out negative NPVs for many of the most exciting strategic opportunities.

The main reason for this shortcoming is that the model can use only information that is already known. That is typically not much, and the resulting uncertainty tends to be reflected in an excessive discount rate. Combining an NPV calculation with decision trees (which assign numerical probabilities to various possible outcomes) may help, but not much. For each branch of the tree, the analyst still has to pick and apply an appropriate discount rate, and that of course was the problem in the first place. More fundamentally, the flaw in the CAPM is that it implicitly assumes that when firms buy new assets, they hold these passively for the life of the project. But they do not. Instead, they employ managers precisely in order to react to events as they unfold. Obviously, this managerial flexibility must be worth something.

Getting Real

To quantify exactly how much it is worth is the point of real-options analysis. It starts by recognising that most investment opportunities have embedded in them a series of managerial options. Take, for instance, an imaginary oil company. Its bosses believe that they have found an oil field, but they know neither how much oil it contains nor what the price of oil will be once they are ready to pump. So, as a first step, they could simply put enough money down to buy or lease the land and explore. If they do not find oil they can cap their outlays at the costs already sunk. If they do strike oil, however, they might invest a bit more and put the drilling gear in place. But suppose the oil price then plummets. Management could put the project on hold and let its field lie fallow. Perhaps it could also switch to producing gas instead of oil. Or it could drop the project and sell the land. If, on the other hand, the oil price goes up, the firm is ready to pump. Since oil prices and other factors are uncertain, in other words, the mere option to produce has value.

Options on "real" assets (and indeed poker bets) behave rather like options on financial assets (puts and calls on shares or currencies, say). The similarities are such that they can, at least in theory, be valued according to the same methodology. In the case of the oil company, for instance, the cost of land corresponds to the premium (or down-payment) on a call option, and the extra investment needed to start production to its strike price (at which the option is exercised). As with financial options, the longer the option lasts before it expires and the more volatile the price of the underlying asset—in this case, oil—the more the option is worth. This is in sharp contrast to the CAPM, which deals harshly with both long time horizons and uncertainty.

There is a snag, of course: sheer complexity. Pricing financial options is daunting, but valuing real options is harder still. Their term, unlike that of financial options, is usually open-ended or undefinable. The volatility of the underlying asset can be difficult to measure or guess, especially since it is not always clear what it is—if, for example, it is yet to be invested. How can one define the appropriate benchmark asset-class in the case of a new drug for a rare disease? And there may be additional variables to consider, such as the strategic benefit of pre-empting a rival.

SUMMARY

- International mergers, acquisitions, and strategic alliances, all face similar challenges: *they must value the target enterprise on the basis of its projected performance in its market.* This process of enterprise valuation combines elements of strategy, management, and finance.

- The process of acquiring an enterprise anywhere in the world has three common elements: (1) identification and valuation of the target; (2) completion of the ownership change transaction (the tender); and (3) the management of the post-acquisition transition.

- A variety of valuation techniques are widely used in international business today, each with its relative merits. In addition to the fundamental methodologies of *discounted cash flow* (DCF) and *multiples* of earnings and cash flows. A variety of industry-specific measures are used that focus on the most significant elements of value in business lines.

- The DCF approach to valuation calculates the value of the enterprise as the present value of all future free cash flows less the cash flows due creditors and minority interest holders. This is termed *sequential valuation.*

- The P/E ratio is an indication of what the market is willing to pay for a currency unit of earnings. It is also an indication of how secure the market's perception is about the future earnings of the firm.

- The *market-to-book ratio* (M/B) is a method of valuing a firm on the basis of what the market believes the firm is worth over and above its capital as recorded on the books of the company.

- In *cross-border valuation*, the home currency of the target firm may or may not be the measure of value. Particularly in emerging markets, cross-border valuations may actually be made in hard currency terms such as dollars to euros.

- *Real-option analysis* (OPT) is an option-based method analyzing investment projects that possess large, identifiable, future decision points regarding investment outcomes. Although extremely valuable in the insights it provides, OPT is difficult to implement on a systematic basis.

QUESTIONS

1. Free Cash Flow versus Profit

Consider the following statement: Academia always focuses on the present value of free cash flow as the definition of value, yet companies seem to focus on "earnings" or "profits."

a. Do you think this statement is true?

b. Explain clearly and precisely what the basic distinction is between cash flow and profit.

c. How do we convert a measure of profit, such as net income on a profit and loss statement into a measure of cash flow?

2. Discounted Cash Flow Valuation

Discounted cash flow (DCF) valuation requires the analyst to estimate and isolate the expected free cash flows that a specific asset or investment will produce in the future. The analyst then must discount these cash flows back to the present.

a. Are the cash flows and discount rate before- or after-tax? Do both need to be the same or should one be before-tax and the other after-tax?

b. How is the discount rate for the investment derived? What assumptions are or should be made about the way the investment will actually be financed?

c. A very common criticism of DCF is that it "punishes future value and therefore is biased against long-term investments." Construct an argument refuting this statement.

3. P/E Valuation of Global.Com

The shares of Global.com (U.S.), a new high-flying worldwide cellular phone company, are valued largely on the bases of price/earnings multiples. Other firms trading on U.S. exchanges in its similar industry segment are currently valued at P/E ratios of 35 to 40. Given the following earnings estimates, what would you estimate the value of Global.Com to be?

Last year's EPS	This year's EPS	Next year's EPS
$(1.20)	$0.75	$1.85

4. Functional Currency and Valuation: P.T. Semen Gresik

Exhibit 15.4 illustrated how the market capitalization of Semen Gresik varied over four different dates in the summer of 1998. If the measure of "value" for this Indonesian company is actually the U.S. dollar and not the Indonesian rupiah, how should the exchange rate between the rupiah and dollar affect the rupiah share price?

5. Bidding on São Paulo Cellular Rights

A consortium of global telecommunication firms is about to submit a bid to purchase the rights to provide cellular telephone services to central São Paulo. The bid must be submitted, and payment made, if awarded the bid, in U.S. dollars, not in Brazilian real (R$). The consortium has finalized the following forecasts of cash flows, exchange rates, and potential discount rates.

	Year-0	Year-1	Year-2	Year-3
Estimated CF (millions of R$):				
Best case	(1,350)	550	2,000	3,800
Moderate case	(1,350)	550	1,600	3,200
Worst case	(1,350)	550	1,000	1,500
Expected exchange rate (R$/$):				
Best case	1.70	1.70	1.70	1.70
Moderate case	1.70	1.80	1.90	2.00
Worst case	1.70	2.00	2.20	2.50
Discount rate (R$ terms)	32.0%			
Discount rate (US$ terms)	18.0%			

Perform a DCF analysis on the potential investment and propose a final bid for submission.

MiniCase: *Private Equity in Latin America - The Soto Group*

Private equity focuses on purchasing small privately held firms, restructuring them with infusions of capital and professional management, and taking them public several years later. This means that their value to the private equity investors is in their terminal value—their value when taken public several years from now.

The Soto Group is a Mexico City-based private equity fund. It is evaluating the prospects for purchasing Guga Avionics (Buenos Aires), an aviation operating and management firm with current business operations throughout Argentina and southern Brazil. The Soto Group has, through its due-diligence process, acquired the needed financial statements, inventory of assets, and assessment of operations. Soto's valuation staff typically values the potential target on both an *a priori* basis (current structure and management strategy) and an *ex post* basis (expected values after capital and management expertise injections).

The second major set of "ifs" associated with acquiring Guga is what it could sell for in three years. The Soto Group has an unbending internal discipline that every firm acquired must be restructured, revitalized, and ready for public sale in three years from deal consummation, or less. Given market multiples on the Buenos Aires Bolsa at this time, a value of 18 to 20 times current free cash flow (year-3) would be considered aggressive.

The a *priori* analysis, acquired from Guga Avionics and adjusted by Soto's own valuation and market experts, appears as follows (millions of Argentine pesos):

	Year-0	Year-1	Year-2	Year-3
Gross revenues	210	235	270	325
Less direct costs	(132)	(144)	(162)	(190)
Gross profit	78	91	108	135
Gross margin	37%	39%	40%	41%
Less G&A	(16)	(17)	(18)	(19)
Less depreciation	(24)	(24)	(24)	(24)
EBIT	38	50	66	92
Less interest	(28)	(30)	(30)	(28)
EBT	10	20	36	64
Less taxes @ 30%	(3)	(6)	(11)	(19)
Net profit	7	14	26	45
Return on sales	3%	6%	9%	14%

The Soto Group believes that it can reduce financing expenses by 25% in years-1 and -2, and 35% in year-3. It also believes that by using its own operational experience, it can reduce direct costs by 15%, 20%, and 25%, in year-1, -2, and -3, respectively. The big question is revenue enhancement. Guga has done a solid job of promoting and expanding service revenues in the past several years. At most, the Soto Group believes it may be able to expand gross revenues by 5% per annum over current forecasts.

Using this data, as the lead member of the Soto Group's valuation staff, answer the following questions:

a. What is the difference between a *priori* and *ex post* earnings and cash flows?

b. What is the difference between a *priori* and *ex post* sale value at the end of year-3?

c. What is Guga Avionics worth?

d. What would you recommend—in addition to the current Soto plan—to enhance the profit and cash flow outlook for Guga if acquired?

WORLD WIDE WEB EXERCISES

W1. Intellectual Property and Valuation

The late 1990s saw the rise of corporate valuations arising from ownership of various forms of intellectual property, rather than the traditional value arising from production and sale of goods or services. Use the following website as a start in preparing a management brief on the current state of valuing intellectual property.

Intellectual Property Valuation   http://valuationcorp.com/

W2. Real Options in Petroleum

The application of options analysis to capital budgeting problems is relatively new. Most of the applications of option analysis to date have been in the area of resource extraction industries such as oil and gas exploration and production. Beginning with the following web site, start building your own information base on the use of options for investment decisions.

Real Options in Petroleum   http://www.puc-rio.br/marco.ind/main.html

W3. Market Capitalization of Brahma of Brazil

Brahma is one of the largest publicly traded firms in Brazil. It is listed on both the Bovespa and the New York Stock Exchange (ADRs). Using historical data that can be found on one of the sources below, answer the following questions.

Hoovers   http://www.hoovers.com
Yahoo   http://www.yahoo.com

a. How did Brahma's share price—in both real and U.S. dollar terms— react to the January 1999 Brazilian real devaluation?

b. Would a firm like Brahma be a more or less attractive target of foreign investors after the real's devaluation?

SUGGESTED READINGS

Bank of America Roundtable on Evaluating and Financing Foreign Direct Investment," *Journal of Applied Corporate Finance*, Fall 1996, Vol. 9, No. 3, pp. 64–79.

Lee, Tung-Jean and Richard E. Caves, "Uncertain Outcomes of Foreign Investment: Determinants of Profits After Large Acquisitions," *Journal of International Business Studies*, Vol. 29, No. 3, Third Quarter 1998, pp. 563–582.

Luehrman, Timothy A., "What's it Worth?: A General Manager's Guide to Valuation," *Harvard Business Review*, May 1997.

Luehrman, Timothy A., "Strategy as a Portfolio of Real Options," *Harvard Business Review*, Sept.–Oct. 1998, pp. 89–99.

NOTES

1. Porter (1996).
2. For example, the P.T. Semen Gresik case presented earlier focuses on the valuation and acquisition of a cement business. In this industry segment, the US$/tonne of installed capacity cost of the business is an industry-specific valuation method frequently employed.
3. *Enterprise value* is defined as the sum of current equity market capitalization (equity share price times shares outstanding) plus the current market value of net debt outstanding.
4. Coca-Cola (U.S.) has long been a prime example of a MNE whose P/E ratio, typically ranging between 35 and 42, is an indicator of how sustainable global earnings and earnings growth are in the eyes of shareholders.
5. One practice growing with the expansion of international mergers and acquisitions is the calculation of separate P/E ratios with earnings measures that include and exclude foreign exchange gains (losses).
6. The M/B ratio is frequently compared to the concept of Tobin's q. However, Tobin's q is actually the ratio of total market value of assets (debt plus equity) to the estimated replacement cost of total assets. The M/B ratio focuses on equity in both the numerator and denominator and is a mix of market value (numerator) and historical accounting value (denominator).

CHAPTER 16

ADJUSTING FOR RISK IN FOREIGN INVESTMENTS

Investors—regardless of whether they are investing internationally in stocks, bonds, acquisitions, or greenfield startups—must estimate the required rate of return on the investment.[1] The investment is made on the basis that the investor expects the return on the investment to exceed the required rate of return. The question remains: How does the investor determine a required rate of return on a foreign investment?

A MNE undertaking foreign direct investment (FDI) must determine the cost of funds and the required returns on the investment.[2] The investment may yield cash flow returns in local currency, the investor's currency, or a third currency. The MNE must weigh the expected cash flow returns and business prospects against the possibilities of political disruption or intervention, political and economic actions that undermine the business environment, or simply restrictions and regulations on the activities of foreign MNEs operating in the country. In short, the MNE must adjust expected returns for expected risk.

Unfortunately, regardless of how sophisticated the theory or how deep the database, risks associated with foreign investments are inherently subjective, or, in other words, relatively more *qualitative* than *quantitative*. But for MNEs, which are putting investments at risk, this risk is a problem that must be addressed. Shareholders worldwide expect the management of the MNE to assess the risks the enterprise undertakes, make informed and consistent judgments, and manage the enterprise responsibly.

This chapter shows how MNEs may go about assessing and adjusting for the risks associated with foreign investments. We begin with a discussion of risk and its various forms and measures, and then we present three critical questions the MNE must address before assessing risk. We follow with a detailed numerical example of the Part IV case (Cemex and P.T. Semen Gresik), illustrating how these risks may be quantified for MNE decision-making. Finally, we return to the motivations for MNEs to go international (Chapter 1) and how these may influence the method of risk adjustment.

DEFINING RISK

Risk is normally defined as "the possibility of suffering harm or loss, or a course involving uncertain danger or hazard." There is, however, no single taxonomy of risk. Chapter 1 introduced the foreign exchange risks and political risks that MNEs must face. However, as we delve deeper into the complexity of MNE activities, it is increasingly difficult to separate economic risks from political risks. The case of Indonesia serves as a classic example. Government economic policies leading to privatization and openness to foreign bidders are most definitely an economic plus. At the same time, growing political opposition by management and labor to the prospects of foreign ownership introduces a level of political risk that many MNEs would find unacceptable.

)))) One-Sided versus Two-Sided Risk

The distinction between *one-sided* or *two-sided risk* can help in isolating what types of quantitative adjustments for risk may be employed.

One-Sided Risk. Traditional definitions of risk emphasize the potential for loss, a form of *one-sided risk*. For a MNE, examples of one-sided risks include the risk of expropriation and the risk of funds blockages. They are termed one-sided risks because management assumes the norm is that ownership and control of foreign affiliates is not threatened and that capital may be moved in and out of the subject country with relative freedom. There is no second side to their impact; maintenance of ownership and movement of capital are considered necessary for the conduct of business in the foreign country.

Although these risks are often described in terms of probabilities of occurrence, they are inherently qualitative in character and may best be thought of as "acceptable" or "unacceptable" by the MNE. They represent decision thresholds for management of the MNE.

Two-Sided Risk. Other risks, however, are *two-sided* in character. The most obvious one for MNEs is foreign exchange risk. A foreign subsidiary manufacturing facility producing in Indonesia may receive international competitive advantages (disadvantages) from having the Indonesian rupiah undervalued (overvalued) by global currency markets. Host government economic policies may be viewed as two-sided, since many governments may undertake economic programs that promote exports (upside) or restrict the activity of foreign firms in their domestic markets (downside). General economic cycles within the host country are also inherently two-sided.

These risks are often approximated through statistical studies of the past or simulations of the future. They lend themselves more directly to quantitative risk measurement and subsequent adjustments. They provide ways in which a MNE can rank-order its investment alternatives once they are categorized as acceptable.

))) Risk-Measurement Origins

The MNE draws upon two distinctly different sets of risk measurements, *measures from the marketplace* and *measures from institutions*.

Measures of Risk from the Market. Measures of risk from the market are typically capital cost components such as credit spreads and sovereign spreads. Their primary attribute is that they reflect the opinions of the marketplace about the probabilities of default or investment results. They are also quantities, lending themselves easily to use in financial analysis. The problem is that little market data exists on the countries in which MNEs are the most interested: the emerging markets of higher perceived risk.

Measures of Risk from Institutions. Measures of risk from institutions are typically constructed indices that rank countries on the basis of their macro-risk fundamentals, particularly their political and economic stability. Although often given numeric values (ordinal rankings more than cardinal in value), they are inherently subjective. They are therefore difficult to utilize in financial analyses and often result in a basic tiering of the country markets by MNEs into the "investment grade" and "speculative grade" categories so common among some of their primary contributors, the credit rating services.

Exhibit 16.1 provides a summary of many of the different measures by source for a selected set of countries. These measures are predominately qualitative in character but quantitative in form. Although many indices are numerical in value, they are formed from either rank-order judgments or ratios with subjective assessment required. If there are internal inconsistencies among rankings, remember that they each have their own individual goals, methodologies, and interpretation. The problem for MNEs is determining which—if any—of the measures is relevant to its foreign investment project, and how to quantify and apply the risk adjustment.

THREE DIMENSIONS OF MANAGERIAL RISK-ADJUSTMENT

A MNE's assessment of the prospects of a specific foreign investment requires managerial philosophy and action in answering three separate yet integrated issues and their associated questions:

1. **Parent viewpoint or project viewpoint**. Are the project's returns and risks to be evaluated on a local level—project viewpoint—or as seen from afar—from the viewpoint of the parent company?

2. **Role of the investment in the MNE's portfolio**. Depending on the nature of the investment and the motivation of the MNE, as introduced in Chapter 1, the way the investment is viewed and valued in the portfolio is critical. Does the investment's value arise from the MNE's entrance into a local market or from its ability to source a resource or produce a product elsewhere?

| Exhibit 16.1 | *Country Risk Ratings for Selected Countries* |

Risk Ratings	Indonesia	Finland	Brazil	Russia	Mexico
Currency:					
Unit	rupiah	euro	real	ruble	peso
Arrangement	floating	EMU	floating	managed float	floating
S&P's Rating	CCC+	AA	B+	SD	BB
Moody's Rating	B3	Aaa	B2	B3	B2
Fitch IBCA	B–	AAA	B	CCC	BB
Economist Intelligence Unit:					
Rating	D	B	D	D	C
Score	67	35	62	79	53
Euromoney:					
Rank	88	12	76	161	47
Score	36.4	90.9	41.7	20.9	55.2
Institutional Investor:					
Rank	86	14	65	104	49
Score	27.9	82.2	37.4	20.0	46.0
Trend	Negative	Positive	Negative	Negative	Positive
International Country Risk Guide:					
Political	42.0	90.0	66.0	54.0	69.0
Financial	22.0	39.0	31.5	25.5	31.0
Economic	18.0	45.5	33.0	18.5	35.0
Milken Institute Capital-Access Index:					
Score	37.8		61.65	57.81	61.65
Quantitative	56.6		52.38	71.15	52.38
Risk measures	26.3		29.41	43.59	31.25
Qualitative	0.0		36.36	31.03	34.76
Overseas Private Investment					
Corporation	Yes	No	Yes	Yes	No

Adapted by authors from the sources listed. All values for March 1999.

3. **Risk adjustment of the cash flows and/or the discount rate**. Should the risks associated with the foreign investment be incorporated in the expected cash flows of the foreign investment or in the discount rate applied to the cash flows?

We will discuss the pros and cons of each of these questions in the following section and then present a numerical illustration of implementing them individually utilizing our Part IV case study of Cemex and P.T. Semen Gresik.

))) Parent versus Project Viewpoints

As illustrated by the numerical analysis in Chapter 14, the prospects from the perspective of the parent MNE and from the project are inherently different. The "foreign risks" of a project from the viewpoint of the parent company are easily identified. These include the risk of goal conflicts with the host government that circumscribe the operations of a foreign firm within its borders—*political risk*; the ability to exercise effective control over the foreign affiliate within the country's legal environment—*governance risk*; the ability to move capital freely and efficiently in and out of the host country—*transfer risk*; and the value of the local currency cash flows generated and remitted to the parent in parent currency terms—*foreign exchange risk*. These risks from the parent perspective are often collectively referred to as *country risk*.

The project viewpoint, however, cannot be overlooked. This encompasses the prospective returns and risks of the project from the perspective of investors based in the foreign host market. From the project point of view, "foreign" risks also exist. A foreign affiliate has foreign exchange exposure on both its imports and its exports. Since the prime purpose of finding a project rate of return is to compare it with alternative opportunities to invest funds locally, the appropriate discount rate should be the one required by local investors for projects of the same business and financial risk class. This approach forces the parent to remember that local inflation and risk must be reflected in the required rate of return for local projects. And finally, it requires the parent company to remember that the "project" or "subsidiary" is a functional business unit operated and directed by professionals with performance and evaluation needs.

)))) Role of the Investment in the MNE's Portfolio

As discussed in Chapter 10, the field of finance has distinguished two different definitions of risk: (1) the risk of the individual security (standard deviation of expected return) and (2) the risk of the individual security as a component of a portfolio (beta). A foreign investment undertaken in order to enter a local or regional market—*market seeking*, as described in Chapter 1—will have returns that are more or less correlated with those of the local market. A portfolio-based assessment of the investment's prospects would then seem appropriate. A foreign investment undertaken for *resource-seeking* or *production-seeking* purposes may have returns related to those of the parent company or units located somewhere else in the world and have little to do with local markets. The decision about which approach is to be used by the MNE in evaluating prospective foreign investments may be the single most important analytical decision it makes. An investment's acceptability may change dramatically from one criteria to the other.

For comparisons within the local host country, a project's actual financing or parent-influenced debt capacity should be overlooked, since these would probably be different for local investors than they are for a multinational owner. In addition, the risks of the project to local investors might differ from those perceived by a foreign multinational owner because of the opportunities a multinational firm has to take advantage of market imperfections. Moreover, the local project may be only one out of an internationally diversified portfolio of projects for the multinational owner, whereas it might have to stand alone, without international diversification, if undertaken by local investors. Since diversification reduces risk, the multinational firm can require a lower rate of return than is required by local investors.

Thus the discount rate used locally must be a hypothetical rate based on a judgment as to what independent local investors would probably demand were they to own the business. Consequently, application of the local discount rate to local cash flows provides only a rough measure of the value of the project as a stand-alone local venture, rather than an absolute valuation.

)))) Adjusting Discount Rates versus Adjusting Cash Flows

When a foreign project is analyzed from the parent's point of view, the additional risk that stems from its "foreign" location can be handled in at least two ways, *adjusting the discount rate* or *adjusting the cash flows*.

Adjusting Discount Rates. The first method is to treat all foreign risk as a single problem by adjusting the discount rate applicable to foreign projects relative to the rate used for domestic projects to reflect the greater foreign exchange risk, political risk, agency costs, asymmetric information, and other uncertainties perceived in foreign operations. However, adjusting the discount rate applied to a foreign project's cash flow to reflect these uncertainties does not penalize net present value in proportion either to the actual amount at risk or to possible variations in the nature of that risk over time.[3] Combining all risks into a single discount rate may cause us to discard much information about the uncertainties of the future.[4] The numerical illustration in the following section illustrates how the discount rate for a foreign investment could be adjusted for risk.

Adjusting Cash Flows. In the second method, foreign risks are incorporated in adjustments to forecasted cash flows of the project. The discount rate for the foreign project is risk-adjusted only for overall business and financial risk, in the same manner as for domestic projects. Simulation-based assessment utilizes scenario development to estimate cash flows arising from the project over time under different alternative economic futures.

Shortcomings of Each. In many cases, however, adjusting neither the discount rate nor cash flows is optimal. For example, political uncertainties are a threat to the entire investment, not just to annual cash flows. Potential loss depends partly on the terminal value of the unrecovered parent investment, which will vary depending on how the project was financed, whether political risk insurance was obtained, and what investment horizon is contemplated. Furthermore, if the political climate were expected to be unfavorable in the near future any investment would probably be unacceptable.[5] Political uncertainty usually relates to possible adverse events that might occur in the more distant future, but that cannot be forseen at the present. Adjusting the discount rate for political risk thus penalizes early cash flows too heavily while not penalizing distant cash flows enough.

In the case of foreign exchange risk, changes in exchange rates have a potential effect on future cash flows because of operating exposure. The direction of the effect, however, can either decrease or increase net cash inflows, depending on where the products are sold and where inputs are sourced. (The variety of outcomes under operating exposure was explained in the Instruments du Rhone example in Chapter 7.) To increase the discount rate applicable to a foreign project, on the assumption that the foreign currency might depreciate more than expected, ignores the possible favorable effect of a foreign currency depreciation on the project's competitive position. Increased sales volume might more than offset a lower value of the local currency. Such an increase in the discount rate also ignores the possibility the foreign currency may appreciate (two-sided risk).[6]

Repercussions to the Investor. Apart from anticipated political and foreign exchange risks, MNEs sometimes worry that taking on foreign projects may increase the firm's overall cost of capital because of investors' perceptions of foreign risk. This worry seemed reasonable if the firm had significant investments in Iran, Russia, Serbia, or Afghanistan in the 1990s. However, the argument loses persuasiveness when applied to diversified foreign investments with a heavy balance in the industrial countries of Canada, Western Europe, Australia, and Asia, where, in fact, the bulk of FDI is located. These countries have a reputation for treating foreign investments by consistent standards, and empirical evidence confirms that a foreign presence in these countries may not increase the cost of capital. In fact, some studies indicate that required returns on foreign projects may even be lower than those for domestic projects.

MNE Practices. Surveys of MNEs over the past 30 years have shown that about half of them adjust the discount rate and half adjust the cash flows. One recent survey indicated a rising utilization of adjusting discount rates over adjusting cash flows. However, the survey also indicated an increasing use of multifactor methods—discount rate adjustment, cash flow adjustment, real options analysis, qualitative criteria—in evaluating foreign investments.[7]

A NUMERICAL ILLUSTRATION:

⟫⟫ Cemex (Mexico) and Semen Gresik (Indonesia)

Cemex, as noted previously in Chapter 14, is a Mexico-based firm that considers its functional currency to be the U.S. dollar. When Cemex makes any investments, it therefore calculates its cost of capital in U.S. dollars. As described in Chapter 10, the customary weighted-average cost of capital formula is as follows:

$$k_{\text{wacc}} = k_e \frac{E}{V} + k_d (1-t) \frac{D}{V}$$

k_e = risk-adjusted cost of equity
k_d = before-tax cost of debt
t = marginal tax rate
E = market value of the firm's equity
D = market value of the firm's debt
V = total market value of the firm's securities $(E + D)$

Cemex's cost of equity is calculated using the capital-asset-pricing model (CAPM):

$$k_e = k_{rf} + (k_m - k_{rf})\, \beta_{Cemex} = 6.00\% + (13.00\% - 6.00\%)1.5 = 16.50\%$$

k_e = risk-adjusted cost of equity,
k_{rf} = risk-free rate of interest (U.S. Treasury intermediate bond yield)
k_m = expected rate of return in U.S. equity markets (large stock)
β_{Cemex} = measure of Cemex's individual risk relative to the market

The calculation assumes the current risk-free rate is 6.00%, the expected return on U.S. equities is 13.00%, and Cemex's beta is 1.5. The result is a cost of equity—required rate of return on equity investment in Cemex—of 16.50%.[8]

The investment will be funded internally by the parent company, roughly in the same debt/equity proportions as the consolidated firm, 40% debt (D/V) and 60% equity (E/V). The current cost of debt for Cemex is 8.00%, and the effective tax rate is 35%. This cost of equity, when combined with the other components, results in a weighted-average cost of capital for Cemex of:

$$k_{wacc} = k_e \frac{E}{V} + k_d (1-t) \frac{D}{V} = (16.50\%)(.60) + (8.00\%)(1-.35)(.40) = 11.98\%$$

Cemex customarily uses this weighted-average cost of capital to discount prospective investment cash flows for project ranking purposes. The Indonesian investment poses a variety of risks, however, that the typical domestic investment does not.

The risks associated with the prospective Indonesian investment can be subdivided into *two-sided risks (symmetric risks)* and *one-sided risks.*[9] Symmetric risks include operating risk, demand markets and pricing risk, and macroeconomic and macro political risks, risk components that can cause the cash flow returns of the investment to be higher or lower than generally expected (most likely). *One-sided risks,* those variables that are likely to result in decreased cash flows only from those expected, include expropriation, cross-border payment restrictions or prohibitions, political chaos, or upheaval. If the prospective Indonesian investment is to be evaluated on a risk-adjusted cost of capital basis, both symmetric and one-sided risks must be incorporated into Cemex's weighted-average cost of capital.

Note that currency risk is not one of the explicit risks mentioned in this framework. Currency risk is assumed eliminated by remeasuring all foreign currency (Indonesian rupiah) cash flows into U.S. dollars at the appropriate forward rates.

Lessard (1996) suggests that both the cost of equity and the cost of debt in the firm's weighted-average cost of capital must be adjusted to appropriately reflect the additional risks posed by the Indonesian investment.[10]

)))) Adjusting Debt Costs (Required Returns)

The simplest and most straightforward estimate of the risk premium on risks associated with debt in Indonesia is based on the Indonesian government's cost of borrowing U.S. dollars. The Indonesian government's risk premium would be that additional interest it pays to borrow U.S. dollars in the Eurobond market above that paid by the U.S. Treasury. Since both parties are committing to repayment in the same currency, U.S. dollars, the differential in their debt costs reflects the higher perceived risk associated with repayment of U.S. dollar-denominated debt by the government of Indonesia. These interest rate spreads are termed *sovereign spreads*.[11] Exhibit 16.2 illustrates sovereign spreads and U.S. dollar borrowing costs by a selected group of emerging market countries, including Indonesia.

The sovereign spread for Indonesia according to Exhibit 16.2 is 400 basis points or 4.00%. The risk-free rate of interest applicable to Cemex's prospective Indonesian investment is then:

$$k_{rf}^{Indo} = k_{rf}^{US} + \text{Indonesian sovereign spread} = 6.00\% + 4.00\% = 10.00\%$$

| Exhibit 16.2 | *The Cost of Borrowing U.S. Dollars by Selected Emerging Market Countries (1996)* | | | |

Country	(1) U.S. Treasury Cost of Funds (basis points)	(2) Country's Sovereign Spread (basis points)	(3) Country's U.S. Dollar Total Cost of Funds (basis points)	(percent)
Argentina	600	718	1318	13.18
Brazil	600	610	1210	12.10
Indonesia	600	400	1000	10.00
Mexico	600	597	1197	11.97
Philippines	600	226	826	8.26
Venezuela	600	811	1411	14.11
United States	600	–	600	6.00

Source: Abstracted by authors from Lessard (1996). Original data from J.P. Morgan and the International Finance Corporation's *Emerging Stock Markets Factbook*, 1996. Column (3) = column (1) + column (2).

If we assume that the project risk of Cemex's prospective Indonesian invest-ment is the same as that of other investments by Cemex, we would add the same credit spread Cemex pays above the risk-free Treasury rate in the United States (200 basis points or 2.00%) to the risk-free rate in Indonesia. This yields a risk-adjusted cost of debt for Cemex's Indonesian investment of:[12]

$$k_d^{Indo} = k_{rf}^{Indo} + \text{credit spread} = 10.00\% + 2.00\% = 12.00\%$$

Although this appears at first glance to be prohibitively high, it does reflect current costs for high-grade Indonesian corporate borrowers in the Eurobond market. And again, this includes the risks associated with borrowing U.S. dollars (the *sovereign-risk premium*) and the risks associated with the project (the *credit-risk premium*).

Adjusting Equity Costs (Required Returns)

Adjusting the required return on equity is not quite as simple as adding a sover-eign spread to an existing corporate cost of debt. Again using the capital-asset pricing model as the theoretical foundation, we need to find what Lessard calls an *offshore project beta*. In our numerical example here, the *offshore project beta* attempts to measure the risk associated with a U.S.-dollar-based company invest-ing in a cement manufacturing facility (the *project* component) in Indonesia (the *offshore* component).

The Offshore Project Beta. In order to create this new beta (it is too specific to have been previously measured), we utilize one of the basic mathematical charac-teristics of betas, that betas are multiplicative (one beta may be multiplied by a second beta). Assuming that the risk of the project relative to the Indonesian market (a cement plant in Indonesia) is the same *relative risk* as that project would represent in the United States market (a cement plant in the United States), we calculate the offshore project beta as the product of Cemex's own beta and the *Indonesia-to-U.S. country beta*.

The *Indonesia-to-U.S. country beta*, β^{Indo}, is rather difficult to estimate empirically because of the limited data on the covariance between U.S. equity markets and Indonesian equity markets. Luckily, an equivalent method of calcu-lating beta is to find the ratio of the standard deviations of each of the individual markets, the United States and Indonesia in this case, and to then simply multiply this ratio by the correlation coefficient between the two markets. The correlation of the Indonesian equity markets to the U.S. equity markets is here assumed to be 0.26 ($\rho_{Indo, USA} = 0.26$). This is then multiplied by the ratio of market standard deviations ($\sigma_{Indo} = 30.55$, $\sigma_{USA} = 10.08$):[13]

$$\beta^{Indo} = \frac{\text{Cov}(k_{Indo}, k_{USA})}{\text{Var}(k_{USA})} = \rho_{Indo,USA} \frac{\sigma_{Indo}}{\sigma_{USA}} = [0.26]\frac{30.55}{10.08} = 0.7880$$

The country beta for Indonesia is found to be 0.7880. We now multiply this country beta with the beta value for Cemex itself, β_{Cemex}, the same 1.5 value used in the parent company's cost of equity calculation. Cemex's *offshore project beta* for Indonesia is now calculated as 1.182:

$$\beta_{Cemex}^{Offshore} = \beta_{Cemex} \cdot \beta^{Indo} = 1.5(0.7880) = 1.182$$

The Equity Risk Premium. The final input to the CAPM approach is the equity risk premium demanded by a U.S. dollar investor on an Indonesian equity investment, RPM_{US}^{Indo}. The offshore project beta calculated in the previous section will now be multiplied by the following risk premium:

$$RPM_{US}^{Indo} = k_m - k_{rf}^{Indo}$$

Empirically, we are confronted with making a choice between two approaches. We could infer that the applicable RPM is that found by subtracting the Indonesian risk-free rate of 10.0% (calculated above) from the U.S. equity return of 13.0%, a premium of 3.0%. Such a small risk premium for the Indonesian market is, however, troubling. Alternatively, we could use the U.S. market's equity risk premium of 13.0% – 6.0% = 7.0% and assume this RPM is what would be demanded by a U.S.-dollar-based investor when establishing the required return on equity investments in the Indonesian marketplace.[14] We choose the latter.

We now have all of the components for estimating the risk-adjusted cost of equity for Cemex's prospective investment in Indonesia:

$$k_e^{Indo} = k_{rf}^{Indo} + (RPM_{US}^{Indo})\beta_{Cemex}^{Offshore} = 10.0\% + (7.0\%) 1.182 = 18.274\%$$

Thus the risk-adjusted cost of equity for Cemex's prospective investment in Indonesia is 18.274%.

The Adjusted Cost of Capital. With all components in place, the weighted-average cost of capital, adjusted for offshore application to Indonesia, can now be calculated as the sum of two components. The first component is the risk-adjusted cost of equity (18.274%) multiplied by the proportion of equity in the investment's financial structure (.60 or 60%). The second component is the risk-adjusted cost of debt (12.000%) after tax (multiplied by 1-tax rate of 35%) multiplied by the proportion of debt in the investment's financial structure:

$$k_{wacc}^{Indo} = (18.274\%)(.60) + (12.000\%)(1 - .35)(.40) = 14.084\%$$

The relatively surprising result is that the Indonesian risk-adjusted weighted-average cost of capital is only 2.104% higher than the parent company's own cost of capital (14.084% – 11.980%). This is substantially less than if the simple sovereign spread of 4.00% were added to the parent's own cost of capital. This is not to say, however, that this will always be the case. This is not a simple cost of capital plus 3% or 6% premium process. Because the costs of equity are adjusted on the basis of relative volatilities and correlations with the home-country capital market, the relative direction and magnitude of the risk-adjusted WACC to that of the parent's is purely an empirical issue on a case-by-case basis.

))) Adjusting Costs of Capital for Cemex's Portfolio of Potential Projects

But what if Cemex wanted to evaluate projects across a number of emerging markets, and not just Indonesia? It would then need to repeat the capital-cost adjustment process just demonstrated for Indonesia across the subject country-set. This calculation, although somewhat cumbersome initially, is quite tractable for Cemex or any other MNE attempting to evaluate a wide spectrum of potential investments globally.

Exhibit 16.3 presents the needed data for a small set of emerging market countries, including Indonesia, used in the Cemex-Indonesia numerical illustration. The data presented in Exhibit 16.3 is generally applicable to any U.S.-based or U.S.-dollar-based MNE. The MNE need only contribute its own cost of capital components, plus the appropriate beta value comparable to the industry-specific beta of the prospective investment. (Under most applications, the MNE parent company will simply use its own beta from its home market as a proxy for this relative measure of risk.)

| Exhibit 16.3 | | | *Risk-Adjustment Component Inputs for Selected Emerging Countries* | | | |

Country	(1) Sovereign Spread (basis points)	(2) Market Volatility (%)	(3) Relative to U.S.	(4) Correlation with U.S.	(5) Country Beta to U.S.	(6) Offshore Beta to U.S. Market
Argentina	718	61.63	6.11	0.32	1.9565	2.935
Brazil	610	60.86	6.04	0.40	2.4151	3.623
Indonesia	400	30.55	3.03	0.26	0.7880	1.182
Mexico	597	37.90	3.76	0.22	0.8272	1.241
Philippines	226	34.16	3.39	0.22	0.7456	1.118
Venezuela	811	60.93	6.04	–0.03	–0.1813	–0.272
United States	–	10.08	1.00	1.00	1.0000	1.500

Columns (1), (2), and (4) are from Lessard (1996). Original data from J.P. Morgan and the International Finance Corporation's *Emerging Stock Markets Factbook*, 1996. Correlations are based on 50 months ending December 1995.
Column (3) is the ratio of the individual country's volatility shown in Column (2) divided by U.S. volatility (10.08) shown in column (2). For example, Argentina's relative volatility of 6.11 = 61.63 ÷ 10.08.
Column (5) = Column (3) × Column (4).
Column (6) = Column (5) × U.S. beta of 1.500.

Exhibit 16.4 summarizes the next step, the calculation of the adjusted cost of equity for Cemex in evaluating prospective investments across the countries listed. As in the previous numerical example, the CAPM approach uses the same basic U.S. Treasury risk-free rate and adds to it the individual country's sovereign risk premium. This country-specific risk-free cost of U.S. dollar debt is then added to the product of the equity market risk premium for the United States (7.000%) and the offshore beta to the U.S. market (Exhibit 16.3). As Exhibit 16.4 illustrates, this results in a wide range of adjusted cost of equity estimates across these countries, with the highest in Brazil (37.458%) and the lowest in Venezuela (12.206%). Note that the reason the Venezuelan adjusted cost of equity is so low is a direct result of the negative correlation the Venezuelan equity markets have with U.S. equity markets.

Finally, with the risk-adjusted costs of debt and equity calculated for each country, it is now possible to calculate the weighted-average cost of capital to be applied to each of the individual emerging market countries. Exhibit 16.5 reports the results of this last step. Clearly this methodology, internally consistent with domestic capital cost estimation, results in substantially different (generally lower) discount rates on foreign projects than the traditional WACC + 3% (or even 6%) rule-of-thumb utilized by many MNEs in the past.

The adjusted costs of Exhibit 16.5 do indeed present some surprises. All but one country's cost ends up higher than that of the parent company's 11.98%. The adjusted cost of equity in one country—Venezuela—is actually lower than that in the United States. This is a result of Venezuela's country beta and a negative cor-

---

Exhibit 16.4   *Cemex's Calculated Risk-Adjusted Cost of Equity for Selected Emerging Market Countries*

Country	(1) Risk-free U.S. Treasury Rate (%)	(2) Sovereign Spread (%)	(3) Adjusted Risk-free Rate (%)	(4) Equity Risk Premium (%)	(5) Offshore Beta (%)	(6) Adjusted Cost of Equity (%)
Argentina	6.00	7.18	13.18	7.00	2.935	33.723
Brazil	6.00	6.10	12.10	7.00	3.623	37.458
Indonesia	6.00	4.00	10.00	7.00	1.182	18.274
Mexico	6.00	5.97	11.97	7.00	1.241	20.655
Philippines	6.00	2.26	8.26	7.00	1.118	16.088
Venezuela	6.00	8.11	14.11	7.00	–0.272	12.206
United States	6.00	–	6.00	7.00	1.500	16.500

Columns (1) and (2) are drawn from Exhibit 16.3.
Column (3) = Column (1) + Column (2).
Column (4) is the same U.S. equity market risk premium used in Exhibit 16.3.
Column (5) is taken from Exhibit 16.3.
Column (6) = Column 3 + [Column (4) × Column (5)].

relation with U.S. equity market returns. It is critical to remember, however, that the adjusted cost of capital in Venezuela is lower *only* when evaluated in the context of Cemex's portfolio of foreign investments and the commensurate correlations with the U.S. dollar markets.

))) The Adjusted Discount Rate and P.T. Semen Gresik

After this rather complex (but doable) process, how do we apply the adjusted discount rate to the prospective Indonesian investment by Cemex, Semen Indonesia, introduced in Chapter 14? The cash flows remitted to the parent company, when converted to U.S. dollars, are now discounted at 14.084% (from above) rather than the 17.980% used previously (11.98% + 6.00%).

Exhibit 16.6 presents the valuation of P.T. Semen Gresik from Chapter 15 (Exhibit 15.2) with two changes:

1. All cash flows have been converted from Indonesian rupiah to U.S. dollars at the series of forward rates listed at the top of the exhibit (not significantly different from the purchasing power parity forecast exchange rates shown); and

2. All U.S. dollar cash flows are discounted at the adjusted discount rate derived in the previous section for Indonesia, 14.084%.

The resulting discounted cash flow (DCF) estimate of fair value per share, $0.28, is significantly less than what Cemex bid, $1.38 per share, for less than controlling interest.

Exhibit 16.5	*Cemex's Calculated Risk-Adjusted Cost of Capital for Selected Emerging Market Countries*			
Country	(1) Adjusted Cost of Debt (%)	(2) Adjusted Cost of Equity (%)	(3) Adjusted Cost of Capital (%)	(4) Spread over U.S. WACC (%)
Argentina	15.180	33.723	24.181	12.201
Brazil	14.100	37.458	26.141	14.161
Indonesia	12.000	18.274	14.084	2.104
Mexico	13.970	20.655	16.025	4.045
Philippines	10.260	16.088	12.321	0.341
Venezuela	16.110	12.206	11.512	–0.468
United States	8.000	16.500	11.980	–

Column (1) and Column (2) from Exhibit 16.4.
Column (3) = [.40 × (1-.35) × Column (1)] + [.60 × Column (2)], where .40 and .60 are the proportions of debt and equity, respectively, in the weighted-average cost of capital, and the tax rate is assumed to be 35%.
Column (4) = the adjusted cost of capital−United States cost of capital. For example, Argentina's spread over U.S. WACC is 24.181 − 11.980 = 12.201.

| Exhibit 16.6 | *Discounted Valuation of P.T. Semen Gresik, Assuming Forward Exchange Rates and Adjusted Discount Rates* |

Project year	0	1	2	3	4
Exchange rate (Rp/$):					
PPP Forecast	10,000	12,621	15,930	20,106	25,376
Forward quotes	10,000	11,105	15,935	21,185	25,945
FCF (Exhibit 15.2):					
Billions of Rp	444.3	561.2	691.8	791.5	19,133.9
FCF (US$ @ forward rate)	$44,426,000	$44,293,847	$33,354,845	$25,161,593	$435,362,263
Discount factor (14.084%)	1.0000	0.8765	0.7683	0.6735	0.5903
PV of FCF (US$)	$44,426,000	$44,293,847	$33,354,845	$25,161,593	$435,362,263
Cumulative PV	$582,598,547				
Enterprise value	$582,598,547				
Less net debt	(411,350,000)				
Less minority interests	(2,310,000)				
Equity value	$168,938,547				
Shares outstanding	593,200,000				
Fair value of equity, per share	$0.28				

How do we explain such a discrepancy in price? In Chapter 15, the estimated fair value per share was calculated to be Rp6,244, which at Rp10,000/$ is $0.62/share. One significant difference in this valuation is that cash flows were converted to dollars prior to discounting and netting (for debt and minority interests). The share price at the time of final bids, Rp10,500/share ($1.05/share), was by all probabilities extremely overvalued given the P/E ratio of 80 and the M/B ratio of 2.34 noted in Chapter 15. Regardless of any adjustment for risk, the price bid by Cemex appears to have been extremely high by DCF and ratio standards. Only in terms of $/tonne capacity does the bid put forth by Cemex appear appropriate (which may be the valuation basis used by Cemex).

))) Reservations on the Country-Beta Approach

The *country-beta approach* has a number of implicit assumptions that need to be appreciated by any MNE considering its application. First, as we mentioned previously, if the purpose of the foreign investment is to either source raw material or natural resources, or produce a product for further processing and sale in some other country market, the returns on the specific investment under consideration may have little association with the host-country market and its observable equity returns and correlations. Secondly, beta values are highly sensitive to leverage. If leverage levels and value differ dramatically in the host market from that of the parent company, resulting equity adjustments will be biased. Finally, MNEs operate in specific industry segments, segments that may or may not be typical of the returns and correlations represented by country-level summary statistics.

ADJUSTING THE CASH FLOWS

Although there is no limit to the number of different methods utilized by MNEs when adjusting cash flows, the predominant method is *simulation-based assessment*.

)))) Simulation-Based Assessment

The degree of certainty regarding the quantity and timing of cash flows in a prospective foreign investment is, as Humphrey Bogart stated in the last lines of *The Maltese Falcon*, "the stuff that dreams are made of." Due to the complexity of economic forces at work in major investment projects, it is paramount that the analyst realizes the subjectivity of the forecast cash flows. Humility in analysis may be another way of putting it.

Most capital budgeting and valuation analyses are derived from sales forecasts. Direct costs, associated overhead expenses, and financing costs are all relatively easier to forecast, at least within general bounds. Sales forecasts can, however, be much more difficult to predict accurately; yet it is their performance that will drive value. The development of scenario-based simulation, in which economic growth rates, income levels, price levels, interest rates, and so on are organized according to story-lines of future events, allows the analyst to establish upper and lower bounds for cash flows.

The actual operating results of foreign investments will literally be a function of how their operating exposures (Chapter 7) change over time. Scenario-based simulation allows the analyst not only to vary exchange rate prospects but also to show how those exchange rate changes may increase or decrease the sales and commensurate operating results of the prospective investment.

The P.T. Semen Gresik case may be an especially good candidate for scenario-based cash flow analysis. Earnings estimates for the 1999–2002 period may be substantially lower than what Cemex believed. And depending on the level of sales growth expected, profit margins associated with higher sales growth may represent significant opportunity for value creation.

PRUDENCE IN PRACTICE

We conclude our discussion of adjusting for risk with a note of caution and humility from a recent essay in the *Harvard Business Review* by Peter Bernstein:

> More than any other development, the quantification of risk defines the boundary between modern times and the rest of history. The speed, power, movement, and instant communication that characterize our age would have been inconceivable before science replaced superstition as a bulwark against risks of all kinds.
>
> It is hubris that we believe that we can put reliable and stable numbers on the impact of a politician's power, on the probability of a takeover boom like the one that occurred in the 1980s, on the return on the stock market over the next 2, 20, or 50 years, or on subjective factors like utility and risk aversion. It is equally silly to

limit our deliberations only to those variables that do lend themselves to quantification, excluding all serious consideration of the unquantifiable. It is irrational to confuse probability with timing and to assume that an event with low probability is therefore not imminent. Such confusion, however, is by no means unusual. And it surely is naive to define discontinuity as anomaly instead of as normality; only the shape and the timing of the disturbances are hidden from us, not their inevitability.

Finally, the science of risk management is capable of creating new risks even as it brings old risk under control. Our faith in risk management encourages us to take risk we otherwise would not take. On most counts, that is beneficial. But we should be wary of increasing the total amount of risk in the system. Research shows that the security of seat belts encourages drivers to behave more aggressively, with the result that the number of accidents rises even as the seriousness of injury in any one accident may diminish.

SUMMARY

- A MNE undertaking foreign direct investment (FDI) must determine the cost of funds and the required returns on the investment. The MNE must weigh the expected cash flow returns and business prospects against the possibilities of political disruption or intervention, political and economic actions that undermine the business environment, or restrictions and regulations on the activities of foreign MNEs operating in the country.

- Risks associated with foreign investments are inherently subjective, *qualitative* not *quantitative*. Shareholders, however, expect the management of the MNE to assess the risks, make informed and consistent judgments, and manage them responsibly.

- Traditional definitions of risk emphasize the potential for loss, a form of *one-sided risk*. For a MNE, examples of these one-sided risks include the risk of expropriation and the risk of funds blockages. Other risks, however, are definitively *two-sided* in character. The most obvious one for MNEs is foreign exchange risk.

- The "foreign risks" of a project from the viewpoint of the parent company include the risk of host government interference—*political risk*; the ability to exercise effective control over the foreign affiliate within the country's legal environment—*governance risk*; the ability to move capital freely and efficiently in and out of the host country—*transfer risk*; and the value of the local currency cash flows generated and remitted to the parent in parent currency terms—*foreign exchange risk*. These risks from the parent perspective are collectively referred to as *country risk*.

- Adjustment for risks associated with foreign investments may be made through the discount rate and/or the cash flows associated with the investment.

- Adjusting the cost of debt on capital invested in a foreign investment requires the use of sovereign spreads, which are based on the market's assessment of the individual country's credit risk for foreign-currency-denominated debt.

- Adjusting the required return on equity invested in a foreign investment is not as simple as adding a sovereign spread to an existing cost of debt. Equity costs need to be adjusted on the basis of what is termed an *offshore project beta*. The offshore project beta acts as a proxy of the covariance between the MNE's existing project risks in its home country with the prospective project risks associated with this new foreign market.

- The primary method for the adjustment of cash flows for foreign investment risk is *simulation-based scenario analysis*.

QUESTIONS

1. The Discount-Rate Dance
The discount rate applied to major investments, domestic or cross-border, is consistently one of the most controversial debates within a firm. How would you assess the following statements, often heard in corporate finance meetings:

a. "DCF analysis is inherently biased against long-term investments."

b. "Foreign investment projects should always have a discount rate that is above that of the parent company to compensate for the additional cross-border risk."

c. "Why should I invest in a foreign project that is discounted at a 16% rate simply because it has a projected NPV greater than a domestic investment that was discounted at only 12%?"

d. "Why should I—because of the latest thinking in portfolio theory—invest in a foreign project that is discounted at only a 12% rate simply because it has a projected NPV greater than a domestic investment that was discounted at a higher rate of 14%?"

2. Rogue River Tractor
Rogue River Tractor (U.S.) is reviewing the methodology of how it analyzes foreign investment opportunities. What data, investment information, and corporate structure information would you request in order to begin the analysis?

3. The Country Beta
This chapter introduced the concept of a *country beta*. How would you explain to your immediate superiors the fact that a country beta may be significantly

lower than the firm's own beta, or that the country beta may actually be negative in value?

4. One-Sided versus Two-Sided Risk

The word "risk" in finance is often measured as the standard deviation of some financial value. But if some risks are indeed *one-sided*, how would you go about incorporating their riskiness in financial analysis?

5. P.T. Semen Gresik

Exhibit 16.1 presents a variety of country-risk ratings for five different countries, including Indonesia, the home country of P.T. Semen Gresik. Utilizing the data presented in this exhibit, compare it with the results of estimating a discount rate of only 14.084%.

a. What would the data in Exhibit 16.1 lead you to believe about investing in Indonesia?

b. How would you—when confronted in a capital allocation committee meeting—explain the rather contradictory ratings versus discount rate?

WORLD WIDE WEB EXERCISES

W1. Sovereign Credit Ratings Criteria

The evaluation of credit risk and all other relevant risks associated with the multitude of borrowers on world debt markets requires a structured approach to international risk assessment. Use Standard and Poor's criteria, described in depth on their web page, to differentiate the various risks (local currency risk, default risk, currency risk, transfer risk, and so on contained in major sovereign ratings worldwide.

Standard and Poor's   http://www.standardpoor.com/ratings/criteria/
(Click on *Sovereigns*)

W2. Milken Capital-Access Index

The Milken Institute's Capital-Access Index (CAI) is one of the most recent informational indices that aids in the evaluation of the accessibility of world capital markets to MNEs and the governments of many emerging market countries. According to the CAI, which countries have seen the largest deterioration in their access to capital in the last two years?

Milken Institute   http://www.milken-inst.org/

W3. Contingency Analysis

There are a number of growing consultancies on the evaluation of risk in business. Beginning with the website below, perform a survey of current risk practices and professionals.

Contingency Analysis Consulting   http://www.contingencyanalysis.com/

SUGGESTED READINGS

Godfrey, Stephen and Ramon Espinosa, "A Practical Approach to Calculating Costs of Equity for Investments in Emerging Markets," *Journal of Applied Corporate Finance*, Vol. 9, No. 3, Fall 1996, pp. 80–89.

Keck, Tom, Eric Levengood, and Al Longfield, "Using Discounted Cash Flow Analysis in an International Setting: A Survey of Issues in Modeling the Cost of Capital," *Journal of Applied Corporate Finance*, Vol. 11, No. 3, Fall 1998, pp. 82–99.

Lessard, Donald R., "Incorporating Country Risk in the Valuation of Offshore Projects," *Journal of Applied Corporate Finance*, Vol. 9, No. 3, Fall 1996, pp. 52–63.

NOTES

1. The authors would like to acknowledge Professor Timothy Luehrman (Thunderbird) and Timothy Magnusson (Cargill, Inc.) for a number of helpful discussions on this topic.
2. International portfolio investors may follow the fundamentals of portfolio theory and the international version of the capital-asset-pricing model (ICAPM), which is covered in detail in Chapter 22.
3. We would be remiss if we did not acknowledge a popular, but extremely flawed, method of adjusting the discount rate for a foreign project: adding an *X*% premium (frequently 3% or 6%) to the firm's own weighted-average cost of capital for foreign investments, without any other consideration for origins or rationality other than "that's the way it's always been done."
4. This is not necessarily true if a different discount rate is used for different periods in the future, much in the tradition of leveraged buyouts (LBOs) in which the discount rate of future cash flows is adjusted for the changing debt/total capitalization structure as debt is reduced.
5. One possible example of periodic or interval risk is what in Mexico is called *seis años* (six years). This term describes the political and economic disruptions surrounding the election of a new President every six years (1982, 1988, 1994, 2000).
6. Lessard (1996) argues that foreign exchange rate risk is most effectively handled by using forward rates. He also notes that these forward rates are assumed to be efficient forecasts of the future spot rate, assuming the interest rates used in their construction have embedded expectations regarding future currency values. Regardless of whether the forward rates are biased or unbiased predictors, indirect exchange rate exposure will still exist via operating and economic condition changes from future unexpected exchange rate movements.
7. Keck, Levengood, and Longfield (1998).
8. Input assumptions are critical. We have roughly based our assumptions on recent empirical results by Ibbotson, Lummer, and Kaplan (1998). For the 1926–1996 period in U.S. equity markets, their results for *large stocks* included a geometric mean return of 10.7%, an arithmetic mean return of 12.7%, and a standard deviation of 20.3%. Similarly for *intermediate-term U.S. government bonds* (for risk-free measures) of 5.2% geometric, 5.4% arithmetic and 5.8% standard deviation.

9. This approach follows that of Lessard (1996) and Godfrey and Espinosa (1996).

10. There are a number of alternative approaches to cost of capital calculations for international projects and investments. See for example Ibbotson (http://www.ibbotson.com) and Erb, Harvey, and Viskanta (1995), or Campbell Harvey's web page (http://www.duke.edu/~charvey/Country_risk).

11. The sovereign spread used here is from J.P. Morgan for issues outstanding on August 30, 1996. Strangely, sovereign spreads are readily available for emerging market countries, but not for the majority of industrialized nations. Emerging market spreads are found most easily by published spreads on Brady bond issuances (see for example the daily *Financial Times*). Industrialized country governments, however, rarely issue dollar-denominated Eurobonds (and definitely not Brady bonds), making their sovereign spreads much harder to capture empirically.

12. This assumption may be a bit heroic. The credit spread of Cemex in the U.S. over U.S. treasuries may not be a good proxy for the credit spread Cemex Indonesia would pay over the dollar risk-free rate in Indonesia.

13. Godfrey and Espinosa (1996) argue that MNEs are often not interested in their investors' ability to diversify internationally, and therefore the correlation coefficient between country markets should be assumed to be equal to 1 in this type of analysis. In our opinion, this would tend to rob the approach to international risk measurement of its theoretical foundations since it would ignore the fact that equity markets in different countries are not perfectly correlated (for example, in this case, the correlation between the United States and Indonesia is 0.26, not 1.00).

14. It should also be noted that the first approach could actually result in a negative premium (for example Brazil/US), which would be even more troubling.

PART 5

MANAGING MULTINATIONAL OPERATIONS

Managing multinational operations is the task that absorbs most of the time and effort of financial managers in MNEs. Even though this task is not as glamorous or theoretically challenging as the activities discussed in the previous Parts, it is a critical part of running a global business as efficiently as possible.

CHAPTER 17 describes the international tax environment, including the tax dimensions of multinational operations. It analyzes the way countries tax a MNE's foreign-source income, including tax implications of repatriating income from offshore affiliates. The chapter also explores the multinational tax management concerns of U.S.-based MNEs.

CHAPTER 18 analyzes how a MNE can reposition funds across borders while overcoming political, foreign exchange, tax, and transaction cost constraints. The key to this process is to unbundle fund transfers from dependence on dividend payments and to utilize license fees, royalties, and overhead contributions. The special problems arising from transfer pricing and blocked funds are also explored.

CHAPTER 19 analyzes working capital management within the globally dispersed multinational operations of the MNE. It details how a MNE should handle cash, accounts receivable, and inventory issues. It also describes the various sources available to finance working capital, including both in-house banks and external international banking offices.

CHAPTER 20 describes how a firm can reduce the risk of nonpayment for an export by utilizing time-proven trade instruments such as a letter of credit and export credit insurance. It describes government programs that help finance exports in addition to privately available financing in the form of bankers' acceptances. It also analyzes countertrade as an alternative to normal trade financing.

CHAPTER 21 analyzes how a MNE can evaluate its overall performance as well as the performance of its foreign affiliates. It details the complexity of differentiating strategy-based concerns with accounting-based financial measures, all in the context of concentrating on utilizing metrics key to maximizing shareholder value.

CHAPTER 17

MULTINATIONAL TAXATION

Tax planning for multinational operations is an extremely complex but vitally important aspect of international business. To plan effectively, MNEs must understand not only the intricacies of their own operations worldwide, but also the different structures and interpretations of tax liabilities across countries. The primary objective of *multinational tax planning* is the maximization of the MNE's income after taxes are paid. This objective, however, must not be pursued without full recognition that decision-making within the firm must always be based on the economic fundamentals of the firm's line of business, and not on convoluted policies undertaken purely for the reduction of tax liability.

Executives with tax responsibility in a MNE should have a background in public finance so that they can understand the principles of tax neutrality, equity, revenue, and morality. They should have experience in tax law in order to be able to follow the various tax rulings as they apply to international business practice, and they should also be able to read a number of foreign languages to keep abreast of foreign tax rulings. Naturally, they should have accounting experience, since a large part of day-to-day tax administration involves making decisions about whether specific transactions are tax-deductible or whether a particular transfer price can be defended as an "arm's length" transaction. Needless to say, the ideal international tax executive probably does not exist. Instead, tax planning is effected by group action, with each group member contributing expertise in one or more of the areas just described.

Because tax planning is so complex, this chapter cannot aim to create tax experts. Rather it sets out to acquaint the reader with the overall international tax environment. At least a minimum of sophisticated knowledge of tax structures is needed by every international financial executive because many decisions require consideration of such factors. As evident from previous chapters, taxes have a major impact on corporate net income and cash flow through their influence on foreign investment decisions, financial structure, determination of the cost of capital, foreign exchange management, working capital management, and financial control.

The sections that follow explain the most important aspects of the international tax environments and specific features that affect multinational operations. Before we explain the specifics of multinational taxation in practice, however, it is necessary to introduce two areas of fundamental importance: *tax morality* and *tax neutrality*.

TAX MORALITY

The MNE faces not only a morass of foreign taxes but also an ethical question. In many countries taxpayers, corporate or individual, do not voluntarily comply with the tax laws. Smaller domestic firms and individuals are the chief violators. The MNE must decide whether to follow a practice of full disclosure to tax authorities or adopt the philosophy of "when in Rome, do as the Romans do." Given the local prominence of most foreign affiliates and the political sensitivity of their position, most MNEs follow the full disclosure practice. Some firms, however, believe that their competitive position would be eroded if they did not avoid taxes to the same extent as their domestic competitors. There is obviously no prescriptive answer to the problem, since business ethics are partly a function of cultural heritage and historical development.

There is also a potential morality problem for the host country. Some countries have imposed what seem to be arbitrary punitive tax penalties on MNEs for presumed violations of local tax laws. Property or wealth tax assessments are sometimes perceived by the foreign firm to be excessively large when compared with those levied on locally owned firms. The problem then is how to respond to tax penalties that are punitive or discriminatory.

TAX NEUTRALITY

When a government decides to levy a tax, it must consider not only the potential revenue from the tax, or how efficiently it can be collected, but also the effect the proposed tax can have on private economic behavior. For example, the U.S. government's policy on taxation of foreign-source income does not have the raising of revenue as its sole objective but rather has multiple and at times conflicting objectives. These include the following:

- The desire to neutralize tax incentives that might favor (or disfavor) U.S. private investment in developed countries.

- The provision of an incentive for U.S. private investment in developing countries.

- The improvement of the U.S. balance of payments by removing the advantages of artificial tax havens and encouraging repatriation of funds.

- The raising of revenue.

The ideal tax should not only raise revenue efficiently but also have as few negative effects on economic behavior as possible. Some theorists argue that the ideal tax should be completely *neutral* in its effect on private decisions and completely *equitable* among taxpayers. However, other theorists claim that national policy objectives such as balance of payments or investment in developing countries should be encouraged through an active *tax incentive policy* rather than require taxes to be neutral and equitable. Most tax systems compromise between these two viewpoints.

One way to view neutrality is to require that the burden of taxation on each dollar, euro, pound, or yen of profit earned in home country operations by a multinational firm be equal to the burden of taxation on each currency-equivalent of profit earned by the same firm in its foreign operations. This is called *domestic neutrality*. A second way to view neutrality is to require that the tax burden on each foreign affiliate of the firm be equal to the tax burden on its competitors in the same country. This is called *foreign neutrality*. The latter interpretation is often supported by MNEs because it focuses more on the competitiveness of the individual firm in individual country markets.

The issue of *tax equity* is also difficult to define and measure. In theory, an equitable tax is one that imposes the same total tax burden on all taxpayers who are similarly situated and located in the same tax jurisdiction. In the case of foreign investment income, the U.S. Treasury argues that since the United States uses the nationality principle to claim tax jurisdiction, U.S.-owned foreign affiliates are in the same tax jurisdiction as U.S. domestic affiliates. Therefore, a dollar earned in foreign operations should be taxed at the same rate and paid at the same time as a dollar earned in domestic operations.

NATIONAL TAX ENVIRONMENTS

Contrary to the fundamental objectives of national tax authorities, it is widely agreed that taxes do affect economic decisions made by MNEs. Tax treaties between nations and differential tax structures, rates, and practices all result in a less than level playing field for the MNEs competing on world markets.

Exhibit 17.1 provides an overview of corporate tax rates as applicable to the United States, Germany, and Japan. The categorizations of income (e.g., distributed versus undistributed profits), the differences in tax rates, and the discrimination in tax rates applicable to income earned in specific countries serve to introduce the critical dimensions of tax planning for the MNE.

))) National Tax Jurisdictions

Nations typically structure their tax systems along one of two basic approaches: the *worldwide approach* or the *territorial approach*. Both approaches are attempts to determine which firms, foreign or domestic by incorporation, or which incomes, foreign or domestic in origin, are subject to the taxation of host country tax authorities.

Exhibit 17.1   *Comparison of Corporate Tax Rates: Japan, Germany, and the United States*

Taxable Income Category	Japan	Germany	United States
Corporate income tax rates:			
Profits distributed to stockholders	37.5%	30%	35%
Undistributed profits	37.5%	45%	35%
Branches of foreign corporations	37.5%	42%	35%
Withholding taxes on dividends (portfolio):			
with Japan	–	15%	15%
with Germany	15%	–	15%
with United States	15%	5%	–
Withholding taxes on dividends (substantial holdings):[a]			
with Japan	–	25%	10%
with Germany	10%	–	5%
with United States	10%	10%	–
Withholding taxes on interest:			
with Japan	–	10%	10%
with Germany	10%	–	0%
with United States	10%	0%	–
Withholding taxes on royalties:			
with Japan	–	10%	10%
with Germany	10%	–	0%
with United States	10%	0%	–

[a] "Substantial holdings" for the United States apply only to intercorporate dividends. In Germany and Japan, "substantial holdings" apply to corporate shareholders of greater than 25%.
Source: Price Waterhouse Coopers, *Corporate Taxes: A Worldwide Summary*, 1999.

The *worldwide approach*, also referred to as the *residential* or *national approach*, levies taxes on the income earned by firms that are incorporated in the host country, regardless of where the income was earned (domestically or abroad). A MNE earning income both at home and abroad would therefore find its worldwide income taxed by its home-country tax authorities. For example, a country like the United States, taxes the income earned by firms based in the United States regardless of whether the income earned by the firm is domestically sourced or foreign-sourced.[1] The primary problem is that this does not address the income earned by foreign firms operating within the United States. Countries like the United States then apply the principle of *territorial taxation* to foreign firms within their legal jurisdiction, taxing all income earned by foreign firms in their borders as well.

The *territorial approach*, also termed the *source approach*, focuses on the income earned by firms within the legal jurisdiction of the host country, not on the country of firm incorporation. Countries like Germany that follow the territorial approach apply taxes equally to foreign or domestic firms on income earned within the country, but in principle not on income earned outside the country. The territorial approach, like the worldwide approach, results in a major gap in coverage if resident firms earn income outside the country, but are not taxed by the country in which the profits are earned. In this case, tax authorities extend tax coverage to income earned abroad if it is not currently covered by foreign tax jurisdictions. Once again, a mix of the two tax approaches is necessary for full coverage of income.

))) Tax Deferral

The worldwide approach to international taxation, if followed to the letter, would end the *tax-deferral* privilege for many MNEs. Foreign affiliates of MNEs pay host-country corporate income taxes, but many parent countries defer claiming additional income taxes on that foreign-source income *until it is remitted to the parent firm*. For example, U.S. corporate income taxes on some types of foreign-source income of U.S.-owned affiliates incorporated abroad are deferred until the earnings are remitted to the United States parent. However, the ability to defer corporate income taxes is highly restricted and has been the subject of many of the tax law changes in the past three decades.

))) Foreign Tax Credits

To prevent double taxation of the same income, most countries grant a *foreign tax credit* for income taxes paid to the host country. Countries differ in the way they calculate the foreign tax credit and the kinds of limitations they place on the total amount claimed. Normally foreign tax credits are also available for withholding taxes paid to other countries on dividends, royalties, interest, and other income remitted to the parent. The value-added tax and other sales taxes are not eligible for a foreign tax credit but are typically deductible from pretax income as an expense.

A *tax credit* is a direct reduction of taxes that would otherwise be due and payable. It differs from a deductible expense, which is an expense used to reduce taxable income before the tax rate is applied. A $100 tax credit reduces taxes payable by the full $100, whereas a $100 deductible expense reduces taxable income by $100 and taxes payable by $100 \times t$, where t is the tax rate. Tax credits are more valuable on a dollar-for-dollar basis than are deductible expenses.

If there were no credits for foreign taxes paid, sequential taxation by the host government and then by the home government would result in a very high cumulative tax rate. To illustrate, assume the wholly owned foreign subsidiary of a MNE earns $10,000 before local income taxes and pays a dividend equal to all its after-tax income. Assume further that the host country income tax rate is 30%, and the home country of the parent taxes at a rate of 35%. For simplicity we will assume no withholding taxes. Total taxation with and without allowances for tax credits is shown in Exhibit 17.2.

If tax credits are not allowed, sequential levying of both a 30% host country tax and then a 35% home country tax on the income that remains results in an

Exhibit 17.2 *Foreign Tax Credits*	Without Foreign Tax Credits	With Foreign Tax Credits
Before-tax foreign income	$10,000	$10,000
Less foreign tax @ 30%	−3,000	−3,000
Available to parent and paid as dividend	$7,000	$ 7,000
Less additional parent-country tax at 35%	−2,450	
Less incremental tax (after credits)		−500
Profit after all taxes	$ 4,550	$ 6,500
Total taxes, both jurisdictions	$ 5,450	$ 3,500
Effective overall tax rate (total taxes paid ÷ foreign income)	54.5%	35.0%

effective 54.5% tax, a cumulative rate that would render many MNEs uncompetitive with single-country local firms. The effect of allowing tax credits is to limit total taxation on the *original* before-tax income to no more than the highest single rate among jurisdictions. In the case depicted in Exhibit 17.2, the effective overall tax rate of 35% with foreign tax credits is equivalent to the higher tax rate of the home country (and is the tax rate that would be payable if the income had been earned at home). The $500 of additional home country tax under the tax credit system in Exhibit 17.2 is the amount needed to bring total taxation ($3,000 already paid plus the additional $500) up to but not beyond 35% of the original $10,000 of before-tax foreign income.

U.S. CALCULATION OF FOREIGN TAX CREDITS

In order to illustrate the specifics of calculating and collecting foreign tax credits, we now describe the method used in the United States. Dividends received from U.S. corporate subsidiaries are fully taxable in the United States at U.S. tax rates but with credit allowed for direct taxes paid on income in a foreign country. The amount of foreign tax allowed as a credit depends on five tax parameters:

1. Foreign corporate income tax rate
2. U.S. corporate income tax rate
3. Foreign corporate dividend withholding tax rate for nonresidents (per the applicable bilateral tax treaty between the specific country and the United States)
4. Proportion of ownership held by the U.S. corporation in the foreign firm
5. Proportion of net income distributed, i.e., the dividend payout rate

The five cases depicted in Exhibit 17.3 are based on a foreign subsidiary of a U.S. corporation that earns $10,000 before local taxes. The U.S. corporate income tax rate is 35%. The foreign tax rate is 30% in cases 1 through 4 and 40% in case 5.

Case 1: Foreign Subsidiary with 100% Payout (No Withholding Tax).
Assuming the foreign subsidiary earns $10,000 before local taxes, it pays $3,000
in foreign taxes (30% foreign tax rate) and distributes all $7,000 of remaining net
income to its U.S. parent (100% payout rate). Because there are no withholding
taxes, the U.S. parent receives a net remittance of the full $7,000.

The U.S. parent corporation takes the *full* before-tax foreign income of the
foreign corporation—apportioned by its proportional ownership in the foreign
corporation (in this case 100%)—into its taxable income. This is called *grossing-up*.

The U.S. parent then calculates a tentative U.S. tax against the grossed-up
foreign income. Assuming a 35% U.S. tax rate, the tentative U.S. tax on a
grossed-up income of $10,000 is $3,500. The U.S. parent is then entitled under
U.S. tax law to reduce this U.S. tax liability by a *deemed-paid foreign tax credit* for
taxes already paid on the same income in the foreign country. The deemed-paid
tax credit is calculated as follows:

$$\text{Deemed-paid credit} = \frac{\text{Dividends received (including withholding tax)} \times \text{Creditable foreign taxes}}{\text{After-tax net profits and earnings of foreign corporation}}$$

Creditable taxes are foreign income taxes that are paid on earnings by a foreign corporation that has paid a dividend to a qualifying U.S. corporation.[2] The
deemed-paid credit in Case 1 is calculated as follows:

$$\text{Deemed-paid credit} = \frac{\$7,000 \times \$3,000}{\$7,000} = \$3,000$$

The U.S. parent owes an additional $500 in U.S. taxes ($3,500 tentative
U.S. tax less the deemed-paid credit of $3,000). The after-tax income earned by
the U.S. parent corporation is $6,500, and the overall tax rate on the foreign
income is 35% (total taxes of $3,500 on total income of $10,000). Note that
although the foreign corporate tax rate was lower (30% to the U.S. 35% rate), the
U.S. corporation ends up paying the higher effective rate.

Case 2: Foreign Subsidiary with 100% Payout (10% Withholding Tax).
Assume that the same foreign corporation earns the same income, but now all
dividends paid to the U.S. parent corporation are subject to a 10% withholding
tax. All other values remain the same as in Case 1. Although the actual net remittance to the U.S. parent is now lower, $6,300 instead of $7,000, the U.S. parent
calculates the tentative U.S. tax on a grossed-up dividend of $7,000.

The tentative U.S. tax liability is again $3,500. The U.S. corporation can
then deduct the amount of the deemed-paid credit ($3,000) and the full amount
of withholding tax ($700) from its U.S. tax liability. Because the total foreign tax
credits of $3,700 are greater than the tentative U.S. tax of $3500, the U.S. par-

| **Exhibit 17.3** | *U.S. Taxation of Foreign-Source Income* |

Baseline Values	Case 1	Case 2	Case 3	Case 4	Case 5
a Foreign corporate income tax rate	30%	30%	30%	30%	40%
b U.S. corporate income tax rate	35%	35%	35%	35%	35%
c Foreign dividend withholding tax rate	0%	10%	10%	10%	10%
d U.S. ownership in foreign firm	100%	100%	100%	40%	40%
e Dividend payout rate of foreign firm	100%	100%	50%	50%	50%
Foreign Affiliate Tax Computation					
1. Taxable income of foreign affiliate	$10,000	$10,000	$10,000	$10,000	$10,000
2. Foreign corporate income taxes (rate *a*)	–3,000	–3,000	–3,000	–3,000	–4,000
3. Net income available for profit distribution	$7,000	$7,000	$7,000	$7,000	$6,000
4. Retained earnings ((1 – rate *e*) × line 3)	0	0	3,500	3,500	3,000
5. Distributed earnings (rate *e* × line 3)	$7,000	$7,000	$3,500	$3,500	$3,000
6. Distribution to U.S. corporation (rate *d* × line 5)	$7,000	$7,000	$3,500	$1,400	$1,200
7. Withholding taxes on dividends (rate *c* × line 6)	0	700	350	140	120
8. Net remittance to U.S. corporation	$7,000	$6,300	$3,150	$1,260	$1,080
U.S. Corporate Tax Computation on Foreign-Source Income					
9. Dividend received (before withholding tax)	$7,000	$7,000	$3,500	$1,400	$1,200
10. Add-back foreign deemed-paid tax (line 6 + line 3 × line 2)	3,000	3,000	1,500	600	800
11. Grossed-up foreign dividend for U.S. taxation	$10,000	$10,000	$5,000	$2,000	$2,000
12. Tentative U.S. tax liability (rate *a* × line 11)	3,500	3,500	1,750	700	700
13. Less credit for foreign taxes:					
a) Foreign income taxes paid	–3,000	–3,000	–1,500	–600	–800
b) Foreign withholding taxes paid	–0	–700	–350	–140	–120
c) Total	–3,000	–3,700	–1,850	–740	–920
14. Additional U.S. taxes due (if line 12 > line 13c)	500	0	0	0	0
15. Excess foreign tax credits (if line 12 < 13c)	0	200	100	40	220
16. After-tax income from foreign affiliate (line 11 + line 13c – line 14)	$6,500	$6,300	$3,150	$1,260	$1,080
Tax Burden Measurement					
17. Total taxes paid (foreign + domestic)	$3,500	$3,700	$1,850	$740	$920
18. Effective tax rate on foreign income (line 17 ÷ line 11)	35%	37%	37%	37%	46%

ent owes no additional U.S. taxes. The U.S. parent has, in fact, an excess foreign tax credit of $200 ($3,700–$3,500), which it can carry back two years or carry forward five years. The effective foreign tax rate is now 37% as a result of the firm's paying higher taxes abroad than it would have theoretically paid at home, including the withholding tax.

Case 3: Foreign Subsidiary with 50% Payout (10% Withholding Tax). In this case it is assumed that all tax rates remain the same, but the foreign corporation chooses to pay out only 50% of net income rather than 100%. As a result, all dividends, withholding taxes, deemed-paid credits, tentative U.S. tax liabilities, foreign tax credits, after-tax income from the foreign subsidiary, and finally total taxes paid are cut in half. The overall effective tax rate is again 37%, higher than what would theoretically have been paid if the income had been earned inside rather than outside the United States.

Case 4: Foreign Affiliate with 50% Payout (10% Withholding Tax). Case 4 illustrates to what degree these cash flows change when the U.S. parent corporation owns only 40% of the foreign corporation. As illustrated in Exhibit 17.3, the 40% ownership acts only as a "scale factor" in apportioning dividends paid, withholding tax withheld, and tax liabilities and credits resulting. Once again, the U.S. parent corporation has excess foreign tax credits as a result of paying more taxes abroad than it is liable for at home. The overall effective tax rate on the reduced after-tax net income for the foreign affiliate of $1,400 is 37%.

Case 5: Foreign Affiliate with 50% Payout (40% Foreign Corporate Tax, 10% Withholding Tax). This fifth and final case illustrates the increasing tax burden on the U.S. parent corporation when the corporate income tax in the foreign country is higher than that in the United States. The combined impact of a 40% foreign income tax and a 10% withholding tax, even after calculation of deemed-paid foreign tax credits, results in a rising excess foreign tax credit and a substantially higher effective tax rate of 46%. Clearly, when the implications of Case 5 are combined with the number of countries with corporate tax rates higher than that of the United States, the tax burden borne by U.S.-based MNEs is a significant competitive concern.

)))) Excess Foreign Tax Credits

If a U.S.-based MNE receives income from a foreign country that imposes higher corporate income taxes than the United States (or combined income and withholding tax), total creditable taxes will exceed U.S. taxes on that foreign income. The result is *excess foreign tax credits*. All firms wish to manage their tax liabilities globally, however, so that they do not end up paying more on foreign-sourced income than they do on domestically sourced income. The proper management of global taxes is not simple, however, and combines three different components: (1) *foreign tax credit limitations*; (2) *tax credit carry-forward/carry-back*; and (3) *foreign tax averaging*.

Foreign Tax Credit Limitation. The amount of credit a taxpayer can use in any year is limited to the U.S. tax on that foreign income. Foreign tax credits *cannot* be used to reduce taxes levied on domestic income. The total foreign tax creditable in any one year is limited according to the following formula:

$$\text{Creditable tax limit} = \frac{\text{Total foreign taxable income}}{\text{Total taxable income}} \times \text{U.S. tax on total income}$$

This requires the consideration of not only foreign source income, but the U.S. tax liabilities associated with the firm's domestic income.

Tax Credit Carry-Forward/Carry-Back. Excess foreign tax credits, like domestic tax credits, may be carried forward five years and carried back two years against similar tax liabilities. Unfortunately, since excess foreign tax credits arise from tax differentials, and tax rates typically change slowly, a firm experiencing an excess FTC one year may experience it year after year.

Tax Averaging. The good news is that under U.S. tax law it is possible to offset foreign tax credits derived from one source against foreign tax liabilities from another source, assuming they are derived from the same type of income. This is termed *tax averaging*. In principle this means that if dividends are received from a high-tax country, creating excess foreign tax credits, these credits can in turn be used against a deficit foreign tax credit position formed from repatriating dividends from a low-tax country.

The primary obstacle to tax averaging is the inability to average across different categories or "baskets" of income. The U.S. tax code specifies a *general limitation income basket*. This is the basket that includes the majority of income derived by U.S. corporations abroad, such as manufacturing, services, and sales income. The U.S. tax code specifies eight other baskets of income into which foreign-source income may fall.[3] The U.S. tax code separates the earnings of foreign corporations into *active* and *passive*. *Active* earnings are those earned from direct business operations such as manufacturing and selling goods or services, and *passive* income is most often investment income earned in the form of dividends, interest, and royalties. A U.S.-based firm cannot average deficit foreign tax credits on active income from a low-tax country against excess foreign tax credits on passive income from a high-tax country. This basket limitation provides fewer incentives for MNEs to position certain types of profits in low-tax countries. Many countries, however, do not restrict the use of foreign tax credits by income category, or they choose to ignore foreign-source income altogether.

CONTROLLED FOREIGN CORPORATIONS AND SUBPART F INCOME

Many countries utilize special rules to prevent tax avoidance on foreign source income. For example, the rule that U.S. shareholders do not pay U.S. taxes on foreign-source income until that income is remitted to the United States was amended in 1962 by the creation of special *Subpart F income*. The revision was designed to prevent the use of arrangements between operating companies and base companies located in tax havens as a means of deferring U.S. taxes and to encourage greater repatriation of foreign incomes. The Tax Reform Act of 1986 retained the concept of Subpart F income but made a number of changes that expanded categories of income subject to taxation, reduced exceptions, and raised or lowered thresholds.

Several definitions are needed to understand Subpart F income:

- A *controlled foreign corporation* is any foreign corporation in which U.S. shareholders, including corporate parents, own more than 50% of the combined voting power or total value.

- A U.S. *shareholder* is a U.S. person owning 10% or more of the voting power of a controlled foreign corporation. A U.S. *person* is a citizen or resident of the United States, a domestic partnership, a domestic corporation, or any nonforeign trust or estate. The required percentages are based on *constructive ownership*, under which an individual is deemed to own shares registered in the names of other family members, trusts, and so on.[4]

Under these definitions a more-than-50% owned "subsidiary" of a U.S. corporation would be a controlled foreign corporation, and the U.S. parent would be taxed on certain undistributed income (Subpart F income) of that controlled foreign corporation.

Subpart F income, which is subject to immediate U.S. taxation *even when not remitted*, is income of a type otherwise easily shifted offshore to avoid current taxation. It includes (1) passive income received by the foreign corporation such as dividends, interest, rents, royalties, net foreign currency gains, net commodities gains, and income from the sale of non-income-producing property; (2) income from the insurance of U.S. risks; (3) financial service income; (4) shipping income; (5) oil-related income; and (6) certain related-party sales and service income.

Subpart F, restated, provides that if a foreign corporation is considered to be a controlled foreign corporation, each U.S. shareholder owning 10% or more of that corporation must include the shareholder's pro rated share of its Subpart F income in the shareholder's gross income. Thus, Subpart F income is subject to current U.S. taxation at the shareholder level even though not remitted to the United States.

TAX TREATIES

A network of bilateral tax treaties, many of which are modeled after one proposed by the Organization for Economic Cooperation and Development (OECD), provides another means of reducing double taxation. Tax treaties normally define whether taxes are to be imposed on income earned in one country by the nationals of another, and if so, how. Tax treaties are bilateral, with the two signatories specifying what rates are applicable to which types of income between themselves alone. Exhibit 17.1's specification of withholding taxes on dividends, interest, and royalty payments between resident corporations of the United States, Germany, and Japan is a classic example of the structure of tax treaties. Note that Germany, for example, imposes a 10% withholding tax on both interest and royalty payments to Japanese investors, while royalty payments to U.S. investors are withheld at a 0% rate.

The individual bilateral tax jurisdictions as specified through tax treaties are particularly important for firms that are primarily exporting to another country rather than doing business there through a "permanent establishment." The latter would be the case for manufacturing operations. A firm that only exports would not want any of its other worldwide income taxed by the importing country. Tax treaties define what is a "permanent establishment" and what constitutes a limited presence for tax purposes.

Tax treaties also typically result in reduced withholding tax rates between the two signatory countries, with the negotiation of the treaty itself serving as a forum for opening and expanding business relationships between the two countries. This practice is important to both MNEs operating through foreign affiliates earning *active income*, and individual portfolio investors simply receiving *passive income* in the form of dividends, interest, or royalties.[5]

TAX TYPES

Taxes are classified on the basis of whether they are applied directly to income, called *direct taxes*, or on the basis of some other measurable performance characteristic of the firm, called *indirect taxes*. Exhibit 17.4 illustrates the wide range of corporate income taxes in the world today.

))) Income Tax

Many governments rely on income taxes, both personal and corporate, for their primary revenue source. Corporate income taxes are widely used today. Some countries impose different corporate tax rates on distributed income versus undistributed income, as in the case of Germany shown in both Exhibit 17.1 and 17.4. Corporate income tax rates vary over a relatively wide range, rising as high as 55% in Kuwait and falling as low as 16.5% in Hong Kong, 15% in the British Virgin Islands, and effectively 0% in a number of offshore tax havens (discussed later in this chapter).

))) Withholding Tax

Passive income (dividends, interest, royalties) earned by a resident of one country within the tax jurisdiction of a second country are normally subject to a withholding tax in the second country. The reason for the institution of withholding taxes is actually quite simple: governments recognize that most international investors will not file a tax return in each country in which they invest and therefore wish to ensure that a minimum tax payment is received. As the term "withholding" implies, the taxes are withheld by the corporation from the payment made to the investor, and the taxes withheld are then turned over to government authorities. Withholding taxes are a major subject of bilateral tax treaties, and generally range between 0 and 25%.

Exhibit 17.4   *Corporate Tax Rates in Selected Countries (percentage of taxable income)*

Country	Tax Rate	Country	Tax Rate	Country	Tax Rate
Antigua & Barbuda	40	Greece	35	Philippines	32
Argentina	33	Guatemala	30	Poland	32
Australia	36	Guyana	45	Portugal	34
Austria	34	Honduras	35	Puerto Rico	20
Azerbaijan	32	Hong Kong	16.5	Qatar	35
Bahamas	0	Hungary	18	Romania	38
Bahrain	0	India	40	Russian Federation	35
Barbados	40	Indonesia	30	St. Lucia	33.33
Belgium	39	Ireland	32	Saudi Arabia	45nr
Belize	35	Isle of Man	20	Singapore	26
Bermuda	0	Israel	36	Senegal	35
Bolivia	25	Italy	37	Slovak Republic	40
Botswana	25/15	Jamaica	33.33	South Africa	35
Brazil	15	Japan	37.5	Spain	35
British Virgin Islands	1/15	Kazakhstan	30	Sri Lanka	30
Brunei Darussalam	30	Kenya	35	Sweden	28
Bulgaria	30	Korea	28	Switzerland	20–45
Cameroon	38.5	Kuwait	55	Taiwan	25
Canada	38	Latvia	25	Tanzania	30
Cayman Islands	0	Liechtenstein	20	Thailand	30
Channel Islands	20	Lithuania	29	Trinidad & Tobago	35
Channel Islands, Jersey	20	Luxembourg	30	Turkey	30
Chile	15/35	Macau	15	Uganda	30
China	30	Malawi	38	Ukraine	30
Colombia	35	Malaysia	28	United Kingdom	31
Congo (formerly Zaire)	nk	Malta	35	United States	35
Costa Rica	30	Mauritius	35	Uruguay	30
Cote d'Ivoire	35	Mexico	34	Vietnam	25
Croatia	35	Morocco	35	Zambia	35
Cyprus	25	Namibia	35	Zimbabwe	37.5
Czech Republic	35	Netherlands	35		
Denmark	34	Netherlands Antilles	39		
Dominican Republic	25	New Caledonia	30		
Ecuador	25	New Zealand	33		
Egypt	40	Nicaragua	30		
El Salvador	25	Nigeria	30		
Estonia	26	Norway	28		
Fiji	35	Oman	50f/7.5r		
Finland	28	Panama	30		
France	33.33	Papua New Guinea	25r/48nr		
Gabon	40	Paraguay	30		
Germany	30d/45u	Peru	30		
Ghana	35				

Notes: Botswana rates depend on manufacturing (*m*) or non-manufacturing (*nm*). British Virgin Islands assess a 1% tax on foreign-source income of incorporate companies. *d* rate applies to distributed profits, *u* to undistributed profits (e.g., Germany and Hungary). Chile imposes a 35% withholding tax on income remitted to foreign residents from domestic operations. Oman tax rates vary depending on the percentage of capital invested held by foreigners (50% if over 65%, falling to a minimum tax with 100% Omani ownership). Papua New Guinea charges different tax rates depending on residents (*r*), non-residents (*nr*); there is no tax on undistributed profits. Representative maximum corporate rates shown only. For actual tax liability calculations see original source. Countries not listed include Iran, Nepal, and Pakistan.
Source: Price Waterhouse Coopers, *Corporate Taxes: A Worldwide Summary*, Information Guide, 1999.

)))) **Value-Added Tax**

One type of tax that has achieved great prominence is the value-added tax. The *value-added tax* is a type of national sales tax collected at each stage of production or sale of consumption goods in proportion to the value added during that stage. In general, production goods such as plant and equipment have not been subject to the value-added tax. Certain basic necessities such as medicines and other health-related expenses, education and religious activities, and the postal service are usually exempt or taxed at lower rates. The value-added tax has been adopted as the main source of revenue from indirect taxation by all members of the European Union, most other countries in Western Europe, a number of Latin American countries, and scattered other countries. A numerical example of a value-added tax computation is shown in Exhibit 17.5.

)))) **Other National Taxes**

There are a variety of other national taxes, that vary in importance from country to country. The *turnover tax* (tax on the purchase or sale of securities in some country stock markets) and the *tax on undistributed profits* were mentioned before. *Property* and *inheritance taxes*, also termed *transfer taxes*, are imposed in a variety of ways to achieve intended social redistribution of income and wealth as much as to raise revenue. There are a number of red-tape charges for public services that are in reality user taxes. Sometimes foreign exchange purchases or sales

---

| **Exhibit 17.5** | *Value-Added Tax Applied to the Sale of a Wooden Fence Post* |

This is an example of how a wooden fence post would be assessed for value-added taxes in the course of its production and subsequent sale. A value-added tax of 10% is assumed.

   The original tree owner sells to the lumber mill, for $0.20, that part of a tree that ultimately becomes the fence post. The grower has added $0.20 in value up to this point by planting and raising the tree. While collecting $0.20 from the lumber mill, the grower must set aside $0.02 to pay the value-added tax to the government. The lumber mill processes the tree into fence posts and sells each post for $0.40 to the lumber wholesaler. The lumber mill has added $0.20 in value ($0.40 less $0.20) through its processing activities. Therefore, the lumber mill owner must set aside $0.02 to pay the mill's value-added tax to the government. In practice, the owner would probably calculate the mill's tax liability as 10% of $0.40, or $0.04, with a tax credit of $0.02 for the value-added tax already paid by the tree owner. The lumber wholesaler and retailer also add value to the fence post through their selling and distribution activities. They are assessed $0.01 and $0.03 respectively, making the cumulative value-added tax collected by the government $0.08, or 10% of the final sales price.

Stage of Production	Sales Price	Value Added	Value-added Tax at 10%	Cumulative Value-added Tax
Tree owner	$0.20	$0.20	$0.02	$0.02
Lumber mill	$0.40	$0.20	$0.02	$0.04
Lumber wholesaler	$0.50	$0.10	$0.01	$0.05
Lumber retailer	$0.80	$0.30	$0.03	$0.08

are in effect hidden taxes, inasmuch as the government earns revenue rather than just regulates imports and exports for balance of payments reasons.

INTERCOMPANY TRANSACTIONS AND TRANSFER PRICES

The problem of intercompany transactions, particularly *transfer pricing*, is a substantial area of concern for the MNE. *Transfer pricing* refers to the prices charged, either domestically or internationally, for goods, services, and technology exchanged between related units. Although the problem is complex enough domestically, internationally it proves an area of continual management attention and government oversight. Because so much of the "business" of a MNE is with other affiliated units, and the nature of the product or service being transferred is so firm-specific, firms can alter their tax liabilities per country through inappropriate or manipulated transfer prices. Transfer pricing is extremely technical and involves a number of issues beyond simply taxation. Chapter 18 will include consideration of transfer pricing in more detail within the more general context of multinational working capital management.

BRANCH VERSUS LOCALLY INCORPORATED AFFILIATE

A MNE normally has a choice of organizing a foreign affiliate as a branch of the parent or as a local corporation. Both tax and nontax consequences must be considered. Nontax factors include the locus of legal liability, public image in the host country, managerial incentive considerations, and local legal and political requirements. Although important, nontax considerations are really outside the scope of this chapter on tax planning.

One major tax consideration is whether the foreign affiliate is expected to run at a loss for several years after start-up. If so, it might be preferable to organize originally as a branch operation to permit these anticipated losses to be consolidated in the parent's income statement for tax purposes. For example, tax laws in the United States and many other countries do not permit a foreign corporation to be consolidated for tax purposes, even though it is consolidated for reporting purposes, but they do permit consolidation of foreign branches for tax purposes.

A second tax consideration is the net tax burden after paying withholding taxes on dividends. A MNE must weigh the benefit of potential tax deferral of home-country taxes on foreign-source income from a fully incorporated foreign unit, versus the total tax burden of paying foreign corporate income taxes and withholding taxes when the income has been distributed to the parent corporation. A foreign branch's income would typically bear the burden of home-country taxation as its income is concurrently consolidated with that of the parent. Foreign income taxes and withholding taxes would also typically apply.

A third tax consideration is important for firms engaged in natural resource exploration and development. Some countries allow exploration costs, and possibly part of development costs, to be written off as a current expense rather than requiring them to be capitalized and amortized over succeeding years. Therefore, many multinational oil and mining firms choose to operate these activities overseas as branches rather than subsidiaries. U.S. natural resource seeking firms have an additional incentive to use the branch form of organization overseas, because this practice permits their use of the special depletion allowances allowed under the U.S. tax laws.

Further complicating the choice of structure are the various special-purpose organization forms permitted or encouraged by some countries. These are normally motivated by a country's desire to increase its exports or to promote development of less developed countries. For example, a U.S. firm can reduce the effective tax on foreign income by establishing a so-called possessions corporation in a U.S. possession such as Puerto Rico, Guam, or Samoa.

TAX-HAVEN AFFILIATES AND INTERNATIONAL OFFSHORE FINANCIAL CENTERS

Many MNEs have foreign affiliates that act as tax havens for corporate funds awaiting reinvestment or repatriation. *Tax-haven affiliates*, categorically referred to as *international offshore financial centers* (IOFCs), are partially a result of tax-deferral features on earned foreign income allowed by some of the parent countries. Tax-haven affiliates are typically established in a country that can meet the following requirements:

- A low tax on foreign investment or sales income earned by resident corporations and a low dividend withholding tax on dividends paid to the parent firm.

- A stable currency, to permit easy conversion of funds into and out of the local currency. This requirement can be met by permitting and facilitating the use of Eurocurrencies.

- The facilities to support financial services for example, good communications, professional qualified office workers, and reputable banking services.

- A stable government that encourages the establishment of foreign-owned financial and service facilities within its borders.

Exhibit 17.6 provides a map of most of the world's major offshore IOFCs.

The typical tax-haven affiliate owns the common stock of its related operating foreign affiliates. There might be several tax-haven affiliates scattered around the world whose equity is typically 100% owned by the parent firm. All transfers of funds might go through the tax-haven affiliates, including dividends and equity financing. Thus the parent country's tax on foreign-source income, which might normally be paid when a dividend is declared by a foreign affiliate, could continue to be deferred until the tax-haven affiliate itself pays a dividend to the parent firm. This event can be postponed indefinitely if foreign operations continue to grow and require new internal financing from the tax-haven affiliate.

Exhibit 17.6   *International Offshore Banking Centers (IOFCs)*

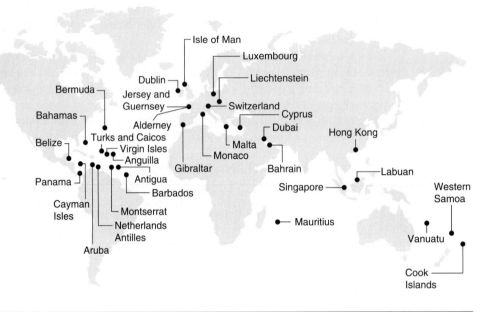

Source: Special Report, *Sunday Morning Post, South China Morning Post,* 4/17/94, p. 7. Reprinted with permission.

Thus, MNEs are able to operate a corporate pool of funds for foreign operations without having to repatriate foreign earnings through the parent country's tax machine.

For U.S. MNEs the tax-deferral privilege operating through a foreign affiliate was not originally a tax loophole. On the contrary, it was granted by the U.S. government to allow U.S. firms to expand overseas and place them on a par with foreign competitors, which also enjoy similar types of tax deferral and export subsidies of one type or another.

Unfortunately, some U.S. firms distorted the original intent of tax deferral into tax avoidance. Transfer prices on goods and services bought from or sold to related affiliates were artificially rigged to leave all the income from the transaction in the tax-haven affiliate. This manipulation could be done by routing the legal title to the goods or services through the tax-haven affiliate, even though physically the goods or services never entered the tax-haven country. This maneuver left no residual tax base for either exporting or importing affiliates located outside the tax-haven country. Needless to say, tax authorities of both exporting and importing countries were dismayed by the lack of taxable income in such transactions.

One purpose of the U.S. Internal Revenue Act of 1962 was to eliminate the tax advantages of these "paper" foreign corporations without destroying the tax-deferral privilege for those foreign manufacturing and sales affiliates that were established for business and economic motives rather than tax motives. Although the tax motive has been removed, some firms have found these affiliates useful as finance control centers for foreign operations.

ILLUSTRATIVE CASE

Offshore Centres' Regulation Under Fire

The European commission's chief fraud-fighter yesterday accused the Channel Islands and the Isle of Man of having "lax regulation even by off-shore standards," making them an ideal location for hiding illegal activities.

The secrecy afforded by Switzerland was also a problem for its European Union neighbors and a "boon to fraudsters," Mr. Per Brix Knudsen, director of the Commission's antifraud coordination unit, told an International Financial Fraud Convention in London. His remarks were publicly challenged by Ms. Jannine Birtwistle, head of compliance at Credit Suisse (Guernsey) and a former regulator on the island. She said Guernsey's regulation had been favourably assessed by the Financial Action Task Force set up by the G7.

But Mr. Knudsen's attack on offshore centres was echoed by Mr. John Moscow, deputy chief of investigations for the New York district attorney's office. After outlining a case involving the Cook Islands, a New Zealand protectorate, Mr. Moscow said: "There are jurisdictions which wish to earn their living protecting crooks." Mr. Knudsen, a Dane, said illicit entry of goods into the EU was alone costing member countries' treasuries Ecu5bn–Ecu6bn ($6.3bn–$7.6bn) in lost revenue each year. Smugglers' potential profit per lorry or container-load ranged from Ecu1m for cigarettes to Ecu100,000 for agricultural produce. The Commission unit was also focusing on fraud in the public sector.

He said: "None of this is exclusive to the European Union. This is a truly worldwide phenomenon." Money acquired illicitly was then hidden in "phantom entities in safe havens and offshore centres." Existing arrangements for international judicial co-operation were "old-fashioned and bureaucratic," Mr. Knudsen said. These needed to be simplified and streamlined, and national law enforcement agencies should integrate their efforts and introduce more specialisation.

Mr. Moscow, whose cases included Bank of Credit and Commerce International, said he was now investigating "a securities dealer in New York who stole in the region of $20m–$50m. He appears to have an account in the Cook Islands," whose law states that no court order can breach its banking secrecy. "Under pressure from the civilized world," he said, traditional offshore centres were changing their laws, but other countries were now offering total secrecy. Mr. Moscow said: "Internal corporate secrecy is the first step towards large-scale international fraud. Bank files have to be accurate and complete. That means you don't have one person who knows the identity and others who comply with subpoenas.

"Little things like the name of the borrower have to be correct. You can look at [BCCI's] files and not have a clue what happened. It would say: "$100m loaned to borrower at your request." Wow, you can kiss that money goodbye." The convention was organised by International Conference Group.

Source: *Financial Times*, December 4, 1996. Reprinted with permission.

SPECIALIZED TAX-SAVING CORPORATIONS

Many countries have established tax incentives that permit the creation of specialized offshore entities that can be utilized by multinational firms, as well as by pure exporters, to reduce the tax burden on exports. The following sections illustrate the U.S. approach to this strategy.

Foreign Sales Corporation

Over the years the United States has introduced into U.S. tax laws special incentives dealing with international operations. To benefit from these incentives, a firm may have to form separate corporations for qualifying and nonqualifying activities. The most important U.S. special corporation is a *foreign sales corporation* (FSC). FSCs were introduced in the Tax Reform Act of 1984 as a device to provide tax-exempt income for U.S. persons or corporations having export-oriented activities.

Exempt foreign trade income of an FSC is not subject to U.S. income taxes. This revenue is income from foreign sources that is not effectively connected with the conduct of a trade or business within the United States. It is a portion of total foreign trade income.

An FSC's total foreign trade income is derived from gross receipts from the sale of *export property*, lease or rental of export property, incidental services provided with the sale or lease of export property, and fees for engineering, architectural, or managerial services. The exempt portion of the FSC's total foreign trade income depends upon the pricing rules used. *Export property* is manufactured, produced, grown, or extracted from the United States by an entity other than the FSC and is sold, leased, or rented outside the United States.

If foreign trade income is based on arm's length pricing between unrelated parties, or between related parties under the rules of Section 482 of the Internal Revenue Code, then exempt foreign trade income is defined as 34% of the income from the transaction. (Section 482 of the U.S. Internal Revenue Code is described in Chapter 18.) If prices are set under special administrative rules established for FSCs, exempt foreign trade income is the fraction 17/23 of income from the transaction. That portion of total foreign trade income that is not exempt is regarded as effectively derived from the conduct of trade or business by a permanent business establishment in the United States and is therefore subject to U.S. income taxes. Exempt income of an FSC may be distributed to its U.S. shareholders on a tax-free basis. Dividends paid from nonexempt income of an FSC are fully taxable to the U.S. parent.

In 1999, however, the World Trade Organization (WTO) ruled that FSCs were an illegal subsidy worth billions of dollars to thousands of U.S. exporters. Although it is unlikely that FSCs will be discontinued, their role in aiding U.S.-based exporters is increasingly controversial.[6]

)))) Possessions Corporation

A business carried on to a substantial extent in a U.S. possession can be carried on by a separate U.S. corporation, which, if it meets the requirements for a possessions corporation, is not subject to U.S. tax on income earned outside the United States unless the income is *received* in the United States. Although technically a U.S. corporation, a possessions corporation is treated like a foreign corporation in nearly every respect.

Requirements. To qualify as a possessions corporation, a corporation must satisfy the following requirements.

1. It is a domestic U.S. corporation.
2. At least 80% of its gross income is derived from within a U.S. possession.
3. At least 75% of its gross income is derived from the active conduct of a trade or business in a U.S. possession.

Exclusion from Gross Income. A corporation meeting the above requirements excludes from U.S. gross income amounts earned outside the United States unless the income is received in the United States. Thus, a possessions corporation should arrange to *receive* income initially outside the United States, although it may subsequently transfer it from a foreign bank account to a bank account in the United States.

The possessions corporation's income is subject to U.S. tax, but a tax-sparing credit is allowed for U.S. taxes on foreign-source income attributable to the conduct of a trade or business in a U.S. possession and qualified possessions-source investment income. The net result is that nonqualified income is subject to U.S. tax but possessions income is exempt from tax. The income qualifying for this credit is as follows:

- Income from foreign sources that is attributable to the conduct of a trade or business in a possession.

- Qualified possessions-source investment income that is defined as investment income (a) from sources within the possession in which the business is carried on, and (b) which the taxpayer establishes is attributable to the funds derived from the business or investment in such possession.

Other investment is taxable in the United States on a current basis. No foreign tax credit is available to possessions corporations except to the extent that a foreign tax is imposed on income subject to U.S. tax but not eligible for the tax-sparing credit. As regards the U.S. parent company of a possessions corporation, foreign taxes paid with respect to distributions from the possessions subsidiary are neither creditable nor deductible.

Dividends from possessions corporations are eligible for the 100% or 85% dividends-received deduction, regardless of when the income was earned. Thus, accumulated earnings from prior years can be repatriated by the possessions corporation to the U.S. parent with little or no U.S. tax.

SUMMARY

- Tax planning for multinational operations is a complex technical subject that requires the inputs of experienced tax and legal counsel in both parent and host countries. Nevertheless, the financial manager of a MNE should be acquainted with the national tax environments in the host countries in which the firm operates. This environment includes the role of local income taxes, value-added taxes, and other indirect taxes, and the less tangible aspects of local tax morality.

- The financial executive must also understand how the parent country taxes foreign-source income in order to organize efficiently for foreign operations. Important considerations include how the parent's country views tax neutrality as well as how it treats tax deferral, foreign tax credits, and intercompany transactions. Bilateral tax treaties may also influence the way foreign operations are structured.

- Finally, the financial manager must choose the specific organization form that would be optimal for each foreign location as well as for the group as a whole. This activity typically involves choosing the branch or corporate form of organization. It also might require use of one or more special-purpose corporations or tax-haven affiliates.

- An illustrative case demonstrated how the United States taxes foreign source income of MNEs. United States tax authorities were shown to tax active income as remitted back to the U.S., while passive or Subpart F income is taxed as earned, regardless of whether it was remitted or not.

- Specialized tax-saving corporations and offshore tax havens are sometimes utilized by MNEs to minimize worldwide taxes.

QUESTIONS

1. U.S. Taxation of Foreign-Source Income
Using the structure for calculating U.S. corporate taxes for foreign-sourced income shown in Exhibit 17.3, assume a foreign subsidiary has $2,750,000 in gross earnings, U.S. and foreign corporate tax rates are 35% and 30%, respectively, and foreign withholding taxes on dividends paid to foreign residents in the United States are 15%.

a. What is the total tax payment, foreign and domestic combined, on this income?

b. What is the effective tax rate paid on this income by the U.S.-based company?

c. What would be the total tax payment and effective tax rate if the foreign corporate tax rate was 45% and there were no withholding taxes on dividends?

2. Tuskeegee Airlines/Hong Kong
Tuskeegee Airlines is a U.S.-based air freight firm with a wholly owned subsidiary in Hong Kong. The subsidiary, Tuskeegee-Hong Kong, has just completed a long-term planning report for the parent company in San Francisco, in which it has estimated the following expected earnings and payout rates for the years 2000–2003.

(millions of U.S. dollars)	Tuskeege–Hong Kong			
	2000	2001	2002	2003
Earnings before interest and taxes (EBIT)	8,000	10,000	12,000	14,000
Less interest expenses	(800)	(1,000)	(1,200)	(1,400)
Earnings before taxes (EBT)	7,200	9,000	10,800	12,600

The current Hong Kong corporate tax rate on this category of income is 16.5%. Hong Kong imposes no withholding taxes on dividends remitted to U.S. investors (per the Hong Kong-United States bilateral tax treaty). The U.S. corporate income tax rate is 35%. The parent company wants to repatriate 75% of net income as dividends annually.

a. Calculate the net income available for distribution by the Hong Kong subsidiary for the years 2000–2003.

b. What is the amount of the dividend which is expected to be remitted to the U.S. parent each year?

c. After gross-up for U.S. tax liability purposes, what is the total dividend after-tax (all Hong Kong and U.S. taxes) expected each year?

d. What is the effective tax rate on this foreign-sourced income per year?

e. What is the effective tax rate if Hong Kong imposes a 15% withholding tax?

f. Which withholding tax rate will make excess foreign tax credits equal to the U.S. tax liability?

3. Stutz of Germany

Stutz is a German-based company that manufactures electronic fuel-injection carburetor assemblies for several large automobile companies in Germany, including Mercedes, BMW, and Opel. The firm, like many firms in Germany today, is revising its financial policies in-line with the increasing degree of disclosure required by firms if they wish to list their shares publicly in or out of Germany.

Stutz's primary problem at the moment is taxation. The German corporate income tax code applies a different income tax rate to income depending on whether it is retained (45%) or distributed to stockholders (30%).

Earnings before interest and taxes (EBIT)	€ 580,000,000
Less interest expenses	(96,500,000)
Earnings before taxes (EBT)	€ 483,500,000
Less corporate income taxes	
Net income	
Retained earnings	
Distributed earnings	

a. If Stutz planned to distribute 50% of its net income, what would be its total net income and total corporate tax bills?

b. If Stutz was attempting to choose between a 40% payout rate and a 60% payout rate to stockholders, what arguments and values would management use in order to convince stockholders which of the two payouts is in everyone's best interest?

4. ZNZ Petroleum

ZNZ Petroleum is a U.S.-based multinational petroleum and petrochemical exploration, production, and distribution company. ZNZ's subsidiary in Zaire, a new promising area of petroleum exploration is expecting a major "find" in the next two-year period. The tax planning staff in the corporate headquarters in Shreveport, Louisiana, wish to estimate tax liabilities and effective tax burdens on this prospective income three years out.

The Zaire currency, the New Zaire (ZRN), is currently trading at ZRN100,000/USD. Although the government claims it is pegged to the dollar, the stability of the currency is highly questionable. Given that inflation in Zaire has been rising (now averaging 20% per year compared to the U.S.'s 3% per year), the tax planning staff would prefer to assume that the currency is likely to weaken over the period.

In addition to the obvious problems with the New Zaire, the government of Zaire requires all petroleum companies operating there to turn over all hard-currency earnings to the government. Since oil is sold on world markets in U.S. dollars, the Zairean subsidiary's income actually begins in U.S. dollars and is then converted to local currency for tax purposes. (When the subsidiary declares a dividend to the parent company, it will have to apply to the government to obtain hard-currency, U.S. dollars, for payment to the U.S. parent.)

ZNZ has estimated the all-in-cost of production per barrel, as well as the estimated barrels produced, for the years 2000–2002. The forecast oil price, which is a company-wide forecast from the corporate headquarters, is used for projecting revenues.

ZNZ—Zaire	*2000*	*2001*	*2002*
Expected price per barrel (US$)	18.50	$19.50	$19.00
Estimated all-in-cost per barrel (US$)	7.50	6.25	4.50
Barrels of oil produced (expected)	1,000,000	10,000,000	15,000,000

The current Zaire corporate income tax rate is 50%. In addition, the Zaire tax authorities impose a 20% withholding tax on dividends and interest remitted to foreign resident investors. Zaire has no current set of bilateral tax treaties, applying the same rates to all foreign investors regardless of country of origin. The parent company plans to repatriate 50% of net income as dividends annually. Complete the following basic income statement in order to answer the following questions.

ZNZ—Zaire	*2000*	*2001*	*2002*
Expected revenues (US$)			
Expected revenues (ZRN)			
Less all-in-costs, production (ZRN)			
Earnings before tax			
Less Zaire corporate income taxes			
Net income of subsidiary			
Retained earnings			
Distributed as dividend to parent			

a. Calculate the expected exchange rate for the 2000 through 2002 period.
b. Calculate the net income available for distribution by the Zaire subsidiary for the years 2000 through 2002, in both Zaire and U.S. dollars (assuming both a fixed and a depreciating Zaire dollar exchange rate).
c. What is the amount of the dividend that is expected to be remitted to the U.S. parent each year, after both income and withholding taxes, in U.S. dollars?

d. After gross-up for U.S. tax liability purposes, what is the total dividend after-tax (all Zaire and U.S. taxes) expected each year?

e. What is the effective tax rate on this foreign-sourced income per year?

5. Gamboa's Tax Averaging

Gamboa, Incorporated, is a relatively new U.S.-based retailer of specialty fruits and vegetables. The firm is vertically integrated with fruit and vegetable-sourcing subsidiaries in Central America, and distribution outlets throughout the southeastern and northeastern regions of the United States. Gamboa's two Central American subsidiaries are in Belize and Costa Rica.

Maria Gamboa, the daughter of the firm's founder, is being groomed to take over the firm's financial management in the near future. Like many firms its size, Gamboa has not possessed a very high degree of sophistication in financial management because of time and cost considerations. Maria, however, has recently finished her MBA and is now attempting to put some specialized knowledge of U.S. taxation practices to work to save Gamboa money. Her first concern is *tax averaging* for foreign tax liabilities arising from the two Central American subsidiaries.

Costa Rican operations are slightly more profitable than Belize, which is particularly good since Costa Rica is a relatively low-tax country. Costa Rican corporate taxes are a flat 30%, and there are no withholding taxes imposed on dividends paid by foreign firms with operations there. Belize has a higher corporate income tax rate, 40%, and imposes a 10% withholding tax on all dividends distributed to foreign investors. The current U.S. corporate income tax rate is 35%.

	Belize	*Costa Rica*
Earnings before taxes	$1,000,000	$1,500,000
Corporate income tax rate	40%	30%
Dividend withholding tax rate	10%	0%

a. If Maria Gamboa assumes a 50% payout rate from each subsidiary, what are the additional taxes due on foreign-sourced income from Belize and Costa Rica individually? How much in additional U.S. taxes would be due if Maria averaged the tax credits/liabilities of the two units?

b. Keeping the payout rate from the Belize subsidiary at 50%, how should Maria change the payout rate of the Costa Rican subsidiary in order to most efficiently manage her total foreign tax bill?

c. What is the minimum effective tax rate which Maria can achieve on her foreign-sourced income?

WORLD WIDE WEB EXERCISES

W1. Official Government Tax Authorities

Tax laws are constantly changing, and a MNE's tax planning and management processes must therefore include a continual updating of tax practices by country. Use the following government tax sites to address specific issues related to those countries.

a. Hong Kong's ownership change to China: http://www.info.gov.hk/eindex.htm
b. Ireland's international financial services center: http://www.revenue.ie/
c. Czech Republic's tax incentives for investment: http://www.czech.cz/homepage/busin.htm

W2. Tax Practices for International Business

Many of the major accounting firms provide online information and advisory services for international business activities as related to tax and accounting practices. Use one of the following web sites to gain up to date information on tax law changes or practices.

Arthur Andersen	http://www.arthurandersen.com/
Ernst and Young	http://www.ey.com/tax/
Deloitte & Touche	http://www.dttus.com/
KPMG	http://www.kpmg.com/
Price Waterhouse Coopers	http://www.pwcglobal.com/

SUGGESTED READINGS

Frisch, Daniel J., Economics of International Tax Policy: Some Old and New Approaches," *Tax Notes*, Apr. 30, 1990, pp. 581–591.

Price Waterhouse Coopers, Corporate Taxes: *A Worldwide Summary*, New York: Price Waterhouse Coopers, 1999.

Scholes, Myron S., and Mark A. Wolfson, *Taxes and Business Strategy: A Planning Approach*, Englewood Cliffs, N.J.: Prentice-Hall, 1992, Ch. 13 and 14.

Weisfelder, Christine J., "Home Country Taxation and the Theory of International Production," *Journal of International Financial Management and Accounting*, Vol. 5, No. 3, Oct. 1994, pp. 193–213.

NOTES

1. In the case of the United States, ordinary foreign-sourced income is taxed only as remitted to the parent firm. As with all questions of tax, however, numerous conditions and exceptions exist.

2. In order to qualify, a U.S. corporation must own at least 10% of the voting power of the distributing foreign corporation. Furthermore, if the 10% owned (first-tier) foreign corporation itself owns 10% or more of another (second-tier) foreign corporation, and the second-tier corporation owns 10% or more of a third-tier corporation, a portion of the second- and third-tier corporations' foreign income taxes will also be creditable to the U.S. taxpayer to the extent that earnings are distributed to the first- and second-tier corporations. However, there must be a minimum indirect ownership of 5% in the second- and third-tier corporations.

3. Under Section 904(d) of the United States Internal Revenue Code, the actual process of foreign-source income categorization begins with the assignment of income to the first eight baskets, with all else falling into the *residual* or *general limitation basket*.

4. Since 10% ownership is required by each U.S. shareholder, a foreign corporation in which six unrelated U.S. citizens and/or corporations each own 9% of the combined voting power or total value would not be a controlled foreign corporation, even though total U.S. ownership is 54%. Nor would a foreign corporation in which U.S. shareholders own exactly 50% be a controlled foreign corporation.

5. Summaries of corporate taxes worldwide and the bilateral treaties in effect between countries are available from a number of sources. One of the most widely used is *Corporate Taxes: A Worldwide Summary*, Information Guide, Price Waterhouse Coopers, updated annually.

6. Boeing (U.S.), the largest user of FSCs, reportedly saved $130 million in U.S. taxes in 1998 by utilizing FSCs, approximately 12% of its total annual earnings.

CHAPTER 18

REPOSITIONING FUNDS

Management of working capital requires both flow and stock decisions. This chapter deals with implementing flows—that is, with techniques to *reposition* liquid cash balances from one currency to another or from one country to another. The motive for repositioning may be to make a payment, as when a U.S. affiliate in Italy uses euros to buy dollars to pay dividends to its U.S. parent or to pay for imports received from its parent. Repositioning also takes place in order to store value in a different currency or in a different geographical location. The Italian affiliate might exchange euro balances for U.S. dollars because U.S. interest rates are higher. Or it might want to transfer euro balances from Italy to a euro account in London as compensation for better bank services.

Techniques to reposition funds are particularly important for operations in countries where exchange controls inhibit free foreign exchange transactions. This chapter looks at repositioning funds via unbundling of fund transfers, dividend remittances, and payment of fees, royalties, and home overhead charges. It also explains the numerous factors that impinge on the choice of transfer prices between related units. Management of blocked funds is required because of the political risk inherent in multinational operations.

This chapter is based on the activities of Lincoln Corporation, a hypothetical U.S. MNE with wholly owned manufacturing affiliates in the United Kingdom, Brazil, and Singapore, plus a wholly owned finance affiliate in the Cayman Islands. The United Kingdom affiliate, in turn, owns 100% of subaffiliates in France, Belgium, and Germany. The Brazilian affiliate manufactures in Brazil for sales throughout South America, Africa, and the Middle East. The Singapore affiliate manufactures for sales in Asia and Australia and also ships components to Europe and the United States. The ownership structure of Lincoln (U.S.) and its affiliates is as shown in Exhibit 18.1. Because Lincoln (U.S.) is a U.S.-based MNE, it measures all of its intra-firm transactions for internal control purposes in U.S. dollars. In this and the next chapter, unless stated otherwise, we will measure Lincoln's internal

Exhibit 18.1   *Lincoln Corporation and Its Foreign Affiliates*

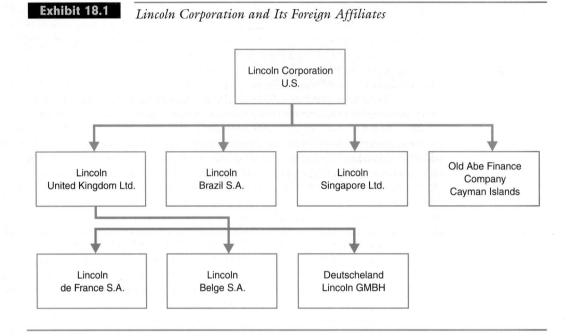

transactions in U.S. dollars even though some would originally be denominated in other currencies.

CONSTRAINTS ON POSITIONING FUNDS

In domestic business, fund flows between units of a large company are generally unimpeded. Cash balance levels are normally determined by desired liquidity in each location, marginal rates of return on short-term investments, gains from operating with minimal cash, and sometimes the temperament and persuasiveness of unit financial managers. With possibly minor exceptions, all funds are denominated in the currency of the home country.

If a firm operates multinationally, political, tax, foreign exchange, and liquidity considerations limit its ability to move funds easily and without cost from one country or currency to another. These constraints are the reason international financial executives must plan ahead for repositioning funds multinationally. Advance planning is essential even when constraints do not exist, for at some future date political events may lead to an unexpected imposition of restrictions. The likelihood of future constraints varies, of course, with the stability of the host country.

))) Political Constraints

Political constraints can block the transfer of funds either overtly or covertly. Overt blockage occurs when a currency becomes inconvertible or is subject to government exchange controls that prevent its transfer at reasonable exchange rates. Covert blockage occurs when dividends or other forms of fund remittances are severely limited, heavily taxed, or excessively delayed by the need for bureaucratic approval.

Tax Constraints

Tax constraints arise because of the complex and possibly contradictory tax structures of various national governments through whose jurisdictions funds might pass. A firm does not want funds in transit eroded by a sequence of nibbling tax collectors in every jurisdiction through which such funds might flow.

Foreign Exchange Transaction Costs

Foreign exchange transaction costs are incurred when one currency is exchanged for another. These costs, in the form of fees and/or the difference between bid and offer quotations, are revenue for the commercial banks and dealers that operate the foreign exchange market. Although usually a small percentage of the amount of money exchanged, such costs become significant for large or frequent transfers. Transaction costs are sufficiently large enough to warrant planning to avoid unnecessary back-and-forth transfers such as would occur if an affiliate remitted a cash dividend to its parent at approximately the same time as the parent paid that affiliate for goods purchased. Sending foreign exchange simultaneously in two directions is obviously a sheer waste of corporate resources, but it sometimes occurs when one part of a firm is not coordinated with another.

Liquidity Needs

Despite the overall advantage of worldwide cash handling, liquidity needs in each individual location must be satisfied and good local banking relationships maintained. The magnitude of appropriate balances is in part a judgmental decision not readily quantifiable. Nevertheless liquidity needs constrain the firm from taking a purely optimal approach to worldwide cash positioning.

UNBUNDLING INTERNATIONAL FUND TRANSFERS

Multinational firms often *unbundle* their transfer of funds into separate flows for specific purposes. Host countries are then more likely to perceive that a portion of what might otherwise be called remittance of profits constitutes an essential purchase of specific benefits that command worldwide values and benefit the host country. Unbundling allows a multinational firm to recover funds from affiliates without piquing host country sensitivities over large "dividend drains." Lincoln Brazil, for example, might transfer funds to Lincoln U.S. by any of the conduits shown in Exhibit 18.2.

Note, however, that these are only techniques that are used to implement more fundamental policy decisions, such as (1) how much money to move from one location to another, (2) when this transfer should be made, and (3) which methods are most appropriate for today's circumstances.

Exhibit 18.2   *Conduits for Moving Funds*

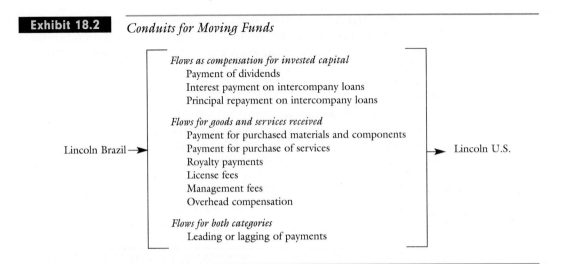

Lincoln Brazil →

Flows as compensation for invested capital
  Payment of dividends
  Interest payment on intercompany loans
  Principal repayment on intercompany loans

Flows for goods and services received
  Payment for purchased materials and components
  Payment for purchase of services
  Royalty payments
  License fees
  Management fees
  Overhead compensation

Flows for both categories
  Leading or lagging of payments

→ Lincoln U.S.

An item-by-item matching of remittance to input, in the form of royalties for patents, fees for advice, and so on, is equitable to host country and foreign investor alike, for it allows each party to see the reason for each remittance and to judge its acceptability independently. Furthermore, if all investment inputs are unbundled, part of what might have been classified as residual profits may turn out to be tax-deductible expenses related to a specific purchased benefit. Unbundling also facilitates allocation of overhead from a parent's international division to each operating affiliate in accordance with a predetermined formula. Predetermination of the allocation method means a host country is less likely to view a given remittance as quixotic and thus inappropriate. Finally, unbundling facilitates the entry of local capital into joint-venture projects, because total remuneration to different owners can be in proportion to the value of the varied contributions of each, rather than only in proportion to the amount of monetary capital they have invested.

For some firms, a negative effect of unbundling is an increase in the transparency of its financial situation to competitors and governments alike. Many firms consider that this information must be kept confidential in order for the firm to survive in a highly competitive world.

In the following sections we consider fund transfer techniques to pay for the bundle of contributions a parent might make to an affiliate and vice versa. Specifically, we examine dividend policy, royalties and fees, contributions to overhead, transfer pricing, and reactions to blocked funds.

INTERNATIONAL DIVIDEND REMITTANCES

Payment of dividends is the classical method by which firms transfer profit back to owners, be those owners individual shareholders or parent corporations. Early economists spoke of returns to land, labor, and capital—the latter meaning the cash investment of owners. Implied in this division was the idea that owners contributed only their capital and nothing more—a view perhaps sustained in the early decades of capitalism by the image of owners (all older males) sitting in red leather lounge chairs in a private London club waiting for the ship they financed to return from one of the colonies. In this view, owners had nothing to do with business guidance of their venture. Contemporary views of ownership responsibilities have changed, and international dividend policy now incorporates tax considerations, political risk, and foreign exchange risk, as well as a return for business guidance and technology.

))) Tax Implications

Host-country tax laws influence the dividend decision. Countries such as Germany tax retained earnings at one rate while taxing distributed earnings at a lower rate. Most countries levy withholding taxes on dividends paid to foreign parent firms and investors. Again, most (but not all) parent countries levy a tax on foreign dividends received but allow a "tax credit" for foreign taxes already paid on that income stream. The tax structure for foreign dividends was discussed in Chapter 17.

))) Political Risk

Political risk may motivate parent firms to require foreign affiliates to remit all locally generated funds in excess of stipulated working capital requirements and planned capital expansions. Such policies, however, are not universal. To enhance the financial self-reliance of Lincoln Brazil, assuming Brazil is perceived to be politically risky, Lincoln U.S. might not require dividend remittances. In many cases neither extreme is followed. Instead, managerial response to potential government restrictions may be to maintain a constant dividend payout ratio so as to demonstrate that an established *policy* is being consistently carried out. In the context of Lincoln Brazil, the Brazilian government is more likely to accept the idea of regular dividend payments because they provide a framework based on precedent against which to judge whether a particular dividend is "normal" or an attempt to transfer liquid funds out of Brazil's currency, to the detriment of Brazil's foreign exchange reserves.

))) Foreign Exchange Risk

If a foreign exchange loss is anticipated, Lincoln may speed up the transfer of funds from Brazil through dividends. This "lead" is usually part of a larger strategy of moving from weak currencies to strong currencies and can include speeding up intra-firm payments on accounts receivable and payable. However, decisions to accelerate dividend payments ahead of what might be normal must take into account interest rate differences and the negative impact on host country relations. Leads and lags were discussed in Chapter 7, Operating Exposure.

⟩⟩⟩ Age and Size of Affiliates

Among other factors that influence dividend policy are the age and size of the foreign affiliate. Older affiliates often provide a greater share of their earnings to their parent, presumably because as the affiliate matures it has fewer reinvestment opportunities.

⟩⟩⟩ Availability of Funds

Dividends are a cash payment to owners equal to all or a portion of earnings of a prior period. To pay dividends, an affiliate needs *both* past earnings and available cash. Affiliates sometimes have earnings without cash, because earnings are measured at the time of a sale but cash is received later when the receivable is collected. Profits of rapidly growing affiliates are often tied up in ever-increasing receivables and inventory. Hence, rapidly growing foreign affiliates may lack the cash to remit a dividend equal to even a portion of earnings.

The reverse may also be true; firms may be receiving cash from the collection of old receivables even when profits are down because current sales have fallen off or current expenses have risen relative to current sales prices. Such firms might want to declare a dividend in order to remove a bountiful supply of cash from a country but lack the earnings against which to charge such payments.

In either of these cases a firm must look at both measured earnings and available cash before settling upon a cash dividend policy. Payment of cash dividends, then, can be considered only in the context of a firm's entire cash budget.

⟩⟩⟩ Joint Venture Factors

Existence of joint-venture partners or local stockholders also influences dividend policy. Optimal positioning of funds internationally cannot dominate the valid claims of independent partners or local stockholders for dividends. The latter do not benefit from the world success of the multinational parent, but only from the success of the particular affiliate in which they own a minority share. Firms might hesitate to reduce dividends when earnings falter. They also might hesitate to increase dividends following a spurt in earnings because of possible adverse reaction to reducing dividends later should earnings decline. Lincoln's affiliates are all 100% owned, so neither Lincoln U.S. nor Lincoln U.K., both of whom own foreign affiliates, is constrained by the wishes of outside shareholders. Many MNEs insist on 100% ownership of affiliates in order to avoid possible conflicts of interest with outside shareholders.

LICENSE FEES, ROYALTY FEES, AND HOME OFFICE OVERHEAD

License fees are remuneration paid to the owners of technology, patents, trade names, and copyrighted material (including moving pictures, video tapes, compact disks, software and books). License fees are usually based on a percentage of the value of the product or on the volume of production. As such they are calculated independently of the amount of sales. Royalty fees are similar compensation for the use of intellectual property belonging to some other party. However, royalty fees are usually a stated percentage of sales revenue paid "off the top," so that the owner is compensated only in proportion to the volume of sales.

When license and royalty fees are paid by independent firms they are a straightforward, arms-length payment for benefits received. However, license and royalty fees are also paid by affiliates to their parents and/or sister affiliates. In these instances they function as another way to reposition funds between affiliates and parent. For the moment we will call all such transfers *intracompany fees*.

Intracompany fees can be differentiated into management fees for general expertise and advice, technical assistance fees for guidance in technical matters, and license fees for use of patented products or processes. Such fees are usually paid for identifiable benefits received by the affiliate, in contrast to overhead charges, discussed below, which are for more general benefits. Management and technical assistance fees are usually a fixed charge, either in total for supplying the services for a stated period of time, or on a time-rate basis varying with the number of billable hours devoted to the affiliate. These fee provisions usually require an affiliate to pay the travel and per diem expenses of the individuals involved.

Home office overhead is a charge to compensate the parent for costs incurred in the general management of international operations and for other corporate overhead that must be recovered by the operating units. Overhead may be charged for regional cash management, research and development, corporate public relations, legal and accounting costs for the entire enterprise, or a share of the salaries and other costs of top management. Home office overhead is often levied throughout an entire company as a predetermined percentage of direct labor costs or of sales. The charge may also be based on pro-rata sharing of specific costs that can be matched to the various units.

ILLUSTRATIVE CASE

Of Mice, Men, and Money

Paris—It looks like being a winter of discontent for Euro Disney. On November 10 the company, which runs a big amusement park outside Paris modeled on American ones owned by its parent firm, Walt Disney, said that it had lost a whopping FFr5.3 billion ($960m) in the year to the end of September. Unless it can solve its problems soon, Euro Disney could end up on the scrap-heap.

Battered by currency changes, stingy visitors and soaring costs, the firm made a net loss before exceptional items of FFr1.7 billion, which was broadly what was expected. However, Euro Disney unexpectedly added a one-off charge of FFr3.6 billion, which mainly represents the start-up costs for the park. The firm had been planning to amortize these over periods of up to 20 years, but has changed its mind. Why?

The most plausible answer is that the new management team that took over Euro Disney in the summer wants to start with a clean sheet. By taking a big hit now, the new regime can blame this year's lousy results on its predecessors. There may be another reason for the red ink, too. Euro Disney is wrangling with its French bankers over a refinancing of its FFr21 billion debt. If the banks are convinced that the worst is behind them, they may be more generous.

Even if it can renegotiate its debts, Euro Disney will still need more cash to get back on its feet. Rebecca Winnington-Ingram, European media analyst at Morgan Stanley in London, puts the amount needed at FFr10 billion. For now, the firm is being kept alive thanks to help from Walt Disney, which says it has made $175m available to Euro Disney to tide it over until the spring.

What then? So far Walt Disney, which owns 49% of Euro Disney, has been steadfastly supportive of its troubled European offspring. Its approach is hardly altruistic. Even when Euro Disney loses money, its parent can still cream off management fees and royalties. (Though it deferred the fees last year, Walt Disney still pocketed FFr262m in royalties.) But if it is asked to dip into its pocket again, some analysts believe it may refuse. If it does, the lights will go out on Euro Disney once and for all. (Ed. Note: After substantial financial and operational restructuring—including the elimination of most of the management fees and royalties to the parent company—Euro Disney is now operating at a marginal profit.)

Source: "Of Mice, Men, and Money," 11/13/93, p. 79 (c) 1993 *The Economist Newspaper* Ltd. Reprinted with permission.

⟫ Licensing Contracts

To preserve the firm's rights to receive funds from affiliates as royalties, fees, or overhead allocations, the contract that establishes the terms and amount of payment must be written carefully. The following points should be addressed in any *licensing contract*.[1]

- **Sales price definition**. If payments are calculated as a percentage of the affiliate's net sales price, *net sales price* must be carefully defined. Ideally, net sales price means invoice price net of any trade discounts and excluding packing charges, sales, excise and use taxes, and allowances for freight if that is billed or credited as a separate item to the customer.

- **Coverage**. The royalty or fee should be defined as a given percentage of the net sales price of *all* licensed products made and used, sold, or otherwise disposed of by the licensee.

- **Time and currency of payment**. A typical arrangement might provide that payments accrue at the time of sale or use, and payment follows on or before the close of the month following the end of the quarter. The currency of payment must be specified so that the location of any foreign exchange risk is clear.

- **Reports**. Each payment should be accompanied by a report describing the number and type of products sold, the customer, and the date of sale. This information is needed to verify the accuracy of the amount remitted and to ensure that licensed products are sold only in those geographic or political areas covered by the licensing agreement.

- **Locus of tax liabilities**. The locus of tax liabilities must be clearly specified. An old example illustrates:[2] In order to help the U.S. balance of payments, and at the urging of the U.S. president, ten Japanese utilities purchased enriched uranium ore in 1972 from the U.S. Atomic Energy Commission for $320 million. By agreement, the uranium was stored on the AEC's premises in Roane County, Tennessee, until needed in the 1980s. In other words, Japan kindly advanced payment for a purchase that would normally have been paid for later in order to help the United States' BOP position.

    The local municipality, discovering that the stored uranium was no longer U.S. government property, sent the Japanese utilities 1974 tax bills totaling $3.8 million. It takes little imagination to understand the difficulty the Japanese had in having to pay such a high tax on a transaction entered into for the purpose of helping the U.S. government! The sales contract had not specified who would pay any unanticipated taxes on the deal.

- **Monitoring costs.** During the period of the license, licensee personnel will probably visit the licenser's plant or office to acquire expertise, and the licenser will probably visit the licensee to monitor the agreement. The license agreement should specify who will pay for the visits, the amount of payments, and the work pattern (days per week, hours per day, and so on) of such visitors.

- **Nonfinancial issues**. The agreement should specify limitations on the exclusiveness of the license in various geographical areas, sublicensing rights, expiration or termination of the agreement, arbitration or litigation procedures in the case of dispute, disposition of products and/or special tools at the end of the license period, and surrender of trademark rights and blueprints. If the agreement is written in two languages, one of the languages should be established as the controlling text.

))) Financial Management Implications

Payment of royalties and fees is especially suitable when unbundling remuneration. In joint ventures the resources contributed by one of the partners may include technology and know-how; the other partner may be the primary supplier of monetary capital. The supplier of technology can readily accept royalty or fee compensation for that input and then accept a smaller proportion of net income as return on its proportionally smaller investment of monetary capital.

Not all companies desire unbundling. Some parents do not want to impair the competitiveness of affiliates with charges for services that could be regarded as remote.

Royalty and fee payments are sometimes allowed by the host country, even when dividend payments are restricted. A company might organize the contractual part of its investment agreements so that, if the free movement of funds via dividends is limited, options for repositioning funds via royalties and fees remain open. This might be desirable for Lincoln Brazil given that Brazil has imposed constraints on dividend payments in years past.

)))) Income Tax Aspects

Royalties and fees may have tax advantages over dividends, especially when host-country combined income and withholding tax rates are above the parent rate. Royalties and fees are usually deductible locally, whereas dividends are normally paid after local income taxes have been calculated, and withholding taxes are paid on the dividend itself. The parent can take a tax credit for local income and withholding taxes paid, but if the affiliate's combined tax rate is above that of the parent, the benefit is lost. The entire benefit is income for tax purposes to the receiving entity when the payment is for royalties and fees.

A company such as Lincoln must be careful to assure itself that each affiliate's royalties and fees can legally be deducted in calculating taxable income. Because a royalty or fee payment from an affiliate in a high-tax jurisdiction to a parent in a lower-tax jurisdiction provides a net gain to the world-wide enterprise, Lincoln U.K. would probably gain if Lincoln Belge and Deutscheland Lincoln moved cash to Lincoln U.K. via royalties and fees instead of dividends. However, to be tax deductible, royalty and fee calculations must usually be constant for all countries; hence the royalty or fee rate assessed Lincoln De France would have to be the same. It is seldom feasible to discriminate between affiliates in setting rates of royalty or fees because most countries' tax authorities share information.

The tax interaction is depicted in Exhibit 18.3. Assume that Lincoln Singapore earns $10,000,000 (measured in U.S. dollars) before remitting cash to Lincoln U.S. and before paying Singaporean income taxes. Lincoln U.S. would like to receive $4,000,000 in cash from Singapore after U.S. taxes. The Singaporean income tax rate is 40% and the U.S. rate is 34%. For simplicity assume no dividend withholding taxes in this example.

Case 1: $4,000,000 dividend only. Case 1 is a "bundled" situation, where only dividends are paid to Lincoln U.S. The $4,000,000 dividend (two-thirds of the amount available for dividends) is "grossed up" by adding back two-thirds of Singaporean taxes. The U.S. tentative tax at 34% of the grossed-up $6,667,000 is $2,267,000. However, this amount is reduced by Singaporean taxes of $2,667,000 already paid on the same income. Because Singapore's tax exceeds the U.S. charge, no additional tax need be paid by Lincoln U.S. Lincoln U.S. receives $4,000,000 in cash, total worldwide taxes are $4,000,000 (all paid in Singapore), and Singapore Lincoln contributes $6,000,000 to worldwide net income in Lincoln U.S.'s consolidated financial statements. Worldwide retention of cash from Singaporean operations is $6,000,000. Of that, $4,000,000 is retained in the U.S. and $2,000,000 in Singapore.

| **Exhibit 18.3** | *Tax Effect, Bundled versus Unbundled Compensation to Lincoln U.S. from Singapore Lincoln (thousands of U.S. dollars)* |

	Case 1	Case 2	Case 3
	Bundled: $4,000 Dividend Only	Unbundled: $2,400 Royalty +$1,600 Dividend	Unbundled: $2,400 Royalty +$2,416 Dividend
SINGAPORE LINCOLN FINANCIAL STATEMENT			
Net income before taxes	$10,000	$10,000	$10,000
Less royalties and fees	–	2,400	2,400
Taxable income in Singapore	10,000	7,600	7,600
Less Singapore tax @ 40%	4,000	3,040	3,040
Available for dividends	6,000	4,560	4,560
Cash dividend to Lincoln U.S.	4,000	1,600	2,416
Reinvested in Singapore	$ 2,000	$ 2,960	$ 2,144
LINCOLN U.S. FINANCIAL STATEMENT			
Dividends received	$ 4,000	$ 1,600	$ 2,416
Add back part of Singapore income tax[a]	2,667	1,067	1,611
Grossed-up dividend in U.S.	6,667	2,667	4,027
Tentative U.S. tax at 34%	2,267	907	1,369
Less credit for Singapore taxes	2,667	1,067	1,611
Additional U.S. tax on dividends	none	none	none
Royalty received	–	2,400	2,400
Less U.S. tax on royalty @ 34%	–	816	816
Royalty received after U.S. tax	–	1,584	1,584
Net dividend after U.S. taxes	4,000	$1,600	2,416
Total cash retained by Lincoln U.S.	$ 4,000	$ 3,184	$ 4,000
WORLDWIDE TAXES PAID			
Taxes paid to Singapore	$ 4,000	$ 3,040	$ 3,040
Taxes paid to U.S. government	–	816	816
Worldwide taxes paid	$ 4,000	$ 3,856	$ 3,856
SINGAPORE CONTRIBUTION TO WORLDWIDE INCOME			
Original income before any taxes	$10,000	$10,000	$10,000
Less total worldwide taxes paid	4,000	3,856	3,856
Contribution to consolidated worldwide income	$ 6,000	$ 6,144	$ 6,144
AFTER-TAX CASH RETAINED			
Retained in the United States	$ 4,000	$ 3,184	$ 4,000
Retained in Singapore	2,000	2,960	2,144
Total, worldwide (from Lincoln Singapore)	$ 6,000	$ 6,144	$ 6,144

[a] Case 1: Dividends of $4,000 are 2/3 of available income of $6,000. Hence 2/3 of taxes of $4,000, or $2,667, is added back.

Case 2: Dividends of $1,600 are 35.1% of available income of $4,560. Hence 35.1% of taxes of $3,040, or $1,067, is added back.

Case 3: Dividends of $2,416 are 53.0% of available income of $4,560. Hence 53.0% of taxes of $3,040, or $1,611, is added back.

Case 2: $2,400,000 royalty plus $1,600,000 dividend, totaling $4,000,000 paid. Case 2 is an "unbundled" situation. A royalty of $2,400,000 is combined with a dividend of $1,600,000 for a total $4,000,000 cash payment to Lincoln U.S., the same total payment as in Case 1. The $1,600,000 dividend (about 35.1% of the amount available for dividends) is grossed up by adding back 35.1% of Singaporean taxes. The U.S. tentative tax is 34% of the grossed-up $2,667,000 or $907,000. Again, because taxes paid on this income in Singapore exceed the U.S. tax charge, no additional taxes are paid in the United States. The royalty, however, is fully taxed at 34% in the United States. (It has been deducted from taxable income in Singapore, reducing Singapore taxes by 40% of the royalty.) After all taxes, Lincoln U.S. retains only $3,184,000 in cash, total worldwide taxes are $3,856,000, and Lincoln Singapore contributes $6,144,000 to consolidated worldwide income. In effect, worldwide income has been increased over what it was in Case 1 by substituting royalties for dividends. Worldwide cash retained ($6,144,000) is also up, but the proportion of that cash held in the United States is down.

Case 3: $2,400,000 royalty plus $2,416,000 dividend, totaling $4,816,000 paid. Case 3 is an alternate "unbundled" situation designed to leave exactly $4,000,000 cash after tax with Lincoln U.S.—the same amount as in Case 1. The royalty of $2,400,000 is combined with a dividend of $2,416,000. The $2,416,000 dividend (about 53.0% of the amount available for dividends) is "grossed up" by adding back 53.0%, or $1,611,000, of Singaporean taxes. The U.S. tentative tax is 34% of the grossed-up $4,027,000, or $1,369,000. Again, nothing is paid in the United States because Singaporean taxes were more than the tentative charge. As before, the royalty is fully taxed at 34%. After all taxes Lincoln U.S. retains $4,000,000, the same as in Case 1. Worldwide taxes are $3,856,000, the same as in Case 2, and Singapore Lincoln contributes $2,144,000 to consolidated world-wide income. Worldwide consolidated income is above that in Case 1 but the same as in Case 2. Cash returned to Lincoln U.S. is more than in Case 2, and worldwide cash retention is $6,144,000, the same as Case 2.

Cases 2 and 3 lead to identical total tax payments and contribution to consolidated worldwide income because the royalty amount is the same, reducing Singaporean taxes by 40% of the royalty, and the Singaporean tax rate is above the U.S. tax rate so that U.S. taxes do not figure in the calculation. If the U.S. tax rate were above the Singaporean rate, results would be quite different.

TRANSFER PRICING

A particularly sensitive problem for multinational firms is establishing a rational method for pricing the transfer of goods, services, and technology between related affiliates in different countries. Even purely domestic firms find it difficult to reach agreement on the best method for setting prices on transactions between affiliates. In the multinational case managers must balance conflicting considerations. These include fund positioning, income taxes, managerial incentives and evaluation, tariffs and quotas, and joint-venture partners.

))) Fund Positioning Effect

Transfer price setting is a technique by which marginally greater or fewer funds may be repositioned within a multinational enterprise. A parent wishing to transfer funds out of a particular country can charge higher prices on goods sold to its affiliate in that country. A foreign affiliate can be financed by the reverse technique, a lowering of transfer prices. Payment by the affiliate for imports from its parent or sister affiliate transfers funds out of the affiliate. A higher transfer price permits funds to be accumulated in the selling country.

Transfer pricing may also be used to transfer funds between sister affiliates. Multiple sourcing of component parts on a worldwide basis allows changes in suppliers from within the corporate family to function as a device to transfer funds.

The flow of funds effect can be illustrated with the data in Exhibit 18.4. This exhibit shows two different results in which Lincoln De France incurs costs of $1,000,000 for goods, which are then sold to Lincoln U.K. Lincoln U.K. resells to an unrelated final customer for $2,000,000. The gross profit for the two companies combined is $1,000,000 under both circumstances. If each affiliate has a 30% income tax rate and if other expenses remain constant, net income on a consolidated basis is $560,000.

The low-markup policy, in which Lincoln De France "charges" Lincoln U.K. $1,400,000 for the goods, results in a cash movement (when the import is paid for) of $1,400,000 from Lincoln U.K. to Lincoln De France. The high-markup policy, where the goods are "sold" at $1,700,000, causes an additional $300,000 of cash to move from the United Kingdom to France. If it were desirable to transfer funds from Lincoln U.K. to Lincoln De France, the high-markup policy would achieve this end. Consolidated profit is unaffected. However, individual profits are altered, a factor discussed below in the section entitled Managerial Incentives and Evaluation.

))) Income Tax Effect

A major consideration in setting a transfer price is the *income tax effect*. Worldwide corporate profits may be influenced by setting transfer prices to minimize taxable income in a country with a high income tax rate and maximize income in a country with a low income tax rate.

The income tax effect is illustrated in Exhibit 18.5, which is identical to Exhibit 18.4 except that the income tax rate in France is assumed to be only 25% while the British income tax rate is 40%. Under the low-markup policy, Lincoln de France pays $75,000 of taxes and Lincoln U.K. pays $200,000 for a total tax bill of $275,000 and consolidated net income of $525,000.

If Lincoln adopts a high-markup policy by "selling" its merchandise at an intracompany sales price of $1,700,000, the same $800,000 of pre-tax consoli-

| Exhibit 18.4 | *Tax-Neutral Impact of Low versus High Transfer Price on Flow of Funds (thousands of U.S. dollars)* |

Assumption: *Lincoln de France and Lincoln U.K. both pay a 30% corporate income tax.*

	Lincoln de France (manufacturing affiliate)	Lincoln U.K. (distribution affiliate)	France and U.K. Combined
LOW-MARKUP POLICY			
Sales	$1,400	$2,000	$2,000
Less cost of goods sold[a]	1,000	1,400	1,000
Gross profit	$ 400	$ 600	$1,000
Less operating expenses	100	100	200
Taxable income	$ 300	$ 500	$ 800
Less income taxes (30%)	90	150	240
Net income	$ 210	$ 350	$ 560
HIGH-MARKUP POLICY			
Sales	$1,700	$2,000	$2,000
Less cost of goods sold[a]	1,000	1,700	1,000
Gross profit	$ 700	$ 300	$1,000
Less operating expenses	100	100	200
Taxable income	$ 600	$ 200	$ 800
Less income taxes (30%)	180	60	240
Net income	$ 420	$ 140	$ 560

[a]Lincoln de France's sales price becomes the cost of goods sold for Lincoln U.K.

dated income is allocated more heavily to low-tax France and less heavily to high-tax United Kingdom. As a consequence, total taxes drop by $45,000 and consolidated net income increases by $45,000 to $570,000.

Lincoln would naturally prefer the high-markup policy for sales from France to Britain. Needless to say, government tax authorities are aware of the potential income distortion from transfer price manipulation. A variety of regulations and court cases exist on the reasonableness of transfer prices, including fees and royalties as well as prices set for merchandise. If a government taxing authority does not accept a transfer price, taxable income will be deemed larger than was calculated by the firm, and taxes will be increased. The problem is illustrated in Exhibit 18.6.

In Exhibit 18.6, the high markup policy of Exhibit 18.5 was used in the tax returns of both France and the United Kingdom. At a later date U.K. tax authorities recalculate U.K. taxes using the original, "valid," transfer price of $1,400,000. This increases taxes in the United Kingdom to $200,000 and causes an additional tax charge of $120,000 over the $80,000 already paid. Lincoln cannot backtrack and revise its French tax filing. A total of $350,000 in taxes is paid,

Exhibit 18.5	*Tax Effect of Low versus High Transfer Price on Net Income (thousands of U.S. dollars)*

Assumption: France's income tax rate is 25% and the United Kingdom's is 40%.

	Lincoln de France (manufacturing affiliate)	Lincoln U.K. (distribution affiliate)	France and U.K. Combined
LOW-MARKUP POLICY			
Sales	$1,400	$2,000	$2,000
Less cost of goods sold[a]	1,000	1,400	1,000
Gross profit	$ 400	$ 600	$1,000
Less operating expenses	100	100	200
Taxable income	$ 300	$ 500	$ 800
Less income taxes[b]	75	200	275
Net income	$ 225	$ 300	$ 525
HIGH-MARKUP POLICY			
Sales	$1,700	$2,000	$2,000
Less cost of goods sold[a]	1,000	1,700	1,000
Gross profit	$ 700	$ 300	$1,000
Less operating expenses	100	100	200
Taxable income	$ 600	$ 200	$ 800
Less income taxes[b]	150	80	230
Net income	$ 450	$ 120	$ 570

[a]Lincoln de France's sales price becomes cost of goods sold for Lincoln U.K.
[b]25% in France; 40% in U.K.

leaving combined net income for the two affiliates at $450,000—lower than the net income of $525,000 (Exhibit 18.5) that would have resulted had transfer prices never been increased in the first place. This, of course, is the consequence of changing transfer prices for tax avoidance reasons and not getting away with it!

Typical of laws circumscribing freedom to set transfer prices is Section 482 of the U.S. Internal Revenue Code. Under this authority the Internal Revenue Service (IRS) can reallocate gross income, deductions, credits, or allowances between related corporations in order to prevent tax evasion or to reflect more clearly a proper allocation of income. Under the IRS guidelines and subsequent judicial interpretation, the burden of proof is on the taxpaying firm to show that the IRS has been arbitrary or unreasonable in reallocating income. This "guilty until proved innocent" approach means that MNEs must keep good documentation of the logic and costs behind their transfer prices. The "correct price" according to the guidelines is the one that reflects an *arm's length price*, that is, the price that would be charged in a sale of the same goods or services to an unrelated customer.

| Exhibit 18.6 | *Disallowal of Transfer Price (based on data in Exhibit 18.5)* *(thousands of U.S. dollars)* |

Assumptions:
- *France's income tax rate is 25% and the United Kingdom's is 40%.*
- *Lincoln uses the high markup policy.*
- *U.K. tax authorities do not recognize the $1,700 transfer price and recalculate U.K. taxes based on a $1,400 transfer price.*

	Lincoln de France (manufacturing affiliate)	Lincoln U.K. (distribution affiliate)	France and U.K. Combined
TAX AUTHORITY CALCULATION		*(After-tax reallocation)*	
Sales	$1,700	$2,000	$2,000
Less cost of goods sold allowed	1,000	1,400	1,000
Gross profit	$ 700	$ 600	$1,000
Less operating expenses	100	100	200
Taxable income	$ 600	$ 500	$ 800
Less income taxes (25% or 40%)[a]	150	200	350
Net income	$ 450	$ 300	$ 450

[a]French tax authorities use $1,700 from Lincoln de France's tax return, but U.K. authorities recalculate gross profit based on the original transfer price of $1,400. Lincoln de France cannot go back and restate its French tax return based on an after-the-fact disallowal in the United Kingdom.

IRS regulations provide three methods to establish arm's length prices: comparable uncontrolled prices, resale prices, and cost-plus calculations. All three of these methods are recommended for use in member countries by the Organization for Economic Cooperation and Development (OECD) Committee on Fiscal Affairs.[3] In some cases combinations of these three methods are used.

Comparable Uncontrolled Price Method. A comparable uncontrolled price is regarded as the best evidence of arm's length pricing. The transfer price is the same as prices of bona fide sales of the same items between the MNE and unrelated customers, or between two unrelated firms. Although such a market-determined price is ideal, in practice it is difficult to apply because of variations in quality, quantity, timing of sale, and proprietary trademarks. Perhaps even more important is the fact that sales between affiliates are often of custom-designed items—a generator sold by Ford U.S. for a European model is unlikely to be sold to, or even usable by, say, General Motors in Europe.

Resale Price Method. This second-best approach to arm's length pricing starts with the final selling price to an independent purchaser and subtracts an appropriate markup for the distribution affiliate. The allowed markup is to cover the distribution affiliate's costs and profits. This price is then used as the intracompany transfer price for similar, but not necessarily identical, items. Nevertheless determination of an appropriate markup is difficult, especially if the distribution affiliate adds value to the item through subsequent processing or packaging.

Cost-Plus Method. This method sets the allowable transfer price by adding an appropriate profit markup to the seller's full cost, where "full cost" is the accounting definition of direct costs plus overhead allocation. This method is often used where semifinished products are sold between affiliates. Nevertheless, allocation of overhead in determining full cost is always a very subjective matter, especially when joint products are involved, so the method allows room for negotiation.

Many tax authorities allow lower transfer prices when a new market is being established. For example, a manufacturing affiliate may cut its price to the distribution affiliate so that the latter can get market penetration. However the price cut *must be passed* on to the final customer; it cannot be used to accumulate more profits in the distribution affiliate. Another approach is to negotiate an *advanced pricing agreement* (APA) with both home country and host country tax authorities. APAs involve time and expense to negotiate, but they do provide the firm with advanced assurance that its transfer pricing policies are acceptable. Without them, a firm may try to follow tax guidelines on transfer prices and still find itself in expensive tax appeals after the fact to defend a decision process it thought conformed to the letter of the tax rule.

Although all governments have an interest in monitoring transfer pricing by MNEs, not all governments use these powers to regulate transfer prices to the detriment of MNEs. In particular, transfer pricing has some political advantages over other techniques of transferring funds. Although the recorded transfer price is known to the governments of both the exporting and importing countries, the underlying cost data are not available to the importing country. Thus, the importing country finds it difficult to judge the reasonableness of the transfer price, especially for nonstandard items such as specialized components.

Additionally, even if cost data could be obtained, some of the more sophisticated governments might continue to ignore the transfer-pricing leak. They recognize that foreign investors must be able to repatriate a reasonable profit by their own standards, even if this profit seems unreasonable locally. An unknown or unproved transfer-price leak makes it more difficult for local critics to blame their government for allowing the country to be "exploited" by foreign investors. Thus, within the potential and actual constraints established by governments, opportunities may exist for MNEs to alter transfer prices away from an arm's length market price. On the other hand, if a host government sours on foreign investment, past transfer-price leaks may be exploited to penalize the foreigners.

)))) Tariff and Quota Effect

Transfer pricing may have an influence on the amount of import duties paid. In the Lincoln example, if Lincoln U.K. pays ad valorem import duties of 10%, and if those duties are levied on the invoice (transfer) price, duties will rise under the high-markup policy. This is shown in Exhibit 18.7, which is derived from Exhibit 18.5.

In Exhibit 18.7, import duties rise by $30,000 from $140,000 to $170,000. Income taxes dip in part because more income is transferred to France, the low-tax jurisdiction, and in part because the increase in import duties itself reduces pre-tax income and hence income taxes. The total interaction is such that the net income is $468,000. This is still more than in the low-markup policy because the additional import duties of $30,000 did not offset the tax reduction of $150,000.

The incidence of import duties is usually opposite to the incidence of income taxes in transfer pricing, but income taxes are usually a heavier burden than import duties. Therefore, transfer prices are more often viewed from an income tax perspective. In some instances, however, import duties are actually levied against internationally posted prices, if such exist, rather than against the stated

| **Exhibit 18.7** | *Income Tax versus Import Duty Effect of Low versus High Transfer Price on Net Income (based on data in Exhibit 18.5) (thousands of U.S. dollars)* |

Assumptions:
- France's income tax rate is 25% and the United Kingdom's is 40%.
- U.K. import duties are 10% of invoice price.

	Lincoln de France (manufacturing affiliate)	Lincoln U.K. (distribution affiliate)	France and U.K. Combined
LOW-MARKUP POLICY			
Sales	$1,400	$2,000	$2,000
Less cost of goods sold[a]	1,000	1,400	1,000
Import duty at 10%		140	140
Gross profit	$ 400	$ 460	$ 860
Less operating expenses	100	100	200
Taxable income	$ 300	$ 360	$ 660
Less income taxes[b]	75	144	219
Net income	$ 225	$ 216	$ 441
HIGH-MARKUP POLICY			
Sales	$1,700	$2,000	$2,000
Less cost of goods sold[a]	1,000	1,700	1,000
Import duty @ 10%		170	170
Gross profit	$ 700	$ 130	$ 830
Less operating expenses	100	100	200
Taxable income	$ 600	$ 30	$ 630
Less income taxes[b]	150	12	162
Net income	$ 450	$ 18	$ 468

[a]Lincoln de France's sales price becomes cost of goods sold for Lincoln U.K. U.K. duties are levied on this price.
[b]25% in France; 40% in U.K.

invoice price. If so, duties will not be influenced by the transfer price policy. Income taxes will still be affected by both the residual location of operating profit and the deductibility of the assessed import duties.

Related to the tariff effect is the ability to lower transfer prices to offset the volume effect of foreign exchange quotas. Should a host government allocate a limited amount of foreign exchange for importing a particular type of good, a lower transfer price on the import allows the firm to bring in a greater quantity. If, for example, the imported item is a component for a locally manufactured product, a lower transfer price may allow production volume to be sustained or expanded and market share increased, albeit at the expense of profits in the supply affiliate.

Managerial Incentives and Evaluation

When a firm is organized with decentralized profit centers, transfer pricing between centers can disrupt evaluation of managerial performance. This problem is not unique to MNEs but is also a controversial issue in the "centralization versus decentralization" debate in domestic circles. In the domestic case, however, a modicum of coordination at the corporate level can alleviate some of the distortion that occurs when any profit center suboptimizes its profit for the corporate good. Also in most domestic cases the company can file a single (for that country) consolidated tax return, so the issue of cost allocation between affiliates is not critical from a tax-payment point of view.

In the multinational case, coordination is often hindered by longer and less-efficient channels of communication, the need to consider the unique variables that influence international pricing, and separate taxation. Even with the best of intent, a manager in one country finds it difficult to know what is best for the firm as a whole when buying at a negotiated price from an affiliate in another country. If corporate headquarters establishes transfer prices and sourcing alternatives, one of the main advantages of a decentralized profit center system disappears: local management loses the incentive to act for its own benefit.

As an example, refer back to Exhibit 18.4, where an increase in the transfer price led to a worldwide income gain: French income rose by an additional $225,000 while U.K. income fell by only $150,000, for a net gain of $75,000. Should the managers of the U.K. affiliate lose their bonuses (or even their jobs) because of their "sub-par" performance? Bonuses are usually determined by a company-wide formula based in part on the profitability of individual affiliates, but in this case Lincoln U.K. "sacrificed" for the greater good of the whole. Arbitrarily changing transfer prices can create measurement problems.

Specifically, transferring profit from high-tax Lincoln U.K. to low-tax Lincoln de France changes the following for one or both affiliates:

- Import tariffs paid (importer only) and hence profit levels
- Measurements of foreign exchange exposure, such as the amount of net exposed assets, because of changes in amounts of cash and receivables

- Liquidity tests, such as the current ratio, receivables turnover, and inventory turnover

- Operating efficiency, as measured by the ratio of gross profit to either sales or to total assets

- Income tax payments

- Profitability, as measured by the ratio of net income to either sales or capital invested

- Dividend payout ratio, in that a constant dividend will show as a varied payout ratio as net income changes. Alternatively, if the payout ratio is kept constant, the amount of dividend is changed by a change in transfer price

- Internal growth rate, as measured by the ratio of retained earnings to existing ownership equity

⟫⟫ Effect on Joint-Venture Partners

Joint ventures pose a special problem in transfer pricing, because serving the interest of local stockholders by maximizing local profit may be suboptimal from the overall viewpoint of the MNE. Often the conflicting interests are irreconcilable. Indeed the local joint-venture partner could be viewed as a potential Trojan horse if it complains to local authorities about the MNE's transfer pricing policy.

ILLUSTRATIVE CASE

The Tax Man and Transfer Prices

TOKYO—Foreign companies in Japan are getting more frequent visits from the Tokyo tax man these days. Tax authorities are clamping down on what they say is a propensity by multinationals to avoid the nation's high corporate taxes by illegally shifting profits off their books in Japan.

Japan's National Tax Administration says it has stepped up its hunt for Japanese units of multinational companies that engage in "transfer pricing," an accounting trick in which a company artificially depresses the profits it reports on its books in one country by moving those profits onto books in another.

Companies caught engaging in transfer pricing often face a whopping bill. In 1994 Coca-Cola Co.'s Japan unit announced it would contest a big claim for back taxes, which was reported to be for $140 million. The Japanese unit of Goodyear Tire and Rubber Co. was hit for roughly 600 million yen in 1994. Tax officials claimed 800 million yen from the Japanese unit of Procter and Gamble Co. in the same year, according to Japanese press reports that P&G faxed to a reporter; P&G wouldn't comment on the report.

Allegations of transfer pricing often arise when tax authorities think the parent company of a foreign concern is overcharging its Japanese unit for the use of its products or trademarks. Coca-Cola's case is typical. Coke's Japan unit sells canned drinks developed especially for Japan, such as canned coffees under the name Georgia. The only indication that Georgia is a Coke product is the tiny Coca-Cola logo on the side of the can.

Tax authorities said the Japan unit paid too much in royalties—for things like the right to use the logo—to the parent company between 1990 and 1992, effectively shifting profits earned in Japan to the United States, where taxes are lower. Coca-Cola's Japan unit argued, in a statement released at the time of the claim, that the royalties it paid were "fair and reasonable, given the unmatched value of the Coca-Cola Company's trademarks, manufacturing, marketing and management know-how."

BLOCKED FUNDS

When a government runs short of foreign exchange and cannot obtain additional funds through borrowing or attracting new foreign investment, it usually limits transfers of foreign exchange out of the country. In theory this does not discriminate against foreign-owned firms because it applies to everyone; in practice foreign firms have more at stake because of their foreign ownership. Depending on the size of a foreign exchange shortage, the host government might simply require approval of all transfers of funds abroad, thus reserving the right to set a priority on the use of scarce foreign exchange in favor of necessities rather than luxuries. In very severe cases the government might make its currency nonconvertible into other currencies, thereby fully blocking transfers of funds abroad. In between these positions are policies that restrict the size and timing of dividends, debt amortization, royalties, and service fees.

MNEs can react to the potential for blocked funds at three stages.

1. Prior to making an investment, a firm can analyze the effect of blocked funds on expected return on investment, the desired local financial structure, and optimal links with affiliates.

2. During operations a firm can attempt to move funds through a variety of repositioning techniques.

3. Funds that cannot be moved must be reinvested in the local country in a manner that avoids deterioration in their real value because of inflation or exchange depreciation.

))) Preinvestment Strategy

Management can consider blocked funds in their capital budgeting analysis, as was done in the example in Chapter 14. Temporary blockage of funds normally reduces the expected net present value and internal rate of return on a proposed investment. Whether the investment should nevertheless be undertaken depends on whether the expected rate of return, even with blocked funds, exceeds the required rate of return on investments of the same risk class. Preinvestment analysis also includes the potential to minimize the effect of blocked funds by financing with local borrowing instead of parent equity, swap agreements, and other techniques to reduce hard currency exposure and thus the need to repatriate funds. Sourcing and sales links with affiliates can be predetermined so as to maximize the potential for moving blocked funds.

))) Moving Blocked Funds

What can a multinational firm do to transfer funds out of countries having exchange or remittance restrictions? Three popular approaches have already been discussed:

1. Unbundling of services, described earlier in this chapter.
2. Transfer pricing, also described earlier in this chapter.
3. Leading and lagging payments, described in Chapter 7.

    Three additional approaches are:

1. Using fronting loans
2. Creating unrelated exports
3. Obtaining special dispensation

Fronting Loans. A *fronting loan* is a parent-to-affiliate loan channeled through a financial intermediary, usually a large international bank. Fronting loans differ from parallel or back-to-back loans, discussed in Chapter 7. The latter are offsetting loans between commercial businesses arranged outside the banking system. Fronting loans are sometimes referred to as *link financing*.

In a direct intracompany loan, a parent or sister affiliate loans directly to the borrowing affiliate, and at a later date the borrowing affiliate repays the principal and interest. In a fronting loan, by contrast, the "lending" parent or affiliate deposits funds in, say, a London bank, and that bank loans the same amount to the borrowing affiliate in the host country. From the London bank's point of view the loan is risk-free, because the bank has 100% collateral in the form of the parent's deposit. In effect the bank "fronts" for the parent—hence the name. Interest paid by the borrowing affiliate to the bank is usually slightly higher than the rate paid by the bank to the parent, allowing the bank a margin for expenses and profit.

The bank chosen for the fronting loan is usually in a neutral country, away from both the lender's and the borrower's legal jurisdiction. Use of fronting loans increases chances for repayment should political turmoil occur between the home and host countries. Government authorities are more likely to allow a local affiliate to repay a loan to a large international bank in a neutral country than to allow the same affiliate to repay a loan directly to its parent. To stop payment to the international bank would hurt the international credit image of the country, whereas to stop payment to the parent corporation would have minimal impact on that image and might even provide some domestic political advantage.

A fronting loan may have a tax advantage. Assume that Lincoln U.S. wants to lend $10,000,000 to Lincoln Belge. Old Abe Finance Company, a wholly owned finance affiliate of Lincoln U.S., located in the Cayman Islands, which is a tax-haven country, is the designated lender. As depicted in Exhibit 18.8, Old Abe Finance deposits $10,000,000 in National Westminster Bank ("NatWest") in London at 8.9% interest, and NatWest, in turn, lends $10,000,000 to Lincoln Belge at 9%. Interest payments net of income tax effect will be as follows:

1. Lincoln Belge pays $900,000 interest to NatWest. Deduction of interest from Lincoln Belge's taxable income at a 39% tax rate results in a net after-tax cost of $549,000.

2. NatWest receives the $900,000, retains $10,000 for its services, and pays $890,000 interest on the deposit of Old Abe Finance.

3. Old Abe Finance receives $890,000 interest on its deposit. This interest may be tax free because Old Abe is located in a tax-haven country.

The overall result is that $890,000 of cash is moved from Lincoln Belge to Old Abe Finance. Because the after-tax cost to Lincoln Belge is only $549,000, the system has been able to move an additional $341,000 out of the country by virtue of the tax shield. If Old Abe Finance, or even Lincoln U.S., had made a

---

Exhibit 18.8   *Tax Aspects of a Fronting Loan*

Old Abe Finance Company is a 100% owned finance subsidiary of Lincoln, U.S., located in the Cayman Islands.

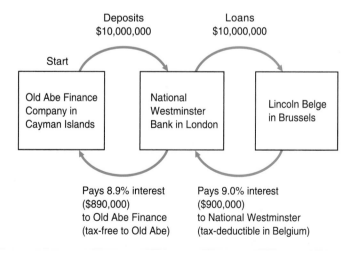

direct loan to Lincoln Belge, the Belgian authorities would be in a position to disallow the interest charge as a tax-deductible bona-fide interest expense by ruling that it was a substantive dividend to the parent disguised as interest. Note that the fronting loan provides no protection against changes in exchange rates.

Creating Unrelated Exports. Another approach to blocked funds that benefits both affiliate and host country is the creation of unrelated exports. Because the main reason for stringent exchange controls is usually a host country's persistent inability to earn hard currencies, anything a MNE can do to create new exports from the host country helps the situation and provides a potential means to transfer funds out.

Some new exports can often be created from present productive capacity with little or no additional investment, especially if they are in product lines related to existing operations. Other new exports may require reinvestment or new funds, although if the funds reinvested consist of those already blocked, little is lost in the way of opportunity costs. If Lincoln U.S., for example, had long-term blocked funds in Brazil, it might locate research and development laboratories in Brazil and pay for them with blocked real, the currency unit of Brazil. Brazilian scientists with advanced degrees from U.S. universities might be happy to return to Brazil at U.S. level salaries paid in blocked real by Lincoln Brazil. Brazilian architectural and engineering firms might be hired separately to provide services for the worldwide enterprise, being paid in real to design plants in France or Singapore.

Export equivalents can also be created with little investment in certain service activities. Lincoln Brazil, for example, could host conventions or other business meetings in Rio de Janeiro for its multinational parent. Employees of Lincoln affiliates worldwide might be sent on company-sponsored vacations to Brazil, and Lincoln employees worldwide might be asked to fly on Varig, the Brazilian national airline, wherever possible. Their tickets would be purchased in Brazil and paid for with real.

Such activities benefit Brazil because they provide export-oriented jobs and earnings. They benefit Lincoln worldwide because they provide a way to effectively use funds otherwise tied up in the Brazilian money market, while at the same time reducing expenses otherwise incurred in U.S. dollars for the same goods or services.

Still another approach for a parent dealing with blocked currency is to arrange barter agreements. A country such as Brazil would probably not allow barter deals involving coffee or other commodities already sold on world markets for hard currencies, but it might permit a barter for exports of goods or services not normally exported. Although Lincoln worldwide has no involvement with textiles, Lincoln Brazil might use its blocked funds to buy Brazilian fabrics, which could be delivered to Lincoln U.S. in return for imports into Brazil of Lincoln components. Lincoln U.S. would arrange the sale of the fabrics in the United States. Countertrade, of which barter is one form, will be discussed in Chapter 20.

Special Dispensation. If all else fails and the multinational firm is investing in an industry that is important to the economic development of the host country, the firm may bargain for special dispensation to repatriate some portion of the funds that otherwise would be blocked. Firms in "desirable" industries such as telecommunications, semiconductor manufacturing, instrumentation, pharmaceuticals, or other research and high-technology industries may receive preference over firms in mature industries. The amount of preference received depends on bargaining among informed parties, the government and the business firm, either of which is free to back away from the proposed investment if unsatisfied with the terms.

Self-fulfilling Prophecies. In seeking "escape routes" for blocked funds—or for that matter in trying to position funds through any of the techniques discussed in this chapter—the MNE may increase political risk and cause a change from partial blockage to full blockage. The possibility of such a self-fulfilling cycle exists any time a firm takes action that, no matter how legal, thwarts the underlying intent of politically authored controls. In the statehouses of the world, as in the editorial offices of the local press and TV, MNEs and their affiliates are always a potential scapegoat.

Forced Reinvestment

If funds are indeed blocked from transfer into foreign exchange, they are by definition "reinvested." Under such a situation the firm must find local opportunities that will maximize rate of return for a given acceptable level of risk.

If blockage is expected to be temporary, the most obvious alternative is to invest in local money market instruments. Unfortunately, in many countries such instruments are not available in sufficient quantity or with adequate liquidity. In some cases government Treasury bills, bank deposits, and other short-term instruments have yields that are kept artificially low relative to local rates of inflation or probable changes in exchange rates. Thus the firm often loses real value during the period of blockage.

If short- or intermediate-term portfolio investments, such as bonds, bank time deposits, or direct loans to other companies, are not possible, investment in additional production facilities may be the only alternative. Often this investment is what the host country is seeking by its exchange controls, even if the fact of exchange controls is by itself counterproductive to the idea of additional foreign investment. Examples of forced direct reinvestment can be cited for Peru, where an airline invested in hotels and in maintenance facilities for other airlines; for Turkey, where a fish canning company constructed a plant to manufacture cans needed for packing the catch; and for Argentina, where an automobile company integrated vertically by acquiring a transmission manufacturing plant previously owned by a supplier.

If investment opportunities in additional production facilities are not available, funds may simply be used to acquire other assets expected to increase in value with local inflation. Typical purchases might be land, office buildings, or commodities that are exported to global markets. Even inventory stockpiling might be a reasonable investment, given the low opportunity cost of the blocked funds.

SUMMARY

- Multinational firms repatriate funds or transfer them between sister affiliates in order to locate those funds where they are needed or where they can be safe against exchange rate changes or currency blockages. All other things being equal, funds not needed in the various affiliates are most likely to be repatriated to the parent.

- The repatriation or movement of funds can be from currency to currency, from country to country with no change of currency, or from one country and currency to another. Limitations on the movement of funds include political and tax constraints, foreign exchange transaction costs, and liquidity needs.

- A variety of techniques are available to move funds. These include the concept of *unbundling remittances*, *dividend remittances*, and the use of *royalties, fees*, and *home-office overhead remuneration*. These techniques result in the rather straightforward movement of funds.

- Funds can also be moved by *transfer pricing* in which the movements occur as a part of the normal movement of funds for purchases and sales between affiliates. Nevertheless, changing transfer prices for the purpose of moving funds involves tradeoffs with other corporate goals, such as tax and tariff minimization and the performance evaluation of both units and individual managers by measuring levels of profits and rates of return.

- Additional techniques available for moving blocked funds include *fronting loans*, creating *unrelated exports*, and obtaining *special dispensation*.

 ## QUESTIONS

1. New Haven Autolock Company, Inc.

The New Haven Autolock Company of Connecticut manufactures automobile door locks that work by a number combination as well as by keys. Manufacturing each lock involves direct labor cost of $20, direct material costs of $10, and manufacturing overhead of $4. A portion of production is sold to Rotterdam Autolock Company of the Netherlands, New Haven's wholly owned European distribution affiliate, for $44 per lock. Amsterdam Autolock incurs an additional $6 of direct costs and resells to European automobile manufacturers for $60 per lock, which price is determined by competition. No other costs are involved except for income taxes. The U.S. tax rate is 30% and the Dutch tax rate is 40%.

New Haven's chief financial manager judges that transfer prices to Europe could be raised or lowered 20% without causing a tax challenge. Hence, he wonders whether New Haven should change the transfer price at which it sells to its affiliates.

What do you recommend?

2. American Wolverine, Inc.

American Wolverine, Inc., of the United States owns 100% of Wolverine-Israel. This year Wolverine-Israel earned 120 million Israeli shekels (Shk) before income taxes, equal to $30,000,000 at the current exchange rate of Shk4.00/$. The exchange rate is not expected to change.

America Wolverine wants to transfer half Wolverine-Israel's post-tax earnings to the United States and wonders whether this sum should be remitted (1) by a cash dividend of the desired amount. The same total amount could also be remitted (2) as a cash dividend equal to half the desired remittance plus a royalty equal to the remainder. Israeli income taxes are 40% and U.S. income taxes are 30%. What do you recommend? Why?

3. Gremlin Games, Inc.

Gremlin Games, Inc., of Los Gatos, California, wants to advance US$4,000,000 to its Chinese manufacturing affiliate, Guangdong Disks, Ltd. Gremlin Games creates, designs, and sells children's computer games throughout North America. The games themselves are manufactured by Guangdong Disks. Gremlin Games owns a wholly owned finance subsidiary in Singapore, which is used to redirect funds between Asia and North America. The current exchange rate is RMB8.00/$. (RMB is the symbol for Chinese yuan, also called "renminbi.")

Gremlin Games might (1) make an equity investment of $4 million in its Singaporean finance affiliate and then have that finance affiliate lend the equivalent in Chinese yuan to Guangdong Disks at 8% per annum, or (2) have its Singaporean finance affiliate deposit $4 million in Standard Chartered Bank in Hong Kong where the funds would earn 7.6%. Standard Chartered Bank would then loan RMB32 million to Guangdong Disks at 8.00%. Standard Chartered would cover its costs and earn its profit on the 0.4% spread. Corporate income taxes are 30% in the United States and 40% in China. No taxes are levied on finance companies in Singapore if those companies do not conduct Singaporean business.

What should Gremlin Games do?

4. Cia. Sevilla de Olivos, S.A.

Cia. Sevilla de Olivos, S.A. (Sevilla Olive Company) sells containers of Spanish olives to its wholly owned distribution affiliate in Frankfurt, Germany. Spanish income tax rates are 25% and German tax rates are 50%. All accounts are kept in euros. At present, profit per container is €60, calculated as follows:

	Sevilla de Olivos	Frankfurt Subsidiary
Direct costs	€200	€320
Overhead	80	20
Total costs	280	340
Desired markup	40	60
Transfer/sales price	€320	€ 400
Less total costs	−280	−340
Taxable income	40	60
Less taxes (25% and 50%)	−10	−30
Post-tax profit	€30	€30
Consolidated profit	€60	

a. What happens to profits if Sevilla de Olivos' transfer price is increased 12.5% to €360?

b. What happens to profits if, after Sevilla de Olivos increases its transfer price to €360, German tax authorities disallow the new transfer price and impose the old €320 price for German tax purposes?

5. Penang Stove Company, Ltd.

Penang Stove Company manufactures propane kitchen stoves for sale to retail outlets in Malaysia and, through a wholly owned distribution subsidiary in neighboring Thailand. Annual capacity of the Penang factory is 18,000 units per year, but present production is only 8,000, of which 4,000 are sold in Malaysia and 4,000 are exported to Thailand. Income tax rates in both Malaysia and Thailand are 30%.

Within Malaysia, Penang Stove sells units to retail outlets for RM1,000 each. (RM stands for Malaysian ringgits.) After-tax profit is RM140 per stove, calculated as follows:

Penang Stove's sales price per unit	RM1,000
less direct labor	180
less direct material	320
less manufacturing overhead	200
Total manufacturing costs	700
Factory margin	RM300
less selling and administrative costs	100
Pre-tax profit per set	RM200
less 30% Malaysian income taxes	60
After-tax profit per unit	RM140

Direct labor consists of hourly payroll costs for assembly workers in Malaysia and of direct material for purchases in Malaysia. Manufacturing overhead is a fixed cost that includes production-line supervision and depreciation. Selling and administrative costs are fixed expenses for management salaries, office expenses, and rent.

Penang Stove sells stoves to its Thai distribution affiliate at a transfer price of RM850, this being Malaysia manufacturing cost of RM700 plus RM150 of margin. Transportation and distribution costs, paid by the Thai subsidiary, add RM50 to the unit cost in Thailand. The stoves are resold to Thai retailers for the Malaysian ringgit equivalent of RM1,050. This Thai sales price was established after estimating elasticity of demand in Thailand as follows: (All prices are in Malaysia ringgits. Thai taxes are credited against Malaysian tax liabilities.)

Unit sales price	950	1,000	1,050	1,100	1,150
less import costs	850	850	850	850	850
less shipping	50	50	50	50	50
Unit profit before tax	50	100	150	200	250
less 30% tax	−15	−30	−45	−60	−75
Unit profit after tax	35	70	105	140	175
Estimated volume	× 3,000	× 2,500	× 2,000	× 1,400	× 1,100
Total profit	105,000	175,000	210,000	196,000	192,500

↑
Maximum

In this calculation, Penang Stove assumed that unit demand in Thailand was a function only of the sales price. Hence it seemed self-evident to Penang's management that a transfer price to Thailand of RM850 maximized the Thai contribution to profits at RM210,000 per year.

a.   Is Penang Stove's present pricing strategy for Thailand optimal?
b.   Assume Penang Stove wants to divide profits on export sales evenly between Malaysia and Thailand so as to avoid difficulties with either tax authority. What final transfer price and unit price in Thailand should the firm adopt for Thai sales?
c.   If Malaysia's income tax rate remains 30%, but Thailand lowers its tax rate to 20%, should a new transfer price be adopted? What policy issues are involved?

WORLD WIDE WEB EXERCISES

W1. Transfer Pricing
A number of international banks and consultancies provide ongoing advisory services on transfer pricing. Visit the following website of KPMG to determine what pricing practices are defensible.

KPMG-United States   http://www.us.kpmg.com/ecs/tp.html

W2. International Offshore Financial Centres (IOFCs)

There are a variety of IOFCs in many parts of the world. Many of these IOFC's are used to re-price intrafirm transfers. Conduct your own survey of their characteristics, qualities, and costs, using the following web sites as a starting point.

British Virgin Islands	http://www.elanbvi.com/bviaffil2.html/
Labuan	http://www.labuan.net/finance/finance.htm
Malta	http://www.u-net.com/metcowww/

W3. NAFTA and Multinational Business

The North American Free Trade Agreement (NAFTA) has enormous impacts on the conduct of business between Canada, the United States, and Mexico. For an update of the variety of regulatory implications and current tariff reduction progress visit the following web site.

NAFTA SECTRETARIAT   http://www.sec-tlcan-mex.org/english/index.htm

SUGGESTED READINGS

Al-Eryani, Mohammad F., Pervaiz Alam, and Syed Akhter, "Transfer Pricing Determinants of U.S. Multinationals," *Journal of International Business Studies*, 3rd Quarter, 1990, pp. 409–425.

Barrett, M. Edgar, "Case of the Tangled Transfer Price," *Harvard Business Review*, May/June 1977, pp. 20-36, 176–178.

Dewenter, Kathryn L., and Vincent A. Warther, "Dividends, Asymmetric Information, and Agency Conflicts: Evidence from a Comparison of the Dividend Policies of Japanese and U.S. Firms," *Journal of Finance*, Vol. 53, No. 3, June 1998, pp. 879–904.

NOTES

1. Holmes (1968).
2. *Wall Street Journal*, October 28, 1975.
3. Recommended by the OECD in 1979.

DECISION CASE

Northwestern Paper Company

"I understand your motivation for wanting to source the pulp from Chile, but it is important for the corporation to act as an integrated team on these issues," Bill Ewing, Vice President of International of Northwestern Paper Company, told Arthur Kim, the Director of Northwestern's South Korean subsidiary.

"Maybe you're right," Kim responded, "but I just don't understand why it would make sense to pay $450/ton for pulp when I can get it for $330/ton from Chile. It's tough enough to submit competitive bids to our customers without that kind of markup on raw materials. Besides, our plant is supposed to be a profit center. Shouldn't we be trying to maximize profits?"

"This is a topic that we will be covering in more detail with the finance people at the upcoming International Directors Meeting," Ewing said. "In the meantime, you need to make sure that you meet your pulp allocation from the Everett (Washington state) mill."

Company Background

Northwestern Paper Company, a Portland, Oregon-based firm, was founded in 1916. From a single pulp and paper mill at the company's inception, Northwestern had expanded substantially over the years, opening additional pulp and paper mills across the country. By the 1950s, the company was one of the largest U.S. producers of pulp and paper products. During the 1960s and 1970s, the company made a big push toward overseas expansion, particularly into Western Europe, where there was high demand for paper products. As that market had become increasingly competitive, however, expansion focused on Latin America and Asia. By early 1994, the company had mills and/or distribution facilities in 20 countries around the world. It was one of the largest United States-based manufacturers of market pulp, paperboard, and uncoated paper with 1993 sales of approximately $5.5 billion.

Market pulp was pulp sold on the open market, rather than being converted into paper at the company's own mills. It was shipped from the mill in bales of dry sheets. Paperboard was used to manufacture folding cartons, milk cartons, disposable cups and plates. Uncoated paper was used in office paper, copier paper, tablets, envelopes, and some printing papers.

The early 1990s had proven difficult for Northwestern and other paper companies in the U.S. and Europe. Many of the industry's problems were attributable to the high level of excess production capacity. Industry growth during the 1980s led paper companies to invest heavily in new mills and paper machines. Starting in 1990, however, demand for paper products declined. In an attempt to absorb the high fixed costs associated with investments in plant and machinery, several firms in the industry had tried to maintain relatively high rates of (plant) capacity utilization. This had resulted in a substantial inventory overhang in several product categories.

At the same time, the environmental movement in the United States successfully lobbied for legislation to limit access to government-owned forest lands and to invoke stricter environmental regulations regarding mill operations.[1] European paper companies had also come under increasing pressure from environmental groups. This resulted in higher prices for U.S. and European paper products. This was particularly true relative to other, less-developed regions of the world.

Pulp is manufactured from wood fibers or recycled paper fibers, which are broken down or separated by using a chemical or mechanical process to dissolve away the lignin (glue) which holds them together. In the world market for pulp, North America had been the low-cost supplier for many years. With less-stringent environmental controls and aggressive promotion of the timber and paper industries, however, South America had assumed that position during the early 1990s. A recent long-term analysis of competition in bleached softwood kraft pulp, for example, indicated that Chile was the low-cost producer in the world, mainly due to low pulpwood costs.[2]

In order to keep capacity utilization of its U.S. mills at adequate levels, Northwestern had directed its foreign-based manufacturing facilities to procure pulp from its U.S. mills whenever possible. The company charged overseas subsidiaries the going market rate for U.S. pulp which, as of late 1993, was $450/ton. Incorporated in that price was an allocation of all production costs and operating expenses, as well as a preset percentage markup. Additionally, given cash constraints in the United States, each subsidiary was also responsible for financing its working capital needs from local sources.

---

1. In fact, the domestic industry's expenditures for environmental protection had been over $1 billion annually from 1989 to 1993. Taken from Anderson-Shaw, Carol, "Overcapacity Plagues Paper Producers," *Standard & Poors Industry Surveys*, August 5, 1993, p B88.

2. Softwood pulp is produced from softwood trees—primarily spruces, firs, hemlocks, and pines. Its fibers are longer than those in hardwood trees, resulting in stronger and more durable products. For many paper products, (i.e., paperboard, softwood and hardwood pulps are mixed together to capitalize on the attributes of both. From Correa, Salvador, "Chile as a World Competitor in Forest Products," *Global Issues and Outlook in Pulp and Paper*, (Seattle, Washington: University of Washington Press); 1988, p. 158.

The South Korean subsidiary, which operated a combination pulp and paperboard mill (a "board plant" in the industry jargon), supplied paperboard to companies located primarily in South Korea and, occasionally, to other countries in the region. The South Korean mill manufactured a portion of the pulp required to produce the paperboard, and sourced the remainder (predominantly softwood pulp) from Northwestern's U.S. pulp mills or from other external sources.

The Bid Conflict and Northwestern's Transfer Pricing System

In early 1994, Suffolk Ltd., an Australian manufacturer, submitted a request for bids for a large quantity of bleached paperboard which they intended to use in manufacturing food cartons.[3] A total of 15 companies submitted bids for the project, including the South Korean subsidiary of Northwestern and another of the company's subsidiaries, which was located in Indonesia. Bids ranged from a low of $640/ton up to $780/ton.

Northwestern's South Korean subsidiary was awarded the contract based on price considerations and quality specifications. In determining the bid price, the South Korean company had calculated the cost of the pulp to be used in manufacture of the paperboard at $330/ton. The pulp was to be acquired from a Chilean supplier, rather than from Northwestern's U.S. mills. On the other hand, the Indonesian subsidiary had developed their bid submission on the basis of raw pulp priced at the $450/ton rate that it was charged by Northwestern's Everett, Washington mill.

Transfer Pricing at Northwestern

Transfer prices between subsidiaries at Northwestern were based on a resale price method in which prices were set at the average sales price charged to unrelated entities. With the majority of Northwestern's market pulp production in the United States, this policy had resulted in pulp prices charged to subsidiaries being set at the prevailing U.S. market rate of $450/ton.

As part of the annual planning process, each of Northwestern's foreign subsidiaries was assigned a certain amount of pulp that it was required to purchase during the year from one of the company's U.S. mills. In evaluating the financial performance of each subsidiary, the Finance Department allocated income generated by the mill in manufacturing and selling the pulp allotment to the subsidiary. The allocation process involved no transfer of funds to the subsidiary; it was merely a book entry made by the corporate office to evaluate the performance of each manufacturing facility or subsidiary.

The mill income applied to the subsidiaries was calculated by taking the sales price of the shipment to the subsidiary less the direct cost and freight charges

---

3. Folding carton was used to package food, milk, toiletries and cosmetics, as well as other consumer goods. Paperboard had to meet strict product specifications with regard to folding and printing characteristics.

Exhibit 1	*Competitive Bids of the South Korean and Indonesian Subsidiaries*	
Subsidiary	**South Korean**	**Indonesian**
Delivered Duty Paid	$655.00	$780.00
Less variable costs:		
Market pulp	(330.00)	(450.00)
Wastage costs (@10%)	(33.00)	(45.00)
Conversion costs	(100.00)	(80.00)
Gross profit or contribution margin	$192.00	$205.00

All values in U.S. dollars per ton of paperboard.

incurred by the mill. In early 1994, the average Northwestern U.S. mill shipped at a price of $450/ton, and had a direct cost of $280/ton, which provided a contribution margin of $170/ton at the U.S. mill.[4] Freight costs to South Korea and Indonesia were $60/ton and $70/ton, respectively, given shipping distances and routes. In the event that the subsidiary did not order its full allotment of pulp during the year, the resulting down-time expense at the mill was also allocated to the subsidiary in determining financial performance.

Comparison of the Bids

South Korean Subsidiary. The South Korean subsidiary won the contract for the paperboard shipment with a bid of $655/ton Delivered Duty Paid (DDP) to Suffolk's Australian plant. Although lower bids had been received by Suffolk's purchasing director, this represented the lowest bid from a firm with the reputation of providing the desired level of quality. In the preparation of the bid package, the Chief Financial Officer at the plant in South Korea calculated that the variable cost relative to the project would be approximately $463/ton, which included acquisition of the raw pulp at $330/ton from the Chilean supplier, a 10% wastage charge on the purchased pulp, and $100/ton in other direct conversion costs. Exhibit 1 provides a breakdown of the bid.

Indonesian Subsidiary. The bid submitted by the Indonesian subsidiary was for delivery of the paperboard at $780/ton DDP to Suffolk's Australian plant. Variable costs were considerably higher than those of the South Korean bid, totaling $575/ton. This variable cost included a $450/ton cost of pulp purchased from the Everett Mill in the United States, a 10% pulp wastage cost applied to the pulp transfer price, and direct conversion costs of $80/ton.[5]

Although not a part of the subsidiary's calculations in determining the bid, in the event that the Indonesian subsidiary had won the contract, its financial per-

---

4. Many of Northwestern's U.S. pulp mills sourced raw wood from the company's wholly owned forest division. Transfer prices were set at market rates.

5. Conversion costs include utilities and other material inputs. Wastage costs are based on the fact that 110 tons of market pulp are consumed for every 100 tons of paperboard produced.

formance measurement would have included the allocation of the U.S. mill contribution margin of $170/ton less delivery costs of $70/ton, adjusted for wastage at the Indonesian location. Had the Indonesian subsidiary gone through the Chilean supplier, the pulp could have been acquired for $320/ton DDP. Due to differentials in shipping distance, the cost quoted by the Chilean pulp supplier for the Indonesian subsidiary was slightly less than that of the South Korean subsidiary.

International Directors Meeting

As Bill Ewing prepared the agenda for the upcoming International Directors Meeting, he penciled in a presentation by representatives of the Finance Department with respect to the issue of transfer pricing at Northwestern. Among the issues that he believed needed clarification were the following:

1. Given the high degree of competition in bidding for contracts that subsidiaries had encountered, should some alteration be made in the process of calculating bids?

2. What were the advantages and disadvantage of the allocation process used by the corporate office in determining subsidiary performance? Was the process fair to the subsidiaries? Was it fair to the company as a whole?

3. Given that some of the subsidiaries were located in low-tax jurisdictions, wouldn't it be logical to set transfer prices from the U.S. to those subsidiaries at lower rates?[6]

As Ewing thought about the system that was in place, he began to empathize with Kim's position. He knew that the recent economic boom in Asia had created a situation in which Northwestern's subsidiaries in that region were growing rapidly (in the 8% per annum range), had high capacity utilization rates, and were operating profitably. Perhaps the company did need to review its approach to transfer pricing. Hopefully, the representatives from the Finance Department would be able to offer some suggestions to resolve the apparent problems.

---

6. As of early 1994, the federal corporate tax rate in the United States was **34%**, with South Korean taxes ranging from 20% to 34%, and Indonesia from 15% to 35%, on a progressive basis.

CHAPTER 19

WORKING CAPITAL MANAGEMENT

Working capital management in a MNE requires managing cash balances, accounts receivable, inventory, and current liabilities when faced with political, foreign exchange, tax, and liquidity constraints. It also encompasses the need to borrow short-term funds to finance current assets from both in-house banks and external local and international commercial banks. The overall goal is to reduce funds tied up in working capital. This should enhance return on assets and equity. It also should improve efficiency ratios and other evaluation of performance parameters.

CASH MANAGEMENT

Cash balances, including marketable securities, are held partly to allow normal day-to-day cash disbursements and partly to protect against unanticipated variations from budgeted cash flows. These two motives are called the *transaction motive* and the *precautionary motive*. Cash may also be held for speculative purposes; however, this aspect is beyond our consideration in this chapter because it does not involve normal day-to-day operations.

Cash disbursed for operations is replenished from two sources: (1) internal working capital turnover, and (2) external sourcing, traditionally short-term borrowing. Short-term borrowing can also be "negative," as when excess cash is used to repay outstanding short-term loans. The cycle operates as illustrated in Exhibit 19.1.

Efficient cash management aims to reduce cash tied up unnecessarily in the system, without diminishing profit or increasing risk, so as to increase the rate of return on invested assets. All firms, both domestic and multinational, engage in some form of the following fundamental steps:

Planning. A financial manager anticipates cash flows over future days, weeks, or months by preparing a comprehensive cash budget showing expected inflows, outflows, and the net of the two. The net flow increases or decreases expected liquidity. Ideally, the cash bud-

Exhibit 19.1   *Cash Management Cycle*

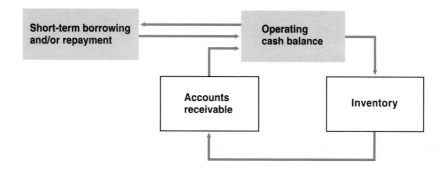

get is prepared on a spreadsheet program to allow simulation of alternate liquidity positions should key variables change. The two most common changing variables are sales volume, leading to changes in the amount of inventories and receivables, and changes in average collection period. MNEs have an added variable: changing exchange rates, which cause the quantity of funds paid or received in one currency to change when measured in another. Three cash budgets can be prepared by a MNE: one for each individual national entity, one for each currency used within the system, and one for the worldwide entity as a whole. The latter necessitates agreement on an intracorporate exchange rate to use for internal budget purposes. This rate is inherently a forecast.

Collection. Cash "on its way" to the firm should be collected as soon as possible. The normal technique is to shorten the time lag between the date on which a customer remits payment and the date on which the funds clear the banking system and are available for disbursement. Domestic examples involve decisions about addresses to which payments are sent and the use of lock boxes, both of which in turn are often determined by the efficiency of the local postal system. Internationally, the country to which payment is directed and the availability of clearing facilities within a multinational banking system are important.

Repositioning. Once cash is collected it must be moved within the worldwide organization to the geographic location and specific currency needed. Techniques to reposition cash were the topic of the previous chapter.

Disbursement. A plan must be designed to disburse cash. Steps include avoiding unnecessary early payment (so as to maintain maximum balances with one's own bank), maximizing float (the time it takes for the firm's own checks to clear), and selecting a disbursement bank that will provide a wide range of services and credit. A MNE must decide whether disbursements are to be handled at each local entity, or whether disbursing should be managed from a central location and routed through a bank. The currency of disbursement must be determined, although this is normally negotiated beforehand.

Covering Cash Shortages. Affiliates in each country have their own needs, determined by their individual cash budgets. Across the MNE, an anticipated or actual cash shortage in one affiliate may be covered by having that affiliate borrow locally or by having another affiliate remit funds to the cash-deficit affiliate. The choice between these two alternatives is often the consequence of the organizational decision to have affiliates "stand on their own two feet" or develop an integrated interaffiliate system of cash management. If short-term borrowing is selected, the currency to be borrowed must be chosen; it could be the currency needed or it could be the currency in which future cash flows will be received. The borrowing entity must also be designated, since one affiliate (presumably in a low real-interest-rate location) can borrow on behalf of a sister affiliate (in a higher real-interest-rate location) and then lend internally to the sister affiliate.

Investing Surplus Cash. If affiliates generate surplus cash, a decision must be made as to whether that affiliate handles its own short-term liquidity (again, "standing on its own two feet") or whether all surplus funds in the organization should be controlled from a central location.

The complexity as well as the opportunity for unique advantages of multinational cash management are illustrated in Exhibit 19.2 and 19.3. Both these charts make use of the idea that a firm keeps both a cash balance for daily operations, maintained at the minimum level needed relative to the firm's attitude toward the risk of running out of operating cash, and a financial pool in which funds not needed immediately are held. In reality, these two cash balances may be commingled.

A domestic-currency-only operation is shown in Exhibit 19.2. Funds for financial purposes may be raised from outside the firm via local borrowing or newly issued shares. Meanwhile, the cash balance for daily operations receives funds from collections on accounts receivable—and from cash sales, if any. A shortage in the cash balance for daily operations is replenished by transferring funds from the financial pool, while any surplus in the cash balance for daily operations can be transferred back to the local currency pool.

The complexity of multinational operations, and the many opportunities for sophisticated global cash management, are shown in Exhibit 19.3. That exhibit is based on an assumed two-home-country, two-home-currency operation plus a central pool. This central pool can be either the parent company or a separately incorporated financial subsidiary that engages only in financial transactions on behalf of the operating affiliates.

Exhibit 19.2   *Flow of Funds in a Domestic-Currency-Only Operation*

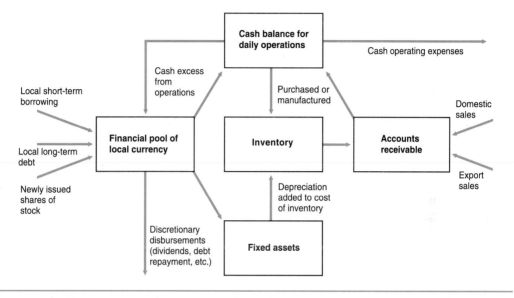

Source: David K. Eiteman, "Financial Sourcing," *Handwörterbuch Export und Internationale Unternehmung* (C.E. Poeschel Verlag Stuttgart, 1989), p. 603–604.

As before, each local financial pool serves as a buffer for its own local cash balance for daily operations. However, other opportunities are created, many of which center around the fact that the central financial pool can easily operate in third-country currency and money markets. As shown in the financial pool of internationally sourced currencies (center left of the chart), funds can be raised in the Eurocurrency market, including third-country currencies that can be swapped into A or B currencies or even "Euro-A" and "Euro-B" markets; local A and B currencies can be borrowed in third-country markets, possibly on better terms because of economies of size and expertise; shares of stock can be sold to third-country investors; and capital can be received from joint venture partners, either directly or via the sale of assets.

Additional possibilities abound. Fixed assets can be acquired by the central pool and then leased to the operating affiliates, setting up a future cash flow for lease payments from affiliates back to the central pool. Excess cash in either operating affiliate's cash for daily operations balance can be transferred to the central financial pool rather than to the local financial pool. Still another possibility, which skips the international central pool, is for either operating affiliate to lend or borrow from its sister affiliate, as shown by the path from A to B that passes beneath the international central pool on the chart. Such intra-affiliate loans may

Exhibit 19.3   *Flow of Funds in a Two-Country Multinational Operation*

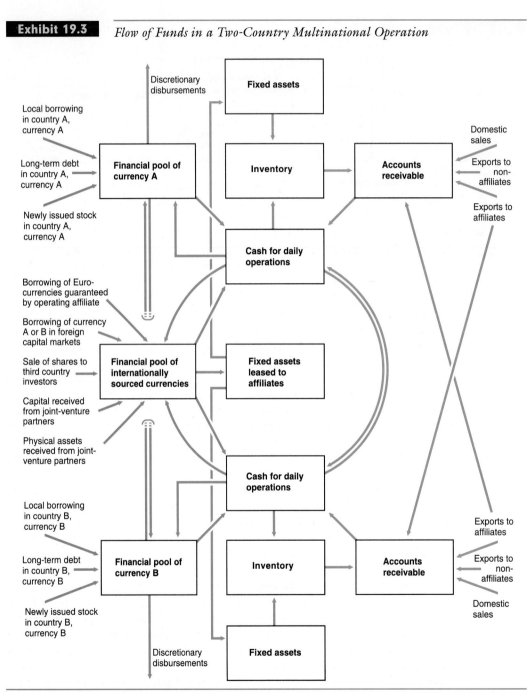

Source: David K. Eiteman, "Financial Sourcing," *Handwörterbuch Export und Internationale Unternehmung* (C.E. Poeschel Verlag Stuttgart, 1989), p. 605–606.

be direct lending and borrowing or they may be de facto lending and borrowing achieved by leads and lags on interaffiliate transactions.

The remainder of this chapter describes the use of techniques to deal with the financing and management of working capital. These techniques include the use of centralized depositories, multilateral netting, managing accounts receivable, managing inventories, and financing working capital. These will be illustrated with the example of Lincoln U.S. introduced in the previous chapter.

CENTRALIZED DEPOSITORIES

Operational benefits can be gained in any business with widely dispersed operating affiliates by centralizing cash management. Internationally, the procedure calls for each affiliate to hold minimum cash for its own transactions and no cash for precautionary purposes. However, the central pool has authority to override this general rule. All excess funds are remitted to a central cash depository, where a single authority invests the funds in such currencies and money market instruments as best serve the worldwide firm as a whole.

Information Advantage. A central depository's size gives it an advantage in obtaining information. It should be located in one of the world's major financial centers so information needed for opinions about the relative strengths and weaknesses of various currencies can easily be obtained. Rate of return and risk information about alternative investments in each currency and facilities for executing orders must also be available. The information logic of centralization is that an office that specializes and operates with larger sums of money can get better information from banks, brokers, and other financial institutions, as well as better service in executing orders.

Funds held in a central pool can be returned quickly to any operating affiliate needing cash. This return can be achieved by wire transfer or by creating a worldwide bank credit line. The money-center bank would wire its branch office in the particular country to advance emergency funds to the local affiliate. Multinational banks can provide same-day credit for deposits from MNEs or their affiliates in the local branches of the banks. Float is reduced and lost payments avoided.

Precautionary Balance Advantage. A second reason for holding all precautionary balances in a central pool is that the total pool, if centralized, can be reduced in size without any loss in the level of protection. Lincoln U.K., for example, has continental affiliates in France, Belgium, and Germany. Assume each of these affiliates maintains its own precautionary cash balance equal to its expected cash needs, plus a safety margin of three standard deviations of historical variability of actual cash demands. Cash needs are assumed to be normally distributed in each country, and the needs are independent from one country to another. Three standard deviations means there exists a 99.87% chance that actual cash needs will be

| Exhibit 19.4 | Decentralized versus Centralized Cash Depositories |

Affiliate	Expected Cash Need (A)	One Standard Deviation (B)	Cash Balance Budgeted for Adequate Protection[a] (A + 3B)
DECENTRALIZED CASH DEPOSITORIES			
Lincoln De France	$10,000,000	$1,000,000	$13,000,000
Lincoln Belge	6,000,000	2,000,000	12,000,000
Deutscheland Lincoln	12,000,000	3,000,000	21,000,000
Total	$28,000,000	$6,000,000	$46,000,000
CENTRALIZED CASH DEPOSITORY			
Lincoln de France	$10,000,000		
Lincoln Belge	6,000,000		
Deutscheland Lincoln	12,000,000		
Total	$28,000,000	$ 3,741,657[b]	$39,224,972

[a]Adequate protection is defined as the expected cash balance plus three standard deviations, assuming that the cash flows of all three individual affiliates are normally distributed.

[b]The standard deviation of the expected cash balance of the centralized depository is calculated as follows:

$$\text{Standard deviation} = \sqrt{(1,000,000)^2 + (2,000,000)^2 + (3,000,000)^2} = \$3,741,657$$

met; that is, there is only a 0.13% chance that any European affiliate will run out of cash.

Cash needs of the individual affiliates, and the total precautionary cash balances held, are shown in Exhibit 19.4 and diagramed in Exhibit 19.5. Total precautionary cash balances held by Lincoln de France, Lincoln Belge, and Deutscheland Lincoln add up to $46,000,000, consisting of $28,000,000 in expected cash needs and $18,000,000 in idle cash balances (the sum of three standard deviations of individual expected cash balances) held as a safety margin.

What would happen if the three Lincoln affiliates maintained all precautionary balances in a single account with Lincoln U.K. in London? Because variances are additive when probability distributions are independent (see footnote b to Exhibit 19.4), cash needed would drop from $46,000,000 to $39,224,972, calculated as follows:

Centralized cash balance	=	Sum of expected cash needs	+	Three standard deviations of expected sum
	=	$28,000,000	+	(3 × $3,741,657)
	=	$28,000,000	+	$11,224,972
	=	$39,224,972		

| **Exhibit 19.5** | *Precautionary Balances* |

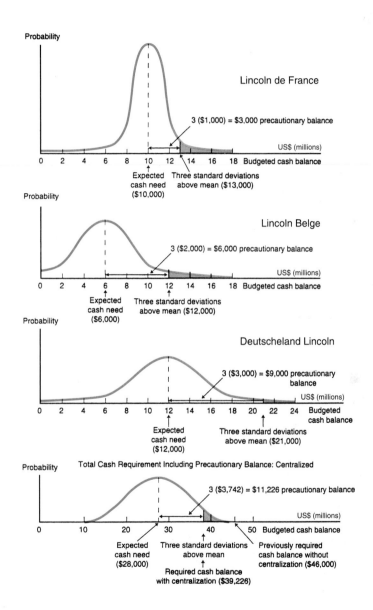

A budgeted cash balance three standard deviations above the aggregate expected cash need requires only $11,224,972 in potentially idle cash, as opposed to the previous cash balance of $18,000,000. Lincoln saves $6,755,028 in cash balances without reducing its safety.

Interest Rate Advantage. A third advantage of centralized cash management is that one affiliate will not borrow at high rates at the same time that another holds surplus funds idle or invests them at low rates. Managers of the central pool can locate the least expensive locations to borrow and the most advantageous returns to be earned on excess funds. When additional cash is needed, the central pool manager determines the location of such borrowing. A local affiliate manager can avoid borrowing at a rate above the minimum available to the pool manager. If the firm has a worldwide cash surplus, the central pool manager can evaluate comparative rates of return in various markets, transaction costs, exchange risks, and tax effects.

Location. Central money pools are usually maintained in major money centers such as London, New York, Zurich, Singapore, and Tokyo. Additional popular locations for money pools include Liechtenstein, Luxembourg, the Bahamas, and Bermuda. Although these countries do not have strong diversified economies, they offer most of the other prerequisites for a corporate financial center: freely convertible currency, political and economic stability, access to international communications, and clearly defined legal procedures. Their additional advantage as so-called tax havens is desirable.

The need for a centralized depository system means that multinational banks have an advantage over single-country banks in designing and offering competitive services. However single-country banks can be incorporated into the system if the desired results can still be achieved, for the essence of the operation is centralized information and decisions. Actual funds may be placed in as many banks as are desired.

MULTILATERAL NETTING

Multilateral netting of payments is useful primarily when a large number of separate foreign exchange transactions occur between affiliates in the normal course of business. Netting reduces the settlement cost of what would otherwise be a large number of crossing spot transactions.

Multilateral netting is an extension of bilateral netting. If Lincoln Belge owes Deutscheland Lincoln $5,000,000 and Deutscheland Lincoln simultaneously owes Lincoln Belge $3,000,000, a bilateral settlement calls for a single payment of $2,000,000 from Belgium to Germany and the cancellation, via offset, of the remainder of the debt.

Exhibit 19.6 *Multilateral Netting Matrix (thousands of U.S. dollars)*

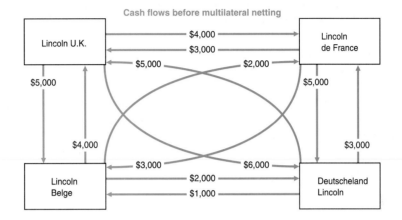

Cash flows before multilateral netting

Calculation of Net Obligation

Receiving Affiliate	Paying Affiliate				Total Receipts	Net Receipts (payments)
	U.K.	Belgium	France	Germany		
Lincoln U.K.	—	$4,000	$3,000	$5,000	$12,000	($3,000)
Lincoln Belge	5,000	—	3,000	1,000	9,000	$1,000
Lincoln de France	4,000	2,000	—	3,000	9,000	($2,000)
Deutscheland Lincoln	6,000	2,000	5,000	—	13,000	$4,000
Total Payments	$15,000	$8,000	$11,000	$9,000	$43,000	—

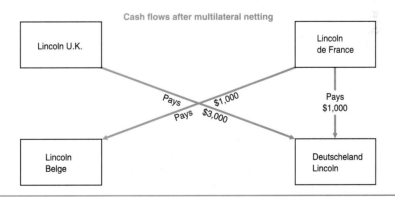

Cash flows after multilateral netting

A multilateral system is an expanded version of this simple bilateral concept. Assume that payments are due between Lincoln's European operations at the end of each month. Each obligation reflects the accumulated transactions of the prior month. These obligations for a particular month might be as shown in the top third of Exhibit 19.6.

Without netting, Lincoln Belge, for example, makes three separate payments and receives three separate receipts at the end of the month. If Lincoln Belge paid its intracompany obligations daily, or even weekly, rather than accumulating a balance to settle at the end of the month, it would generate a multitude of costly small bank transactions every day. The daily totals would add up to the monthly accumulated balances shown in the diagram.

In order to reduce bank transaction costs, such as the spread between foreign exchange bid and ask quotations and transfer fees, some MNEs such as Lincoln establish in-house multilateral netting centers. Other firms contract with banks to manage their netting system. Assume that Lincoln Europe's net intracompany obligations for a given month are as shown in the top of Exhibit 19.6. These can be summarized as in the table in the middle of the same exhibit.

Note that payment obligations and expected receipts both add up to $43,000,000 because one affiliate's debts are another's receivables. If the cost of foreign exchange transactions and transfer fees was 0.5%, the total cost of settlement would be $215,000. Using information from the netting matrix in the middle of Exhibit 19.6, the netting center at Lincoln U.K. can order three payments to settle the entire set of obligations. Lincoln U.K. will itself remit $3,000,000 to Deutscheland Lincoln, and Lincoln de France will be instructed to send $1,000,000 each to Lincoln Belge and Deutscheland Lincoln. Total foreign exchange transfers are reduced to $5,000,000, and transaction costs at 0.5% are reduced to $25,000.

Some countries limit or prohibit netting, while others permit netting on a "gross payment" basis only. For a single settlement period all payments may be combined into a single payment, and all receipts will be received as a single transfer. However, these two amounts may not be netted. Thus, two large payments must pass through the local banking system. The reason for such a requirement is usually a desire to subsidize local banks by forcing firms with a significant international business (often these are foreign rather than domestic firms) to pay for unnecessary transactions.

MANAGING RECEIVABLES

A firm's operating cash flow is derived primarily from collecting its accounts receivable. Multinational accounts receivable are created by two separate types of transactions: sales to related affiliates and sales to independent buyers having no ownership relationship with the selling firm.

))) Independent Customers

Management of accounts receivable from independent customers involves two types of decisions: In what currency should the transaction be denominated, and what should be the terms of payment? Domestic sales are almost always denominated in the local currency. At issue is whether export sales should be denominated in the currency of the exporter, the currency of the buyer, or a third-country currency. Competition or custom will often dictate the answer, but if negotiating room exists, the seller prefers to price and to invoice in the strongest currency. However an informed buyer prefers to pay in the weakest currency. Since both parties are likely to be equally well informed about the risk involved, the usual result is a tradeoff in which a price or a terms-of-payment concession is granted by the seller in order to obtain the sale in a hard currency. Alternatively, the buyer pays more or pays sooner if payment in a soft currency is desired.

Parties to the transaction are likely to deviate from this straightforward bargaining position only if they have different opinions about the relative strengths of the currencies involved or if their own financial situation is strong enough to absorb the weak currency position. For example, a seller is more willing to price and invoice in a weak currency if that seller already has debts in that currency, for the sales proceeds can be used to retire the debt without any obvious loss. From an opportunity cost point of view, that seller nevertheless forgoes an exchange gain. The buyer may be willing to pay in a hard currency if the buyer intends to resell the merchandise in a hard currency.

))) Payment Terms

Terms of payment are another bargaining factor. Considered by themselves, receivables from sales in weak currencies should be collected as soon as possible to minimize loss of exchange value between sales date and collection date. Accounts receivable resulting from sales in hard currencies may be allowed to remain outstanding longer. In fact, if the seller is expecting an imminent devaluation of its home currency, it might want to encourage slow payment of its hard currency receivables, especially if the home government requires immediate exchange of foreign currency receipts into the home currency. An alternative, if legal, would be for the seller to accept the proceeds abroad and keep them on deposit abroad rather than return them to the home country.

In some economies accounts receivable are used as a basis for short-term financing in preference to inventory financing. This situation occurs most often in inflationary economies and in economies in which the banking system is institutionally oriented toward discounting paper rather than financing merchandise.

In inflationary economies the demand for credit usually exceeds the supply. Often, however, a large business (be it multinational or a large local concern) has better access to the limited, cheaper credit that is available locally than do smaller domestic businesses, such as local distributors, retail merchants, or smaller manufacturers. Assume, for example, that the cost of local credit to Lincoln Brazil is 30% per annum, in part because it is affiliated with a large, presumably creditworthy, MNE. The cost of credit to customers of Lincoln Brazil, which are smaller and which might be other manufacturers or retailers, is 50% per annum. Both Lincoln and its customers will benefit by maximizing sales volume to the final customer if Lincoln Brazil finances the transactions as long as possible and adds the financing costs (at 30%) to the sales price. In other words, it is better for Lincoln Brazil to finance its customers' inventory at 30% per annum in the form of long-term receivables than for the customers to finance their own inventory at 50% per annum.

))) Self-liquidating Bills

Some banking systems, often for reasons of tradition, have a predilection toward self-liquidating, discountable bills. In many European countries it is easier to borrow from a bank on the security of bills (receivables in negotiable form) generated from sales than on the security of physical inventory. Napoleon is alleged to have had a philosophy that no good French merchant should be required to wait for funds if good merchandise has been sold to good people, provided a document exists showing sales of the items. The document must have the signature of the buyer and the endorsement of the seller and the rediscounting bank. Thus, in France it is often possible to reduce net investment in receivables to zero by selling entirely on trade acceptances that can be discounted at the bank.

The European predilection for discountable bills has a very real rationale behind it. According to European commercial law, which is based on the Code Napoleon, the claim certified by the signature of the buyer on the bill is separated from the claim based on the underlying transaction. For example, a bill is easily negotiable because objections about the quality of the merchandise by the buyer do not affect the claim of the bill holder. In addition, defaulted bills can be collected through a particularly speedy judicial process that is much faster than the collection of normal receivables. Thus, there is nothing mystical about the preference of European countries for commercial bills, and retail buyers often finance their entire inventory with receivable financing from the manufacturer/seller.

))) Other Terms

In many countries government bodies facilitate inventory financing in the guise of receivable financing by extending export credit or by guaranteeing export credit from banks at advantageous interest rates. When the term of the special export financing can be extended to match the payment of the foreign purchaser, the foreign purchaser is in effect able to finance its inventory through the courtesy of the exporter's government.

In some environments credit terms extended by manufacturers to retailers are of such long maturities as to constitute "purchase" of the retailer, such "purchase" being necessary to build an operational distribution system between manufacturer and ultimate customer. In Japan, for example, customer payment terms of 120 days are fairly common, and a manufacturer's sales effort is not competitive unless sufficient financial aid is provided to retailers to make it possible or beneficial for them to buy the manufacturer's product. Financial aid is reported to take the form of outright purchase of the retailer's capital stock, working capital loans, equipment purchase, subsidy or loan, and consideration of payment terms. Such manufacturer-supplied financing is a normal way of doing business in

Japan—and contributes to the lack of domestic competition prevalent in that country.

In summary, MNEs often manufacture or sell a product in a credit-short or inflationary economy, in a country where the banking system is oriented toward self-liquidating bills, or in locations where competition causes suppliers to finance their commercial customers. Longer collection periods have implications not only for the amount of financing that must be budgeted for a venture but also for the criteria by which the performance of local managers is evaluated.

)))) Payment Practices

The experience of getting paid for goods or services rendered varies considerably around the world. Typical credit terms and actual payment period (for they are not the same thing) differ widely by both region and country, creating substantial problems for multinational firms attempting to reduce the size of current assets (cash, accounts receivable outstanding, inventories, and work in progress).

European Payment Practices. For example, Exhibit 19.7 provides survey results on average payment periods in Europe for 10 Western European countries in rank order from longest—Italy at 90 days—to best—the Netherlands, averaging 47 days.

The variance across countries, even in a Europe that is moving toward more open internal commerce and common regulatory practices, standards, tariffs, and even a single currency, still presents significant problems for companies managing cross-border. No matter how difficult and costly, the MNE operating throughout the European Union in the future will more than likely be faced with continued differences in expected credit terms and payment practices between customers. These practices may result in continued distortions in payment and credit terms, and serve to once again support the long-forgotten principle that business practices of all kinds, including financial practices, may still be deeply ensconced in local business attitudes and practices that are culturally determined.

Exhibit 19.7	*Average Payment Periods in Europe (average period in days)*						
Ranking	Country	1993	1992	Ranking	Country	1993	1992
1	Italy	90	90	6	Portugal	63	76
2	Spain	80	74	7	Belgium	57	45
3	Greece	73	69	8	Ireland	56	56
4	France	70	67	9	United Kingdom	49	52
5	Luxembourg	66	58	10	Netherlands	47	48

Source: "The Check Is in the Mail," *International Business*, July 1994, p. 41.

Latin American and Asian-Pacific Payment Practices. Although summary data is difficult to find, average payment terms for most cross-border transactions into much of Latin America vary between 90 and 180 days. In many Latin American business ventures importers have been known to profit more from *financing arbitrage* (investing capital received for goods imported and sold prior to paying the original exporter because of extended payment terms) than on the actual business line itself.[1] In a number of the emerging markets of Asia, credit terms of 60 to 90 days in-country are not unusual, while cross-border payment terms vary from a relatively short 180 days to as long as 360 days.

INVENTORY MANAGEMENT

Operations in inflationary, devaluation-prone economies sometimes force management to modify its normal approach to inventory management. In some cases management may choose to maintain inventory and reorder levels far in excess of what would be called for in a typical inventory management system.

Under conditions where local currency devaluation is likely, management must decide whether to build up inventory of imported items in anticipation of the expected devaluation. After the devaluation, imported inventory will cost more in local currency terms. One tradeoff is a higher holding cost because of the bloated level of inventory and high local interest rates, which normally reflect the expected devaluation. A less obvious tradeoff is the possibility that local government will enforce a price freeze following devaluation. This freeze would prevent the imported inventory from being sold for an appropriate markup above its now-higher replacement value. Still worse, the devaluation may not occur as anticipated, leaving management holding an excessive level of inventory until it can be worked down. Disposing of excessive inventory will be particularly painful if competitors have followed the same strategy of speculating on imported inventory.

))) Anticipating Price Freezes

To circumvent an anticipated price freeze, management can establish the local currency price of an imported item at a high level, with actual sales being made at a discount from this posted price. In the event of a devaluation, sales continue at the posted prices but discounts are withdrawn. This technique circumvents the price freeze only if that freeze is expressed in terms of posted rather than effective price. In any event it provides no protection against competitive price squeezes. An alternative is to sell at the posted price but increase selling, promotion, or other marketing mix activities, which can later be reduced.

If imported inventory is a commodity, another strategy is to purchase the commodity in the forward market. Then if local prices are frozen, the forward contract can be sold abroad for the same currency in which it is denominated. On the other hand, if local price controls are based on a fixed markup over cost, the forward contract can be exercised and the commodity imported at the now-higher local currency cost, which becomes the basis for the markup. If options on the commodity are available, the same benefit can be achieved. The certain cost of the option should be compared with the uncertain trading gain or loss on the forward contract.

))) Free-Trade Zones and Free Industrial Zones

A free-trade zone combines the old idea of duty-free ports with legislation that reduces or eliminates customs duties to retailers or manufacturers who structure their operations to benefit from the technique. Income taxes may also be reduced for operations in a free-trade zone. The old duty-free ports were typically in the dock area of major seaports, where goods were held, duty free, until the owner was ready to deliver them within the country. Modern free-trade zones, by comparison, are often located away from a port area. For example, the Italian firm of Olivetti has such a zone in Harrisburg, Pennsylvania.

Free-trade zones function in several ways. As mentioned, they may be a place to off-load merchandise for subsequent sale within the country where the zone is located. An example of such a zone is a storage area for imported Toyota automobiles in the Port of Los Angeles. A large quantity of differentiated models can be held until sold by a dealer, at which time the cars are "imported" into the United States from the free-trade zone. The advantage of such an arrangement is that a variety of models can be kept near the point of sale for quick delivery, but import duties need be paid only when the merchandise passes from the zone into California.

A second type of zone involves the assembly of components for subsequent sale within the country where the zone is located. An example is the Mercedes assembly line in Alabama. Components are imported into the free-trade zone where assembly work is finished. The import duty is paid only when the finished car is removed from the zone. Furthermore, the duty is lower than it would be for a finished car because the charges on components are less than the charge on a finished vehicle.

A third type of zone is a full-fledged manufacturing center with a major portion of its output re-exported out of the country. Two examples are Penang, Malaysia, and Madagascar, where such zones are officially designated *free industrial zones*. In Penang, companies as diverse as Dell Computers, National Semiconductor, Sony, Bosch, and Trane Air Conditioning manufacture final products. A major portion of production is re-exported, avoiding Malaysian customs altogether—but, of course, providing jobs for Malaysian workers and engineers. The portion of production sold in Malaysia is assessed duties only on the components originally imported. However, the variety of firms permits one to buy from another; Dell buys Pentium chips from Intel and disk drives from Seagate, both of which are located less than a mile from the Dell plant.[2]

WORKING CAPITAL MAINTENANCE UNDER INFLATION

As diagramed earlier, the basic working capital structure is for cash to be used to acquire or manufacture inventory, which is then sold for an account receivable; this receivable is eventually collected to provide cash for the next cycle. Continued operations depend on a steady inflow of cash. Operations in a high-inflation country often make this difficult if not impossible, and income taxes levied as a percent of accounting income compound the problem. Preserving cash flow to feed the working capital cycle under hyperinflation conditions can be illustrated with an example.

Assume that Lincoln Brazil in turn owns Carioca, S.A., a department store, which purchases merchandise on January 1 for R$240,000 (Brazilian real) at a time when the price index is 100. Carioca also invests R$200,000 in display counters, cash registers, and leasehold improvements; these purchases and improvement have an expected life of four years. Carioca's only sale of merchandise is made on December 31 at the end of the year at a price of R$500,000, by which time the price level in Brazil has risen to 150. During the year general operating expenses of R$160,000 are paid. Income taxes are 25%.

Lincoln Brazil's, and indeed Lincoln U.S.'s, cash management problem is to determine whether Carioca sold the merchandise at a sufficiently high price and whether it can continue to survive. Carioca's cost-based income statement is in the left columns of Exhibit 19.8.

Exhibit 19.8   *Carioca, S.A. Income Calculations (in Brazilian real)*

	Cost-based Accounting	Price-level Accounting	Free Cash Flow for Next Year
Price-index	100	150	
Sales proceeds	500,000	500,000	500,000
Cost of goods sold	240,000	360,000[a]	360,000[a]
Administrative expenses	160,000	160,000[b]	240,000[c]
Depreciation	50,000	75,000	
Pre-tax profit	50,000	(95,000)	
Income taxes (25% of profit on historic cost basis)	12,500	12,500	12,500[d]
Net profit (loss)	37,500	(107,500)	
Free cash flow for next year, after replacing inventory and in anticipation of administrative costs rising 50%			(112,500)

Notes:

[a] The real, year end, value of the inventory sold was 50% above its costs, or R$360,000. Next year's inventory, if purchased on January 1, would have this cost.

[b] R$160,000 was the actual cost of administrative expenses for the year just finished.

[c] Next year, administrative expenses can reasonably be expected to be 50% higher, at R$240,000.

[d] This R$12,500 represents the cash outflow for the past year's taxes, which reduces cash available to finance next year's operations.

As we can see, original cost accounting indicates a pre-tax profit of R$50,000, against which a 25% income tax of R$12,500 was levied, leaving "profit" of R$37,500. Lincoln U.S. might think its Brazilian subaffiliate is doing well and might even consider requesting Lincoln Brazil to have Carioca declare dividends, either for Lincoln Brazil to finance its expansion or to include in a dividend back to Lincoln, U.S.

In fact, in real terms Carioca lost R$95,000, in part because the replacement cost (real value) of the inventory sold was R$360,000 rather than R$240,000, and in part because income taxes were levied on book income rather than real income.

Carioca's cash position for the following year is even worse. As shown in the rightmost column, the sale produced a cash inflow of R$500,000. From this cash inflow an income tax of R$12,500 must still be paid (taxes are paid from cash flow, not from earnings), leaving R$487,500 for continued operations. A new cycle of inventory will cost R$360,000 if purchased right away, and if administrative expenses follow the trend of costs (which is reasonable), next year they will be R$240,00. Thus, R$600,000 will be needed to continue operations next year at the level of last year. This shortfall equals R$112,500, even before considering any needs for additional equipment and leasehold improvements. The shortfall of R$112,500 includes depreciation, which is a non-cash expense.

Managers of MNEs with a home base in North America, Europe, Japan, and some other countries may not be fully aware what happens to their cash working capital when they own an affiliate in a hyperinflation country. This lack of alertness often causes an otherwise well-conceived FDI to fail. The practical choices available to the foreign parent are either to keep on pumping in additional cash, year after year, in spite of the original cost financial statements that report the affiliate to be making a profit, or to raise sales prices faster than the rate of inflation so as to "keep ahead." The latter option may not be feasible, either because the host government finds ways to penalize foreign firms that raise prices faster than the rate of inflation or because the market cannot afford to buy such products.

FINANCING WORKING CAPITAL CHOICES

All firms need to finance working capital. The normal sources of funds for financing short-term working capital come from accounts payable to suppliers and borrowing against bank credit lines. In some countries, such as the United States, the firm borrows by issuing notes payable to banks and other creditors. In other countries short-term borrowing is done on an "overdraft" basis. A firm is allowed to overdraw its checking account up to the limit of its credit line. No compensating deposit balances are required, in contrast to the U.S. system that expects compensating deposit balances. In all cases, permanent working capital requirements, as opposed to seasonal needs, are at least partially financed with long-term debt and equity.

The MNE enjoys a much greater choice of banking sources to fund its working capital needs than do domestic firms. Banking sources available to MNEs include in-house banks funded by unrepatriated capital, international banks, and local banks where subsidiaries are located. In-house banks and the various types of external commercial banking offices are described in the remainder of this chapter.

IN-HOUSE BANKS

Some MNEs have found that their financial resources and needs are either too large or too sophisticated for the financial services available in many locations where they operate. One solution to this has been the establishment of an *in-house* or *internal bank* within the firm. Such an in-house bank is not a separate corporation; rather, it is a set of functions performed by the existing Treasury department. Acting as an independent entity, the central Treasury of the firm transacts with the various business units of the firm on an arms-length basis. The purpose of the in-house bank is to provide banking-like services to the various units of the firm. The in-house bank may be able to provide services that are not available in many countries or that are higher cost when they are. In addition to traditional banking activities, the in-house bank may be able to offer services to units of the firm that aid in the management of ongoing transaction exposures. Lastly, because it is in-house, credit analysis is not a part of decision-making.

Exhibit 19.9 illustrates how the in-house bank of Lincoln Europe could work with Lincoln Belge and Deutscheland Lincoln. Lincoln Belge sells all its receivables to the in-house bank as they arise, reducing some of its domestic working capital needs. Additional working capital needs are supplied by the in-house bank

| **Exhibit 19.9** | *An In-House Bank of Lincoln Europe* |

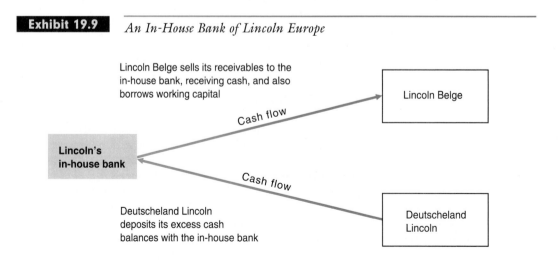

directly to Lincoln Belge. Because the in-house bank is part of the same company, interest rates it charges may be significantly lower than what Lincoln Belge could obtain on its own. The source of funds for the in-house bank may arise from the deposits of excess cash balances from Deutscheland Lincoln.

If the in-house bank can pay Deutscheland Lincoln a higher deposit rate than it could obtain on its own in Germany, and if the in-house bank can lend these funds to Lincoln Belge at an interest rate lower than it could obtain on its own in Belgium, then both operating units benefit. Assuming the loan rate is greater than the deposit rate, the in-house bank profits by the margin between the two, but this margin or spread must be smaller than would be available from a commercial bank.

How can the in-house bank operate with a smaller spread than a regular commercial bank? First, its costs are lower because it does not have to conform to the stringent capital requirements imposed on commercial banks worldwide. Second, in-house banks do not have the large overhead costs of supporting large dealing rooms, branch networks, retail "store fronts," and other services required for commercial bank competitiveness. Third, they need not assess the creditworthiness of the corporate units with which they deal, since the units are all in the same family. Nor need they provide for credit losses, or deposit insurance.

In addition to providing financing benefits, in-house banks allow for more effective currency risk management. In the case of Lincoln Belge, the sale of foreign currency receivables to the in-house bank shifts transaction exposure to the bank. The in-house bank is better equipped to deal with currency exposures and has a greater volume of international cash flows, allowing Lincoln Europe overall to gain from more effective use of netting and matching. This approach frees the units of the firm from struggling to manage transaction exposures and allows them to focus on their primary business activities.

There are a variety of different structures used for in-house banks. Many firms allow their units to use outside banks if the same services are available at lower cost. This forces the in- house bank to be operationally competitive. In this case, the in-house bank cannot rely on captive customers for its business but must compete with commercial banks openly. Many firms, however, require their units to use the in-house bank in order to ensure the bank of having an adequate level of activity to take advantage of economies of scale.

TYPES OF COMMERCIAL BANKING OFFICES

MNEs depend on their commercial banks to handle most of their trade financing needs, such as letters of credit, but also to provide advice about government support, country-risk assessment, introductions to foreign firms and banks, and general financing availability. MNEs interface with their banks through a variety of different types of banking offices, many of which perform specialized functions. Therefore, it is important for financial managers to understand which bank offices provide which kinds of activities. The main points of bank contact are with correspondent banks, representative offices, branch banks, subsidiaries, and affiliates. In the United States, a more specialized banking facility is available: the Edge Act corporation, which is discussed later in this chapter.

Correspondent Banks

Most major banks of the world maintain correspondent banking relationships with local banks in each of the important foreign cities of the world. The two-way link between such banks is essentially one of correspondence via fax, cable, and mail and a mutual deposit relationship. For example, a U.S. bank may have a correspondent bank in Kuala Lumpur, Malaysia, and the U.S. bank will in turn be the correspondent bank for the Malaysian bank. Each will maintain a deposit in the other in local currency.

Correspondent services include accepting drafts, honoring letters of credit, and furnishing credit information. Services are centered around collecting or paying foreign funds, often because of import or export transactions. However, a visiting business person can use the home bank's introduction to meet local bankers.

Under a correspondent banking relationship, neither of the correspondent banks maintains its own personnel in the other country. Direct contact between the banks is usually limited to periodic visits between members of the banks' management.

For the business person the main advantage of banking at home with a bank having a large number of foreign correspondent relationships is the ability to handle financial matters in a large number of foreign countries through local bankers whose knowledge of local customs should be extensive. The disadvantages are the lack of ability to deposit in, borrow from, or disburse from a branch of one's own home bank, as well as the possibility that correspondents will put a lower priority on serving the foreign banks' customer than on serving their own permanent customers.

Representative Offices

A bank establishes a representative office in a foreign country primarily to help parent bank clients when they are doing business in that country or in neighboring countries. It also functions as a geographically convenient location from which to visit correspondent banks in its region rather than sending bankers from the parent bank at greater financial and physical cost. A representative office is not a "banking office." It cannot accept deposits, make loans, commit the parent bank to a loan, or deal in drafts, letters of credit, or the Eurocurrency market. Indeed, a tourist cannot even cash a travelers check from the parent bank in the representative office.

The basic function of a representative office is to provide information, advice, and local contacts for the parent bank's business clients and to provide a location where business persons from either country can initiate inquiries about the parent bank's services. Representative offices introduce visiting executives to local banks, and they watch over correspondent banking relationships. They put parent bank customers in contact with local business firms interested in supplying, purchasing, or marketing products or services, and they arrange meetings with government officials if that is needed to obtain permissions, approvals, or government help. They provide credit analysis of local firms and economic and political intelligence about the country.

A representative office is usually small, often one executive, two or three assistants, and clerical help, all of whom work in an office that does not resemble a banking office in the physical sense. The representative and the assistants may have come to the office from the home country, but it is equally likely that they are citizens or permanent residents of the host country. The major advantage of a representative office is that the local representative will have a more precise understanding of the needs of home-country clients than might local correspondents and can thus provide data and advice more suitable to their needs. The local representative will be bilingual, if that is needed, and can advise visitors about local customs and procedures.

If the parent bank eventually decides to open a local general banking office, the existence of a representative office for some prior period usually provides a valuable base of contacts and expertise to facilitate the change. However, representative offices are not necessarily a prelude to a general banking office, nor need an eventual general banking office be the major reason for opening a representative office. In some countries, such as Mexico, foreign banks are precluded from opening new general banking offices. Thus, representative offices are the only possible presence in such countries.

The essential disadvantage of the representative office to the business firm is that it cannot conduct general banking activities. Although it can facilitate such transactions with local correspondents, the process may be slower or more cumbersome than a business firm might wish. Because a representative office is usually small, physical limitations do exist on the services that can be supplied to home office clients.

))) Branch Banks

A foreign branch bank is a legal and operational part of the parent bank, with the full resources of that parent behind the local office. A branch bank does not have its own corporate charter, its own board of directors, or any shares of stock outstanding. Although for managerial and regulatory purposes it will maintain its own set of books, its assets and liabilities are in fact those of the parent bank. However, branch deposits are not subject to reserve requirements or FDIC insurance, in the case of U.S. banks, unless the deposits are reloaned to the U.S. parent bank.

Branch banks are subject to two sets of banking regulations. As part of the parent, they are subject to home-country regulations. However, they are also subject to regulations of the host country, which may provide any of a variety of restrictions on their operations.

The major advantage to a business of using a branch bank is that the branch will conduct a full range of banking services under the name and legal obligation of the parent. A deposit in a branch is a legal obligation of the parent. Services to customers are based on the worldwide value of the client relationship rather than just on the relationship to the local office. Legal loan limits are a function of the size of the parent, not of the branch.

From the point of view of a banker, the profits of a foreign branch are subject to immediate taxation at home, and losses of a foreign branch are deductible against taxable income at home. A new office expected to have losses in its early years creates a tax advantage if it is initially organized as a branch, even if eventually the intent is to change it to a separately incorporated subsidiary. From an organizational point of view, a foreign branch is usually simpler to create and staff than is a separately incorporated subsidiary.

The major disadvantage of a branch bank is one that accrues to the bank rather than to its customers. The parent bank (not just the branch) may be sued at the local level for debts or other activities of the branch.

Branch banking has been the most important way for U.S. banks to conduct their foreign activities. Foreign branches account for about one-half of all international banking assets held by U.S. banks.[3] Europe is the most important location of U.S. branches with respect to size of assets and historical development. The Caribbean shell branches are also important, but their growth has leveled off in recent years. Asia is growing in importance at the same time as Latin America is declining in importance in terms of assets held.[4]

)))) Banking Subsidiaries

A subsidiary bank is a separately incorporated bank, owned entirely or in major part by a foreign parent, which conducts a general banking business. As a separate corporation, the banking subsidiary must comply with all the laws of the host country. Its lending limit is based on its own equity capital rather than that of the parent bank. This limits its ability to service large borrowers, but local incorporation also limits the liability of the parent bank to its equity investment in the subsidiary.

A foreign banking subsidiary often appears as a local bank in the eyes of potential customers in host countries and is thus often able to attract additional local deposits. This will especially be true if the bank was independent prior to being purchased by the foreign parent. Management may well be local, giving the bank greater access to the local business community. A foreign-owned bank subsidiary is more likely to be involved in both domestic and international business than is a foreign branch, which is more likely to appeal to the foreign business community but may well encounter difficulty in attracting banking business from local firms.

Sometimes foreign banks are not allowed to operate branches in a host country but are allowed to operate a locally incorporated subsidiary. Tax laws may favor subsidiaries over branches, both from the local perspective and from the parent-country perspective.

Subsidiaries are the second most important organization form for U.S. banks, with about 20% of all international assets held by U.S. banks located in subsidiaries. Over half the assets of these subsidiaries are located in Europe, particularly in the United Kingdom.[5]

))) Affiliates

A banking affiliate is a locally incorporated bank owned in part, but not necessarily controlled, by a foreign parent. The remainder of the ownership may be local, or it may be other foreign banks. The affiliated bank itself may be newly formed, or it may be a local bank in which a foreign bank has purchased a part interest.

The major advantage of an affiliated banking relationship derives from the nature of a joint venture between parties of different nationalities. The bank acquires the expertise of two or more sets of owners. It maintains its status as a local institution with local ownership and management, but it has continuing and permanent relations with its foreign part-owner, including an ability to draw upon the international expertise of that part-owner. The major disadvantage is also common to joint ventures; the several owners may be unable to agree on particular policies important to the viability of the bank.

))) Edge Act Corporations

Edge Act corporations are subsidiaries of U.S. banks, incorporated in the United States under Section 25 of the Federal Reserve Act as amended, to engage in international banking and financing operations. Not only may such subsidiaries engage in general international banking, they may also finance commercial, industrial, or financial projects in foreign countries through long-term loans or equity participation. Such participation, however, is subject to the day-to-day practices and policies of the Federal Reserve System.

Edge Act corporations are physically located in the United States. Because U.S. banks cannot have branches outside their own state, Edge Act corporations are usually located in other states in order to conduct international banking activities. Growth in Edge Act banking was greatly facilitated in 1979 when the Federal Reserve Board issued new guidelines that permitted interstate branching by Edge Act corporations. Previously an Edge Act corporation had to be separately incorporated in each state. By increasing their interstate penetration through Edge Act corporations, the large money-center banks are establishing a physical presence in most of the important regional financial centers in order to prepare for the day when interstate branching will also be permitted for domestic business.

Edge Act corporations generally engage in two types of activities: direct international banking, including acting as a holding company for the stock of one or more foreign banking subsidiaries, and financing development activities not closely related to traditional banking operations.

International Banking Activities. Edge Act corporations may accept demand and time deposits from outside the United States (as well as from within, if such deposits are incidental to or for the purpose of transactions in foreign countries).

Each corporation can also make loans, although commitments to any one borrower cannot exceed 10% of capital and surplus. They can issue or confirm letters of credit; make loans or advances to finance foreign trade, including production loans; create bankers' acceptances; receive items for collection; offer such services as remittance of funds abroad, or buying, selling, or holding securities for safekeeping; issue guarantees; act as paying agent for securities issued by foreign governments or foreign corporations; and engage in spot and forward foreign exchange transactions.

Edge Act subsidiaries whose primary activity is international banking may also function as holding companies by owning shares of foreign banking subsidiaries and affiliates. Domestic banks may have branches abroad, but they may not themselves own shares of foreign banking subsidiaries. Thus the Edge Act route permits U.S. banks to own foreign banking subsidiaries, either as wholly owned subsidiaries via an intermediary Edge Act corporation, or as part of a joint venture with foreign or domestic banks or with other nonbanking institutions.

International Financing Activities. Edge Act corporations differ from other U.S. banks in their ability to make portfolio-type investments in the equity of foreign commercial and industrial firms, either directly or through the intermediary of official or semi-official development banks or corporations. Direct investment in a wide variety of local businesses can be made by intermediate-term loans, by purchase of shares of stock, or by a combination of these two methods.

Some longer-term development projects are typically initiated in the foreign country by local business and are referred to the Edge Act corporation by the parent bank. Edge Act corporations engaged only in financing may invest up to 50% of their capital and surplus in a single venture. However, if the Edge Act corporation is also engaged in general banking, the limit is 10% of capital and surplus.

SUMMARY

Financial managers of MNEs must control international liquid assets in order to maintain adequate liquidity in a variety of currencies while also minimizing political and foreign exchange risk.

- The basic steps in international cash management include cash planning, collection, mobilization, and disbursement, as well as covering cash shortages and investing cash surpluses. A MNE must perform all the tasks required of a domestic firm in each foreign location, and in addition it must consider other techniques that arise because of its international position.

- Cash balances are held to provide planned disbursements and to protect the firm against unanticipated variations from budgeted cash flows in an array of currencies. Techniques of cash management include the use of centralized depositories and multilateral netting.

- Accounts receivable management can be viewed in terms of receivables from independent customers and payment practices.

- Inventory management provides ways to protect inventory values in the face of adverse exchange rate changes and anticipated price freezes. Free-trade zones are useful because they can postpone tariff payment until goods are sold.

- When a foreign affiliate operates in a hyperinflation country, cash working capital problems abound. Parents of such affiliates must, at a minimum, be aware their affiliate may be decapitalized. If they cannot raise sales prices faster than the rate of inflation, they must be prepared to invest follow-up capital, year after year until the inflation rate diminishes.

- MNEs can finance working capital needs through in-house banks, international banks, and local banks where subsidiaries are located.

- International banks finance MNEs and service these accounts through representative offices, correspondent banking relationships, branch banks, banking subsidiaries, affiliates, and Edge Act corporations (U.S. only).

QUESTIONS

1. Piñon Corporation

Piñon Corporation (U.S.) operates subsidiaries in Brazil and Indonesia. In the United States Piñon typically requires $1,000,000 in accounts receivable and $162,500 in inventory to support $12,000,000 in sales. Piñon's gross markup over inventory cost is 33 1/3%. A similar markup is used by the two affiliates.

Piñon's marketing department reports that the firm should be able to sell an additional $2,400,000 in Brazil and an additional $1,500,000 in Indonesia next year. Before preparing operating budgets for its Brazilian and Indonesian affiliates, Piñon's chief financial officer asked chief financial officers in the two countries to report on local payment customs and inventory needs. The Brazilian officer reported that customers in Brazil normally took three months to pay, and that a two-month supply of inventory was necessary because of the possibility of shipping delays due to strikes by longshoremen. In Indonesia the average collection period was reported to be four months, and a three-month supply of inventory was necessary.

Net working capital is defined here to mean current assets (cash, accounts receivable, and inventory) less current liabilities (accounts payable).

	United States	Brazil	Indonesia
Sales	$12,000,000	$2,400,000	$1,500,000
Cash	$400,000	$80,000	$50,000
A/R	$1,000,000	3 months	4 months
Inventory	$162,500	2 months	3 months
A/P	$800,000	3 months	6 months

a. What are the days sales outstanding (DSO) of the three different units?
b. What is the required net working capital position of the three units?
c. What is the fundamental working capital difference among the three countries?
d. What additional investment, if any, will be needed for the following year in the two affiliates?

2. Southern Cross Ski Company

Southern Cross Ski Company of Santiago de Chile has sales and service centers in Argentina and Peru and also maintains a corporate wide account in dollars in Miami. Accounts are maintained in the currency of each country, but because of exchange rate volatility in the country in which it operates, Southern Cross uses the U.S. dollar for internal control purposes. Southern Cross maintains separate operating cash balance in each country at a level equal to two standard deviations above expected needs. Expected operating cash needs and one standard deviation of those needs, measured in dollars, are:

	Expected cash need	One standard deviation
Chile	$ 5,000,000	$ 1,000,000
Argentina	3,000,000	400,000
Peru	2,000,000	300,000
Bolivia	800,000	40,000
	$ 10,800,000	$ 1,740,000

Southern Cross's Miami bank suggested the same level of safety could be maintained with less cash if all precautionary balances were combined in a central account. This would necessitate a South America-wide cash management system, which the Miami bank could provide.

a. How much lower would Southern Cross Ski company's total cash balances be if all precautionary balances were combined? Assume cash needs in each country are normally distributed and are independent of each other.

b. What other advantages might accrue to Southern Cross Ski Company from centralizing its cash holdings? Are these advantages realistic?

3. Coldcase Appliances, Inc.

Coldcase Appliances manufactures household refrigerators and freezers in Mexico, Spain, and California. Each affiliate has monthly unsettled balances due to or from other affiliates. At the end of March, unsettled intracompany debts in U.S. dollars were:

Coldcase, Mexico:	Owes $8 million to Spanish affiliate.
	Owes $9 million to California parent.
Coldcase, Spain:	Owes $5 million to Mexican affiliate.
	Owes $6 million to California parent.
Coldcase, California:	Owes $4 million to Mexican affiliate.

Foreign exchange transaction spreads average 0.3% of funds transferred.

a.   How should Coldcase net these intracompany debts? How much would be saved in transaction expenses over the no-netting alternative?

b.   Before settling the above accounts, Coldcase decides to invest $6,000,000 of parent funds in a new hard-disk-drive plant in a new Free Industrial Zone in Penang, Malaysia. How can this decision be incorporated into the settlement process? What would be total bank charges? Explain.

WORLD WIDE WEB EXERCISES

W1. Working Capital Management

Many major multinational banks provide a variety of working capital and multinational cash management services described in this chapter. Using the web sites of a variety of these cross-border banks, search out the banks that offer multinational cash management services that combine banking with foreign exchange management. Which banks provide specific services through regional or geographic service centers?

Bank of America	http://corp.bankofamerica.com/
Bank of Montreal	http://www.bmo.com/
	(Select *Cash Management* under *Corporate*)

W2. Clearing-House Associations

The actual process of moving and crediting funds between banks and between firms is often overlooked in academic discussions. Associations like the New York Clearing-House Association have, however, played major roles in the international financial system for centuries. Use the following web sites to prepare a two-page executive briefing on the role of clearing houses in history and in contemporary finance. Use the web site for the Clearing-House Interbank Payments System (CHIPS) to estimate the volume of international financial transactions.

New York Clearinghouse Association	http://www.theclearinghouse.org/
Clearing House Interbank Payments System	http://www.chips.org/

SUGGESTED READINGS

Gentry, James A., Dileep R. Mehta, S. K. Bhattacharya, Robert Cobbaut, and Jean-Louis Scaringella, "An International Study of Management Perceptions of the Working Capital Process," *Journal of International Business Studies*, Spring-Summer 1979, pp. 28–38.

Houpt, James V., "International Trends for U.S. Banks and Banking Markets," Staff Study of the Board of Governors of the Federal Reserve System, No. 156, May 1988.

Srinivasan, VenKat, Susan E. Moeller, and Yong H. Kim, "International Cash Management: State-of-the-Art and Research Directions," *Advances in Financial Planning and Forecasting*. Vol. 4, part B, 1990, pp. 161–194.

NOTES

1. This is actually an example of *uncovered interest arbitrage* (see Chapter 3) if the importer is receiving, say, Brazilian real, reinvesting locally at relatively high interest rates, prior to paying the original exporter in some hard currency such as U.S. dollars.
2. Eiteman (1997).
3. Houpt (1988).
4. Ibid, p. 8.
5. Ibid, p. 11.

DECISION CASE

The Far East Trading Company (Abridged)

"We have worked 30 to 40 years to develop our countries to this level, but along comes a man with a few billion dollars, and who in a period of just two weeks, has undone most of the work we have done. As a result, the people of our countries suffer. You talk about human rights and protecting people. But they must be protected from people like Soros who has so much money and so much power and totally thoughtless because he is not only hurting the people of Myanmar, but the poor people in Indonesia, Malaysia, the Philippines and Thailand."

—Prime Minister Datuk Seri Dr. Mahathir Mohamad of Malaysia
New Straits Times, Kuala Lumpur, July 27, 1997

For Thailand to blame Mr Soros for its plight is rather like condemning an undertaker for burying a suicide.

—*The Economist*, August 2, 1997, p. 57.

Jan Karl Karlsen, CFO of The Far East Trading Company Ltd. A/B, hurried down the Kuala Lumpur hotel corridor to his meeting with the financial controllers of many of the company's regional operating units. His task this morning was to explain personally the profit warning reported by the company in a press release the previous Friday, November 21, 1997, in Stockholm. This had been the second official profit warning of the year, and FETC's shares on the Stockholm Stock Exchange had once again fallen.

Karlsen's thoughts on the flight from Stockholm to Kuala Lumpur had been dominated by what he considered the three critical factors facing FETC's management: *cash flow*, *confidence*, and *control*. FETC was expected to suffer significant losses from the current Asian currency crisis. Operating units throughout East Asia were already reeling from currency exposures, working capital financing shortfalls, and the general economic slowdown spreading out from the currency crisis which had begun in July in Thailand. With losses came increasing criticism of management and increasing influence of the company's creditors. Ultimately, control of the company could be at stake.

The Company

The Far East Trading Company Ltd. A/S was incorporated in Stockholm, Sweden, on March 27, 1897, by H. N. Johansson. Johansson, an experienced sea captain, had established a trading house in Bangkok, Thailand, in 1884, and wished to establish a trading company in Sweden which could serve as a financial base for continuous trade between the Far East and Europe. In the early years the Far East Company made markets in rice, oilseed, spice, and timber. As the company expanded with the turn of the century, FETC opened trade routes to Africa, the Indies, North America, and Australia, eventually making shipping itself a major part of its business.

What differentiated the Far East Trading Company in 1897 was still significant in 1997. It was a global trading company which had no real domestic business base, but instead, served to provide a cultural and corporate center for the conduct of global trade. For the next century, no matter what market or business it was involved in, the continuity of Swedish management was the only constant. Throughout the 20th century, the company prospered and faltered, like so many others, but persevered and maintained its corporate charter in Stockholm.

The firm was a loosely knit collection of independent country-units from its very beginnings. The individual businesses were under the direct and active management of the country manager assigned from the Swedish home office. The decentralized organizational structure produced what many came to call *country kingdoms*. The individual country-based operating units were inherently entrepreneurial, entering into any business which offered profit potential.

Although FETC was a Swedish corporation, Managing Director Jesper Erickson focused on the fact that nearly 75% of the firm's earnings were in the Far East. FETC was currently organized along along two different lines, *FETC Core Businesses* and *FETC Businesses*. Erickson's long term strategy called for the concentration of FETC's activities in fewer business areas.

The FETC Core Businesses

FETC's strength—and future prospects in the eyes of management—was in three core areas of identified competence: *Consumer Products*, *Foods*, and *Graphics*. These three areas were expected to make up over 70% of FETC's turnover in the coming decade. The company's plan was to organize activities around these business areas across countries rather than by country. Exhibit 1 shows the 1995 and 1996 financial results by business areas.

- The *Consumer Products* segment was made up of two major sub-segments: marketing services and nutritional products. The Marketing Services Group provided marketing, sales, distribution, and merchandising services to consumer product firms in the ASEAN countries[1] and Greater China. The *Nutritions Group* was largely composed of a newly operational state-of-the-art dairy plant in Shanghai, China, producing dry and liquid infant and baby nutritional products.

---

1. ASEAN, the Association of Southwest Asian Nations, is a regional economic and trade organization, including Brunei, Indonesia, Malasia, Philippines, Singapore, and Thailand.

| **Exhibit 1** | FETC Turnover and Operating Profit Margins, 1995–1996 (millions of SKK) |

	1996 Sales	%	1996 Profits	%	1995 Sales	%	1995 Profits	%
FETC Core Businessses								
Consumer Products	6,809	60	7	3	5,113	45	65	20
Marketing Services	6,085		(26)		4,504		24	
Nutrition	724		33		609		41	
Logistics	–		–					
Foods	966	9	84	30	1,217	11	116	35
Graphics	3,574	31	187	67	3,085	27	151	45
Total Core	11,349	100	278	100	9,415	100	352	100
FETC Businesses								
Timber	979	19	26	8	900	18	16	5
Wool	803	16	19	6	816	17	(27)	–9
Shipping	737	14	(8)	–3	778	16	12	4
Technical	825	16	71	23	702	14	85	28
Other activities	1,761	34	202	65	1,744	35	217	72
Total Businesses	5,105	100	310	100	4,940	100	303	100
Core Businesses	11,349	69	278	47	9,415	66	352	52
Businesses	5,105	31	310	53	4,940	34	303	48
Total FETC Group	16,454	100	588	100	14,355	100	655	100

Source: *FETC Annual Reports, 1995, 1996.*

- The *Foods* segment, was the newest of the three core business segments. Unique for FETC, Foods was purely South American in composition. It was headquartered in Caracas, Venezuela. Serving the Andean Region, the Foods Group focused on meats and meat products.

- The *Graphics* business segment, the third of the FETC core businesses, provided material and service solutions to the graphic arts industry in East Asia. This included the importation and distribution of equipment, services, and consumables to this rapidly growing sector of Asia.

FETC Businesses

When Jesper Erickson reorganized much of FETC in 1992, all of those Group interests which did not fall into the three FETC Core Businesses were collected under *FETC Businesses*. Erickson believed these businesses were the leftovers of the earlier era in which country managers were allowed to follow entrepreneurial instincts, not the proven competency of the organization. The result was a steady liquidation of non-core businesses.

FETC Businesses included timber (procured in Southeast Asia, Ghana, and Brazil, and traded through a central trading unit in London), wool, shipping, and technical services. All shipping unit businesses were scheduled for divestment and liquidation. The Chemicals Group, part of Technical Services, was a marketer and distributor of specialty chemicals to a variety of manufacturing industries. *Other activities* included unallocated expenses related to the Corporate Center in Stockholm and other regional centres in Asia.

In FETC's half-year report (for the January–June period) published in August (see Exhibit 2), problems were apparent. Although sales were up by 12% in Swedish krona terms, operating income was down by a full 26%. Sales were up in all three Core Businesses and four of the seven FETC Businesses, but the operating results of most core businesses were down. Jan Karlsen believed the causes were a combination of operating and financing cost problems.

Operations. The report noted specifically that cost-control and utilization issues in Asian market segments were largely to blame. The core business units in Thailand had experienced significant theft of inventories and accounting fraud (postponed orders had continued to be booked as current sales) since the first of the year. Unit management had been quickly replaced, but the declining Thai market continued to put pressure on management performance. Days sales outstanding

Exhibit 2	FETC Net Sales and Operating Results, Half-Year Report, 1997 *(millions of SKK)*				

| | Net Sales | | | Operating Result | | |
Segment	Actual 1997	Actual 1996	Chg in %	Actual 1997	Actual 1996	Chg in %
Graphics	1,747	1,618	8	78	67	16
Consumer Products	3,949	3,169	25	−15	34	−144
Foods	554	464	19	9	39	−77
Total Core Business	6,250	5,251	19	72	140	−49
Chemicals	342	323	6	52	54	−4
Technical business	509	349	46	34	34	0
Timber	592	471	26	20	9	122
Wool	277	428	−35	3	17	−82
Shipping	121	402	−70	17	−19	189
Plumrose Germany	325	–	–	−6	–	–
Other Activities	270	529	−49	28	40	−30
Total FETC Businesses	2,436	2,502	3	148	135	10
Total FETC	8,686	7,753	12	220	275	−20
Administrative expenses[a]	–	–	–	−85	−93	−9
Total	8,686	7,753	12	135	182	−26

[a]Administrative expenses are predominantly composed of unallocated overheads of corporate centers.

on receivables were stretching out, and many suppliers had simultaneously begun drawing-in their credit terms. Although sales had grown, the cost of doing business was increasing.

Financing. Financing expenses were significantly higher than in the previous year. The parent company had provided minimal equity investment in the beginning. Additional funding needs were supplied over time through retained earnings and debt. FETC's long history in the region had allowed it to build bank relations over time. The reliance on debt had risen as profits had declined.

In 1995 and 1996 many of the Asian units had moved to reduce financing expenses by financing working capital financing needs offshore in U.S. dollars. The stable currencies of the region allowed the firm to borrow dollars offshore at an average interest rate of 9% in 1996, as opposed to 14% for Malaysian ringgit or 18% for Thai baht. The parent company had also encouraged the individual units to decrease capital needs through improved inventory turns and reduced cycle times. But in June the dollar had strengthened leading to rising debt service expenses and foreign exchange losses.

FETC had concluded its half-year report to stockholders in August with a profit warning that "... it is expected that 1997 full-year operating profits will be lower than in 1996." FETC's share price suffered another setback, and Jan Karlsen was spending more and more of his time meeting with both institutional investors and the major creditors of the company.

Asian Crisis Impact

Thailand's key role in heralding in the emerging market crises of 1997–1998 was described in an illustrative case in Chapter 2. The falling value of Asian currencies was reflected in a series of impacts on The FETC Group's financial results. First, individual Asian business units suffered currency *transaction losses* associated with exposures (mostly accounts payable or debt obligations in U.S. dollars). Local management, however, argued that although the Swedish krona value of these units was diminished, they were continuing to make significant progress and take growing market shares.

Secondly, the FETC Group would suffer currency *translation losses* in both earnings and asset values on a consolidated basis. These translation losses would include not only the reduced Swedish krona value of Asian currency financial results, but also the reduced equity value of the Asian businesses themselves. This was the reduced Swedish krona value of the firm's original equity investments in its Asian businesses as recorded in consolidated equity.

FETC had pursued a relatively common practice of hedging its (corporate) net equity investment in its subsidiaries (an asset) by borrowing in the currency of the subsidiary (a liability). But FETC had borrowed U.S. dollars, not Thai baht or Malaysian ringgit, in the belief that these currencies would maintain their pegs to the U.S. dollar. However, FETC was now realizing substantial equity losses.

Third, the *operating exposure* of the firm, the firm's changing long term competitiveness as a result of the currency changes, was still unknown. The currency crisis had already caused the World Bank and IMF to intervene in the region in the hopes of preventing a general recession. Regardless, it appeared East Asia was headed for recession. The consumer product and graphics units were already finding themselves squeezed as a result of rising import costs. And local competitors were gaining lost market share.

Of immediate need in the eyes of Karlsen was the firming-up of the Group's many working capital lines with banks. The banks were repeatedly denying expanded working capital lines, even for units with growing sales. The Kuala Lumpur and Singapore units had both started lagging intra-firm payments due to capital shortfalls. Currency charges were also rising as all intra-firm payments were required to be in U.S. dollars. More scheduled payments were not occurring as promised.

FETC's Second Profit Warning: November 21, 1997

Jan Karlsen concluded that with the continually declining earnings in the Core Business segments there was little choice but to go public with a second profit warning.

> FETC's Management has evaluated the consequences of the crisis in a number of Asian financial markets, and the impact the recession in several Asian countries has on FETC's businesses. Assuming that conditions in our main markets are unchanged for the balance of the year, FETC expects a loss after tax of about SKK 300 million in 1997.

It now appeared that management had no choice but to take rather drastic measures if FETC was to have hopes of returning to profitability within the near term. Erickson and Karlsen returned to a topic of constant debate between them, the potential liquidation of FETC's non-core businesses. Erickson wanted to liquidate them immediately, at any price. This would generate additional capital for the reduction of corporate debt loads and signal shareholders that management was taking positive actions in the crisis. Karlsen was more reluctant to sell-off these other units quite yet.

An emergency meeting between the senior management team and institutional investors had concluded with the agreed expectation that the Group would return positive results by the second half of 1998. The first profit warning of the year had left the share price at about SKK80 (see Exhibit 3). As Jan Karl Karlsen entered the Kuala Lumpur hotel meeting room, still focusing on the three C's of *cash flow, confidence,* and *control,* he consciously changed his thoughts from Swedish to English. He knew there were two sets of issues he had to address: (1) what FETC's corporate outlook was from the Stockholm perspective; and (2) what actions were needed immediately in the regional business units.

Exhibit 3   *FETC's Share Price on the Stockholm Stock Exchange, 1988–96 (end of year)*

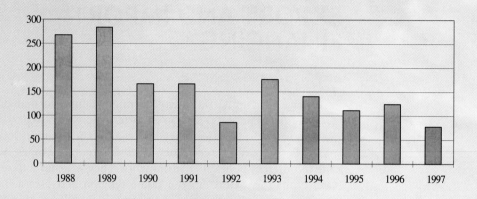

Note: 1997 share price as of November 21, 1997.

CHAPTER 20

EXPORT AND IMPORT FINANCING

International trade must work around a fundamental dilemma. Imagine an importer and an exporter who would like to do business with one another. They live in different countries located far apart. They have never met. They speak different languages. They operate in different political environments. They worship different gods (each capitalizes "God" in the home religion and uses a lowercase "god" for foreign religions!). They come from cultures that have different standards for honoring obligations to other persons and different ways to settle disputes. They both know that if they default on an obligation, the other party will have a hard time catching up to seek redress. Although it might be too harsh to say they don't trust one another, each has perfectly valid reasons for being very cautious in dealing with the other.

Because of the distance between the two, it is not possible to simultaneously hand over goods with one hand and accept payment with the other. The importer would prefer the arrangement at the top of Exhibit 20.1, while the exporter's preference is shown at the bottom.

The fundamental dilemma of being unwilling to trust a stranger in a foreign land is solved by using a highly respected bank as intermediary. A greatly simplified view is described in Exhibit 20.2. In this simplified view, the importer obtains the bank's promise to pay on its behalf, knowing that the exporter will trust the bank. The bank's promise to pay is called a *letter of credit*.

The exporter ships the merchandise to the importer's country. Title to the merchandise is given to the bank on a document called an *order bill of lading*. The exporter asks the bank to pay for the goods, and the bank does so. The document to request payment is a *sight draft*. The bank, having paid for the goods, now passes title to the importer, whom the bank trusts. At that time or later, depending on their agreement, the importer reimburses the bank.

Financial managers of MNEs must understand these three basic documents—in part because their firms will often trade with unaffiliated

| Exhibit 20.1 | *The Mechanics of Import and Export* |

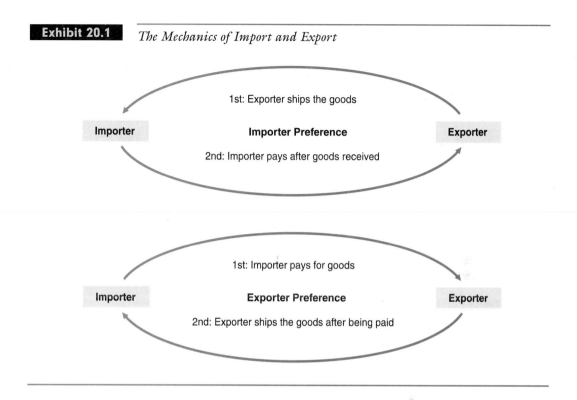

parties, but also because the system of documentation provides a source of short-term capital that can be drawn upon even when shipments are to sister affiliates.

BENEFITS OF THE SYSTEM

The three key documents and their interaction will be described in the following pages. They constitute a system developed and modified over centuries to protect both importer and exporter from the risk of noncompletion and foreign exchange risk, as well as to provide a means of financing.

⑂ Protection against Risk of Noncompletion

As stated above, once importer and exporter agree on terms, the seller usually prefers to maintain legal title to the goods until paid, or at least until assured of payment. The buyer, however, will be reluctant to pay before receiving the goods, or at least before receiving title to them. Each wants assurance that the other party will complete its portion of the transaction. The letter of credit, sight draft, and bill of lading are part of a system carefully constructed to determine who bears the financial loss if one of the parties defaults at any time.

| Exhibit 20.2 | *The Bank as the Import/Export Intermediary* |

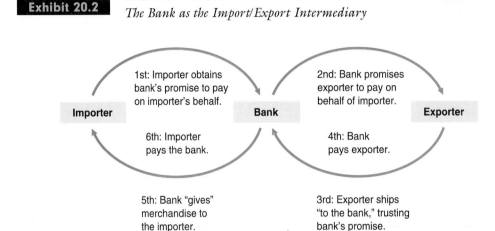

))) Protection against Foreign Exchange Risk

In international trade, foreign exchange risk arises from transaction exposure. If the transaction requires payment in the exporter's currency, the importer carries the foreign exchange risk. If the transaction calls for payment in the importer's currency, the exporter has the foreign exchange risk.

Transaction exposure can be hedged by the techniques described in Chapter 6, but in order to hedge, the exposed party must be certain that payment of a specified amount will be made on a particular date. The three key documents described in this chapter ensure both amount and time of payment and thus lay the groundwork for effective hedging.

The risk of noncompletion and foreign exchange risk are most important when the international trade is episodic, with no outstanding agreement for recurring shipments and no sustained relationship between buyer and seller. When the import/export relationship is of a recurring nature, as in the case of manufactured goods shipped weekly or monthly to a final assembly or retail outlet in another country, and when it is between countries whose currencies are considered strong, the exporter may well bill the importer on open account after a normal credit check. Banks provide credit information and collection services outside of the system of processing drafts drawn against letters of credit.

))) Financing the Trade

Most international trade involves a time lag during which funds are tied up while the merchandise is in transit. Once the risks of noncompletion and of exchange rate changes are disposed of, banks are willing to finance goods in transit. A bank can finance goods in transit, as well as goods held for sale, based on the key documents, without exposing itself to questions about the quality of the merchandise or other physical aspects of the shipment.

In the remainder of this chapter we will examine the letter of credit, the draft, the bill of lading, and a few additional documents that support these key documents. We will also discuss government programs to encourage exports and countertrade, which is a type of barter system.

LETTER OF CREDIT

A *letter of credit*, abbreviated L/C, is an instrument issued by a bank at the request of an importer, in which the bank promises to pay a beneficiary upon presentation of documents specified in the letter of credit. In international trade a letter of credit is sometimes referred to as a *commercial letter of credit*, a *documentary letter of credit*, or simply a *credit*. A letter of credit reduces the risk of noncompletion, since the bank agrees to pay against documents rather than actual merchandise. The relationship between the three parties can be seen in Exhibit 20.3.

))) Typical Transaction

Although details vary, depending on the type of letter of credit and its provisions, the following transaction is typical. An importer (buyer) and exporter (seller) agree on a transaction and the importer applies to its local bank for the issuance of a letter of credit. The importer's bank issues a letter of credit based on its assessment of the importer's creditworthiness, or the bank might require a cash deposit

| Exhibit 20.3 | *Parties of a Letter of Credit* |

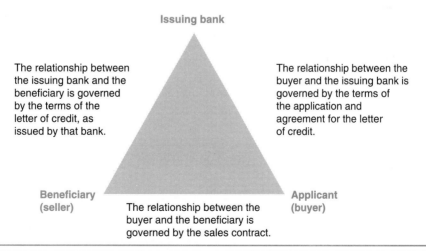

Source: First National Bank of Chicago, *Financing U.S. Exports*, compiled by Patricia A. Ferris, January 1975, p. 21.

or other collateral from the importer in advance. The importer's bank will want to know the type of transaction, the amount of money involved, and what documents must accompany the draft that will be drawn against the letter of credit.

If the importer's bank is satisfied with the credit standing of the applicant, it will issue a letter of credit guaranteeing to pay for the merchandise if shipped in accordance with the instructions and conditions contained in the credit. Exhibit 20.4 shows a letter of credit issued by Bank of America (Asia), Ltd., in Hong Kong on the application of Shing Hing Paper Merchants, Ltd. The letter of credit is for the importing into Hong Kong of a shipment of I.P. bleached MF bag paper worth US$33,400.00, being purchased from ABC Electronics Corporation in Palisades Park, New Jersey. The letter of credit specifies the documents that must accompany a draft drawn against the credit: commercial invoice in triplicate, packing list issued by beneficiary, a full set of original clean shipped "on board" ocean bills of lading issued by a shipping company, plus two non-negotiable copies made out to the order of Bank of America (Asia), Ltd.

At this point the credit of Bank of America (Asia) has been substituted for that of the Shing Hing Paper Merchants, and the letter of credit becomes a financial contract between Bank of America (Asia) and the designated beneficiary, ABC Electronics Corporation of New Jersey. This financial contract is a separate transaction from the sale of the merchandise. If the terms of the letter of credit are met, any payment problems that develop at a later date are of concern only to the importer and the issuing bank. All other parties to the transaction may rely on the bank's credit without regard to the financial status of the importer.

The importer's bank issuing the letter of credit sends the document to an "advising bank" in the exporter's country, in this case to BankAmerica International in New York City, which will advise the exporter (the beneficiary) of the establishment of a letter of credit in the beneficiary's name. Procedures also exist for letters of credit to be sent by tele-transmission. In such cases, the tele-transmission is deemed to be the operative letter of credit unless a statement to the contrary is included. Such a contrary statement might be, "Full details to follow."

After shipping the merchandise, the exporter draws a draft against the issuing bank in accordance with the terms of the letter of credit, attaches the required documents, and presents the draft to its own bank for payment. At this point different combinations of events are possible. In the most straightforward case, the exporter's bank will receive the draft and accompanying documents and forward them to the bank of the importer that issued the credit. If all the terms and conditions expressed on the letter of credit have been complied with and the required documents are attached, the importer's bank will honor the draft, paying the exporter's bank or promising to pay after a period of time (60 days in the example in Exhibit 20.4). When the exporter's bank receives the funds, it passes them on to the exporter.

The importer's bank, in turn, collects from the importer in accordance with the terms agreed upon at the time the letter of credit was opened. The importer

Exhibit 20.4   *Letter of Credit*

美 國 亞 洲 銀 行
Bank of America (Asia) Ltd.   PAGE   1   Date 02NOV1993

CREDIT NUMBER OF ISSUING BANK YLC35666
CREDIT NUMBER OF ADVISING BANK

ADVISING BANK   BANKAMERICA INTERNATIONAL
                335 MADISON AVENUE
                NEW YORK U.S.A.

BENEFICIARY   ABC ELECTRONICS CORPORATION
                123 GRAND AVENUE
                PALISADES PARK
                NEW JERSEY 07650 U.S.A.

APPLICANT   SHING HING PAPER MERCHANTS LTD.
                168 PRINCE EDWARD ROAD
                KOWLOON HONG KONG

AMOUNT USD*****33,400.00 U.S. DOLLARS THIRTY THREE THOUSAND
                        FOUR HUNDRED ONLY

EXPIRY DATE DECEMBER 29 1993   IN THE COUNTRY OF BENEFICIARY

LATEST SHIPMENT DATE DECEMBER 15 1993

WE HEREBY ISSUE IN YOUR FAVOUR THIS IRREVOCABLE DOCUMENTARY
CREDIT WHICH IS AVAILABLE BY NEGOTIATION OF YOUR DRAFT(S) AT
60 DAYS SIGHT DRAWN ON L/C ISSUING BANK
BEARING THE CLAUSE DRAWN UNDER DOCUMENTARY CREDIT NO. YLC35666
OF BANK OF AMERICA (ASIA) LTD., HONG KONG ACCOMPANIED BY
THE FOLLOWING DOCUMENTS :

SIGNED COMMERCIAL INVOICE IN TRIPLICATE.

PACKING LIST ISSUED BY BENEFICIARY.

FULL SET OF ORIGINAL CLEAN SHIPPED 'ON BOARD' OCEAN BILLS OF
LADING ISSUED BY SHIPPING COMPANY PLUS TWO NON-NEGOTIABLE COPIES
MADE OUT TO ORDER OF BANK OF AMERICA (ASIA) LTD., HONG KONG
MARKED 'FREIGHT PREPAID' AND NOTIFY APPLICANT. FORWARDER'S B/L
NOT ACCEPTABLE.

EVIDENCING SHIPMENT OF
I.P. BLEACHED MF BAG PAPER, DIAMETER : 40'', CORE : 3''
@USD835.00 PER MT COMPRISING :
1) 5MT SUBSTANCE : 81GSM
2) 10MT SUBSTANCE : 98GSM
3) 25MT SUBSTANCE : 114GSM
AS PER SALE CONTRACT NO. IM-228

SHIPMENT FROM U.S.A. TO HONG KONG   C AND F
PARTIAL SHIPMENTS PROHIBITED
TRANSHIPMENT PROHIBITED

SPECIAL INSTRUCTIONS :

ALL BANKING CHARGES OUTSIDE HONG KONG ARE FOR ACCOUNT OF
BENEFICIARY.

ORIGINAL FOR BENEFICIARY

                    2   ..... TO BE CONTINUED ON PAGE   2.....
This document consists of   pages.
Bills Department: 31/F, 9 Queen's Road Central, Hong Kong. • SWIFT: SPAB HK HH • Telex: 73471 BOFAA HX • Cable Address: "BOFAAHK" • Fax: 845 307

Exhibit 20.4   *Letter of Credit (continued)*

美 國 亞 洲 銀 行
Bank of America (Asia) Ltd.   PAGE   2   Date 02NOV1993

THIS PAGE IS ATTACHED TO AND FORMS PART OF CREDIT NO   YLC35666

INSURANCE TO BE COVERED BY BUYER.

SHIPMENT DATE PRIOR TO L/C ISSUING DATE NOT ACCEPTABLE.

5 PCT MORE OR LESS BOTH IN QUANTITY OF EACH ITEM OF GOODS
AND CREDIT AMOUNT ACCEPTABLE.

UNLESS OTHERWISE STATED, ALL DOCUMENTS MUST BE MANUALLY SIGNED
AND DOCUMENTS IN PHOTOCOPIES NOT ACCEPTABLE.

THIS CREDIT IS NOT RESTRICTED TO ANY BANK FOR NEGOTIATION.

AT MATURITY, WE SHALL REMIT THE FACE AMOUNT OF DRAFT TO
THE NEGOTIATING BANK ACCORDING TO THEIR INSTRUCTIONS.

ALL DOCUMENTS MUST BE SENT TO BANK OF AMERICA (ASIA) LTD.
HONG KONG BY ONE REGISTERED AIRMAIL.

A DISCREPANCY FEE OF USD30.00 WILL BE DEDUCTED FROM THE
PROCEEDS ON EACH SET OF DOCUMENTS PRESENTED WITH
DISCREPANCY(IES), EVEN IF THE L/C INDICATES THAT ALL BANKING
CHARGES ARE FOR ACCOUNT OF APPLICANT.

WE HEREBY ENGAGE WITH DRAWERS AND/OR BONA FIDE HOLDERS THAT
DRAFTS DRAWN AND NEGOTIATED IN CONFORMITY WITH THE TERMS OF THIS
CREDIT AND SUBSEQUENT AMENDMENT(S) IF ANY WILL BE DULY HONOURED
ON PRESENTATION AND THAT DRAFTS ACCEPTED WITHIN THE TERMS OF THIS
CREDIT WILL BE DULY HONOURED AT MATURITY.
THE AMOUNT OF EACH DRAFT MUST BE ENDORSED ON THE REVERSE OF THIS
CREDIT BY THE NEGOTIATING BANK.   EXCEPT SO FAR AS OTHERWISE
EXPRESSLY STATED, THIS DOCUMENTARY CREDIT IS SUBJECT TO THE
'UNIFORM CUSTOMS AND PRACTICE FOR DOCUMENTARY CREDITS' (1993
REVISION) BY THE INTERNATIONAL CHAMBER OF COMMERCE PUBLICATION
NO. 500.
THE ADVISING BANK IS REQUESTED TO NOTIFY THE BENEFICIARY
WITHOUT ADDING THEIR CONFIRMATION.

AUTHORIZED SIGNATURE(S)

ORIGINAL FOR BENEFICIARY

SAMPLE COPY

This document consists of   2   pages.

Bills Department: 31/F, 9 Queen's Road Central, Hong Kong • SWIFT: SPAB HK HH • Telex: 73471 BOFAA HX • Cable Address: "BOFAAHK" • Fax: 845 3073 might pay at once in order to obtain the documents, including the order bill of lading that is needed to obtain physical possession of the merchandise. Alternatively, the bank may release the documents to the importer, and the importer may promise to pay at some later date, usually under a trust receipt arrangement.

))) Essence of the Agreement

The essence of a letter of credit is the promise of the issuing bank to pay *against specified documents*, which must accompany any draft drawn against the credit. The letter of credit is not a guarantee of the underlying commercial transaction. Indeed, the letter of credit is a separate transaction from any sales or other contracts on which it might be based. In a true letter-of-credit transaction, the following five conditions will all hold with respect to the issuing bank:

1. The issuing bank must receive a fee or other valid business consideration for issuing the letter of credit.

2. The bank's letter of credit must contain a specified expiration date or a definite maturity.

3. The bank's commitment must have a stated maximum amount of money.

4. The bank's obligation to pay must arise only on the presentation of specific documents, and the bank must not be called on to determine disputed questions of fact or law.

5. The bank's customer must have an unqualified obligation to reimburse the bank on the same condition as the bank has paid.

))) Variations in the Terms of a Letter of Credit

Most commercial letters of credit are *documentary*, meaning that certain documents must be included with any drafts drawn under their terms. Required documents usually include an order bill of lading, a commercial invoice, and any of the following: consular invoice, insurance certificate or policy, certificate of origin, weight list, certificate of analysis, packing list. Commercial letters of credit are also classified as follows.

Irrevocable versus Revocable. An irrevocable letter of credit obligates the issuing bank to honor drafts drawn in compliance with the credit and can be neither canceled nor modified without the consent of all parties, including in particular the beneficiary (exporter). A revocable letter of credit can be canceled or amended at any time before payment; it is intended to serve as a means of arranging payment but not as a guarantee of payment.

Confirmed versus Unconfirmed. A letter of credit issued by one bank can be confirmed by another, in which case both banks are obligated to honor drafts drawn in compliance with the credit. An unconfirmed letter of credit is the obligation only of the issuing bank. An exporter is likely to want a foreign bank's letter of credit confirmed by a domestic bank when the exporter has doubts about the foreign bank's ability to pay. Such doubts can arise when the exporter is unsure of the financial standing of the foreign bank, or when political or economical conditions in the foreign country are unstable.

Revolving versus Nonrevolving. Most letters of credit are nonrevolving; they are valid for one transaction only. Under some circumstances, a revolving credit is issued. A $10,000 revolving weekly credit means that the beneficiary is authorized to draw drafts up to $10,000 each week until the credit expires. The period of a revolving credit might be daily, weekly, or monthly. Because the maximum exposure under an irrevocable revolving credit is very great (the buyer cannot stop its obligation to pay for future shipments even if it is dissatisfied with the merchandise), most revolving credits are issued in revocable form. A revolving credit may be noncumulative, in which case any amount not used by the beneficiary during the specified period may not be drawn against in a later period, or it may be *cumulative*, in which case undrawn amounts carry over to future periods.

⟫⟫ Issuers of Letters of Credit

From an exporter's point of view, a documentary letter of credit is one of the following:

1. An irrevocable letter of credit issued by a domestic bank.
2. An irrevocable letter of credit issued by a foreign bank and confirmed irrevocably by a domestic bank, or on occasion confirmed by a third-country foreign bank.
3. An irrevocable letter of credit issued by a foreign bank without the confirmation of a domestic bank. In this situation the domestic bank simply transmits information (when the letter is opened) and forwards drafts for collection but does not guarantee payment.
4. A revocable letter of credit established to arrange for payment.

Exporters naturally prefer types 1 and 2 above, because they need look no further than a bank in their own country for compliance with the terms of the letter of credit. Although a letter of credit issued by a foreign bank alone (type 3) might well be of the highest esteem, many exporters, especially smaller firms, are not in a position to evaluate or deal with foreign banks directly if difficulties arise.

Every irrevocable letter of credit must indicate an expiration date beyond which documents for payment or acceptance will not be accepted. Documents, such as drafts or bills of lading, must be presented within a reasonable time after issue, for if there is undue delay, the bank may refuse to accept them.

⟫⟫ Advantages and Disadvantages of Letters of Credit

The primary advantage of a letter of credit is that the exporter can sell against a bank's promise to pay, rather than the promise of a commercial firm. The exporter is also in a more secure position as to the availability of foreign exchange to pay for the sale; banks are more likely to be aware of foreign exchange conditions and rules than is the importing firm itself. If the importing country should change its foreign exchange rules during the course of a transaction, the government is likely to allow already outstanding bank letters of credit to be honored for fear of throwing its own domestic banks into international disrepute. Of course, if the letter of credit is confirmed by a bank in the exporter's country, the exporter avoids any problem of blocked foreign exchange.

An exporter may find that an order backed by an irrevocable letter of credit will facilitate obtaining domestic pre-export financing. If the exporter's reputation for delivery is good, a local bank may lend funds to process and prepare the merchandise for shipment. Once the merchandise has been shipped in compliance with the terms and conditions of the credit, payment for the business transaction is made and funds will be generated to repay the pre-export loan.

The major advantage to the importer of a letter of credit is that the importer need not pay out funds until the documents have arrived at a local port or airfield and unless all conditions stated in the credit have been fulfilled. The main disadvantages are the fee charged by the importer's bank for issuing its letter of credit and the possibility that the letter of credit reduces the importer's borrowing line of credit from its bank.

))) Liabilities of Banks under Letters of Credit

When banks issue letters of credit they incur certain obligations that are specified in detail in *Uniform Customs and Practices for Documentary Credits*, published by the International Chamber of Commerce.[1]

The basic nature of a letter of credit is that the bank is obligated to pay against documents, not actual goods. Thus, banks must carefully examine all documents to be sure that they are in accordance with the original terms and conditions of the letter of credit. Banks are not liable for defects in the documents themselves, however, as long as any defect was not apparent on the face of the document. Thus, for example, the bank is not responsible for detecting false documents; for verifying that the quantities, quality, weights, or condition of the goods are other than what is stated on the documents; or for validating the good faith and performance of any of the parties to the underlying transaction. The bank is not responsible if messages are delayed, lost, or mistranslated, and it is not responsible for the consequences of such events as strikes, lockouts, riots, or war.

DRAFT

A *draft*, sometimes called a *bill of exchange (B/E)* or *first of exchange*, is the instrument normally used in international commerce to effect payment. A draft is simply an order written by an exporter (seller) instructing an importer (buyer) or its agent to pay a specified amount of money at a specified time. (A personal check is another type of draft; the drawer writes an order to a bank to pay a specified amount of money on demand to the order of a designated beneficiary.)

The person or business initiating the draft is known as the *maker, drawer,* or *originator.* Normally, this is the exporter who sells and ships the merchandise. The party to whom the draft is addressed is the *drawee.* The drawee is asked to *honor* the draft, that is, to pay the amount requested according to the stated terms. In commercial transactions the drawee is either the buyer, in which case the draft is called a *trade draft,* or the buyer's bank, in which case the draft is called a *bank draft.* Bank drafts are usually drawn according to the terms of a letter of credit. A draft may be drawn as a bearer instrument, or it may designate a person to whom payment is to be made. This person, known as the payee, may be the drawer itself or it may be some other party such as the drawer's bank.

Negotiable Instruments

If properly drawn, drafts can become *negotiable instruments.* As such, they provide a convenient instrument for financing the international movement of the merchandise. To become a negotiable instrument, a draft or bill of exchange must conform to the following requirements:[2]

- It must be in writing and signed by the maker or drawer.
- It must contain an unconditional promise or order to pay a definite sum of money.
- It must be payable on demand or at a fixed or determinable future date.
- It must be payable to order or to bearer.

If a draft is drawn in conformity with the above requirements, a person receiving it with proper endorsements becomes a "holder in due course." This is a privileged legal status that enables the holder to receive payment despite any personal disagreements between drawee and maker about the underlying commercial transaction. If the drawee dishonors the draft, payment must be made to any holder in due course by any prior endorser or by the maker. This clear definition of the rights of parties who hold a negotiable instrument as a holder in due course has contributed significantly to the widespread acceptance of various forms of drafts, including personal checks.

Types of Drafts

Drafts are of two types: sight drafts and time drafts. A *sight draft* is payable on presentation to the drawee; the drawee must pay at once or dishonor the draft. A *time draft,* also called a *usance draft,* allows a delay in payment. It is presented to the drawee, who accepts it by writing or stamping a notice of acceptance on its face. Once accepted, the time draft becomes a promise to pay by the accepting party. When a time draft is drawn on and accepted by a bank, it becomes a *banker's acceptance.* When a time draft is drawn on and accepted by a business firm, it becomes a *trade acceptance.*

A time draft drawn by ABC Electronics Corporation of New Jersey for its export of bleached paper bag against the letter of credit shown earlier is illus-

| **Exhibit 20.5** | *Time Draft and Stamp Indicating Acceptance by Bank* |

No: ___ABC-9330___

Exchange for ___USD33,400.00 U.S.A.___   ___December 10, 1993.___

_____–60–_____ days after sight of this First of Exchange

(Second Unpaid) pay to the order of CHEMICAL BANK, NEW YORK

the sum of Thirty-three thousands four hundred only._____

Value received DRAWN UNDER BANK OF AMERICA (ASIA) LTD.

LETTER OF CREDIT NO. YLC35666 DATED NOVEMBER 2, 1993.

TO: BANK OF AMERICA (ASIA) LTD.   ABC ELECTRONICS CORP.

      HONG KONG   _____

                                        Managing Director

ACCEPTED ON DECEMBER 15, 1993
DUE ON FEBRUARY 15, 1994
PAYABLE AT BANK OF AMERICA (ASIA) LTD.
          HONG KONG

_____
        Authorized Signature

This chop (stamp) on the face of the draft represents the L/C issuing bank's acceptance.

---

trated in Exhibit 20.5. ABC Corporation is instructing Bank of America (Asia) to pay to Chemical Bank, New York, the sum of US$33,400.00 60 days after the draft is first presented to Bank of America (Asia). Chemical Bank is ABC's U.S. banker. When the draft is presented to Bank of America (Asia), that bank will check to see that all terms of the letter of credit have been complied with and will then stamp the face of the draft with the acceptance inscription shown with the draft in Exhibit 20.5. A bank officer will sign, and the draft becomes a bankers' acceptance maturing in 60 days. Because the draft in Exhibit 20.5 was accepted on December 15, 1993, it will mature on February 15, 1994.

The time period of a draft is referred to as its *tenor* or *usance*. For the draft to qualify as a negotiable instrument, and so be attractive to a holder in due course, it must be payable on a fixed or determinable future date. For example, 60 days after sight is a determinable date, such a maturity being established precisely at the time the draft is accepted. However, payment "on arrival of goods" is not determinable, since the date of arrival cannot be known in advance. Indeed, there is no assurance that the goods will arrive at all. Third parties would have no interest in investing in it because they could not be certain they would ever be paid. Note, however, that a non-negotiable acceptance is still a legal device to obtain payment unless a defect exists in the underlying commercial transaction. Thus a non-negotiable draft creates a legal obligation between the original parties without giving third parties (holders in due course) any privileged claim.

Drafts are also classified as clean or documentary. A *clean draft* is an order to pay unaccompanied by any other documents. When it is used in trade, the seller has usually sent the shipping documents directly to the buyer, who thus obtains possession of the merchandise independent of its payment (on a clean sight draft) or acceptance (on a clean time draft). Clean drafts are often used by multinational firms shipping to their own affiliates because matters of trust and credit are not involved. Clean drafts are also used for nontrade remittances, for example, when collection of an outstanding debt is sought. Use of a clean draft puts pressure on a recalcitrant debtor by forcing it to convert an open-account obligation into documentary form. Failure to pay or accept such a draft when presented through a local bank can damage the drawee's reputation.

Most drafts in international trade are *documentary drafts*, which means that various shipping documents are attached to the draft. Payment (for sight drafts) or acceptance (for time drafts) is required to obtain possession of those documents, which are needed in turn to obtain the goods involved in the transaction. If documents are to be delivered to the buyer on payment of the draft, it is known as a "D/P draft"; if the documents are delivered on acceptance, the draft is called a "D/A draft."

))) Bankers' Acceptances

When a draft is accepted by a bank, it becomes a *bankers' acceptance*. As such it is the unconditional promise of that bank to make payment on the draft when it matures. In quality the bankers' acceptance is practically identical to a marketable bank certificate of deposit (CD). The holder of a bankers' acceptance need not wait until maturity to liquidate the investment but may sell the acceptance in the money market, where constant trading in such instruments occurs.

The first owner of the bankers' acceptance created from an international trade transaction will be the exporter, who receives the accepted draft back after the bank has stamped it "accepted." The exporter may hold the acceptance until maturity and then collect. On an acceptance of, say, $100,000 for six months, the exporter would receive the face amount less the bank's acceptance commission of 1.5% per annum:

Face amount of the acceptance	$100,000
Less 1.5% per annum commission for 6 months	−750
Amount received by exporter in 6 months	$ 99,250

Alternatively, the exporter may "discount"—that is, sell at a reduced price—the acceptance to its bank in order to receive funds at once. The exporter will then receive the face amount of the acceptance less both the acceptance fee and the going market rate of discount for bankers' acceptances. If the discount rate were 7% per annum, the exporter would receive the following:

Face amount of the acceptance	$100,000
Less 1.5% per annum commission for 6 months	−750
Less 7% per annum discount rate for 6 months	−3,500
Amount received by exporter at once	$ 95,750

The discounting bank may hold the acceptance in its own portfolio, earning for itself the 7% per annum discount rate, or the acceptance may be resold in the acceptance market to portfolio investors. Investors buying bankers' acceptances provide the funds that finance the underlying commercial transaction.

BILL OF LADING

The third key document for financing international trade is the *bill of lading*, or B/L. The bill of lading is issued to the exporter by a common carrier transporting the merchandise. It serves three purposes: as a receipt, a contract, and a document of title.

As a receipt, the bill of lading indicates that the carrier has received the merchandise described on the face of the document. The carrier is not responsible for ascertaining that the containers hold what is alleged to be their contents, so descriptions of merchandise on bills of lading are usually short and simple. If shipping charges are paid in advance, the bill of lading will usually be stamped "freight paid" or "freight prepaid." If merchandise is shipped collect—a less common procedure internationally than domestically—the carrier maintains a lien on the goods until freight is paid.

As a contract, the bill of lading indicates the obligation of the carrier to provide certain transportation in return for certain charges. Common carriers cannot disclaim responsibility for their negligence through inserting special clauses in a bill of lading. The bill of lading may specify alternative ports in the event that delivery cannot be made to the designated port, or it may specify that the goods will be returned to the exporter at the exporter's expense.

As a document of title, the bill of lading is used to obtain payment or a written promise of payment before the merchandise is released to the importer. The bill of lading can also function as collateral against which funds may be advanced to the exporter by its local bank prior to or during shipment and before final payment by the importer.

)))) Characteristics of the Bill of Lading

Bills of lading are either straight or to order. A *straight bill of lading* provides that the carrier deliver the merchandise to the designated consignee. It is not title to the goods and is not required for the consignee to obtain possession. Because a straight bill of lading is *not* title, it is not good collateral for loans. Therefore, a straight bill of lading is used when the merchandise has been paid for in advance, when the transaction is being financed by the exporter, or when the shipment is to an affiliate.

An *order bill of lading* directs the carrier to deliver the goods to the order of a designated party. An additional inscription may request the carrier to notify someone else of the arrival. The order bill of lading grants title to the merchandise only to the person to whom the document is addressed, and surrender of the order bill of lading is required to obtain the shipment.

The order bill of lading is typically made payable to the order of the exporter, who thus retains title to the goods after they have been handed to the carrier. Title to the merchandise remains with the exporter until payment is received, at which time the exporter endorses the order bill of lading (which is negotiable) in blank or to the party making the payment, usually a bank. The most common procedure would be for payment to be advanced against a documentary draft accompanied by the endorsed order bill of lading. After paying the draft, the exporter's bank forwards the documents through bank clearing channels to the bank of the importer. The importer's bank, in turn, releases the documents to the importer after payment (sight drafts), after acceptance (time drafts addressed to the importer and marked D/A), or after payment terms have been agreed upon (drafts drawn on the importer's bank under provisions of a letter of credit).

))) Variations in the Bill of Lading

A *clean* bill of lading indicates that the goods were received by the carrier in apparently good condition. The carrier is not obligated to check the condition of the merchandise beyond external visual appearance. A *foul* bill of lading indicates that the merchandise appeared to have suffered some damage before being received for shipment. A foul bill of lading lacks complete negotiability.

An *on-board* bill of lading indicates that the merchandise has been placed on board the vessel whose name is designated on the document. This form is preferred to a *received-for-shipment* bill of lading, which allows for the possibility that the goods are sitting on the dock and might remain there for some time. A received-for-shipment bill of lading is not an acceptable document unless it has been specifically authorized in the letter of credit. Similarly, unless authorized otherwise by the letter of credit, banks will refuse to accept *on-deck* bills of lading, indicating that the goods have been stowed on deck. Received-for-shipment bills of lading may be issued when goods are first received on the carrier's premises; they can be converted to an on-board form by an appropriate stamp showing the name of the vessel, the date, and the signature of an official of the carrier.

ADDITIONAL DOCUMENTS

The draft, the bill of lading, and the letter of credit are the major documents required in most international transactions. However, additional documents may be needed as a condition of the letter of credit for honoring a draft. The more common additional documents include those described below.

A signed *commercial invoice* is issued by the seller and contains a precise description of the merchandise. Unit prices, financial terms of sale, and amount due from the buyer are indicated, as are shipping conditions related to charges, such as "FOB" (free on board), "FAS" (free alongside), "C & F" (cost and freight), or "CIF" (cost, insurance, freight).

Insurance documents must be as specified in the letter of credit and must be issued by insurance companies or their agents. The insurance may be issued to the exporter, who must then endorse the policy to the importer, or it may be issued in the name of the importer. The document must be expressed in the same currency as the credit and must not be dated later than the date of shipment carried on the face of the shipping documents. Insurance must be of types and for risks specified in the letter of credit.

Consular invoices are issued by the consulate of the importing country to provide customs information and statistics for that country and to help prevent false declarations of value. The consular invoice may be combined with a certificate of origin of the goods.

Certificates of analysis may be required to ascertain that certain specifications such as weight, purity, sanitation have been met. These conditions may be required by health or other officials of the importing country—especially in the case of foods and drugs—or they may be insisted on by the importer as assurance that it is receiving what it ordered. The certificates may be issued by government or private organizations, as specified in the letter of credit.

Packing lists may be required so that the contents of containers can be identified, either for customs purposes or for importer identification of the contents of separate containers.

An *export declaration* is a document prepared by the exporter to assist the government to prepare export statistics.

DOCUMENTATION IN A TYPICAL TRADE TRANSACTION

A trade transaction could conceivably be handled in many ways. The transaction that would best illustrate the interactions of the various documents would be an export financed under a documentary commercial letter of credit, requiring an order bill of lading, with the exporter collecting via a time draft accepted by the importer's bank. Such a transaction is illustrated in Exhibit 20.6

1. Importer places an order for the goods with Exporter, inquiring if Exporter would be willing to ship under a letter of credit.

Exhibit 20.6   *Typical Trade Transaction*

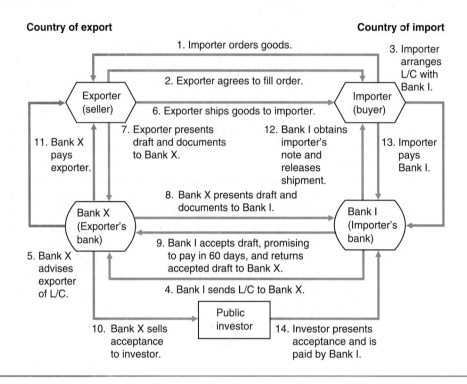

Country of export

Country of import

1. Importer orders goods.

2. Exporter agrees to fill order.

3. Importer arranges L/C with Bank I.

Exporter (seller)

6. Exporter ships goods to importer.

Importer (buyer)

11. Bank X pays exporter.

7. Exporter presents draft and documents to Bank X.

12. Bank I obtains importer's note and releases shipment.

13. Importer pays Bank I.

8. Bank X presents draft and documents to Bank I.

Bank X (Exporter's bank)

Bank I (Importer's bank)

9. Bank I accepts draft, promising to pay in 60 days, and returns accepted draft to Bank X.

5. Bank X advises exporter of L/C.

4. Bank I sends L/C to Bank X.

Public investor

10. Bank X sells acceptance to investor.

14. Investor presents acceptance and is paid by Bank I.

2. Exporter agrees to ship under a letter of credit and specifies relevant information such as prices and terms.

3. Importer applies to its bank, Bank I, for a letter of credit to be issued in favor of Exporter for the merchandise Importer wishes to buy.

4. Bank I issues the letter of credit in favor of Exporter and sends it to Bank X, Exporter's bank, or to a correspondent bank in the country of export.

5. Bank X advises Exporter of the opening of a letter of credit in the Exporter's favor. Bank X may or may not confirm the letter of credit to add its own guarantee to the document.

6. Exporter ships the goods to Importer.

7. Exporter presents a time draft to Bank X, drawn on Bank I in accordance with Bank I's letter of credit and accompanied by such other documents as required, including the order bill of lading. Exporter endorses the order bill of lading in blank so that title to the goods goes with the holder of the documents—Bank X at this point in the transaction.

8. Bank X presents the draft and documents to Bank I. Bank I accepts the draft, taking possession of the documents and promising to pay the now-accepted draft at maturity (60 days).

9. Bank I returns the accepted draft to Bank X. Alternatively, Bank X could have asked Bank I to accept and discount the draft; then Bank I would have returned cash less a discount fee rather than the accepted draft to Bank X.

10. Bank X, having received back the accepted draft, now a bankers' acceptance, must choose between several alternatives. Bank X may sell the acceptance in the open market at a discount to a portfolio investor. The investor will typically be a corporation or financial institution with excess cash it wants to invest for a short period of time. Bank X may also hold the acceptance in its own portfolio.

11. If Bank X has discounted the acceptance with Bank I (mentioned in step 9 above) or has discounted it in the local money market, Bank X will transfer the proceeds less any fees and discount to Exporter. Another possibility would be for Exporter itself to take possession of the acceptance, hold it for 60 days, and present it for collection. Normally, however, exporters prefer to receive the discounted cash value of the acceptance at once rather than wait for the acceptance to mature and receive a slightly greater amount of cash.

12. Bank I notifies Importer of the arrival of the documents. Importer signs a note or makes some other agreed plan to pay the bank for the merchandise in 60 days, and Bank I releases the underlying documents so that Importer can obtain physical possession of the shipment.

13. In 60 days Bank I receives from Importer funds to pay the maturing draft.

14. On the same day—the 60th day after acceptance—the holder of the matured acceptance presents it for payment and receives its face value. The holder may present it directly to Bank I, as in the diagram, or return it to Bank X and have Bank X collect it through normal banking channels.

GOVERNMENT PROGRAMS TO HELP FINANCE EXPORTS

Governments of most export-oriented industrialized countries have special financial institutions that provide some form of subsidized credit to their own national exporters. These export finance institutions offer terms that are better than those generally available from the competitive private sector. Thus, domestic taxpayers are subsidizing lower financial costs for foreign buyers in order to create employment and maintain a technological edge. The most important institutions usually offer export credit insurance and a government supported bank for export financing.

))) Export Credit Insurance

The exporter who insists on cash or letter of credit payment for foreign shipments is likely to lose orders to competitors from other countries that provide more favorable credit terms. Better credit terms are often made possible by means of *export credit insurance,* which provides assurance to the exporter or the exporter's bank that, should the foreign customer default on payment, the insurance company will pay for a major portion of the loss. Because of the availability of export credit insurance, commercial banks are willing to provide medium- to long-term financing (five to seven years) for exports.

Importers prefer that the exporter purchase export credit insurance to pay for nonperformance risk by the importer. In this way the importer does not need to pay to have a letter of credit issued and does not reduce his or her credit line.

Since credit has become an increasingly competitive component of the terms of export selling, governments of at least 35 countries have established entities that insure credit risks for exports. Details of these systems appear in the various editions of the *World's Principal Export Credit Insurance Systems,* published by the International Export Credits Institute, New York.

Competition between nations to increase exports by lengthening the period for which credit transactions can be insured could lead to a credit war and to unsound credit decisions. To prevent such an unhealthy development, a number of leading trading nations joined together in 1934 to create the Berne Union (officially, the Union d'Assureurs des Credits Internationaux) for the purpose of establishing a voluntary international understanding on export credit terms. The Berne Union recommends maximum credit terms for many items, including, for example, heavy capital goods (five years), light capital goods (three years), and consumer durable goods (one year).

Export Credit Insurance in the United States

In the United States, export credit insurance is provided by the Foreign Credit Insurance Association (FCIA). This is an unincorporated association of private commercial insurance companies operating in cooperation with the Export-Import Bank, an independent agency of the U.S. government.

The FCIA provides policies protecting U.S. exporters against the risk of nonpayment by foreign debtors as a result of commercial and political risks. Losses due to commercial risk are those that result from the insolvency or protracted payment default of the buyer. Political losses arise from actions of governments beyond the control of buyer or seller. FCIA political coverage generally protects against the following events.

- A buyer's inability to legally obtain U.S. dollars or other approved currencies and to transfer those funds to the insured

- Loss of transportation or insurance charges incurred after shipment because of the politically caused interruption of a voyage outside the United States, when it is not practical to recover the charges from the buyer

- The occurrence after shipment of any of the following, when it is not the fault of the buyer, issuing bank, or the insured or its agents:

1. Cancellation or nonrenewal of an export license, or the imposition of restrictions on the export of products that were not subject to license or restriction prior to shipment

2. Cancellation of authority to import the products of the buyer's country

3. Imposition of laws that prevent import of the products into the buyer's country, or that prevent exchange of local currency into U.S. dollars or some other approved currency

- The occurrence of any of the following after shipment but on or before the date of default:

    1. War, hostilities, civil war, rebellion, revolution, insurrection, civil commotion, or similar disturbances

    2. Governmentally authorized requisition, expropriation, confiscation of, or intervention in, the specific business of the buyer, issuing bank, or guarantors

Foreign Credit Insurance Association (FCIA) Policies

The FCIA offers short-term policies, involving payment terms up to 180 days, and medium-term policies, with payment terms from 181 days to 5 years. Coverage up to seven years may be arranged on a case-by-case basis for aircraft, marine, and other sales, if necessary to meet government-supported foreign competition. Coverage is for U.S. goods produced and shipped from the United States during the policy period and applies to credit sales to a foreign buyer or to export letters of credit opened by a foreign issuing bank.

Generally, commercial coverage ranges from 90% to 95% and political coverage ranges from 95% to 100%, depending on the type of policy and options chosen by the exporter. Premiums depend on a number of variables, including the length of credit terms being offered, the exporter's previous experience with export sales, the risk associated with the countries to which goods are shipped or services are rendered, and the spread of risk covered by the policy.

Export-Import Bank

The Export-Import Bank (also called Eximbank) is an independent agency of the U.S. government, established in 1934 to stimulate and facilitate the foreign trade of the United States. Interestingly, the Eximbank was originally created primarily to facilitate exports to the Soviet Union.

In 1945 the Eximbank was rechartered "to aid in financing and to facilitate exports and imports and the exchange of commodities between the United States and any foreign country or the agencies or nationals thereof." The bank has $1 billion of nonvoting stock paid in by the U.S. Treasury and has the option of borrowing an additional $6 billion from the Treasury if and when needed.

The Eximbank facilitates the financing of U.S. exports through various loan guarantee and insurance programs. The Eximbank guarantees repayment of medium-term (181 days to 5 years) and long-term (5 years to 10 years) export loans extended by U.S. banks to foreign borrowers.

The Eximbank's medium- and long-term, direct-lending operation is based on participation with private sources of funds. Essentially, the Eximbank lends dollars to borrowers outside the United States for the purchase of U.S. goods and services. Proceeds of such loans are paid to U.S. suppliers. The loans themselves are repaid with interest in dollars to the Eximbank. The Eximbank requires private participation in these direct loans in order to: (1) ensure that it complements rather than competes with private sources of export financing; (2) spread its resources more broadly; and (3) ensure that private financial institutions will continue to provide export credit.

The Eximbank also guarantees lease transactions; finances the costs involved in the preparation by U.S. firms of engineering, planning, and feasibility studies for non-U.S. clients on large capital projects; and supplies counseling for exporters, banks, or others needing help in finding financing for U.S. goods.

COUNTERTRADE

The word *countertrade* refers to a variety of international trade arrangements in which goods and services are exported by a manufacturer with compensation linked to that manufacturer accepting imports of other goods and services. In other words, an export sale is tied by contract to an import. The countertrade may take place at the same time as the original export, in which case credit is not an issue; or the countertrade may take place later, in which case financing becomes important.

Conventional wisdom is that countertrade takes place with countries having strict foreign exchange controls, countertrade being a way to circumvent those controls; and that countertrade is more likely to take place with countries having low creditworthiness. One study found to the contrary.[3] The authors found that (1) countries that ban inward foreign direct investment have a significantly higher propensity to engage in countertrade, (2) the higher the level of political risk (i.e., environmental volatility) perceived by foreign investors, the higher the level of countertrade, and (3) the more extensive the degree of state planning, the greater the level of countertrade.

Exhibit 20.7 organizes countertrade into two broad categories—transactions that avoid the use of money, shown along the bottom on the right, and transactions that use money or credit but impose reciprocal commitments, shown along the bottom on the left.

Three types of transactions avoid the use of money:

Simple Barter. *Simple barter* is a direct exchange of physical goods between two parties. It is a one-time transaction carried out under a single contract that specifies both the goods to be delivered and the goods to be received. The two parts of the transaction occur at the same time, and no money is exchanged. Money

Exhibit 20.7   *Classification of Forms of Countertrade*

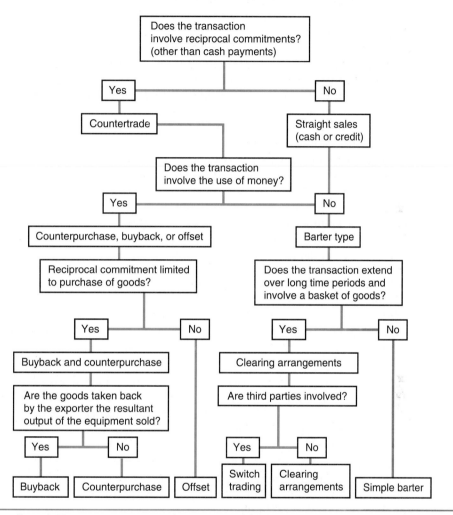

Source: Jean-François Hennart, "Some Empirical Dimensions of Countertrade." *Journal of International Business Studies*, Second Quarter 1990, p. 245. Reprinted with permission.

may, however, be used as the numeraire by which the two values are established and the quantities of each good are determined.

Clearing Arrangements. In a *clearing arrangement*, each party agrees to purchase a specific (usually equal) value of goods and services from the other, with the cost of the transactions debited to a special account. At the end of the trading period any residual imbalances may be cleared by shipping additional goods or by a hard currency payment. In effect, the addition of a clearing agreement to a barter scheme allows for a time lag between barter components. Thus, credit facilitates eventual matching of the transactions.

Switch Trading. *Switch trading* involves transferring use of bilateral balances from one country to another. For example, an original export from, say, Canada to Romania is paid for with a balance deposited in a clearing account in Romania. Although the clearing account may be measured in Canadian dollars or any other currency, the balance can be used only to purchase goods from Romania. The original Canadian exporter might buy unrelated goods from Romania, or it might sell the clearing balance at a discount to a "switch trader" who in turn purchases goods from Romania for sale elsewhere.

Three types of transactions use money or credit but impose reciprocal commitments:

Buyback or Compensation Agreement. A *compensation agreement*, also called a *buyback transaction*, is an agreement by an exporter of plant or equipment to take compensation in the form of future output from that plant. Such an arrangement has attributes that make it, in effect, an alternative form of direct investment. The value of the goods received back usually exceeds the value of the original sale, as would be appropriate to reflect the time value of money.

Counterpurchase. A *counterpurchase* involves an initial export, but with the exporter receiving back merchandise that is unrelated to items the exporter manufactures. A widely publicized early example was the export of jet aircraft by McDonnell Douglas to Yugoslavia with payment partly in cash and partly in Zagreb hams, wines, dehydrated vegetables and even some power transmission towers designated eventually for the City of Los Angeles. McDonnell Douglas had the responsibility for reselling the goods received.

Offset. *Offset* refers to the requirement of importing countries that their purchase price be offset in some way by the seller. The exporter may be required to source some of the production locally, to increase imports from the importing country, or to transfer technology.

))) Reasons for the Growth of Countertrade

In theory, countertrade is a movement away from free multilateral trade. It is a slow, expensive, and convoluted way of conducting trade that often forces firms to set up operations to deal in products very remote from their expertise. The basic problem is that the agreement to take back goods in some form of barter suggests these goods cannot be sold in the open market for as high a price as is being locked into the countertrade agreement.

Nevertheless, several reasons are advanced in support of countertrade. First, from the perspective of a centrally planned economy, countertrade reduces the risk of fluctuations in export receipts by ensuring that future exports will provide foreign exchange roughly equivalent to the cost of the original import.[4] Centrally planned economies have never been competent at marketing their products in foreign countries, perhaps because marketing was not necessary at home. Production plans in these countries are made by a central authority, and the production system does not respond well to sudden changes in export demand. Countertrade provides an assured market for a period of time and can be negotiated by governmental officials who set economic production quotas, rather than by the managers of individual plants who do not control the availability of resources.

Second, countertrade exports avoid domestic price controls and base prices set by international cartels or commodity agreements. In the case of barter, goods change hands without the explicit use of prices. Consequently, any domestic price controls are passed over. Goods can be "sold" abroad at "prices" that are substantially below those charged to local customers. Nigeria, Iran, Libya, Indonesia, Iraq, Qatar, and Abu Dhabi are reported to have used barter deals to sell oil below the OPEC cartel agreed-upon price.[5]

Third, because foreign exchange is not created, it need not be turned over to a central bank. Yet the entity that pays for its original imports with mandated countertrade exports in effect earns foreign exchange that it is able to keep to itself to pay for the import.

Fourth, countertrade enables a country to export merchandise of poor design or quality. The merchandise is often sold at a major discount in world markets. Whether or not this constitutes a discount on the original sale, or even dumping, depends on how that original sale was priced. To the extent that communist and former communist countries have a reputation for poor quality, the fact that the goods are marketed in foreign countries by reputable firms gives buyers some assurance of quality and after-sale service.

Survey research indicates that countertrade was most successful for large firms experienced in exporting large, complex products; for firms vertically integrated or that could accommodate countertrade take backs; and for firms that traded with countries having inappropriate exchange rates, rationed foreign exchange, and import restrictions. Importers who were relatively inexperienced in assessing technology or in export marketing also enjoyed greater success.[6]

SUMMARY

- Over many years, established procedures have arisen to finance international trade. The basic procedure rests on the interrelationship between three key documents, the *letter of credit*, the *draft*, and the *bill of lading*. Variations in each of these three key documents provide a variety of ways to accommodate any type of transaction.

- In the simplest transaction, in which all three documents are used and in which financing is desirable, an importer applies for and receives a letter of credit from its bank. In the letter of credit, the bank substitutes its credit for that of the importer and promises to pay if certain documents are submitted to the bank. The exporter may now rely on the promise of the bank rather than on the promise of the importer.

- The exporter typically ships on an order bill of lading, attaches the order bill of lading to a draft ordering payment from the importer's bank, and presents these documents, plus any of a number of additional documents, through its own bank to the importer's bank. If the documents are in order, the importer's bank either pays the draft (a *sight draft*) or accepts the draft (a *time draft*). In the latter case the bank promises to pay in the future. At this step the importer's bank acquires title to the merchandise through the bill of lading, and it then releases the merchandise to the importer against payment or promise of future payment.

- If a sight draft is used, the exporter is paid at once. If a time draft is used, the exporter receives the accepted draft, now a bankers' acceptance, back from the bank. The exporter may hold the bankers' acceptance until maturity or sell it at a discount in the money market.

- The process of international trade is facilitated by various national programs to provide *export credit insurance* and direct financial support.

- *Countertrade* provides an alternative to traditional importing and exporting. In countertrade, a seller provides a buyer with goods or services and promises in return to take back (barter) or purchase (other forms of countertrade) goods or services in partial or full payment.

QUESTIONS

1. Michigan Medical Company

Michigan Medical Company has received an order for medical equipment to be exported to Turkey under the terms of a letter of credit issued by London Bank Corporation on behalf of the Turkish importer. The letter of credit specifies that the face value of the shipment, $12,000,000, will be paid nine months after London Bank Corporation accepts a draft drawn by Michigan Medical in accordance with the terms of the letter of credit.

The current discount rate on nine-month acceptances is 8% per annum, and Michigan Medical judges its weighted average cost of capital to be 16%. The commission for selling in the discount market is 1.5% of the face amount.

How much cash can Michigan Medical expect from the sale if it holds the acceptance until maturity? Alternatively, should Michigan Medical sell the acceptance at once at a discount in the U.S. money market?

2. Honka Homes of Finland

Prefabricated log cabins from Finland are very popular with homebuilders in the mountains of the western United States. A Flagstaff developer has just ordered one such cabin for a client. The terms of agreement are such that Honka Homes of Finland, the manufacturer, drew a six-month draft against a letter of credit issued by Wells Fargo Bank, Los Angeles, on behalf of the Flagstaff developer in the amount of $300,000. After the cabin was shipped and all documentation completed, Honka Homes presented the draft to its local bank for forwarding to Los Angeles, where Wells Fargo Bank stamped it "Accepted. Payable six months from today," dated the stamp May 10 (the current date), and returned it to Honka Homes of Finland.

Market rates today, the day of acceptance, are as follows:

Spot exchange rate:	$1.1000/€
Six-month forward exchange rate:	$1.1200/€
Discount rate on six-month euro-denominated money market instruments:	8% p.a.
Discount rate on six-month U.S. dollar bankers' acceptances:	7% p.a.
Treasury bill rate in the United States	6% p.a.
Euro deposit rates available in Helsinki, six-month maturity	5% p.a.

Honka Homes has no immediate need for cash within its business but wants funds in six months to finance a seasonal expansion of its production line. Honka Homes does not want to expose itself to any exchange risk. What should Honka Homes do? (You may ignore transaction cost and taxes.)

3. Documenting an Export

Explain and diagram the steps involved in an export of wine from California to Japan, using a confirmed letter of credit, payment to be made 90 days from sight.

4. Confirmed Letter of Credit

Explain why an exporter might want a confirmed letter of credit rather than an unconfirmed one. What are its advantages and disadvantages?

WORLD WIDE WEB EXERCISES

W1. Letter of Credit Services

Commercial banks worldwide provide a variety of services to aid in the financing of foreign trade. Contact any of the many major multinational banks (a few are listed below) and determine what types of letter of credit services and other trade financing services they are able to provide.

Bank of America	http://corp.bankofamerica.com/
Citibank	http://www.citibank.com/
Barclays	http://www.barclays.com/
Deutsche Bank	http://www.deutschebank.com/
Union Bank of Switzerland	http://www.ubs.com/
Swiss Bank Corporation	http://www.ubswarburg.com

W2. Export-Import Bank of the United States

The Eximbank of the United States provides financing for U.S.-based exporters. Like most major industrial country trade-financing organizations, it is intended to aid in the export sale of products in which the buyer needs attractive financing terms. Use the Eximbank's web site to determine the current country limits, fees, and other restrictions that currently apply. (The Eximbank of the United States' web page provides some of the best web site links in international business and statistics.)

Export-Import Bank of the United States   http://www.exim.gov/

SUGGESTED READINGS

Dominguez, Luis V., and Carlos G. Sequeira, "Determinants of LDC Exporters' Performance: A Cross-National Study," *Journal of International Business Studies*, 1st Quarter 1993, pp. 19–40.

Hennart, Jean-François, "Some Empirical Dimensions of Countertrade," *Journal of International Business Studies*, 2nd Quarter 1990, pp. 243–270.

Lecraw, Donald J., "The Management of Countertrade: Factors Influencing Success," *Journal of International Business Studies*, Spring 1989, pp. 41–59.

NOTES

1. *Uniform Customs and Practice for Documentary Credits, 1993 Revision*. ICC Publication No. 500, issued in May 1993. The address of the International Chamber of Commerce is 38, Cours Albert 1er, 75008 Paris, France. Fax (1) 49.53.28.62. The United States office is at 156 Fifth Avenue, Suite 820, New York, N.Y. 10010, USA. Fax (212) 633-6025. The ICC has offices in most major cities around the world.
2. Uniform Commercial Code, Section 3104(1).
3. Hennart and Anderson, 1993.
4. Hennart (1990), p. 247.
5. Ibid., p. 249, quoting *Petroleum Economist*, May 1984.
6. Lecraw (1989), p. 57.

CHAPTER 21

EVALUATION OF PERFORMANCE

A MNE must be able to set specific financial goals, monitor progress by all units of the enterprise toward those goals, and evaluate results. It must be able to measure the performance of each of its affiliates on a consistent basis, and managers of affiliates must be given unambiguous objectives against which they will be judged. The criteria for internal evaluation and control should be designed for the specific purposes of the firm and not be the byproduct of reports or statements that were initially designed and prepared for financial accounting or for local reporting and tax purposes.

Evaluation is carried out not only by internal management for planning and control purposes, but also by outsiders. Outside evaluation centers around analysis of a firm's official financial statements. Comparing a firm's financial statements with those of its competitors helps managers evaluate their own performance or learn how policies of their firms differ from those of other firms. Bankers and rating agencies use financial statements to assess relative strengths and weaknesses of applicants for credit. Security analysts, portfolio managers, and investors use them to help select among competing securities. Government officials use them for a variety of regulatory purposes.

This chapter provides a brief overview of how multinational firms can apply these tools of evaluation to financial performance measurement and management for shareholder wealth maximization.

THE FINANCIAL GOALS OF THE MULTINATIONAL ENTERPRISE

The MNE, because it is a collection of many business units operating in a multitude of economic environments, must determine for itself the proper balance among three operating financial objectives:

1. Maximization of consolidated after-tax income
2. Minimization of the firm's effective global tax burden
3. Correct positioning of the firm's income, cash flows, and available funds

These goals—as seen throughout this book—are frequently inconsistent; the pursuit of one goal may result in a less desirable outcome in regard to another. Management must continually make decisions about the proper tradeoffs for the MNE. These tradeoffs exist not only among the three goals listed above, but also between goals to be pursued now and those that belong to the future.

Consider once again our U.S.-based multinational Lincoln Corporation. The explicit goal of management is to maximize shareholder wealth, which within the confines of corporate headquarters is typically interpreted as the maximization of earnings and earnings per share (EPS) growth. Chapter 18 described the various methods by which management may reposition the funds of the firm to maximize earnings and minimize the global tax liability of the MNE. But repositioning profits, by definition, means reducing the profits of one individual unit for the benefit of the whole—and logically increasing profits for another unit. How does the MNE design and maintain a performance management system that recognizes the impacts of these "sacrifices" by the individual unit for the benefit of the MNE in total?

)))) Domestic versus Multinational Control

Managers of foreign affiliates must be able to run their own operations efficiently according to achievable objectives. Higher-level management should evaluate their personal success according to criteria that are both clear in a quantitative sense and equitable in regard to the nonquantifiable factors of operating in a foreign environment. Furthermore, the criteria by which managers are to be judged must be congruent with the goals of the firm so that managerial action furthers the best long-run interests of the firm. This strategy is much easier said than done, however.

All firms expand and modify their domestic profitability measures when applying them to foreign affiliates. In addition, some firms establish foreign affiliates for objectives not related to normal corporate profit-oriented goals. Such exceptions include ensuring sources of supply, maintaining a presence in a given market, and conforming with government regulations. Although these goals have some very long-run focus on profits, performance measurement in the short run is not meaningful.

There are four purposes of an internal evaluation system. In order of importance they are as follows.

1. *To ensure adequate profitability*. This goal clearly provides the primary directive of the MNE; profits are the single biggest driver of shareholder wealth creation. All other purposes are secondary to the basic corporate goal of profitability.

2. *To have an early-warning system if something is wrong*. Although intuitively appealing, this goal is difficult to implement in practice because failure to meet targeted results may be due to valid and nonrecurring problems unique to international operations or to the fact that the original target was unrealistic.

3. *To have a basis for allocating resources.* This goal arises primarily in the context of requests from foreign affiliates for new funds that total more than the parent firm has available. Top management needs a fair and equitable means of rationing limited resources while serving overall corporate goals.

4. *To evaluate individual managers.* Managers are often evaluated by criteria in addition to profit contribution, such as their success in developing organizations or in expanding product lines.

)))) Complexities of International Performance Evaluation

Internal financial evaluation of foreign affiliates is both unique and difficult. Use of one foreign exchange translation method, in an attempt to measure results in the home currency, will present a different measure of success or of compliance with predetermined goals than use of some other translation method. Even though an internal control system stands independent of such accounting rules as FAS #52, evidence suggests that most firms start with the translation system used for financial reporting. Such a starting point is probably inappropriate when the goal is an effective control system, but it does lessen the cost of an entirely separate reporting procedure.

The results of any control system must be judged against distortions of performance caused by widely differing national business environments. Because many foreign direct investments are made to enhance strategic interaction with the rest of the worldwide system, we cannot evaluate such investments as if they stand alone.

Costs often not attributed to affiliates in a formal measurement system include implied costs to the parent of guaranteeing affiliate loans or holding safety inventory in the home country to serve foreign affiliates. Benefits to the worldwide system include profits to the parent or related affiliates from additional exports, royalties and management fees, keeping the parent abreast of technological developments in other countries, preempting markets, enlarging economies of scale, and denying such benefits to competing firms.

International measurement systems are distorted by decisions to benefit the world system at the expense of a specific local affiliate. For example, an affiliate in a low-interest country may finance another affiliate in a high-interest country. Although the system benefits, the first affiliate will have excess interest charges and the second will save on interest. Positioning of funds sometimes requires artificial transfer prices between related affiliates for tax, foreign exchange, or liquidity reasons. Management must devise a fair and consistent method of adjusting the basic reports to reflect the "self-sacrifice" of one affiliate for another.

Additional variables that may invalidate comparisons of reports from affiliates in separate countries include nationally imposed barriers on fund remittances, differential rates of inflation, requirements for certain levels of legal reserves financed via earnings retention, customs that call for profit sharing with workers, differing standards between countries over primary corporate goals, and variations in the work ethic and/or labor productivity. By and large, these variables are not significant in differentiating among domestic affiliates, but a company that seeks to extend a domestic control system abroad must ponder the significance of the financial data obtained under these variables.

FINANCIAL PERFORMANCE MEASUREMENT

How does management actually *manage* the firm in order to provide the greatest opportunity for adding value to shareholder wealth? What specific *goals* or *metrics* are the keys to maximizing shareholder value? Should management attempt to maximize net income (NI), earnings per share (EPS) or earnings per share growth, return on assets (ROA), or some other measure of financial performance? The single biggest problem facing financial managers today may be determining the proper measure of financial performance to use.

> Financial theory provides the framework for thinking about value creation, but it falls short of providing specific tools for management decisions. The challenge, therefore, is to translate financial theory into practical tools that effectively focus attention on value creation in different business situations and company cultures. These tools need to be simple enough to be useful to the line manager for planning and comprehensive enough for use by the chief financial officer (CFO) for high stakes decisions.[1]

Management is left with a significant dilemma. The value of managers to shareholders is in their ability to add income and capital gains to shareholder wealth. Management, however, has to continually struggle to determine what it is that these shareholders really want (market share, EPS growth, changes in leverage, right-sizing, contribution margin, core competencies, or other goal) in order for share prices to increase. Everyone likes to criticize management, but no one seems to know what to tell them to focus on. This has led to the development of new metrics that combine the financial information and data available from the traditional accounting-based financial statements with the theoretical principles of free cash flow-based value creation. This chapter incorporates the new metrics as tools for evaluating the multinational firm's performance. We use Nokia, a Finnish-based multinational firm, as an illustrative case.

))))) Measures of Financial Performance

There are a variety of measures, or *metrics*, of financial performance. Ultimately, firm profitability and success is measured by *total shareholder return* (TSR), which combines share price appreciation from beginning-of-year (boy) to end-of-year (eoy) with current income paid to stockholders in the form of dividends:[2]

$$TSR = \frac{\text{Share price}_{\text{eoy}} - \text{Share price}_{\text{boy}} + \text{Dividends}}{\text{Share price}_{\text{boy}}}$$

This is the measure of performance by equity investors in the firm, and therefore the ultimate measure of performance for management. Unfortunately, share prices are determined by the market, not by management. Management must therefore choose other measures, measures that are more within their more limited sphere of influence, to serve as their guide.[3]

The selection of the proper benchmark for financial performance is not, however, a trivial problem.[4] There are several very practical issues related to the selection of the firm's financial performance measure.

- **Focus**. Management must be sure that the measures it is communicating within the organization are truly what it wishes emphasized; many measures may have unintended consequences as a result of a singular focus. For example, firms that emphasize earnings growth often find that the goal of greater earnings is achieved through overinvestment, leading to poor shareholder returns, as capital is poured into the business at a greater rate than earnings are enhanced.

- **Complexity**. There is a wide range of measures, each with its associated complexity. Measures that are highly complex may require the reconstruction of many financial statements and may be difficult to communicate widely throughout the organization. In many cases there may be a direct tradeoff between efficiency and complexity.

- **Divisibility**. Many firms would prefer a measure that is useful on the business unit level. Measures that require a high degree of financial detail regarding individual financial or operational activities are often unwieldy on the unit level. The firm must decide how important it is for the measure to be implemented successfully at lower and lower levels of the organization.

- **Incentive**. Financial management is in many ways more *management* than *finance*. Not only must the members of the organization understand the performance measurements, they must be rewarded on the basis of their success in achieving the stated goals. This requires that management not only fully understand the measure employed, but it must also have the ability to alter the key value drivers of the measure.

The traditional measures of financial performance, used by management for decades, can be calculated directly from the firm's financial statements. The three traditional financial statements, the income statement, the balance sheet, and the statement of cash flows, provide most of the traditional inputs for corporate financial management. These financial statements are organized and presented in accordance with generally accepted accounting practices (GAAP) to allow the investor a clear picture of the firm's status. It remains to be seen, however, whether the financial information required for disclosure purposes, is the same as that information most appropriate for the ongoing management of the business.

Although some of the measures described here are often employed in *financial statement analysis*, that is not the express purpose of *financial performance measurement*. Whereas the first is an analytical process undertaken by outside experts and analysts attempting to determine relative financial health, the latter is intended as an internal indicator—a *compass*—of the management of the business.

Return on sales (ROS), return on investment or assets (ROA), and return on equity (ROE), are some of the most widely recognized measures.[5] Although markets are known to react to earnings announcements, these are purely accounting-based estimates of income and make no reference to the level of investment required to generate that income.

ILLUSTRATIVE CASE

Nokia (Finland)

Nokia is a Finnish multinational firm famous today for its cellular phones and general telecommunication expertise. We will use the financial statements of Nokia in Exhibit 21.1 to illustrate the various measures of performance.[6] Nokia's home currency is the Finnish markka (FIM).

- Return on Sales (ROS). Return on sales is by far the roughest and least accurate of the measures that follow. Because industries are so different in their structure, cost, and profitability, ROS is nothing more than an internal measure for comparison of year-to-year performance.

$$ROS = \frac{\text{Profit from continuing operations}}{\text{Net sales}} = \frac{\text{FIM4,087}}{\text{FIM36,810}} = 11.1\%$$

- Return on Investment (ROI) or Return on Assets (ROA). These two measures are essentially the same, assuming that assets represent the total investment. Return is profit from continuing operations, which excludes income from nonrecurring sources. As with all the following measures, it is assumed that current earnings are derived from average assets, in this case, the average of 1994 and 1995 total assets.

$$ROA = \frac{\text{Profit from continuing operations}}{\text{Average total assets}} = \frac{\text{FIM4,087}}{\dfrac{\text{FIM32,761} + \text{FIM28,849}}{2}} = 13.5\%$$

If ROA is then linked to the financial measurement linkages developed by E. I. DuPont de Nemours and Company (the *DuPont System*), the relationship between ROI and profit margin on sales (earnings/net sales) and turnover (net sales/average total assets) is apparent:

$$ROA = \frac{\text{Profit from continuing operations}}{\text{Net sales}} \times \frac{\text{Net sales}}{\text{Average total assets}}$$

Exhibit 21.1   *Nokia's Financial Statements, 1991-1995 (millions of Finnish markka)*

	1995	1994	1993	1992	1991
Profit and Loss Account, IAS					
Net sales	36.810	30.177	23.697	18.168	15.457
Cost of goods sold	(29.973)	(25.572)	(21.236)	(16.960)	(15.553)
Depreciation	(1.825)	(1.009)	(996)	(920)	–
Operating profit	5.012	3.596	1.465	288	(96)
Share of results of associated companies	85	22	28	(5)	9
Net interest and other financial income/expenses	(154)	66	(213)	(316)	(237)
Exchange gains and losses	(10)	450	(134)	(125)	–
Profit before tax and minority expenses	4.933	4.134	1.146	(158)	(324)
Tax	(769)	(932)	(299)	(167)	(231)
Minority interests	(77)	(75)	(80)	(88)	(49)
Profit from continuing operations	4.087	3.127	767	(413)	(604)
Discontinued operations	(2.340)	–	–	–	–
Profit from ordinary activities before cum effect of change in accounting policies	1.747	3.127	767	(413)	(604)
Cumulative prior year effect (after tax) of change in accounting policies	485	–	–	–	–
Profit from ordinary activities	2.232	3.127	767	(413)	(604)
Extraordinary items	–	944	(1.917)	(310)	393
Net profit	2.232	4.071	(1.150)	(723)	(211)
Balance Sheet Items					
Fixed assets and other noncurrent assets	9.047	7.943	7.994	7.630	8.263
Inventories	9.982	6.803	5.129	3.840	3.409
Accounts receivable and prepaid expenses	9.518	7.835	6.227	6.650	4.754
Cash and cash equivalents	4.214	5.268	3.297	3.118	3.727
Total current assets	23.714	19.906	14.653	13.608	11.890
Total assets	32.761	27.849	22.647	21.238	20.153
Shareholders' equity	13.806	12.418	6.511	6.727	7.393
Minority shareholders' interests	422	555	536	695	600
Long-term debts	2.121	3.071	3.397	3.124	3.896
Other long-term liabilities	457	486	683	581	477
Total long-term liabilities	2.578	3.557	4.080	3.705	4.373
Short-term borrowings	4.332	2.453	3.435	3.835	2.797
Current portion of long-term loans	187	278	139	1.221	1.086
Accounts payable and accrued liabilities	9.388	8.086	5.976	4.314	3.389
Advance payments	396	502	534	399	202
Discontinuity/restructuring provisions	1.652	–	1.436	342	313
Total current liabilities	15.955	11.319	11.520	10.111	7.787
Total liabilities and net worth	32.761	27.849	22.647	21.238	20.153
Other Key Items					
Earnings per share, continuing operations, FIM	14.36	10.97	3.07	neg	neg
Dividends per share, FIM	3.00	2.50	7.00	0.50	0.50
Share price:					
K (common), year-end	172	174	72	23	16
K (common), average	221	120	47	18	20
A (preferred), year-end	171	174	72	20	12
A (preferred), average	220	123	46	17	14

$$= \frac{\text{FIM4,087}}{\text{FIM36,810}} \times \frac{\text{FIM36,810}}{\text{FIM30,305}} = 13.5\%$$

ROA, when expressed in this way, highlights that operationally a business unit is performing better if earnings can be maximized relative to sales, as well as if sales can be maximized relative to total assets (turnover).

This is also an excellent opportunity to discuss the divisibility of the performance measurement for the business units of the multinational firm. Making relevant adjustments to this concept to give it multinational validity requires deciding where and how foreign exchange management and other system-improving decisions should be made. The three key variables in the DuPont system are: (1) sales; (2) earnings; and (3) underlying investment.

1. What the foreign affiliate of a MNE like Nokia sells may differ from what the same affiliate would sell if it were independent. For reasons of strategy or economies of scale, particular products might be either assigned or denied to the product line of any particular affiliate; export sales might be invoiced in any of a number of currencies in order to minimize exchange risk or position funds; and credit terms to customers might be dictated by the firm's decisions to lead or lag the flow of funds between countries. In addition, sales to related customers may be influenced by transfer price decisions intended to benefit the system worldwide as well as by lead- or lag-induced changes in credit terms.

2. The most immediate international variable in determining the relevant level of earnings is whether foreign exchange gains/losses will be included. If earnings are measured before netting foreign exchange gains/losses, local operating managers are in essence relieved of direct responsibility for minimizing currency losses. Alternatively, such responsibility can be assigned to local managers by a variation in the calculation of earnings for control purposes. Taxes, interest, and other financial costs may, likewise, be included or excluded when calculating earnings for control purposes.

3. The MNE and its various foreign affiliates and units must also determine the relevant measure of assets. As indicated by the equation above, as assets increase, all other components held constant, the return on investment falls. In a MNE like Nokia, however, the level of current assets in the various foreign affiliates may be altered by exchange rate changes, particularly when a significant portion of the unit's sales are invoiced in foreign currencies.

Ultimately, it is important that the management of the multinational business unit be judged and rewarded only on those variables that management in the individual unit can influence.

- **Return on Equity (ROE).** If the primary interest in measuring financial performance is to determine the return to shareholders and shareholder investment, ROE attempts to provide returns to the equity capital employed in the firm.

$$ROE = \frac{\text{Profit from continuing operations}}{\text{Average shareholders equity}} = \frac{\text{FIM4,087}}{\dfrac{\text{FIM13,806} + \text{FIM12,418}}{2}} = 31.2\%$$

ROE is typically higher than ROI when the firm utilizes a sizable amount of debt in its financial structure. ROE equals ROI for an all-equity firm.

- **Return on Net Assets (RONA).** Return on net assets is a slightly more sophisticated measure that attempts to correct for the fact that many of the firm's current assets and current liabilities are spontaneous; they are automatically created as a result of the operation of the business. The capital base is therefore fixed assets plus net working capital (total current assets less total current liabilities). In the case of Nokia,

$$RONA = \frac{\text{Profit from continuing operations}}{\text{Fixed assets} + \text{Net working capital}}$$

$$= \frac{\text{FIM4,087}}{\text{FIM9,047} + (\text{FIM23,714} - \text{FIM15,955})} = 24.3\%$$

RONA has grown more popular for financial measurement as more firms have focused on their net investment positions in current assets and liabilities. Many modern operation management philosophies such as just-in-time (JIT) inventory management have a favorable impact on RONA performance measures.

- **Return on Capital Employed (ROCE).** The returns used in all the previous measurements were returns to shareholders exclusively—that is, returns to equity investors only. If the returns were widened to include those to all investors—both creditors and equity investors—the numerator of the formula must be amended to include the payments to debt providers, including interest payments. Similarly, the investment base in the denominator is adjusted to a more refined capital investment measure—capital employed—to include those sources of capital that have an explicit required return, both interest-bearing debt and equity:

$$ROCE = \frac{\text{Profit from operations} + \text{Net interest} + \text{Exchange gains/losses}}{\text{Shareholder equity} + \text{Long-term debt} + \text{Interest-bearing short-term debt}}$$

If we substitute the appropriate values for Nokia in 1995, the ROCE is as follows (without averaging the capital base in this instance; current portion of long-term debt is included here with interest-bearing short-term debt):

$$ROCE = \frac{FIM4,087 + FIM154}{FIM13,806 + FIM2,578 + FIM187} = 20.3\%$$

The track record of these measures of financial performance—ROE, RONA, and ROCE—is not good. They have not proven to be very good barometers for management attempting to build shareholder wealth. All the measures shown above suffer from the same two basic deficiencies in the eyes of financial professionals: (1) a reliance on book values as reported and carried on historically valued balance sheets; and (2) the use of accounting-based income measures rather than measures of cash flow.

The New Metrics

The *new metrics*, as they are often called, return to the theoretical foundations of value—market-based values arising from cash flow. Financial theory advocates value creation through *free cash flow* generation. Although many firms are now paying more attention to free cash flow, its primary use remains in the valuation of potential investments such as in capital budgeting and mergers and acquisition. Here we demonstrate two of the better-known metrics now embraced by many MNEs: *economic value added* (EVA) and *cash flow return on investment* (CFROI).

Economic Value Added (EVA). The exclusive trademarked property of Stern Stewart and Company, a New York-based management consultancy, EVA is currently one of the most hotly debated financial metrics. Whereas the previous measures attempted to determine returns to specific capital providers, usually equity investors, EVA attempts to determine whether management has in fact added value to the enterprise over and above what the providers of capital to the firm *require*.

EVA charges the earnings of the firm for both debt and equity, rather than calculating a measure of return to equity providers. The numerator, net operating profit after tax (NOPAT), focuses on the continuing profits of the business itself, without reducing the earnings for payments to providers of capital of any kind.

EVA = [Net operating profit after tax] – [*WACC* × Capital employed]

For Nokia, using the average costs and relative weights of debt and equity illustrated in Exhibit 21.2, the WACC at the end of 1994, to raise the capital to generate the operating profits for 1995, is approximately 12.9%. Notice that WACC must be recalculated each year if the firm's capital structure or associated capital cost components are changing. The resulting EVA measure is then:

$$EVA = [FIM5,012 - FIM769] - [0.129 \times FIM64,533] = (FIM4,084)$$

According to this calculation, Nokia actually destroyed economic value in 1995. This measure of *economic profit*, also termed *residual income* in the economic literature, provides a clear indication of whether the firm has made enough profit in a year to satisfy both creditors and equity holders.[7] In this case, Nokia did not.[8]

The weighted-average cost of capital is a significant element of added complexity to this measure not employed in the previous measures. Determination of the firm's WACC (see Chapter 10), which is ordinarily utilized elsewhere in the firm in internal financial studies like capital budgeting (described in Chapter 16), estimates what the current costs of raising capital are for both debt and equity.[9] And like the WACC calculation employed in Chapter 16, the preferred measure of required return to shareholders is found using the capital-asset-pricing model (CAPM). Note also that EVA is a monetary value, and not a percentage return.

A second important distinction is that EVA no longer relies on traditional accounting-based measures such as historical cost or book value. The calculation of the weighted-average cost of capital is shown in Exhibit 21.2, and it utilizes the CAPM. For expository purposes only, the beta for Nokia has been assumed to be 1.0. The capital measure is derived from market value of outstanding debt (which is typically close to face value) and market capitalization of equity outstanding.

Stern Stewart also recommends that the financial components used in the EVA calculation be from a cash-flow-based set of financial statements, and not on the traditional accounting measurements required under GAAP in most countries. For example, in the case of Nokia, research and development expenses (R&D) in 1995 were approximately FIM2,531 million, and they are listed under International Accounting Standards as a deductible expense of the firm. Stern Stewart argues that R&D is actually *investment* in the firm's business future and should be included in the capital-employed component of the calculation, and not as a reduction to its net operating profit.

In addition to EVA, Stern Stewart has created a measure of cumulative shareholder wealth called *market value added* (MVA). MVA is the total stockholder wealth added over time by management. It is calculated as the difference between total equity capitalization and the cumulative value of all cash investments made in the firm including retained earnings.

Cash Flow Return on Investment (CFROI). One of the most complex measures of financial performance, cash flow return on investment (CFROI) is also one whose calculation is most widely debated. As you might guess, a fundamental distinction of CFROI is its use of cash flow generated by the firm, rather than income or earnings derived from financial statements, as the "return." In the case of Nokia, profit from continuing operations is supplemented by depreciation to approximate cash flow returns from the business. Like EVA, CFROI moves away from historical accounting measures of capital. In the case of CFROI, the capital base is termed *cash investment* and represents actual replacement cost of capital employed.

$$CFROI = \frac{\text{Profit from continuing operations} - \text{Cash taxes} + \text{Depreciation}}{\text{Cash investment}}$$

If we substitute values from Nokia's financial statements listed in Exhibit 21.1, CFROI for Nokia in 1995 becomes:

$$CFROI = \frac{\text{FIM4,087} - \text{FIM769} + \text{FIM1,825}}{\text{FIM64,533}} = 8.0\%$$

Here we have used the same estimate of total capital employed as in EVA. Most practitioners of the CFROI art, however, like the Boston Consulting Group, have their own distinct and detailed methodology for the estimation of cash investment.[10] Other firms that utilize CFROI, like Mc Kinsey, have a detailed and distinct methodology for estimating the free cash flows derived from the continuing business activities of the firm.

One of the strongest arguments in favor of CFROI over most of the other competitive measures is its reliance on the theoretical foundations of valuation arising from capital budgeting and the subsequent conclusion that many cash investments undertaken by a firm in an individual year will not produce their free cash flow returns for some years into the future. EVA, although there are a number of different methods in practice, emphasizes what earnings are derived from the investment this period, not in future periods.

Metric Summary. The area of financial performance measurement is currently in hot debate. Competitive measures are all vying for corporate attention, while the academic community struggles to catch up with the measures through empirical testing.

The academic community's judgment is still out, but it is safe to say that those firms that are utilizing some of the newer financial metrics are striving to accomplish what shareholders want—the use of the management compass that will provide the correct signals to increase shareholder wealth.

FOREIGN EXCHANGE RATES AND PERFORMANCE EVALUATION

How are we to determine the impact of exchange rate movements on the measured performance of foreign affiliates? That is one of the single largest dilemmas facing management of the MNE. Chapter 8 described the process of translating foreign affiliate foreign-currency-denominated financial statements into the home currency of the parent company. As a result of translation, however, it is possible that financial measures of performance may not give true signals as to the profitability—or general success—of the foreign affiliate.

Consider the two-year income statement summary of Lincoln Brazil S.A., described in Exhibit 21.2. By all financial indications on the local level—in Brazilian real—the affiliate showed good growth in earnings (+14%), earnings before interest, taxes, depreciation, and amortization—EBITDA (+15%), and income (+38%). The unit's gross margin was maintained at 42%, its return on sales rose from 5% to 6%, all in the face of a tumultuous economic environment that gave rise to a 34% depreciation of the Brazilian real (from R$1.20/$ to R$1.82/$).

But from the U.S. parent company's point of view, because of the depreciation of the real, the income generated by the Brazilian affiliate in U.S. dollar terms fell 9% from the previous year. The evaluation of the performance of a MNE affiliate like this one involves three different evaluation dimensions:

1. **Management Evaluation**. If the unit is essentially local currency functional, the weight of performance evaluation of local management should be conducted in local currency terms. Growth of sales, control of costs, and maintenance of margins all rely upon the work effort and commitment of local

---

Exhibit 21.2   *Profit and Loss Items, Lincoln Brazil S.A., January 31, 1998 and 1999 (in thousands of Brazilian real)*

Income Items	1998	1999	% Change
Sales	358,640	410,500	14%
Less cost of goods sold	(208,600)	(238,400)	14%
Gross operating profit	150,040	172,100	15%
Gross margin	42%	42%	
Less G&A expenses	(38,600)	(44,380)	
EBITDA	111,440	127,720	15%
Less depreciation and amortization	(58,000)	(58,000)	
EBIT	53,400	69,720	30%
Less interest	(28,000)	(34,500)	
EBT	25,440	35,220	38%
Less Brazilian income tax @ 30%	(7,632)	(10,566)	
Net income	17,808	24,654	38%
Return on sales	5%	6%	
Exchange rate (R$/$)	1.20	1.82	−34%
Net income (US$)	$14,840	$13,546	−9%

management. If, however, significant operating costs or financing costs are directed from the parent company, either for better or for worse, the performance evaluation system will have to adjust for these corporate-driven decisions that impact financial performance.

2. **Affiliate Evaluation**. The evaluation of the affiliate itself as seen through the eyes of the parent company requires a focus on competitiveness in the local market. This is similar to the *project viewpoint* described in the capital budgeting analysis of Chapter 14. Maintenance of gross margin, sales growth, and market share, as compared to similar margins and shares of local competitors, provides a measure of competitiveness on the local level.

3. **Strategic Evaluation**. The role the foreign affiliate plays within the portfolio of the MNE requires senior management of the parent company level to take the parent viewpoint. This, however, is frequently extremely difficult, requiring management to trade off short-term profitability, here measured in U.S. dollars, against long-term shareholder wealth creation, as realized in Brazilian real in the business itself. Regardless of local currency performance, the flat earnings in dollar terms will result in flat consolidated profits as reported to shareholders. If the MNE's major competitors do not have a similar Brazilian exposure (that is, they have different operating exposures), Lincoln is seen to be underperforming its competitors. Shareholders, and possibly creditors, will require explanations of this underperformance. Senior strategic and financial management will then have to determine whether the affiliate is to be liquidated, maintained, or possibly expanded, depending on their perceptions and aspirations for future Brazilian real and U.S. dollar performance.

These three different levels of performance evaluation are inextricably intertwined. By standing in the shoes of local affiliate management, senior corporate management, and shareholders, it is easy for us to see how difficult evaluating the performance of foreign affiliates is within the MNE. This complexity is compounded by the growth of affiliates into more and more emerging markets with their commensurate currency volatility.

Regardless of complexity, however, the ultimate test of a performance measurement system is whether it enables the firm to create shareholder value. If not, the shareholders' expectations will not be met and the share price will underperform the market.

SUMMARY

- Traditional financial ratios such as ROS, ROI, ROE, and even relatively more recent versions such as RONA and ROCE utilize book values as measures of capital invested. This tendency, combined with the fact that most of these measures record accounting income and not cash flow, has led to the development of a number of new measures of financial performance.

- Economic value added (EVA) and cash flow return on investment (CFROI) are two of the most widely used *new metrics* of financial performance. Each attempts to provide managers with financial criteria that provide a truer direction to building shareholder value. Although each is thought to have a higher correlation with shareholder wealth, both measures are more complex for calculation and interpretation than the traditional financial statement ratios.

- In the illustrative case of Nokia (Finland), each of the potential performance measures was illustrated by using Nokia data. Although each measure provided some useful information, each was also seen to be somewhat misleading if used in isolation.

- The performance evaluation of a foreign affiliate consists of three different levels of analysis: (1) management performance; (2) affiliate performance (local viewpoint); (3) affiliate performance (parent viewpoint).

QUESTIONS

1. EVA and the Cost of Capital
One of the major issues firms must confront when implementing EVA on the business unit level is whether or not to differentiate the cost of capital per unit by the riskiness of its business. Business units operating in business segments that are of higher risk would be charged a higher cost of capital. Many firms, however, raise capital centrally and provide the capital at the same basic cost to each individual unit, regardless of risk. Prepare a one-page briefing for management on the pros and cons of differentiating the cost of capital when implementing an EVA system.

2. Financial Metrics and Compensation
Many firms and management consultants believe that in order for a firm's managers to buy into a financial performance metric, they must be compensated on the basis of their performance as measured by that metric. What problems could you forsee resulting from a firm's implementing EVA or CFROI as a management compensation program? Would its singular pursuit of these measures help or hinder the firm's pursuit of shareholder wealth-building?

3. Working Capital Management and Financial Metrics
Working capital, the current assets and liabilities of the firm, is often considered something of a necessary evil of conducting business. But many management strategies today focus on minimizing the amount of capital that is tied up in working capital and encouraging firms to minimize inventories, reduce receivables, and at the same time utilize extended payment terms at every opportunity.

a. What are the pros and cons of instituting a financial management system in which working capital is intentionally downsized?

b. If the firm were exporting products to buyers in many different countries, countries in which standard business practices include extensive credit terms, how would these sales be financed? At what potential cost?

MINICASE: *Computer Data Corporation's St. Petersburg Subsidiary*

Computer Data Corporation (CDC), a New York-based business computing services firm, is attempting to revise its foreign affiliate evaluation system. Of particular focus is its existing Russian subsidiary, a 100%-owned business unit in St. Petersburg. The 1998 collapse of the ruble, and the economic depression following the ruble's collapse, have caused the subsidiary's own management to request a revision in what is known in the MNE itself as *affiliate performance criteria* (APC).

Although sales grew dramatically from 1997 to 1998, gross margin declined marginally, and interest expenses rose rapidly as a result of the ruble's falling value and rising inflation. CDC-St. Petersburg had roughly half its debt in local currency, so rising inflation rates led to rising interest rates, and subsequently higher interest expenses. No additional capital investment in the subsidiary had been allowed by corporate management since 1996 as a result of the fears that eventually were realized—of ruble collapse.

		CDC-St. Petersburg	
(Thousands of Rubles)	*1997*	*1998*	*1999*
Sales	680,245	750,250	635,280
Less cost of goods sold	(450,266)	(501,220)	(448,000)
Gross operating profits	229,979	249,030	187,280
Gross margin	34%	33%	29%
Less G&A expenses	(48,630)	(44,650)	(44,380)
EBITDA	181,349	204,380	142,900
Less depreciation	(65,000)	(65,000)	(65,000)
EBIT	116,349	139,380	77,900
Less interest	(32,000)	(38,000)	(35,000)
EBT	84,349	101,380	42,900
Less Russian taxes @ 30%	(25,305)	(30,414)	(12,870)
Net income	59,044	70,966	30,030
Exchange rate, Rb/$ (eoy)	6.30	22.0	26.0
Net income, US$	$9,372	$3,226	$1,155
Total assets, rubles	1,250,000	1,185,000	1,120,000
Total assets, US$	$198,413	$156,440	$143,200
Return on Assets, rubles (%)	4.7%	6.0%	2.7%
Return on Assets, US$ (%)	4.7%	2.1%	0.8%

Although many of the financial impacts of ruble's collapse hit the financial statements by end-of-year 1998 (consolidation practices including translation), the subsequent Russian recession hit 1999's sales and operating performance even harder.

CDC's corporate evaluation system APC differentiated between what affiliate management truly controlled—the upper half of the profit and loss statement, and what they did not directly control—the lower half of the P&L, which focused on financing and taxation. Financing was directed by corporate, who arranged both local debt with Russian banks and intracompany debt with loans from the parent company. Taxation was similarly managed by corporate, with internal transfer prices on both debt and corporate services and software.

Affiliate Performance Criteria	Weight	Score
Gross margin performance, growth	1/3	1–5
EBITDA performance, growth	1/3	1–5
Net income performance	1/3	1–5

Scoring was on the basis of 5 as highest. What was particularly difficult for local management of any affiliate was the fact that all three components were measured in U.S. dollars, not local currency. Local management felt it was unreasonable to penalize them for an exchange rate that was completely out of their control. Corporate management, while sympathetic, argued that shareholders were not quite so understanding and demanded performance in the functional currency of the parent company, the U.S. dollar.

CDC has brought your management consulting firm in to evaluate the current system and make recommendations. What do you propose?

WORLD WIDE WEB EXERCISES

W1. Treasury Management Association (TMA)

The Treasury Management Association (TMA) is a U.S.-based organization that publishes a journal, organizes and presents conferences, and pursues a number of other professional development activities in the field of Treasury management. Use TMA's Website to find out the latest developments in Treasury information technology.

Treasury Management Association   http://www.afponline.org
(Association for Financial Projessionals)

W2. Treasury Management Advisory Services

There are a growing number of associations, trade groups, and management consultants in the area of international treasury management. KPMG-Canada publishes an annual report on cross-border mergers and acquisitions. Use the following Website to find out which investment banking firms dominated the market in 1998 and 1999.

KPMG   http://www.kpmg.ca/trm

SUGGESTED READINGS

Hamilton, Robert D. and Roger J. Kashlak, "National Influences on Multinational Corporation Control System Selection," *Management International Review*, Feb. 1999, pp. 167–189.

Hanson, Bruce B., "What You Need to Know About Economic Value Added," *Compensation and Benefits Review*, Mar./Apr. 1995, pp. 33–36.

O'Donnell, Sharon, "Compensation Design as a Tool for Implementing Foreign Subsidiary Strategy," *Management International Review*, Feb. 1999, pp. 149–166.

Olsen, Eric E., and James A. Knight, "Managing for Value," in the *Handbook of Modern Finance*, Dennis E. Logue, ed., New York: Warren, Gorharn & Lamont, 1996, p. E 10-2.

Rappaport, Alfred, "Linking Competitive Strategy and Shareholder Value Analysis," *Journal of Business Strategy*, Spring 1987, pp. 58–67.

NOTES

1. Olsen and Knight (1996).
2. A similar measurement of performance, total business return (TBR), can be constructed for the privately held firm. This metric requires a valuation of the firm's shares against publicly traded comparables.
3. There are a growing number of surveys of financial performance measurements. See for example, Olsen and Knight (1996), and Myers (1996).
4. The search for the perfect measure of financial performance may rival that of the search for the Holy Grail, and like the epic pursuit by the Knights of the Round Table, it may require the services of a magician. There is today no shortage of magicians or consultants who stand at the ready to aid the firm in its quest.
5. The following formulas are far from the last word. Each of these measures is calculated a number of different ways; here we present some of the more traditional forms.
6. Nokia's willingness to report financial performance according to Finnish Accounting Standards, U.S. GAAP, and International Accounting Standards makes it particularly attractive as an example.
7. A number of management consultants such as KPMG (U.S.) actually refer to their form of this measure as *economic profit*. For an overview of the historical development of economic profit see Rappaport (1986).
8. One author (Hanson, 1995) has noted that "At this point EVA—"economic value added"—may sound too good to be true. It is, but not because it doesn't work. The fundamental problem is that it sounds to compensation managers like a Finance 302 final exam for a course where they never went to class and they lost the notes they borrowed."
9. The charge for equity capital will generally be much larger in an EVA measure because firms generally have share capital that is more valuable than what is recorded on their books at historical value.
10. The Boston Consulting group's version of CFROI, termed *spot cash return on investment* (SCROI), emphasized that the investment measure should be defined in a parallel fashion to the cash flow numerator and is therefore equivalent to cash investment.

PART 6 contains advanced topics that are particularly relevant for financial executives and students majoring in Finance. However, these topics may be too complex for someone interested primarily in a survey of the main elements of multinational financial management.

PART 6

ADVANCED TOPICS IN MULTINATIONAL FINANCE

CHAPTER 22 analyzes the risk-reduction benefits of international diversification, both from the viewpoint of a MNE and from the viewpoint of an international portfolio investor. This chapter builds on traditional domestic portfolio theory but adds the foreign exchange risk of holding foreign-currency-denominated securities. It also analyzes the use of a global-asset pricing model (global beta) compared to a domestic-asset pricing model (domestic beta).

CHAPTER 23 analyzes advanced topics in currency risk management. This includes defining the optimal hedge ratio, cross-hedging, delta-hedging, and other financial engineering topics dealing with currency risk management. Special emphasis is placed on option-based instruments.

CHAPTER 24 analyzes advanced topics in interest rate risk management, building on the framework previously presented in Chapter 9. Special emphasis is again placed on option-based instruments. Advanced topics include interest rate caps, floors, and collars, as well as option and swap combinations (swaptions).

CHAPTER 22

INTERNATIONAL PORTFOLIO THEORY AND THE MNE

I n Chapter 10 we emphasized the critical importance for a firm to attract international portfolio investors in order to achieve a global cost of capital. In this chapter we explain in detail how international portfolio investors benefit from international portfolio diversification. This requires a basic knowledge of portfolio theory and its interplay with foreign exchange rate risk. Portfolio theory is also applicable to the MNE itself, both with respect to the composition of its asset portfolio and its cash flows.[1] In the first part of the chapter we illustrate the extension of portfolio theory from the domestic to the international business environment. From this we show how the foreign exchange risks of a portfolio, whether it be a securities portfolio or the general portfolio of activities of the MNE, are reduced through international diversification. The second part of the chapter details the theory and application of international portfolio theory and presents recent empirical results of the risk-return tradeoffs of internationally diversified portfolios.

PORTFOLIO RISK REDUCTION FROM INTERNATIONAL DIVERSIFICATION

Portfolio risk reduction is shown graphically in Exhibit 22.1. The upper line shows how a portfolio's risk can be reduced by adding domestic securities (U.S. stocks, in this example) to a domestic-only portfolio. Note that as more stocks are added, the curve flattens out. The lowest portion of that line is a proxy for the beta of the U.S. stock market as a whole, which is defined as beta equals 1.0. We can add more and more stocks, but no further risk reduction occurs because all that is left is the systematic risk of the market itself. The lowest line in Exhibit 22.1 (international stocks) represents a portfolio in which foreign securities have been added. It has the same overall shape as the portfolio of U.S. stocks, but a lower portfolio beta. This situation arises because the returns on the foreign stocks are not closely correlated with returns on U.S. stocks, but rather with a global beta.

| **Exhibit 22.1** | *Portfolio Risk Reduction from International Diversification* |

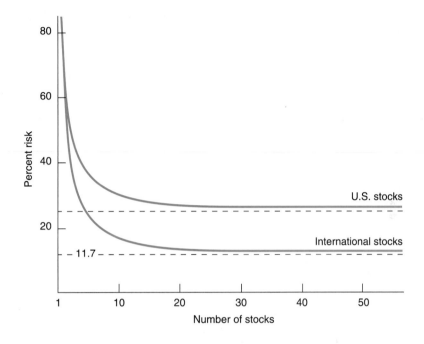

))) **International Portfolio Construction and Foreign Exchange Risk**

The construction of *internationally diversified portfolios* is both the same as and different from the creation of a traditional domestic portfolio. Internationally diversified portfolios are the same in principle, because the investor is attempting to combine assets that are less than perfectly correlated, reducing the total risk of the portfolio. In addition, by the addition of assets outside the home market, assets that previously were not available to be averaged into the portfolio's expected returns and risks, the investor has now tapped into a larger pool of potential investments.

But international portfolio construction is also different in that when the investor acquires assets or securities outside his or her home-country market, the investor may also be acquiring a foreign-currency-denominated asset.[2] Thus, the investor has actually acquired *two* additional assets—the currency of denomination and the asset subsequently purchased with the currency—two assets in one, in principle, but in expected returns and risks, two.

A numerical example can illustrate the difficulties associated with international portfolio diversification and currency risk. A U.S.-based investor takes US$1,000,000 on January 1, 2000, and invests in a share traded on the Tokyo Stock Exchange (TSE). On January 1, 2000, the spot exchange rate is ¥100.00/$. The US$1million therefore yields ¥100,000,000. The ¥100,000,000 is then used to acquire shares on the Tokyo Stock Exchange at ¥20,000 per share, acquiring 5,000 shares. The investor holds the shares for one year.

At the end of one year the investor sells the 5,000 shares at the market price, which is now ¥25,000 per share; the shares have risen ¥5,000 per share in price. The 5,000 shares at ¥25,000 per share yield proceeds of ¥125,000,000. The Japanese yen are then changed back into the investor's home currency, the U.S. dollar, at the spot rate in effect on January 1, 2001 of ¥120.00/$. This results in total U.S. dollar proceeds of $1,041,666.67. The total return on the investment is then:

$$\frac{US\$1,041,666.67 - US\$1,000,000}{US\$1,000,000} = 4.167\%$$

The total U.S. dollar return is actually a combination of the return on the Japanese yen (which in this case was negative) and the return on the shares listed on the Tokyo Stock Exchange (which was positive). This value is expressed by isolating the percentage change in the share price (r^{shares}) in combination with the percentage change in the currency value ($r^{¥/\$}$):

$$R^\$ = [(1 + r^{¥/\$})(1 + r^{shares,¥})] - 1$$

In this case the value of the Japanese yen, in the eyes of a U.S.-based investor, fell 16.67%, while the shares traded on the Tokyo Stock Exchange rose 25.0%. The total investment return in U.S. dollars is therefore

$$R^\$ = [(1 + r^{¥/\$})(1 + r^{shares})] - 1 = [(1 - .1667)(1 + .2500)] - 1 = .04167 \approx 4.167\%$$

Obviously the risk associated with international diversification, when it includes currency risk, is inherently more complex than that of domestic investments. It should also be apparent, however, that the presence of currency risk may alter the correlations associated with securities in different countries and currencies, providing portfolio composition and diversification possibilities that domestic investment and portfolio construction may not. We can state the following, however:

- International diversification benefits induce investors to demand foreign securities.

- If the addition of a foreign security to the portfolio of the investor aids in the reduction of risk for a given level of return, or increases the expected return for a given level of risk, then the security adds value to the portfolio.

- Securities that add value will be demanded by investors. Given the limits of the potential supply of securities, increased demand will bid up the price of the security, resulting in a lower cost of capital for the issuing firm.
- The firm issuing the security is therefore able to raise capital at a lower cost.

THE CASE FOR INTERNATIONAL PORTFOLIO DIVERSIFICATION

In this section we explain why investors should diversify their portfolios internationally. The first section will review the principles of domestic portfolio diversification, which is then followed by the theory and evidence in support of international diversification of the investor's portfolio.

Principles of Portfolio Diversification

It is generally known that an investor may reduce investment risk by holding risky assets in a portfolio. As long as the asset returns are not perfectly positively correlated, risk reduction can be achieved because some of the fluctuations of the asset returns will offset each other. For a simple illustration, consider a portfolio consisting of two risky assets. If the weights of investment in the two assets are w_1 and w_2, respectively, and $w_1 + w_2 = 1$, the risk of the portfolio (σ_p), usually expressed in terms of the standard deviation of the portfolio's expected return, is given by the following equation:

$$\sigma_p = \sqrt{w_1^2\sigma_1^2 + w_2^2\sigma_2^2 + 2w_1 w_2 \rho_{12}\sigma_1\sigma_2}$$

where σ_1^2 and σ_2^2 are the variances of the expected returns of risky assets 1 and 2, respectively, σ_1 and σ_2 are their respective standard deviations, and ρ_{12} is the correlation coefficient between the two assets' returns. The portfolio expected return can be obtained with the following equation:

$$E\left(R_p\right) = w_1 E\left(R_1\right) + w_2 E\left(R_2\right)$$

where $E(R_p)$, $E(R_1)$, and $E(R_2)$ are the expected returns of the portfolio, asset 1, and asset 2, respectively.

For example, assume that the expected returns of risky assets 1 and 2 are, respectively, 14% and 18%. Their standard deviations are 15% and 20%, respectively. The correlation coefficient is 0.5. If an investor invests 0.4 in asset 1 and 0.6 in asset 2, the risk of the investment portfolio will be

$$\sigma_p = \sqrt{(0.4)^2(0.15)^2 + (0.6)^2(0.20)^2 + 2(0.4)(0.6)(0.5)(0.15)(0.20)}$$

which, when reduced, becomes

$$\sqrt{0.0036 + 0.0144 + 0.0072} = 0.159 \approx 15.9\%$$

The expected return of the portfolio will be

$$E(R_p) = (0.4)(0.14) + (0.6)(0.18) = 0.164 \approx 16.4\%$$

Note that the portfolio risk is *not* the weighted average of the risks of the individual assets. As long as the correlation coefficient (ρ_{12}) is smaller than 1.0, some of the fluctuations of the asset returns will offset each other, resulting in risk reduction. The lower the correlation coefficient, the greater the opportunity for risk diversification.

The equations above can be generalized to the case when a portfolio consists of multiple assets. The portfolio risk is

$$\sigma_p = \sqrt{\sum_{i=1}^{N} w_i^2 \sigma_j^2 + \sum_{i=1}^{N-1} \sum_{j=i+1}^{N} w_i w_j \, \rho_{ij} \sigma_i \sigma_j}$$

and the portfolio expected return is

$$E(R_p) = \sum_{i=1}^{N} w_i E(R_i)$$

where N stands for the total number of assets included in the portfolio.

))) Efficient Frontiers

In a given country (for example, the United States), there are usually a substantial number of assets from which an investor can choose. A large number of possible portfolios can be formed by combining these assets with different sets of weights. Each of the resulting portfolios will have its own expected return, $E(R_p)$, and risk, σ_p. The performance of the portfolios can be plotted in a graph as in Exhibit 22.2, with σ_p as the *x*-axis quantity and $E(R_p)$ as the *y*-axis quantity. Each dot on the graph represents the score of a portfolio. A risk-averse investor will welcome a dot that is higher (with greater expected return) and closer to the left (with lower portfolio risk). However, the dots will all stay below and to the right of the boundary line *ABC*. *ABC* is known as the *efficient frontier*. Rational investors will choose portfolios along the efficient frontier; any portfolio below the line will have higher risk (given the same expected return) or lower expected return (given the same level of risk). However, investors in domestic portfolios are limited to the efficient frontier for domestic investors.

If the investor is willing and allowed to go beyond his or her home country boundary and include foreign assets in the portfolio, the efficient frontier will shift up and to the left to a new boundary line, *DEF*. The line *DEF* is the *efficient frontier for an international investor*. Allowing investors to hold foreign assets substantially enlarges the feasible set of investments; higher return can be obtained at a given level of risk, or lower risk can be attained at the same level of return.

| **Exhibit 22.2** | *Gains from International Portfolio Diversification* |

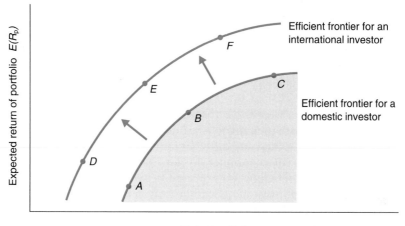

| **Exhibit 22.3** | *Summary Statistics of the Monthly Returns for 18 Major Stock Markets, 1977-1996 (All returns are converted into U.S. dollars and include all dividends paid)* |

	Mean Return (%)	Standard Deviation (%)	Beta (β_i)	Sharpe Measure (SHP$_i$)	Treynor Meausure (TRN$_i$)
Australia	1.00	7.44	1.02	0.078	0.0057
Austria	0.77	6.52	0.54	0.055	0.0066
Belgium	1.19	5.53	0.86	0.141	0.0091
Canada	0.82	5.34	0.93	0.076	0.0044
Denmark	0.99	6.25	0.68	0.092	0.0085
France	1.18	6.76	1.08	0.113	0.0071
Germany	0.97	6.17	0.84	0.089	0.0065
Hong Kong	1.50	9.61	1.09	0.113	0.0100
Italy	0.96	7.57	0.89	0.071	0.0061
Japan	1.08	6.66	1.21	0.099	0.0055
Netherlands	1.39	4.93	0.89	0.197	0.0109
Norway	1.00	7.94	1.02	0.073	0.0057
Singapore	1.09	7.50	1.01	0.090	0.0057
Spain	0.83	6.81	0.94	0.060	0.0044
Sweden	1.37	6.67	0.97	0.143	0.0099
Switzerland	1.10	5.39	0.86	0.127	0.0080
United Kingdom	1.35	5.79	1.06	0.162	0.0089
United States	1.01	4.16	0.82	0.143	0.0072
Average	1.09	6.51	0.93	0.107	0.0073

The results are computed with stock market data from Morgan Stanley's *Capital International Perspectives*, monthly.

))) National Equity Market Performance

Exhibit 22.3 presents the performance of the individual country stock markets from 1977 to 1996. Note that the return is that of a market index, a portfolio that is already well diversified within that market. For instance, in the case of Australia, if a U.S. investor had invested in nothing but the Australian index fund for the entire period, that investor received an average monthly return of 1.0% (or about 12% a year) in dollar terms. Of the 18 stock markets, the Hong Kong market yielded the highest return (1.5%), followed by the Netherlands (1.39%) and Sweden (1.37%).

Risk reduction is possible through international diversification because the returns of different stock markets around the world are not perfectly positively correlated. Because there are different industrial structures in different countries, and because different economies do not follow exactly the same business cycle, smaller return correlations are expected between investments in different countries than between investments within a given country. Exhibit 22.4 reports the relatively low correlation coefficients among returns of 18 major stock markets around the world in the 20-year period of 1977–1996, indicating great potential for international diversification. The returns are monthly and, for the sake of comparison, have all been converted to the same currency basis (in this case the U.S. dollar).

))) The Sharpe and Treynor Performance Measures

However, investors should not examine returns in isolation, but rather the amount of return per unit of risk accepted. With the highest return, the Hong Kong market also had the highest risk, a standard deviation of 9.61%. A major contributing factor to its high volatility was, perhaps, political uncertainty about the future of the former British colony after 1997.

To consider both risk and return in evaluating portfolio performance, we introduce two measures, the *Sharpe measure* (SHP) and the *Treynor measure* (TRN). The *Sharpe measure* calculates the average return over and above the risk-free rate of return per unit of portfolio risk:

$$SHP_i = \frac{\overline{R}_i - R_f}{\sigma_i}$$

where R_i is the average return for portfolio i during a specified time period, R_f is the average risk-free rate of return, and σ_i is the risk of portfolio i. The *Treynor measure* is very similar, but instead of using the standard deviation of the portfolio's total return as the measure of risk, it utilizes the portfolio's beta, β_i, the systematic risk of the portfolio, as measured against the world market portfolio:

$$TRN_i = \frac{\overline{R}_i - R_f}{\beta_i}$$

Exhibit 22.4   *Correlation Coefficients among Monthly Returns of 18 Major Stock Markets, 1977-1996 (All returns are converted to U.S. dollars)*

Correlation Coefficients

Stock Market	AU	AS	BE	CA	DE	FR	GE	HK	IT	JA	NE	NO	SI	SP	SD	SW	UK
Australia (AU)																	
Austria (AS)	0.18																
Belgium (BE)	0.33	0.42															
Canada (CA)	0.59	0.19	0.37														
Denmark (DE)	0.19	0.28	0.37	0.22													
France (FR)	0.34	0.45	0.63	0.40	0.34												
Germany (GE)	0.29	0.62	0.61	0.42	0.42	0.60											
Hong Kong (HK)	0.46	0.26	0.33	0.29	0.18	0.28	0.33										
Italy (IT)	0.23	0.29	0.35	0.39	0.33	0.42	0.38	0.29									
Japan (JA)	0.25	0.20	0.42	0.31	0.37	0.41	0.33	0.22	0.40								
Netherlands (NE)	0.40	0.43	0.61	0.24	0.41	0.57	0.65	0.47	0.33	0.37							
Norway (NO)	0.46	0.31	0.48	0.55	0.31	0.45	0.40	0.34	0.26	0.19	0.54						
Singapore (SI)	0.49	0.23	0.36	0.47	0.24	0.24	0.29	0.55	0.21	0.26	0.41	0.36					
Spain (SP)	0.37	0.32	0.42	0.42	0.33	0.41	0.40	0.34	0.40	0.42	0.39	0.31	0.30				
Sweden (SD)	0.40	0.29	0.39	0.32	0.31	0.33	0.40	0.36	0.34	0.39	0.45	0.44	0.37	0.45			
Switzerland (SW)	0.37	0.49	0.58	0.35	0.40	0.55	0.67	0.35	0.29	0.40	0.64	0.47	0.34	0.36	0.48		
United Kingdom (UK)	0.52	0.33	0.51	0.42	0.37	0.53	0.47	0.44	0.35	0.38	0.65	0.48	0.44	0.44	0.44	0.54	
United States (US)	0.46	0.14	0.40	0.70	0.21	0.44	0.34	0.35	0.23	0.21	0.57	0.45	0.49	0.33	0.41	0.43	0.53

The correlation coefficients are calculated with data from Morgan Stanley's *Capital International Perspectives*. The average of the 153 correlation coefficients is 0.39.

The Sharpe measure indicates on average how much excess return (above risk-free rate) an investor is rewarded per unit of portfolio risk the investor bears. Though the equations of the Sharpe and Treynor measures look similar, the different measure of risk is important. If a portfolio is perfectly diversified (without any unsystematic risk), the two measures give similar rankings because the total portfolio risk is equivalent to the systematic risk. If a portfolio is poorly diversified, it is possible for it to show a high ranking on the basis of the Treynor measure, but a lower ranking on the basis of the Sharpe measure. The difference is attributable to the low level of portfolio diversification. The two measures, therefore, provide complementary but different information.

Take Hong Kong as an example. The mean return was 1.5%. Assume the average risk-free rate was 5% per annum or 0.42% per month over this period. The Sharpe measure was $(0.015 - 0.0042)/0.0961 = 0.113$. For each unit (%) of portfolio total risk an investor bore, the Hong Kong market rewarded the investor with a monthly excess return of 0.113% in 1977–1996. Alternatively, the Treynor measure was $(0.015 - 0.0042)/1.09 = 0.01$.

Though the Hong Kong market had the second highest Treynor measure, its Sharpe measure was ranked eighth, indicating that the Hong Kong market portfolio was not very well diversified from the world market perspective. Instead, the highest ranking belonged to the Netherlands market, which had the highest Sharpe (0.197) and Treynor (0.0109) measures. Does this mean that a U.S. investor would have been best rewarded by investing in the Netherlands market over this historical period? The answer is yes if the investor was allowed to invest in only one of these markets. It would definitely have been better than staying home in the U.S. market, which had a Sharpe measure of 0.143 for the period. However, if the investor was willing to combine these markets in a portfolio, the performance would have been even better. Since these market returns were not perfectly positively correlated, further risk reduction was possible through diversification across markets.

Exhibit 22.4 reports the correlation coefficients among the monthly returns of 18 major stock markets in 1977–1996. Of the 153 correlations reported, the highest was the coefficient between Canada and the United States (0.70). This comes as no surprise since Canada, being a neighboring country and the largest U.S. trading partner, has strong business linkages with the United States. Furthermore, fluctuations of the Canadian dollar to U.S. dollar exchange rates are usually mild relative to the fluctuations of other exchange rates. The next highest correlation was found between the Swiss and the German markets (0.67). Given the strong linguistic and economic ties between the countries, the high correlation is not surprising. On the contrary, the lowest correlations were found between the United States and the Austrian markets (0.14), between the Australian and the Austrian markets (0.18), and between the Hong Kong and the Danish markets (0.18). Situated in different continents and with few economic linkages, these countries have relatively low correlations, which is not surprising. In fact, they provide ample opportunities for portfolio diversification.

The correlation coefficient matrix as a whole also conveys a similar message: there were plenty of portfolio diversification opportunities among various stock markets. Out of 153 correlations, 129 (84%) were below 0.5. The average of the coefficients was 0.39, which is quite low. The potential for risk reduction was great.

Are Markets Increasingly Integrated?

It is often said that as capital markets around the world become more and more integrated over time, the benefits of diversification will be reduced. To test this prediction, we break the 20-year sample period into two halves: 1977–1986 and 1987–1996.[3] Exhibit 22.5 reports correlation coefficients for each subperiod. The means of the correlation coefficients in these two subperiods were, respectively, 0.34 and 0.46, with an average increase of 0.12. The biggest increase was seen between the Singapore and Spanish markets, from 0.04 in 1977–1986 to 0.58 in 1987–1996. The largest decrease was between the Swiss and German markets, dropping from 0.77 to 0.57. Of the 153 pairs of correlations, 115 (75%) showed an increase.

The overall picture is that the correlations have increased over time. Nevertheless, 91 of the 153 correlations (59%) and the overall mean (0.46) were still below 0.5 in 1987–1996. The answer to the question, "Are markets increasingly integrated?" is yes. However, although capital market integration has decreased some benefits of international portfolio diversification, the correlation coefficients between markets are still far from 1.0. There are still plenty of risk-reducing opportunities for international portfolio diversification out there.

The Optimal International Portfolio

To support this argument, we compute an *optimal international portfolio* using the return data of this latter subperiod. In estimating the optimal portfolio weights, we assume that (1) the investors measure returns in their own currencies; (2) the monthly risk-free rate was 0.417% (or 5% per annum); and (3) the investors can buy or short-sell stocks. As an illustration, we choose investors of three countries—Germany, Japan, and the United States.

The optimal portfolio weights are shown in Exhibit 22.6. Notice that the weights are different for the three investors; what was optimal from the Japanese perspective was not necessarily optimal in the United States. The difference is due to the fact that the stock market returns are measured in different home currencies. Since parity conditions do not hold well in reality (at least not in the short run), real exchange risks exist. The effective return of a foreign stock will be different to investors residing in different countries.

Exhibit 22.6 also shows the changes of the Sharpe and Treynor measures when an investor moves from a domestic portfolio to the optimal international portfolio. For example, if a German investor invested only in the domestic market portfolio, the Sharpe measure was 0.024 in 1987–1996. If that same German investor invested in the optimal international portfolio instead, the Sharpe mea-

Exhibit 22.5 *Correlation Coefficients among Monthly Returns of 18 Major Stock Markets, 1977–1986 (All returns are converted to U.S. dollars)*

Stock Market	Correlation Coefficients																
	AU	AS	BE	CA	DE	FR	GE	HK	IT	JA	NE	NO	SI	SP	SD	SW	UK
Australia (AU)																	
Austria (AS)	0.09																
Belgium (BE)	0.23	0.52															
Canada (CA)	0.55	0.18	0.27														
Denmark (DE)	0.28	0.31	0.46	0.27													
France (FR)	0.27	0.49	0.58	0.36	0.30												
Germany (GE)	0.24	0.62	0.60	0.25	0.47	0.54											
Hong Kong (HK)	0.31	0.19	0.22	0.22	0.22	0.19	0.29										
Italy (IT)	0.23	0.21	0.35	0.30	0.31	0.43	0.28	0.33									
Japan (JA)	0.25	0.28	0.44	0.20	0.30	0.42	0.43	0.27	0.40								
Netherlands (NE)	0.33	0.43	0.58	0.52	0.48	0.52	0.64	0.42	0.33	0.40							
Norway (NO)	0.41	0.26	0.47	0.46	0.37	0.45	0.34	0.30	0.19	0.11	0.52						
Singapore (SI)	0.30	0.03	0.20	0.26	0.23	0.07	0.12	0.37	0.09	0.14	0.26	0.22					
Spain (SP)	0.25	0.26	0.29	0.22	0.22	0.33	0.30	0.19	0.38	0.39	0.29	0.15	0.04				
Sweden (SD)	0.29	0.24	0.33	0.29	0.40	0.25	0.30	0.28	0.26	0.31	0.39	0.31	0.20	0.28			
Switzerland (SW)	0.36	0.56	0.63	0.42	0.52	0.56	0.77	0.32	0.30	0.42	0.68	0.48	0.20	0.25	0.41		
United Kingdom (UK)	0.44	0.27	0.46	0.54	0.38	0.49	0.43	0.32	0.36	0.31	0.59	0.40	0.24	0.33	0.30	0.51	
United States (US)	0.35	0.09	0.27	0.66	0.26	0.37	0.24	0.13	0.24	0.16	0.51	0.38	0.31	0.15	0.32	0.38	0.40

The correlation coefficients are computed with data from Morgan Stanley's *Capital International Perspectives*. The average of the 153 correlation coefficients is 0.34.

Exhibit 22.5 *Correlation Coefficients among Monthly Returns of 18 Major Stock Markets, 1987–1996 (All returns are converted to U.S. dollars)*

Correlation Coefficients

Stock Market	AU	AS	BE	CA	DE	FR	GE	HK	IT	JA	NE	NO	SI	SP	SD	SW	UK
Australia (AU)																	
Austria (AS)	0.25																
Belgium (BE)	0.43	0.35															
Canada (CA)	0.65	0.22	0.52														
Denmark (DE)	0.14	0.26	0.32	0.19													
France (FR)	0.43	0.42	0.71	0.46	0.42												
Germany (GE)	0.33	0.62	0.63	0.35	0.40	0.68											
Hong Kong (HK)	0.62	0.34	0.49	0.65	0.16	0.42	0.38										
Italy (IT)	0.23	0.36	0.35	0.34	0.36	0.40	0.49	0.25									
Japan (JA)	0.25	0.14	0.41	0.29	0.42	0.42	0.25	0.19	0.41								
Netherlands (NE)	0.49	0.44	0.65	0.60	0.38	0.65	0.67	0.55	0.33	0.36							
Norway (NO)	0.51	0.36	0.50	0.49	0.27	0.45	0.47	0.38	0.35	0.26	0.55						
Singapore (SI)	0.68	0.40	0.54	0.63	0.26	0.47	0.45	0.78	0.36	0.37	0.59	0.52					
Spain (SP)	0.50	0.39	0.52	0.46	0.43	0.53	0.50	0.52	0.44	0.47	0.52	0.50	0.58				
Sweden (SD)	0.49	0.34	0.45	0.42	0.25	0.43	0.49	0.45	0.43	0.45	0.52	0.57	0.54	0.62			
Switzerland (SW)	0.38	0.45	0.53	0.43	0.32	0.54	0.57	0.38	0.28	0.39	0.60	0.45	0.48	0.49	0.54		
United Kingdom (UK)	0.60	0.38	0.56	0.59	0.38	0.59	0.52	0.58	0.33	0.45	0.74	0.58	0.66	0.59	0.60	0.59	
United States (US)	0.56	0.18	0.56	0.77	0.18	0.55	0.42	0.61	0.23	0.26	0.65	0.52	0.66	0.53	0.50	0.47	0.67

The correlation coefficients are computed with data from Morgan Stanley's *Capital International Perspectives*. The average of the 153 correlation coefficients is 0.46.

Exhibit 22.6 | *Weights of International Optimal Portfolio for German, Japanese, and United States Investors, 1987–1996*

Stock Markets	No Short Selling			Short Selling Allowed		
	German Investor	Japanese Investor	U.S. Investor	German Investor	Japanese Investor	U.S. Investor
Australia	0.0	0.0	0.0	−0.299	−0.263	−0.025
Austria	0.0	0.0	0.0	−0.428	−0.264	0.082
Belgium	0.0	0.0	0.0	2.417	1.816	0.626
Canada	0.0	0.0	0.0	−5.016	−3.778	−0.867
Denmark	0.113	0.126	0.116	1.903	1.441	0.456
France	0.0	0.0	0.0	−0.753	−0.526	−0.244
Germany	0.0	0.0	0.0	−3.355	−2.701	−0.815
Hong Kong	0.104	0.164	0.052	1.795	1.225	0.242
Italy	0.0	0.0	0.0	−1.201	−0.940	−0.145
Japan	0.0	0.0	0.0	−2.300	−1.695	−0.409
Netherlands	0.777	0.694	0.512	5.092	4.086	1.209
Norway	0.0	0.0	0.0	−0.233	−0.254	−0.132
Singapore	0.0	0.0	0.0	−0.476	−0.248	−0.199
Spain	0.0	0.0	0.0	−0.883	−0.563	−0.171
Sweden	0.006	0.016	0.027	2.306	1.733	0.469
Switzerland	0.0	0.0	0.0	0.294	0.352	0.137
United Kingdom	0.0	0.0	0.0	−0.277	−0.217	−0.148
United States	0.0	0.0	0.292	2.413	1.795	0.933
Optimal International Portfolio						
Mean Monthly Return (%)	1.195	1.176	1.251	10.760	8.241	2.801
Standard Deviation (%)	5.296	5.337	4.029	33.337	24.960	6.887
Beta (β)	0.841	0.956	0.785	1.183	0.883	0.455
Sharpe Measure	0.147	0.142	0.207	0.310	0.313	0.346
Treynor Measure	0.010	0.008	0.011	0.087	0.089	0.052
Domestic Portfolio						
Mean Monthly Return (%)	0.462	0.012	1.120	0.462	0.012	1.120
Standard Deviation (%)	5.951	5.337	4.207	5.951	5.337	4.207
Beta (β)	0.612	0.942	0.740	0.612	0.942	0.740
Sharpe Measure	0.008	−0.063	0.167	0.008	−0.063	0.167
Treynor Measure	0.001	−0.004	0.010	0.001	−0.004	0.010
Gains from International Diversification						
Sharpe Measure	0.139	0.205	0.040	0.302	0.376	0.179
Treynor Measure	0.009	0.012	0.001	0.087	0.093	0.043

The results are computed with stock market data from Morgan Stanley's *Capital International Perspectives*. The returns are measured in terms of the investor's home currency.

sure was 0.096. This is an improvement of 0.072, which means that for every percentage of total risk the German investor bore, that investor would have been rewarded by 0.072% more per month for switching to the international portfolio. The increase is quite attractive. The Treynor measure also showed a significant increase (from 0.0057 to 0.0085). In fact, significant improvement in the measures was seen for all three investors. These results confirm the earlier argument that although capital markets are increasingly integrated, there are still ample opportunities for international diversification.

A note of caution should be added. When investors implement international portfolio diversification, they may encounter some obstacles. These obstacles may include higher transaction and information costs, foreign exchange and political risks, discriminatory taxation, legal restrictions on foreigners' ownership of domestic securities, and other market frictions that impede cross-border flow of capital. In recent years, government deregulations and capital market integration have reduced these obstacles significantly. If investors make portfolio decisions when investment barriers exist, they should balance the benefits of international diversification against the extra costs resulting from these barriers. Nevertheless, the potential gains from international diversification generally outweigh the costs. Investors who are willing to invest beyond their national boundaries will be rewarded.[4]

ILLUSTRATIVE CASE

British Pension Funds and International Diversifications

A typical British pension fund has more money invested in BP Amoco than in the entire U.S. stock market. Moreover, even a fund that simply wants to take a neutral position on the British stock market ends up holding fully 6% of its British equity portfolio in this single share. This makes pension-fund trustees unhappy. Not only does it explain why they have missed out on much of Wall Street's bull market; it also burdens them with enormous stock-specific risk. But pension funds have little choice. "Best practice" rules oblige them to match assets to liabilities, that is, to invest mostly in their home market. That home market suddenly includes a U.S. company, Amoco, since it merged with BP last year. And so their local stock market index, the FTSE All-Share, tells British investors that 6% is a proper weighting.

The example points to a growing problem facing investors and index-calculators: how to deal with a world in which capital markets are skipping national boundaries and becoming global. One solution, proposed by Barclays Global Investors (BGI), the world's largest institutional money manager, and Bacon & Woodrow (B&W), an actuarial consultancy, is to create a new asset class of *footloose multinational companies*—and a new index to go with it. FTSE International, the firm that calculates Britain's FTSE All-Share and FTSE 100 indices, plans to launch such a product. Standard & Poor's, a U.S. rival, is thinking similarly. But some say such an index would miss the point.

Pension funds use indices to define the classes of assets in which they invest, and hence the mandates that they give to their fund managers. So one manager running, say, a U.S. equity portfolio uses the Russell 1000 or S&P 500 indices as his benchmark; another invests only in British shares and tries to beat the FTSE All-Share. Or a manager might be hired to replicate an index, not to outperform it. This means that, for trustees, choosing the right indices is at least as important as picking good managers.

But what if the indices no longer provide diversification? The United States, home to about half the world's total stock market capitalization, has relatively little to worry about. Even huge companies such as Microsoft represent less than 5% of the overall market, the weight at which investment consultants start worrying about stock-specific risk.

But more and more trustees and fund managers in the United States and Europe are wondering whether the indices they track still paint a good picture of the asset classes they are supposed to represent. B&W reckons that 20% of U.S. stock market capitalization, and 40% of Europe's, is made up of companies whose operations are too global to be considered "American" or "European."

So B&W and BGI propose to strip multinationals out of their geographical indices and group them in a new global index. This action would be instantly appealing as a benchmark because over the past decade, multinationals have provided the best returns with the lowest volatility. And, with fewer foreign components, local stock indices should become less correlated with each other and allow pension funds to diversify more effectively.

One problem is how to define a multinational. BGI and B&W reckon that any company with more than half its turnover abroad fits the description. But this definition would exclude Microsoft and General Electric. It would include Diageo, a British-based food and drinks maker, but not if Diageo happened to be registered in the United States. Frank Russell, an investment consultancy (and rival to B&W), reckons this makes the proposed index just as arbitrary as those it would replace.

SUMMARY

- The foreign exchange risks of a portfolio, whether it be a securities portfolio or the general portfolio of activities of the MNE, are reduced through international diversification.

- Investors construct *internationally diversified portfolios* in an attempt to combine assets which are less than perfectly correlated, reducing the total risk of the portfolio. In addition, by adding assets outside the home market, the investor has now tapped into a larger pool of potential investments.

- Empirical tests of the application of international portfolio theory indicate that there are significant risk-reduction benefits from international diversification despite increasing global capital market integration.

- The potential gains from international diversification generally outweigh the costs. Investors who are willing to invest beyond their national boundaries will be rewarded.

- Investors should not examine returns in isolation, but rather the amount of return per unit of risk accepted. To consider both risk and return in evaluation of portfolio performance, the Sharpe and Treynor measures were introduced and illustrated.

- The calculation of an optimal international portfolio—specifically the optimal portfolio weights—was shown to depend upon the home country of the investor. This is because market returns must be measured in different home currencies.

QUESTIONS

1. International Diversification and Currency Risk

As the newest member of the asset allocation team in your firm, you constantly find yourself being quizzed by your fellow group members. The topic this morning is international diversification. One analyst asks you the following question:

> Security prices are driven by a variety of factors, but corporate earnings are clearly one of the primary drivers. And corporate earnings—on average—follow business cycles. Exchange rates, as they taught you back in college, reflect the market's assessment of the growth prospects for the economy behind the currency. So if securities go up with the business cycle, and currencies go up with the business cycle, why do we see currencies and securities prices across the globe not going up and down together?

How would you answer?

2. Investing on the DAX

Giri Iyer is European analyst and strategist for Tristar Funds, a New York-based mutual fund company. Mr. Iyer is currently evaluating the recent performance of shares in Pacific Wietz, a publicly traded specialty chemical company in Germany that is listed on the Frankfurt DAX. He gathers the following quotes:

Element	Jan 1 Purchase	Dec 31 Sale	Distributions
Share price	€135.00	€157.60	€15.00
Exchange rate	$1.0660/€	$1.1250/€	—

a.   What was the return on the security in local currency terms?
b.   What was the return on the security in U.S. dollar terms?
c.   Does this mean it was a good investment for a local investor, a U.S.-based investor, or both?

3. Are MNEs Global Investments?

Firms with operations and assets across the globe, true MNEs, are in many ways as international in composition as the most internationally diversified portfolio of unrelated securities. Why do investors not simply invest in MNEs traded on their local exchanges and forgo the complexity of purchasing securities traded on foreign exchanges?

4. Portfolio Risk and Return: Boeing and Unilever

An investor is evaluating a two-asset portfolio of the following two securities:

Security	Expected Return (percent)	Std. Dev. (percent)
Boeing (U.S.)	18.6	22.8
Unilever (U.K.)	16.0	24.0

a.   If the two securities have a correlation of +.6, what is the expected risk and return for a portfolio that is equally weighted?
b.   If the two securities have a correlation of +.6, what is the expected risk and return for a portfolio that is 70% Boeing and 30% Unilever?
c.   If the two securities have a correlation of +.6, what is the expected risk and return for a portfolio that is optimally weighted? (You have to determine the weights that minimize the combined risk.)

5. ADRs versus Direct Holdings

When you are constructing your portfolio, you know you want to include Cementos de Mexico (Mexico) in it, but you cannot decide whether you wish to hold it in the form of ADRs traded on the NYSE or directly through purchases on the Mexico City Bolsa.

a.   Does it make any difference in regard to currency risk?
b.   List the pros and cons of ADRs compared to direct purchases.
c.   What would you recommend if you were an asset investor for a corporation with no international operations or internationally diversified holdings?

6. Monthly Returns for Major Markets

Exhibit 22.3 presented summary statistics for monthly returns on 18 major stock markets across the globe. All returns have been converted to U.S. dollars. In this form, which investors does this data apply most directly to, and who does it not really serve effectively?

7. Sharpe and Treynor Performance Measures

Assume the following U.S. dollar returns (monthly averages) for these Baltic republics. Calculate the Sharpe and Treynor measures of market performance.

Country	Mean Return	Standard Deviation	Risk-Free Rate	Beta
Estonia	1.12%	16.00%	0.42%	1.65
Latvia	0.75%	22.80%	0.42%	1.53
Lithuania	1.60%	13.50%	0.42%	1.20

a. In comparing these measures with those presented in Exhibit 22.3, what was the excess return of the three country markets?

b. Comparing to the averages in Exhibit 22.3, how do these three countries stack up?

WORLD WIDE WEB EXERCISES

W1. International Diversification via Mutual Funds

All major mutual fund companies now offer a variety of internationally diversified mutual funds. The degree of international composition across funds, however, differs significantly. Use the web sites listed below, and any others of interest.

a. Distinguish between international funds, global funds, worldwide funds, and overseas funds.

b. Determine how international funds have been performing, in U.S. dollar terms, relative to mutual funds offering purely domestic portfolios.

Fidelity	http://www.fidelity.com/funds/
T. Rowe Price	http://www.troweprice.com/
Merrill Lynch	http://www.ml.com/
Scudder	http://www.scudder.com/
Kemper	http://www.kemper.com/

W2. Center for Latin American Capital Markets Research

Although most of the Latin American markets suffered significant falls in trading following the Mexican peso crisis of December 1994, many of these markets may still be some of the most "undervalued" markets in the world. If you were given the task of investing US$ 1 million in a single equity market in Latin America, which one would you invest in? Use the World Wide Web to find recent market performance statistics to support your choice.

Center for Latin American Capital	http://www.netrus.net/users/gmorles/

SUGGESTED READINGS

Bekaert, Gert, and Campbell R. Harvey, "Emerging Equity Market Volatility," *Journal of Financial Economics*, Vol. 43, No. 1, Jan. 1997, pp. 29–77.

Brennan, Michael J., and H. Henry Cro, "International Portfolio Investment Flows," *The Journal of Finance*, Vol. 52, No. 5, Oct. 1997, pp. 1851–1880.

De Santis, Giorgio, and Bruno Gerard, "International Asset Pricing and Portfolio Diversification with Time-Varying Risk," *The Journal of Finance*, Vol. 52, No. 5, Oct. 1997, pp. 1881–1912.

Errunza, Vihang, and Ked Hogan, "Macroeconmic Determinants of European Stock Market Volatility, *European Financial Management*, Vol. 4, No. 3, Nov. 1998, pp. 361–378.

Fama, Eugene, and Kenneth R. French, "Value Versus Growth: The International Evidence," *The Journal of Finance*, Vol. 53, No. 6, Dec. 1998, pp. 1975–1999.

Guffin, John M., and G. Andrew Karolyi, "Another Look at the Role of the Industrial Structure of Markets for International Diversification Strategies," *Journal of Financial Economics*, Vol. 50, No. 3, Dec. 1998, pp. 351–373.

Kim, E. Han, and Vijay Singal, "Are Open Markets Good for Foreign Investors and Emerging Nations?," *Journal of Applied Corporate Finance*, Fall 1997, Vol. 10, No. 3, pp. 18–33.

Smith, Roy C., and Ingo Walter, "Risks and Rewards in Emerging Market Investments," *Journal of Applied Corporate Finance*, Fall 1997, Vol. 10, No. 3, pp. 8–17.

NOTES

1. This chapter is largely the work of Professor Chuck C.Y. Kwok, University of South Carolina. Reprinted with permission.
2. This is not always the case. For example, many U.S.-based investors routinely purchase and hold Eurodollar bonds (on the secondary market only; it is illegal during primary issuance), which would not possess currency risk to the U.S.-based investor for they are denominated in the investor's home currency.
3. The choice of 1986 as a dividing date coincided with the official movement toward a Single Europe. At this time most European Union countries deregulated their securities markets or began the process of removing remaining restrictions on the free flow of capital cross-border.
4. The introduction of the euro on January 1, 1999, has, however, rendered historical data on market correlations between European participants obsolete. The euro has not yet had enough of a track record to be used in this form of analysis.

CHAPTER 23

ADVANCED TOPICS IN CURRENCY RISK MANAGEMENT

his chapter provides a more rigorous presentation of a number of topics introduced in previous chapters, including the determination of the optimal currency hedge ratio, cross-currency "proxy" hedging, delta-neutral hedging strategies, and the construction and use of a number of increasingly accepted second-generation option products such as range forwards and participating forwards.

This chapter is optional. Only those interested in more detailed theoretical foundations and additional knowledge in the use of complex options for risk management need read further.

THE CURRENCY HEDGE RATIO

Chapter 6's discussion of transaction exposure management assumed —without discussion—a *hedge ratio* of 1.0. The *hedge ratio*, frequently termed *beta* (β), is the percentage of an individual exposure's nominal amount covered by a financial instrument such as a forward contract or currency option. *Beta* is then defined as follows:

$$\beta = \frac{\text{Value of currency hedge}}{\text{Value of currency exposure}}$$

This section describes the theoretical methodology for the determination of the optimal hedge ratio, the optimal beta.

))) The Optimal Hedge

The value of an individual currency position can be expressed as a portfolio of two assets, a spot asset (the exposure) and a hedge asset (a forward, future, or option). The hedge is constructed so that whatever spot value is lost as a result of adverse exchange rate movements (ΔS) is replaced by an equal but opposite change in the value of the hedge asset, the futures position (ΔF):

$$\Delta \text{ Position value} = \Delta \text{ Spot} - \Delta \text{ Futures} \approx 0$$

The goal is to formulate the effective hedge that will indeed result in no change in the value of the total position.

The *optimal currency hedge* can be found by minimizing the terminal (end-of-period) variance of the two-asset portfolio.[1] The hedge asset amount as a percentage of the exposure is altered to minimize the terminal portfolio variance.

For example, a multinational firm is expecting a foreign-currency-denominated payment, an account receivable at a future date, time t_1, which is termed here the spot or *cash position*. The amount of the hedge, however, must be determined now, at time t_0. We can then specify the *expected value* of this receivable at the future date as

$$E(X_1^\$) = X_1 \times E(S_1)$$

where $E(X_1^\$)$ is the expected value of the foreign currency receivable at time 1;

   X_1 is the amount of the foreign currency to be received (in foreign-currency);

   $E(S_1)$ is the expected spot rate to occur at time 1; $E(S_1)$ is presently unknown.

Note that the *present* spot rate is not a part of the expected value at the end of the period.

Because it does not know what the exchange rate will actually be on the future date, the firm would like to hedge its foreign currency exposure. It can sign a forward contract that would guarantee it a specific exchange rate for U.S. dollars per unit of foreign currency at time t_1, for whatever amount of foreign currency it wishes. The firm then forms a portfolio of this cash position above and a forward contract as a hedge asset. The expected value of the portfolio, $E(P_1)$, at the end of the period, is

$$E(P_1^\$) = X_1 E(S_1) + X_f[E(F_1) - F_0]$$

where X_f is the amount of foreign currency sold forward at time 0

   F_0 is the current price of the futures contract

   $E(F_1)$ is the expected futures price at time 1

This is the expectation now of the portfolio's total value when the receivable is paid in 90 days.

The expected spot rate in 90 days is the only true unknown. The *decision variable* is the amount of the foreign currency that it chooses to sell forward. The question is, what is the specific (mathematical) goal that the firm is pursuing when it chooses the amount of the hedge? Answer: The firm's goal is to minimize the variance of the expected return. This would translate mathematically into selecting the X_f value that results in the minimum variance of the portfolio's final value.

The variance of the expected portfolio value is

$$\text{var}[E(P_1^\$)] = X^2\text{var}(S_1) + X_f^2\,\text{var}(F_1) + 2XX_f\text{cov}(S_1,F_1)$$

Thus, the quantitative problem at hand is the *minimization of this variance* with respect to the decision variable, X_f:

$$\underset{X_f}{\text{MIN}} \quad \text{var}[E(P_1^\$)] = X^2 \text{var}(S_1) + X_f^2 \text{var}(F_1) + 2XX_f \text{cov}(S_1, F_1)$$

Differentiating the total variance with respect to X_f, and setting the results equal to zero yields the following:[2]

$$2X_f \text{var}(F_1) = -2X \text{cov}(S_1, F_1)$$

If this equation is then solved for the amount of foreign currency to be sold forward (X_f) to minimize the portfolio's terminal variance:

$$X_f = \frac{-2X \text{cov}(S_1, F_1)}{2 \text{var}(F_1)} = \frac{-X \text{cov}(S_1, F_1)}{\text{var}(F_1)}$$

Finally, if this equation is rearranged to determine the relative size of the optimal hedge amount to the amount of the original exposure, the optimal hedge ratio, *beta*, is found.

$$\frac{X_f}{X} = \beta = \frac{-\text{cov}(S_1, F_1)}{\text{var}(F_1)}$$

))) Optimal Hedge Calculation Example

What are the implications in practice for this theoretical model of the optimal hedge? Assume a U.S.-based firm expects the receipt of DM1,000,000 in 90 days. With this model, the only values necessary for the determination of the optimal hedge percentage, beta, are the variance of the 90-day forward, .005573, and the covariance between the spot rate ($/DM) and the forward rate ($/DM) of .0054998.[3] The optimal hedge ratio is

$$\beta = \frac{X_f}{X} = \frac{-0.0054998}{0.005573} = -.986865 \approx 98.69\%$$

This optimal hedge ratio indicates that if the firm wishes to minimize the expected value of the two-asset portfolio (spot position and forward position) at the end of the 90 days, it should sell 98.68% of the DM exposure forward, or .9868 × DM1,000,000 = DM986,865.

A beta of 1.0 would imply that the entire amount of the exposure (100%) should be sold forward, yet the theoretical model implies a value that is slightly less than 1. Why is that? The reason is that the spot rate and the futures rate are not perfectly correlated. This less-than-perfect correlation is called *basis risk*. Given that the spot and forward rates for most major currencies typically indicate similar high hedge ratios (.97 and up), hedgers generally do not bother to evaluate and hedge less than the beta of 1.0 when selling currency forward to eliminate exchange rate risk.

))) Cross-Hedging

Sometimes there are no available futures or forward markets for currencies. In these cases, the risk manager may wish to use a substitute or *proxy* for the underlying currency which is available. The methodology used for the determination of the optimal hedge ratio in the previous section is also helpful in the analysis of *proxy-hedging* or *cross-hedging*.

The cross-hedger would likely go through a simple two-step process to determine the optimal cross-hedge: first, find the currency future that is most highly correlated with the actual currency of exposure; second, find the optimal hedge ratio using the covariance between the proxy futures and the actual currency, as in the above model. This would then tell the risk manager the amount of the proxy future that should be purchased to hedge the currency exposure.

The Deutschemark (DM) has long been used as a proxy for the hedging of all European Monetary System (EMS) currencies. This currency will now be replaced by the euro. A U.S.-resident firm with long currency positions in many EMS currencies could effectively hedge all positions at once using the DM as a proxy future. The validity of the proxy hedge, however, depends on the covariance and variance of the recent past applying to the future (as in the case of volatility in options). In periods in which the fundamental relations between EMS currencies change, as in September 1992 or July 1993, the proxy hedge may prove suboptimal.

Many of the emerging market countries of Latin America and Asia are just now beginning to allow the formation of derivative markets (forwards, futures, and options) in their currencies. It is clear, however, that for many MNEs that are exposed to these currencies, cross-hedging will continue to be utilized to manage the currency risks arising as these derivative markets slowly develop.

)))) Delta Hedging

A slightly more sophisticated currency hedging strategy than the traditional one demonstrated in Chapter 6 is called delta hedging. The objective of **delta hedging** is to construct a position—the combined exposure and hedging instrument—whose *market values* (not terminal values) will change in opposite directions with changes in the spot exchange rate; it is the value of the position at all times that is being managed, not the value of the position only at termination.

Suppose we return to the basic position valuation principle introduced at the beginning of this chapter. If the hedge is constructed so that the changes in the spot position and hedge position are equal and opposite in currency value at all times in the life-span of the exposure, it is termed *delta-neutral*.

$$\Delta \text{ Position value} = \Delta \text{ Spot} - \Delta \text{ Futures} \approx 0$$

What is lost (gained) on the spot position as a result of exchange rate changes is exactly offset by the gain (loss) in the market value of the hedge instrument.

A numerical example helps in differentiating this strategy from the generic hedging we have described up to now. Assume a U.S.-based firm has an account payable in 90 days in the amount of £1,000,000. The current exchange rate and interest rate values are the same as those used in Chapter 5 in the explanation of currency option valuation and its corresponding "Greeks."

Spot rate	= $1.7000/£
90-day forward	= $1.7000/£
Strike rate	= $1.7000/£
U.S. dollar interest rate	= 8.00% (per annum)
British pound interest rate	= 8.00% (per annum)
Time (days)	= 90
Standard deviation (volatility)	= 10.00 %

This call option on British pounds, with strike price of $1.70/£ (forward at-the-money), has a premium of 3.3 cents/£. The delta of this option is 0.5. This means that the value of the option, the option premium, will change by (0.5) × (change in spot rate). For example, if the spot rate moves from $1.70/£ to $1.71/£, the option premium changes by:

$$\Delta \text{ Option premium} = 0.5 \times (\$1.71/£ - \$1.70/£) = \$0.005/£$$

This delta is the focal point of a delta-hedging strategy.

Exhibit 23.1 illustrates how a delta-neutral hedge would be constructed for this exposure. The firm that is short in a foreign currency fears a foreign currency appreciation versus the domestic currency. If the spot rate were to rise to $1.71/£, while all other values remained the same, the expected cost in U.S. dollars of making the payment would rise from $1,700,000 to $1,710,000, an increase of $10,000.

At the same time, the value of the call option on British pounds—the market price of the option—would rise from 3.3 cents/£ to 3.8 cents/£; or one half-cent per pound purchased. Since the cost of the foreign currency payable has increased one cent per pound, and the option's value changes by only one-half cent per pound, if the value of the option position is to offset the change in the

---

Exhibit 23.1   *Construction and Valuation of a Delta-Neutral Hedging Strategy*

(1) Spot Rate	(2) Value of Exposure	(3) US$ Value of Exposure[a]	(4) Call Option Premium[b]	(5) Option Contract[c]	(6) Market Value of Option[d]
$1.70/£	£1,000,000	$1,700,000	$0.033/£	£2,000,000	$66,000
$1.71/£	£1,000,000	$1,710,000	$0.038/£	£2,000,000	$76,000
Change in value:		$10,000	$0.005/£		+ $10,000

[a]Column (3) = column (1) × column (2).
[b]Call option strike price of $1.70/£, 90-day maturity, volatility of 10% per annum, delta = 0.5.
[c]Option contract size for delta-neutral hedge = exposure/delta = £1,000,000/0.5 = £2,000,000. The delta of the same call option (strike price $1.70/£) rises to .546 after spot rate moves to $1.71/£.
[d]Column (6) = column (4) × column (5).

exposure, the option contract would need to be for twice the amount of the exposure, or £2,000,000. An option for £2,000,000 would increase from the purchase price of $66,000 to $76,000 in market value after the spot rate changes. The impact of the exchange rate change has been neutralized by the combined position.

Delta-hedging strategies utilize the *total value* of the option (the market value, which includes both intrinsic value and time value) as the hedge instrument's value, not simply the intrinsic value, which has been utilized throughout previous chapters. Although this is more theoretically correct, delta hedging has two major drawbacks:

1. Delta-neutral positions such as the example shown here require the purchase of option or other financial derivative contracts, which are often substantially larger in currency amount than the exposure itself. In this case the option contract is for £2,000,000 in order to hedge an exposure of £1,000,000. Many firms believe this is inherently speculative and overly expensive in capital outlays.

2. Delta-neutral positions must be constantly monitored and frequently rebalanced. For example, after the spot rate in the previous example has moved to $1.71/£, the delta of the option has now risen to approximately 0.55 from 0.50. In order to maintain a delta-neutral position, the firm needs currency coverage of only £1,818,182 (£1,000,000 ÷ .55). It would sell part of the existing option position down to the new delta-neutral position. This requires active management and more frequent transactions, which many firms do not wish to undertake.

FINANCIAL ENGINEERING AND RISK MANAGEMENT

Financial engineering has come to mean very different things to different people. Probably one of the best definitions is that provided by John Finnerty, himself one of the innovators in this field:

> Financial engineering involves the design, the development, and the implementation of innovative financial instruments and processes, and the formulation of creative solutions to problems in finance.[4]

We use "financial engineering" here to describe the use of the basic financial building blocks (spot positions, forwards, options) to construct positions that provide the user with desired risk and return characteristics. The number of combinations and deviations is indeed infinite.

The following techniques are, however, simply tools. They are a means to an end, foreign currency risk management, and not an end in themselves. The purpose of this section is to demonstrate the mechanics of their construction and to highlight the types of currency exposures for which they may be appropriate. Many of these products have been developed for a specific risk-management problem, a problem that may or may not be applicable to all firms. With a few notable exceptions, the following products can either be acquired as risk-management products from financial institutions or be constructed by the firm itself.

Dayton Manufacturing: U.S.-Based Firm with £1,000,000 90-Day Account Receivable

Exhibit 23.2 illustrates the problem that is used throughout the remainder of this chapter. Dayton possesses a long £1,000,000 exposure—an account receivable—to be settled in 90 days. The firm believes that the exchange rate will move in its favor over the 90-day period (the British pound will appreciate versus the U.S. dollar). This is a movement to the right along the horizontal axis of Exhibit 23.2. Although it has this *directional view* or *currency expectation*, the firm wishes to have downside protection in the event the pound were to depreciate instead. Exhibit 23.2 also lists the assumptions and option values used throughout the remainder of the chapter.[5]

The exposure management zones that are of most interest to the firm are the two opposing *triangles* formed by the uncovered and forward rate profiles. The firm would like to retain all potential area in the upper-right triangle but minimize its own potential exposure to the bottom-left triangle. The put option's kinked profile is consistent with what the firm wishes if it believes the pound will appreciate (the dollar will depreciate).

The firm could consider any number of different put option strike prices, depending on the minimum assured value—degree of self-insurance—the firm is willing to accept. Exhibit 23.2 illustrates two different put option alternatives, a forward-ATM put of strike price $1.4700/£, and a forward-OTM put with strike price $1.4400/£.[6] The forward-OTM put provides protection at lower cost, but also at a lower level of protection.

The Synthetic Forward

At a forward rate of $1.4700/£, the proceeds of the forward contract in 90 days will yield $1,470,000. A second alternative for the firm would be to construct a *synthetic forward* using options. The *synthetic forward* requires the firm to combine three different elements:

1. Maintain a long position in £ (A/R of £1,000,000);
2. Buy a put option on £ bought at a strike price of $1.4700/£, paying a premium of $0.0318/£;
3. Sell a call option on £ at a strike price of $1.4700/£, earning a premium of $0.0318/£.

The purchase of the put option requires a premium payment, whereas the sale of the call option earns the firm the premium payment. If both options are struck at the forward rate (forward-ATM), the premiums should be identical and the net premium payment a value of zero.

Exhibit 23.2   *Dayton Manufacturing's Assumptions and Option Values*

Spot rate:	$1.4790/£	90-day forward rate:	$1.4700/£
A/R due:	90 days	90/day euro-dollar interest rate:	3.250%
$/£ volatility:	11.0%	90-day euro-pound interest rate:	5.720%

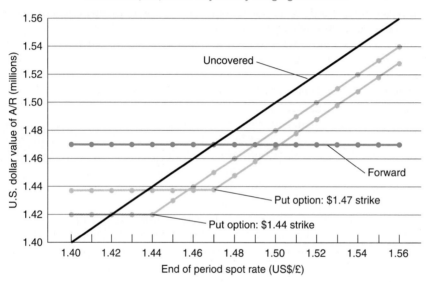

Value of £1,000,000 90-day A/R by hedging alternative

Strike Price ($/£)	Put Premium ($/£)	Put Premium (%)	Call Premium ($/£)	Call Premium (%)	
$1.4000	$0.0079	0.6	$0.0774	5.5	
1.4200	0.0125	0.9	0.0621	4.4	
1.4400	0.0188	1.3	0.0486	3.4	
1.4500	0.0226	1.6	0.0425	2.9	
1.4600	0.0269	1.8	0.0369	2.5	
1.4700	0.0318	2.2	0.0318	2.2	"Forward-ATM"
1.4800	0.0371	2.5	0.0272	1.8	
1.4900	0.0429	2.9	0.0231	1.6	
1.5000	0.0491	3.3	0.0194	1.3	
1.5200	0.0630	4.1	0.0134	0.9	
1.5400	0.0784	5.1	0.0089	0.6	

All premiums are for European-style options and are calculated using the currency option pricing spreadsheet "OPTION.XLS" introduced in Chapter 5. All premiums are rounded to the nearest hundredth of a cent. Premiums are stated both in absolute terms of $/£ and as a percentage of the strike price (industry practice).

Exhibit 23.3 illustrates the uncovered position, the basic forward rate hedge, and the individual profiles of the put and call options for the chapter problem. The outcome of the combined position is easily confirmed by simply tracing what would happen at all exchange rates to the left of $1.4700/£, and what would happen to the right of $1.4700/£.

At all exchange rates to the left of $1.4700/£, the following would be true:

1. The firm would receive £1,000,000 in 90 days.

2. The call option on pounds sold by the firm would expire out of the money.

3. The firm would exercise the put option on pounds to sell the pounds received at $1.4700/£.

Exhibit 23.3   *Construction of a Synthetic Forward for a Long FX Position*

Instruments	Strike Rates	Premium	Amount (£)
Buy a put	$1.4700/£ (OTM)	$0.0318/£	£1,000,000
Sell a call	$1.4700/£ (OTM)	$0.0318/£	£1,000,000

At all exchange rates below $1.4700/£, the U.S.-based firm would earn $1,470,000 from the receivable. At all exchange rates to the right of $1.4700/£, the following would be true:

1. The firm would receive £1,000,000 in 90 days;

2. The put option on pounds purchased by the firm would expire out of the money;

3. The firm would turnover the £1,000,000 received to the buyer of the call who now exercises the call option against the firm. The firm receives $1.4700/£ from the call option buyer.

Thus, at all exchange rates above or below $1.4700/£, the U.S.-based firm nets $1,470,000 in domestic currency. The combined spot-option position has behaved identically to that of a forward contract. A firm with the exact opposite position, £1,000,000 payable 90 days in the future, could similarly construct a synthetic forward using options.[7]

But why would a firm undertake this relatively complex position in order simply to create a forward contract? The answer is found by looking at the option premiums earned and paid. We have assumed that the option strike prices used were precisely forward-ATM rates, and the resulting option premiums paid and earned were exactly equal. But this need not be the case. If the option strike prices (remember they must be identical for both options, bought and sold) are not precisely on the forward-ATM, the two premiums may differ by a slight amount. The net premium position may then end up as a net premium earning or a net premium payment. If positive, this amount would be added to the proceeds from the receivable to result in a higher total dollar value received.[8]

SECOND-GENERATION CURRENCY RISK MANAGEMENT PRODUCTS

Second-generation risk management products are constructed from the two basic derivatives used throughout this book: the forward and the option. We will subdivide them into two groups: (1) the *zero-premium option products,* which focus on pricing in and around the forward rate, and (2) the *exotic option products* (for want of a better name), which focus on alternative pricing targets. Although all the following derivatives are sold as financial products by risk management firms, we will present each as simply the construction of the position from common building blocks, or LEGO®s as they have been termed, used in traditional currency risk management, forwards and options.[9] As a group, they are collectively referred to as *complex options.*

))) Zero-Premium Option Products

The primary problem with the use of options for risk management in the eyes of the firms is the up-front premium payment. Although the premium payment is only a portion of the total payoff profile of the hedge, many firms view the expenditure of substantial funds for the purchase of a financial derivative as prohibitively expensive. In comparison, the forward contract, which eliminates currency risk, requires no out-of-pocket expenditure by the firm (and requires no real specification of expectations regarding exchange rate movements).

Zero-premium option products (or financially engineered derivative combinations) are designed to require no out-of-pocket premium payment at the initiation of the hedge. This set of products includes what are most frequently labeled the *range forward* and the *participating forward*.[10] Both these products: (1) are priced on the basis of the forward rate; (2) are constructed to provide a zero-premium payment up front; (3) allow the hedger to take advantage of expectations of the direction of exchange rate movements.

For the case problem at hand in which the U.S.-resident firm possesses a long position in British pounds, this means that all the following products are applicable to an expectation that the U.S. dollar will depreciate versus the pound. If the hedger has no such view, it should turn back now (and buy a forward, or nothing at all)!

))) Ratio Spreads

Before w : describe the most widely accepted second-generation option products, it is helpful to demonstrate one of the older methods of obtaining a zero-premium option combination, an alternative that leaves the hedger with a large uncovered exposure.

The U.S.-based firm in our chapter problem decides that it wishes to establish a floor level of protection by purchasing a $1.4700/£ put option (forward-ATM) at a cost of $0.0318/£ (total cost of $31,800). This is a substantial outlay of capital upfront for the option premium, and the firm's risk-management division has no budget funding expenditures of this magnitude. The firm, feeling strongly that the dollar will depreciate against the pound, decides to finance the purchase of the put with the sale of an OTM call option. The firm reviews market conditions and considers a number of call option strike prices that are significantly OTM, strike prices of $1.5200/£, $1.5400/£, or further out.

It is decided that the $1.5400/£ call option, with a premium of $0.0089/£, is to be written and sold to earn the premium and finance the put purchase. However, because the premium on the OTM call is so much smaller than the forward-ATM put premium, the size of the call option written must be larger. The firm determines the amount of the call by solving the simple problem of premium equivalency:

Cost of put premium = Earnings call premium

Substituting in the put and call option premiums yields

$$\$0.0318/£ \times £1{,}000{,}000 = \$0.0089/£ \times £ \text{ call}$$

Solving for the size of the call option to be written, we obtain:

$$\frac{\$31,800}{\$0.0089/\pounds} = \pounds 3,573,034$$

The reason that this strategy is called a *ratio spread* is that the final position, call option size to put option size, is a ratio greater than 1 ($\pounds 3,573,034 \div \pounds 1,000,000$ or a ratio of about 3.57).[11]

As a number of firms using this strategy have learned the hard way, however, that if the expectations of the hedger prove incorrect and the spot rate moves past the strike price of the call option written, the firm is faced with delivering a foreign currency that it does not have. In this example, if the spot rate moved above $1.5400/\pounds, the firm would have to cover a position of $\pounds 2,573,034$.

)))) The Range Forward

The basic *range forward* has been marketed under a variety of other names, including the *collar*, *flexible forward*, *cylinder option*, *option fence*, or simply *fence*, *mini-max*, or *zero-cost tunnel*. The range forward is constructed in two steps:

1. Buying a put option with a strike rate *below* the forward rate, for the full amount of the long currency exposure (100% coverage)

2. Selling a call option with a strike rate *above* the forward rate, for the full amount of the long currency exposure (100% coverage)

The hedger chooses one side of the "range" or spread, normally the downside (put strike rate), which then dictates the strike rate at which the call option will be sold. The call option must be chosen at a distance as far from the forward rate as the put option strike price is from the forward rate. If the hedger believes there is a significant possibility that the currency will move in the firm's favor, and by a sizable degree, the put-floor rate may be set relatively low in order for the ceiling to be higher or further out from the forward rate and still enjoy a zero net premium.[12]

Exhibit 23.4 illustrates the final outcome of a range forward constructed by buying a put with strike price $1.4500/\pounds, paying a premium of $0.0226/\pounds, combined with selling a call option with strike price $1.4900/\pounds, earning a premium of $0.0231/\pounds. The hedger has bounded the range over which the firm's A/R value moves as an uncovered position, with a put option floor and a sold call option ceiling.

A number of variations on the basic range forward exist. If both strike prices are the same, it is a *synthetic forward* as described in the previous section. If both strike prices chosen are equal to the actual forward rate, the synthetic equals the actual forward contract. This synthetic forward should theoretically have a near-zero net premium.[13] If the strike rates of the options are selected independently of the desire for an exact zero net premium up front (it must still bracket the forward rate), it is termed an *option collar* or *cylinder option*.

Exhibit 23.4	*The Range Forward*

Instruments	Strike Rates	Premium	Amount(£)
Buy a put	$1.4500/£ (OTM)	$0.0226/£	£1,000,000
Sell a call	$1.4900/£ (OTM)	$0.0231/£	£1,000,000

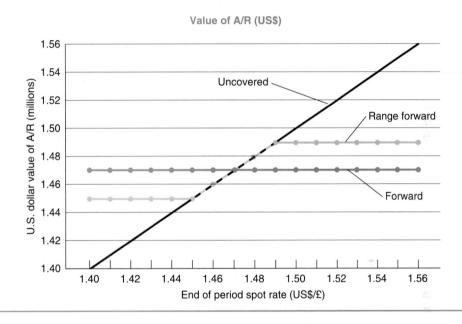

The Participating Forward

The *participating forward*, also called a *zero-cost ratio option* and *forward participation agreement*, is an option combination that allows the hedger to take a position that will share in potential upside movements in the exchange rate, while providing option-based downside protection, all at a zero net premium. The participating forward is constructed via two steps:

1. Buying a put option with a strike price *below* the forward rate, for the *full amount* of the long currency exposure (100% coverage)

2. Selling a call option with a strike price *that is the same as the put option*, for a *portion* of the total currency exposure (less than 100% coverage).

As in the case of the range forward, the buyer of a participating forward will normally choose the put option strike rate first. Because the call option strike rate is the same as the put, all that remains is to determine the participation rate, the proportion of the exposure sold as a call option.

Exhibit 23.5	The Participating Forward

Instruments	Strike Rates	Premium	Amount (£)
Buy a put	$1.4500/£ (OTM)	$0.0262/£	£1,000,000
Sell a call	$1.4500/£ (ITM)	$0.0425/£	£532,000

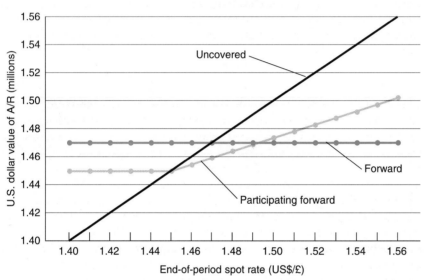

Exhibit 23.5 illustrates the construction of a participating forward for the chapter problem. The firm first chooses the put option protection level, in this case $1.4500/£, with a premium of $0.0226/£. A call option sold with the same strike rate of $1.4500/£ would earn the firm $0.0425/£. The call premium is substantially higher than the put premium because the call option is already in the money.

The percentage cover for the call option is then determined so that call premium earnings exactly offset put premiums paid.

$$\text{Put premium} = \text{Percent cover} \times \text{Call premium}$$

Using the chapter problem premiums, we find the percent cover

$$\text{Percent cover} = \frac{\$0.0226/£}{\$0.0425/£} = .5318 \approx 53.2\%$$

The firm must sell a call option of .532 × £1,000,000, or £532,000, in order to achieve a zero net premium.

The *participation rate* is the residual percentage of the exposure that is not covered by the sale of the call option. For example, if the percent cover is 53.2%, the participation rate would be 100% – the percent cover, or 46.8%. This means that for all favorable exchange rate movements, those above $1.4500/£, the hedger would "participate" in or enjoy 46.8% of the differential. However, as with all option-based hedges, downside exposure is bounded by the put option strike rate.

The expectations of the buyer are similar to those in the case of the range forward, only the degree of foreign currency bullishness is greater. For the participating forward to be superior in outcome to the range forward, it is necessary for the exchange rate to move farther in the favorable direction than for the range forward.

EXOTIC OPTIONS

This second set of instruments offers alternative pricing, timing, or exercise provisions of the product. All these have in some way altered the valuation principles of the basic option-pricing model, hence the term *exotic*.[14] These products are therefore products only and not easily independently reproducible by the corporate risk manager. Their pricing is generally complex and they are generally produced and sold by risk management departments of major multinational banks.

Most exotic options are European-style options whose values change with the direction and the *path* the spot rate follows over their life span (they are in fact often referred to as path-dependent in value). We briefly discuss a few of these exotics: the *knock-out option*, the *average rate option*, *compound option*, and the *chooser option*. This is only a sampling of some of these increasingly complex—even bizarre—option-based instruments. We continue discussing each of these currency derivative products in the context of a U.S.-based firm with a long British pound exposure. But, as they warn spectators during daredevil exhibitions, "Don't try this at home."

))) The Knock-Out Option

The *knock-out option*, also often referred to as the *down and out option (DAOO)*, *barrier option*, *extinguishable option*, or *activate/deactivate option*, differs markedly from previous products covered. The knock-out option is designed to behave like any option, offering downside protection, but to offer only a limited upside range before crossing a previously specified *barrier* or *knock-out level*, at which it automatically expires. Because the knock-out level is in the upside direction, the automatic expiration of the option would occur only after the exchange rate has moved in the expected direction of the hedger (a favorable movement). In return for giving up the full maturity period coverage, the premium of the option—being a shorter-term option—is smaller.[15]

Exhibit 23.6 depicts the knock-out option for Dayton (U.S.) and compares its basic profile with that of the standard put option (strike price $1.4700/£ at premium $0.0318/£). The knock-out strike price is also $1.4700/£ (forward-

ATM), with a barrier of $1.4900/£. The premium of the barrier option is significantly lower, only $0.0103/£.[16] As illustrated, the knock-out appears to be the obviously better choice with the same strike price at a lower premium. The problem, however, is that the diagram is not able to illustrate the possibility that the spot rate could rise in the early days of the exposure to $1.4900/£ or higher, crossing the barrier, and therefore canceling the option protection. The exposure would still have many days left until maturity, during which the spot rate could easily rise or fall in essentially unlimited magnitudes. The standard put option, although higher in premium, will not expire prior to the maturity of the exposure. In the end, the cheaper cost of the knock-out option may prove to be an added cost for a final protection level of zero.

)))) The Average Rate Option

The *average rate option* is the most recent second-generation (possibly third-generation) currency derivative. These options are normally classified as "path-

Exhibit 23.6	The Knock-Out Option

Instruments	Strike Rates	Premium	Amount (£)
Buy a put	$1.4700/£ (ATM) Barrier: $1.4900/£	$0.0103/£	£1,000,000

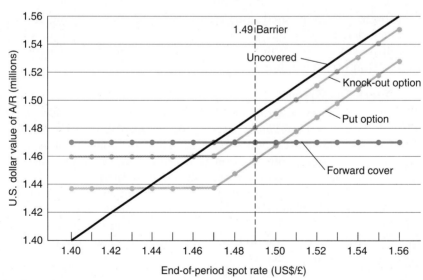

dependent" currency options because their values depend on averages of spot rates over some prespecified period of time. Here we describe two examples of path-dependent options, the *average rate option* and the *average strike option*:

1. The *average rate option* (ARO), also known as an *Asian option*, sets the option strike rate up front and is exercised at maturity if the average spot rate over the period (as observed by scheduled sampling) is less than the preset option strike rate.

2. The *average strike option* (ASO), establishes the option strike rate as the average of the spot rate experienced over the option's life and is exercised if the strike rate is greater than the end-of-period spot rate.

Like the knock-out option, the average rate option is difficult to depict because its value depends not on the ending spot rate; instead, the path the spot rate takes over its specified life span. For example, an average rate option with strike price $1.4700/£ would have a premium of only $0.0186/£. The average rate would be calculated by weekly observations (12 full weeks, the first observation occurring 13 days from purchase) of the spot rate. Numerous different averages or paths of spot rate movement obviously exist. A few different scenarios aid in understanding how the ARO differs in valuation.

1. The spot rate moves very little over the first 70 to 80 days of the period, with a sudden movement in the spot rate below $1.4700/£ in the days prior to expiration. Although the final spot rate is below $1.4700/£, the average for the period is above $1.4700, so the option cannot be exercised. The receivable is exchanged at the spot rate (below $1.4700/£) and the cost of the option premium is still incurred.

2. The dollar slowly and steadily depreciates versus the pound, the rate rising from $1.4790/£ to $1.48, $1.49, and on up. At the end of the 90-day period the option expires out of the money, the receivable is exchanged at the favorable spot rate, and the firm has enjoyed average rate option protection at substantially lower premium expense.

A variety of different types of average rate currency option products are sold by banking institutions, each having a distinct payoff structure. Because of the intricacy of the path-dependent option's value, care must be taken in the use of these instruments. As in all markets, buyer beware.[17]

)))) The Compound Option

The *compound option* is an option to either buy or sell an option on a specific future date. Also referred to as *options on options*, a call compound option gives the buyer the right to buy a specific option on a future date, while a put compound option gives the buyer the right to sell a specific option on a future date. The underlying option—the option the first option is written upon—is fully defined in terms of premium, strike price, amount, and maturity. Because the first option is an option on an option, the up-front premium is substantially smaller.

It is ironic that these "third-generation" currency risk-management products are focused on contingent currency exposures, the same exposure for which only a few years ago the simple put and call options were thought appropriate.[18] For example, a firm making a bid on a contract that will result in a substantial exposure in terms of foreign currency cash flows, positive or negative, may be able to cover the bid exposure with a smaller initial premium payment than a standard option would require. It must be remembered, however, that the first premium is to maintain the right to pay (receive) the second premium if the right is exercised. The hedger must be careful and clear as to what cash flows and premiums will be required at what points in time if the compound option is purchased.

The compound option has two different points in time of maturity. The first, the *near-date* or *first-date*, is the date on which the buyer of the compound option must decide whether the right is to be exercised to buy or sell the underlying option. The second point in time is the *last-date* or *second-date*, on which the actual underlying option expires. Because of this sequencing of time periods, the compound option may in the future be one method firms may use for distant currency exposures that are highly contingent without committing substantial quantities of corporate capital to the payment of option premiums.

The Chooser Option

A final alternative—final for the moment—offers the extreme of option flexibility. The *chooser option* allows the buyer to lock-in a specific option strike price, amount, and maturity now, and choose at a later date ("chooser date") whether the option is to be a call option or put option. The use of such a hedge instrument is primarily in cases in which the exposure's final net long or net short position is unknown until further into the life of the exposure.

SUMMARY

- The determination of the *optimal hedge ratio* for an individual exposure can be derived by constructing a two-asset portfolio and minimizing its expected terminal value.

- Alternative hedging methodologies such as *delta hedging* and *proxy hedging* are often useful and necessary when dealing with exotic currencies or exposures.

- The rapidly developing field of financial engineering allows the corporate Treasurer to construct financial positions with financial derivatives that possess desired risk-return profiles to match and manage complex exposures and detailed market expectations.

- Second-generation option products like *range forwards*, and *participating forwards* allow hedgers to acquire option protection with a zero net up-front premium payment.

■ Exotic option products, sometimes called *third-generation products*, are options constructed to provide values and protection that are functions of the path the spot rate takes over the life span of the option, and not simply based on the value at expiration (ending spot rate). The primary benefit is the reduction of the option premium paid by the buyer.

QUESTIONS

1. Delta-Neutral Hedging
Which is more appropriate for the MNE's accounting purposes, the typical end-of-period currency hedging strategy or the continuing market-value hedging strategy used in delta-neutral hedging?

2. Financial Derivatives: Engineering in Emerging Markets
The number of countries allowing domestic banks and other financial service providers to create and sell financial derivatives for risk management is continually growing. Many emerging markets, however, are still confronted with both lack of financial breadth in financial products and regulatory restrictions limiting derivative construction.

a. What basic financial products and markets are needed to create the currency risk-management derivatives described in this chapter?
b. Why do you think many emerging markets do not possess these elements?
c. Why do you think the governments of many emerging markets still prohibit or restrict the growth of either the necessary products and markets or the derivatives themselves?

3. Synthetic Forwards
Assume the same identical values hold as in the case of Dayton in the chapter, with the single exception that the £1,000,000 exposure is a 90-day account payable, not account receivable.

a. Explain precisely how to construct a synthetic forward to cover the exposure.
b. Diagram the construction.
c. Explain how you would construct a "synthetic forward" whose strike prices are set so that the firm would have a positive net premium to pay up front, but would enjoy a slightly better constructed forward rate.

4. Tiffany's Yen Exposure (A)
Tiffany & Co., the prestigious U.S. luxury item retailer, sells all merchandise to its Japanese retail representative, Matsusoka. Matsusoka has recently changed its purchasing patterns with its suppliers like Tiffany from an as-

ordered basis to a strategy of building substantial inventories of merchandise. Matsusoka's reasoning is that, particularly for many luxury items, consumers buy on impulse and not based on price, taking into consideration that the goods are expensive to begin with, and that therefore they want to be able to buy and carry on the same day.

Tiffany invoices all sales to Matsusoka in Japanese yen, a standard policy of the firm. It believes it that it is best carrying the currency risk and allowing firms like Matsusoka to focus on sales rather than risk management. The new inventory purchase pattern means that Tiffany will now have a 90-day account receivable of ¥270 million.

Tiffany wishes to consider the use of currency options to manage this exposure. Due to the limited budget of the Finance and Treasury divisions, it will need to finance these option purchases by writing offsetting positions. Current market conditions are as follows:

Spot exchange rate:	¥108.20/$
90-day forward rate:	¥107.88/$
90-day Eurodollar deposit rate:	3.3750%
90-day Euroyen deposit rate:	2.1875%
90-day yen/dollar volatility quote:	11.8%

Construct and diagram a range forward that is ± 2% around the forward rate.

a. What precisely would Tiffany like the spot rate to be at the end of the 90-day period?
b. What would be the U.S. dollar proceeds, net of all premiums, if this spot rate did occur?
c. What would be the minimum dollar proceeds if the spot rate moved against Tiffany?

Construct and diagram a range forward that is ± 5% around the forward rate.

a. What precisely would Tiffany like the spot rate to be at the end of the 90-day period?
b. What would be the U.S. dollar proceeds, net of all premiums, if this spot rate did occur?
c. What would be the minimum dollar proceeds if the spot rate moved against Tiffany?

5. Tiffany's Yen Exposure (B)

Using the same assumptions as in the previous question, construct a participating forward with a 65% participation rate.

a. What is the size of the call option that must now be sold to yield a net-zero up front premium?
b. Why are the notional principals of the call option and put option different?

c.   What is the maximum and minimum dollar proceeds from this position for the yen receivable?

6. Lopez Motor Works (Spain)

Lopez Motor Works of Bilbao, Spain, builds automotive transmission sub-assemblies for a variety of major auto manufacturers in Europe. It imports a critical computerized "brain-chip" for the transmissions from a Japanese subsidiary of NEC (Japan). Shipments of the chips occur quarterly, with 90-day payment terms. Lopez is invoiced in yen, and the shipments average ¥150 million. Lopez's Treasury wishes to utilize options in its risk management of this short yen position but does not wish to pay out substantial currency option premiums. It therefore wishes to consider a variety of net-zero complex option positions. Current market conditions are as follows:

Spot exchange rate:	¥118.157/€
90-day forward exchange rate:	¥117.450/€
90-day Euroyen interest rate:	0.7500%
90-day Euroeuro interest rate:	3.1250%
90-day yen/euro volatility quote:	12.50%

a.   Construct a range forward that is ± 3% around the forward rate. What is the maximum and minimum euro proceeds to be expected by Lopez from this position in 90 days?

b.   Construct a range forward that is ± 5% around the forward rate. What is the maximum and minimum euro proceeds to be expected by Lopez from this position in 90 days?

WORLD WIDE WEB EXERCISES

W1. Options and Futures Pricing in Emerging Markets

The growth of financial derivatives and financial engineering-related risk management services is growing rapidly, even in emerging markets. Use the following websites to begin your assessment of what opportunities are available to manage long positions arising from your firm's exporting to firms in these markets and accepting local currency payment.

Emerging Markets Companion	http://www.emgmkts.com/pricing/optfut.htm
Numa Web for Financial Derivatives	http://www.numa.com/
Derivatives Links	http://www.ftmanagement.com/

W2. Statistics Tutorial

Use the following website, one of many that provides some basic instruction in probability and statistical methods, to find the calculation formula for volatility.

Learning Modules   http://www.cne.gmu.edu/modules/dau/stat

SUGGESTED READINGS

Finnerty, John D., "Financial Engineering in Corporate Finance: An Overview," *Financial Management*, Winter 1988, p. 14.

Géczy, Christopher, Bernadette A. Minton, and Catherine Schrand, "Why Firms Use Currency Derivatives," *The Journal of Finance*, Vol. 52, No. 4, Aug. 1997, pp. 1323–1354.

Kerkvliet, Joe, and Michael H. Moffett, "The Hedging of an Uncertain Future Foreign Currency Cash Flow," *Journal of Financial and Quantitative Analysis*, Vol. 26, No. 4, Dec. 1991, pp. 565–578.

Tompkins, Robert, "Behind the Mirror," in *From Black-Scholes to Black Holes: New Frontiers in Options*, London: Risk Management Ltd., 1992, pp. 129–133.

NOTES

1. Kerkvliet and Moffett (1991).
2. Differentiation of the entire equation with respect to X_f results in the left-hand side equaling zero, and the first term on the right-hand side also equaling zero. The remaining terms would appear as:
$$0 = 0 + 2X_f \operatorname{var}(F_1) + 2X \operatorname{cov}(S_1, F_1)$$
3. Variance and covariance are for the U.S. dollar/Deutschemark for the 1981 to 1987 period.
4. Finnerty (1988), p. 14.
5. Values are roughly those in existence on December 31, 1993. Note that the euro-pound interest rate has been set so that the forward rate is exactly $1.4700/£ (interest rate parity holds).
6. Because foreign currency options are actually priced about the forward rate (see Chapter 5), not the spot rate, the correct specification of whether an option, put or call, is ITM, ATM, or OTM, is in reference to the same maturity forward rate.
7. A U.S.-resident firm possessing a future foreign-currency-denominated payment of £1,000,000 could construct a synthetic forward in the following way:
   1. The firm would pay £1,000,000 in 90 days.
   2. The firm would buy a call option on pounds at a strike price of $1.4700/£.
   3. The firm would sell a put option on pounds at a strike price of $1.4700/£.
8. An additional possibility is that the firm finds, for the moment at which the position is taken, that the call option premium earned may actually slightly exceed the put option premium paid. This means that the options market is temporarily out of equilibrium (parity). This is quite possible given the judgment required in the pricing of options (different banks pricing options do not necessarily use the identical volatilities at all times) and the inherent decentralized structure of the currency and currency option markets.
9. One of the original works in this field is Smithson (1987).

10. This zero-premium section draws on Sam Srinivasulu, "Second-Generation Forwards: A Comparative Analysis," *Business International Money Report*, September 21, 1987, pp. 297–299, 303. There are, in fact, a number of other products such as the *break forward* and the *deferred premium option* that are used to a much lesser extent.

11. An alternative form of the ratio spread is the *calendar spread*. The calendar spread combines the 90-day put option with the sale of an OTM call option with a maturity that is longer, for example, 120 or 180 days. The longer maturity of the call option written earns the firm larger premium earnings requiring a smaller "ratio."

12. How far down the downside protection should be set is a difficult issue for the firm to determine. Often the firm's treasurer will determine at what bottom exchange rate the firm would be able to recover the minimum necessary margin on the business underlying the cash flow exposure, called the *budget rate* (see Chapter 6).

13. Although the put and call option premiums are in this case not identical, they are close enough to result in a near-zero net premium:

$$\text{Net premium} = (\$0.0226/\pounds - \$0.0231/\pounds) \times \pounds1,000,000 = -\$500$$

The benefits of the combined position are readily observable, given that the put option premium alone amounts to $22,600.

14. The term *exotic* is not to be confused with its occasional usage as the collective term for currencies of the Asian-Pacific countries.

15. For a more detailed evaluation of the pro and con arguments on the use of knock-out options see Martyn Turner, "Break-even Analysis of Knock-Out Options," *Corporate Finance*, September 1993, pp. 43–45.

16. The premium of the barrier option is quite sensitive to the specification of the barrier level. The further the barrier is from the forward rate, the less likely the barrier will be crossed and therefore the more likely the option will not automatically expire. In that case, the premium must rise to compensate the writer of the knock-out option for the probability of providing coverage for a longer period of time.

17. A variation on the average rate is the *lookback option, with strike* and *without strike*. A *lookback option with strike* is a European-style option with a preset strike rate that on maturity is valued versus the highest or lowest spot rate reached over the option life. A *lookback option without strike* is typically a European-style option that sets the strike rate at maturity as the lowest exchange rate achieved over the period for a call option, or the highest exchange rate experienced over the period for a put option, and is exercised on the basis of this strike rate versus the ending spot rate.

18. For a more detailed illustration of the use of compound options, including a description of an additional variety known as the *installment option*, see Stephanie Mon, "Hedging Bids Made in Foreign Currencies," *Treasury*, Fall 1991, pp. 46–47.

CHAPTER 23 APPENDIX A

Currency Option Pricing Theory

The foreign currency option model presented here, the European-style option, is the result of the work of Black and Scholes (1973), Cox and Ross (1976), Cox, Ross, and Rubinstein (1979), Garman and Kohlhagen (1983), and Bodurtha and Courtadon (1987). Although we do not explain the theoretical derivation of the following option-pricing model, the original model derived by Black and Scholes is based on the formation of a riskless hedged portfolio composed of a long position in the security, asset, or currency and a European call option. The solution to this model's expected return yields the option premium.

The basic theoretical model for the pricing of a European call option is:

$$C = e^{-r_f T} S N(d1) - E e^{-r_d T} N(d2)$$

where

C	premium on a European call
e	continuous time discounting
S	spot exchange rate (\$/fc)
E	exercise or strike rate
T	time to expiration
N	cumulative normal distribution function
r_f	foreign interest rate
r_d	domestic interest rate
σ	standard deviation of asset price (volatility)
ln	natural logarithm

The two density functions, $d1$ and $d2$, are defined:

$$d1 = \frac{\ln\left(\dfrac{S}{E}\right) + \left(r_d - r_f + \dfrac{\sigma^2}{2}\right) T}{\sigma\sqrt{T}}$$

and

$$d2 = d1 - \sigma\sqrt{T}$$

This expression can be rearranged so the premium on a European call option is written in terms of forward rates:

$$C = e^{-r_d T} F N(d_1) - e^{-r_d T} E N(d_2)$$

where the spot rate and foreign interest rate have been replaced with the forward rate, F, and both the first and second terms are discounted over continuous time, e. If we now slightly simplify, we find the option premium is the present value of the difference between two cumulative normal density functions:

$$C = [FN(d1) - EN(d2)]e^{-r_dT}$$

The two density functions are now defined:

$$d1 = \frac{\ln\left(\dfrac{F}{E}\right) + \left(\dfrac{\sigma^2}{2}\right)T}{\sigma\sqrt{T}}$$

and

$$d2 = d1 - \sigma\sqrt{T}$$

Solving each of these equations for $d1$ and $d2$ allows the determination of the European call option premium. The premium for a European put option, P, is similarly derived:

$$P = [F(N(d1) - 1) - E(N(d2) - 1)]e^{-r_dT}$$

The European Call Option: Numerical Example

The actual calculation of the option premium is not as complex as it appears from the preceding set of equations. Assuming the following basic exchange rate and interest rate values, computation of the option premium is relatively straightforward:

Spot rate:	$1.7000/£
90-day forward:	$1.7000/£
Strike rate:	$1.7000/£
U.S. dollar interest rate:	8.00% (per annum)
Pound sterling interest rate:	8.00% (per annum)
Time (days):	90
Standard deviation (volatility):	10.00%
e (infinite discounting):	2.71828

The value of the two density functions are first derived:

$$d1 = \frac{\ln\left(\dfrac{F}{E}\right) + \left(\dfrac{\sigma^2}{2}\right)T}{\sigma\sqrt{T}} = \frac{\ln\left(\dfrac{1.7000}{1.7000}\right) + \left(\dfrac{.1000^2}{2}\right)\dfrac{90}{365}}{.1000\sqrt{\dfrac{90}{365}}} = .025$$

and

$$d2 = .025 - .1000 \sqrt{\frac{90}{365}} = -.025$$

The values of $d1$ and $d2$ are then found in the cumulative normal probability table (see Appendix 23B):

$$N(d1) = N(.025) = .51; \quad N(d2) = N(-.025) = .49$$

The premium of the European call with a forward ATM strike rate is

$$C = [(1.7000)(.51) - (1.7000)(.49)] \, 2.71828^{-.08(90/.365)} = \$0.033/\pounds$$

CHAPTER 23 APPENDIX B

Cumulative Normal Probability Tables

The probability that a drawing from a unit normal distribution will produce a value less than the constant d is

$$\text{Prob}(\tilde{z} < d) = \int_{-\infty}^{d} \frac{1}{\sqrt{2\pi}} e^{-z^2/2} dz = N(d)$$

Range of d: $-2.49 \leq d \leq 0.00$

d	−0.00	−0.01	−0.02	−0.03	−0.04	−0.05	−0.06	−0.07	−0.08	−0.09
−2.40	0.00820	0.00798	0.00776	0.00755	0.00734	0.00714	0.00695	0.00676	0.00657	0.00639
−2.30	0.01072	0.01044	0.01017	0.00990	0.00964	0.00939	0.00914	0.00889	0.00866	0.00842
−2.20	0.01390	0.01355	0.01321	0.01287	0.01255	0.01222	0.01191	0.01160	0.01130	0.01101
−2.10	0.01786	0.01743	0.01700	0.01659	0.01618	0.01578	0.01539	0.01500	0.01463	0.01426
−2.00	0.02275	0.02222	0.02169	0.02118	0.02068	0.02018	0.01970	0.01923	0.01876	0.01831
−1.90	0.02872	0.02807	0.02743	0.02680	0.02619	0.02559	0.02500	0.02442	0.02385	0.02330
−1.80	0.03593	0.03515	0.03438	0.03362	0.03288	0.03216	0.03144	0.03074	0.03005	0.02938
−1.70	0.04457	0.04363	0.04272	0.04182	0.04093	0.04006	0.03920	0.03836	0.03754	0.03673
−1.60	0.05480	0.05370	0.05262	0.05155	0.05050	0.04947	0.04846	0.04746	0.04648	0.04551
−1.50	0.06681	0.06552	0.06426	0.06301	0.06178	0.06057	0.05938	0.05821	0.05705	0.05592
−1.40	0.08076	0.07927	0.07780	0.07636	0.07493	0.07353	0.07215	0.07078	0.06944	0.06811
−1.30	0.09680	0.09510	0.09342	0.09176	0.09012	0.08851	0.08691	0.08534	0.08379	0.08226
−1.20	0.11507	0.11314	0.11123	0.10935	0.10749	0.10565	0.10383	0.10204	0.10027	0.09853
−1.10	0.13567	0.13350	0.13136	0.12924	0.12714	0.12507	0.12302	0.12100	0.11900	0.11702
−1.00	0.15866	0.15625	0.15386	0.15150	0.14917	0.14686	0.14457	0.14231	0.14007	0.13786
−0.90	0.18406	0.18141	0.17879	0.17619	0.17361	0.17106	0.16853	0.16602	0.16354	0.16109
−0.80	0.21186	0.20897	0.20611	0.20327	0.20045	0.19766	0.19489	0.19215	0.18943	0.18673
−0.70	0.24196	0.23885	0.23576	0.23270	0.22965	0.22663	0.22363	0.22065	0.21770	0.21476
−0.60	0.27425	0.27093	0.26763	0.26435	0.26109	0.25785	0.25463	0.25143	0.24825	0.24510
−0.50	0.30854	0.30503	0.30153	0.29806	0.29460	0.29116	0.28774	0.28434	0.28096	0.27760
−0.40	0.34458	0.34090	0.33724	0.33360	0.32997	0.32636	0.32276	0.31918	0.31561	0.31207
−0.30	0.38209	0.37828	0.37448	0.37070	0.36693	0.36317	0.35942	0.35569	0.35197	0.34827
−0.20	0.42074	0.41683	0.41294	0.40905	0.40517	0.40129	0.39743	0.39358	0.38974	0.38591
−0.10	0.46017	0.45620	0.45224	0.44828	0.44433	0.44038	0.43644	0.43251	0.42858	0.42465
0.00	0.50000	0.49601	0.49202	0.48803	0.48405	0.48006	0.47608	0.47210	0.46812	0.46414

Range of d: $0.00 \leq d \leq 2.49$

d	0.00	0.01	0.02	0.03	0.04	0.05	0.06	0.07	0.08	0.09
0.00	0.50000	0.50399	0.50798	0.51197	0.51595	0.51994	0.52392	0.52790	0.53188	0.53586
0.01	0.53983	0.54380	0.54776	0.55172	0.55567	0.55962	0.56356	0.56749	0.57142	0.57535
0.20	0.57926	0.58317	0.58706	0.59095	0.59483	0.59871	0.60257	0.60642	0.61026	0.61409
0.30	0.61791	0.62172	0.62552	0.62930	0.63307	0.63683	0.64058	0.64431	0.64803	0.65173
0.40	0.65542	0.65910	0.66276	0.66640	0.67003	0.67364	0.67724	0.68082	0.68439	0.68793
0.50	0.69146	0.69497	0.69847	0.70194	0.70540	0.70884	0.71226	0.71566	0.71904	0.72240
0.60	0.72575	0.72907	0.73237	0.73565	0.73891	0.74215	0.74537	0.74857	0.75175	0.75490
0.70	0.75804	0.76115	0.76424	0.76730	0.77035	0.77337	0.77637	0.77935	0.78230	0.78524
0.80	0.78814	0.79103	0.79389	0.79673	0.79955	0.80234	0.80511	0.80785	0.81057	0.81327
0.90	0.81594	0.81859	0.82121	0.82381	0.82639	0.82894	0.83147	0.83398	0.83646	0.83891
1.00	0.84134	0.84375	0.84614	0.84850	0.85083	0.85314	0.85543	0.85769	0.85993	0.86214
1.10	0.86433	0.86650	0.86864	0.87076	0.87286	0.87493	0.87698	0.87900	0.88100	0.88298
1.20	0.88493	0.88686	0.88877	0.89065	0.89251	0.89435	0.89617	0.89796	0.89973	0.90147
1.30	0.90320	0.90490	0.90658	0.90824	0.90988	0.91149	0.91309	0.91466	0.91621	0.91774
1.40	0.91924	0.92073	0.92220	0.92364	0.92507	0.92647	0.92785	0.92922	0.93056	0.93189
1.50	0.93319	0.93448	0.93574	0.93699	0.93822	0.93943	0.94062	0.94179	0.94295	0.94408
1.60	0.94520	0.94630	0.94738	0.94845	0.94950	0.95053	0.95154	0.95254	0.95352	0.95449
1.70	0.95543	0.95637	0.95728	0.95818	0.95907	0.95994	0.96080	0.96164	0.96246	0.96327
1.80	0.96407	0.96485	0.96562	0.96637	0.96712	0.96784	0.96856	0.96926	0.96995	0.97062
1.90	0.97128	0.97193	0.97257	0.97320	0.97381	0.97441	0.97500	0.97558	0.97615	0.97670
2.00	0.97725	0.97778	0.97831	0.97882	0.97932	0.97982	0.98030	0.98077	0.98124	0.98169
2.10	0.98214	0.98257	0.98300	0.98341	0.98382	0.98422	0.98461	0.98500	0.98537	0.98574
2.20	0.98610	0.98645	0.98679	0.98713	0.98745	0.98778	0.98809	0.98840	0.98870	0.98899
2.30	0.98928	0.98956	0.98983	0.99010	0.99036	0.99061	0.99086	0.99111	0.99134	0.99158
2.40	0.99180	0.99202	0.99224	0.99245	0.99266	0.99286	0.99305	0.99324	0.99343	0.99361

Source: Hans R. Stoll and Robert E. Whaley, *Futures and Options*, Southwestern Publishing, 1993, pp. 242–243. Reprinted with permission.

CHAPTER 24

ADVANCED TOPICS IN INTEREST RATE RISK MANAGEMENT

These advanced topics in *interest rate risk management* build on the foundation established in Chapter 9 (Interest Rate Exposure and Swaps). We extend that foundation to explore the potential offered by option-based instruments and techniques.

Interest rate option instruments differ by their market, which may be exchange-traded or interbank (over-the-counter). Interest rate options that are exchange-traded are actually options on interest rate futures contracts. Interest rate options that are traded or written over-the-counter are termed *caps*, *floors*, and *collars*.

INTEREST RATE CAPS AND FLOORS

An *interest rate cap* is an option to fix a ceiling or maximum short-term interest rate payment. The contract is written such that the buyer of the cap will receive a cash payment equal to the difference between the actual market interest rate and the cap strike rate on the notional principal, if the market rate rises above the strike rate. As with any option, the buyer of the cap pays an up-front premium to the seller of the cap for this right. The premium is normally stated as an annual percentage consistent with that of the strike rate. An *interest rate floor* gives the buyer the right to receive the compensating payment (cash settlement) when the reference interest rate falls below the strike rate of the floor.

Exhibit 24.1 lists interest rate cap and floor quotations for the U.S. dollar three-month LIBOR rate and the Deutschemark six-month LIBOR. The quotes provide alternative maturities, 2, 3, or 5 years, and alternative cap rates for the two shorter maturities, with a single cap and floor rate for the five-year maturity. Each cap and floor has bid and offer quotations so that a buyer could either buy or sell (write) the cap or floor.

))) Cap and Floor Currencies

The U.S. dollar cap market started in 1985 with the issuance by banks of over $2.75 billion worth of *floating rate notes* (FRNs). These notes had an internal cap rate, like all floating rate mortgages,

| Exhibit 24.1 | *Interest Rate Cap and Floor Quotations* |

Maturity	U.S. Dollar Caps vs 3m LIBOR		U.S. Dollar Floors vs 3m LIBOR	
	Cap Rate	Bid-Offer	Floor Rate	Bid-Offer
2 years	5.00 %	42–46	4.00 %	42–47
	6.00 %	15–19	5.00 %	149–154
3 years	6.00 %	69–79	4.00 %	54–62
	7.00 %	35–42	5.00 %	190–200
5 years	7.00 %	147–165	5.00 %	245–261

Maturity	Deutschemark Caps vs 6m LIBOR		Deutschemark Floors vs 6m LIBOR	
	Cap Rate	Bid-Offer	Floor Rate	Bid-Offer
2 years	6.00 %	35–40	5.50 %	57–63
	6.50 %	19–24	6.00 %	101–107
3 years	6.00 %	93–99	5.50 %	89–96
	6.50 %	60–65	6.00 %	156–161
5 years	6.75 %	172–185	5.50 %	122–145

Source: Adapted from *International Financing Review*, July 31, 1993, Issue 990, p. 83. Bid-offer spreads are stated in basis points. For example, "42–46" is 0.42%–0.46% of the notional principal per annum.

which was eventually stripped from the notes and resold separately. The British pound sterling cap market took off in the late 1980s with increasing conditions of interest rate uncertainty. The Deutschemark interest rate cap market was initiated in 1989. The reunification of Germany, which required massive government spending and borrowing, added upward pressure to interest rates in Germany. German firms demanded some protection from these rising rates, and the cap filled the need. Although some development of yen-denominated interest rate caps started in 1989, most of these were issued by Japanese financial institutions that wished to benefit from speculative views; there has been no substantial market demand to date for a yen product. The fact that yen-denominated interest rates rarely have risen above 7% or 8% in the past two decades may also be a major factor. In addition, some market activity exists in caps denominated in Swiss francs, French francs, and Italian lira, and a growing market exists in Spanish peseta caps, but these will soon be replaced by euro caps.

))) **Maturities and Structure**

No theoretical limit exists to the specification of caps and floors. Most currency cap markets are liquid out to ten years in the over-the-counter market, though the majority of trading falls between one and five years. There is an added distinction that is important to understanding cap maturity. It is not the total maturity that is singularly important, but the number of interest rate *resets* involved. For example, a common interest rate cap would be a two-year cap on the three-month LIBOR. This means that the total cap agreement will last for two years, in which there will be a total of seven three-month LIBOR interest rate reset dates, or *fixings*. No reset exists for the first three-month period. There are two major types of interest rate caps:

1. *Interest rate guarantee* (IRG), which provides protection to the buyer for a single period only. Protection is provided to the borrower in the event of a single major variable rate refunding or reinvestment.

2. *Interest rate cap,* which provides protection for an extended period of time, for example two to five years, on some interest rate reset. The subperiod reset—for example, the three-month LIBOR or six-month LIBOR—is called the cap's *tenor.* This protection is discrete, meaning that protection is for the interest rate put into effect on a reset date, and not just any day over the period in which the actual market rate may creep up over the strike rate.

The interest rate cap is the more common of the two and is the subject of the following numerical example.

))) Cap Valuation

A typical cap written over-the-counter by a bank for a firm would appear as follows:

1. Maturity: 3 years

2. Strike rate: 6.00%

3. Reference rate: three-month U.S. dollar LIBOR

4. Total number of periods: 12 (four per year for three years)

5. Notional principal: $10,000,000

6. Premium: 79 basis points (0.79%)

7. Fixed borrowing rate: 7.00%

This agreement establishes a cap on all quarterly reset dates for three years. The cap rate is 6.00% per annum. All interest payments made are calculated on the basis of a notional principal of $10,000,000. The up-front cost of the cap, the premium, is 79 basis points. If the firm were to borrow at fixed interest it would pay 7.00%.

The value of a capped interest payment such as this one is actually composed of three different elements: (1) the actual three-month interest payment; (2) the amount of the cap payment to the cap buyer if the reference rate rises above the cap rate; and (3) the annualized cost of the cap. To demonstrate how the cap would work in practice, let us assume that the three-month LIBOR rate on the reset date (the actual reset rate is normally determined two days prior to the next actual payment date) has risen above the strike rate of 6.00% to 6.50%.

1. **Interest rate payment**. Regardless of whether the cap is activated, the buyer of the cap is responsible for making the normal interest payment. The firm owes a payment of three-month U.S. dollar LIBOR of 6.50% on a three-month period (actual 90 days) on a notional principal of $10,000,000:

$$\$10,000,000 \times .0650 \times \frac{90}{360} = \$162,500$$

2. **Receive cap cash flow**. If the three-month LIBOR rate has risen above the cap rate on the reset date, the cap is activated and the buyer of the cap receives a cash payment from the cap seller equal to the difference between the actual three-month LIBOR rate of 6.50% and the cap rate of 6.00%; a cash payment of the following amount:

$$\$10,000,000 \times \left[(.0650 - .0600) \times \frac{90}{360} \right] = \$12,500$$

3. **Amortized cap premium payment**. But, alas, such flexibility and protection comes at a cost, the premium. The cap premium of 0.79% is a single lump-sum payment made at the beginning of the three-year period, and it must therefore be annualized in order to calculate the total cost of the capped payment. The fixed rate of interest at which this firm could borrow is 7.00%, and this is therefore the rate of interest used in the amortization of the cap premium over 12 reset periods.

   The amortized premium for 12 periods, discounted at a rate of 7.00% per annum (1.75% per quarter), is found by using the standard loan amortization formula used in calculating mortgage payments of all kinds:

$$\text{Quarterly premium} = \frac{0.7900\%}{\left[\dfrac{1}{.0175} - \dfrac{1}{.0175 \times (1.0175)^{12}} \right]} = .07356\%$$

This is .07356% on a quarterly basis, .2942% on an annual basis.[1]

The resulting total or all-in-cost (AIC) of the capped interest payment is 6.2942%, or a maximum of $157,356 every three months.

Cap Component	Annualized Interest Cost	Quarterly Cash Payments
#1: Interest payment outflow	6.5000%	$ 162,500
#2: Cap cash payment inflow	6.0000%–6.5000%	−12,500
#3: Cap premium payment outflow	0.2942%	+7,356
Total Cost or All-in-Cost	6.2942%	$157,356

The firm has limited or *capped* its potential interest payments. If three-month LIBOR is below the cap rate of 6.00% on the next reset date, the firm's all-in-cost would be the actual LIBOR payment plus its quarterly premium payment of 0.294%. The premium payment will be made for the life of the cap regardless of whether the cap is exercised or not.

When the cap is exercised like this, the payment resembles the exchange of a floating-fixed-interest payment, a swap. However, unlike the case for a swap, when the reference rate does not rise above the strike rate, the firm continues to make regular interest payments and is not restricted to the swap rate.

In order to understand the motivation of the buyer of the interest rate guarantee or cap, it is useful to see the expected interest payment over a wide range of potential three-month LIBOR rates at the time of the cap agreement initiation. Exhibit 24.2 compares the unhedged interest payment with the cap-hedged interest payment over a range of potential three-month LIBOR rates. Note that although the effective cap interest payment is slightly higher than 6.00% because of the cap premium that must be paid, it is still significantly cheaper than the unhedged interest payment if three-month LIBOR rates were to rise significantly above the strike rate of 6.00%. If the LIBOR does not rise above the cap's strike rate, the presence of the premium of course increases the total cost of debt service above the totally uncovered position.

Exhibit 24.2 *Profile of an Interest Rate Cap*

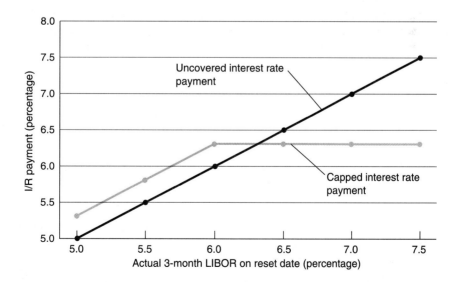

If, however, the firm had swapped its three-month LIBOR floating payment for a fixed-interest payment of 6.00%, regardless of the actual LIBOR rate on the original reset date it would be locked into a 6.00% interest payment. The interest rate cap provides the buyer with insurance against a rise in interest rates, while allowing the firm the opportunity to enjoy lower interest payments if actual market rates do not rise. As was the case with the use of foreign currency options in the management of currency transaction exposures in Chapter 6, a firm would only purchase this insurance, this cap, if it expects not to use it. If the firm held a strong expectation that interest rates would rise above 6.00% by the reset date, it would be better off swapping the floating- for a fixed-rate payment.

)))) Interest Rate Floors

Interest rate caps are basically call options on an interest rate, and equivalently, interest rate floors are put options on an interest rate. A *floor* guarantees the buyer of the floor option a minimum interest rate to be received (rate of return on notional principal invested) for a specified reinvestment period or series of periods.

For example, if a firm knows that it will receive a cash inflow in three months, which it must invest, it will want to invest at the highest possible rate. If it fears that interest rates will fall by that time, it may wish to purchase a floor. The floor will guarantee the firm a minimum effective rate of investment. If, when the date of investment arrives, the actual market rate of interest is less than the floor rate, the holder of the floor will receive from the writer of the floor a cash settlement equal to the difference between the actual reference rate and the floor rate.

)))) Floor Valuation

The pricing and valuation of an interest rate floor are the same as for the interest rate cap. Assume a German firm purchases a two-year interest rate floor of 6.00% as listed in Exhibit 24.1. The specifications of the firm and its floor would be:

1. Maturity: 2 years
2. Strike rate: 6.00%
3. Reference rate: six-month DM LIBOR
4. Total number of periods: 4 (semi-annually for two years)
5. Notional principal: DM 5,000,000
6. Floor premium: 107 basis points (1.07%)
7. Fixed investment rate: 6.50%

The firm does not expect interest rates (investment rates available to it) to fall below 6.00%, but it wishes some insurance against the possibility. If, at the end of a six-month period, however, the six-month DM LIBOR rate has indeed fallen below the floor rate of 6.00% to 5.80%, the interest rate floor is activated (exercised). The valuation of the floor would be decomposed into the same three basic elements as the cap.

1. **Interest rate payment/yield**. Regardless of whether the floor is activated, the firm that bought the floor will invest its funds at the market rate of interest. The firm therefore will earn 5.80%, the six-month DM LIBOR rate, on a notional principal of DM5,000,000

$$DM5,000,000 \times .0580 \times \frac{180}{360} = DM145,000$$

2. **Receive floor cash flow**. The reference rate (six-month DM LIBOR) has fallen below the floor strike rate, so the floor is activated. The buyer of the floor receives the difference between the floor rate and the reference rate in cash of

$$DM5,000,000 \times \left[\left(.0600 - .0580\right) \times \frac{180}{360} \right] = DM5,000$$

3. **Amortized floor premium payment**. Regardless of whether the floor is activated, the firm must pay for the floor option. The single lump-sum payment of 1.07% made up front is amortized over the two-year period of six-month reset periods. The rate of interest used for the amortization is the fixed rate of interest available to the firm at the beginning of the period, in this case 6.50%. The premium expense per semi-annual period is

$$\text{Semi-annual premium} = \frac{1.07\%}{\left[\dfrac{1}{.0325} - \dfrac{1}{.0325 \times (1.0325)^4} \right]} = .2896\%$$

This is 0.2896% on a semi-annual basis, or 0.5792% on an annual basis.

The all-in-cost of the floor-covered interest instrument is then 5.421% per annum, or a minimum return of DM135,520 each six months on a notional principal of DM5,000,000 for the two-year period.

Floor Component	Annualized Interest Yield	Quarterly Cash Flows
#1: Interest payment inflow	5.800%	DM 145,000
#2: Floor cash payment inflow	6.000 %–5.800%	5,000
#3: Floor premium payment outflow	0.579%	–14,480
Total Yield or All-in-Yield	5.421%	$ 135,520

Exhibit 24.3 illustrates this floor valuation over a range of potential reference rates (six-month DM LIBOR) at the time of the semi-annual reset. Note that although the firm had placed a floor of 6.00% on its reinvestment of DM cash flows, its actual effective yield when the reference rate falls below the floor of

6.00% is 5.421% per annum. This rate is due to the annualized premium expense. Once again, if the firm truly believed that interest rates would fall far enough to require the use of the floor, it would be better off investing at the fixed rate of 6.50% at the start of the period, rather than purchasing the floor as protection.

))) Interest Rate Collars

An *interest rate collar* is the simultaneous purchase (sale) of a cap and sale (purchase) of a floor. The firm constructing the collar earns a premium from the sale of one side to cover in part or in full the premium expense of purchasing the other side of the collar. If the two premiums are equal, the position is often referred to as a *zero-premium collar*.

Interest rate collars allow the firm to retain some of the benefit of declining rates while removing the unpleasantness of paying an up-front option premium for the cap. This unpleasantness can be mitigated—or totally eliminated in the case of a zero-cost collar—by the firm's simultaneously selling a floor option of a suitable strike rate. For example, using the cap and floor quotations of Exhibit 24.1, a firm could fund the purchase of a cap against three-month U.S. dollar LIBOR rising above 5.00% in the next two years (paying a premium of 0.46%) by selling a 4.00% floor on the three-month U.S. dollar LIBOR for the same two-year maturity (earning a premium of 0.42%). Although not precisely a zero net

---

Exhibit 24.3   *Profile of an Interest Rate Floor*

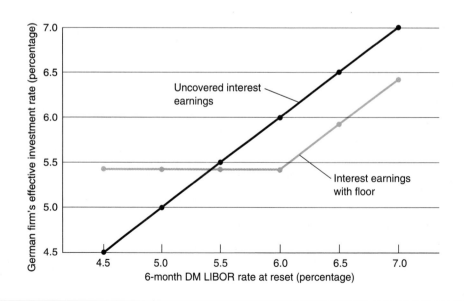

cost, the up-front net cost of the position is extremely small (0.46% – 0.42% = 0.04%). This interest rate collar is illustrated in Exhibit 24.4.

The risk of increased rates has been eliminated by forsaking the advantage of rates declining below the floor, at zero cost. It is important to remember that this means *zero initial cost*, for the firm will still be called on to make payments to the collar seller if rates fall below the floor level. Because the firm may be called on to make payments to the seller, each party to the transaction has credit exposure to the other like a swap. In the extreme case of a zero-cost collar of zero width, the collar becomes a swap. The foreign exchange equivalent of a collar is the simultaneous purchase of a call option and the sale of a put option on the short currency (a synthetic forward for a short foreign currency position).

))) Swaptions

The purchase of a swap option—a *swaption*—gives the firm the right but not the obligation to enter into a swap on a predetermined notional principal at some defined future date at a specified strike rate.[2] The firm's Treasurer would typically purchase a *payer's swaption*, giving the Treasurer the right to enter a swap in which the fixed rate is paid and the floating rate is received. The Treasurer would exercise this option if rates had risen above the strike level of the swaption, otherwise, the Treasurer would allow the option to expire and take advantage of the lower-rate environment.

Exhibit 24.4	*Profile of an Interest Rate Collar*

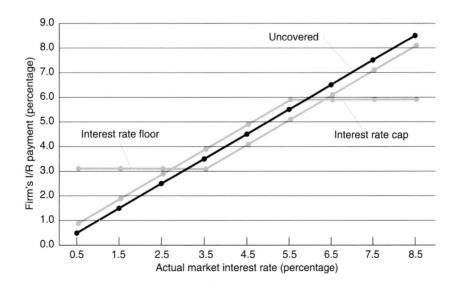

If exercised, the swaption may be *swap-settled*, settled for cash. In this case, the firm would receive a payment reflecting the intrinsic value of the swap. In the case of cash settlement, this eliminates the ongoing mutual counterparty risk. As with any option, the maximum downside risk for the firm is the initial premium exposure.

Many multinationals increasingly sell swaptions. A U.K.-resident firm would sell a swaption, termed a *receiver's swaption*, struck at an acceptable fixed rate, giving the purchasing bank the right to receive the fixed rate from the firm. The bank would exercise this option if rates had declined below the strike rate.

SUMMARY

- Option-based instruments and techniques are commonly employed for *interest rate risk management*.

- An *interest rate cap* is an option to fix a ceiling or maximum short-term interest rate payment.

- An *interest rate floor* gives the buyer of the floor option a minimum interest rate to be received (rate of return on notional principal invested) for a specified reinvestment period or series of periods.

- An *interest rate collar* is the simultaneous purchase (sale) of a cap and sale (purchase) of a floor.

- The purchase of a swap option—a *swaption*—gives the firm the right but not the obligation to enter into a swap on a predetermined notional principal at some defined future date at a specified strike rate.

QUESTIONS

1. Interest Rate Risk: Pricing Resets
Differentiate the nature and frequency of the interest rate risk associated with the following alternative forms of a three-year loan agreement:
- **a.** three-year fixed rate loan (no price resets)
- **b.** three-year floating-rate loan (annual price reset)
- **c.** three one-year loan agreements, each at a fixed rate for one-year (annual price reset)

2. Interest Rate Cap Valuation
Use the same assumptions as in the cap valuation demonstrated in the chapter, with the exception that the three-month U.S. dollar LIBOR is 6.250% (not 6.000%). State each answer in both annualized interest and quarterly cash flow.
- **a.** What is the actual interest rate payment due?
- **b.** What is the interest rate cap cash flow if activated?
- **c.** What is the premium payment due for the cap?
- **d.** What is the total yield or all-in-yield on the position?

3. Interest Rate Floor Valuation

Use the same assumptions as in the floor valuation demonstrated in the chapter, with the exception that the six-month DM LIBOR is 5.500% (not 6.000%). State each answer in both annualized interest and quarterly cash flow.

a. What is the actual interest rate payment inflow?
b. What is the floor cash payment inflow?
c. What is the premium payment due for the floor?
d. What is the total yield or all-in-yield on the position?

4. Chipolte Properties (A)

Chipolte Properties has just purchased the following interest rate cap agreement:

Maturity:	2 years
Strike rate:	7.000%
Reference rate:	three-month U.S. dollar LIBOR
Total periods:	8 (four per year for two years)
Notional principal:	$3,600,000
Premium:	66 basis points (0.66%)
Fixed borrowing rate:	8.000%

Using the assumption that the actual three-month U.S. dollar LIBOR rate is 7.25% at the time of the next quarterly interest payment, answer the following questions:

a. What is the interest payment outflow on an annualized interest cost basis and a quarterly cash payment basis?
b. What is the interest cap cash payment on an annualized interest cost basis and a quarterly cash payment basis?
c. What is the cap premium outflow on an annualized interest cost basis and a quarterly cash payment basis?
d. What is the total yield or all-in-cost of the position?

5. Sun City Pension Management

Sun City is a U.S. pension fund management firm. It must, by law, hold a minimum percentage of its assets in highly liquid interest-bearing deposits of 360 days maturity or less. It can and does hold foreign-currency-denominated securities. Because of the recent continuing decline in Euromarket interest rates, Sun City has purchased a floor agreement for the entirety of its euro-denominated money market portfolio, approximately €3,600,000.

Maturity:	2 years
Strike rate:	6.000%
Reference rate:	six-month euro LIBOR (5.80%)
Total periods:	4 (two per year for two years)
Notional principal:	€3,600,000
Premium:	107 basis points (1.07%)
Fixed borrowing rate:	6.500%

a. What is the interest payment inflow (annualized yield and cash flow)?
b. What is the floor cash payment inflow (annualized yield and cash flow)?
c. What is the floor premium outflow (annualized yield and cash flow)?
d. What is the total yield or all-in-yield on the position?

WORLD WIDE WEB EXERCISES

W1. Interest Rate Futures Trading: Emerging Markets
The predominant interest rate futures contracts are traded on the Chicago Mercantile Exchange (CME). There are now a variety of contracts on fixed income and other debt securities traded for emerging markets, but trading is still quite thin. Visit the CME's website and assess the liquidity of emerging markets (e.g., Mexico, Brazil) by noting the actual open interest on positions by maturity dates.

Chicago Mercantile Exchange   http://www.cme.com

W2. Treasury Management at the Bank of Ireland
Use the following website at the Bank of Ireland to survey the types of interest rate risk-management services available to firms operating within Ireland and the European Union.

Bank of Ireland Treasury   http://www.treasury.boi.ie/

SUGGESTED READINGS

Brown, Keith C., and Donald J. Smith, "Default Risk and Innovations in the Design of Interest Rate Swaps," *Financial Management*, Vol. 22, No. 2, Summer 1993, pp. 94–105.

Howton, Shawn D. and Steven B. Perfect, "Currency and Interest Rate Derivatives Use in U.S. Firms," *Financial Management*, Vol. 27, No. 4, Winter 1998, pp. 111–121.

Smith, Clifford W., Jr., Charles W. Smithson, and Lee MacDonald Wakeman, "The Market for Interest Rate Swaps," *Financial Management*, Winter 1988, pp. 34–44.

NOTES

1. This is the calculation formula for amortized loan payments for a fixed rate of interest. The formula itself is

$$\text{Period payment} = \frac{\text{Present value}}{\left[\dfrac{1}{r} - \dfrac{1}{r \times (1+r)^t}\right]}$$

where the present value is the current loan amount, t is the number of periods, and r is the rate of interest per period. The resulting amortized mortgage payment services both principal and interest in a single constant cash payment per period.

2. One of the best introductions to swaptions is "Behind the Mirror" by Robert Tompkins, in *From Black-Scholes to Black Holes: New Frontier in Options*, Risk Magazine Ltd, London, 1992, pp. 129–133.

BIBLIOGRAPHY

Abbott, Ashok B., and K. Victor Chow, "Cointegration Among European Equity Mar-kets," *Journal of Multinational Financial Management*, Vol. 2, No. 3/4, 1993, pp. 167–184.

Abuaf, Niso, "The Nature and Management of Foreign Exchange Risk," *Midland Corporate Fin-ance Journal*, Fall 1986, pp. 30–44.

Abuaf, Niso, and Philippe Jorion, "Purchasing Power Parity in the Long Run," *Journal of Finance*, Mar 1990, pp. 157–174.

Adams, Paul D., and Steve B. Wyatt, "On the Pricing of European and American Foreign Currency Call Options," *Journal of International Money and Finance*, Vol. 6, No. 3, Sep 1987, pp. 315–338,

Adhikari, Ajay, and Rasoul H. Tondkar, "Environmental Factors Influencing Accounting Disclosure Requirements of Global Stock Exchanges," *Journal of International Financial Management and Accounting*, Vol. 4, No. 2, Summer 1992, pp. 75–105.

Adler, Michael, "The Cost of Capital and Valuation of a Two-Country Firm," *Journal of Finance*, Mar 1974, pp. 119–132.

Adler, Michael, and Bernard Dumas, "International Portfolio Choice and Corporation Finance: A Synthesis," *Journal of Finance*, Jun 1983, pp. 925–984.

Adler, Michael, and Bernard Dumas, "Exposure to Currency Risk: Definition and Measurement," *Financial Management*, Spring 1984, pp. 41–50.

Agénor, Pierre-Richard, *Parallel Currency Markets in Developing Countries: Theory, Evidence, and Policy Implications*, Essays in International Finance, No. 188, Princeton: International Financial Section, Department of Economics, 1992.

Aggarwal, Raj, "International Differences in Capital Structure Norms: An Empirical Study of Large European Companies," *Management International Review*, 1981/1, pp. 75–88.

Aggarwal, Raj, "Capital Structure Differences Among Large Asian Companies," *ASEAN Economic Bulletin*, Vol. 7, No. 1, Jul 1990, pp. 39–53.

Aggarwal, Raj, "Distribution of Spot and Forward Exchange Rates: Empirical Evidence and Investor Valuation of Skewness and Kurtosis," *Decision Sciences*, Summer 1990, pp. 588–595.

Aggarwal, Raj, "The Distribution of Exchange Rates and Forward Risk Premia," *Advances in Financial Planning and Forecasting*, Vol. 4, 1990. pp. 43–54.

Aggarwal, Raj, and Luc A. Soenen, "Corporate Use of Options and Futures in Foreign Exchange Management," *Journal of Cash Management*, Nov/Dec 1989, pp. 61–66.

Aggarwal, Reena, Ricardo Leal, and Leonardo Hernandez, "The Aftermarket Performance of Initial Public Offerings in Latin America," *Financial Management*, Spring 1993, pp. 42–53.

Ahkam, Sharif N., "A Model for the Evaluation of and Response to Economic Exposure Risk by Multinational Companies," *Managerial Finance*, Vol. 21, No. 4, 1995, pp. 7–22.

Ahtiala, Pekka, and Yair E. Orgler, "The Optimal Pricing of Exports Invoiced in Different Currencies," *Journal of Banking and Finance*, Vol. 19, No. 1, Apr 1995, pp. 61–77.

Akhter, Syed H., and Robert F. Lusch, "Environmental Determinants of U.S. Foreign Direct Investment in Developed and Developing Countries: A Structural Analysis," *The International Trade Journal*, Vol. 5, No. 3, Spring 1991, pp. 329–360.

Al-Eryani, Mohammad F., Pervaiz Alam, and Syed Akhter, "Transfer Pricing Determinants of U.S. Multinationals," *Journal of International Business Studies*, 3rd Quarter, 1990, pp. 409–425.

Alexander, Gordon J., Cheol S. Eun, and S. Janakiramanan, "Asset Pricing and Dual Listing on Foreign Capital Markets: A Note," *Journal of Finance*, Mar 1987, pp. 151–158.

Alexander, Gordon J., Cheol S. Eun, and S. Janakiramanan, "International Listings and Stock Returns: Some Empirical Evidence," *Journal of Financial and Quantitative Analysis*, Vol. 23, No. 2, Jun 1988, pp. 135–151.

Aliber, R. Z., and C. P. Stickney, "Accounting Measures of Foreign Exchange Exposure: The Long and Short of It," *Accounting Review*, Jan 1975, pp. 44–57.

Allen, Linda, and Christos Pantzalis, "Valuation of the Operating Flexibility of Multinational Corporation, *Journal of International Business Studies*, Vol. 27, No. 4, Fourth Quarter 1996, pp. 633–653.

Amin, Kaushik, and Robert A. Jarrow, "Pricing Foreign Currency Options Under Stochastic Interest Rates," *Journal of International Money and Finance*, Sep 1991, pp. 310-329.

Anderson, R. W., and J. P. Danthine, "Cross-Hedging," *Journal of Political Economy*, Dec 1981, pp. 1182–1196.

Ang, James S., and Ali M. Fatemi, "A Test of the Rationality of Forward Exchange Rate," *Advances in Financial Planning and Forecasting*, Vol. 4, 1990, pp. 3–22.

Ang, James S., and Tsong-Yue Lai, "A Simple Rule for Multinational Capital Budgeting," *Global Finance Journal*, Fall 1989, pp. 71–75.

Anvari, M., "Efficient Scheduling of Cross-Border Cash Transfers," *Financial Management*, Summer 1986, pp. 40–49.

Aoi, Joichi, "To Whom Does the Company Belong?: A New Management Mission for the Information Age," *Journal of Applied Corporate Finance*, Winter 1994. pp. 25–31.

Arnold, Jerry L., and William W. Holder, *Impact of Statement 52 on Decisions, Financial Reports, and Attitudes*, Morristown, NJ: Financial Executives Research Foundation, 1986.

Arpan, Jeffrey S., "International Intracorporate Pricing: Non-American Systems and Views," *Journal of International Business Studies*, Spring 1972, pp. 1–18.

Arshanapalli, Bala, and John Doukas, "Integration of Euro-Money Markets," *Journal of Multinational Financial Management*, Vol. 2, No. 3/4, 1993, pp. 107–126.

Arshanapalli, Bala, Jongmo Jay Choi, E. Tyler Clagget, Jr., and John Doukas, "Explaining Premiums and Discounts on Closed-End Equity Country Funds," *Journal of Applied Corporate Finance*, Vol. 9, No. 3, Fall 1996, pp. 109–117.

Babbel, David F., "Determining the Optimum Strategy for Hedging Currency Exposure," *Journal of International Business Studies*, Spring/Summer 1983, pp. 133–139.

Baker, James C., and Laurence J. Beardsley, "Multinational Companies' Use of Risk Evaluation and Profit Measurement for Capital Budgeting Decisions," *Journal of Business Finance*, Spring 1973, pp. 38–43.

Ball, Ray, "Making Accounting International: Why, How, and How Far Will It Go?" *Journal of Applied Corporate Finance*, Vol. 8, No. 3, Fall 1995, pp. 19–29.

Bank for International Settlements, Annual Report, annual issues, Basle.

Bank for International Settlements Economic Paper No. 41 and *Financial Markets, Institu-tions and Instru-ments*, Volume 4, No. 1, 1995.

Bank of America Roundtable on Evaluating and Financing Foreign Direct Investment," *Journal of Applied Corporate Finance*, Fall 1996, Vo. 9, No. 3, pp. 64–79.

Bank of America, "Corporate America: FX Risk Management 1996," Global Capital Markets Group, Monograph 78, Winter 1996–1997.

Barrett, M. Edgar, "Case of the Tangled Transfer Price," *Harvard Business Review*, May/Jun 1977, pp. 20–36, 176–178.

Batten, Jonathan, Robert Mellor, and Victor Wan, "Foreign Exchange Risk Management Practices and Products Used by Australian

Firms," *Journal of International Business Studies*, third Quarter 1993, pp. 557–573.

Bauman, Joseph, Steve Saratore, and William Liddle, "A Practical Framework for Corporate Exposure Management," *Journal of Applied Corporate Finance*, Vol. 7, No. 3, Fall 1994, pp. 66–72.

Baumol, William J., and Burton G. Malkiel, "Redundant Regulation of Foreign Security Trad-ing and U.S. Competitiveness," *Journal of Applied Corporate Finance*, Winter 1993, pp. 19–27.

Bavishi, Vinod B., "Capital Budgeting Practices at Multinationals," *Management Accounting*, Aug. 1981, pp. 32–35.

Bekaert, Gert and Campbell R. Harvey, "Emerging Equity Market Volatility," *Journal of Financial Economics*, Vol. 43, No. 1, Jan. 1997, pp. 29–77.

Belk, P. A., and M. Glaum, "The Management of Foreign Exchange Risk in UK Multinationals: An Empirical Investigation," *Accounting and Business Research*, Vol. 21, No. 81, 1990, pp. 3–13.

Benito, Gabriel R. G., "Ownership Structures of Norwegian Foreign Subsidiaries in Manufac-tur-ing," *The International Trade Journal*, Vol. 10, No. 2, Summer 1996, pp. 157–198.

Bergendahl, Göran, "Multi-Currency Netting in a Multi-National Firm," in *International Financial Management*, Göran Bergendahl, ed., Stockholm: Norstedts, 1982, pp. 149–173.

Berkman, Henk, Michael E. Bradley, and Stephen Magan, "An International Comparison of Derivatives Use," *Financial Management*, Vol. 26, No. 4, Winter 1997, pp. 69–73.

Bessembinder, Hendrik, "Forward Contracts and Firm Value: Investment Incentive and Contracting Effects," *Journal of Financial and Quantitative Analysis*, Vol. 26, No. 4, Dec 1991, pp. 519–532.

Biddle, Gary C., and Shahrokh M. Saudagaran, "The Effects of Financial Disclosure Levels on Firms' Choices Among Alternative For-

eign Stock Exchange Listings," *Journal of International Financial Management and Accounting*, Vol. 1, No. 1, Spring 1989, pp. 55–87.

Bilson, John F.O., "The Evaluation and Use of Foreign Exchange Rate Forecasting Services," in R.J. Herring, ed., *Management of Foreign Exchange Risk*, Cambridge, U.K.: Cambridge University Press, 1984, pp. 149–179.

Black, Fischer, and Myron Scholes, "The Pricing of Options and Corporate Liabilities," *Journal of Political Economy*, May/Jun 1973, pp. 637–659.

Bodnar, Gordon M., "1998 Wharton Survey of Financial Risk Management by U.S. Non-Financial Firms," *Financial Management*, Volume 24, No. 4, Winter 1998, pp. 70–91.

Bodurtha, James N., D. Chinhyung Cho, and Lemma W. Senbet, "Economic Forces in the Stock Market: An International Perspective," *Global Finance Journal*, Fall 1989, pp. 21–46.

Bodurtha, James N., Jr., and Georges R. Courtadon, "Efficiency Tests of the Foreign Currency Options Market," *Journal of Finance*, Mar 1986, pp. 151–162.

Bodurtha, James N., Jr., and Georges R. Courtadon, "Tests of an American Option Pricing Model on the Foreign Currency Options Market," *Journal of Financial and Quantitative Analysis*, Jun 1987, pp. 153–168.

Bonser-Neal, Catherine, Greggory Brauer, Robert Neal, and Simon Wheatley, "International Investment Restrictions and Closed-End Country Fund Prices," *Journal of Finance*, Jun 1990, pp. 523–548.

Booth, Laurence, and Wendy Rotenberg, "Assessing Foreign Exchange Exposure: Theory and Application using Canadian Firms," *Journal of International Financial Management and Accounting*, Vol. 2, No. 1, Spring 1990, pp. 1–22.

Booth, Laurence David, "Taxes, Funds Positioning, and the Cost of Capital for Multinationals," *Advances in Financial Planning and Forecasting,* Vol. 4, part B, 1990, pp. 245–270.

Boris, C. E. V., "Leverage and Financing of Non-Financial Companies: An International Perspective," *BIS Economic Papers,* No. 27, May 1990.

Boubakri, Narjess and Jean Claude Cosset, "The Financial and Operating Performance of Newly Privatized Firms: Evidence from Developing Countries," *Journal of Finance,* Vol. 53, No. 3, Jun 1998, pp. 1081–1110.

Braas, Alberic, and Charles N. Bralver, "An Analysis of Trading Profits: How Most Trading Rooms Really Make Money," *Journal of Applied Corporate Finance,* Winter 1990, pp. 85–90.

Bradley, Finbarr, "An Analysis of Call Strategy in the Eurodollar Bond Market," *Journal of International Financial Management and Accounting,* Vol. 2, No. 1, Spring 1990, pp. 23–46.

Brealey, Richard A., Ian A. Cooper, and Michael A. Habib, "Using Project Finance to Fund Infrastruc-ture Investments," *Journal of Applied Corporate Finance,* Fall 1996, Volume 9, No. 5, pp. 25–38.

Brennan, Michael J. and H. Henry Cro, "International Portfolio Investment Flows," *Journal of Finance,* Vol. 52, No. 5, Oct. 1997, pp. 1851–1880.

Brewer, Thomas L., "Government Policies, Market Imperfections, and Foreign Direct Investment," *Journal of International Business Studies,* 1st Quarter 1993, pp. 101–120.

Briys, Eric, and Francois de Varenne, "Optimal Hedging and the Partial Loss Offset," *European Financial Management,* Vol. 4, No. 3, November 1998, pp. 321–334.

Briys, Eric, and Michel Crouhy, "Creating and Pricing Hybrid Foreign Currency Options," *Financial Management,* Winter 1988, pp. 59–65.

Brown, Keith C., and Donald J. Smith, "Default Risk and Innovations in the Design of Inter-

est Rate Swaps," *Financial Management,* Vol. 22, No. 2, Summer 1993, pp. 94–105.

Buckley, Peter J., "The Limits of Explanation: Testing the Internalization Theory of the Multinational Enterprise," *Journal of International Business Studies,* Summer 1988, pp. 181–193.

Buckley, Peter J., and Mark Casson, "An Economic Model of International Joint Venture Strategy," *Journal of International Business Studies,* Volume 27, Number 5, Special Issue 1996, pp. 849–876.

Burgman, Todd A., "An Empirical Examination of Multinational Corporate Capital Structure," *Journal of International Business Studies,* Third Quarter 1996, pp. 553–570.

Cantor, Richard and Frank Packer, "Sovereign Risk Assessment and Agency Credit Ratings," *European Financial Management,* Vol. 2, 1996.

Capel, Jeanette, "A Real Options Approach to Economic Exposure Management," *Journal of International Financial Management and Accounting,* Vol. 8, No. 2, 1997, pp. 87–113.

Caves, Richard E., "International Corporatons: The Industrial Economics of Foreign Investment," *Economica,* February 1971, pp. 1–27.

Carney, William J., "Large Bank Stockholders in Germany: Saviors or Substitutes?," *Journal of Applied Corporate Finance,* Vol. 9, No. 4, Winter 1997, pp. 74–81.

Chan, Su Han, John W. Kensinger, Arthur Keown, and John D. Martin, "When Do Strategic Alliances Create Shareholder Value," *Journal of Financial Economics,* 1997.

Chan, Su Han, John W. Kensinger, Arthur Keown, and John D. Martin, "When Do Strategic Alliances Create Shareholder Value," *Journal of Applied Corporate Finance,* Spring 1999, Vol. 12, No. 1, pp. 82–87.

Chang, Rosita P., Peter E. Koveos, and S. Ghon Rhee, "Financial Planning for International Long-Term Debt Financing," *Advances in*

Financial Planning and Forecasting, Vol. 4, part B, 1990, pp. 33–58.

Chase, Carmen D., James L. Kuhle, and Carl H. Walther, "The Relevance of Political Risk in Direct Foreign Investment," *Management International Review*, Vol. 28, No. 3, 1988, pp. 31–38.

Chen, Andrew H., and Sumon C. Mazumdar, "Interest Rate Linkages Within the EMS and Bank Credit Supply," *European Financial Management*, Vol. 1, No. 1, Mar 1995, pp. 37–48.

Chen, Charles J.P., C. S. Agnes Cheng, Jia He, and Jawon Kim, "An Investigation of the Relationship Between International Activities and Capital Structure," *Journal of International Business Studies*, Third Quarter, 1997, pp. 563–577.

Chen, Howin and Tain-Jy Chen, "Network Linkages and Location Choice in Foreign Direct Investment," *Journal of International Business Studies*, Vol. 29, No. 3, Third Quarter, 1998, pp. 445–468.

Chen, T. J., K. C. John Wei, "Risk Premiums in Foreign Exchange Markets: Theory and Evidence," *Advances in Financial Planning and Forecasting*, Vol. 4, 1990, pp. 23–42.

Chesney, Marc, and Louis Scott, "Pricing European Currency Options: A Comparison of the Modified Black-Scholes Model and a Random Variance Model," *Journal of Financial and Quantitative Analysis*, Sep 1989, pp. 267–284.

Chiang, Thomas C., "Empirical Analysis on the Predictors of Future Spot Rates," *Journal of Financial Research*, Summer 1986, pp. 153–162.

Choi, Frederick D. S., "International Data Sources for Empirical Research in Financial Management," *Financial Management*, Summer 1988, pp. 80–98.

Choi, Frederick D. S., and Arthur Stonehill, "Foreign Access to U.S. Securities Markets: The Theory, Myth and Reality of Regulatory Barriers," *The Investment Analyst*, Jul 1982, pp. 17–26.

Choi, Frederick, Hisaaki Hino, Sang Kee Min, Sang Oh Nam, Junishi Ujiie, and Arthur Stonehill, "Analyzing Foreign Financial Statements: The Use and Misuse of International Ratio Analysis, " *Journal of International Business Studies*, Spring/Summer 1983, pp. 113–131.

Choi, Jongmoo Jay, "A Model of Firm Valuation with Exchange Exposure," *Journal of International Business Studies*, Summer, 1986, pp. 145–152.

Choi, Jongmoo Jay, "Diversification, Exchange Risk, and Corporate International Investment," *Journal of International Business Studies*, Spring 1989, pp. 145–155.

Choi, Jongmoo Jay, "Accounting Valuation and Economic Hedging of Foreign Inventory Under Exchange and Inflation Risk," in *Advances in Work-ing Capital Management*, Vol. 2, JAI Press, 1991.

Choi, Jongmoo Jay, and Richard Ajayi, "The Effect of Foreign Debt on Currency Values," *Journal of Economics and Business*, 45, Aug/Oct l993, pp. 331–340.

Choi, Jongmoo Jay, and Shmuel Hauser, "The Effects of Domestic and Foreign Yield Curves on the Value of American Currency Call Options," *Journal of Banking and Finance*, 14, Mar 1990, pp. 41–53.

Choi, Jongmoo Jay and Murli Rajan, "A Joint Test of Market Segmentation and Exchange Risk Factor in International Capital Markets," *Journal of International Business Studies*, Volume 28, No. 1, First Quarter 1997, pp. 29–49.

Choi, Jongmoo Jay, and Alan Severn, "On the Effects of International Risk, Segmentation and Diversification on the Cost of Equity Capital: A Critical Review and Synthesis," *Journal of Multinational Financial Management*, Vol. 1, issue 3, 1991, pp. 1–19.

Clark, Terry, Masaaki Kotabe, and Dan Rajaratnam, "Exchange Rate Pass-Through and International Pricing Strategy: A Conceptual Framework and Research Propositions," *Journal of International Business Studies*, Vol.

30, No. 2, Second Quarter 1999, pp. 249–268.

Coase, R. H., "The Nature of the Firm," *Economica*, No. 4, 1937, pp. 386–405.

Cochran, Steven J., and Robert H. Defina, "Can Purchasing Power Parity Help Forecast the Dollar?" *Journal of Forecasting*, Vol. 14, No. 6, Nov 1995, pp. 523–532.

Cochrane, James L., "Helping to Keep U.S. Capital Markets Competitive: Listing World-Class Non-U.S. Firms on U.S. Exchanges," *Journal of International Financial Management and Ac-counting*, Vol. 4, No. 2, Summer 1992, pp. 163–170.

Codogne, Lorenzo, "Assessing Bond Market Developments Post-Euro," *Journal of Applied Corporate Finance*, Fall 1998, Vol. 11, No. 3, pp. 66–81.

Cohen, Stephen S., and John Zysman, "Countertrade, Offsets, Barter and Buybacks," *California Management Review*, Winter 1986, pp. 41–56.

Cohn, Richard A., and John J. Pringle, "Imperfections in International Financial Markets: Implications for Risk Premia and the Cost of Capital to Firms," *Journal of Finance*, Mar 1973, pp. 59–66.

Collier, Paul A., E. W. Davis, J. B. Coates, and S. G. Longden, "Policies Employed in the Management of Currency Risk: A Case Study Analysis of US and U.K.," *Managerial Finance*, Vol. 18, No. 3, 1992, pp. 41–52.

Collins, J. Markham, "A Market Performance Comparison of U.S. Firms Active in Domestic, Developed and Developing Countries," *Journal of International Business Studies*, Second Quarter 1990, pp. 271–287.

Collins, J. Markham, and William S. Sekely, "The Relationship of Headquarters, Country, and Industry Classification to Financial Structure," *Financial Management*, Autumn 1983, pp. 45–51.

Constand, Richard L., Lewis P. Freitas, and Michael J. Sullivan, "Factors Affecting Price Earnings Ratios and Market Values of Japanese Firms," *Financial Management*, Winter 1991, pp. 68–79.

Contractor, Farok J., "Ownership Patterns of U.S. Joint Ventures Abroad and the Liberalization of Foreign Government Regulations in the 1980s: Evidence from the Benchmark Surveys," *Journal of International Business Studies*, First Quarter 1990, pp. 55–73.

Cooper, Ian, and Evi Kaplanis, "Home Bias and the Cost of Capital for Multinational Firms," *Journal of Applied Corporate Finance*, Vol. 8, No. 3, Fall 1995, pp. 95–104.

Copeland, Thomas, and Yash Joshi, "Why Derivatives Do Not Reduce FX Risk," *Corporate Finance*, May 1996, pp. 35–41.

Cosset, Jean-Claude, and Jean-Marc Suret, "Political Risk and the Benefits of International Portfolio Diversification, *Journal of International Business Studies*, Vol. 26, No. 2, Second Quarter 1995, pp. 301–318.

Cox, J. C., and S. A. Ross, "The Valuation of Options for Alternative Stochastic Processes," *Journal of Financial Economics*, Vol. 3, 1976, pp. 145–166.

Cox, J. C., S. A. Ross, and M. Rubinstein, "Option Pricing: A Simplified Approach," *Journal of Financial Economics*, Vol. 7, 1979, pp. 229–263.

Crum, Roy L., and Lee A. Tavis, "Allocating Multinational Resources When Objectives Conflict: A Problem of Overlapping Systems, *Advances in Financial Planning and Forecasting*, Vol. 4, part B, 1990, pp. 271–294.

Culp, Christopher L., Steve H. Hanke, and Merton H. Miller, "The Case for an Indonesian Currency Board," *Journal of Applied Corporate Finance*, Volume 2, No. 4, Winter 1999, pp. 57–64.

Cumby, Robert E., and Maurice Obstfeld, "A Note on Exchange-Rate Expectations and Nominal Interest Differentials: A Test of the Fisher Hypothesis," *Journal of Finance*, Jun 1981, pp. 697–703.

De Santis, Giorgio and Bruno Gerard, "International Asset Pricing and Portfolio Diversification with Time-Varying Risk," *Journal of Finance*, Volume 52, No. 5, October 1997, pp. 1881–1912.

Dewenter, Kathryn L. and Paul H. Malatesta, "Public Offerings of State-Owned and Privately-Owned Enterprises: An International Comparison," *Journal of Finance*, Vol. 52, No. 4, Aug 1997, pp. 1659–1670.

Dewenter, Kathryn L. and Vincent A. Warther, "Dividends, Asymmetric Information, and Agency Conflicts: Evidence from a Comparison of the Dividend Policies of Japanese and U.S. Firms," *Journal of Finance*, Vol. 53, No. 3, Jun 1998, pp. 879–904.

Dixit, Avinash K., and Robert S. Pindyck, "The Options Approach to Capital Investment," *Harvard Business Review*, May/Jun 1995, pp. 105–115.

Dodd, Mikel T., and James A. Millar, "Financial Structure in Japanese and American Firms: An Indirect Test of Agency Relationships," *Journal of International Financial Management and Accounting*, Vol. 2, nos. 2 and 3, Summer & Autumn 1990, pp. 131–144.

Dominguez, Luis V., and Carlos G. Sequeira, "Determinants of LDC Exporters' Performance: A Cross-National Study," *Journal of International Business Studies*, First Quarter 1993, pp. 19–40.

Domowitz, Ian, Jack Glen, and Ananth Madhavan, "Market Segmentation and Stock Prices: Evidence from an Emerging Market," *Journal of Finance*, Vol. 52, No. 3, June 1997, pp. 1059–1085.

Domowitz, Ian, Jack Glen, and Ananth Madhavan, "International Cross Listing and Order Flow Migration: Evidence from an Emerging Market," *Journal of Finance*, Vol. 53, No. 6, Dec 1998, pp. 2001–2027.

Donaldson, Gordon, "The Corporate Restructuring of the 1980s-and its Import for the 1990s," *Journal of Applied Corporate Finance*, Winter 1994, pp. 55–69.

Dotan, Amihud, and Arie Ovadia, "A Capital-Budgeting Decision-The Case of a Multinational Corporation Operating in High-Inflation Countries," *Journal Of Business Research*, Oct 1986, pp. 403–410.

Doukas, John, "Syndicated Euro-Credit Sovereign Risk Assessments, Market Efficiency and Contagion Effects," *Journal of International Business Studies*, Summer 1989, pp. 255–267.

Doukas, John, and Nickolaos G. Travlos, "The Effect of Corporate Multinationalism on Shareholders' Wealth: Evidence from International Acquisi-tions," *Journal of Finance*, Dec 1988, pp. 1161–1175.

Doukas, John and Christos Pantzalis, "Multinational Firms' Agency Cost of Debt," 1998.

Dufey, Gunter, "Corporate Finance and Exchange, Rate Variations," *Financial Management*, Summer 1972, pp. 51–57.

Dufey, Gunter, and Ian H. Giddy, "International Financial Planning: The Use of Market-Based Forecasts," *California Management Review*, Fall 1978, pp. 69–81; reprinted in Heide V. Wortzel and Lawrence Wortzel, eds., *Strategic Manage-ment of Multinational Corporations: The Essentials*, second ed., New York: Wiley, 1991.

Dufey, Gunter, and S. L. Srinivasulu, "The Case for Corporate Management of Foreign Exchange Risk," *Financial Management*, Winter 1983, pp. 54–62.

Dunning, John H., "Trade Location of Economic Activity and the MNE: A Search for an Eclectic Approach," in *The International Allocation of Economic Acitivty*, Bertil Ohlin, Per-Ove Hesselborn, and Per Magnus Wijkman, eds., New York: Holmes and Meier, 1977, pp. 395–418.

Dunning, John H., "The Eclectic Paradigm of International Production: A Restatement and Some Possible Extensions," *Journal of Interna-tional Business Studies*, Spring 1988, pp. 1–32.

Dunning, John H., "Location and the Multinational Enterprise: A Neglected Factor?," *Journal of International Business Studies*, Vol. 29, No. 1, First Quarter 1998, pp. 45–66.

Dunning, John H., and Alan M. Rugman, "The Influence of Hymer's Dissertation on the Theory of Foreign Direct Investment," *American Economic Review*, May 1985, pp. 228–232.

Eaker, Mark R., "The Numeraire Problem and Foreign Exchange Risk," *Journal of Finance*, May 1981, pp. 419–427.

Eaker, Mark R., and Dwight Grant, "Optimal Hedging of Uncertain and Long-Term Foreign Exchange Exposure," *Journal of Banking and Finance*, Jun 1985, pp. 222–231.

Eaker, Mark R., and Dwight M. Grant, "Cross-Hedging Foreign Currency Risk," *Journal of International Money and Finance*, Mar 1987, pp. 85–105.

Economist, "A Survey of Corporate Risk Management," Feb 10, 1996.

Eiteman, David K., "A Model for Expropriation Settlement: The Peruvian-IPC Controversy," *Business Horizons*, Apr 1970, pp. 85–91.

Eiteman, David K., "Multinational Firms and the Development of Penang, Malaysia," *The International Trade Journal*, Vol. XI, No. 2, 1997.

Engel, Charles, and James D. Hamilton, "Long Swings in the Dollar: Are They in the Data and Do Markets Know It?" *American Economic Review*, Sept 1990, pp. 689–713.

Eriksson, Kent, Jan Johanson, Anders Majkgård, and D. Deo Sharma, "Experiential Knowledge and Cost in the Internationalization Process," *Journal of International Business Studies*, Vol. 28, No. 2, Second Quarter 1997, pp. 337–360.

Errunza, Vihang R., "Determinants of Financial Structure in the Central American Common Market," *Financial Management*, Autumn 1979, pp.72–77.

Errunza, Vihang R., "Financing MNC Subsidiaries in Central America," *Journal of International Business Studies*, Fall 1979, pp. 88–93.

Errunza, Vihang, and Ked Hogan, "Macroeconomic Determinants of European Stock Market Volatility, *European Financial Management*, Vol. 4, No. 3, Nov 1998, pp. 361–378.

Errunza, Vihang R., and Lemma W. Senbet, "International Corporate Diversification, Market Valuation, and Size-Adjusted Evidence," *Journal of Finance*, Jul 1984, pp. 727–743.

Errunza, Vihang R., and Lemma W. Senbet, "The Effects of International Operations on the Market Value of the Firm: Theory and Evidence," *Journal of Finance*, May 1981, pp. 401–417.

Eun, Cheol S., and S. Janakiramanan, "Bilateral Cross-Listing and the Equilibrium Security Prices," *Advances in Financial Planning and Forecasting*, Vol. 4, part B, 1990, pp. 59–74.

Fama, Eugene F., "Forward Rates as Predictors of Future Spot Rates," *Journal of Financial Economics*, Oct 1976, pp. 361–377.

Fama, Eugene F., "Forward and Spot Exchange Rates," *Journal of Monetary Economics*, Vol. 14, 1984, pp. 319–338.

Fama, Eugene, and Kenneth R. French, "Value Versus Growth: The International Evidence," *Journal of Finance*, Vol. 53, No. 6, Dec 1998, pp. 1975–1999.

Fatemi, Ali M., "The Effect of International Diversification on Corporate Financing Policy," *Journal of Business Research*, Vol. 16, No. 1, Jan 1988, pp.17–30.

Feiger, George, and Bertrand Jacquillat, "Currency Option Bonds, Puts and Calls on Spot Exchange and the Hedging of Contingent Foreign Earnings," *Journal of Finance*, Dec 1979, pp. 1129–1139.

Finnerty, John D., "Financial Engineering in Corporate Finance: An Overview," *Financial Management*, Winter 1988, pp. 14–32.

Fletcher, Donna J., and Larry W. Taylor, "A Non-Parametric Analysis of Covered Interest Parity in Long-Date Capital Markets," *Journal of International Money and Finance*, Vol. 13, No. 4, Aug 1994, pp. 459–475.

Flood, Eugene, Jr., and Donald R. Lessard, "On the Measurement of Operating Exposure to Exchange Rates: A Conceptual Approach," *Financial Management*, Spring 1986, pp. 25–36.

Foerster, Stephen R. and G. Andrew Karolyi, "The Effects of Market Segmentation and Investor Recognition on Asset Prices: Evidence From Foreign Stock Listing in the United States," *Journal of Finance*, Volume 54, No. 3, June 1999, pp. 981–1013.

Folks, William R., Jr., "Decision Analysis for Exchange Risk Management," *Financial Management*, Winter 1972, pp. 101–112.

Folks, William R., Jr., "Optimal Foreign Borrowing Strategies with Operations in the Forward Exchange Markets," *Journal of Financial and Quantitative Analysis*, Jun 1978, pp. 245–254.

Folks, William R., and Stanley R. Stansell, "The Use of Discriminant Analysis in Forecasting Exchange Risk Movements," *Journal of International Business Studies*, Spring 1975, pp. 33–50.

Fowler, D. J., "Transfer Prices and Profit Maximization in Multinational Enterprise Operations," *Journal of International Business Studies*, Winter 1978, pp. 9–26.

Frankel, J. A., "The Japanese Cost of Finance: A Survey," *Financial Management*, Spring 1991, pp. 95–127.

Frankel, Jeffrey, and Alan MacArthur, "Political vs. Currency Premia in International Real Interest Rate Differentials: A Study of Forward Rates for 24 Countries," *European Economic Review*, Vol. 32, No. 5, Jun 1988, pp. 1083–1114.

Frankel, Allen, and John Montgomery, "Financial Structure: An International Perspective," *Brookings Papers on Economic Activity*, Vol. 1, 1991, pp. 257–297.

Franks, Julian and Colin Mayer, "Corporate Ownership and Control in the U.K., Germany, and France," *Journal of Applied Corporate Finance*, Winter 1997, Vol. 9, No.4, pp. 30–45.

Frenkel, Jacob A., and Richard M. Levich, "Covered Interest Arbitrage: Unexploited Profits?" *Journal of Political Economy*, Apr 1975, pp. 325–338.

Frenkel, Jacob A., and Richard M. Levich, "Transaction Costs and Interest Arbitrage: Tranquil versus Turbulent Periods," *Journal of Political Economy*, Nov/Dec 1977, pp. 1209–1226.

Friend, Irwin, and Ichiro Tokutsu, "The Cost of Capital to Corporations in Japan and the U.S.A.," *Journal of Banking and Finance*, Vol. 11, No. 2, Jun 1987, pp. 313–328.

Frisch, Daniel J., Economics of International Tax Policy: Some Old and New Approaches," *Tax Notes*, Apr 30, 1990, pp. 581–591.

Fry, Clifford, Insup Lee, and Jongmoo Jay Choi, "International Listing and Valuation: The Case of the Tokyo Stock Exchange," *Review of Quantitative Finance and Accounting*, Mar 1994.

Ganitsky, Joseph, and Gerardo Lema, "Foreign Investment Through Debt-Equity Swaps," *Sloan Management Review*, Vol. 29, No. 2, Winter 1988, pp. 21–29.

Garman, Mark B., and Steven W. Kohlhagen, "Foreign Currency Option Values," *Journal of International Money and Finance*, Dec 1983, pp. 231–237.

Géczy, Christopher, Bernadette A. Minton, and Catherine Schrand, "Why Firms Use Currency Derivatives," *Journal of Finance*, Vol. 52, No. 4, Augt 1997, pp. 1323–1354.

Gentry, James A., Dileep R. Mehta, S. K. Bhattacharya, Robert Cobbaut, and Jean-Louis Scaringella, "An International Study of Management Perceptions of the Working Capital Process," *Journal of International Business Studies*, Spring–Summer 1979, pp. 28–38.

Geringer, J, Michael, and Louis Hebert, "Control and Performance of International Joint Ventures," *Journal of International Business*

Studies, Summer 1989, pp. 235–254.

Ghertman, Michel, "Foreign Subsidiary and Parents' Roles During Strategic Investment and Divestment Decisions," *Journal of International Business Studies,* Spring 1988, pp. 47–68.

Giddy, Ian H., "An Integrated Theory of Exchange Rate Equilibrium," *Journal of Financial and Quantitative Analysis,* Dec 1976, pp. 863–892,

Giddy, Ian H., "Exchange Risk: Whose View?" *Financial Management,* Summer 1977, pp. 23–33.

Giddy, Ian H., and Gunter Dufey, "The Random Behavior of Flexible Exchange Rates," *Journal of International Business Studies,* Spring 1975, pp. 1–32.

Giddy, Ian H., and Gunter Dufey, "Uses and Abuses of Currency Options," *Journal of Applied Corporate Finance,* Vol. 8, No. 3, Fall 1995, pp. 49–57.

Glassman, Debra, "Exchange Rate Risk and Transactions Costs: Evidence from Bid-Ask Spreads," *Journal of International Money and Finance,* Vol. 6, No. 4, Dec 1987, pp. 479–491.

Glaum, Martin, "Strategic Management of Exchange Rate Risks," *Long Range Planning,* Vol. 23, No. 4, 1990, pp. 65–72.

Gleason, Kimberly C., Ike Mathur, and Lynette Knowles Mathur, "Shareholders' Gains from Corporate Expansion to the Republics of the Former Soviet Union," *Financial Management,* Vol. 28, No. 1, Spring 1999, pp. 61–74.

Godfrey, Stephen, and Ramon Espinosa, "A Practical Approach to Calculating Cost of Equity for Investments in Emerging Markets," *Journal of Applied Corporate Finance,* Vol. 9, No. 3, Fall 1996, pp. 80–89.

Gonzalez, Manolete V., and Edwin Villanueva, "Steering a Subsidiary Through a Political Crisis," *Risk Management,* Oct 1992, pp. 16–27.

Goodman, Stephen, "Foreign Exchange Forecasting Techniques: Implications for Business and Policy," *Journal of Finance,* May 1979, pp. 415–427.

Goodwin, Barry K., Thomas Grennes, and Michael K. Wohlgenant, "Testing the Law of One Price When Trade Takes Time," *Journal of International Money and Finance,* May 1990, pp. 21–40.

Grabbe, J. Orlin, "The Pricing of Call and Put Options on Foreign Exchange," *Journal of International Money and Finance,* Dec 1983, pp. 239–253.

Granick, David, "National Differences in the Use of Internal Transfer Prices," *California Management Review,* Summer 1975, pp. 28–40.

Gruber, W., D. Mehta, and R. Vernon, "The R&D Factor in International Trade and Investment of United States Industries," *Journal of Political Economy,* Feb 1967, pp. 20–37.

Guffin, John M. and G. Andrew Karolyi, "Another Look at the Role of the Industrial Structure of Markets for International Diversification Strategies," *Journal of Financial Economics,* Vol. 50, No. 3, Dec 1998, pp. 351–373.

Gultekin, Mustafa N., N. Bulent Gultekin, and Alessandro Penati, "Capital Controls and International Capital Market Segmentation: The Evidence from the Japanese and American Stock Markets," *Journal of Finance,* Sep 1989, pp. 849–869.

Hamilton, Robert D. and Roger J. Kashlak, "National Influences on Multinational Corporation Control System Selection," *Management International Review,* 2/99, pp. 167–189.

Hanson, Bruce B., "What You Need to Know About Economic Value Added," *Compensation and Benefits Review,* Mar/Apr 1995, pp. 33–36.

Harris, Trevor S., Nahun D. Melumad, and Toshi Shibano, "An Argument Against Hedging by

Matching the Currency of Costs and Revenues," *Journal of Applied Corporate Finance*, Fall 1996, Volume 9, No. 3, pp. 90–97.

Harvard Business School, "A Note on Private Equity in Developing Countries," Boston, Ma: Harvard Business School Publishing, Mar 1997.

He, Jia and Lilian Ng, "The Foregin Exchange Exposure of Japanese Multinational Corporations," *Journal of Finance*, Vol. 53, No. 2, April 1998, pp. 733–753.

Hedlund, Gunner, "A Model of Knowledge Management and the N-form Corporation," *Strategic Management Journal*, No. 15, 1994, pp. 73–90.

Hedlund, Gunner, "The Hypermodem MNC-A Heterarchy?" *Human Resource Management*, Vol. 25, No. 1, pp. 9–35.

Hekman, Christine R., "A Financial Model of Foreign Exchange Exposure." *Journal of International Business Studies*, Summer 1985, pp. 83–99.

Hekman, Christine R., "Don't Blame Currency Values for Strategic Errors," *Midland Corporate Finance Journal*, Fall 1986, pp. 45–55.

Hennart, Jean-Francois, "Internalization in Practice: Early Foreign Direct Investment in Malaysian Tin Mining," *Journal of International Business Studies*, Summer 1986. pp. 131–144.

Hennart, Jean-Francois, "Some Empirical Dimensions of Countertrade," *Journal of International Business Studies*, second Quarter 1990, pp. 243–270.

Hennart, Jean-Francois and Erin Anderson, "Countertrade and the Minimization of Transaction Costs: An Empirical Examination," *Journal of Law, Economics, and Organization*, Oct 1993, pp. 290–313.

Hill, Claire A., "Securitization: A Financing Strategy for Emerging Market Firms," *Journal of Applied Corporate Finance*, Fall 1998, Vol. 11, No. 3, pp. 55–65.

Hirsch, Se'ev, "Multinationals: How Different Are They?" in *The Growth of The Large Multinational Corporation*, G. Y. Bertin, ed., Paris: Centre Nationale de la Recherche Scientifique, 1973.

Ho, T.S., Richard C. Stapleton, and Marti G. Subrahmanyam, "The Risk of a Currency Swap: A Multivariate Binomial Methodology, *European Financial Management*, Vol. 4, No. 1, March 1998, pp. 9–28.

Hodder, James E., "Evaluation of Manufacturing Investments: A Comparison of U.S. and Japanese Practices," *Financial Management*, Spring 1986, pp. 17–24.

Hodder, James E., and Adrian E. Tschoegl, "Some Aspects of Japanese Corporate Finance," *Journal of Financial and Quantitative Analysis*, Jun 1985, pp. 173–191.

Hodder, James E., and Lemma W. Senbet, "International Capital Structure Equilibrium," *Journal of Finance*, Dec 1990, pp. 1495–1516.

Hogue, W. Dickerson, "The Foreign Investment Decision Making Process," *Association for Education in International Business Proceedings*, Dec 29, 1967, pp.1–2.

Holmes, M.C., "Check list for Foreign Licensing," *Business Lawyer*, Nov 1968, pp. 281–289.

Horaguchi, Haruo, and Brian Toyne, "Setting the Record Straight: Hymer, Internalization Theory and Transaction Cost Economics," *Journal of International Business Studies*, Third Quarter 1990, pp. 487–494.

Houpt, James V., "International Trends for U.S. Banks and Banking Markets," Staff Study of the Board of Governors of the Federal Reserve System, No. 156, May 1988.

Houston, Carol Olson, "Translation Exposure Hedging Post SFAS No. 52," *Journal of International Financial Management and Accounting*, Vol. 2, Nos. 2 and 3, Summer and Autumn 1990, pp. 145–170.

Howton, Shawn D. and Steven B. Perfect, "Currency and Interest Rate Derivatives Use in

U.S. Firms," *Financial Management*, Vol. 27, No. 4, Winter 1998, pp. 111–121.

Howe, John S., and Kathryn Kelm, "The Stock Price Impacts of Overseas Listings," *Financial Management*, Autumn 1987, pp. 51–56.

Hu, Henry T.C., "Behind the Corporate Hedge: Information and the Limits of 'Shareholder Wealth Maximization,'" *Journal of Applied Corporate Finance*, Vol. 9, No. 3, Fall 1996, pp. 39–51.

Huang, Roger D., "Expectations of Exchange Rates and Differential Inflation Rates: Further Evidence on Purchasing Power Parity in Efficient Markets," *Journal of Finance*, Mar 1987, pp. 69–79.

Huang, Roger D., and Hans R. Stoll, *Major World Equity Markets: Current Structure and Prospects for Change*, New York: New York University Salomon Center; Monograph Series in Finance and Economics, No. 3, 1991.

Huckins, Nancy White, and Anoop Rai, "Market Risk for Foreign Currency Options: Basle's Simplified Model," *Financial Management*, Vol. 28, No. 1, Spring 1999, pp. 99–109.

Hughes, John S., Dennis E. Logue, and Richard J. Sweeney, "Corporate International Diversification and Market Assigned Measures of Risk and Diversification," *Journal of Financial and Quantitative Analysis*, Nov 1975, pp. 627–637.

Hull, John, and Alan White, "Hedging the Risks from Writing Foreign Currency Options," *Journal of International Money and Finance*, Jun 1987, pp. 131–152.

Hymer, Stephen, and Robert Rowthorn, "Multinational Corporations and International Oligopoly: The Non-American Challenge," in *The International Corporation: A Symposium*, Charles P. Kindleberger, ed., Cambridge, Mass.: MIT Press, 1970, pp. 57–91.

Investing, Licensing and Trading Conditions Abroad, New York: Business International, a reference service that is continually updated.

Jacque, Laurent, and Gabriel Hawawini, "Myths and Realities of the Global Capital Market: Lessons for Financial Managers," *Journal of Applied Corporate Finance*, Fall 1993, pp. 81–90.

Jadlow, Janice Wickstead, "Market Assessment of the Eurodollar Default Risk Premium," *Advances in Financial Planning and Forecasting*, Vol. 4, part A, 1990, pp. 105–122.

Jayaraman, Narayanan, Kuldeep Shastri, and Kishore Tandon, "The Impact of International Cross Listings on Risk and Return: The Evidence from American Depositary Receipts," *Journal of Banking and Finance*, No. 17, pp. 91–103.

Jennergren, L. Peter, and Bertil Nëslund, "Models for the Valuation of International Convertible Bonds," *Journal of International Financial Management and Accounting*, Vol. 2, nos. 2 and 3, Summer and Autumn 1990, pp. 93–110.

Jensen, Michael C., "Agency Cost of Free Cash Flow, Corporate Finance and Takeovers, *American Economic Review*, 76, 1986, pp. 323–329.

Jensen, Michael and W. Meckling, "Theory of the Firm: Managerial Behavior, Agency Costs, and Ownership Structure," *Journal of Financial Economics*, No. 3, 1976, pp. 305–360.

Jesswein, Kurt R., Chuck C. Y. Kwok, and William R. Folks, Jr., "Corporate Use of Innovative Foreign Exchange Risk Management Products," *Columbia Journal of World Business*, Vol. 30, No. 3, Fall 1995, pp. 70–82.

Johansen, John, and F. Weidersheim-Paul, "The Internationalization of the Firm: Four Swedish Case Studies," *Journal of Management Studies*, Vol. 12, No. 3, 1975.

Johansen, John, and Jan Erik Vahlne, "The Internationalization of the Firm: A Model of Knowledge Development and Increasing Foreign Market Commitments," *Journal of International Business Studies*, Vol. 8, No. 1, 1977.

John, Kose, Lemma Senbet, and Anant Sundaram, "Cross-border Liability of Multinational Enterprises, Border Taxes, and Capital Structure," *Financial Management*, Winter 1991.

Johnson, Greg and Thomas Funkhouser, "Yankee Bonds and Cross-Border Private Placements," *Journal of Applied Corporate Finance*, Fall 1999, Vol. 10, No. 3, pp. 34–45.

Johnson, Robert, and Luc Soenen, "Evaluating the Impact of Investment Projects on the Firm's Currency Exposure," *Managerial Finance*, Vol. 20, No. 7, 1994, pp. 51–58.

Jorion, Philippe and William N. Goetzmann, "Global Stock Markets in the Twentieth Century," *Journal of Finance*, Vol. 54, No. 3, Jun 1999, pp. 953–980.

Jorion, Philippe, "The Exchange-Rate Exposure of U.S. Multinationals," *Journal of Business*, Vol. 63, No. 3, Jul 1990, pp. 331–345.

Jorion, Philippe, and Neal M. Stoughton, "An Empirical Investigation of the Early Exercise Premium of Foreign Currency Options," *Journal of Futures Markets*, Oct 1989, pp. 365–375.

Kaen, Fred R., Evangelos 0. Simos, and George A. Hachey, "The Response of Forward Exchange Rates to Interest Rate Forecasting Errors," *Journal of Financial Research*, Winter 1984, pp. 281–290.

Kanas, Angelos, "Exchange Rate Economic Exposure When Market Share Matters and Hedging Using Currency Options," *Management International Review*, Vol. 36, No. 1, First Quarter 1996, pp. 67–84.

Kaplan, Steven N., "Corporate Governance and Incentives in German Companies: Evidence From Top Executive Turnover and Firm Performance, *European Financial Management*, Vol. 1, No. 1, Mar 1995, pp. 23–36.

Kaplan, Steven, "Corporate Governance and Corporate Performance: A Comparison of Germany, Japan, and the U.S.," *Journal of Applied Corporate Finance*, Winter 1997, Vol. 9, No.4, pp. 86–93.

Karolyi, G. Andrew, "Sourcing Equity Internationally With Depositary Receipt Offerings:

Two Exceptions That Prove The Rule," *Journal of Applied Corporate Finance*, Winter 1998, Vol. 10, No. 4, pp. 90–101.

Kaufold, Howard, and Michael Smirlock, "Managing Corporate Exchange and Interest Rate Exposure," *Financial Management*, Autumn 1986, pp. 64–72.

Kawaller, Ira G., "The Imperative of Interest Rate Risk Management," *Treasury Management Association (THA) Journal*, Vol. 15, No. 6, Nov/Dec 1996, pp. 4–7.

Keck, Tom, Eric Levengood, and Al Longfield, "Using Discounted Cash Flow Analysis in an International Setting," *Journal of Applied Corporate Finance*, Fall 1998, Vol. 11, No. 3, pp. 82–99.

Kelly, Marie E. Wicks, and George C. Philippatos, "Comparative Analysis of the Foreign Investment Evaluation Practices by U.S.-Based Manufacturing Multinational Corporations," *Journal of International Business Studies*, Winter 1982, pp. 19–42.

Kemna, Antzellen G. Z., "Case Studies in Real Options," *Financial Management*, Autumn 1993, pp. 259–270.

Kerkvliet, Joe, and Michael H. Moffett, "The Hedging of an Uncertain Future Foreign Currency Cash Flow," *Journal of Financial and Quantitative Analysis*, Vol. 26, No. 4, Dec 1991, pp. 565–578.

Kester, W. Carl, "Capital and Ownership Structure: A Comparison of United States and Japanese Manufacturing Corporations," *Financial Management*, Spring 1986, pp. 5–16.

Khouri, Sarkis J., and K. Hung Chan, "Hedging Foreign Exchange Risk: Selecting the Optimal Tool," *Midland Corporate Finance Journal*, Winter 1988, pp. 40–52.

Kim, E. Han, "Globalization of Capital Markets and the Asian Financial Crisis," *Journal of Applied Corporate Finance*, Fall 1998, Vol. 11, No. 3, pp. 30–39.

Kim, E. Han and Vijay Singal, "Are Open Markets Good for Foreign Investors and Emerging

Nations?," *Journal of Applied Corporate Finance*, Fall 1997, Vol. 10, No. 3, pp. 18–33.

Kim, Wi Saeng, and Esmerelda 0. Lyn, "FDI Theories and the Performance of Foreign Multinationals Operating in the U.S.," *Journal of International Business* Studies, First Quarter 1990, pp. 41–54.

Kimura, Yui, "Firm-Specific Strategic Advantages and Foreign Direct Investment Behavior of Firms: The Case of Japanese Semiconductor Firms," *Journal of International Business Studies*, Summer 1989, pp. 296–314.

Kobrin, Stephen J., "The Environmental Determinants of Foreign Direct Manufacturing Investment: An Ex-Post Empirical Analysis," *Journal of International Business Studies*, Fall/Winter 1976, pp. 29–42.

Kobrin, Stephen J., "Political Risk: A Review and Reconsideration," *Journal of International Business Studies*, Spring/Summer 1979, pp. 67–80.

Kogut, Bruce, and Harbir Singh, "The Effect of National Culture on the Choice of Entry Mode," *Journal of International Business Studies,* Fall 1988, pp. 411–432.

Kogut, Bruce, and Udo Zander, "Knowledge of the Firm and the Evolutionary Theory of the Multinational Corporation," *Journal of International Business Studies*, Fourth Quarter, 1993, pp. 625–645.

Kohlhagen, Stephen W., *The Behavior of Foreign Exchange Markets—Critical Survey of the Empirical Literature*, New York: New York University Monograph Series in Finance and Economics, No. 3, 1978.

Kohlhagen, Steven W., "A Model of Optimal Foreign Exchange Hedging Without Exchange Rate Projections," *Journal of International Business Studies*, Fall 1978, pp. 9–19.

Kopits, George F., "Intra-Firm Royalties Crossing Frontier, and Transfer–Pricing Behaviour," *Economic Journal*, Dec 1976, pp. 791–805.

Koveos, Peter, and Bruce Seifert, "Purchasing Power Parity and Black Markets," *Financial Management*, Autumn 1985, pp. 40–46.

Kulatilaka, Nalin, and Alan J. Marcus, "Hedging Foreign Project Risk," *Journal of International Financial Management & Accounting*, Vol. 5, No. 2, Jun 1994, pp. 142–156.

Kunz, Roger M., "Factors Affecting the Value of the Stock Voting Right: Evidence from the Swiss Equity Market," *Financial Management*, Vol. 25, No. 3, Autumn 1996, pp. 7–21.

Kwok, Chuck C. Y., "Hedging Foreign Exchange Exposures: Independent vs. Integrative Approaches," *Journal of International Business Studies*, Summer 1987, pp. 33–52.

Kwok, Chuck C. Y., and LeRoy D. Brooks, "Examining Event Study Methodologies in Foreign Exchange Markets," *Journal of International Business Studies*, Second Quarter 1990, pp. 189–224.

Kwok, Chuck C. Y., and David M. Reeb, "Internationalization, Financial Leverage, and Risks of the Multinational Corporation: An Upstream-Downstream Hypothesis," Paper Presented at the Academy of International Business Annual Conference, Vienna, Austria, 1998.

Laurence, Martin, Francis Cai, and Sun Qian, "Weak-Form Efficiency and Causality Tests in Chinese Stock Markets," *Multinational Finance Journal*, Vol. 1, No. 4, Dec 1997, pp. 291–307.

Lecraw, Donald J., "The Management of Countertrade: Factors Influencing Success," *Journal of International Business Studies*, Spring 1989, pp. 41–59.

Lee, Kwang Chul, and Chuck C.Y. Kwok, "Multinational Corporations vs. Domestic Corporations: International Environmental Factors and Determinants of Capital Structure," *Journal of International Business Studies*, Summer 1988, pp. 195–217.

Lee, Suk Hun, "Relative Importance of Political Instability and Economic Variables on Perceived Country Creditworthiness," *Journal of International Business Studies*, Fourth Quarter, 1993, pp. 801–812.

Lee, Tung-Jean, and Richard E. Caves, "Uncertain Outcomes of Foreign Investment: Determinants of Profits After Large Acquisitions," *Journal of International Business Studies*, Vol. 29, No. 3, Third Quarter 1998, pp. 563–582.

Lee, W. Y., and K. S. Sachdeva, "The Role of the Multinational Firm in the Integration of Segmented Capital Markets," *Journal of Finance,* May 1977, pp. 479–492.

Lessard, Donald R., "Incorporating Country Risk in the Valuation of Offshore Projects," *Journal of Applied Corporate Finance*, Vol. 9, No. 3, Fall 1996, pp. 52–63.

Lessard, Donald R., "Evaluating International Projects: An Adjusted Present Value Approach," in *International Financial Management: Theory and Application*, Donald R. Lessard, ed., New York: Wiley, 1985, pp. 570–584.

Lessard, Donald R., "Finance and Global Competition: Exploiting Financial Scope and Coping with Volatile Exchange Rates," *Midland Corporate Finance Journal,* Fall 1986, pp. 6–29.

Lessard, Donald R., "Global Competition and Corporate Finance in the 1990's," *Journal of Applied Corporate Finance*, Winter 1991, pp. 59–72.

Lessard, Donald R., and S. B. Lightstore, "Volatile Exchange Rates Can Put Operations at Risk," *Harvard Business Review,* Jul/Aug 1986, pp.107–114.

Levi, Maurice D., and Piet Sercu, "Erroneous and Valid Reasons for Hedging Foreign Exchange Rate Exposure," *Journal of Multinational Financial Management*, Vol. 1, No. 2, 1991, pp. 19–28.

Levich, Richard M., "Tests of Forecasting Models and Market Efficiency in the International Money Market," in Jacob A. Frenkel and Harry G. Johnson, eds., *The Economics of Exchange Rates*, Reading, MA: Addison-Wesley, 1978, pp.129–158.

Levich, Richard M., "Are Forward Exchange Rates Unbiased Predictors of Future Spot Rates?" *Columbia Journal of World Business*, Winter 1979, pp. 49–61.

Levich, Richard M., "Analyzing the Accuracy of Foreign Exchange Forecasting Services: Theory and Evidence," in Clas Wihlborg and Richard Levich, eds., *Exchange Risk and Exposure: Current Developments in International Financial Development*, Lexington, Mass.: D.C. Heath, 1980.

Lewent, Judy C., and A. John Kearney, "Identifying, Measuring, and Hedging Currency Risk at Merck," *Journal of Applied Corporate Finance*, Winter 1990, pp. 19–28.

Lin, James Wuh, and Jeff Madura, "Optimal Debt Financing for Multinational Projects," *Journal of Multinational Financial Management*, Vol. 3, Nos. 1/2, 1993, pp. 63–73.

Logue, Dennis E., "First We Kill All the Currency Traders," *Journal of Business Strategy*, Vol. 17, No. 2, Mar/Apr 1996, pp. 12–13.

Luehrman, Timothy A., "The Exchange Rate Exposure of a Global Competitor," *Journal of International Business Studies*, Vol. 21. No. 2, 1990, pp. 225–242.

Luehrman, Timothy A., "What's it Worth?: A General Manager's Guide to Valuation," *Harvard Business Review*, May 1997.

Luehrman, Timothy A., "Strategy as a Portfolio of Real Options," *Harvard Business Review*, Sept–Oct 1998, pp. 89–99.

Macey, Jonathan R., and Geoffrey P. Miller, "Universal Banks are not the Answer to America's Corporate Governance 'Problem': A Look at Germany, Japan, and the U.S.," *Journal of Applied Corporate Finance*, Vol. 9, Winter 1997, No. 4, pp. 57–73.

Magee, Stephen P., "Currency Contracts, Pass-Through, and Devaluation," *Brookings Papers on Economic Activity*, Vol. 1, 1973, pp. 303–325.

Magee, Stephen P., "U.S. Import Prices in the Currency-Contract Period," *Brookings Papers on Economic Activity*, Vol. 1, 1974, pp. 117–164.

Magee, Stephen P., "Contracting and Spurious Deviations from Purchasing Power Parity," in Jacob A. Frenkel and Harry G. Johnson, eds., *The Economics of Exchange Rates*, Reading, MA: Addison Wesley, 1978, pp. 67–74.

Mahajan, Arvind, and Dileep Mehta, "Swaps, Expectations, and Exchange Rates," *Journal of Banking and Finance*, Mar 1986, pp. 7–20.

Malindretos, John, and Demetri Tsanacas, "Hedging Preferences and Foreign Exchange Exposure Management," *Multinational Business Review*, Vol. 3, No. 2, Fall 1995, pp. 56–66.

Malliaropulos, Dimitrios, "Excess Stock Returns and News: Evidence from European Markets," *European Financial Management*, Vol. 4, No. 1, Mar 1998, pp. 29–46.

Mann, Catherine L., "Prices, Profit Margins, and Exchange Rates," *Federal Reserve Bulletin*, Jun 1986, pp. 366–379.

Manzur, Meher, "An International Comparison of Prices and Exchange Rates: A New Test of Purchasing Power Parity," *Journal of International Money and Finance*, Mar 1990, pp. 75–91.

Marr, M. Wayne, Robert W. Rogowski, and John L. Trimble, "The Competitive Effects of U.S. and Japanese Commercial Bank Participation in Eurobond Underwriting," *Financial Management*, Winter 1989, pp. 47–54.

Marr, M. Wayne, John L. Trimble, and Raj Varma, "On the Integration of International Capital Markets: Evidence from Euroequity Offerings," *Financial Management*, Winter 1991, pp. 11–21.

Masson, Dubos J., "Planning and Forecasting of Cash Flows for the Multinational Firm: International Cash Management," *Advances in Financial Planning and Forecasting*, Vol. 4, Part B. 1990, pp. 195–228.

McCauley, R. N., and S. A. Zimmer, "Explaining International Differences in the Cost of Capital," *Federal Reserve Bank of New York Quarterly Review*, Summer 1989, pp. 7–28.

Meese, Richard, and Kenneth Rogoff, "Was It Real? The Exchange Rate-Interest Differential Relation over the Modern Floating-Rate Period," *Journal of Finance*, Sep 1988, pp. 933–948.

Megginson, William L., Robert C. Nash, and Matthias Ian Randenbough, "The Financial and Operating Performance of Newly Privatized Firms: An International Empirical Analysis," *Journal of Finance*, Jun 1994, pp. 403–452.

Melino, Angelo, and Stuart M. Turnbull, "Misspecification and the Pricing and Hedging of Long-Term Currency Options," *Journal of International Money and Finance*, Vol. 14, No. 3, Jun 1995, pp. 373–393.

Mian, Shehzad L., "Evidence on Corporate Hedging Policy," *Journal of Financial and Quantitative Analysis*, Vol. 31, No. 3, Sep 1996, pp. 419–439.

Michel, Allen, and Israel Shaked, "Multinational Corporations vs. Domestic Corporations: Financial Performance and Characteristics," *Journal of International Business Studies*, Fall 1986, pp. 89–100.

Miller, Darius P., "The Market Reaction to International Cross-Listings: Evidence from Depositary Receipts," *Journal of Financial Economics*, 51, 1999, pp. 103–123.

Miller, Kent D. and Jeffrey J. Reuer, "Firm Strategy and Economic Exposure to Foreign Exchange Rate Movements," *Journal of International Business Studies*, Vol. 29, No. 3, Third Quarter, 1998, pp. 493–514.

Miller, Merton H., "Some Reflections on Recent Monetary Turmoil in Eastern Europe," *Journal of Applied Corporate Finance*, Vol. 11, No. 3, 1998, pp. 49–54.

Miller, Merton H., "Is American Corporate Governance Fatally Flawed?" *Journal of Applied Corporate Finance*, Winter 1994, pp. 32–39.

Miller, Merton H., "Financial Markets and Economic Growth," *Journal of Applied Corporate Finance*, Fall 1998, Vol. 11, No. 3, pp. 8–15.

Millman, Gregory J., "Financing the Uncreditworthy: New Financial Structures for

LDCs," *Journal of Applied Corporate Finance*, Vol. 3, No. 4, Winter 1991, pp. 83–89.

Minor, Michael, "Changes in Developing Country Regimes for Foreign Direct Investment: The Raw Materials Sector, 1968–1985," *Essays in International Business*, No. 8, Columbia: University of South Carolina, Sep 1990.

Mirus, Rolf, and Bemard Yeung, "The Relevance of the Invoicing Currency in Intra-Firm Trade Transactions," *Journal of International Money and Finance*, Vol. 6, No. 4. Dec 1987, pp. 449–464.

Mishra, Chandra S. and David H. Gobeli, "Managerial Incentives, Internalization, and Market Valuation of Multinational Firms, " *Journal of International Business Studies*, Vol. 29, No. 3, Third Quarter 1998, pp. 583–598.

Miyamoto, Arnold, and Stephen Godfrey, "Foreign Exchange Budget Rates: How They Can Affect the Firm," *Journal of Applied Corporate Finance*, Vol. 8, No. 3, Fall 1995, pp. 115–120.

Moffett, Michael H., "The J-Curve Revisited: An Empirical Examination for the United States," *Journal of International Money and Finance*, 1989, pp. 425–444.

Moffett, Michael H., and Jan Karl Karlsen, "Managing Foreign Exchange Rate Economic Exposure," *Journal of International Financial Management and Accounting*, Vol. 5, No. 2, Jun 1994, pp. 157–175.

Moffett, Michael H., and Douglas J. Skinner, "Issues in Foreign Exchange Hedge Accounting," *Journal of Applied Corporate Finance*, Vol. 8, No, 3, Fall 1995, pp. 82–94.

Moxon, Richard W., "The Motivation for Investment in Offshore Plants: The Case of the U.S. Electronics Industry," *Journal of International Business Studies,* Spring 1975, pp. 51–66.

Myers, Randy, "Keeping Score: Where Strategy and Performance Metrics Meet," *CFO*, Oct 1996, pp. 25–50.

Nance, Deana R., Clifford W. Smith, Jr., and Charles W. Smithson, "On the Determinants of Corporate Hedging," *Journal of Finance*, Mar 1993, pp. 267–284.

Nigh, Douglas, "The Effect of Political Events on United States Direct Foreign Investment: A Pooled Time Series Cross-Sectional Analysis," *Journal of International Business Studies*, Spring 1985, pp. 1–17.

Oblak, David J., and Roy J. Helm, Jr., "Survey and Analysis of Capital Budgeting Methods Used by Multinationals," *Financial Management*, Winter 1980, pp. 37–41.

O'Brien, Thomas J., "International Production Location and Pro Forma Financial Hedging of Exchange Rate Risk," *Journal of Applied Corporate Finance*, Fall 1998, Vol. 11, No. 3, pp. 100–108.

O'Donnell, Sharon, "Compensation Design as a Tool for Implementing Foreign Subsidiary Strategy," *Management International Review*, 2/99, pp. 149–166.

Ohmae, Kenichi, "Lies, Damned Lies, and Statistics: Why the Trade Deficit Doesn't Matter in a Borderless World," *Journal of Applied Corporate Finance*, Vol. 3, No. 4, Winter 1991, pp. 98–106.

Ohno, Kenichi, "Exchange Rate Fluctuations, PassThrough, and Market Share," *IMF Staff Papers*, Vol. 37, No. 2, Jun 1990, pp. 294–310.

Olsen, Eric E., and James A. Knight, "Managing for Value," in the *Handbook Of Modern Finance*, Dennis E. Logue, ed., New York: Warren, Gorharn & Lamont, 1996, p. E 10-2.

Oxelheim, Lars, and Clas Wihlborg, "Corporate Strategies in a Turbulent World Economy," *Management International Review*, Vol. 31, No. 4,1991, pp. 293–315.

Oxelheim, Lars, and Clas Wihlborg, "Managing Foreign Exchange Exposure," *Journal of Applied Corporate Finance*, Vol. 3, No. 4, Winter 1991, pp. 73–82.

Oxelheim, Lars, and Clas Wihlborg, "Measuring Macroeconomic-Exposure: The Case of

Volvo Cars," *European Financial Management*, Vol. 1, No. 3, 1995, pp. 241–263.

Pan, Ming-Shiun, Angela Y. Liu, and Hamid Bastin, "An Examination of the Short-Term and Long-Term Behavior of Foreign Exchange Rates," *Financial Review*, Vol. 31, No. 3, Aug 1996, pp. 603–622.

Park, Yoon S., "Currency Swaps as a Long-Term International Financing Technique," *Journal of International Business Studies*, Winter 1984, pp. 47–54.

Pedersen, Torben, and Steen Thomsen, "European Patterns of Corporate Ownership," *Journal of International Business Studies*, Vol. 28, No. 4, Fourth Quarter, 1997, pp. 759–778.

Plasschaert, S. R. F., "Transfer Pricing Problems in Developing Countries," in *Multinationals and Transfer Pricing*, A. M. Rugman and L. Eden, eds., New York: St. Martin's Press, 1985, pp. 247–266.

Popper, Helen, "Long-Term Covered Interest Parity: Evidence from Currency Swaps," *Journal of International Money and Finance*, Aug 1993, pp. 439–448.

Prahalad, C.K., "Corporate Governance or Corporate Value Added?: Rethinking the Primacy of Shareholder Value," *Journal of Applied Corporate Finance*, Winter 1994, pp. 40–50.

Pringle, John J., "A Look at Indirect Foreign Exchange Exposure," *Journal of Applied Corporate Finance*, Vol. 8, No. 3, Fall 1995, pp. 75–81.

Prowse, Stephen D., "Institutional Investment Patterns and Corporate Financial Behavior in the U.S. and Japan," *Journal of Financial Economics* 27, Sept 1990, pp. 43–66.

Prowse, Stephen D., "Corporate Governance in an International Perspective: A Survey of Corporate Control Mechanisms Among Large Firms in the U.S., U.K., Japan, and Germany," Geneva: *Bank for International Settlements Economic Paper No. 41*, and *Financial Markets, Institutions, and Instruments*, Vol. 4, No. 1, 1995.

Rajan, Raghuram, and Luigi Zingales, "Debt, Folklore, and Cross-Country Differences in Financial Structure," *Journal of Applied Corporate Finance*, Winter 1998, Vol. 10, No. 4, pp. 102–107.

Rajan, Raghuram G., and Luigi Zingales, "Which Capitalism? Lessons From the East Asia Crisis," *Journal of Applied Corporate Finance*, Fall 1998, Vol. 11, No. 3, pp. 40–48.

Rajan, Raghuram G., and Luigi Zingales, "What Do We Know About Capital Structure? Some Evidence From International Data," *Journal of Finance*, Vol. 1, No. 1, December 1995, pp. 1421–1460.

Rappaport, Alfred, "Linking Competitive Strategy and Shareholder Value Analysis," *Journal of Business Strategy*, Spring 1987, pp. 58–67.

Ravichandran, R., and J. Michael Pinegar, "Risk Shifting in International Licensing Agreements: A Note," *Journal of International Financial Management and Accounting*, Vol. 2, nos. 2 and 3, Summer and Autumn 1990, pp. 181–195.

Reeb, David M., Chuck C. Y. Kwok, and H. Young Baek, "Systematic Risk of the Multinational Corporation," *Journal of International Business Studies*, Second Quarter 1998, pp. 263–279.

Remmers, Lee, Arthur Stonehill, Richard Wright, and Theo Beekhuisen, "Industry and Size as Debt Ratio Determinants for Manufacturing Internationally," *Financial Management*, Summer 1974, pp. 24–32.

Rezaee, Zabihollah, R. P. Malone, and Russell F. Briner, "Capital Market Response to SFAS Nos. 8 and 52; Professional Adaptation," *Journal of Accounting, Auditing & Finance*, Vol. 8, No. 3, Summer 1993, pp. 313–332.

Rhee, S. Ghon, Rosita P. Chang, and Peter E. Koveos, "The Currency-of-Denomination Decision for Debt Financing," *Journal of In-*

ternational Business Studies, Fall 1985, pp. 143–150.

Rivoli, Pietra, and Eugene Salorio, "Foreign Direct Investment and Investment Under Uncertainty," *Journal of International Business Studies*, Vol. 27, No. 2, Second Quarter 1996, pp. 335–357.

Rogoff, Kenneth, "The Purchasing Power Parity Puzzle," *Journal of Economic Literature*, Vol. 34, No. 2, Jun 1996, pp. 647–668.

Roll, Richard W., and Bruno H. Solnik, "A Pure Foreign Exchange Asset Pricing Model," *Journal of International Economics*, May 1977, pp. 161–179.

Rugman, Alan, "Internalization Is Still a General Theory of Foreign Direct Investment," *Weltwirtschaftliches Archiv*, Sep 1985.

Rugman, Alan, "Internalization as a General Theory of Foreign Direct Investment: A Reappraisal of the Literature," *Weltwirtschaftliches Archiv*, Vol. 116, No. 2, June 1980, pp. 368–369.

Ruland, Robert G., and Timothy S. Doupnik, "Foreign Currency Translation and the Behavior of Exchange Rates," *Journal of International Business Studies*, Fall 1988, pp. 461–476.

Rummel, R. J., and David A. Heenan, "How Multinationals Analyze Political Risk," *Harvard Business Review*, Jan/Feb 1978, pp. 67–76.

Rutenberg, David P., "Maneuvering Liquid Assets in a Multinational Company: Formulation and Deterministic Solution Procedures," *Management Science*, Jun 1970, pp. B-671–684.

Saá-Requejo, Jesus, "Financing Decisions: Lessons from the Spanish Experience," *Financial Management*, Vol. 25, No. 3, Autumn 1996, pp. 44–56.

Sarathy, Ravi, and Sangit Chatterjee, "The Divergence of Japanese and U.S. Corporate Financial Structure," *Journal of International Business Studies*, Winter 1984, pp. 75–89.

Saudagaran, Shahrokh M. and Gary C. Biddle, "Foreign Listing Location: A Study of MNEs and Stock Exchanges in Eight Countries," *Journal of International Business Studies*, Vol. 26, No. 2, Second Quarter 1995, pp. 319–341.

Scott, Robert Haney, "Pegged Exchange Rate System of Macao and Hong Kong," *Multinational Finance Journal*, Vol. 1, No. 2, Jun 1997, pp. 153–168.

Sekely, William S., and J. Markham Collins, "Cultural Influences on International Capital Structure," *Journal of International Business Studies*, Spring 1988, pp. 87–100.

Selling, Thomas I., and George H. Sorter, "FASB Statement No. 52 and its Implications for Financial Statement Analysis," *Financial Analysts Journal*, May/Jun 1983, pp. 3–8.

Shao, Lawrence Peter, and Alan T. Shao, "Capital Budgeting Practices Employed by European Affiliates of U.S. Transnational Companies," *Journal of Multinational Financial Management*, Vol. 3. Nos. 1/2, 1993, pp. 95–109.

Shapiro, Alan C., "Optimal Inventory and Credit Granting Strategies Under Inflation and Devaluation," *Journal of Financial and Quantitative Analysis*, Jan 1973, pp. 37–46.

Shapiro, Alan C., "Evaluating Financing Costs for Multinational Subsidiaries," *Journal of International Business Studies*, Fall 1975, pp. 25–32.

Shapiro, Alan C., "Capital Budgeting for the Multinational Corporation," *Financial Management*, Spring 1978, pp. 7–16.

Shapiro, Alan C., "Financial Structure and Cost of Capital in the Multinational Corporation," *Journal of Financial and Quantitative Analysis*, Jun 1978, pp. 211–226.

Shastri, Kuldeep, and Kishore Tandon, "Valuation of Foreign Currency Options: Some Empirical Tests," *Journal of Financial and Quantitative Analysis*, Jun 1986, pp. 145–160.

Sherman, H. Arnold, "Managing Taxes in the Multinational Corporation," *The Tax Executive*, Winter 1987, pp. 171–181.

Singal, Vijay, "Floating Currencies, Capital Controls, or Currency Boards: What's the Best Remedy for the Currency Crises," *Journal of Applied Corporate Finance*, Vol. 11, Winter 1999, No. 4, pp. 49–56.

Smith, Clifford W., Jr., and Charles W. Smithson, "Financial Engineering: An Overview," in *The Handbook of Financial Engineering*, Clifford W. Smith, Jr., and Charles W. Smithson, eds., New York: Harper & Row, 1990, pp. 3–29.

Smith, Clifford W., Jr., Charles W. Smithson, and Lee MacDonald Wakeman, "The Market for Interest Rate Swaps," *Financial Management*, Winter 1988, pp. 34–44.

Smith, Clifford W., Jr., Charles W. Smithson, and D. Sykes Wilford, "Financial Engineering: Why Hedge?" in *The Handbook of Financial Engineering*, Clifford W. Smith, Jr., and Charles W. Smithson, eds., New York: Harper Business, 1990, pp. 126–138.

Smith, Clifford W., and Rene M. Stulz, "The Determinants of Firms' Hedging Policies," *Journal of Financial and Quantitative Analysis*, Vol. 20, No. 4, Dec 1985, pp. 390–405.

Smith, Roy C. and Ingo Walter, "Risks and Rewards in Emerging Market Investments," *Journal of Applied Corporate Finance*, Fall 1997, Vol. 10, No. 3, pp. 8–17.

Smithson, Charles W., "A LEGO Approach to Financial Engineering: An Introduction to Forwards, Futures, Swaps, and Options," *Midland Corporate Finance Journal*, Vol. 4, No. 4, 1987, pp. 16–28.

Soenen, L. A., "International Cash Management: A Study of Practices of U.K.-Based Companies," *Journal of Business Research*, Aug 1986, pp. 345–354.

Soenen, L. A., and Raj Aggarwal, "Corporate Foreign Exchange and Cash Management Practices," *Journal of Cash Management*, Mar/Apr 1987, pp. 62–64.

Soenen, Luc A., and Jeff Madura, "Foreign Exchange Management-A Strategic Approach," *Long Range Planning*, Vol. 24, No. 5, Oct 1991, pp. 119–124.

Solnik, Bruno, "Swap Pricing and Default Risk: A Note," *Journal of International Financial Management and Accounting*, Vol. 2, No. 1, Spring 1990, pp. 79–91.

Srinivasan, VenKat, Susan E. Moeller. and Yong H. Kim, "International Cash Management: State-of-the-Art and Research Directions," *Advances in Financial Planning and Forecasting*. Vol. 4. part B, 1990. pp. 161–194.

Stanley, Marjorie T., "Capital Structure and Cost of Capital for the Multinational Firm," *Journal of International Business Studies*, Spring/Summer 1981, pp. 103–120.

Stanley, Marjorie, and Stanley Block, "An Empirical Study of Management and Financial Variables Influencing Capital Budgeting Decisions for Multinational Corporations in the 1980s," *Management International Review*, No. 3, 1983.

Stapleton, Richard C., and Marti Subrahmanyam, "Market Imperfections, Capital Asset Equilibrium, and Corporation Finance," *Journal of Finance*, May 1977, pp. 307–319.

Stonehill, Arthur, and Kåre Dullum, "Corporate Wealth Maximization, Takeovers, and the Market for Corporate Control," *Nationaløkonomisk Tidsskrift* (Denmark), No. 1, 1990, p. 76–96.

Stonehill, Arthur, and Leonard Nathanson, "Capital Budgeting and the Multinational Corporation, *California Management Review*, Summer 1968, pp. 39–54.

Stonehill, Arthur, and Thomas Stitzel, "Financial Structure and Multinational Corporations," *California Management Review*, Fall 1969, pp. 91–96.

Stonehill, Arthur I., Niels Ravn, and Kåre Dullum, "Management of Foreign Exchange Economic Exposure," in *International Financial Management*, Göran Bergendahl, ed., Stockholm: Norstedts. 1982, pp. 128–148.

Stonehill, Arthur, Theo Beekhuisen, Richard Wright, Lee Remmers, Norman Toy, Antonio Parés, Alan Shapiro, Douglas Egan, and Thomas Bates, "Financial Goals and Debt Ratio Determinants: A Survey of Practice in Five Countries," *Financial Management,* Autumn 1975, pp. 27–41.

Stulz, Rene M, "On the Effects of Barriers to International Investment," *Journal of Finance,* Sep 1981, pp. 923–933.

Stulz, Rene M., "Optimal Hedging Policies," *Journal of Financial and Quantitative Analysis,* Vol. 19, No. 2, Jun 1984, pp. 127–140.

Stulz, Rene M, "The Cost of Capital in Internationally Integrated Markets: The Case of Nestlé," *European Financial Management,* Vol. 1, No. 1, Mar 1995, pp. 11–22.

Stulz, Rene M., "Globalization of Capital Markets and the Cost of Capital: The Case of Nestlé," *Journal of Applied Corporate Finance,* Vol. 8, No. 3, Fall 1995, pp. 30–38.

Stulz, Rene M., "Does the Cost of Capital Differ Across Countries? An Agency Perspective," *European Financial Management*, volume 2, 1996.

Stulz, Rene M., "Rethinking Risk Management," *Journal of Applied Corporate Finance*, Vol. 9, No. 3, Fall 1996, pp. 8–24.

Sundaram, Anant, "International Financial Markets," in the *Handbook of Modern Finance,* Dennis Logue, ed., Warren, Gorham, and Lamont, New York, 1994.

Sundaram, Anant K., and Dennis E. Logue, "Valuation Effects of Foreign Company Listings on U.S. Exchanges," *Journal of International Business Studies,* Vol. 27, No. 1, First Quarter 1996, pp. 67–88.

Swamidass, Paul M., "A Comparison of the Plant Location Strategies of Foreign and Domestic Manufacturers in the U.S," *Journal of International Business Studies,* Second Quarter 1990, pp. 301–317.

Swanson, Peggy E., and Stephen C. Caples, "Hedging Foreign Exchange Risk Using Forward Foreign Exchange Markets: An Extension," *Journal of International Business*

Studies, Spring 1987, pp. 75–82.

Sweeney, Richard J., "Beating the Foreign Exchange Market," *Journal of Finance,* March 1986, pp. 163–182.

Sweeney, Richard J., and Edward J. Q. Lee, "Trading Strategies in Forward Exchange Markets," *Advances in Financial Planning and Forecasting,* Vol. 4, 1990, pp. 55–80.

Tallman, Stephen B., "Home Country Political Risk and Foreign Direct Investment in the United States," *Journal of International Business Studies,* Summer 1988, pp. 219–234.

Taussig, Russell A., "Impact of SFAS No. 52 on the Translation of Foreign Financial Statements of Companies in Highly Inflationary Economies," *Journal of Accounting, Auditing and Finance,* Winter 1983, pp. 142-156.

Terpstra, Vern, and Chwo-Ming Yu, "Determinants of Foreign Investment of U.S. Advertising Agencies," *Journal of International Business Studies,* Spring 1988. pp. 33–46.

Thomadakis, Stavros, and Nilufer Usmen, "Foreign Project Financing in Segmented Capital Markets: Equity Versus Debt," *Financial Management,* Winter 1991, pp. 42–53.

Tompkins, Robert, "Behind the Mirror," in *From Black-Scholes to Black Holes: New Frontiers in Options,* London: Risk Management Ltd., 1992, pp. 129–133.

Toy, Norman, Arthur Stonehill, Lee Remmers, Richard Wright, and Theo Beekhuisen, "A Comparative International Study of Growth, Profitability and Risk as Determinants of Corporate Debt Ratios in the Manufacturing Sector," *Journal of Financial and Quantitative Analysis,* Nov 1974, pp. 875–886.

Trevino, Len J., and John D. Daniels, "The Preconditions for Manufacturing Foreign Direct Investment in the United States: An Empirical Assessment," *The International Trade Journal,* Vol. 10, No. 2, Summer 1996, pp. 223–246.

Tucker, Alan, "Foreign Exchange Option Prices as Predictors of Equilibrium Forward Exchange Rates," *Journal of International Money and Finance*, Vol. 6, No. 3, Sep 1987, pp. 283294.

Vernon, Raymond, "International Investment and International Trade in the Product Cycle," *Quarterly Journal of Economics*, May 1966, pp. 190–207.

Vernon, Raymond, "The Product Cycle Hypothesis in a New International Environment," *Oxford Bulletin of Economics and Statistics*, Vol. 41, 1979, pp. 255–267.

Wald, John K., "How Firm Characteristics Affect Capital Structure: An International Comparison," *The Journal of Financial Research*, Vol. *xxii*, No. 2, Summer 1999, pp. 161–187.

Weinstein, David, E., and Yishay Yafeh, "On the Costs of a Bank-Centered Financial System: Evidence from the Changing Main Bank Relations in Japan," *Journal of Finance*, Vol. 53, No. 2, April 1998, pp. 635–672.

Weisman, Lorenzo, "The Advent of Private Equity in Latin America," *The Columbia Journal of World Business*, Spring 1996, pp. 60–98.

Wells, Louis T., Jr., "Multinationals and the Developing Countries," *Journal of International Business Studies*, Volume 29, No. 1, First Quarter, 1998, pp. 101–114.

Weisfelder, Christine J., "Home Country Taxation and the Theory of International Production," *Journal of International Financial Management and Accounting*, Vol. 5, No. 3, Oct. 1994, pp. 193–213.

Wheatley, S., "Some Tests of International Equity Integration," *Journal of Financial Economics,* Sep 1989, pp. 177–212.

Wright, Richard, and Sadahiko Suzuki, "Financial Structure and Bankruptcy Risk in Japanese Companies," *Journal of International Business Studies,* Spring 1985, pp. 97–110.

Wyatt, Steve B., "On the Valuation of Puts and Calls on Spot, Forward, and Future Foreign Exchange: Theory and Evidence," *Advances in Financial Planning and Forecasting*, Vol. 4, 1990, pp. 81–104.

Yang, Ho C., James W. Wansley, and William R. Lane, "A Direct Test of the Diversification Service Hypothesis of Foreign Direct Investment," *Advances in Financial Planning and Forecasting*, Vol. 4, Part A, 1990, pp. 215–238.

Zaheer, Srilata, "Circadian Rhythms: The Effects of Global Market Integration on the Currency Trading Industry," *Journal of International Business Studies*, Vol. 26, No. 4, Fourth Quarter 1995, pp. 699–728.

Zhang, Peter G., "Professional Forum: An Introduction to Exotic Options," *European Financial Management*, Vol. 1, No. 1, Mar 1995, pp. 87–95.

Books

Agmon, Tamir, Robert G. Hawkins, and Richard M. Levich, eds., *The Future of the International Monetary System*, Lexington, MA: Lexington Books, 1984.

Aharoni, Yair, *The Foreign Investment Decision Process*, Boston: Harvard Graduate School of Business Administration. Division of Research, 1966.

Ahm, Mark J., and William D. Falloon, *Strategic Risk Management: How the Global Corporations Manage Financial Risk for Competitive Advantage*, Chicago: Probus, 1991.

Aliber, Robert Z., *The International Money Game*, 5th ed., New York: Basic Books. 1987.

Aliber, Robert Z., *Handbook of International Financial Management*, Homewood, IL: Dow Jones-Irwin, 1989.

Amihud Y. and R. Levich, eds, *Exchange Rates and Corporate Performance*, Burr Ridge, Ill: Irwin, 1994.

Andersen, Torben Juul, *Currency and Interest Rate Hedging*, 2nd ed., New York: New York Institute of Finance, 1993.

Anderson, Torben Juul, *Euromarket Instruments: A Guide to the World's Large Debt Market*, New York: New York Institute of Finance, 1990.

Balling, Morten, *Financial Management in the New Europe*, Oxford, UK: Blackwell, 1993.

Beidleman, Carl R., *Financial Swaps*, Homewood, IL: Dow Jones-Irwin, 1985.

BenDaniel, David J., and Arthur H. Rosenbloom, *The Handbook of International Mergers & Acquisitions*, Englewood Cliffs, NJ: Prentice-Hall, 1990.

Bergsten, Fred C., and Shafique Islam, *The United States as a Debtor Country*, Washington, D.C.: Institute of International Economics, 1990.

Bernstein, Peter L., *Against the Gods: The Remarkable Story of Risk*, New York: John Wiley Sons, Inc., 1996.

Bishop, Paul, and Don Dixon, *Foreign Exchange Handbook: Managing Risk and Opportunity in Global Currency Markets*, New York: McGraw-Hill, 1992.

Brewer, Thomas L., *Political Risks in International Business*, New York: Praeger, 1985.

Brown, Brendan, *The Flight of International Capital: A Contemporary History*, New York and London: Croom Helm, 1987.

Buckley, Adrian, *International Investment Value Creation and Appraisal: A Real Options Approach*, Copenhagen: Copenhagen Business School Press, 1998.

Buckley, Adrian, *Multinational Finance*, 2nd edition, Hemel Hempstead, Hertfordshire: UK: Prentice-Hall International (UK), Ltd., 1992.

Buckley, Peter J., and Jeremy Clegg, *Multinational Enterprises in Less Developed Countries*, New York: St. Martin's Press, 1991.

Buckley, Peter J., and Mark Casson, *The Future of the Multinational Enterprise*, London: Macmillan. 1976.

Buckley, Peter J., and Mark Casson, eds., *Multinational Enterprises in the World Economy: Essays in the Honour of John Dunning*, Aldershot, Hants, England: Edward Elgar, 1992.

Business International, *Automating Global Financial Management*, Morristown, NJ: Financial Executives Research Foundation, 1988.

Butler, Kirt C., *Multinational Finance*, second edition, Cincinnati, OH: Southwestern, 1999.

Carvounis, Chris C., *The United States Trade Deficit of the 1980s*, Westport, CT: Quorum Books, 1987.

Casson, Mark, *The Firm and the Market: Studies on Multinational Enterprises and the Scope of the Firm*, Cambridge, MA: MIT Press, 1987.

Caves, Richard E., *Multinational Enterprises and Economic Analysis*, 2nd ed., Cambridge U.K.: Cambridge University Press, 1996.

Celi, Louis J., and I. James Czechowicz, Export Financing, *A Handbook of Sources and Techniques*, Morristown, NJ: Financial Executives Research Foundation, 1985.

Chance, Don M., *An Introduction to Derivatives*, 3rd Edition, Harcourt Brace Publishers, Ft. Worth, 1995.

Chew, Donald H., editor, *Studies in International Corporate Finance and Governance Systems: A Comparison of the U.S., Japan, and Europe*, Oxford, U.K.: Oxford University Press, 1997.

Choi, Jongmoo Jay, and Shmuel Hauser, "Forward Foreign Exchange in Continuous-Time Derivative Asset Framework," *Research in Finance*, JAI Press, 1994.

Chorafas, Dimitris N., *Treasury Operations and The Foreign Exchange Challenge*, New York: Wiley, 1992.

Claassen, Emil-Maria, *International and European Monetary Systems*, New York: Praeger, 1990.

Coffey, Peter, *The European Monetary, System Past, Present and Future*, 2nd ed., Dordrecht, Netherlands; Lancaster, U.K.: Kluwer Academic Publishers, 1987.

Coninx, Raymond G. F., *Foreign Exchange Dealer's Handbook*, 2nd ed., Homewood, IL: Dow Jones-Irwin, 1986.

Cooper, Richard N., *The International Monetary System: Essays in World Economics*, Cambridge, MA: MIT Press, 1987.

Copeland, Laurence S., *Exchange Rates and International Finance*, 2nd ed., Workingham, England: Addison-Wesley, 1994.

Copeland, Tom, Tim Koller, and Jack Murrin, *Valuation: Measuring and Managing the Value of Companies*, 2nd ed., New York: Wiley, 1994.

de Vries, Margaret Garritsen, *Balance of Payments Adjustment, 1945-1986: The IMF Experience*, Washington, D.C.: IMF, 1987.

Derivatives Week, *Learning Curves, Volume II: The Guide to Understanding Derivatives, Editors of Derivatives Week*, Institutional Investor, Inc., New York, 1995.

Derivatives Week, *Learning Curves: The Guide to Understanding Derivatives, Editors of Derivatives Week*, Institutional Investor, Inc., New York, 1994.

DeRosa, David F., *Managing Foreign Exchange Risk*, Chicago: Probus, 1991.

Dixit, Avinash K., *Investment Under Uncertainty*, Princeton University Press. Princeton, NJ, 1994.

Donaldson, Gordon, and Jay W. Lorsch, *Decision Making At the Top: The Shaping of Strategic Direction*, New York: Basic Books, 1983.

Donaldson, Gordon, *Managing Corporate Wealth: The Operation of a Comprehensive Goals System*, New York: Praeger, 1984.

Donaldson, Gordon, *Strategy for Financial Mobility*, Boston: Graduate School of Business Administration, Harvard University, 1969.

Dufey, Gunter, and Ian Giddy, *50 Cases in International Finance*, 2nd ed., Reading, MA: Addison-Wesley, 1992.

Dufey, Gunter, and Ian H. Giddy, *The International Money Market*, 2nd ed., Prentice Hall, Englewood Cliffs, NJ, 1994.

Dunning, John H., ed., Multinational Enterprises, *Economic Structure, and International Competitiveness*, New York: Wiley, 1985.

Dunning, John H., *Explaining International Production*, Winchester. MA: Unwin Hyman, 1988.

Eaker, Mark R., Frank J. Fabozzi, and Dwight Grant, *International Corporate Finance*, Ft. Worth: The Dryden Press, 1996.

Eichengreen, Barry, and Peter H. Lindert, *The International Debt Crisis in Historical Perspective*, Cambridge, MA: MIT Press, 1990.

Elfstrom, Gerard, *Moral Issues and Multinational Corporations*, New York: St. Martin's Press, 1991.

Eun, Cheol S. and Bruce G. Resnick, *International Financial Management*, Boston: Irwin McGraw-Hill, 1998.

Financial Accounting Standards Board, *Foreign Currency Translation, Statement of Financial Accounting Standards No. 52*, Dec 1981, Stamford, CT: Financial Accounting Standards Board, 1981.

Forsgren, Mats, *Managing the Internationalization Process: The Swedish Case*, London: Routledge. 1989.

Forsgren, Mats and Jan Johanson, editors, *Managing Networks in International Business*, Philadelphia: Gordon and Breach, 1992.

Francis, Dick, *The Countertrade Handbook*, Westport, CT: Quorum Books, 1987.

Friedman, Irving, *Reshaping the Global Money System*, Lexington, MA: Lexington Books, 1987.

Ghadar, Fariborz, *New Financial Instruments: Horizons for Risk Management*, Center for Global Business Studies, Pennsylvania State University, 1996.

Giddy, Ian H., *Global Financial Markets*, Lexington, MA: D.C. Heath, 1994.

Gordon, Sara L., and Francis A. Lees, *Foreign Multinational Investment in the United States: Struggle for Industrial Supremacy*, Westport, CT: Quorum Books, 1986.

Grabbe, J. Orlin, *International Financial Markets*, 2nd ed., New York: Elsevier, 1991.

Graham, Edward, and Paul Krugman, *Foreign Direct Investment in the United States*, Washington, D.C.: Institute for International Economics, 1989.

Haendel, Dan, *Foreign Investment and the Management of Political Risk*, Boulder, CO: Westview Press, 1979.

Hawawini, Gabriel, and Eric Rajendra, *The Transformation of the European Financial Services Industry: From Fragmentation to Integration*, New York: New York University Salomon Center; Monograph Series in Finance and Economics, No. 4, 1989.

Hirsch, Se'ev, *Location of Industry and International Competitiveness*, Oxford: Oxford University Press, 1967.

Holland, John, *International Financial Management*, 2nd ed., New York and Oxford, U.K.: Basil Blackwell. 1992.

Howcroft, Barry, and Christopher Storey, *Management and Control of Currency and Interest Rate Risk*, Chicago: Probus. 1989.

Howe, Donna M., *A Guide to Managing Interest Rate Risk*, New York: New York Institute of Finance, 1991.

Hufbauer, Gary Clyde, Diane T. Berliner, and Kimberly Ann Elliott, *Trade Protection in the United States: 31 Case Studies*, Washington, D.C.: Institute for International Economics, 1986.

Hymer, Stephen H., *The International Operations of National Firms: A Study of Direct Foreign Investment*, Cambridge, MA: MIT Press, 1976.

Ibbotson, Roger G., and Gary P. Brinson, *Global Investing: The Professional Guide to the World's Capital Markets*, McGraw-Hill, Inc., New York, 1993.

Jacque, Laurent, *Management and Control of Foreign Exchange Risk*, Boston: Kluwer, 1996.

Kester, Carl W., *Japanese Takeovers: The Global Contest for Corporate Control*, Boston: Harvard Business School Press, 1991.

Klein, Robert A. and Jess Lederman, *Derivatives Risk and Responsibility*, Chicago: Irwin Professional Publishing, 1996.

Knickerbocker, Fred T., *Oligopolistic Reaction and the Multinational Enterprise*, Boston: Harvard Graduate School of Business Administration, 1973.

Kobrin, Stephen J., *Managing Political Risk Assessment: Strategic Response to Environmental Change*, Berkeley: University of California Press, 1982.

Korth, Christopher M., ed., *International Counter-trade*, Westport. CT: Quorum Books, 1987.

Krugman, Paul R., and Maurice Obstfeld, *International Economics: Theory and Policy*, Third Edition, New York: Harper Collins, 1994.

Lessard, Donald R., *International Financial Management, Theory, and Application*, 2nd ed., New York: Wiley, 1987.

Levi, Maurice, *International Finance: Financial Management and the International Economy*, 3rd ed., New York: McGraw-Hill, 1996.

Levich, Richard, *International Financial Markets: Prices and Policies*, Boston: Irwin McGraw-Hill, 1998.

Madura, Jeff, *International Financial Management*, 5th ed., St. Paul, MN: West, 1998.

Madura, Jeff, *Global Portfolio Management for Institutional Investors*, Quorum Books, Westbury, CT, 1996.

Marshall, John F., and Vipul K. Bansal, *Financial Engineering: A Complete Guide to Financial Innovation*, New York: New York Institute of Finance, 1992.

Millar, William, and Brad Asher, *Strategic Risk Management*, New York: Business International, Jan 1990.

Mueller, Gerhard G., Helen Gernon, and Gary Meek, *Accounting: An International Perspective*, Homewood, Ill.: Richard D. Irwin, 1987.

Murphy, John J., *Intermarket Technical Analysis: Trading Strategies for the Global Stock, Bond, Commodity, and Currency Markets*, New York: Wiley, 1991.

Murray, Alan I., and Caren Siehl, *Joint Ventures and Other Alliances: Creating a Successful Cooperative Linkage*, New York: Financial Executive Research Foundation, 1989.

O'Brien, Thomas J., *Global Financial Management*, John Wiley & Sons, Inc.: New York, 1996.

Oxelheim, Lars, *International Financial Integration*, Berlin: Springer-Verlag, 1990.

Oxelheim, Lars, *The Global Race for Foreign Direct Investment: Prospects for the Future*, Berlin: Springer-Verlag, 1993.

Oxelheim, Lars, *Financial Markets in Transition-Globalization, Investment and Economic Growth*, London and New York: Routledge, 1996.

Oxelheim, Lars, and Clas Wihlborg, *Managing in the Turbulent World Economy-Corporate Performance and Risk Exposure*, Chichester and New York: John Wiley, 1997.

Oxelheim, Lars, and Clas Wihlborg, *Macroeconomic Uncertainty: International Risks and Opportuni-ties for the Corporation*, Chichester, U.K.: Wiley, 1987.

Oxelheim, Lars, Arthur Stonehill, Trond Randøy, Kaisa Vikkula, Kåre Dullum, and Karl-Markus Modén, *Corporate Strategies for Internationaliz-ing the Cost of Capital*, Copenhagen: Copenhagen Business School Press, 1998.

Phylaktis, Kaate, and Mahmeed Pradhan, eds., *International Finance and the Less Developed Countries*, Basingstoke, U.K.: Macmillan, in association with the Department of Banking and Finance, City University Business School, 1990.

Porter, Michael, *The Competitive Advantage of Nations*, London: Macmillan Press, 1990.

Price Waterhouse Coopers, *Corporate Taxes: A Worldwide Summary*, New York: Price Waterhouse Coopers, 1999.

Rappaport, Alfred, *Creating Shareholder Value*, New York: The Free Press: Macmillan, 1986.

Riahi-Belkaoui, Ahmed, *Multinationality and Firm Performance*, London: Quorum Books, 1996.

Rogers, Jerry, ed., *Global Risk Assessments: Issues, Concepts and Applications*, Riverside, CA: Global Risk Assessments, Inc., 1988.

Rugman, A.M. and L. Eden, Editors, *Multinationals and Transfer Pricing*, New York: St. Martins Press, 1985.

Scholes, Myron S. and Mark A. Wolfson, *Taxes and Business Strategy: A Planning Approach*, Englewood Cliffs, N.J.: Prentice-Hall, 1992, Chapters 13 and 14.

Schwartz, Robert J. and Clifford W. Smith, Jr., editors, *Currency and Interest Rate Risk Management*, New York Institute of Finance, 1990.

Shapiro, Alan C., *Multinational Financial Man-age-ment*, 6th ed., Boston: Prentice-Hall, 1999.

Simon, Herbert, *Administrative Behavior*, New York: Macmillan, 1947.

Smith, Clifford W., Jr., Charles W. Smithson, and D. Sykes Wilford, *Managing Financial Risk, Institutional Investor Series in Finance*, New York: Harper & Row, 1990.

Smith, Roy C., and Ingo Walter, *Global Financial Services*, New York: Harper-Business, 1990.

Solnik, Bruno, *International Investments*, 4th ed., Reading, MA: Addison-Wesley Longman, 1999.

Stewart, G. Bennet, III, *The Quest of Value*, Harper Business, 1991.

Stoll, Hans R., and Robert E. Whaley, *Futures and Options: Theory and Applications, Current Issues in Finance*, Cincinnati: Southwestern, 1993.

Stonehill, Arthur, and Kåre B. Dullum, *Internationalizing the Cost of Capital in Theory and Practice: The Novo Experience and National Policy Implications*, Copenhagen: Nyt Nordisk Forlag Arnold Busck, 1982; and London: Wiley, 1982.

Sutton, William H., *Trading in Currency Options*, New York Institute of Finance, New York: Simon & Schuster, 1988.

Tavis, Lee A., ed., *Rekindling Development: Multinational Firms and World Debt*, Notre Dame, IN: Notre Dame Press, 1988.

Tucker, Alan L., Jeff Madura, and Thomas C. Chiang, *International Financial Markets*, St. Paul, MN, 1991.

Vanden Bulcke, D., and J. J. Boddewyn, *Investment and Divestment Policies in Multinational Corporations in Europe*, London: Saxon/Teakfield: New York: Praeger, 1979.

Venedikian, Harry M., and Gerald A. Warfield, *Export-Import Financing*, 2nd ed., New York: Wiley, 1986.

Walmsley, Julian, *The Foreign Exchange and Money Markets Guide*, New York: Wiley, 1992.

Williamson, John, *Equilibrium Exchange Rates: An Update*, Washington, D.C.: Institute for International Economics, 1990.

Williamson, John, *Voluntary Approaches to Debt Relief*, Washington, D.C.: Institute for International Economics, 1988.

Williamson, John, and Donald Lessard, eds., *Capital Flight and Third World Debt*, Washington, D.C.: Institute for International Economics, 1987.

Williamson, Oliver, *Markets and Hierarchies*, New York: Free Press, 1975.

Williamson, Oliver, *The Economic Institutions of Capitalism*, New York: Free Press, 1985.

Wunnicke, Diane B., David R. Wilson, and Brooke Wunnicke, *Corporate Financial Risk Management*, New York: Wiley, 1992.

GLOSSARY

A.B. *Aktiebolag.* Swedish word for incorporated or stock company.

A.G. *Aktiengesellschaft.* German word for incorporated or stock company.

Accounting exposure. The potential for an accounting-derived change in owners' equity resulting from exchange rate changes and the need to restate financial statements of foreign affiliates in the single currency of the parent corporation so as to create a consolidated financial statement. Also called "translation exposure."

Adjusted present value. A type of present value analysis in capital budgeting in which operating cash flows are discounted separately from (1) the various tax shields provided by the deductibility of interest and other financial charges, and (2) the benefits of project-specific concessional financing. Each component cash flow is discounted at a rate appropriate for the risk involved.

ADR. *See* American Depositary Receipt.

Ad valorem duty. A customs duty levied as a percentage of the assessed value of goods entering a country.

Affiliate. A foreign operation, formed as either a branch or a foreign-incorporated subsidiary.

Agency for International Development (AID). A unit of the U.S. government dealing with foreign aid.

AID. *See* Agency for International Development.

All-equity discount rate. A discount rate in capital budgeting that would be appropriate for discounting operating cash flows if the project were financed entirely with owners' equity.

American Depositary Receipt (ADR). A certificate of ownership, issued by a U.S. bank, representing a claim on underlying foreign securities. ADRs may be traded in lieu of trading in the actual underlying shares.

American option. An option that can be exercised at any time up to and including the expiration date.

American selling price (ASP). For customs purposes, the use of the domestic price of competing merchandise in the United States as a tax base for determining import duties. The ASP is generally higher than the actual foreign price, so its use is a protectionist technique.

American terms. Foreign exchange quotations for the U.S. dollar, expressed as the number of U.S. dollars per unit of non-U.S. currency.

A/P. In international trade documentation, abbreviation for "authority to purchase" or "authority to pay." In accounting, abbreviation for "accounts payable."

Appreciation. In the context of exchange rate changes, a rise in the foreign exchange value of a currency that is pegged to other currencies or to gold. Also called "revaluation."

Arbitrage. A trading strategy based on the purchase of a commodity, including foreign exchange, in one market at one price while simultaneously selling it in another market at a more advantageous price, in order to obtain a risk-free profit on the price differential.

Arbitrageur. An individual or company which practices arbitrage.

Arm's-length price. The price at which a willing buyer and a willing unrelated seller freely agree to carry out a transaction. In effect, a free market price. Applied by tax authorities in judging the appropriateness of transfer prices between related affiliates.

Ask price. The price at which a dealer is willing to sell foreign exchange, securities or commodities. Also called "offer price."

ASP. *See* American selling price.

"Aussie." Foreign exchange dealers' nickname for the Australian dollar.

Back-to-back loan. A loan in which two companies in separate countries borrow each other's currency for a specific period of time, and repay the other's currency at an agreed maturity. Sometimes the two loans are chan-nelled through an intermediate bank. Back-to-back financing is also called "link financing."

Balance of payments. A financial statement summa-rizing the flow of goods, ser-vices, and invest-ment funds between residents of a given country and residents of the rest of the world.

Balance of trade. An entry in the balance of payments measuring the difference be-tween the monetary value of merchandise exports and mer-chandise imports.

Balance on current account. *See* Current account.

Bank for International Settlements. (BIS) A bank in Basle, Switzerland, that functions as a bank for European central banks.

Bank rate. The interest rate at which central banks for var-ious countries lend to their own monetary institutions.

Bankers' acceptance. An unconditional promise of a bank to make payment on a draft when it matures. The ac-ceptance is in the form of the bank's endorsement ("accep-tance") of a draft drawn against that bank in accord-ance with the terms of a letter of credit issued by the bank.

Barter. International trade conducted by the direct ex-change of physical goods, rather than by separate pur-chases and sales at prices and exchange rates set by a free market.

Basic Balance. In a coun-try's balance of payments, the net of exports and imports of goods and services, unilateral transfers, and long-term capi-tal flows.

Basis point. One one-hun-dredth of one percentage point, often used in quota-tions of spreads between inter-est rates or to describe changes in yields in securities. 0.01% is one basis point.

Basis risk. That type of in-terest rate risk in which the in-terest rate base is mismatched.

B/E. *See* Bill of exchange.

Bearer bond. Corporate or governmental debt in bond form that is not registered to any owner. Possession of the bond implies ownership, and interest is obtained by clipping a coupon attached to the bond. The advantage of the bearer form is easy transfer at the time of a sale, easy use as collateral for a debt, and what some cynics call "taxpayer anonymity," meaning that governments find it hard to trace interest payments in or-der to collect income taxes. Bearer bonds are common in Europe, but are seldom issued any more in the United States. The alternate form to a bearer bond is a registered bond.

Beta. Second letter of Greek alphabet, used as a statistical measure of risk in the Capital Asset Pricing Model. Beta is the covariance between re-turns on a given asset and re-turns on the market portfolio, divided by the variance of re-turns on the market portfolio.

Bid. The price which a dealer is willing to pay for (i.e., buy) foreign exchange or a security.

BID. *Banco Interamericano de Desarrollo.* Spanish name for the Inter-American Development Bank.

Bid-ask spread. The differ-ence between a bid (buy) and an ask (offer) quotation.

Big Bang. The October 1986 liberalization of the London capital markets.

Bill of exchange (B/E). A written order requesting one party (such as an importer) to pay a specified amount of money at a specified time to the order of the writer of the bill of exchange. Also called a "draft." *See* Sight draft.

Bill of lading (B/L). A con-tract between a common car-rier and a shipper to transport goods to a named destination. The bill of lading is also a re-ceipt for the goods. Bills of lading are usually negotiable, meaning they are made to the order of a particular party and can be endorsed to transfer ti-tle to another party.

BIS. *See* Bank for International Settlements.

B/L. *See* Bill of lading.

Black market. An illegal foreign exchange market.

Blocked funds. Funds in one country's currency that may not be exchanged freely for foreign currencies because of exchange controls.

Border tax adjustments. The fiscal practice, under the General Agreement on Tariffs and Trade, by which imported goods are subject to some or all of the tax charged in the importing country and reexported goods are exempt from some or all of the tax charged in the exporting country.

Branch. A foreign operation not incorporated in the host country, in contradistinction to a "subsidiary."

Bretton Woods Conference. An international conference in 1944 that established the international monetary system in effect from 1945 to 1971. The conference was held in Bretton Woods, New Hampshire, USA.

Bridge financing. Short-term financing from a bank, used while a borrower obtains medium- or long-term fixed-rate financing from capital markets.

Broker. An individual or firm that buys or sells foreign exchange, or securities, on a commission basis, without itself taking title to what was purchased, on behalf of a customer. A broker is an alternative to a "dealer." *See* Dealer.

Bulldogs. British pound-denominated bonds issued within the United Kingdom by a foreign borrower.

Cable. The U.S. dollar per British pound crossrate.

Call option. The right, but not the obligation, to buy foreign exchange or some other financial contract at a specified price within a specified time. *See* Option.

Capital account. A section of the balance of payments accounts. Under the revised format of the International Monetary Fund, the capital account measures capital transfers and the acquisition and disposal of non-produced non-financial assets. Under traditional definitions, still used by many countries, the capital account measures public and private international lending and investment. Most of the traditional definition of the capital account is now incorporated in IMF statements as the "financial account."

Capital Asset Pricing Model (CAPM). A theoretical model that relates the return on an asset to its risk, where risk is the contribution of the asset to the volatility of a portfolio. Risk and return are presumed determined in competitive and efficient financial markets.

Capital budgeting. The analytical approach used to determine whether investment in long-lived assets or projects is viable.

Capital flight. Movement of funds out of a country because of political risk.

Capital markets. The financial markets in various countries in which various types of long-term debt and/or ownership securities, or claims on those securities, are purchased and sold.

Capital mobility. The degree to which private capital moves freely from country to country seeking the most promising investment opportunities.

Cash budgeting. The planning for future receipts and disbursements of cash.

Cash flow return on investment (CFROI). A measure of corporate performance in which the numerator is profit from continuing operations less cash taxes and depreciation. This is divided by "cash investment" which is taken to mean the replacement cost of capital employed.

CAPM. *See* Capital Asset Pricing Model.

Certificate of Deposit (CD). A negotiable receipt issued by a bank for funds deposited for a certain period of time. CDs can be purchased or sold prior to their maturity in a secondary market, making them an interest-earning marketable security.

CFC. *See* Controlled foreign corporation.

CFROI. *See* Cash flow return on investment.

C&F. *See* Cost and freight.

CHIPS. *See* Clearinghouse Interbank Payments System.

Cia. *Companía.* Spanish word for company.

CIF. *See* Cost, insurance, and freight.**Closing rate method.** Another name for the current rate method of creating consolidated financial statements. *See* Current rate method.

CKD. "Completely knocked down." International trade term for components shipped into a country for assembly there. Often used in the automobile industry.

Clearing house. An institution through which financial obligations are cleared by the process of netting obligations of various members.

Clearinghouse Interbank Payments System (CHIPS). A New York-based computerized clearing system used by banks to settle interbank foreign exchange obligations (mostly U.S. dollars) between members.

Collar option. The simultaneous purchase of a put option and sale of a call option, or vice versa. Thus a form of hybrid option.

Commercial risk. In banking, the likelihood that a foreign debtor will be unable to repay its debts because of business (as distinct from political) events.

Common market. An association through treaty of two or more countries that agree to remove all trade barriers between themselves. The best known is the European Common Market, now called the European Union.

Comparative advantage. A theory that everyone gains if each nation specializes in the production of those goods that it produces relatively most efficiently and imports those goods that other countries produce relatively most efficiently. The theory supports free trade arguments.

Concession agreement. An understanding or contract between a foreign corporation and a host government defining the rules under which the corporation may operate in that country.

Consolidated financial statement. A corporate financial statement in which accounts of subsidiaries and the parent are added together to produce a statement which reports the status of the worldwide enterprise as if it were a single corporation. Inter-affiliate obligations are eliminated in consolidated statements.

Consolidation. In the context of accounting for multinational corporations, the process of preparing a single "reporting currency" financial statement that combines financial statements of affiliates that are in fact measured in different currencies.

Consortium bank. A banking joint venture, owned by two or more individual banks often of different nationalities. Consortium banks are formed in order to offer loans that are larger than the capacity of any one single bank, as well as to engage in other aspects of international banking.

Contagion. A form of financial panic, in which the devaluation of exchange rates by one country leads to similar devaluations at about the same time by other, often nearby, countries.

Controlled foreign corporation (CFC). A foreign corporation in which U.S. shareholders own more than 50% of the combined voting power or total value. Under U.S. tax law, U.S. shareholders may be liable for taxes on undistributed earnings of the controlled foreign corporation.

Convertible bond. A bond or other fixed-income security which may be exchanged for a number of shares of common stock.

Convertible currency. A currency that can be exchanged freely for any other currency without government restrictions.

Corporate wealth maximization. The corporate goal of maximizing the total wealth of the corporation itself rather than just the shareholders' wealth. Wealth is defined to include not just financial wealth but also the technical, marketing and human resources of the corporation.

Correspondent bank. A bank that holds deposits for and provides services to another bank, located in another geographic area, on a reciprocal basis.

Cost and freight (C&F). Price, quoted by an exporter, that includes the cost of transportation to the named port of destination.

Cost, insurance, and freight (CIF). Exporter's quoted price including the cost of packaging, freight or carriage, insurance premium, and other charges paid in respect of the goods from the time of loading in the country of export to their arrival at the named port of destination or place of transshipment.

Cost of capital. *See* Weighted average cost of capital.

Counterparty. The opposite party to a double transaction; that is, to a transaction involving an exchange of financial instruments or obligations now and a reversal of that same transaction at some agreed-upon later date.

Countertrade. A type of international trade in which parties exchange goods directly rather than for money. Hence a type of barter.

Countervailing duty. An import duty charged to offset an export subsidy by another country.

Country risk. In banking, the likelihood that unexpected events within a host country will influence a client's or a government's ability to repay a loan. Country risk is often divided into sovereign (political) risk and foreign exchange (currency) risk.

Covered interest arbitrage. The process whereby an investor earns a risk-free profit by (1) borrowing funds in one currency, (2) exchanging those funds in the spot market for a foreign currency, (3) investing the foreign currency at interest rates in a foreign country, (4) selling forward, at the time of original investment, the investment proceeds to be received at maturity, (5) using the proceeds of the forward sale to repay the original loan, and (6) having a remaining profit balance.

Covering. A transaction in the forward foreign exchange market or money market which protects the value of future cash flows. Covering is another term for hedging. *See* Hedge.

Crawling peg. A foreign exchange rate system in which the exchange rate is adjusted very frequently to reflect prevailing rate of inflation.

Crosslisting. The listing of shares of common stock on two or more stock exchanges.

Cross rate. An exchange rate between two currencies derived by dividing each cur-

rency's exchange rate with a third currency. For example, if ¥/$ is 140 and DM/$ is 1.5000, the cross rate between ¥ and DM is ¥140/$ 4 DM1.5000 = ¥93.3333/DM.

CTA account. *See* Cumulative translation adjustment account.

Cumulative translation adjustment (CTA) account. An entry in a translated balance sheet in which gains and/or losses from translation have been accumulated over a period of years.

Currency basket. The value of a portfolio of specific amounts of individual currencies, used as the basis for setting the market value of another currency. Also called currency cocktail.

Currency cocktail. *See* Currency basket.

Currency swap. A transaction in which two counterparties exchange specific amounts of two different currencies at the outset and then repay over time according to an agreed upon contract which reflects interest payments and possibly amortization of principal. In a currency swap, the cash flows are similar to those in a spot and forward foreign exchange transaction. *Also see* Swaps.

Current account. In the balance of payments, the net flow of goods, services, and unilateral transfers (such as gifts) between a country and all foreign countries.

Current rate method. A method of translating the financial statements of foreign affiliates into the parent's reporting currency. All assets and liabilities are translated at the current exchange rate.

Current/noncurrent method. A method of translating the financial statements of foreign affiliates into the parent's reporting currency. All current assets and current liabilities are translated at the current rate, and all noncurrent accounts at their historical rates.

D/A. "Documents against acceptance." International trade term.

Dealer. An individual or firm that buys or sells foreign exchange, or securities, for its own account, usually buying at one price and reselling at a higher price to a customer in order to make a profit on the spread between the buying and selling price. A dealer is an alternative to a "broker." *See* Broker. A dealer does not charge a commission for its efforts.

Deemed-tax paid. That portion of taxes paid to a foreign government that is allowed as a credit (reduction) in taxes due to a home government.

Delta. The change in an Option's price divided by the change in the price of the underlying instrument. Hedging strategies are based on delta ratios.

Demand deposit. A bank deposit that can be withdrawn or transferred at any time without notice, in contradistinction to a time deposit where (theoretically) the bank may require a waiting period before the deposit can be withdrawn. Demand deposits may or may not earn interest. A "time deposit" is the opposite of a demand deposit.

Depreciate. In the context of foreign exchange rates, a drop in the spot foreign exchange value of a floating currency; i.e., a currency the value of which is determined by open market transactions. *See* Devaluation. In the context of accounting, a periodic charge (expense) that represents the allocation of the cost of a fixed asset to various time periods.

Devaluation. A drop in the spot foreign exchange value of a currency that is pegged to other currencies or to gold. *See* Depreciate.

Direct quote. The price of a unit of foreign exchange expressed in the home country's currency. The term has meaning only when the "home country" is specified.

"Dirty" float. A system of floating (i.e., market-determined) exchange rates in which the government intervenes from time to time to influence the foreign exchange value of its currency.

Discount (in foreign exchange market). The amount by which a currency is cheaper for future delivery than for spot (immediate) delivery. The opposite of "discount" is "premium."

DISC. *See* Domestic International Sales Corporation.

Domestic International Sales Corporation (DISC). Under the U.S. tax code, a type of subsidiary formed to export U.S.-produced goods. A portion of the earnings and profits of DISCs is not taxed to the DISC but is instead taxed directly to its shareholders.

D/P. "Documents against payment." International trade term.

Draft. An unconditional written order requesting one party (such as an importer) to pay a specified amount of money at a specified time to the order of the writer of the draft. Also called a "bill of exchange." Personal checks are one type of draft.

Dragon bond. A U.S. dollar de-nominated bond sold in the so-called "Dragon" economies of Asia, such as Hong Kong, Taiwan, and Singapore.

D/S. "Days after sight." International trade term.

Dumping. The practice of offering goods for sale in a foreign market at a price that is lower than that of the same product in the home market or a third country. As used in GATT, a special case of "differential pricing."

EBITDA. Earnings before interest, taxes, depreciation, and amortization.

Economic exposure. Another name for operating exposure. *See* Operating exposure.

Economic Value Added (EVA). The corporate goal of increasing the value of the capital that investors and shareholders have vested in the operations of the business. "EVA" is a registered trademark of Stern Stewart & Company.

ECU. *See* European Currency Unit.

Edge Act and Agreement Corporation. Subsidiary of a U.S. bank incorporated under federal law to engage in various international banking and financing operations, including equity participations which are not allowed to regular domestic banks. The Edge Act subsidiary may be located in a state other than that of the parent bank.

EEC. *See* European Economic Community.

Effective exchange rate. An index measuring the change in value of a foreign currency determined by calculating a weighted average of bilateral exchange rates. The weighting reflects the importance of each foreign country's trade with the home country.

Efficient market. A market in which all relevant information is already reflected in market prices. The term is most frequently applied to foreign exchange markets and securities markets.

EFTA. *See* European Free Trade Association.

EMS. *See* European Monetary System.

EOM. "End of month." International trade term.

Euro. The single currency adopted by the 11 members of the European Monetary Union on January 1, 1999, to replace their national currencies. The change over from national currencies to euros takes place over three years, so that by January 1, 2002, the individual national currencies will have been phased out.

Eurobank. A bank, or bank department, which bids for time deposits and makes loans in currencies other than that of the country where the bank is located.

Eurobond. A bond originally offered outside the country in whose currency it is denominated. For example, a dollar-denominated bond originally offered for sale to investors outside of the United States.

Euro-Commercial Paper. Short-term notes (30, 60, 90, 120, 180, 270, and 360 days) sold in international money markets.

Eurocurrency. A currency deposited in a bank located in a country other than the country issuing the currency.

Eurodollar. A U.S. dollar deposited in a bank outside the United States. A Eurodollar is one type of Eurocurrency.

Euronote. Short- to medium-term debt instruments sold in the Eurocurrency market.

European Currency Unit (ECU). Composite currency created by the European Monetary System to function as a reserve currency numeraire. The ECU is used as the numeraire for denominating a number of financial instruments and obligations.

European Economic Community (EEC). The European common market composed of Belgium, Denmark, France, Germany, Greece, Ireland, Italy, Luxembourg, the Netherlands, Portugal, Spain, and the United Kingdom. Officially renamed the European Union (EU) January 1, 1994.

European Free Trade Association (EFTA). European countries not part of the EEC (EU) but having no internal tariffs. EFTA consists of Austria, Iceland, Finland, Sweden, and Switzerland.

European Monetary System (EMS). A monetary alliance of fifteen European countries (same members as the European Union), formed to maintain member exchange rates within specified margins about fixed central rates. As of July 1994, the United

Kingdom and Italy are not active members.

European option.   An option that can be exercised only on the day on which it expires.

European terms.   Foreign exchange quotations for the U.S. dollar, expressed as the number of non-U.S. currency units per U.S. dollar.

European Union (EU). The official name of the former European Economic Community (EEC) as of January 1, 1994.

EVA.   *See* Economic Value Added.

Exchange rate.   The price of a unit of one country's currency expressed in terms of the currency of some other country.

Exchange Rate Mechanism (ERM).   The means by which members of the EMS maintain their currency exchange rates within an agreed upon range with respect to the other member currencies.

Exchange risk.   *See* Foreign exchange risk.

Ex dock.   followed by the name of a port of import. International trade term in which seller agrees to pay for the costs (shipping, insurance, customs duties, etc.) of placing the goods on the dock at the named port.

Exim Bank.   *See* Export-Import Bank.

Export-Import Bank (Eximbank).   A U.S. government agency created to finance and otherwise facilitate imports and exports.

Expropriation.   Official government seizure of pri-vate property, recognized by international law as the right of any sovereign state provided expropriated owners are given prompt comp-ensation and fair market val-ue in convertible currencies.

FAF.   "Fly away free." International trade term.

FAQ.   "Free at quay." International trade term.

FAS.   *See* Free alongside.

FASB 8.   A regulation of the Financial Accounting Standards Board requiring U.S. companies to translate foreign affiliate financial statements by the temporal method. FASB was in effect from 1976 to 1981.

FASB 52.   A regulation of the Financial Accounting Standards Board requiring U.S. companies to translate foreign affiliate financial statements by the current rate (closing rate) method. FASB 52 became effective in 1981.

FCIA.   *See* Foreign Credit Insur- ance Association.

FDI.   *See* Foreign direct investment.

FI.   "Free in." International trade term meaning that all expenses for loading into the

hold of a vessel are for the account of the consignee.

FIFO.   "First in, first out." An inventory valuation approach in which the cost of the earliest inventory purchases is charged against current sales. The opposite is LIFO, or "last in, first out."

Financial account.   A section of the balance of payments accounts. Under the revised format of the International Monetary Fund, the financial account measures long-term financial flows including direct foreign investment, portfolio investments, and other long- term movements. Under the traditional definition, still used by many countries, items in the financial account were included in the capital account.

Financial engineering. Those basic building blocks, such as spot positions, forwards, and options, used to construct positions that provide the user with desired risk and return characteristics.

Fisher Effect.   A theory that nominal interest rates in two or more countries should be equal to the required real rate of return to investors plus compensation for the expected amount of inflation in each country.

Fixed exchange rates. Foreign exchange rates tied to the currency of a major country (such as the United States), to gold, or to a basket of currencies such as Special Drawing Rights.

Flexible exchange rates. The opposite of fixed exchange rates. The foreign exchange rate is adjusted periodically by the country's monetary authorities in accordance with their judgment and/or an external set of economic indicators.

Floating exchange rates. Foreign exchange rates determined by demand and supply in an open market that is presumably free of government interference.

Floating rate note (FRN). Medium-term securities with interest rates pegged to LIBOR and adjusted quarterly or semiannually.

FOB. "Free on board." International trade term in which exporter's quoted price includes the cost of loading goods into transport vessels at a named point.

Foreign bond. A bond issued by a foreign corporation or government for sale in the domestic capital market of another country, and denominated in the currency of that country.

Foreign Corrupt Practices Act of 1977. A U.S. law that punishes companies and their executives if they pay bribes or make other improper payments to foreigners.

Foreign Credit Insurance Association (FCIA). Private

U.S. insurance association that insures exporters in conjunction with Exim Bank.

Foreign currency translation. The process of restating foreign currency accounts of subsidiaries into the reporting currency of the parent company in order to prepare a consolidated financial statement.

Foreign direct investment (FDI). Purchase of physical assets, such as plant and equipment, in a foreign country, to be managed by the parent corporation. FDI is in contradistinction to foreign portfolio investment.

Foreign exchange broker. An individual or firm which arranges foreign exchange transactions between two parties, but is not itself a principal in the trade. Foreign exchange brokers earn a commission for their efforts.

Foreign exchange option. *See* Option.

Foreign exchange risk. The likelihood that an unexpected change in exchange rates will alter the home currency value of foreign currency cash payments expected from a foreign source. Also, the likelihood that an unexpected change in exchange rates will alter the amount of home currency needed to repay a debt denominated in a foreign currency.

Foreign exchange dealer (or trader). An individual or firm that buys foreign ex-

change from one party (at a "bid" price), and then sells it (at an "ask" price) to another party. The dealer is a principal in two transactions and makes a profit on the spread between its buying and selling prices.

Foreign exchange rate. The price of one country's currency in terms of another currency, or in terms of a commodity such as gold or silver. *See also* Exchange rates *and* Foreign exchange.

Foreign sales corporation (FSC). Under U.S. tax code, a type of foreign corporation that provides tax-exempt or tax-deferred income for U.S. persons or corporations having export-oriented activities.

Foreign tax credit. The amount by which a domestic firm may reduce (credit) domestic income taxes for income tax payments to a foreign government.

Forfaiting. A technique for arranging nonrecourse medium-term export financing, used most frequently to finance imports into Eastern Europe. A third party, usually a specialized financial institution, guarantees the financing.

Forward contract. An agreement to exchange currencies of different countries at a specified future date and at a specified forward rate.

Forward differential. The difference between spot and

forward rates, expressed as an annual percentage.

Forward discount or premium.   The same as "forward differential."

Forward rate.   An exchange rate quoted today for settlement at some future date. The rate used in a forward transaction.

Forward transaction.   A foreign exchange transaction agreed upon today but to be settled at some specified future date, often one, two, or three months after the transaction date.

Free alongside (FAS).   An international trade term in which the seller's quoted price for goods includes all costs of delivery of the goods alongside a vessel at the port of embarkation.

Freely floating exchange rates.   Exchange rates determined in a free market without government interference, in contradistinction to "dirty" float.

Free trade zone.   An area within a country into which foreign goods may be brought duty free, often for purposes of additional manufacture, inventory storage, or packaging. Such goods are subject to duty only when they leave the duty-free zone to enter other parts of the country.

FRN.   *See* Floating rate note.

Fronting loan.   A parent-to-affiliate loan channeled through a financial intermediary such as a large international bank in order to reduce political risk. Presumably government authorities are less likely to prevent a foreign affiliate repaying an established bank than repaying the affiliate's corporate parent.

FSC.   *See* Foreign sales corporation.

Functional currency.   In the context of translating financial statements, the currency of the primary economic environment in which a foreign affiliate operates and in which it generates cash flows.

Futures, or futures contracts.   Exchange-traded agreements calling for future delivery of a standard amount of any good, e.g., foreign exchange, at a fixed time, place, and price.

Gamma.   A measure of the sensitivity of an option's delta ratio to small unit changes in the price of the underlying security.

Gap risk.   That type of interest rate risk in which the timing of maturities is mismatched.

GATT.   *See* General Agreement on Tariffs and Trade.

General Agreement on Tariffs and Trade (GATT).   A framework of rules for nations to manage their trade policies, negotiate lower international tariff barriers, and settle trade disputes.

Glasnost.   Russian language word for the political reform policies of President Mikhail S. Gorbachev in the Soviet Union.

G.m.b.H.   *Gesellschaft mit beschraenkter Haftung.* German term for limited liability company.

Gold standard.   A monetary system in which currencies are defined in terms of their gold content, and payment imbalances between countries are settled in gold.

Gross up.   *See* Deemed tax paid.

Group of Five.   France, Japan, United Kingdom, United States, and Germany. Central bankers and finance ministers of these countries met in the mid-1980s to discuss coordinating economic policies.

Group of Seven.   Canada, France, Germany, Italy, Japan, United Kingdom, and the United States. Political leaders of these countries met in 1990 and 1991 to discuss, among other topics, economic aid to the Soviet Union and whether to intervene in the foreign exchange markets to try to stop the rise in the international value of the U.S. dollar.

Group of Ten.   Germany, France, Belgium, the Netherlands, Italy, the United Kingdom, Sweden, Canada, Japan, and the United States. These countries pledged in 1962 to stand ready to lend their currencies to the International Monetary Fund. They have been active in the design and operation of the world's international monetary system.

Hard currency. A freely convertible currency that is not expected to depreciate in value in the foreseeable future.

Hedge. The purchase of a contract (including forward foreign exchange) or tangible good that will rise in value and offset a drop in value of another contract or tangible good. Hedges are undertaken to reduce risk by protecting an owner from loss.

Hedge accounting. An accounting procedure specifying that gains and losses on hedging instruments be recognized in earnings at the same time as the effects of changes in the value of the items being hedged are recognized.

Hijo(s). Spanish word for son(s).

Historical exchange rate. In accounting, the exchange rate in effect when an asset or liability was acquired.

Hermanos (Hnos). Spanish word for brothers.

Hot money. Money which moves internationally from one currency and/or country to another in response to interest rate differences, and moves away immediately when the interest advantage disappears.

Hybrid foreign currency options. Purchase of a put op-

tion and the simultaneous sale of a call (or vice versa) so that the overall cost is less than the cost of a straight option.

Hyperinflation countries. Countries with a very high rate of inflation. Under United States FASB 52, these are defined as countries where the cumulative three-year inflation amounts to 100% or more.

IBF. *See* International Banking Facility.

IBRD. *See* International Bank for Reconstruction and Development.

IMF. *See* International Monetary Fund.

IMM. International Monetary Market. A division of the Chicago Mercantile Exchange.

Inc. "Incorporated." American English word for a business formed as a corporation. *Also see* Limited.

Indirect quote. The price of a unit of a home country's currency expressed in terms of a foreign country's currency.

Interest equalization tax. A 1963 U.S. tax imposed on U.S. residents who purchased foreign securities. The law was repealed in 1973. The purpose of the tax was to penalize U.S. residents who invested outside of the United States, and so help the U.S. balance of payments.

Interest rate parity. A theory that the differences in na-

tional interest rates for securities of similar risk and maturity should be equal to but opposite in sign to the forward exchange rate discount or premium for the foreign currency.

Interest rate swap. A transaction in which two counterparties exchange interest payment streams of different character (such as floating vs. fixed), based on an underlying notional principal amount.

Internal rate of return (IRR). A capital budgeting approach in which the discount rate is found that matches the present value of expected future cash inflows with the present value of outflows.

Internalization. A theory that the key ingredient for maintaining a firm-specific competitive advantage in international competition is the possession of proprietary information and control of human capital that can generate new information through expertise in research, management, marketing, or technology.

International Bank for Reconstruction and Development (IBRD, or World Bank). International development bank owned by member nations that makes development loans to member countries.

International Banking Facility (IBF). A department within a U.S. bank that may accept foreign deposits and make loans to foreign borrowers as if it were a foreign subsidiary. IBFs are free of U.S. reserve requirements, deposit insurance, and interest rate regulations.

International Fisher Effect. A theory that the spot exchange rate should change by an amount equal to the difference in interest rates between two countries.

International Monetary Fund (IMF). An international organization created in 1944 to promote exchange rate stability and provide temporary financing for countries experiencing balance of payments difficulties.

International Monetary Market (IMM). A branch of the Chicago Mercantile Exchange which specializes in trading currency and financial futures contracts.

International monetary system. The structure within which foreign exchange rates are determined, international trade and capital flows are accommodated, and balance of payments adjustments made.

IRR. *See* Internal rate of return.

Joint venture. A business venture that is owned by two or more other business ventures. Often the several business owners are from different countries.

Jumbo loans. Loans of $1 billion or more.

Kangaroo bonds. Australian dollar-denominated bonds issued within Australia by a foreign borrower.

"Kiwi." Foreign exchange dealers' nickname for the New Zealand dollar.

KK. *Kabushiki-Kaishi.* Japanese term for stock company.

Lag. In the context of leads and lags, payment of a financial obligation later than is expected or required.

Lambda. A measure of the sensitivity of an option premium to a unit change in volatility.

L/C. *See* Letter of credit.

Lead. In the context of leads and lags, payment of a financial obligation earlier than is expected or required.

Letter of credit (L/C). An instrument issued by a bank, in which the bank promises to pay a beneficiary upon presentation of documents specified in the letter of credit.

LIBOR. *See* London Interbank Offered Rate.

LIFO. "Last in, first out." An inventory valuation approach in which the cost of the latest inventory purchases is charged against current sales. The opposite is FIFO, or "first in, first out."

Limited (Ltd). British

English word for a business formed as a corporation.

Link financing. *See* Back-to-back loan.

Lombard rate. The interest rate on a "Lombard loan," which is an advance against the collateral of specified European securities.

London Interbank Offered Rate (LIBOR). The deposit rate applicable to interbank loans in London. LIBOR is used as the reference rate for many international interest rate transactions.

Long position. A position in which foreign currency assets exceed foreign currency liabilities to deliver. The opposite of a long position is a short position.

"Loonie." Foreign exchange dealer's nickname for the Canadian dollar.

Ltd. *See* Limited.

Maastricht Treaty. A treaty among the 12 European Union countries which specified a plan and timetable for the introduction of a single European currency, to be called the "Euro."

Managed float. *See* "Dirty" float.

Margin. A deposit made as security for a financial transaction otherwise financed on credit.

Merchant bank. A bank that specializes in helping corporations and governments finance by any of a variety of market and/or traditional techniques. In Europe, merchant banks combine in one institution what in the United States are separated into commercial banks or in-vestment banks. European merchant banks are sometimes differentiated from clearing banks, which tend to focus on bank deposits and clearing balances for the majority of the population.

MFN.   *See* Most-favored-nation treatment.

Monetary/nonmonetary method.   A method of translating the financial statements of foreign affiliates into the parent's reporting currency. All monetary accounts are translated at the current rate, and all nonmonetary accounts are translated at their historical rates. Sometimes called "temporal method" in the United States.

Money market hedge.   Use of foreign currency borrowing to reduce transaction or accounting foreign exchange exposure.

Money Markets.   The financial markets in various countries in which various types of short-term debt instruments, including bank loans, are purchased and sold.

Monetary assets or liabilities.   Assets in the form of cash or claims to cash (such as accounts receivable), or liabilities payable in cash. Monetary

assets minus monetary liabilities are called "net monetary assets."

m.n.   *Moneda nacional.* Spanish language term for "national money," the local currency.

Most-favored-nation status. A term meaning the same as "normal trade status." *See* Normal trade status.

NAFTA.   *See* North American Free Trade Agreement.

Negotiable instrument.   A draft or promissory note that is in writing, signed by the maker or drawer, contains an unconditional promise or order to pay a definite sum of money on demand or at a determinable future date, and is payable to order or to bearer. A "holder in due course" of a negotiable instrument is entitled to payment despite any personal disagreements between drawee and maker.

Nepotism.   The practice of showing favor to relatives in preference to other qualified persons in conferring such benefits as the awarding of contracts, granting of special prices, promotions to various ranks, etc.

Net present value.   A capital budgeting approach in which the present value of expected future cash inflows is subtracted from the present value of outflows to determine the "net" present value.

Netting.   The mutual offsetting of sums due between two business entities. If "A" owes "B" $100, and "B"owes "A" $60, a single payment of $40 from "A" to "B" would eliminate both debts. This would be "netting."

Nominal exchange rate. The actual foreign exchange quotation, in contradistinction to "real exchange rate," which is adjusted for changes in purchasing power.

Nontariff barrier.   Trade restrictive practices other than custom tariffs. Examples are import quotas, "voluntary" restrictions, variable levies, and special health regulations.

Nordic.   A word used to describe collectively the countries of Norway, Sweden, Denmark, Finland, and Iceland.

Normal trade status.   The term currently used to describe what economists used to call "most-favored nation" status. Normal trade status is the application by a country of import duties on the same (i.e., "most favored") basis to all countries accorded such treatment. Any tariff reduction granted in a bilateral negotiation to a specific country will be automatically extended to all other nations that have been granted normal trade status.

North American Free Trade Agreement (NAFTA). Atreaty allowing free trade and investment between Canada, the United States, and Mexico.

Note issuance facility (NIF). An agreement by which a syndicate of banks indicates a willingness to accept short-term notes from borrowers and resell those notes in the Eurocurrency markets. The discount rate is often tied to LIBOR.

NPV. *See* Net present value.

N.V. *Naamloze vennootschap*. Dutch term for stock company or corporation.

O/A. "Open account." Arrangement in which the importer (or other buyer) pays for the goods only after the goods are received and inspected. The importer is billed directly after shipment, and payment is not tied to any promissory notes or similar documents.

Offer. The price at which a trader is willing to sell for- eign exchange, securities, or commodities. Also called "ask."

Offshore finance subsidiary. A foreign financial subsidiary owned by a corporation in another country. Offshore finance subsidiaries are usually located in tax-free or low-tax jurisdictions to enable the parent multinational firm to finance international operations without being subject to home country taxes or regulations.

OPEC. *See* Organization of Petroleum Exporting

Countries.

Operating exposure. The potential for a change in expected cash flows, and thus in value, of a foreign affiliate as a result of an unexpected change in exchange rates. Also called "economic exposure."

OPIC. *See* Overseas Private Investment Corporation.

Option. In foreign exchange, a contract giving the purchaser the right, but not the obligation, to buy or sell a given amount of foreign exchange at a fixed price per unit for a specified time period. Options to buy are "calls" and options to sell are "puts."

Order bill of lading. A shipping document through which possession and title to the shipment reside with the owner of the order bill of lading.

Organization of Petroleum Exporting Countries (OPEC). An alliance of most major crude oil producing countries, formed for the purpose of allocating and controlling production quotas so as to influence the price of crude oil in world markets.

OTC market. *See* Over-the-counter market.

Outright quotation. The full price, in one currency, of a unit of another currency. *See* Points quotation.

Overseas Private Investment Corporation (OPIC). A U.S. government-owned in-

surance company that insures U.S. corporations against various political risks.

Over-the-counter market. A market for share of stock, options (including foreign currency options), or other financial contracts conducted via electronic connections between dealers. The over-the-counter market has no physical location or address, and is thus differentiated from organized exchanges which have a physical location where trading takes place.

Parallel loan. Another name for a back-to-back loan, in which two companies in separate countries borrow each other's currency for a specific period of time, and repay the other's currency at an agreed maturity.

Parallel market. An unofficial foreign exchange market tolerated by a government but not officially sanctioned. The exact boundary between a parallel market and a black market is not very clear, but official tolerance of what would otherwise be a black market leads to use of the term parallel market.

"Paris." Foreign exchange dealers' nickname for the French franc.

Parity conditions. In the context of international finance, a set of basic economic relationships which provide for equilibrium between spot and forward foreign exchange rates, interest rates, and inflation rates.

Participating forward. A complex option position which combines a bought put and a sold call option at the same strike price to create a net zero position. Also called *zero-cost option* and *forward participation agreement.*

Phi. The expected change in an option premium caused by a small change in the foreign interest rate (interest rate for the foreign currency).

P/N. "Promissory note."

Points. A "point" is the smallest unit of price change quoted, given a conventional number of digits in which a quotation is stated. Deutschemarks per dollar are usually quoted to four decimal points, DM1.5624/$. In this quote, a change from 1.5624 to 1.5625 would be an increase of one point. A 12 point increase would bring the quote to 1.5636.

Points quotation. A forward quotation expressed only as the number of decimal points (usually four decimal points) by which it differs from the spot quotation.

Political risk. The possibility that political events in a particular country will have an influence on the economic well-being of firms in that country. *Also see* Sovereign risk.

Portfolio investment. Purchase of foreign stocks and bonds, in contradistinction to "foreign direct investment."

Possessions Corporation. A U.S. corporation, the sub-sidiary of another U.S. corporation, which for tax purposes is treated as if it were a foreign corporation.

Premium (in foreign exchange market). The amount by which a currency is more expensive for future delivery than for spot (immediate) delivery. The opposite of "premium" is "discount."

Protectionism. A political attitude or policy intended to inhibit or prohibit the import of foreign goods and services. The opposite of "free trade" policies.

Pty. Ltd. "Proprietary Limited." Term used in Australia, Singapore, and other countries for a privately owned corporation.

Purchasing power parity. A theory that the price of internationally traded commodities should be the same in every country, and hence the exchange rate between the two currencies should be the ratio of prices in the two countries.

Put. An option to sell foreign exchange or financial contracts. *See* Option.

Quota. A limit, mandatory or "voluntary," set on the import of a product.

Quotation. In foreign exchange trading, the pair of prices (bid and ask) at which a dealer is willing to buy or sell foreign exchange.

Range forward. A complex option position which combines the purchase of a put option and the sale of a call option with strike prices equidistant from the forward rate. Also called *flexible forward, cylinder option, option fence, mini-max,* and *zero-cost tunnel.*

Real exchange rate. An index of foreign exchange adjusted for relative price level changes since a base period. Sometimes referred to as "real effective exchange rate," it is used to measure purchasing-power-adjusted changes in exchange rates.

Registered bond. Corporate or governmental debt in a bond form in which the owner's name appears on the bond and in the issuer's records, and interest payments are mailed to the owner. Transfer, as at the time of sale or if the bond is being possessed as collateral for a loan in default, requires power of attorney and the return of the physical bond to a transfer agent. The transfer agent replaces the old bond with a new one registered to the new owner.

Reinvoicing center. A central financial subsidiary used by a multinational firm to reduce transaction exposure by having all home country exports billed in the home currency and then reinvoiced to each operating affiliate in that affiliate's local currency.

Rembrandt bonds. Dutch guilder-denominated bonds issued within the Netherlands by a foreign borrower.

Reporting currency. In the context of translating financial statements, the currency in which a parent firm prepares its own financial statements. Usually this is the parent's home currency.

Revaluation. A rise in the foreign exchange value of a currency that is pegged to other currencies or to gold. Also called "appreciation."

Rho. The expected change in an option premium caused by a small change in the domestic interest rate (interest rate for the home currency).

"Rules of the Game." The basis of exchange rate determination under the international gold standard during most of the 19th and early 20th centuries. All countries agreed informally to follow the "rule" of buying and selling their currency at a fixed and predetermined price against gold.

SA. *Sociedad Anónima* (Spanish), or *Societe Anonyme* (French). Term meaning corporation.

SACI or SAIC. *Sociedad Anónima de Capital e Industria.* Spanish term for company of capital and industry.

Samurai bonds. Yen-denominated bonds issued within Japan by a foreign borrower.

SARL. *Società a Responsabilità Limitada* (Italian), or *Société a Responsabilité Lim-itée* (French). Term for company with limited liability.

S/D. "Sight draft." International trade term.

S/D-B/L. "Sight draft and bill of lading attached." International trade term.

SDR. *See* Special drawing right.

S. de R.L. *Sociedad de Responsabilidad Limitada.* Spanish term for limited partnership.

Section 482. The set of U.S. Treasury regulations governing transfer prices.

S. en C. *Sociedad en Comandita.* Spanish term for silent partnership.

Shareholder wealth maximization. The corporate goal of maximizing the total value of the shareholders' investment in the company.

Shogun bonds. Foreign currency-denominated bonds issued within Japan by Japanese corporations.

Short position. *See* Long position.

SIBOR. Singapore interbank offered rate.

Sight draft. A bill of exchange (B/E) that is due on demand; i.e., when presented to the bank. *Also see* Bill of exchange.

SIMEX. Singapore International Monetary Exchange.

"Sing dollar." Foreign exchange dealers' nickname for the Singapore dollar.

Snake. Informal name for European Narrow Margins (or

Joint Float) Agreement, in which European governments agreed to keep their currencies within a plus or minus 2.25% trading band around an agreed central value. Superceded by the adoption of the euro and so, is no longer in effect.

Society for Worldwide Interbank Financial Telecommunications (SWIFT). A dedicated computer network providing funds transfer messages between member banks around the world.

Soft currency. A currency expected to drop in value relative to other currencies. Free trading in a currency deemed soft is often restricted by the monetary authorities of the issuing country.

Sovereign risk. The risk that a host government may unilaterally repudiate its foreign obligations or may prevent local firms from honoring their foreign obligations. Sovereign risk is often regarded as a subset of political risk.

SPA. *Societa per Azioni.* Italian term for corporation.

Special Drawing Right (SDR). An international reserve asset, defined by the International Monetary Fund as the value of a weighted basket of five currencies.

Speculation. An attempt to make a profit by trading on expectations about future prices.

Spot rate. The price at which foreign exchange can be purchased (its bid) or sold (its ask) in a spot transaction. *See* Spot transaction.

Spot transaction. A foreign exchange transaction to be settled (paid for) on the second following business day.

Spread. The difference between the bid (buying) quote and the ask (selling) quote.

Strategic alliance. A formal relationship, short of a merger or acquisition, between two companies, formed for the purpose of gaining synergies because in some aspect the two companies complement each other.

Stripped bonds. Bonds issued by investment bankers against coupons or the maturity (corpus) portion of original bearer bonds, where the original bonds are held in trust by the investment banker. Whereas the original bonds will have coupons promising interest at each interest date (say June and December for each of the next twenty years), a given stripped bond will represent a claim against all interest payments from the entire original issue due on a particular interest date. A stripped bond is in effect a zero coupon bond manufactured by the investment banker.

Subpart F. A type of foreign income, as defined in the U.S. tax code, which under certain conditions is taxed in the United States even though it has not been repatriated to the United States.

Subsidiary. A foreign operation incorporated in the host country and owned 50% or more by a parent corporation. Foreign operations that are not incorporated are called "branches."

Sushi bonds. Eurodollar, or other non-yen denominated, bonds issued by a Japanese corporation for sale to Japanese investors.

Swap. This term is used in many contexts. In general it is the simultaneous purchase and sale of foreign exchange or securities, with the purchase being effected at once and the sale back to the same party to be carried out at a price agreed upon today but to be completed at a specified future date. Swaps include interest rate swaps, currency swaps, and credit swaps. A "swap rate" is a forward foreign exchange quotation expressed in terms of the number of points by which the forward rate differs from the spot rate.

SWIFT. *See* Society for Worldwide Interbank Financial Telecommunications.

"Swissie." Foreign exchange dealers' nickname for the Swiss franc.

Syndicated loan. A large loan made by a group of banks to a large multinational firm or government. Syndicated loans allow the participating banks to maintain diversification by not lending too much to a single borrower.

Synthetic forward. A complex option position which combines the purchase of a put option and the sale of a call option, or vice versa, both at the forward rate.

Systematic risk. The risk of the market itself, i.e., risk that cannot be diversified away.

T/A. "Trade acceptance." International trade term.

Tariff. A duty or tax on imports that can be levied as a percentage of cost or as a specific amount per unit of import.

Tax haven. A country with either no or very low tax rates that uses its tax structure to attract foreign investment or international financial dealings.

Temporal method. In the United States, term for a codification of a translation method essentially similar to the "monetary/nonmonetary method."

Terms of trade. The weighted average exchange ratio between a nation's export prices and its import prices, used to measure gains from trade. Gains from trade refers to increases in total consumption resulting from production specialization and international trade.

Theta. The expected change in an option premium caused by a small change in the time to expiration.

Total Shareholder Return (TSR). A measure of corporate performance based on the sum of share price appreciation and current dividends.

Trade acceptance. A draft accepted by a commercial enterprise, instead of by a bank.

Transaction exposure. The potential for a change in the value of outstanding financial obligations entered into prior to a change in exchange rates but not due to be settled until after the exchange rates change.

Transfer pricing. The setting of prices to be charged by one unit (such as a foreign affiliate) of a multiunit corporation to another unit (such as the parent corporation) for goods or services sold between such related units.

Translation exposure. Another name for accounting exposure. *See* Accounting exposure.

TSR. See Total Shareholder Return.

Unbiased predictor. A theory that spot prices at some future date will be equal to today's forward rates.

Unbundling. Dividing cash flows from an affiliate to a parent into their many separate components, such as royalties, lease payments, dividends, etc., so as to increase the likelihood that some fund flows will be allowed during economically difficult times.

Unsystematic risk. In a portfolio, the amount of risk that can be eliminated by diversification.

Value-added tax. A type of national sales tax collected at each stage of production or sale of consumption goods, and levied in proportion to the value added during that stage.

Value date. The date when value is given (i.e., funds are deposited) for foreign exchange transactions between banks.

Value today. A spot foreign exchange transaction in which delivery and payment are made on the same day as the contract. Normal delivery is two business days after the contract.

Value tomorrow. A spot foreign exchange transaction in which delivery and payment are made on the next business day after the contract. Normal delivery is two business days after the contract.

VAT. *See* Value-added tax.

WACC. *See* Weighted average cost of capital.

Weighted average cost of capital (WACC). The sum of the proportionally weighted costs of different sources of capital, used as the minimum acceptable target return on new investments.

World Bank. *See* International Bank for Reconstruction and Development.

Yankee bonds. Dollar-denominated bonds issued within the United States by a foreign borrower.

World Trade Organization (WTO). The intra-governmental organization which applies rules to international trade and hears complaints filed by countries that a particular rule has been violated. The World Trade Agreement replaced the General Agreement on Trade and Tariffs (GATT).

WTO. *See* World Trade Organization.

Yield to maturity. The rate of interest (discount) which equates future cash flows of a bond, both interest and principal, with the present market price. Yield to maturity is thus the time-adjusted rate of return earned by a bond investor.

Y.K. *Yugen-Kaisha*. Japanese term for limited liability company.

Zero coupon bond. A bond which pays no periodic interest, but simply returns a given amount of principal at a stated maturity date. Zero coupon bonds are sold at a discount from the maturity amount to provide the holder a compound rate of return for the holding period.

AUTHOR INDEX

SUBJECT INDEX

Currencies of the World

Country	Currency	Symbol	Subdivision	ISO-4217 Code
Afghanistan	afghani	Af	100 puls	AFA 004
Albania	lek	L	100 qindarka (qintars)	ALL 008
Algeria	dinar	DA	100 centimes	DZD 012
American Samoa	see United States of America			
Andorra	Andorran Peseta (1/1 to Spanish Peseta) and Andorran Franc (1/1 to French Franc)			
Angola	kwanza	Kz	100 lwei	AOK —
Angola	new kwanza (kwanza reajustado)	Kz	100 lwei	AON 024
Anguilla	dollar	EC$	100 cents	XCD 951
Antarctica	each Antarctic base uses the currency of its home country			
Antigua and Barbuda	dollar	EC$	100 cents	XCD 951
Argentina	austral (-1991)	double dashed A	100 centavos	ARA —
Argentina	peso (1991-)	$	100 centavos	ARS 032
Armenia	dram		100 luma	AMD 051
Aruba	guilder (a.k.a. florin or gulden)	Af.	100 cents	AWG 533
Australia	dollar	A$	100 cents	AUD 036
Austria	Schilling	S	100 groschen	ATS 040
Azerbaijan	manat		100 gopik	AZM 031
Bahamas	dollar	B$	100 cents	BSD 044
Bahrain	dinar	BD	1,000 fils	BHD 048
Bangladesh	taka	Tk	100 paisa (poisha)	BDT 050
Barbados	dollar	Bds$	100 cents	BBD 052
Belarus	ruble	BR		BYB 112
Belgium	franc	BF	100 centimes	BEF 056
Belize	dollar	BZ$	100 cents	BZD 084
Belorussia	old name of Belarus			
Benin	franc	CFAF	100 centimes	XOF 952
Bermuda	Dollar	Bd$	100 cents	BMD 060
Bhutan	ngultrum	Nu	100 chetrum	BTN 064
Bolivia	boliviano	Bs	100 centavos	BOB 068
Bosnia-Herzegovina (-1999)	B.H. dinar		100 para	BAD 070
Bosnia-Herzegovina (1999+)	convertible mark	KM	100 fennig	BAM 977
Botswana	pula	P	100 thebe	BWP 072
Bouvet Island	see Norway			
Brazil	cruzeiro (-1993)		100 centavos	BRE 076
Brazil	cruzeiro (1993-94)		100 centavos	BRR 076
Brazil	real (1994-)	R$	100 centavos	BRL 076
British Indian Ocean Territory	legal currency is GBP, but mostly USD is used			
British Virgin Islands	see United States			
Brunei	ringgit (a.k.a. Bruneian dollar)	B$	100 sen (a.k.a. 100 cents)	BND 096
Bulgaria	leva	Lv	100 stotinki	BGL 100
Burkina Faso	franc	CFAF	100 centimes	XOF 952
Burma	now Myanmar			

Country	Currency	Symbol	Subdivision	ISO-4217 Code
Burundi	franc	FBu	100 centimes	BIF 108
Cambodia	new riel	CR	100 sen	KHR 116
Cameroon	franc	CFAF	100 centimes	XAF 950
Canada	dollar	Can$	100 cents	CAD 124
Canton and Enderbury Islands	see Kiribati			
Cape Verde Island	escudo	C.V.Esc.	100 centavos	CVE 132
Cayman Islands	dollar	CI$	100 cents	KYD 136
Central African Republic	franc	CFAF	100 centimes	XAF 950
Chad	franc	CFAF	100 centimes	XAF 950
Chile	peso	Ch$	100 centavos	CLP 152
China	yuan renminbi	Y	10 jiao = 100 fen	CNY 156
Christmas Island	see Australia			
Cocos (Keeling) Islands	see Australia			
Columbia	peso	Col$	100 centavos	COP 170
Comoros	franc	CF		KMF 174
Congo	franc	CFAF	100 centimes	XAF 950
Congo, Dem. Rep.	franc		100 centimes	CDF 180
Cook Islands	see New Zealand			
Costa Rica	colon	slashed C	100 centimos	CRC 188
Côte d'Ivoire	franc	CFAF	100 centimes	XOF 952
Croatia	kuna	HRK	100 lipas	HRK 191
Cuba	peso	Cu$	100 centavos	CUP 192
Cyprus	pound	£C	100 cents	CYP 196
Cyprus (Northern)	see Turkey			
Czechoslovakia	split into Czech Republic and Slovak Republic on January 1, 1993			
Czech Republic	koruna	Kc (with hacek on c)	100 haleru	CZK 203
Denmark	krone (pl. kroner)	Dkr	100 øre	DKK 208
Djibouti	franc	DF	100 centimes	DJF 262
Dominica	dollar	EC$	100 cents	XCD 951
Dominican Rep.	peso	RD$	100 centavos	DOP 214
Dronning Maud Land	see Norway			
East Timor	see Indonesia			
Ecuador	sucre	S/	100 centavos	ECS 218
Egypt	pound	£E	100 piasters or 1,000 milliemes	EGP 818
El Salvador	colon	¢	100 centavos	SVC 222
Equatorial Guinea	franc	CFAF	100 centimos	GQE 226
Eritrea	nakfa	Nfa	100 cents	ERN 232
Estonia	kroon (pl. krooni)	KR	100 senti	EEK 233
Ethiopia	birr	Br	100 cents	ETB 231
European Currency Unit (-1998)	ecu			XEU 954
European Union (1999-)	Euro[1]	€	100 euro-cents	EUR 978
Faeroe Islands (Foroyar)	see Denmark			
Falkland Islands	pound	£F	100 pence	FKP 238
Fiji	dollar	F$	100 cents	FJD 242

[1]See http://pacific.commerce.ubc.ca/xr/euro/

Currencies of the World (continued)

Country	Currency	Symbol	Subdivision	ISO-4217 Code
Finland	markka (pl. markkaa)	mk	100 penniä (sg. penni)	FIM 246
France	franc	F	100 centimes	FRF 250
French Guiana	see France			
French Polynesia	franc	CFPF	100 centimes	XPF 953
Gabon	franc	CFAF	100 centimes	XAF 950
Gambia	dalasi	D	100 butut	GMD 270
Gaza	see Israel and Jordan			
Georgia	lari		100 tetri	GEL 268
Germany	deutsche mark	DM	100 pfennig	DEM 280
Ghana	new cedi	¢	100 pesewas	GHC 288
Gibraltar	pound	£G	100 pence	GIP 292
Great Britain	see United Kingdom			
Greece	drachma	Dr	100 lepta (sg. lepton)	GRD 300
Greenland	see Denmark			
Grenada	dollar	EC$	100 cents	XCD 951
Guadeloupe	see France			
Guam	see United States			
Guatemala	quetzal	Q	100 centavos	GTQ 320
Guernsey	see United Kingdom			
Guinea-Bissau (-Apr1997)	peso	PG	100 centavos	GWP 624
Guinea-Bissau (May1997-)	franc	CFAF	100 centimes	XAF 950
Guinea	syli	FG	10 francs, 1 franc = 100 centimes	GNS 324
Guinea	franc		(no longer used)	GNF 324
Guyana	dollar	G$	100 cents	GYD 328
Haiti	gourde	G	100 centimes	HTG 332
Heard and McDonald Islands	see Australia			
Honduras	lempira	L	100 centavos	HNL 340
Hong Kong	dollar	HK$	100 cents	HKD 344
Hungary	forint	Ft	-none-	HUF 348
Iceland	króna	IKr	100 aurar (sg. aur)	ISK 352
India	rupee	Rs	100 paise	INR 356
Indonesia	rupiah	Rp	100 sen (not used)	IDR 360
International Monetary Fund	Special Drawing Right[2]	SDR		XDR 960
Iran	rial	Rls	10 rials = 1 toman	IRR 364
Iraq	dinar	ID	1,000 fils	IQD 368
Ireland	punt or pound	IR£	100 pingin or pence	IEP 372
Isle of Man	see United Kingdom			
Israel	new shekel	NIS	100 new agorot	ILS 376
Italy	lira (pl. lire)	Lit	no subdivision in use	ITL 380
Ivory Coast	see Côte d'Ivoire			
Jamaica	dollar	J$	100 cents	JMD 388
Japan	yen	¥	100 sen (not used)	JPY 392
Jersey	see United Kingdom			
Johnston Island	see United States			
Jordan	dinar	JD	1,000 fils	JOD 400
Kampuchea	see Cambodia			

[2]See http://pacific.commerce.ubc.ca/xr/SDR.html

Country	Currency	Symbol	Subdivision	ISO-4217 Code
Kazakhstan	tenge		100 tiyn	KZT 398
Kenya	shilling	K Sh	100 cents	KES 404
Kiribati	see Australia			
Korea, North	won	Wn	100 chon	KPW 408
Korea, South	won	W	100 chon	KRW 410
Kuwait	dinar	KD	1,000 fils	KWD 414
Kyrgyzstan	som		100 tyyn	KGS 417
Laos	new kip	KN	100 at	LAK 418
Latvia	lat	Ls	100 santims	LVL 428
Lebanon	pound (livre)	£L	100 piastres	LBP 422
Lesotho	loti, pl., maloti	L, pl., M	100 lisente	LSL 426
Liberia	dollar	$	100 cents	LRD 430
Libya	dinar	LD	1,000 dirhams	LYD 434
Liechtenstein	see Switzerland			
Lithuania	litas, pl., litai		100 centu	LTL 440
Luxembourg	franc	LuxF	100 centimes	LUF 442
Macao (Macau)	pataca	P	100 avos	MOP 446
Macedonia (Former Yug. Rep.)	denar	MKD	100 deni	MKD 807
Madagascar	ariayry = 5 francs	FMG	1 franc = 100 centimes	MGF 450
Malawi	kwacha	MK	100 tambala	MWK 454
Malaysia	ringgit	RM	100 sen	MYR 458
Maldives	rufiyaa	Rf	100 lari	MVR 462
Mali	franc	CFAF	100 centimes	MLF 466
Malta	lira, pl, liri	Lm	100 cents	MTL 470
Martinique	see France			
Mauritania	ouguiya	UM	5 khoums	MRO 478
Mauritius	rupee	Mau Rs	100 cents	MUR 480
Micronesia	see United States			
Midway Islands	see United States			
Mexico	peso	Mex$	100 centavos	MXP 484
Moldova	leu, pl., lei			MDL 498
Monaco	see France			
Mongolia	tugrik (tughrik?)	Tug	100 mongos	MNT 496
Montserrat	dollar	EC$	100 cents	XCD 951
Morocco	dirham	DH	100 centimes	MAD 504
Mozambique	metical	Mt	100 centavos	MZM 508
Myanmar	kyat	K	100 pyas	MMK 104
Nauru	see Australia			
Namibia	dollar	N$	100 cents	NAD 516
Nepal	rupee	NRs	100 paise	NPR 524
Netherlands Antilles	guilder (a.k.a. florin or gulden)	Ant.f. or NAf.	100 cents	ANG 532
Netherlands	guilder (a.k.a. florin or gulden)	f.	100 cents	NLG 528
New Caledonia	franc	CFPF	100 centimes	XPF 953
New Zealand	dollar	NZ$	100 cents	NZD 554
Nicaragua	gold cordoba	C$	100 centavos	NIC 558
Niger	franc	CFAF	100 centimes	XOF 952
Nigeria	naira	double-dashed N	100 kobo	NGN 566
Niue	see New Zealand			
Norfolk Island	see Australia			
Norway	krone (pl. kroner)	NKr	100 øre	NOK 578